THE

top10★

OF EVERYTHING

2000

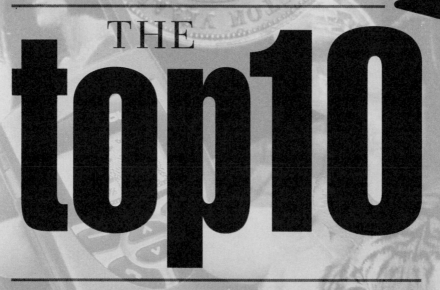

THE top10

OF EVERYTHING

2000

RUSSELL ASH

DK PUBLISHING, INC.

CONTENTS

A DK PUBLISHING BOOK

www.dk.com

Senior Editor Adèle Hayward
Senior Designer Tassy King
Project Editor David Tombesi-Walton
US Editors Barbara Minton, Chuck Wills,
Michael Wise

DTP Designer Jason Little
Production Controller Silvia La Greca

Managing Editor Jonathan Metcalf
Managing Art Editor Nigel Duffield

Produced for Dorling Kindersley by
Cooling Brown, 9–11 High Street, Hampton,
Middlesex TW12 2SA

Editor Alison Bolus
Designers Tish Mills, Elaine Hewson,
Pauline Clarke
Creative Director Arthur Brown

First American Edition, 1999
2 4 6 8 10 9 7 5 3 1

Published in the United States by DK Publishing Inc.,
95 Madison Avenue, New York, New York 10016

DK Publishing books are available at special discounts for bulk
purchases for sales promotions or premiums. Special editions,
including personalized covers, excerpts of existing guides, and
corporate imprints can be createdin large quantities for specific needs.
For more information, contact Special Markets Dept./DK Publishing
Inc./95 Madison Ave./New York, NY 10016/Fax: 800-600-9098.

Library of Congress Cataloging-in-Publication Data
Ash, Russell.
    The Top 10 of everything 2000 / Russell Ash. -- 1st American ed.
    p. cm.
    ISBN 0-7894-4892-0 (hardcover). -- ISBN 0-7894-4632-4 (pbk.)
    1. Curiosities and wonders. 2. World records--Miscellanea.
I. Title. II. Title: Top ten of everything 2000.
AG243.A69 1999
031.02--dc21   99-23292
                                                    CIP

Reproduction by Colourpath, London.
Printed and bound in the United States by World Color.

INTO THE NEW MILLENNIUM

Now in its 11th year, *The Top 10 of Everything* celebrates the end of the 20th century and the start of the 21st by presenting more lists than ever! The book's radical redesign has enabled us to expand the content and to introduce a millennium section in which a time line and 50 historical lists survey the past 1,000 years. In total there are more than 1,000 Top 10 lists, which encompass many categories. These lists are supplemented by quiz questions, SnapShot features, and "Did You Know?" entries.

WHY LISTS?

Many of us make what might be called "lists for life," the kind of lists you compile to organize yourself, such as shopping lists. Lists of all types are becoming an increasingly prominent feature of the "Information Age": as we are bombarded with information – from newspapers and magazines, radio, television, and the Internet – lists provide a shorthand way of presenting what might otherwise be an impenetrable mass of data. Lists have become a way of simplifying our awareness of the world around us in a form that we can easily absorb.

ENTRY RULES

When I started compiling *The Top 10 of Everything*, I set myself the rule that all the lists should be of things that can be quantified. The book focuses on superlatives in numerous categories, but also contains a variety of "firsts" or "latests," which recognize the pioneers and the most recent achievers in various fields of endeavor. Top 10 lists of films are based on worldwide box-office income, and those on topics such as recorded music, videos, and books are based on sales, unless otherwise stated.

INFORMATION RETRIEVAL

Of all the questions I am asked about *The Top 10 of Everything*, the most common is, "Where do you get all the information?" There is no simple answer, as my sources are diverse. I delve into obscure and specialized books, and I use government and other official statistics. Individuals, especially enthusiasts in specialized fields, provide me with information, and I would like to pay tribute not only to them, but also to those readers who have taken the trouble to write to me with helpful suggestions and corrections.

FACTS ARE FUN

Even after over a decade's involvement with *The Top 10 of Everything*, I remain enthusiastic and excited by it. Working on the book has led me into innumerable discoveries that I would not otherwise have made. Through countless broadcast interviews, talks, and bookstore presentations, I have met many interesting people. The book has also inspired a successful children's television series that, like the book, conveys to its audience the message that facts are fun.

DATES AND DEADLINES

I endeavor to ensure that all the information in *The Top 10 of Everything* is as up to date as possible. However, some organizations compile statistics slowly: by the time I use them they may be up to two years old. Conversely, many lists, such as those based on sports records or movie box-office receipts, rely on information that changes frequently. This makes updating the lists an ongoing pursuit, but one that continues to fascinate me, and will, I hope, inform and entertain you, too.

GET IN CONTACT

If you have any list ideas or comments, please write to me c/o the publishers or email me directly at ash@pavilion.co.uk

Other DK Publishing books by Russell Ash:
The Factastic Book of Comparisons
The Factastic Book of 1,001 Lists
Factastic Millennium Facts

SPECIAL FEATURES FOR THIS EDITION

- A millennium section featuring a time line and 50 historical lists charting 1,000 years of world history and take a tentative look into the next century.

- More than 1,000 lists give you the most comprehensive *Top 10 of Everything* ever.

- Illustrated SnapShot features provide entertaining supplementary information.

- Challenging quiz questions with multiple-choice answers are scattered throughout the book.

- "Did You Know?" entries offer surprising and unusual facts on many of the subjects explored.

- 121 thematic spreads in 10 categories bring together lists on related topics.

- Sources for many Top 10 lists are displayed at the foot of the lists.

- For many of the lists, explanatory text expands on the data provided.

MILLENNIUM MILESTONES

IT IS HARD TO IMAGINE what the world was like a thousand years ago. In this age of space travel, instant global communication, virtual reality, and genetic engineering, it is sometimes impossible to believe that this is the same planet our ancestors inhabited. Things that seemed miraculous even a hundred years ago are now commonplace. Exclusive to this special edition of *The Top 10 of Everything*, the Millennium Milestones section puts the past into perspective, looking at the events that shaped the world over the last thousand years.

MILLENNIUM MILESTONES

BATTLES OF THE FIRST CRUSADE

	LOCATION	TYPE	RESULT	YEAR
1	Nicaea	City siege	Crusader victory	1097
2	Dorylaeum	Battle	Crusader victory	1097
3	Tarsus	City siege	Crusader victory	1097
4	Antioch	City siege	Crusader victory	1098
5	Jerusalem	City siege	Crusader victory	1099
6	Ashkelon	Battle	Crusader victory	1099
7	Melitene	Battle	Crusader defeat	1100
8	Mersivan	Battle	Crusader defeat	1101
9	Eregli	Ambush/battle	Crusader defeat	1101
10	Ramleh	Battle	Crusader defeat	1102

1066
BATTLE OF HASTINGS

The events that led to the bloody Battle of Hastings in 1066, culminating in the death of King Harold, are depicted in the Bayeux Tapestry, completed in 1080.

1097
CHRISTIAN SOLDIERS

The first victory for the Crusaders occurred in 1097 when they laid siege to the city of Nicaea in Asia Minor.

1148 The arrival of sugar
Sugar, previously almost unknown in Europe, was brought back by the Crusaders returning from the Middle East.

1000 |

1050 |

1199 |

1000 The first journey to North America
Leif Ericsson set sail from his Viking settlement in Greenland, and sighted North America.

1088
BOLOGNA UNIVERSITY

This was the first teaching institution in Europe to act independently of the Church. It became famous for its modern approach to teaching law.

1192 Shogun
Minamoto Yoritomo became Shogun (great general). This title was given to him by the Emperor of Japan for restoring peace after a long civil war.

BOLOGNA UNIVERSITY

OLDEST UNIVERSITIES IN THE WORLD

	UNIVERSITY/COUNTRY	YEAR FOUNDED
1	Quaraouyine, Fez, Morocco	859
2	Al-Azhar, Cairo, Egypt	970
3	Parma, Italy	1064
4	Bologna, Italy	1088
5	Modena, Italy	1175
6 =	Paris, France	1200
=	Perugia, Italy	1200
8	Padua, Italy	1222
9	Naples, Italy	1224
10	Siena, Italy	1240

THE CAPTURE OF CONSTANTINOPLE, 4TH CRUSADE, 1203–4

TOP 10 ★
OLDEST NATIONAL LIBRARIES

	LIBRARY/LOCATION	YEAR FOUNDED
1	National Library of the Czech Republic, Prague	1366
2	National Library of Austria, Vienna	1368
3	Biblioteca Nazionale Marciana, Venice	1468
4	National Library of France, Paris	1480
5	National Library of Malta, Valetta	1555
6	Bayericsche Staatsbibliothek, Munich	1558
7	National Library of Belgium, Brussels	1559
8	National Library of Croatia, Zagreb	1606
9	National Library of Finland, Helsinki	1640
10	National Library of Denmark, Copenhagen	1653

1206 Birth of the Mongol Empire
After being elected as supreme leader, Genghis Khan increased the size of the Mongol Empire to include parts of Europe and most of Central Asia.

1271 Marco Polo
Marco Polo was only a teenager when he set out for China. He spent 17 years there, and was offered the position of governor by the Mongol Emperor.

1366
HISTORIC LIBRARY
The oldest library in the world was founded when Charles IV donated a set of codices to Prague University.

1368 The Ming Dynasty
After defeating the Mongols and driving them out of China, Hong Wu became the new leader of the country and the founder of the Ming Dynasty.

|1250 |1300 |1350 |**1399**

1202
NATURAL DISASTER
Violent earthquakes cause devastation through the collapse of structures and generate catastrophic tidal waves. The worst-ever earthquake occurred in 1202 and killed over 1 million people.

1300 Invention of the clock
The first mechanical clocks introduced in Europe were not fully accurate and had to be reset every day with the help of a sundial.

1347 The Black Death
The plague, spread by fleas living on rats, started in India at the end of the 1200s. It spread through Asia and reached Europe in the mid-14th century.

1378
MOORISH LEGACY
The Alhambra Palace built in Grenada was the stronghold of the last Moorish rulers of Spain.

THE 10 ★
WORST EARTHQUAKES

	LOCATION	DATE	APPROX. NO. OF DEATHS
1	Near East/Mediterranean	May 20, 1202	1,100,000
2	Shenshi, China	Feb 2, 1556	820,000
3	Calcutta, India	Oct 11, 1737	300,000
4	Antioch, Syria	May 20, 526	250,000
5	Tang-shan, China	Jul 28, 1976	242,419
6	Nan-Shan, China	May 22, 1927	200,000
7	Yeddo, Japan	(date unknown) 1703	190,000
8	Kansu, China	Dec 16, 1920	180,000
9	Messina, Italy	Dec 28, 1908	160,000
10	Tokyo/Yokohama, Japan	Sep 1, 1923	142,807

Did You Know? The earliest known illustration of a pair of eyeglasses appeared in a fresco painted in Treviso, Italy, in 1352.

Millennium Milestones

THE 10 ★
LONGEST WARS OF ALL TIME

	WAR/COMBATANTS	DATES	DURATION (YEARS)
1	**Hundred Years War**, France v England	1338–1453	115
2 =	**Wars of the Roses**, Lancaster v York	1455–85	30
=	**Thirty Years War**, Catholic v Protestant	1618–48	30
4	**Peloponnesian War**, Peloponnesian League (Sparta, Corinth, etc) v Delian League (Athens, etc)	431–404BC	27
5 =	**First Punic War**, Rome v Carthage	264–241BC	23
=	**Napoleonic Wars**, France v other European countries	1792–1815	23
7 =	**Greco-Persian Wars**, Greece v Persia	499–478BC	21
=	**Second Great Northern War**, Russia v Sweden and War Baltic states	1700–21	21
9	**Vietnam War**, South Vietnam (with US support) v North Vietnam	1957–75	18
10	**Second Punic War**, Rome v Carthage	218–201BC	17

EARLY PRINTING PRESS

1431 Joan of Arc was executed
Joan of Arc, leader of the rebel forces fighting for French independence, was burned at the stake by the English.

1400	1410	1420	1430	1440

1418 Exploration of Africa
Prince Henry the Navigator of Portugal encouraged exploration of the African coast by creating a navigation school and sponsoring maritime enterprises. By the time of Henry's death, the Portuguese had explored the whole of the west coast of Africa.

1439 COMPLETION OF NOTRE DAME
Although construction of the Notre Dame Cathedral in Strasbourg started in 1015, it was not until 1439 that the spire was completed.

TOP 10 ★
TALLEST BUILDINGS IN THE MEDIEVAL WORLD

	BUILDING/LOCATION	YEAR	FT	M
1	**Lincoln Cathedral**, England	*c.*1307	525	160
2	**Rouen Cathedral**, France	1530	512	156
3	**St. Pierre Church**, Beauvais, France	1568	502	153
4	**St. Peter's Church**, Louvain, Flanders (Belgium)	1497	500	152
5	**St. Paul's Cathedral**, London, England	1315	489	149
6	**Great Pyramid**, Giza, Egypt	*c.*2580BC	481	146
7	**Notre Dame Cathedral**, Strasbourg, France	1439	466	142
8	**St. Stephen's Cathedral**, Vienna, Austria	1433	440	136
9	**Amiens Cathedral**, France	1260	440	134
10	**Chartres Cathedral**, France	1513?	427	130

THE 10 ★
FIRST CITIES TO HAVE PRINTING PRESSES

	CITY/COUNTRY	YEAR
1	**Mainz**, Germany	1450
2	**Rome**, Italy	1467
3	**Pilsen**, Bohemia	1468
4	**Venice**, Italy	1469
5 =	**Paris**, France	1470
=	**Nuremberg**, Germany	1470
=	**Utrecht**, Netherlands	1470
8 =	**Milan**, Italy	1471
=	**Naples**, Italy	1471
=	**Florence**, Italy	1471

THE 10 ★
FIRST KNOWN EXPLORERS TO LAND IN THE AMERICAS

	EXPLORER/NATIONALITY	DISCOVERY/EXPLORATION	YEAR
1	**Christopher Columbus**, Italian	West Indies	1492
2	**John Cabot**, Italian/English	Nova Scotia/Newfoundland	1497
3	**Alonso de Hojeda**, Spanish	Brazil	1499
4	**Vicente Yañez Pinzón**, Spanish	Amazon	1500
5	**Pedro Alvarez Cabral**, Portuguese	Brazil	1500
6	**Gaspar Corte Real**, Portuguese	Labrador	1500
7	**Rodrigo de Bastidas**, Spanish	Central America	1501
8	**Vasco Nuñez de Balboa**, Spanish	Panama	1513
9	**Juan Ponce de León**, Spanish	Florida	1513
10	**Juan Díaz de Solís**, Spanish	Río de la Plata	1515

1450
FIRST PRINTING PRESS
After developing a movable type, Johannes Gutenberg printed the first large book in Europe: a Bible.

1462 Ivan III became Prince of Russia
The reign of Ivan III was the first step toward turning Russia into one of the greatest powers in Europe. He declared himself "Tsar of all the Russias" in 1480.

1478 Start of the Renaissance
After becoming Lord of Florence in 1469, Lorenzo de'Medici started a program of renewal of the city which marked the beginning of the Renaissance. Under his rule, Florence became a center of artistic and intellectual excellence.

1450 | 1470 | 1480 | 1490 | 1499

1453
HUNDRED YEARS WAR ENDS
The war began with England's claims over France. It ended in 1453 after France recaptured most of its territories.

1478 Spanish Inquisition begins
On the orders of Pope Sixtus IV (1471–84), heretics (initially Jews) were hunted down and punished. Many people were burned to death.

1492
DISCOVERY OF AMERICA
In the search for a more direct route to Asia, Christopher Columbus on the Santa Maria reached the Americas.

TOP 10 ★
MOST EXPENSIVE RENAISSANCE PAINTINGS EVER SOLD AT AUCTION

	PAINTING/ARTIST/SALE	PRICE ($)
1	*Portrait of Duke Cosimo I de Medici*, Jacopo da Carucci (Pontormo), Christie's, New York, May 31, 1989	32,000,000
2	*Adoration of the Magi*, Andrea Mantegna, Christie's, London, Apr 18, 1985	9,525,000
3	*Venus and Adonis*, Titian, Christie's, London, Dec 13, 1991	8,250,000
4	*Study for Head and Hand of an Apostle*, Raphael, Christie's, London, Dec 13, 1996	7,920,000
5	*Argonauts in Colchis*, Bartolomeo di Giovanni, Sotheby's, London, Dec 6, 1989	7,268,000
6	*Christ and Woman of Samaria*, Michelangelo, Sotheby's, New York, Jan 28, 1998	6,800,000
7	*Departure of the Argonauts*, Master of 1487, Sotheby's, London, Dec 6, 1989	6,636,000
8	*Meeting of Infant St. John with Holy Family*, Michelangelo, Christie's, London, July 6, 1993	5,586,000
9	*Etude de Draperie*, Leonardo da Vinci, Sotheby's, Monaco, Dec 1, 1989	5,249,000
10	*La Flagellation du Christ*, Master of the Karlsruhe Passion, Cornette de St. Cyr, Paris, Dec 9, 1998	4,455,000

SANTA MARIA

Did You Know? Golf was banned in England in 1457 because it was considered a distraction from the serious pursuit of archery.

1504 MICHELANGELO'S DAVID

The colossal marble statue of David (14 ft 3 in/4.34 m) was Michelangelo's first public commission. It became the symbol of Florence and was placed outside the Palazzo Signoria. In the 19th century the statue was moved to the Accademia.

THE 10 ★
FIRST PEOPLE TO DISCOVER ELEMENTS*

	DISCOVERER/COUNTRY	ELEMENT	YEAR
1	Julius Caesar Scaliger (1484–1558), Italy	Platinum	1557
2	Hennig Brand (?–c.1692), Germany	Phosforus	1669
3	Georg Brandt (1694–1768), Sweden	Cobalt	1735/39
4	Andreas Marggraf (1709–82), Germany	Zinc	1746
5	Axel Cronstedt (1722–65), Sweden	Nickel	1751
6	Henry Cavendish (1731–1810), England	Hydrogen	1766
7	Daniel Rutherford (1749–1819), Scotland	Nitrogen	1772
8 =	Carl Wilhelm Scheele (1742–86), Sweden	Chlorine	1774
=	Johan Gahn (1745–1818), Sweden	Manganese	1774
=	Joseph Priestley (1733–1809), England; Carl Wilhelm Scheele (1742–86), Sweden	Oxygen	1774

* Named discoverers, 16th century onward

1519–21 End of the Aztec Empire
Conquistador Hernán Cortés, welcomed by Emperor Montezuma of Mexico as a reincarnated Aztec god, later killed the emperor and declared himself governor.

1536 Dissolution of the Monasteries
Henry VIII – who assumed full control of the English Church in 1534 – began the dissolution of the monasteries in 1536. This decree led to severe hardship for the nation's poor.

1500 | 1510 | 1520 | 1530 | 1540 |

1506 Work on St. Peter's Basilica began
Construction of St. Peter's Basilica in Rome took over a century, reaching completion in 1612. It remains one of the largest Christian churches in the world.

1522 First circumnavigation of the world
Sebastian del Cano completed the around-the-world voyage begun by Ferdinand Magellan, who was killed in the Philippines.

1545 GREAT GARDENS

Botanical gardens provide an environment where plants from around the world can be grown, studied, and displayed to the public.

THE GARDENS AT PADUA

THE 10 ★
FIRST BOTANICAL GARDENS

	CITY/COUNTRY	YEAR
1	**Padua**, Italy	1545
2	**Montpelier**, France	1558
3	**Leyden**, Netherlands	1577
4	**Leipzig**, Germany	1580
5	**Oxford**, England	1621
6	**Paris**, France	1624
7	**Jena**, Germany	1629
8	**Uppsala**, Sweden	1657
9	**Edinburgh**, Scotland	1670
10	**Chelsea**, London, England	1673

THE 10 ★
FIRST BRITISH AMERICAN COLONIES

	COLONY	MODERN STATE	FOUNDER	DATE
1	Roanoke	North Carolina	Sir Walter Raleigh	July 1585
2	Jamestown	Virginia	John Smith	May 1607
3	Plymouth	Massachusetts	William Bradford	Dec 1620
4	New Amsterdam	New York	Peter Minuit*	May 1626
5	New Hampshire	–	John Mason	Nov 1629
6	Massachusetts Bay	Massachusetts	John Winthrop	June 1630
7	Maryland	–	George Calvert	Feb 1634
8	Connecticut	–	Thomas Hooker	May 1636
9	Rhode Island	–	Roger Williams	June 1636
10	Delaware	–	Peter Minuit*	Mar 1638

* Founded by Holland (No. 4) and Sweden (No. 10), but later ceded to Britain

THE 10 ★
FIRST SHAKESPEARE PLAYS

	PLAY	APPROX. YEAR WRITTEN
1	Titus Andronicus	1588–90
2	Love's Labour's Lost	1590
3	Henry VI, Parts I–III	1590–91
4=	The Comedy of Errors	1591
=	Richard III	1591
=	Romeo and Juliet	1591
7	The Two Gentlemen of Verona	1592–93
8	A Midsummer Night's Dream	1593–94
9	Richard II	1594
10	King John	1595

1557 PLATINUM DISCOVERED
Platinum is renowned as the world's noblest metal: it resists tarnishing and is highly durable.

PLATINUM

1585 THE LOST COLONY
Roanoke, founded by Sir Walter Raleigh in 1585, was not revisited until 1590, when, mysteriously, no trace was found of the settlers.

1588 SHAKESPEARE'S FIRST PLAY
William Shakespeare, universally regarded as the greatest playwright that ever lived, began work on Titus Andronicus in 1588.

|1550 |1560 |1570 |1580 |1590 |1599

1558 Elizabeth I crowned Elizabeth I, daughter of Henry VIII, was Queen of England until her death in 1603. She turned England into one of the world's most powerful nations.

1572 St. Bartholomew's Day Massacre Catholic King Charles IX instigated the murder of thousands of Protestants who had come to Paris for the wedding of Henry of Navarre.

1588 SPANISH ARMADA
Phillip II of Spain's "Invincible Armada" was scattered by the English fleet led by Francis Drake. After fleeing to the North Sea, many of the ships were wrecked by storms.

THE 10 ★
WORST PRE-20TH-CENTURY MARINE DISASTERS

	DATE/INCIDENT	NO. KILLED
1	Aug–Oct 1588, Spanish Armada destroyed off the British coast	c.4,000
2=	Aug 22, 1711, Eight British ships sank in storms off Labrador	over 2,000
=	Dec 4, 1811, British warships St. George, Defence, and Hero stranded off the Jutland coast	over 2,000
4	Apr 27, 1865, Sultana, a Mississippi River steamboat, destroyed by a boiler explosion near Memphis, Tennessee	1,547
5	July 31, 1715, Two Spanish treasure vessels sank in a hurricane at Capitanas	over 1,000
6	Aug 29, 1782, British warship Royal George wrecked off the British coast	over 900
7	Sept 3, 1878, Pleasure steamer Princess Alice collided with the Bywell Castle on the Thames River near Woolwich, London	786
8	Mar 17, 1800, British warship Queen Charlotte caught fire in Livorno Harbor, Italy	over 700
9	Sept 19, 1890, Turkish frigate wrecked at Ertogrul, off the Japanese coast	587
10	Mar 17, 1891, British steamer Utopia collided with British warship Amson off Gibraltar	576

1610
GALILEO

Galileo's discovery of the four satellites of Jupiter proved for the first time that there were celestial bodies rotating around a body other than the Earth.

THE 10 ★
FIRST PLANETARY MOONS TO BE DISCOVERED

	MOON	PLANET	DISCOVERER/COUNTRY	YEAR
1	Moon	Earth	–	Ancient
2=	Io	Jupiter	Galileo Galilei, Italy	1610
=	Europa	Jupiter	Galileo Galilei	1610
=	Ganymede	Jupiter	Galileo Galilei	1610
=	Callisto	Jupiter	Galileo Galilei	1610
6	Titan	Saturn	Christian Huygens, Holland	1655
7	Iapetus	Saturn	Giovanni Cassini, Italy/France	1671
8	Rhea	Saturn	Giovanni Cassini	1672
9=	Tethys	Saturn	Giovanni Cassini	1684
=	Dione	Saturn	Giovanni Cassini	1684

1612 Tobacco introduced in America
Tobacco was planted in Virginia by Englishman John Rolfe. This led to a successful export trade, affluence for Virginia, and eventually slavery.

1633 Galileo sentenced by the Inquisition
Galileo's theory that the Earth moves round the Sun enraged the Catholic Church, which forced him to deny his beliefs.

1642 Discovery of New Zealand
Dutch sailor Abel Tasman discovered Tasmania and also New Zealand.

1600| **1620|**   **1630|**   **1640|**

1605
LEO XI

During Pope Leo XI's coronation on April 17, 1605, he caught the cold that was to cost him his life after just 26 days in office.

1620 Mayflower
The Pilgrims – English religious refugees – set sail for America aboard the *Mayflower*. They landed at what is today Plymouth, Massachusetts.

1636
HARVARD UNIVERSITY

Harvard University was named in 1638 after John Harvard, who left his library and half his estate to the institution.

TOP 10 ★
SHORTEST-SERVING POPES

	POPE	YEAR IN OFFICE	DURATION (DAYS)
1	Urban VII	1590	12
2	Valentine	827	c.14
3	Boniface VI	896	15
4	Celestine IV	1241	16
5	Sisinnius	708	20
6	Sylvester III	1045	21
7	Theodore II	897	c.21
8	Marcellus II	1555	22
9	Damasus II	1048	23
10=	Pius III	1503	26
=	Leo XI	1605	26

TOP 10 ★
OLDEST UNIVERSITIES AND COLLEGES IN THE US

	UNIVERSITY/LOCATION	YEAR CHARTERED
1	Harvard University, Massachusetts	1636
2	College of William & Mary, Virginia	1692
3	Yale University, Connecticut	1701
4	University of Pennsylvania, Pennsylvania	1740
5	Moravian College, Pennsylvania	1742
6	Princeton University, New Jersey	1746
7	Washington & Lee University, Virginia	1749
8	Columbia University, New York (originally Kings' College)	1754
9	Brown University, Rhode Island	1764
10	Rutgers, the State University of New Jersey	1766

Source: *National Center For Educational Statistics*

Did You Know? Popcorn was first eaten by Europeans in 1621, when settlers at Plymouth received a deerskin bag of "popped corn" from Native American Quadequina.

1669
REMBRANDT'S DEATH

Although Rembrandt had been Holland's foremost artist, with a constant flow of important commissions, by the early 1660s he had to auction his house and goods to pay some of his debts.

TOP 10 ★
MOST EXPENSIVE REMBRANDT PAINTINGS EVER SOLD AT AUCTION

PAINTING/SALE	PRICE ($)	PAINTING/SALE	PRICE ($)
1 *Portrait of a Girl Wearing a Gold-trimmed Cloak*, Sotheby's, London, Dec 10, 1986	9,372,000	**6** *Aristotle Contemplating the Bust of Homer*, Parke-Bernet Galleries, New York, Nov 15, 1961	2,300,000
2 *Portrait of Bearded Man in Red Coat*, Sotheby's, New York, Jan 30, 1998	8,250,000	**7** *Portrait of the Artist's Son Titus*, Christie's, London, Mar 19, 1965	2,234,400
3 *Portrait of Johannes Uyittenbogaert*, Sotheby's, London, July 8, 1992	7,296,000	**8** *The Ramparts near the Bulwark beside the St. Anthonlespoort*, Christie's, London, July 6, 1987	2,012,500
4 *Cupid Blowing a Soap Bubble*, Sotheby's, London, Dec 6, 1995	5,320,000	**9** *Self-portrait*, Christie's, London, June 27, 1969	1,990,400
5 *Bust-length Portrait of Old Man with Beard*, Sotheby's, New York, Jan 30, 1997	2,700,000	**10** *View of Houtewaal near the St. Anthonlespoort*, Sotheby's, New York, Nov 17, 1986	870,392

1652 Cape Town founded
Jan Van Riebeeck founded this trading post for ships traveling between Europe and Asia.

1679 First European to see the Niagara Falls
Father Hennepin, a Jesuit missionary, witnessed the beauty of the falls.

|1660 |1670 |1680 |1690 |**1699**

1653
TAJ MAHAL COMPLETED

The Taj Mahal was commissioned in 1630 by Shah Jehan in honor of his beloved wife Mumtaz, who had died in childbirth.

1687
NEWTON'S THEORY

Isaac Newton published his theory on gravity, according to which all bodies gravitate toward the center of a celestial body such as the Earth or the Moon.

MILLENNIUM MILESTONES

1711
ST. PAUL'S FINISHED

Although the first service in St. Paul's Cathedral, London, was held in 1697, work on the building's construction went on until 1711. It took a total of 35 years to build the cathedral, which was designed by Sir Christopher Wren.

ST. PAUL'S CATHEDRAL, LONDON

MOZART

1703 Birth of St. Petersburg
Peter the Great celebrated the new wealth and political stability of his country by creating a new capital on the Baltic coast – St. Petersburg.

1716 Yoshimune became Shogun
Yoshimune was an enlightened and capable administrator who lifted the ban on traveling abroad and making contact with foreign states, and brought European influences into Japan.

1700	1710	1720	1730	1740	1749

1709 Invention of the piano
Florentine harpsichord maker Bartolomeo Cristofori invented the piano. It proved immediately popular, and soon supplanted all its predecessors.

1715
LOUIS XIV DIED

Louis XIV, also known as the Sun King, was an enthusiastic patron of the arts, and also encouraged scientific and technological research.

1747 Cure for scurvy discovered
James Lind, an English naval surgeon, discovered that a high consumption of citrus fruit was instrumental in preventing scurvy, the disease that killed sailors on long voyages.

A PORTRAIT OF LOUIS XIV

TOP 10 ★
LONGEST-REIGNING MONARCHS

	MONARCH/COUNTRY	REIGN	YEARS
1	**Louis XIV**, France	1643–1715	72
2	**John II**, Liechtenstein	1858–1929	71
3	**Franz-Josef**, Austria–Hungary	1848–1916	67
4	**Victoria**, Great Britain	1837–1901	63
5	**Hirohito**, Japan	1926–89	62
6	**Kangxi**, China	1662–1722	61
7	**Qianlong**, China	1736–96	60
8	**George III**, Great Britain	1760–1820	59
9	**Louis XV**, France	1715–74	59
10	**Pedro II**, Brazil	1831–89	58

Some authorities claim a 73-year reign for Alfonso I of Portugal, but he ruled as count before becoming king in 1139, and so reigned for just 46 years.

18

Did You Know? Louis XV was the first person to use an elevator: in 1743 his "flying chair" carried him between the floors of Versailles palace.

THE 10 ★
FIRST MOZART WORKS*

	TITLE/KOCHEL NO.	KEY
1	Minuet for Harpsichord, 1	G Major
2	Andante for Harpsichord, 1	C Major
3	Allegro for Harpsichord, 1b	C Major
4	Allegro for Harpsichord, 1c	F Major
5	Minuet for Harpsichord, 1d	F Major
6	Minuet for Harpsichord, 1e	G Major
7	Minuet for Harpsichord, 1f	C Major
8	Minuet for Harpsichord, 2	F Major
9	Allegro for Harpsichord, 3	B Flat Major
10	Minuet for Harpsichord, 4	F Major

* Based on order of Kochel catalogue numbers

1783
FIRST MANNED BALLOON FLIGHT

Joseph and Etienne Montgolfier's balloon was launched in Paris on September 21, 1783. It was not flown by the brothers themselves, but by Pilâtre de Rozier and François Laurent.

EXECUTION OF LOUIS XVI IN 1793, ON CHARGES OF COUNTER-REVOLUTION

1789
FRENCH REVOLUTION

On July 14, 1789, an angry mob stormed the Bastille prison, symbol of the monarchic tyranny.

1756
MOZART'S BIRTH

Wolfgang Amadeus Mozart was born in Salzburg. A child prodigy, he completed his first compositions at the age of 4.

|1750 |1760 |1770 |1780 |1790 |1799

1776
US INDEPENDENCE

On July 4, 1776, the Declaration of Independence was signed by all 13 US states. It pronounced the 13 rebellious colonies to be "free and independent states."

1799 Rosetta Stone found
This Egyptian artifact, which had different languages carved on it, enabled linguists to decipher two ancient scripts written in hieroglyphics.

THE 10 ★
YOUNGEST TO SIGN THE DECLARATION OF INDEPENDENCE

	SIGNER/BIRTHDATE	AGE AT SIGNING
1	Edward Rutledge, Nov 23, 1749	26
2	Thomas Lynch, Jr., Aug 5, 1749	26
3	Thomas Heyward, Jr., July 28, 1746	29
4	Benjamin Rush, Dec 24, 1745	30
5	Elbridge Gerry, July 17, 1744	31
6	Thomas Jefferson, Apr 13, 1743	33
7	Thomas Stone*, 1743	33
8	James Wilson, Sept 14, 1742	33
9	William Hooper, June 28, 1742	34
10	Arthur Middleton, June 26, 1742	34

* Precise birthdate unknown

TOP 10 ★
MOST HIGHLY POPULATED COUNTRIES, 1800

	COUNTRY	POPULATION
1	China	295,753,000
2	India	131,000,000
3	Russia	33,000,000
4	France	27,349,000
5	Germany	24,833,000
6	Turkey	20,912,000
7	Vietnam	17,000,000
8	Japan	15,000,000
9	Italy	14,134,000
10	Indonesia	13,476,000

THE 10 ★
FIRST DINOSAURS TO BE NAMED

	NAME	MEANING	NAMED BY	YEAR
1	Megalosaurus	Great lizard	William Buckland	1824
2	Iguanodon	Iguana tooth	Gideon Mantell	1825
3	Hylaeosaurus	Woodland lizard	Gideon Mantell	1832
4	Macrodontophion	Large tooth snake	A. Zborzewski	1834
5 =	Thecodontosaurus	Socket-toothed lizard	Samuel Stutchbury and H. Riley	1836
=	Palaeosaurus	Ancient lizard	Samuel Stutchbury and H. Riley	1836
7	Plateosaurus	Flat lizard	Hermann von Meyer	1837
8 =	Cladeiodon	Branch tooth	Richard Owen	1841
=	Cetiosaurus	Whale lizard	Richard Owen	1841
10	Pelorosaurus	Monstrous lizard	Gideon Mantell	1850

1800
POPULATION GROWTH
The vast populations of both China and India dwarfed those of all the other countries in the world.

1812 *Grimms' Fairy Tales*
Jakob and Wilhelm Grimm, German brothers, started writing down some of the world's best-known fairy tales including *Hansel and Gretel* and *Snow White*.

1800   1805 | 1810 | 1815 | 1819 |

1804
FIRST AUSTRALIAN CITIES
Although Sydney was founded in 1788, extensive civic developments did not start in Australia until the 1800s.

1804 Napoleon declared himself Emperor of France
Napoleon Bonaparte expanded France's empire as far as the Russian border, and introduced the Napoleonic code of law.

1815
BATTLE OF WATERLOO
Napoleon's imperialistic invasions came to an end near Waterloo, in Belgium, where the French army was defeated by British and German forces.

THE 10 ★
FIRST CITIES IN AUSTRALIA

	CITY/STATE	FOUNDED
1	**Sydney**, New South Wales	Jan 26, 1788
2	**Hobart**, Tasmania	Feb 26, 1804
3	**Newcastle**, New South Wales	Apr 19, 1804
4	**Brisbane**, Queensland	Sept 28, 1824
5	**Canberra**, Australian Capital Territory	May 3, 1825
6	**Perth**, Western Australia	Aug 12, 1829
7	**Bathurst**, New South Wales	Jan 23, 1833
8	**Wollongong**, New South Wales	Nov 28, 1834
9	**Adelaide**, South Australia	Aug 21, 1836
10	**Geelong**, Victoria	Mar 8, 1837

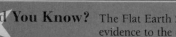

Did You Know? The Flat Earth Society was founded in 1800. Today, despite 200 years of evidence to the contrary, its members continue to believe that the Earth is flat.

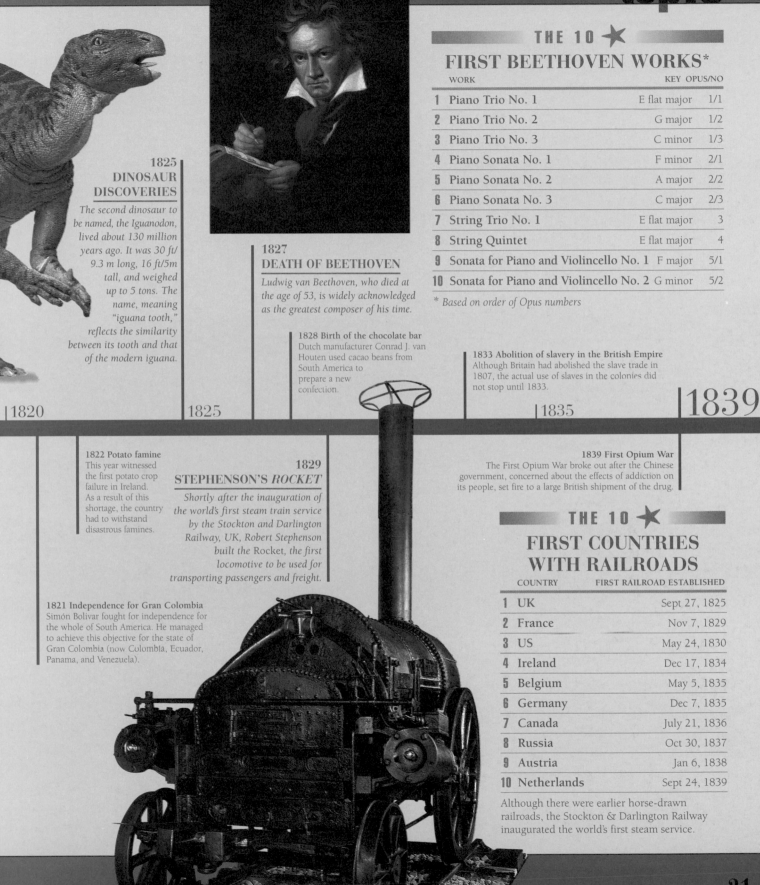

THE 10 ★
FIRST BEETHOVEN WORKS*

	WORK	KEY	OPUS/NO
1	Piano Trio No. 1	E flat major	1/1
2	Piano Trio No. 2	G major	1/2
3	Piano Trio No. 3	C minor	1/3
4	Piano Sonata No. 1	F minor	2/1
5	Piano Sonata No. 2	A major	2/2
6	Piano Sonata No. 3	C major	2/3
7	String Trio No. 1	E flat major	3
8	String Quintet	E flat major	4
9	Sonata for Piano and Violincello No. 1	F major	5/1
10	Sonata for Piano and Violincello No. 2	G minor	5/2

* Based on order of Opus numbers

1825
DINOSAUR DISCOVERIES

The second dinosaur to be named, the Iguanodon, lived about 130 million years ago. It was 30 ft/ 9.3 m long, 16 ft/5m tall, and weighed up to 5 tons. The name, meaning "iguana tooth," reflects the similarity between its tooth and that of the modern iguana.

1827
DEATH OF BEETHOVEN

Ludwig van Beethoven, who died at the age of 53, is widely acknowledged as the greatest composer of his time.

1828 Birth of the chocolate bar
Dutch manufacturer Conrad J. van Houten used cacao beans from South America to prepare a new confection.

1833 Abolition of slavery in the British Empire
Although Britain had abolished the slave trade in 1807, the actual use of slaves in the colonies did not stop until 1833.

1820 **1825** **1835** **1839**

1822 Potato famine
This year witnessed the first potato crop failure in Ireland. As a result of this shortage, the country had to withstand disastrous famines.

1829
STEPHENSON'S *ROCKET*

Shortly after the inauguration of the world's first steam train service by the Stockton and Darlington Railway, UK, Robert Stephenson built the Rocket, the first locomotive to be used for transporting passengers and freight.

1821 Independence for Gran Colombia
Simón Bolivar fought for independence for the whole of South America. He managed to achieve this objective for the state of Gran Colombia (now Colombia, Ecuador, Panama, and Venezuela).

1839 First Opium War
The First Opium War broke out after the Chinese government, concerned about the effects of addiction on its people, set fire to a large British shipment of the drug.

THE 10 ★
FIRST COUNTRIES WITH RAILROADS

	COUNTRY	FIRST RAILROAD ESTABLISHED
1	UK	Sept 27, 1825
2	France	Nov 7, 1829
3	US	May 24, 1830
4	Ireland	Dec 17, 1834
5	Belgium	May 5, 1835
6	Germany	Dec 7, 1835
7	Canada	July 21, 1836
8	Russia	Oct 30, 1837
9	Austria	Jan 6, 1838
10	Netherlands	Sept 24, 1839

Although there were earlier horse-drawn railroads, the Stockton & Darlington Railway inaugurated the world's first steam service.

	COUNTRY	STAMPS FIRST ISSUED
1	Great Britain	1840
2	US (New York City)	1842
3	Switzerland (Zurich)	1843
4	Brazil	1843
5	Mauritius	1847
6	Bermuda	1848
7	France	1849
8	Belgium	1849
9	Germany (Bavaria)	1849
10	Spain	1850

ROME

1840
WORLD'S FIRST STAMP

The first postage stamp ever printed, the Penny Black, portrayed Queen Victoria; it was placed on sale on May 1, 1840.

1848 *The Communist Manifesto*
Karl Marx and Friedrich Engels published this book, in which they advocated the rebellion of the working class against capitalists, and the birth of a classless society based on sharing.

1850
POPULATION EXPANSION

Rome passed the 1 million population mark in ancient times. In the 1850s–70s, many more cities grew to reach this size.

1840   1845 | 1850   1854 |

1840
BIRTH OF MONET

Claude Monet's painting Impression, Sunrise is regarded as the major influence on the development of the artistic movement known as Impressionism.

1849 California Gold Rush
Gold was found at Sutter's Mill, California, in 1848. The following year, thousands of prospectors moved to the area hoping to make their fortunes.

1853
CRIMEAN WAR

The Crimean War broke out between Turkey and Russia over the protection of the holy places in Palestine. Medical developments, such as the use of anesthesia, were features of this war, and Florence Nightingale remains famous for her nursing work.

TOP 10 ★
MOST EXPENSIVE MONET PAINTINGS EVER SOLD AT AUCTION

	PAINTING/SALE	PRICE ($)
1	*Bassin aux nymphéas et sentier au bord de l'eau*, Sotheby's, London, June 30, 1998	29,520,000
2	*Dans la prairie*, Sotheby's, London, June 30, 1998	21,840,000
3	*Le Parlement, coucher de soleil*, Christie's, New York, May 10, 1989	13,000,000
4=	*Nymphéas*, Christie's, New York, Nov 13, 1996	12,000,000
=	*Le jardin de l'artist à Vétheuil*, Christie's, New York, Nov 13, 1996	12,000,000
6	*Le Pont du Chemin de Fer à Argenteuil*, Christie's, London, Nov 28, 1988	11,594,000
7=	*Le basin aux nymphéas*, Christie's, New York, Nov 11, 1992	11,000,000
=	*La Grand Canal*, Sotheby's, New York, May 13, 1998	11,000,000
9	*La Cathédrale de Rouen, effet d'après-midi, plein soleil*, Christie's, London, June 26, 1995	10,971,000
10=	*Nymphéas*, Christie's, New York, Nov 14, 1989	10,500,000
=	*La Grand Canal*, Sotheby's, New York, Nov 15, 1989	10,500,000

THE "LETHEON" ETHER INHALER OF 1847, USED TO ADMINISTER ANESTHETIC

Did You Know? The first jeans were made in 1849 by Bavarian immigrant Levi Strauss as hard-wearing attire for California gold-miners.

THE 10 ★
FIRST CITIES IN THE WORLD WITH POPULATIONS OF MORE THAN ONE MILLION

	CITY	COUNTRY	APPROX. DATE
1	Rome	Italy	133BC
2	Alexandria	Egypt	30BC
3	Angkor	Cambodia	900
4	Hangchow	China	1200
5	London	UK	1810
6	Paris	France	1850
7	Peking	China	1855
8	Canton	China	1860
9	Berlin	Prussia	1870
10	New York	US	1874

1862 Pasteurization
French chemist Louis Pasteur's discovery of the micro-organisms that sour wine and milk resulted in the pasteurization process.

1865 Antiseptic surgery
Joseph Lister adopted the antiseptic principles being used in other areas of medicine and applied them to surgery.

|1860

1865

|1869

1856
NEANDERTHAL MAN
The Neander Valley in Germany yielded the fossilized remains of a man from prehistoric times.

1861
START OF US CIVIL WAR
The war started when southern states separated from the Union in protest at Abraham Lincoln's election.

1864 Red Cross established
Jean Henri Dunant, concerned for the lack of care and assistance for war victims, established an international volunteer aid organization – the Red Cross.

THE 10 ★
WORST CIVIL WAR BATTLES

	BATTLE	DATE	CASUALTIES*
1	Gettysburg	July 1–3, 1863	51,116
2	Seven Days Battles	June 25–July 1, 1862	36,463
3	Chickamauga	Sept 19–20, 1863	34,624
4	Chancellorsville	May 1–4, 1863	29,609
5	The Wilderness#	May 5–7, 1862	25,416
6	2nd Bull Run (2nd Manassas)	Aug 27–Sept 2, 1862	25,340
7	Murfreesboro (Stone's River)	Dec 31, 1862–Jan 1, 1863	24,645
8	Shiloh (Pittsburg Landing)	Apr 6–7, 1862	23,741
9	Antietam	Sept 17, 1862	22,726
10	Fredericksburg	Dec 13, 1862	17,962

* Killed, missing, and wounded
\# Confederate totals estimated

THE BATTLE OF GETTYSBURG

1874
FIRST IMPRESSIONIST EXHIBITION

Rejected by the Salon des Artistes, a group of French artists including Monet, Pissarro, and Renoir organized their own exhibition. Some critics saw the potential of the paintings on show, and encouraged the "Impressionists" to hold further exhibitions.

THE 10 ★
FIRST "FASTEST MEN ON EARTH"*

	ATHLETE	COUNTRY	DATE	TIME SECS
1	Luther Cary	US	July 4, 1891	10.8
2	Emil Ketterer#	Germany	July 9, 1911	10.5
3	Charles Paddock#	US	June 18, 1921	10.2
4	Armin Harry	East Germany	June 21, 1960	10.0
5	Jim Hines	US	Oct 14, 1968	9.95
6	Carl Lewis	US	Sept 24, 1988	9.92
7	Leroy Burrell	US	June 14, 1991	9.90
8	Carl Lewis	US	Aug 25, 1991	9.86
9	Leroy Burrell	US	July 6, 1994	9.85
10	Donovan Bailey+	Canada	July 27, 1996	9.74

* To run 100 meters

\# Unofficial record   + Current record-holder

CHARLES PADDOCK

1877 Porfirio Diaz becomes Mexican President
A leader who brought stability and prosperity to the country, Diaz also put a stop to banditry.

1870

1870 Discovery of Troy
After analyzing Homer's *Iliad*, German archaeologist Heinrich Schliemann led an expedition to find the remains of the ancient city of Troy. He finally located it in Turkey.

1880

1879
ELECTRIC LIGHT

American Thomas Edison developed the first commercially practical incandescent lamp.

THE 10 ★
FIRST DAIMLER/BENZ CARS

	CAR	TOP SPEED MPH	KM/H	DATE
1	Benz Patent Motor Car	10	16	1886
2	Daimler Motor Carriage	11	18	1886
3	Daimler Wire Wheel Car	11	18	1889
4	Benz Viktoria	11	18	1893
5	Benz Velo	12.5	20	1894
6	Daimler Belt-Driven Car	11	18	1894
7	Daimler Phoenix	not known		1897
8	Benz Dos-à-Dos	21.5	35	1899
9	Benz Elegant	25	40	1900
10	Daimler Mercedes	43.5	70	1901

BENZ PATENT MOTOR CAR

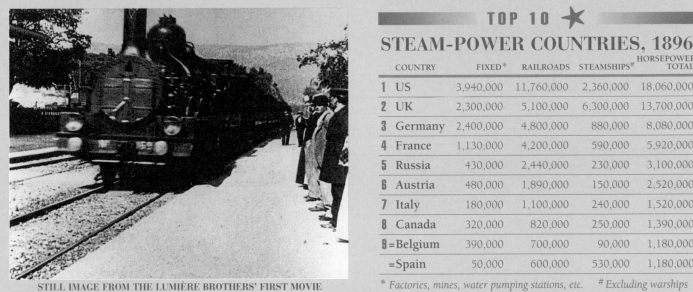

STILL IMAGE FROM THE LUMIÈRE BROTHERS' FIRST MOVIE

TOP 10 ★
STEAM-POWER COUNTRIES, 1896

	COUNTRY	FIXED*	RAILROADS	STEAMSHIPS#	HORSEPOWER TOTAL
1	US	3,940,000	11,760,000	2,360,000	18,060,000
2	UK	2,300,000	5,100,000	6,300,000	13,700,000
3	Germany	2,400,000	4,800,000	880,000	8,080,000
4	France	1,130,000	4,200,000	590,000	5,920,000
5	Russia	430,000	2,440,000	230,000	3,100,000
6	Austria	480,000	1,890,000	150,000	2,520,000
7	Italy	180,000	1,100,000	240,000	1,520,000
8	Canada	320,000	820,000	250,000	1,390,000
9	=Belgium	390,000	700,000	90,000	1,180,000
	=Spain	50,000	600,000	530,000	1,180,000

* Factories, mines, water pumping stations, etc.   # Excluding warships

1891
TOP SPEED
In 1891, Luther Cary became the first person to be officially recognized as the fastest man on Earth.

1896
STEAM POWER
By now steam power was playing a major role in manufacturing and transportation during the Industrial Revolution.

|1885 |1890 |1895 |1899

1889 Eiffel Tower
The Eiffel Tower was built by French engineer Gustave Eiffel for the Paris Exposition.

1895
INVENTION OF MOVIES
French brothers Louis and Auguste Lumière developed the world's first motion-picture camera and used it to record a train approaching a station.

1896
FIRST MODERN OLYMPICS
It was Pierre de Coubertin, a young French nobleman, who revived the Olympic Games. At the first games, 13 countries competed against one other in 9 different sports, including cycling, fencing, swimming, and wrestling.

1886
FIRST MOTOR CAR
The world's first gasoline-powered automobile was invented by German engineer Karl Benz. It was a three-wheeler and received its first public testing in Mannheim on July 3, 1886.

THE 10 ★
FIRST OLYMPIC GAMES

	SITE/LOCATION	NUMBER	YEAR
1	**Athens**, Greece	I	1896
2	**Paris**, France	II	1900
3	**St. Louis**, US	III	1904
4	**Athens**, Greece	–	1906
5	**London**, UK	IV	1908
6	**Stockholm**, Sweden	V	1912
7	**Antwerp**, Belgium	VII	1920
8	**Paris**, France	VIII	1924
9	**Amsterdam**, Netherlands	IX	1928
10	**Los Angeles**, US	X	1932

The so-called Intermediate or Intercalated Games of 1906 were the only ones not to be numbered.

MARATHON DAY AT THE 1896 ATHENS OLYMPICS

Did You Know? Britain's shortest-ever war broke out in 1896: it was declared against Zanzibar and ended 38 minutes later.

MOST HIGHLY POPULATED COUNTRIES, 1900

	COUNTRY	POPULATION
1	China	303,241,969
2	India	289,187,316
3	Russia	129,211,113
4	US	62,981,000
5	Germany	52,244,503
6	Austria	41,345,329
7	Japan	40,072,020
8	UK	39,824,563
9	Turkey	39,500,000
10	France	38,517,975

1900

1900
POPULATION GROWTH
China topped the 300 million mark, with India close behind.

1904 Work started on the Panama Canal
The canal created a shortcut between the Pacific and the Caribbean.

1911
MELBOURNE
Established in 1835, Melbourne became Australia's second largest city thanks to the discovery of gold there in 1851.

1914
START OF WORLD WAR I
Trench warfare dominated this war, in which millions of soldiers died.

1905|

1910|

1900
PARK ROW BUILDING
At the dawn of the 20th century, the Park Row Building in New York City was the world's tallest building.

1911 China becomes a republic
The Chinese population rebelled against the Manchu dynasty which had been in power since 1644 and declared the country a republic.

FIRST "WORLD'S TALLEST BUILDINGS" IN THE PAST 100 YEARS

	BUILDING/LOCATION	YEAR	STORYS	FT	M
1	Park Row Building, New York City	1899	29	386	118
2	City Hall, Philadelphia	1901	7	511	155
3	Singer Building*, New York City	1908	34	656	200
4	Metropolitan Life, New York City	1909	50	700	212
5	Woolworth Building, New York City	1913	59	792	241
6	40 Wall Street (with spire), New York City	1929	71	927	282
7	Chrysler Building (with spire), New York City	1930	77	1,046	319
8	Empire State Building (with spire), New York City	1931	102	1,472	449
9	World Trade Center (with spire), New York City	1973	110	1,710	521
10	Sears Tower (with spire), Chicago	1974	110	1,707	520

* Demolished 1970

MOST HIGHLY POPULATED TOWNS IN AUSTRALIA, 1911

	TOWN/STATE	POPULATION
1	Sydney, New South Wales	637,102
2	Melbourne, Victoria	591,830
3	Adelaide, South Australia	192,294
4	Brisbane, Queensland	141,342
5	Perth, Western Australia	84,580
6	Newcastle, New South Wales	65,500
7	Ballarat, Victoria	44,000
8	Bendigo, Victoria	42,000
9	Hobart, Tasmania	38,055
10	Broken Hill, New South Wales	31,000

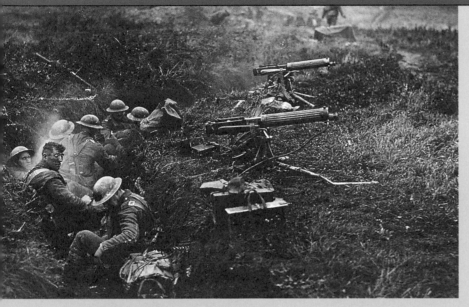

BATTLE OF CAMBRAI, WORLD WAR I

THE 10 ★
LARGEST ARMED FORCES
OF WORLD WAR I

	COUNTRY	PERSONNEL*
1	Russia	12,000,000
2	Germany	11,000,000
3	British Empire	8,904,467
4	France	8,410,000
5	Austria-Hungary	7,800,000
6	Italy	5,615,000
7	US	4,355,000
8	Turkey	2,850,000
9	Bulgaria	1,200,000
10	Japan	800,000

* Total at peak strength

1917 Russian Revolution
A simple protest for better working conditions ended with Lenin's Bolshevik party seizing power and the tsar and his family brutally killed.

1920 Gandhi's passive protest
Mahatma Gandhi took control of the Indian National Congress Party and preached a peaceful approach to independence.

1926 Invention of TV
John Logie Baird invented the first television, leading the way for the electronic models developed in the 1930s.

1929 The Great Depression
A dramatic fall in stock prices led to the collapse of the New York Stock Exchange, leaving millions bankrupt.

1915   1920   1925   1929

1915
SUCCESSFUL SILENT MOVIE

*In spite of its explicit racism, director D.W. Griffith's
The Birth of a Nation was one of the biggest box-
office money-makers in movie history.*

1928
DISCOVERY OF PENICILLIN

*Bacteriologist Alexander Fleming discovered an
antibacterial mold that he named penicillin. He was
awarded a Nobel Prize in 1945 for his work.*

TOP 10 ★
MOVIES OF THE
SILENT ERA

	MOVIE	YEAR
1	The Birth of a Nation	1915
2	The Big Parade	1925
3	Ben Hur	1926
4	The Ten Commandments	1923
5 =	The Covered Wagon	1923
=	What Price Glory?	1926
7 =	Hearts of the World	1918
=	Way Down East	1921
9 =	The Four Horsemen of the Apocalypse	1921
=	Wings	1927

Did You Know? In 1916, to revolutionize trench warfare, Jones Wister of Philadelphia invented a rifle for shooting around corners. It had a curved barrel and periscopic sights.

MILLENNIUM MILESTONES

FIRST HOSTS OF THE SOCCER WORLD CUP

	HOST COUNTRY	FINAL (WINNER FIRST)	SCORE	YEAR
1	Uruguay	Uruguay–Argentina	4-2	1930
2	Italy	Italy–Czechoslovakia	2-1	1934
3	France	Italy–Hungary	4-2	1938
4	Brazil	Uruguay–Brazil	1-2	1950
5	Switzerland	West Germany–Hungary	3-2	1954
6	Sweden	Brazil–Sweden	5-2	1958
7	Chile	Brazil–Czechoslovakia	3-1	1962
8	England	England–West Germany	4-2	1966
9	Mexico	Brazil–Italy	4-1	1970
10	West Germany	West Germany–Netherlands	2-1	1974

1930
FIRST SOCCER WORLD CUP

Following the success of the soccer matches at the 1924 Paris Olympics, the first World Cup was held in Uruguay in 1930 and attracted 13 competing nations.

FIRST ELVIS PRESLEY SINGLES RELEASED IN THE US

	TITLE	CAT. NO.	RELEASED
1	That's All Right, Mama/Blue Moon of Kentucky	Sun 209	July 1954
2	Good Rockin' Tonight/I Don't Care if the Sun Don't Shine	Sun 210	Sept 1954
3	You're a Heartbreaker/Milkcow Blues Boogie	Sun 215	Jan 1955
4	Baby Let's Play House/I'm Left, You're Right, She's Gone	Sun 217	Apr 1955
5	I Forgot to Remember to Forget/Mystery Train	Sun 223	Aug 1955
6 =	I Forgot to Remember to Forget/Mystery Train	RCA 6357	Dec 1955
=	That's All Right, Mama/Blue Moon of Kentucky	RCA 6380	Dec 1955
=	You're a Heartbreaker/Milkcow Blues Boogie	RCA 6382	Dec 1955
=	Baby Let's Play House/I'm Left, You're Right, She's Gone	RCA 6383	Dec 1955
10	Heartbreak Hotel/I Was the One	RCA 6420	Jan 1956

1930   **1935**   **1940**

1933 Nazi Germany
Adolf Hitler became Chancellor, and then *Führer* (leader) of Germany. He soon turned the country into a dictatorship, banning other political parties and persecuting minorities.

1936 Spanish Civil War
Franco led a revolt against the Republican government. By 1939, he had seized complete power over Spain.

1939
WORLD WAR II

World War II started with Hitler's invasion of Poland in 1939. France and Britain reacted against Germany's military policy and declared war. In the following year, Germany occupied Denmark, Norway, Belgium, Holland, and France. On Dec 7, 1941, Japan came in on Germany's side, and the US on the side of the Allies.

COUNTRIES SUFFERING THE GREATEST MILITARY LOSSES IN WORLD WAR II

	COUNTRY	NO. KILLED
1	USSR	13,600,000*
2	Germany	3,300,000
3	China	1,324,516
4	Japan	1,140,429
5	British Empire# (UK 264,000)	357,116
6	Romania	350,000
7	Poland	320,000
8	Yugoslavia	305,000
9	US	292,131
10	Italy	279,800

* Total, of which 7,800,000 battlefield deaths

 # Including Australia, Canada, India, New Zealand, etc.

ELVIS PRESLEY

THE 10 ★
FIRST ARTIFICIAL SATELLITES

	SATELLITE	COUNTRY OF ORIGIN	LAUNCH DATE
1	Sputnik 1	USSR	Oct 4, 1957
2	Sputnik 2	USSR	Nov 3, 1957
3	Explorer 1	US	Feb 1, 1958
4	Vanguard 1	US	Mar 17, 1958
5	Explorer 3	US	Mar 26, 1958
6	Sputnik 3	USSR	May 15, 1958
7	Explorer 4	US	July 26, 1958
8	SCORE	US	Dec 18, 1958
9	Vanguard 2	US	Feb 17, 1959
10	Discoverer 1	US	Feb 28, 1959

1953
ELVIS CUTS HIS FIRST RECORD

Arguably the most influential figure of modern popular music, Elvis Presley first entered a recording studio on July 18 to record the song My Happiness. Pictured above is the cover of Elvis's eponymous debut album, released on RCA three years after that momentous date.

1948 South African apartheid
South Africa's National Party came to power and immediately established apartheid, a policy of racial segregation and white supremacy. Apartheid was finally abolished in 1991.

1957 Laika in space
Russia became the first country to send a living creature into space in the shape of a dog called Laika.

1957
FIRST SPACE LAUNCH

Sputnik 1, the first Russian satellite, made about 1,400 orbits before burning up.

|1945 |1950 |1955 |**1959**

1945
FIRST ATOMIC BOMB

On August 6, the US dropped the world's first atomic bomb on the Japanese city of Hiroshima. About 150,000 people were killed outright, but many more died in subsequent years because of radiation exposure. The total number of victims is estimated to be 200,000.

1953 Everest conquered
On May 29, New Zealander Edmund Hillary and Nepalese Sherpa Tenzing Norgay became the first to climb Mount Everest, the highest mountain in the world at 29,028 ft (8,847 m) high.

1953
THE DISCOVERY OF DNA

Dr. James Watson, Dr. Francis Crick, and Dr. Maurice Wilkins discovered the structure of DNA and were rewarded with the Nobel Prize for Medicine in 1962.

1959
AUSTRALIAN IMMIGRANTS

After World War II, Australia started an immigration program to increase the population and boost economic strength.

TOP 10 ★
COUNTRIES OF ORIGIN OF IMMIGRANTS TO AUSTRALIA, 1959–60

	COUNTRY	IMMIGRANTS
1	UK and Ireland	37,851
2	Italy	16,126
3	West Germany	9,406
4	Netherlands	9,328
5	Yugoslavia	6,319
6	Greece	6,214
7	Austria	2,025
8	Finland	1,935
9	Poland	1,836
10	Malta	1,818

Did You Know? In 1959 – after its 1957 success with the Frisbee – the Wham-O company introduced the Hula Hoop and sold 25 million hoops in four months.

29

THE 10 ★
FIRST MOONWALKERS

	NAME/SPACECRAFT	MISSION DATES
1	Neil Armstrong, *Apollo 11*	July 16–24, 1969
2	Edwin E. Aldrin, *Apollo 11*	July 16–24, 1969
3	Charles Conrad Jr., *Apollo 12*	Nov 14–24, 1969
4	Alan L. Bean, *Apollo 12*	Nov 14–24, 1969
5	Alan B. Shepard, *Apollo 14*	Jan 31–Feb 9, 1971
6	Edgar Mitchell, *Apollo 14*	Jan 31–Feb 9, 1971
7	David R. Scott, *Apollo 15*	July 26–Aug 7, 1971
8	James B. Irwin, *Apollo 15*	July 26–Aug 7, 1971
9	John W. Young, *Apollo 16*	Apr 16–27, 1972
10	Charles M. Duke, *Apollo 16*	Apr 16–27, 1972

1969
MAN ON THE MOON

The world held its breath as Apollo 11 neared the Moon's surface. With the words "The Eagle has landed," Neil Armstrong announced to the world that he and Buzz Aldrin had arrived safely on the Moon.

1960 | 1965 | 1970

1963 JFK assassinated
President John Fitzgerald Kennedy was shot dead during a motorcade through the city of Dallas. Lee Harvey Oswald was accused of being the assassin.

1966 Chinese Cultural Revolution
Mao Zedong's Cultural Revolution was based on a rejection of old ideas, old culture, old customs, and old habits. Those who did not agree with these principles were publicly humiliated and punished by Mao's Red Guards.

1973 End of the Vietnam War
American troops withdrew from Vietnam, conceding defeat in a war that lasted eight years and cost the lives of about 2.5 million people.

1961
BERLIN WALL

In order to prevent the people of East Germany from fleeing to the West, communist authorities built a wall across Berlin. It divided the city until 1989.

THE 10 ★ FIRST APPLE COMPUTERS

	COMPUTER	LAUNCHED
1	Apple I	Mar 1976
2	Apple II	Apr 1977
3	Apple II+	June 1979
4	Apple III	Sept 1980
5	Apple IIe	Jan 1983
6	Apple Lisa	Jan 1983
7	Apple III+	Dec 1983
8	Apple Macintosh	Jan 1984
9	Apple Macintosh 128K	Jan 1984
10	Apple IIc	Apr 1984

1976
BIRTH OF THE APPLE I
The brainchild of high school friends Steven Wozniak and Steven Jobs, the first Apple computer, Apple I, was created in 1976.

1985
GORBACHEV ELECTED
Mikhail Gorbachev provided a new policy of openness and freedom of information (glasnost).

1978 First test-tube baby
The first IVF baby was born in Britain.

1989 Tiananmen square
Hundreds of thousands of students gathered in Beijing's main square to demand democratic reforms. The peaceful protest was crushed by government soldiers, and a massacre followed.

|1975 |1980 |1985   1989

1979 Khomeini in power
Ayatollah Khomeini organized a coup to depose the Shah of Iran, who had ruled since 1941. Khomeini reintroduced strict Islamic laws and turned Iran into an Islamic republic.

1980
OLDEST PRESIDENT
Ronald Reagan, pictured here with UK Prime Minister Margaret Thatcher, was the fortieth and oldest US president. He was elected in 1980 and remained in office for two terms.

1984 Ethiopian famine
After 10 years of civil war, Ethiopia was struck by a drought that led to extensive crop damage. Thousands of people died of starvation in the ensuing famine.

1989 Nintendo Gameboy
The Japanese company Nintendo introduced a hand-held video game. Today one-third of all American and Japanese homes have one.

1976 CONCORDE
The first civilian Concorde flight took place in January. The aircraft, equipped with four Rolls Royce engines, could reach a speed of 1,338 mph/ 2,155 km/h.

TOP 10 ★ OLDEST US PRESIDENTS

	PRESIDENT	AGE ON TAKING OFFICE YEARS	DAYS
1	Ronald W. Reagan	69	349
2	William H. Harrison	68	23
3	James Buchanan	65	315
4	George H.W. Bush	64	223
5	Zachary Taylor	64	100
6	Dwight D. Eisenhower	62	98
7	Andrew Jackson	61	354
8	John Adams	61	125
9	Gerald R. Ford	61	26
10	Harry Truman	60	339

TOP 10 ★

MOST RECENT
INDEPENDENT STATES

	STATE	DATE
1	Palau	Oct 1, 1994
2	Eritrea	May 24, 1993
3 =	Czech Republic	Jan 1, 1993
=	Slovakia	Jan 1, 1993
5	Federal Republic of Yugoslavia	Apr 11, 1992
6	Bosnia and Herzegovina	Apr 5, 1992
7	Kazakhstan	Dec 16, 1991
8	Ukraine	Dec 1, 1991
9	Turkmenistan	Oct 27, 1991
10	Armenia	Sept 23, 1991

1999 War in Kosovo
On March 24, in order to put an end to Serbian violence against the Albanian population of Kosovo, Nato started a program of military action against Serbia.

1990
RELEASE OF MANDELA
After 28 years in prison, Nelson Mandela became a free man. An inspirational figure to the world, Mandela was awarded the 1993 Nobel Peace Prize.

1994
MOST RECENT STATE
Palau, an archipelago in the West Pacific, became the world's most recent independent state in 1994.

1997 Hong Kong returned
On July 1, Britain honored an agreement signed in 1898 and handed the colony of Hong Kong back to China.

1990

1995|

1999

1991 Gulf War
The United Nations reacted to the invasion of Kuwait by Iraqi military forces by authorizing war on Saddam Hussein, leader of Iraq.

1993 Peace in the Middle East
President Bill Clinton brought together two historical enemies, Israel and Palestine, when he acted as mediator for a peace agreement between them.

1995 End of war in Bosnia
After three and a half years of war between several Balkan states, an agreement was finally reached at Dayton, Ohio.

1997
DEATH OF DIANA
A sea of flowers commemorated the death of Diana, Princess of Wales, in a car accident.

INTO THE FUTURE

As we enter the third millennium, we find the future is full of amazing possibilities. We can only speculate on where human innovation will take us next.

MOST POPULATED COUNTRIES IN 2050

	COUNTRY	1998	2050*
1	India	982,223,000	1,528,853,000
2	China	1,255,698,000	1,477,730,000
3	US	274,028,000	349,318,000
4	Pakistan	148,166,000	345,484,000
5	Indonesia	206,338,000	311,857,000
6	Nigeria	106,409,000	244,311,000
7	Brazil	165,851,000	244,230,000
8	Bangladesh	124,774,000	212,495,000
9	Ethiopia	59,649,000	169,446,000
10	Dem. Rep. of Congo	49,139,000	160,360,000
	World total	5,901,054,000	8,909,095,000

* Estimated population   Source: United Nations

2005 Mars visit?
The first Martian soil samples may be brought to Earth by the *Mars Surveyor*.

2022 Extinct animals cloned?
Scientists hope to unveil the first "revived" animal species, brought back from extinction through the cloning of *genetic* material.

2035 Brain stimulation?
Electrical stimulation of the brain, presently used by the medical profession, may become a widespread training technique.

2050
INDIA OVERTAKES CHINA?

By the year 2050, it is estimated that India will have a larger population than China.

2000
2010
2020
2030
2040
2050

2000
GENETIC REPLICAS

Since the arrival of Dolly the sheep, cloning technology has progressed rapidly. It seems that the new millennium marks the beginning of a clone-filled future.

2000
GOING SOLAR?

At the dawn of an era of clean transportation, scientists and engineers are increasing their efforts to create a reliable, zero-emission, solar-powered car.

2019
MAN ON MARS?

NASA plans to launch a manned mission to Mars, scheduled to land in 2019, beginning a new era of human presence on the red planet.

2045 Human clone?
Despite current legislation in some nations banning experimentation in the area of genetic modification, by 2045 scientists may be able to to create the first human clone.

The Universe & the Earth

STAR GAZING

SOLAR FLARE

The core of the Sun reaches a temperature of 27,720,000°F/ 15,400,000°C. Columns of gas, each the size of France, flare away from the fiery surface at five-minute intervals.

LARGEST BODIES IN THE SOLAR SYSTEM

	BODY	MAXIMUM DIAMETER	
		MILES	KM
1	Sun	865,036	1,392,140
2	Jupiter	88,846	142,984
3	Saturn	74,898	120,536
4	Uranus	31,763	51,118
5	Neptune	30,778	49,532
6	Earth	7,926	12,756
7	Venus	7,520	12,103
8	Mars	4,222	6,794
9	Ganymede	3,274	5,269
10	Titan	3,200	5,150

Most of the planets are visible with the naked eye and have been observed since ancient times. The exceptions are Uranus, discovered on March 13, 1781, by the British astronomer Sir William Herschel; Neptune, found by German astronomer Johann Galle on September 23, 1846; and, outside the Top 10, Pluto, located using photographic techniques by American astronomer Clyde Tombaugh. Its discovery was announced on March 13, 1930; its diameter is uncertain but is thought to be approximately 1,430 miles/ 2,302 km. Mercury, also outside the Top 10, has a diameter of 3,032 miles/4,880 km.

LONGEST DAYS IN THE SOLAR SYSTEM

	BODY	LENGTH OF DAY*		
		DAYS	HOURS	MINS
1	Venus	244	0	0
2	Mercury	58	14	0
3	Sun	25#	0	0
4	Pluto	6	9	0
5	Mars		24	37
6	Earth		23	56
7	Uranus		17	14
8	Neptune		16	7
9	Saturn		10	39
10	Jupiter		9	55

* Period of rotation, based on 23'56 Sidereal day
# Variable

BODIES FARTHEST FROM THE SUN*

	BODY	AVERAGE DISTANCE FROM THE SUN	
		MILES	KM
1	Pluto	3,675,000,000	5,914,000,000
2	Neptune	2,794,000,000	4,497,000,000
3	Uranus	1,784,000,000	2,871,000,000
4	Chiron	1,740,000,000	2,800,000,000
5	Saturn	887,000,000	1,427,000,000
6	Jupiter	483,600,000	778,300,000
7	Mars	141,600,000	227,900,000
8	Earth	92,900,000	149,600,000
9	Venus	67,200,000	108,200,000
10	Mercury	36,000,000	57,900,000

* In the Solar System, excluding satellites and asteroids

Chiron, a "mystery object" that may be either a comet or an asteroid, was discovered on November 1, 1977, by American astronomer Charles Kowal. It measures 124–186 miles/ 200–300 km in diameter.

TOP 10 STARS NEAREST TO THE EARTH*

	STAR	LIGHT YEARS	MILES (MILLIONS)	KM (MILLIONS)
1	Proxima Centauri	4.22	24,792,500	39,923,310
2	Alpha Centauri	4.35	25,556,250	41,153,175
3	Barnard's Star	5.98	35,132,500	56,573,790
4	Wolf 359	7.75	73,318,875	45,531,250
5	Lalande 21185	8.22	48,292,500	77,765,310
6	Luyten 726-8	8.43	49,526,250	79,752,015
7	Sirius	8.65	50,818,750	81,833,325
8	Ross 154	9.45	55,518,750	89,401,725
9	Ross 248	10.40	61,100,000	98,389,200
10	Epsilon Eridani	10.80	63,450,000	102,173,400

* Excluding the Sun

A spaceship traveling at 25,000 mph/40,237 km/h – which is faster than any human has yet reached in space – would take more than 113,200 years to reach the Earth's closest star, Proxima Centauri. While the nearest stars in this list lie just over four light years away from the Earth, others within the Milky Way lie at a distance of 2,500 light years.

TOP 10 ★
GALAXIES NEAREST TO THE EARTH

	GALAXY	DISTANCE (LIGHT YEARS)
1	Large Cloud of Magellan	169,000
2	Small Cloud of Magellan	190,000
3	Ursa Minor dwarf	250,000
4	Draco dwarf	260,000
5	Sculptor dwarf	280,000
6	Fornax dwarf	420,000
7 =	Leo I dwarf	750,000
=	Leo II dwarf	750,000
9	Barnard's Galaxy	1,700,000
10	Andromeda Spiral	2,200,000

These and other galaxies are members of the so-called "Local" Groups, although with vast distances such as these, "local" is clearly a relative term.

BLACK HOLE

The largest blue spot on this "false color" X-ray image of the Large Cloud of Magellan is LMC X-1, a binary system thought to consist of a black hole gulping material from its ordinary stellar companion.

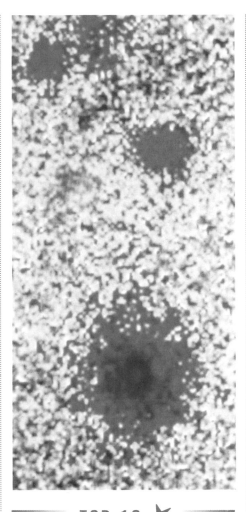

TOP 10 ★
MOST MASSIVE BODIES IN THE SOLAR SYSTEM*

	BODY	MASS#
1	Sun	332,800.000
2	Jupiter	317.828
3	Saturn	95.161
4	Neptune	17.148
5	Uranus	14.536
6	Earth	1.000
7	Venus	0.815
8	Mars	0.10745
9	Mercury	0.05527
10	Pluto	0.0022

* Excluding satellites

 # Compared with the Earth = 1; the mass of Earth is approximately 80,000,000,000,000 tons

TOP 10 ★
LONGEST YEARS IN THE SOLAR SYSTEM

	BODY	LENGTH OF YEAR* YEARS	DAYS
1	Pluto	247	256
2	Neptune	164	298
3	Uranus	84	4
4	Saturn	29	168
5	Jupiter	11	314
6	Mars		687
7	Earth		365
8	Venus		225
9	Mercury		88
10	Sun		0

* Period of orbit around the Sun, in Earth years/days

TOP 10 BRIGHTEST STARS*

(Star/constellation/apparent magnitude)

1 **Sirius**, Canis Major, -1.46 **2** **Canopus**, Carina, -0.73 **3** **Alpha Centauri**, Centaurus, -0.27 **4** **Arcturus**, Boötes, -0.04 **5** **Vega**, Lyra, +0.03 **6** **Capella**, Auriga, +0.08 **7** **Rigel**, Orion, +0.12 **8** **Procyon**, Canis Minor, +0.38 **9** **Achernar**, Eridanus, +0.46 **10** **Beta Centauri**, Centaurus, +0.61

* Excluding the Sun

Based on apparent visual magnitude as viewed from the Earth – the lower the number, the brighter the star. At its brightest, the star Betelgeuse is brighter than some of these, but because it is variable its average brightness disqualifies it from the Top 10. The absolute magnitude of Cygnus OB2 No. 12, discovered in 1992, may make it the brightest star in the galaxy, but it is 5,900 light years away.

GIANT PLANET

Jupiter is bigger than all the other planets in the Solar System put together and has 16 moons of its own.

ASTEROIDS, METEORITES & COMETS

COMETS COMING CLOSEST TO THE EARTH

	COMET	DATE*	DISTANCE AU#
1	Lexell	Jul 1, 1770	2.3
2	Tempel-Tuttle	Oct 26, 1366	3.4
3	Halley	Apr 10, 1837	5.0
4	Biela	Dec 9, 1805	5.5
5	Grischow	Feb, 8 1743	5.8
6	Pons-Winnecke	Jun 26, 1927	5.9
7	La Hire	Apr 20, 1702	6.6
8	Schwassmann-Wachmann	May 31, 1930	9.3
9	Cassini	Jan 8, 1760	10.2
10	Schweizer	Apr 29, 1853	12.6

* Of closest approach to the Earth

Astronomical Units: 1 AU = mean distance from the Earth to the Sun (92,955,900 miles/149,598,200 km)

HEAVENLY OBSERVATIONS

The most famous recorded sighting of Halley's comet occurred in 1066, when William the Conqueror regarded it as a sign of his imminent victory over King Harold at the Battle of Hastings.

MOST RECENT OBSERVATIONS OF HALLEY'S COMET

1 1986
The Japanese *Suisei* probe passed within 93,827 miles/151,000 km of its 9-mile/15-km nucleus on March 8, 1986, revealing a whirling nucleus within a hydrogen cloud emitting 20–50 tons of water per second. The Soviet probes *Vega 1* and *Vega 2* passed at within 5,524 miles/8,890 km and 4,990 miles/ 8,030 km respectively. The European Space Agency's *Giotto* passed as close as 370 miles/596 km on March 14. All were heavily battered by dust particles, and it was concluded that Halley's comet is composed of dust bonded by water and carbon dioxide ice.

2 1910
Predictions of disaster were widely published, with many people convinced that the world would come to an end. Mark Twain, who was born at the time of the 1835 appearance and believed that his fate was linked to that of the comet, died when it reappeared.

3 1835
Widely observed, but noticeably dimmer than in 1759.

4 1759
The comet's first return, as predicted by Halley, thus proving his calculations correct.

5 1682
Observed in Africa and China and extensively in Europe, where it was observed on September 5–19 by Edmund Halley, who predicted its return.

6 1607
Seen extensively in China, Japan, Korea, and Europe, described by German astronomer Johannes Kepler, and its position accurately measured by amateur Welsh astronomer Thomas Harriot.

7 1531
Observed in China, Japan, and Korea and in Europe from August 13–23 by Peter Appian, German geographer and astronomer who noted that comets' tails point away from the Sun.

8 1456
Observed in China, Japan, and Korea and by the Turkish army that was threatening to invade Europe. The Turks were defeated by Papal forces, and the comet was interpreted as a portent of this outcome.

9 1378
Observed in China, Japan, Korea, and Europe.

10 1301
Seen in Iceland, parts of Europe, China, Japan, and Korea.

Before Edmund Halley (1656–1742) studied and predicted the return of the famous comet that now bears his name, no one had succeeded in proving that comets travel in predictable orbits. The dramatic return in 1759, precisely as Astronomer Royal Halley had calculated, of the comet he had observed in 1682, established the science of cometary observation.

TOP 10 MOST FREQUENTLY SEEN COMETS

(Comet/years between appearances)

1 Encke, 3.302 2 Grigg-Skjellerup, 4.908
3 Honda-Mrkós-Pajdusáková, 5.210
4 Tempel 2, 5.259 5 Neujmin 2, 5.437
6 Brorsen, 5.463 7 Tuttle-Giacobini-Kresák, 5.489 8 Tempel-L. Swift, 5.681
9 Tempel 1, 5.982 10 Pons-Winnecke, 6.125

MASSIVE METEORITE

At 9 x 8 ft/2.73 x 2.43 m, the Hoba West meteorite was found on a South African farm in 1920. It consists of 82 percent iron and 16 percent nickel.

TOP 10 ★
LARGEST METEORITES EVER FOUND

	LOCATION	ESTIMATED WEIGHT TONS
1	Hoba West, Grootfontein, South Africa	60.0
2	Ahnighito ("The Tent"), Cape York, West Greenland	34.1
3	Bacuberito, Mexico	29.8
4	Mbosi, Tanganyika	28.7
5	Agpalik, Cape York, West Greenland	22.2
6	Armanti, Western Mongolia	22.0
7	Mundrabilla*, Western Australia	19.4
8 =	Willamette, Oregon	15.4
=	Chupaderos, Mexico	15.4
10	Campo del Cielo, Argentina	14.3

* In two parts – 12.7 and 6.7 tons

Meteorites have been known since early times: fragments have been found mounted in a necklace in an Egyptian pyramid and in ancient American Indian burial sites. The number of meteorites falling has been calculated to amount to some 500 a year across the whole globe, although many fall in the ocean and in unpopulated areas where their descent goes unnoticed. Apart from occasional unfounded legends, there is no record of anyone being killed by a meteorite, although animals are occasional victims.

TOP 10 ★
LARGEST ASTEROIDS TO BE DISCOVERED

	NAME	YEAR DISCOVERED	DIAMETER MILES	KM
1	Ceres	1801	582	936
2	Pallas	1802	377	607
3	Vesta	1807	322	519
4	Hygeia	1849	279	450
5	Euphrosyne	1854	229	370
6	Interamnia	1910	217	349
7	Davida	1903	200	322
8	Cybele	1861	192	308
9	Europa	1858	179	288
10	Patientia	1899	171	275

The first and largest to be discovered was Ceres, which was found by Giuseppi Piazzi (1746–1826), director of the observatory in Palermo, Sicily, on New Year's Day, 1801. Since then over 6,000 have been found, 26 larger than 124 miles/200 km in diameter. The total mass of all the asteroids is less than that of the Moon.

DAMAGED ASTEROID

This color-coded elevation map of Vesta shows a giant crater, suggesting that the asteroid has suffered a large impact.

THE 10 ★
FIRST ASTEROIDS TO BE DISCOVERED

	ASTEROID/DISCOVERER	DISCOVERED
1	Ceres, Giuseppe Piazzi	Jan 1, 1801
2	Pallas, Heinrich Olbers	Mar 28, 1802
3	Juno, Karl Ludwig Harding	Sep 1, 1804
4	Vesta, Heinrich Olbers	Mar 29, 1807
5	Astraea, Karl Ludwig Hencke	Dec 8, 1845
6	Hebe, Karl Ludwig Hencke	Jul 1, 1847
7	Iris, John Russell Hind	Aug 13, 1847
8	Flora, John Russell Hind	Oct 18, 1847
9	Metis, A. Graham	Apr 25, 1848
10	Hygeia, Annibale de Gasparis	Apr 12, 1849

Asteroids, sometimes known as "minor planets," are fragments of rock orbiting between Mars and Jupiter. There are perhaps 45,000 of them, but fewer than 10 percent have been named.

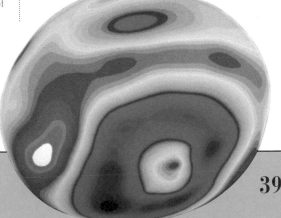

Did You Know? An asteroid that collided with the Earth 65 million years ago may have caused the extinction of the dinosaurs.

SPACE EXPLORATION

OLDEST US ASTRONAUTS*

	ASTRONAUT	LAST FLIGHT	AGE#
1	John H. Glenn	Nov 6, 1998	77
2	F. Story Musgrave	Dec 7, 1996	61
3	Vance D. Brand	Dec 11, 1990	59
4	Karl G. Henize	Aug 6, 1985	58
5	Roger K. Crouch	Jul 17, 1997	56
6	William E. Thornton	May 6, 1985	56
7	Don L. Lind	May 6, 1985	54
8	Henry W. Hartsfield	Nov 6, 1988	54
9	John E. Blaha	Dec 7, 1996	54
10	William G. Gregory	Mar 18, 1995	54

* Including payload specialists, etc., to Jan 1, 1999

 # Those of apparently identical age have been ranked according to their precise age in days at the time of their last flight

At 53, Shannon W. Lucid (born Jan 14, 1943; last flight Mar 31, 1996) holds the record as the oldest woman in space.

PENSIONER IN SPACE

At 77, Glenn became the oldest astronaut by a considerable margin, when he re-entered space aboard the Space Shuttle STS-95 Discovery in 1998.

YOUNGEST US ASTRONAUTS*

	ASTRONAUT	FIRST FLIGHT	AGE#
1	Janice E. Voss	Jun 21, 1993	27
2	Kenneth D. Bowersox	Jun 25, 1984	28
3	Sally K. Ride	Jun 18, 1983	32
4	Tamara E. Jernigan	Jun 5, 1991	32
5	Eugene A. Cernan	Jun 3, 1966	32
6	Eoichi Wakata	Jan 11, 1996	32
7	Steven A. Hawley	Aug 30, 1984	32
8	Mary E. Weber	Jul 13, 1995	32
9	Kathryn D. Sullivan	Oct 5, 1984	33
10	Ronald E. McNair+	Feb 3, 1984	33

* To Jan 1, 1999

 # Those of apparently identical age have been ranked according to their precise age in days at the time of their first flight

+ Killed in Challenger disaster, Jan 28, 1986

COUNTRIES WITH MOST SPACEFLIGHT EXPERIENCE*

	COUNTRY	ASTRONAUTS	TOTAL DURATION OF MISSIONS			
			DAYS	HRS	MINS	SECS
1	USSR/Russia#	88	13,723	19	28	19
2	US	244	6,331	18	09	49
3	Kazakhstan	2	341	09	55	23
4	Germany	9	298	11	30	13
5	France	8	158	12	44	05
6	Canada	7	89	00	50	33
7	Japan	5	64	02	39	16
8	Italy	3	39	10	35	47
9	Switzerland	1	34	12	53	58
10	Ukraine	1	15	16	34	4

* To Jan 1, 1999

 # Russia became a separate independent state on Dec 25, 1991

The USSR, now called Russia, has clocked up its considerable lead on the rest of the world (with 65 percent of the total time spent by humans in space) largely through the long-duration stays of its cosmonauts on board the *Mir* space station, which has been occupied since 1986.

MOST EXPERIENCED SPACEMEN*

	SPACEMAN	MISSIONS	TOTAL DURATION OF MISSIONS			
			DAYS	HRS	MINS	SECS
1	Valeri V. Polyakov	2	678	16	33	18
2	Anatoli Y. Solovyov	5	651	00	11	25
3	Musa K. Manarov	2	541	00	29	38
4	Alexander S. Viktorenko	4	489	01	35	17
5	Sergei K. Krikalyov	4#	483	09	37	26
6	Yuri V. Romanenko	3	430	18	21	30
7	Alexander A. Volkov	3	391	11	52	14
8	Vladimir G. Titov	5#	387	00	51	03
9	Vasily V. Tsibliev	2	381	15	53	02
10	Yuri V. Usachyov	2	375	19	34	36

* To Jan 1, 1999

 # Including flights aboard US Space Shuttles

All the missions listed were undertaken by the USSR (Russia). The record-holder, Polyakov, gained 241 days' experience as a USSR *Mir* space station astronaut in 1988, and spent his second mission – and the longest-ever residence in space – aboard *Mir* from Jan 8, 1994 until Mar 26, 1995. In recent years, a number of US astronauts have added to their space logs by spending time on board the rapidly aging *Mir*.

*Background image: **MIR SPACE STATION***

THE 10 ★
FIRST PLANETARY PROBES

	PROBE/COUNTRY	PLANET	ARRIVAL*
1	*Venera 4*, USSR	Venus	Oct 18, 1967
2	*Venera 5*, USSR	Venus	May 16, 1969
3	*Venera 6*, USSR	Venus	May 17, 1969
4	*Venera 7*, USSR	Venus	Dec 15, 1970
5	*Mariner 9*, US	Mars	Nov 13, 1971
6	*Mars 2*, USSR	Mars	Nov 27, 1971
7	*Mars 3*, USSR	Mars	Dec 2, 1971
8	*Venera 8*, USSR	Venus	Jul 22, 1972
9	*Venera 9*, USSR	Venus	Oct 22, 1975
10	*Venera 10*, USSR	Venus	Oct 25, 1975

* *Successfully entered orbit or landed*

This list excludes "fly-bys" – probes that passed by, but did not land on, the surface of another planet – such as the US's *Pioneer 10*, which flew past Jupiter on Dec 4, 1973. *Venera 4* was the first unmanned probe to land on a planet, and *Venera 9* the first to transmit pictures from a planet's surface. *Mariner 9* was the first to orbit another planet; earlier and later *Mariners* are now either in orbit around the Sun or have traveled beyond the Solar System.

THE 10 ★
FIRST SPACEMEN AND WOMEN TO CELEBRATE BIRTHDAYS IN SPACE

	SPACEMAN/WOMAN	AGE	BIRTHDAY
1	Viktor I. Patsayev	38	Jun 19, 1971
2	Charles Conrad	43	Jun 2, 1973
3	William R. Pogue	44	Jan 23, 1974
4	Vitali I. Sevastyanov	40	Jul 8, 1975
5	Pyotr I. Klimuk	33	Jul 10, 1975
6	Alexandr S. Ivanchenkov	38	Sep 28, 1978
7	Vladimir A. Lyakhov	38	Jul 20, 1979
8	Valeri V. Ryumin	40	Aug 16, 1979
9	Valeri V. Ryumin	41	Aug 16, 1980
10	Leonid I. Popov	35	Aug 31, 1980

THE 10 FIRST PEOPLE TO ORBIT THE EARTH

	NAME/SPACECRAFT	COUNTRY OF ORIGIN	DATE
1	**Yuri A. Gagarin**, *Vostok I*	USSR	Apr 12, 1961
2	**Gherman S. Titov**, *Vostok II*	USSR	Aug 6–7, 1961
3	**John H. Glenn**, *Friendship 7*	US	Feb 20, 1962
4	**M. Scott Carpenter**, *Aurora 7*	US	May 24, 1962
5	**Andrian G. Nikolayev**, *Vostok III*	USSR	Aug 11–15, 1962
6	**Pavel R. Popovich**, *Vostok IV*	USSR	Aug 12–15, 1962
7	**Walter M. Schirra**, *Sigma 7*	US	Oct 3, 1962
8	**L. Gordon Cooper**, *Faith 7*	US	May 15–16, 1963
9	**Valeri F. Bykovsky**, *Vostok V*	USSR	Jun 14–19, 1963
10	**Valentina V. Tereshkova**, *Vostok VI*	USSR	Jun 16–19, 1963

Yuri Gagarin, at the age of 27, orbited the Earth once, taking 1 hour 48 minutes. Titov, the youngest-ever astronaut at 25 years 329 days, performed 17 orbits during 25 hours. The first American to orbit the Earth, John Glenn, is the oldest on this list at 40; he has since gone on to become the oldest astronaut ever. Bykovsky spent the longest time in space – 119 hours – and Tereshkova was the first woman in space. Among early pioneering flights, neither Alan Shepard (May 5, 1961, *Freedom 7*) nor Gus Grissom (July 21, 1961, *Liberty Bell 7*) actually orbited, achieving altitudes of only 115 miles/185 km and 118 miles/190 km respectively, and neither flight lasted longer than 15 minutes.

THE 10 FIRST ANIMALS IN SPACE
(Name/animal/ country/date)

SPACE DOGS
On August 19, 1960, these four-legged cosmonauts from the USSR, Belka and Strelka, were the first animals to return safely after orbiting the Earth.

1 Laika, dog, USSR, Nov 3, 1957
2 = **Laska** and **Benjy**, mice, US, Dec 13, 1958
4 = **Able**, female rhesus monkey, and **Baker**, female squirrel monkey, US, May 28, 1959
6 = **Otvazhnaya**, female Samoyed husky, and an unnamed rabbit, USSR, July 2, 1959
8 Sam, male rhesus monkey, US, Dec 4, 1959 **9 Miss Sam**, female rhesus monkey, US, Jan 21, 1960 **10** = **Belka** and **Strelka**, female Samoyed huskies, USSR, Aug 19, 1960

Which planet has the longest years in the Solar System?
see p.37 for the answer
A Pluto
B Uranus
C Mars

WATERWORLD

TOP 10 ★

HIGHEST WATERFALLS

	WATERFALL	LOCATION	TOTAL DROP FT	M
1	Angel	Venezuela	3,212	979*
2	Tugela	South Africa	3,107	947
3	Utigård	Norway	2,625	800
4	Mongefossen	Norway	2,540	774
5	Yosemite	California	2,425	739
6	Østre Mardøla Foss	Norway	2,152	656
7	Tyssestrengane	Norway	2,120	646
8	Cuquenán	Venezuela	2,000	610
9	Sutherland	New Zealand	1,904	580
10	Kjellfossen	Norway	1,841	561

* Longest single drop 2,648 ft/807 m

MIGHTY FALLS

The cascades of the Yosemite Falls can be viewed from all over Yosemite Valley. They are best seen in late spring, when the creek that forms them is at its fullest. By September they have often dried up.

TOP 10 ★

COUNTRIES WITH THE GREATEST AREAS OF INLAND WATER

	COUNTRY	PERCENTAGE OF TOTAL AREA	WATER AREA SQ MILES	SQ KM
1	Canada	7.60	291,573	755,170
2	India	9.56	121,391	314,400
3	China	2.82	104,460	270,550
4	US	2.20	79,541	206,010
5	Ethiopia	9.89	46,680	120,900
6	Colombia	8.80	38,691	100,210
7	Indonesia	4.88	35,908	93,000
8	Russia	0.47	30,657	79,400
9	Australia	0.90	26,610	68,920
10	Tanzania	6.25	22,799	59,050

Large areas of some countries are occupied by major rivers and lakes. Lake Victoria, for example, raises the water area of Uganda to 15.39 percent of its total. In Europe, three Scandinavian countries have considerable percentages of water: Sweden 8.68 percent, Finland 9.36 percent, and Norway 5.05 percent.

TOP 10 ★

DEEPEST OCEANS AND SEAS

	OCEAN OR SEA	GREATEST DEPTH FT	M	AVERAGE DEPTH FT	M
1	Pacific Ocean	35,837	10,924	13,215	4,028
2	Indian Ocean	24,460	7,455	13,002	3,963
3	Atlantic Ocean	30,246	9,219	12,880	3,926
4	Caribbean Sea	22,788	6,946	8,685	2,647
5	South China Sea	16,456	5,016	5,419	1,652
6	Bering Sea	15,659	4,773	5,075	1,547
7	Gulf of Mexico	12,425	3,787	4,874	1,486
8	Mediterranean Sea	15,197	4,632	4,688	1,429
9	Japan Sea	12,276	3,742	4,429	1,350
10	Arctic Ocean	18,456	5,625	3,953	1,205

The deepest point in the deepest ocean is the Marianas Trench in the Pacific at a depth of 35,837 ft/10,924 m, according to a recent survey, although the slightly lesser depth of 35,814 ft/10,916 m was recorded on January 23, 1960, by Jacques Piccard and Donald Walsh in their 58-ft/17.7-m long bathyscaphe *Trieste 2* during the deepest-ever ocean descent. The Pacific is so vast that it contains more water than all the world's other seas put together.

TOP 10 ★

LONGEST RIVERS

	RIVER	LOCATION	LENGTH MILES	KM
1	Nile	Tanzania/Uganda/Sudan/Egypt	4,145	6,670
2	Amazon	Peru/Brazil	4,007	6,448
3	Yangtze–Kiang	China	3,915	6,300
4	Mississippi–Missouri–Red Rock	US	3,710	5,971
5	Yenisey–Angara–Selenga	Mongolia/Russia	3,442	5,540
6	Huang Ho (Yellow River)	China	3,395	5,464
7	Ob'–Irtysh	Mongolia/Kazakhstan/Russia	3,362	5,410
8	Congo	Angola/Dem. Rep. of Congo	2,920	4,700
9	Lena–Kirenga	Russia	2,734	4,400
10	Mekong	Tibet/China/Myanmar (Burma)/Laos/Cambodia/Vietnam	2,703	4,350

FROZEN NORTH

The island of Novaya Zemlya in the Russian Arctic is almost entirely covered by ice. The main Novaya Zemlya Glacier subdivides into smaller ones, including the Brounov Glacier at Mack's Bay, shown here.

Did You Know? The eight deepest ocean trenches would be deep enough to submerge Mount Everest, which is 29,022 ft/8,846 m above sea level.

TOP 10 ★
LARGEST LAKES IN NORTH AMERICA

	LAKE	LOCATION	APPROX. AREA SQ MILES	SQ KM
1	Superior	Canada/US	31,820	82,413
2	Huron	Canada/US	23,010	59,596
3	Michigan	US	22,400	58,016
4	Great Bear	Canada	12,030	31,150
5	Great Slave	Canada	11,030	28,570
6	Erie	Canada/US	9,930	25,719
7	Winnipeg	Canada	9,094	24,553
8	Ontario	Canada/US	7,520	19,477
9	Athabasca	Canada	3,058	7,920
10	Reindeer	Canada	2,444	6,330

TOP 10 ★
LARGEST FRESHWATER LAKES IN THE US*

	LAKE	LOCATION	APPROX. AREA SQ MILES	SQ KM
1	Michigan	Illinois/Indiana/ Michigan/Wisconsin	22,400	58,016
2	Iliamna	Alaska	1,000	2,590
3	Okeechobee	Florida	700	1,813
4	Becharof	Alaska	458	1,186
5	Red	Minnesota	451	1,168
6	Teshepuk	Alaska	315	816
7	Naknek	Alaska	242	627
8	Winnebago	Wisconsin	215	557
9	Mille Lacs	Minnesota	207	536
10	Flathead	Montana	197	510

* Excluding those partly in Canada

TOP 10 ★
DEEPEST FRESHWATER LAKES

	LAKE	LOCATION	GREATEST DEPTH FT	M
1	Baikal	Russia	5,371	1,637
2	Tanganyika	Burundi/ Tanzania/Dem. Rep. of Congo/Zambia	4,825	1,471
3	Malawi	Malawi/ Mozambique/Tanzania	2,316	706
4	Great Slave	Canada	2,015	614
5	Matana	Celebes, Indonesia	1,936	590
6	Crater	Oregon, US	1,932	589
7	Toba	Sumatra, Indonesia	1,736	529
8	Hornindals	Norway	1,686	514
9	Sarez	Tajikistan	1,657	505
10	Tahoe	California/ Nevada, US	1,645	501

TOP 10 ★
DEEPEST DEEP-SEA TRENCHES

	TRENCH/OCEAN	DEEPEST POINT FT	M
1	Marianas, Pacific	35,837	10,924
2	Tonga*, Pacific	35,430	10,800
3	Philippine, Pacific	34,436	10,497
4	Kermadec*, Pacific	32,960	10,047
5	Bonin, Pacific	32,786	9,994
6	New Britain, Pacific	32,609	9,940
7	Kuril, Pacific	31,985	9,750
8	Izu, Pacific	31,805	9,695
9	Puerto Rico, Atlantic	28,229	8,605
10	Yap, Pacific	27,973	8,527

*Some authorities consider these parts of one feature

TOP 10 ★
LARGEST LAKES

	LAKE	LOCATION	APPROX. AREA SQ MILES	SQ KM
1	Caspian Sea	Azerbaijan/ Iran/Kazakhstan/ Russia/Turkmenistan	143,205	371,000
2	Superior	Canada/US	31,820	82,413
3	Victoria	Kenya/ Tanzania/Uganda	26,570	68,800
4	Huron	Canada/US	23,010	59,596
5	Michigan	US	22,400	58,016
6	Aral Sea	Kazakhstan/ Uzbekistan	15,444	40,000
7	Tanganyika	Burundi/ Tanzania/Dem. Rep. of Congo/Zambia	13,860	32,900
8	Great Bear	Canada	12,030	31,150
9	Baikal	Russia	11,775	30,500
10	Great Slave	Canada	11,030	28,570

TOP 10 ★
LONGEST GLACIERS

	GLACIER	LOCATION	LENGTH MILES	KM
1	Lambert-Fisher	Antarctica	320	515
2	Novaya Zemlya	Russia	260	418
3	Arctic Institute	Antarctica	225	362
4	Nimrod-Lennox-King	Antarctica	180	290
5	Denman	Antarctica	150	241
6	=Beardmore	Antarctica	140	225
	=Recovery	Antarctica	140	225
8	Petermanns	Greenland	124	200
9	Unnamed	Antarctica	120	193
10	Slessor	Antarctica	115	185

ISLANDS OF THE WORLD

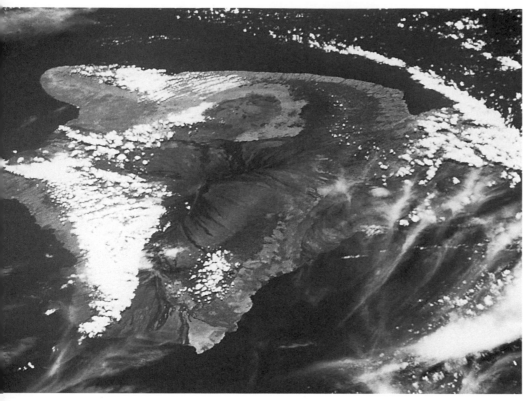

HAWAII

This infrared image from Space Shuttle Columbia *shows Hawaii's forested areas (dark red), cultivated land (lighter red and pink), vegetated volcanic summits (green-gray), and recent lava flows (black).*

ISLAND/LOCATION	AREA SQ MILES	SQ KM
1 Great Britain, North Atlantic	84,186	218,041
2 Iceland, North Atlantic	39,769	103,000
3 Ireland, North Atlantic	32,342	83,766
4 West Spitsbergen, Arctic Ocean	15,200	39,368
5 Sicily, Mediterranean Sea	9,807	25,400
6 Sardinia, Mediterranean Sea	9,189	23,800
7 North East Land, Barents Sea	5,792	15,000
8 Cyprus, Mediterranean Sea	3,572	9,251
9 Corsica, Mediterranean Sea	3,367	8,720
10 Crete, Mediterranean Sea	3,189	8,260

TOP 10 ⭐
LARGEST ISLANDS

ISLAND/LOCATION	APPROX. AREA* SQ MILES	SQ KM
1 Greenland	840,070	2,175,600
2 New Guinea, Papua New Guinea/Indonesia	312,190	789,900
3 Borneo, Indonesia/ Malaysia/Brunei	289,961	751,000
4 Madagascar	226,674	587,041
5 Baffin Island, Canada	195,926	507,451
6 Sumatra, Indonesia	163,011	422,200
7 Honshu, Japan	88,839	230,092
8 Great Britain	84,186	218,041
9 Victoria Island, Canada	83,896	217,290
10 Ellesmere Island, Canada	75,767	196,236

* Mainlands, including areas of inland water, but excluding offshore islands

Australia is regarded as a continental land mass rather than an island; otherwise it would rank first, at 2,941,517 sq miles/7,618,493 sq km, or 35 times the size of Great Britain.

TOP 10 ⭐
LARGEST ISLANDS IN THE US

ISLAND/LOCATION	AREA SQ MILES	SQ KM
1 Hawaii	4,037	10,456
2 Kodiak, Alaska	3,672	9,510
3 Puerto Rico	3,459	8,959
4 Prince of Wales, Alaska	2,587	6,700
5 Chicagof, Alaska	2,085	5,400
6 Saint Lawrence, Alaska	1,710	4,430
7 Admiralty, Alaska	1,649	4,270
8 Nunivak, Alaska	1,625	4,210
9 Unimak, Alaska	1,606	4,160
10 Baranof, Alaska	1,598	4,140

Long Island, New York (1,396 sq miles/ 3,630 sq km) falls just outside the Top 10.

TOP 10 ⭐
LARGEST ISLANDS IN THE UK

ISLAND/LOCATION	POPULATION	AREA SQ MILES	SQ KM
1 Lewis and Harris, Outer Hebrides	23,390	859.19	2,225.30
2 Skye, Inner Hebrides	8,139	643.27	1,666.08
3 Mainland, Shetland	22,184	373.36	967.00
4 Mull, Inner Hebrides	2,605	347.20	899.25
5 Ynys Môn (Anglesey), Wales	69,800	275.60	713.80
6 Islay, Inner Hebrides	3,997	246.64	638.79
7 Isle of Man, England	69,788	220.72	571.66
8 Mainland, Orkney	14,299	206.99	536.10
9 Arran, Inner Hebrides	4,726	168.08	435.32
10 Isle of Wight, England	126,600	147.10	380.99

Did You Know? The smallest island with country status is Pitcairn in Polynesia, at just 1.75 sq miles/4,53 sq km.

TOP 10 ★
MOST DENSELY POPULATED ISLANDS*

ISLAND/LOCATION	AREA SQ MILES	SQ KM	POPULATION#	POPULATION PER SQ MILE	SQ KM
1 **Manhattan**, New York	22	57	1,487,536	67,615	26,316
2 **Salsette**, India	246	637	13,000,000	52,846	20,408
3 **Hong Kong**, China	29	75	1,330,000	45,862	17,733
4 **Singapore**	210	543	3,476,000	16,552	6,317
5 **Montreal Island**, Canada	201	521	1,800,000	8,955	3,455
6 **Long Island**, New York	1,402	3,630	6,840,000	4,879	1,884
7 **Dakhin Shahbazbur**, Bangladesh	614	1,590	1,700,000	2,769	1,069
8 **Okinawa**, Japan	471	1,220	1,200,000	2,548	984
9 **Java**, Indonesia	49,807	129,000	109,000,000	2,188	845
10 **Sardinia**, Italy	919	2,380	1,640,000	1,785	689

* Includes only islands with populations of more than 1 million

Latest available year

Source: *United Nations*

TOP 10 ★
MOST DENSELY POPULATED ISLAND COUNTRIES

ISLAND	AREA SQ MILES	SQ KM	POPULATION*	POPULATION PER SQ MILE	SQ KM
1 **Malta**	122	316	382,000	3,131	1,209
2 **Bermuda**	21	53	63,000	3,000	1,189
3 **Maldives**	115	298	310,000	2,695	1,040
4 **Bahrain**	268	694	642,000	2,395	925
5 **Mauritius**	720	1,861	1,141,000	1,545	598
6 **Taiwan**	13,800	35,742	22,211,000	1,609	622
7 **Barbados**	166	430	260,000	1,566	605
8 **Tuvalu**	10	25	11,000	1,100	440
9 **Marshall Islands**	70	181	68,000	971	376
10 **Japan**	143,939	372,801	126,582,000	879	340

* Estimated for the year 2000

Source: *United Nations*

TOP 10 HIGHEST ISLANDS
(Island/location/highest elevation in ft/m)

① **New Guinea**, Papua New Guinea/Indonesia, 16,503/5,030 ② **Akutan**, Alaska, US, 14,026/4,275 ③ **Borneo**, Indonesia/Malaysia/Brunei, 13,698/4,175 ④ **Hawaii**, US, 13,796/4,205 ⑤ **Formosa**, China, 13,114/3,997 ⑥ **Sumatra**, Indonesia, 12,480/3,804 ⑦ **Ross**, Antarctica, 12,448/3,794 ⑧ **Honshu**, Japan, 12,388/3,776 ⑨ **South Island**, New Zealand, 12,349/3,764 ⑩ **Lombok**, Lesser Sunda Islands, Indonesia, 12,224/3,726

Source: *United Nations*

TOP 10 ★
LARGEST VOLCANIC ISLANDS

ISLAND/LOCATION	TYPE	AREA SQ MILES	SQ KM
1 **Sumatra**, Indonesia	Active volcanic	171,068.7	443,065.8
2 **Honshu**, Japan	Volcanic	87,182.0	225,800.3
3 **Java**, Indonesia	Volcanic	53,588.5	138,793.6
4 **North Island**, New Zealand	Volcanic	43,082.4	111,582.8
5 **Luzon**, Philippines	Active volcanic	42,457.7	109,964.9
6 **Iceland**	Active volcanic	39,315.2	101,826.0
7 **Mindanao**, Philippines	Active volcanic	37,656.5	97,530.0
8 **Hokkaido**, Japan	Active volcanic	30,394.7	78,719.4
9 **New Britain**, Papua New Guinea	High volcanic	13,569.4	35,144.6
10 **Halmahera**, Indonesia	Active volcanic	6,965.1	18,039.6

Source: *United Nations*

BAY OF ISLANDS

The North Island of New Zealand has several active volcanoes. One of New Zealand's biggest lakes, Lake Taupo, lies in a volcanic crater.

THE FACE OF THE EARTH

HIGHEST MOUNTAINS

MOUNTAIN/LOCATION	HEIGHT* FT	M
1 Everest, Nepal/Tibet	29,022	8,846
2 K2, Kashmir/China	28,250	8,611
3 Kangchenjunga, Nepal/Sikkim	28,208	8,598
4 Lhotse, Nepal/Tibet	27,890	8,501
5 Makalu I, Nepal/Tibet	27,790	8,470
6 Dhaulagiri I, Nepal	26,810	8,172
7 Manaslu I, Nepal	26,760	8,156
8 Cho Oyu, Nepal	26,750	8,153
9 Nanga Parbat, Kashmir	26,660	8,126
10 Annapurna I, Nepal	26,504	8,078

* Height of principal peak; lower peaks of the same mountain are excluded

Dhaulagiri was once believed to be the tallest mountain until Kangchenjunga was surveyed and declared to be even higher. Everest later topped them all when its height was computed.

THE HIGHEST HEIGHTS

Mount Everest was named in 1865 as a tribute to Sir George Everest, the Surveyor General of India who led the 19th-century Great Trigonometrical Survey of India that was to accord Everest its No. 1 position.

DEEPEST DEPRESSIONS

DEPRESSION/LOCATION	MAXIMUM DEPTH BELOW SEA LEVEL FT	M
1 Dead Sea, Israel/Jordan	1,312	400
2 Turfan Depression, China	505	154
3 Qattâra Depression, Egypt	436	133
4 Poluostrov Mangyshlak, Kazakhstan	433	132
5 Danakil Depression, Ethiopia	383	117
6 Death Valley, US	282	86
7 Salton Sink, US	235	72
8 Zapadny Chink Ustyurta, Kazakhstan	230	70
9 Prikaspiyskaya Nizmennost', Kazakhstan/Russia	220	67
10 Ozera Sarykamysh, Turkmenistan/Uzbekistan	148	45

The shore of the Dead Sea is the lowest exposed ground below sea level, but the bed of the sea actually reaches 2,388 ft/728 m below sea level. Much of Antarctica is also below sea level.

LONGEST CAVES

CAVE/LOCATION	TOTAL KNOWN LENGTH MILES	KM
1 Mammoth cave system, Kentucky	352	567
2 Optimisticeskaja, Ukraine	125	201
3 Jewel Cave, South Dakota	108	174
4 Hölloch, Switzerland	103	166
5 Lechuguilla Cave, New Mexico	100	161
6 Siebenhengsteholen-system, Switzerland	87	140
7= Fisher Ridge cave system, Kentucky	78	126
= Wind Cave, South Dakota	78	126
9 Ozernay, Ukraine	69	111
10 Gua Air Jernih, Malaysia	68	109

Source: *Tony Waltham, BCRA, 1999*

DEEPEST CAVES

CAVE SYSTEM/LOCATION	DEPTH FT	M
1 Lampreschtsofen, Austria	5,354	1,632
2 Gouffre Mirolda, France	5,282	1,610
3 Réseau Jean Bernard, France	5,256	1,602
4 Shakta Pantjukhina, Georgia	4,948	1,508
5 Sistema Huautla, Mexico	4,839	1,475
6 Sistema del Trave, Spain	4,737	1,444
7 Boj Bulok, Uzbekistan	4,642	1,415
8 Puerto di Illamina, Spain	4,619	1,408
9 Lukina Jama, Croatia	4,567	1,392
10 Sistema Cheve, Mexico	4,547	1,386

Which is the highest island in the world?
see p.45 for the answer
A New Guinea
B Hawaii
C Sumatra

TOP 10 ★
HIGHEST ACTIVE VOLCANOES

	VOLCANO	LOCATION	LATEST ACTIVITY	FT	HEIGHT M
1	Guallatiri	Chile	1987	19,882	6,060
2	Lascar	Chile	1991	19,652	5,990
3	Cotopaxi	Ecuador	1975	19,347	5,897
4	Tupungatito	Chile	1986	18,504	5,640
5	Popocatépetl	Mexico	1995	17,887	5,452
6	Ruiz	Colombia	1992	17,716	5,400
7	Sangay	Ecuador	1988	17,159	5,230
8	Guagua Pichincha	Ecuador	1988	15,696	4,784
9	Purace	Colombia	1977	15,601	4,755
10	Kliuchevskoi	Russia	1995	15,584	4,750

This list includes all volcanoes that have been active at some time during the 20th century. The tallest currently active volcano in Europe is Mt. Etna, Sicily (10,855 ft/3,311 m), which was responsible for numerous deaths in earlier times. Although still active, Etna's last major eruption took place on March 11, 1669; the lava flow engulfed the town of Catania.

TOP 10 ★
COUNTRIES WITH THE HIGHEST ELEVATIONS*

	COUNTRY	PEAK	FT	HEIGHT M
1	Nepal#	Everest	29,022	8,846
2	Pakistan	K2	28,250	8,611
3	India	Kangchenjunga	28,208	8,598
4	Bhutan	Khula Kangri	24,784	7,554
5	Tajikistan	Mt. Garmo (formerly Kommunizma)	24,590	7,495
6	Afghanistan	Noshaq	24,581	7,499
7	Kyrgystan	Pik Pobedy	24,406	7,439
8	Kazakhstan	Khan Tengri	22,949	6,995
9	Argentina	Cerro Aconcagua	22,834	6,960
10	Chile	Ojos del Salado	22,588	6,885

* Based on the tallest peak in each country

 # Everest straddles Nepal and Tibet, which, now known as Xizang, is a province of China

TOP 10 ★
STATES WITH THE HIGHEST ELEVATIONS IN THE US

	STATE	PEAK	FT	HEIGHT M
1	Alaska	Mount McKinley	20,320	6,194
2	California	Mount Whitney	14,494	4,418
3	Colorado	Mount Elbert	14,433	4,399
4	Washington	Mount Rainier	14,410	4,392
5	Wyoming	Gannett Peak	13,804	4,207
6	Hawaii	Mauna Kea	13,796	4,205
7	Utah	Kings Peak	13,528	4,123
8	New Mexico	Wheeler Peak	13,161	4,011
9	Nevada	Boundary Peak	13,140	4,005
10	Montana	Granite Peak	12,799	3,901

TOP 10 ★
LARGEST DESERTS

	DESERT	LOCATION	APPROX. AREA SQ MILES	SQ KM
1	Sahara	North Africa	3,500,000	9,000,000
2	Australian	Australia	1,470,000	3,800,000
3	Arabian	Southwest Asia	502,000	1,300,000
4	Gobi	Central Asia	400,000	1,036,000
5	Kalahari	Southern Africa	201,000	520,000
6	Turkestan	Central Asia	174,000	450,000
7	Takla Makan	China	125,000	327,000
8 =	Namib	Southwest Africa	120,000	310,000
=	Sonoran	US/Mexico	120,000	310,000
10 =	Somali	Somalia	100,000	260,000
=	Thar	Northwest India/Pakistan	100,000	260,000

SAHARAN WILDERNESS

Contrary to popular image of endless stretches of sand, 80 percent of the Sahara is, in fact, composed of smooth rock and rubble. The average annual rainfall here is a mere 6–7 in/15–18 cm.

Background image: **A NASA COMPUTER-GENERATED TOPOGRAPHIC IMAGE OF THE CONTINENTS OF THE EARTH**

THE 10 DEGREES OF HARDNESS*

(Mohs Scale no./substance)

1 Talc   **2** Gypsum   **3** Calcite   **4** Fluorite   **5** Apatite   **6** Orthoclase

7 Quartz   **8** Topaz   **9** Corundum   **10** Diamond

* According to the Mohs Scale in which No. 1 is the softest mineral and No. 10 is the hardest

TOP 10 ★
MOST VALUABLE TRADED METALLIC ELEMENTS

ELEMENT*	PRICE PER KG ($)
1 Rhodium	28,300
2 Osmium	12,860
3 Iridium	12,541
4 Platinum	11,673
5 Palladium	11,271
6 Gold	9,170
7 Rhenium	1,400
8 Ruthenium	1,254
9 Germanium	1,100
10 Gallium	450

* Based on 10–100 kg quantities of minimum 99.9% purity; excluding radioactive elements, isotopes, and rare earth elements traded in minute quantities

Source: *London Metal Bulletin/Lippman Walton & Co.*

The price of traded metals varies enormously according to their rarity, changes in industrial uses, fashion, and popularity as investments. The price of market-leader rhodium has increased by some 66 per cent in a year. Rhenium, which is used in airplane engines, has also risen in price.

RUSSIAN WEALTH
Today platinum is used in oil refining and in reducing car exhaust pollution, but in times past it was used for coinage in several countries, including Russia.

TOP 10 ★
PRINCIPAL COMPONENTS OF AIR

COMPONENT	VOLUME PERCENT
1 Nitrogen	78.110
2 Oxygen	20.953
3 Argon	0.934
4 Carbon dioxide	0.01–0.10
5 Neon	0.001818
6 Helium	0.000524
7 Methane	0.0002
8 Krypton	0.000114
9 = Hydrogen	0.00005
= Nitrous oxide	0.00005

TOP 10 ★
MOST COMMON ELEMENTS IN THE UNIVERSE

ELEMENT	PARTS PER 1,000,000
1 Hydrogen	739,000
2 Helium	240,000
3 Oxygen	10,700
4 Carbon	4,600
5 Neon	1,340
6 Iron	1,090
7 Nitrogen	970
8 Silicon	650
9 Magnesium	580
10 Sulfur	440

TOP 10 ★
MOST EXTRACTED NONMETALLIC ELEMENTS

ELEMENT	ESTIMATED ANNUAL EXTRACTION (TONS)
1 Hydrogen	385,808,950,000
2 Carbon*	17,857,440,000
3 Phosphorus	6,283,000,000
4 Chlorine	185,180,000
5 Sulfur	59,520,000
6 Nitrogen	48,500,000
7 Oxygen	11,020,000
8 Silicon#	4,282,000
9 Boron	1,102,000
10 Argon	771,000

* Carbon, natural gas, oil, and cbal

 # Various forms

TOP 10 ★
METALLIC ELEMENTS WITH THE GREATEST RESERVES

ELEMENT	ESTIMATED GLOBAL RESERVES (TONS)
1 Iron	121,254,200,000
2 Magnesium	22,046,200,000
3 Potassium	11,023,100,000
4 Aluminum	6,613,800,000
5 Manganese	3,968,300,000
6 Zirconium	>1,102,300,000
7 Chromium	1,102,300,000
8 Barium	496,000,000
9 Titanium	485,000,000
10 Copper	341,700,000

This list includes accessible reserves of commercially mined metallic elements, but excludes two, calcium and sodium, that exist in such vast quantities that their reserves are considered "unlimited" and unquantifiable. In contrast, there are relatively small amounts of certain precious metals: the world's silver reserves are put at 1,102,300 tons, mercury at 650,400 tons, and gold at 16,500 tons.

Did You Know? The metallic element gallium is used in LEDs (light-emitting diodes), its compounds creating the colors seen on computer screens.

IRON MINING

Iron (right) has been mined in Britain since c.750 BC and is still present in vast reserves. A tough metal that is easy to work, it can be cast, forged, machined, rolled, and alloyed.

TOP 10 ⭐
MOST EXTRACTED METALLIC ELEMENTS

	ELEMENT	ESTIMATED ANNUAL EXTRACTION (TONS)
1	Iron	789,247,000
2	Aluminum	16,535,000
3	Copper	7,209,000
4	Manganese	6,856,000
5	Zinc	5,534,000
6	Lead	3,086,000
7	Nickel	562,000
8	Magnesium	358,000
9	Sodium	220,000
10	Tin	182,000

Certain metallic minerals are extracted in relatively small quantities, whereas compounds containing these elements are major industries: contrasting with 220,500 tons of metallic sodium, 185 million tons of salt are extracted annually; metallic calcium is represented by about 2,210 tons, contrasting with some 123 million tons of lime (calcium carbonate), and 220 tons of the metal potassium contrast with 56 million tons of potassium salts.

TOP 10 ⭐
LIGHTEST ELEMENTS*

	ELEMENT	YEAR DISCOVERER/COUNTRY	DISCOVERED	DENSITY#
1	Lithium	J.A. Arfvedson, Sweden	1817	0.533
2	Potassium	Sir Humphry Davy, UK	1807	0.859
3	Sodium	Sir Humphry Davy	1807	0.969
4	Calcium	Sir Humphry Davy	1808	1.526
5	Rubidium	R.W. Bunsen/G. Kirchoff, Germany	1861	1.534
6	Magnesium	Sir Humphry Davy	1808+	1.737
7	Phosphorus	Hennig Brandt, Germany	1669	1.825
8	Beryllium	F. Wöhler, Germany/ A.A.B. Bussy, France	1828★	1.846
9	Caesium	R.W. Bunsen/G. Kirchoff	1860	1.896
10	Sulfur	– Prehistoric		2.070

* Solids only # Grams per cu cm at 20°C + Recognized by Joseph Black, 1755, but not isolated ★ Recognized by Nicholas Vauquelin, 1797, but not isolated

TOP 10 ⭐
HEAVIEST ELEMENTS

	ELEMENT	YEAR DISCOVERER/COUNTRY	DISCOVERED	DENSITY*
1	Osmium	S. Tennant, UK	1804	22.59
2	Iridium	S. Tennant	1804	22.56
3	Platinum	J.C. Scaliger#, Italy/France	1557	21.45
4	Rhenium	W. Noddack et al., Germany	1925	21.01
5	Neptunium	Edwin M. McMillan/ Philip H. Abelson, US	1940	20.47
6	Plutonium	G.T. Seaborg et al., US	1940	20.26
7	Gold	– Prehistoric		19.29
8	Tungsten	J.J. and F. Elhuijar, Spain	1783	19.26
9	Uranium	M.J. Klaproth, Germany	1789	19.05
10	Tantalum	A.G. Ekeberg, Sweden	1802	16.67

* Grams per cu cm at 20°C

 # Earliest reference to this element

WORLD WEATHER

TOP 10 ★
HOTTEST INHABITED PLACES

WEATHER STATION/LOCATION	AVERAGE TEMPERATURE °F	°C
1 Djibouti, Djibouti	86.0	30.0
2 =Timbuktu, Mali	84.7	29.3
=Tirunelevi, India	84.7	29.3
=Tuticorin, India	84.7	29.3
5 =Nellore, India	84.6	29.2
=Santa Marta, Colombia	84.6	29.2
7 =Aden, South Yemen	84.0	28.9
=Madurai, India	84.0	28.9
=Niamey, Niger	84.0	28.9
10 =Hudaydah, North Yemen	83.8	28.8
=Ouagadougou, Burkina Faso	83.8	28.8
=Thanjavur, India	83.8	28.8
=Tiruchirapalli, India	83.8	28.8

TWIN TEMPERATURES

A hygrometer is used to measure the moisture content of a gas. The type most often used to gauge air humidity is the dry- and wet-bulb psychrometer.

TOP 10 ★
HOTTEST CITIES IN THE US

CITY/STATE	AVERAGE ANNUAL TEMPERATURE °F	°C
1 Key West, Florida	77.8	25.4
2 Miami, Florida	75.9	24.2
3 West Palm Beach, Florida	74.7	23.7
4 =Fort Myers, Florida	74.4	23.3
=Yuma, Arizona	74.4	23.3
6 Brownsville, Texas	73.8	23.1
7 =Tampa, Florida	72.4	22.4
=Vero Beach, Florida	72.4	22.4
9 Corpus Christi, Texas	71.6	22.3
10 Daytona Beach, Florida	70.4	21.3

Source: *National Climatic Data Center*

TOP 10 ★
DRIEST CITIES IN THE US

CITY/STATE	MEAN ANNUAL PRECIPITATION IN	MM
1 Yuma, Arizona	3.17	80.5
2 Las Vegas, Nevada	4.13	104.9
3 Bishop, California	5.37	136.4
4 Bakersfield, California	5.72	145.3
5 Reno, Nevada	7.53	191.3
6 Alamosa, Colorado	7.57	192.3
7 Phoenix, Arizona	7.66	194.6
8 Yakima, Washington	7.97	202.4
9 Winslow, Arizona	8.04	204.2
10 Winnemucca, Nevada	8.23	209.0

Source: *National Climatic Data Center*

TOP 10 ★
COLDEST INHABITED PLACES

WEATHER STATION/LOCATION	AVERAGE TEMPERATURE °F	°C
1 Norilsk, Russia	12.4	−10.9
2 Yakutsk, Russia	13.8	−10.1
3 Yellowknife, Canada	22.3	−5.4
4 Ulan-Bator, Mongolia	23.9	−4.5
5 Fairbanks, Alaska	25.9	−3.4
6 Surgut, Russia	26.4	−3.1
7 Chita, Russia	27.1	−2.7
8 Nizhnevartovsk, Russia	27.3	−2.6
9 Hailar, Mongolia	27.7	−2.4
10 Bratsk, Russia	28.0	−2.2

TOP 10 ★
COLDEST PLACES IN THE US

WEATHER STATION/STATE	MEAN TEMPERATURE °F	°C
1 International Falls, Minnesota	36.8	2.67
2 Duluth, Minnesota	38.5	3.61
3 Caribou, Maine	38.8	3.78
4 Marquette, Michigan	39.1	3.94
5 Sault St. Marie, Michigan	39.7	4.28
6 Fargo, North Dakota	41.0	5.00
7 Alamosa, Colorado	41.1	5.05
8 =Saint Cloud, Minnesota	41.5	5.28
=Williston, Maryland	41.5	5.28
10 Bismark, North Dakota	41.6	5.33

Source: *National Climatic Data Center*

TOP 10 ★
WETTEST CITIES IN THE US

CITY/STATE	MEAN ANNUAL PRECIPITATION IN	MM
1 Quillayute, Washington	105.18	2,672
2 Astoria, Oregon	66.40	1,687
3 Tallahassee, Florida	65.71	1,669
4 Mobile, Alabama	63.96	1,625
5 Pensacola, Florida	62.25	1,581
6 New Orleans, Louisiana	61.88	1,572
7 Baton Rouge, Louisiana	60.89	1,547
8 West Palm Beach, Florida	60.75	1,543
9 Meridian, Mississippi	56.71	1,440
10 Tupelo, Mississippi	55.87	1,419

Source: *National Climatic Data Center*

What is the longest river in the world?
see p.42 for the answer
A Nile
B Mississippi
C Amazon

TOP 10 ★
DRIEST INHABITED PLACES

	WEATHER STATION/LOCATION	AVERAGE ANNUAL RAINFALL IN	MM
1	Aswan, Egypt	0.02	0.5
2	Luxor, Egypt	0.03	0.7
3	Arica, Chile	0.04	1.1
4	Ica, Peru	0.09	2.3
5	Antofagasta, Chile	0.19	4.9
6	Minya, Egypt	0.20	5.1
7	Asyut, Egypt	0.21	5.2
8	Callao, Peru	0.47	12.0
9	Trujilo, Peru	0.54	14.0
10	Fayyum, Egypt	0.75	19.0

The total annual rainfall of the Top 10 inhabited places, as recorded over extensive periods, is just 2½ in/64.8 mm – the average length of an adult little finger.

TOP 10 ★
WETTEST INHABITED PLACES

	WEATHER STATION/LOCATION	AVERAGE ANNUAL RAINFALL IN	MM
1	Buenaventura, Colombia	265.47	6,743
2	Monrovia, Liberia	202.01	5,131
3	Pago Pago, American Samoa	196.46	4,990
4	Moulmein, Myanmar	191.02	4,852
5	Lae, Papua New Guinea	182.87	4,645
6	Baguio, Luzon Island, Philippines	180.04	4,573
7	Sylhet, Bangladesh	175.47	4,457
8	Conakry, Guinea	170.91	4,341
9 =	Padang, Sumatra Island, Indonesia	166.34	4,225
=	Bogor, Java, Indonesia	166.34	4,225

The total annual rainfall of the Top 10 locations is equivalent to more than 26 adults, each measuring 6 ft/1.83 m, standing on top of each other.

TOP 10 ★
HIGHEST TEMPERATURES RECORDED IN THE US

	WEATHER STATION/STATE*	DATE	TEMPERATURE °F	°C
1	Greenland Ranch, California	July 10, 1913	134	56.7
2	Lake Havasu City, Arizona	June 29, 1994	128	53.3
3	Laughlin, Nevada	June 29, 1994	125	51.7
4	Waste Isolation Pilot Plant, New Mexico	June 27, 1994	122	50.0
5 =	Alton, Kansas	July 24, 1936	121	49.5
=	Steele, North Dakota	July 6, 1936	121	49.5
7 =	Ozark, Arkansas	Aug 10, 1936	120	48.9
=	Tipton, Oklahoma	June 27, 1994	120	48.9
=	Gannvalley, South Dakota	July 5, 1936	120	48.9
=	Seymour, Texas	Aug 12, 1936	120	48.9

* Extreme high for each state

Source: *National Climatic Data Center*

TOP 10 ★
LOWEST TEMPERATURES RECORDED IN THE US

	WEATHER STATION/STATE*	DATE	TEMPERATURE °F	°C
1	Prospect Creek, Alaska	Jan 23, 1971	-80	-62.2
2	Rogers Pass, Montana	Jan 20, 1954	-70	-56.7
3	Peteris Sink, Utah	Feb 1, 1985	-69	-56.1
4	Riverside Ranger Station, Wyoming	Feb 9, 1933	-66	-54.4
5	Maybell, Colorado	Feb 1, 1985	-61	-51.7
6 =	Island Park Dam, Idaho	Jan 18, 1943	-60	-51.1
=	Parshall, North Dakota	Feb 15, 1936	-60	-51.1
=	Tower, Minnesota	Feb 2, 1996	-60	-51.1
9	McIntosh, South Dakota	Feb 17, 1936	-58	-50.0
10 =	Seneca, Oregon	Feb 10, 1933	-54	-47.8
=	Danbury, Wisconsin	Jan 24, 1922	-54	-47.8

* Extreme low for each state

Source: *National Climatic Data Center*

PREPARING FOR STORMY WEATHER

A monsoon is a strong seasonal wind that occurs mostly in South Asia, the tropics, and subtropics, bringing with it heavy rain. This picture shows a young child in the Philippines taking cover under a huge leaf.

NATURAL DISASTERS

THE 10 ★
WORST EPIDEMICS OF ALL TIME

	EPIDEMIC	LOCATION	DATE	ESTIMATED NO. KILLED
1	Black Death	Europe/Asia	1347–51	75,000,000
2	Influenza	Worldwide	1918–20	21,640,000
3	Bubonic plague	India	1896–1948	12,000,000
4	AIDS	Worldwide	1981–	6,400,000
5	Typhus	Eastern Europe	1914–15	3,000,000
6 =	"Plague of Justinian"	Europe/Asia	541–90	millions*
=	Cholera	Worldwide	1846–60	millions*
=	Cholera	Europe	1826–37	millions*
=	Cholera	Worldwide	1893–94	millions*
10	Smallpox	Mexico	1530–45	>1,000,000

* No precise figures available

THE 10 ★
WORST AVALANCHES AND LANDSLIDES OF THE 20TH CENTURY*

	LOCATION	INCIDENT	DATE	ESTIMATED NO. KILLED
1	Yungay, Peru	Landslide	May 31, 1970	17,500
2	Italian Alps	Avalanche	Dec 13, 1916	10,000
3	Huarás, Peru	Avalanche	Dec 13, 1941	5,000
4	Nevada Huascaran, Peru	Avalanche	Jan 10, 1962	3,500
5	Medellin, Colombia	Landslide	Sep 27, 1987	683
6	Chungar, Peru	Avalanche	Mar 19, 1971	600
7	Rio de Janeiro, Brazil	Landslide	Jan 11, 1966	550
8 =	Northern Assam, India	Landslide	Feb 15, 1949	500
=	Grand Riviere du Nord, Haiti	Landslide	Nov 13/14, 1963	500
10	Blons, Austria	Avalanche	Jan 11, 1954	411

* Excluding those where most deaths resulted from flooding, earthquakes, etc., associated with landslides

THE 10 ★
WORST FLOODS AND STORMS OF THE 20TH CENTURY

	LOCATION/DATE	ESTIMATED NO. KILLED
1	Huang He River, China, Aug 1931	3,700,000
2	Bangladesh, Nov 13, 1970	300–500,000
3	Henan, China, Sept 1939	over 200,000
4	Chang Jiang River, China, Sept 1911	100,000
5	Bengal, India, Nov 15–16, 1942	40,000
6	Bangladesh, June 1–2, 1965	30,000
7	Bangladesh, May 28–29, 1963	22,000
8	Bangladesh, May 11–12, 1965	17,000
9	Morvi, India, Aug 11, 1979	5–15,000
10 =	Hong Kong, Sept 18, 1906	10,000
=	Bangladesh, May 25, 1985	10,000

BANGLADESHI FLOODS

The summer monsoon rains, vital for watering the crops, can easily bring disaster, causing devastating floods that wash away people and buildings alike.

THE 10 ★
WORST EARTHQUAKES OF THE 20TH CENTURY

	LOCATION	DATE	ESTIMATED NO. KILLED
1	Tang-shan, China	July 28, 1976	242,419
2	Nan-Shan, China	May 22, 1927	200,000
3	Kansu, China	Dec 16, 1920	180,000
4	Messina, Italy	Dec 28, 1908	160,000
5	Tokyo/Yokohama, Japan	Sept 1, 1923	142,807
6	Kansu, China	Dec 25, 1932	70,000
7	Yungay, Peru	May 31, 1970	66,800
8	Quetta, India*	May 30, 1935	50–60,000
9	Armenia	Dec 7, 1988	over 55,000
10	Iran	June 21, 1990	over 40,000

* Now Pakistan

DEVASTATED YOKOHAMA

The worst earthquake ever to hit Japan leveled towns and cities for hundreds of miles around the epicenter of Tokyo, leaving millions homeless.

THE 10 ★
WORST TSUNAMIS OF THE 20TH CENTURY

	LOCATIONS AFFECTED	DATE	ESTIMATED NO. KILLED
1	Agadir, Morocco*	Feb 29, 1960	12,000
2	Papua New Guinea	July 18, 1998	8,000
3=	Philippines	Aug 17, 1976	5,000
	=Chile/Pacific islands/Japan	May 22, 1960	5,000
5	Japan/Hawaii	Mar 2, 1933	3,000
6	Japan*	Dec 21, 1946	1,088
7	Kii, Japan	Dec 4, 1944	998
8	Lomblem Island, Indonesia	July 18, 1979	539
9	Hawaii/Aleutians/ California	Apr 1, 1946	173
10	Colombia/ Ecuador*	Dec 12, 1979	133

* Combined effect of earthquake and tsunamis

Tsunamis are powerful waves caused by undersea earthquakes or volcanic eruptions.

TOP 10 ★
WORST VOLCANIC ERUPTIONS OF ALL TIME

LOCATION/DATE/INCIDENT	EST. NO. KILLED
1 Tambora, Indonesia, Apr 5–12, 1815	92,000

The eruption on the island of Sumbawa killed about 10,000 islanders immediately, with 82,000 more dying subsequently from disease and famine.

| **2 Miyi-Yama**, Java, 1793 | 53,000 |

The volcano dominating the island of Kiousiou erupted, engulfing all the local villages in mudslides and killing most of the rural population.

| **3 Mont Pelée**, Martinique, May 8, 1902 | 40,000 |

After lying dormant for centuries, Mont Pelée began to erupt in April 1902.

| **4 Krakatoa**, Sumatra/Java, Aug 26–27, 1883 | 36,380 |

Krakatoa exploded with what may have been the biggest bang ever heard by humans, audible up to 3,000 miles/4,800 km away.

| **5 Nevado del Ruiz**, Colombia, Nov 13, 1985 | 22,940 |

The hot steam, rocks, and ash ejected from Nevado del Ruiz melted its icecap, resulting in a mudslide that completely engulfed the town of Armero.

| **6 Mt. Etna**, Sicily, Mar 11, 1669 | over 20,000 |

Europe's largest volcano has erupted frequently, but the worst instance occurred in 1669, when the lava flow engulfed the town of Catania.

| **7 Laki**, Iceland, Jan–June 1783 | 20,000 |

Many villages were engulfed in a river of lava up to 50 miles/80 km long and 100 ft/30 m deep, releasing poisonous gases that killed those who escaped the lava. This was the largest ever recorded lava flow.

| **8 Vesuvius**, Italy, Aug 24, 79 | 16–20,000 |

The Roman city of Herculaneum was engulfed by a mud flow, while Pompeii was buried under a vast and preserving layer of pumice and volcanic ash.

| **9 Vesuvius**, Italy, Dec 16–17, 1631 | up to 18,000 |

Lava and mudflows gushed down onto the surrounding towns, including Naples.

| **10 Mt. Etna**, Sicily, 1169 | over 15,000 |

Large numbers died in Catania cathedral where they believed they would be safe, and more were killed when a tidal wave caused by the eruption hit the port of Messina.

Did You Know? The eruption of Tambora in 1815 sent 1,700,000 tons of ash into the atmosphere, blocking out the sunlight and affecting the weather. The resulting brilliantly colored sunsets are captured in J.M.W. Turner's paintings of the period.

LIFE ON EARTH

EXTINCT & ENDANGERED

MOST ENDANGERED BIG CATS*

1	Amur leopard
2	Anatolian leopard
3	Asiatic cheetah
4	Eastern puma
5	Florida cougar
6	North African leopard
7	Siberian tiger
8	South Arabian leopard
9	South China tiger
10	Sumatran tiger

In alphabetical order

Source: *International Union for Conservation of Nature*

All 10 of these big cats are classed by the International Union for Conservation of Nature as being "critically endangered," that is, facing an extremely high risk of extinction in the wild in the immediate future.

TOP 10 ★

MOST ENDANGERED MAMMALS

	MAMMAL	ESTIMATED NO.
1 =	Tasmanian wolf	?
=	Halcon fruit bat	?
=	Ghana fat mouse	?
4	Javan rhinoceros	50
5	Iriomote cat	60
6	Black lion tamarin	130
7	Pygmy hog	150
8	Kouprey	100–200
9	Tamaraw	200
10	Indus dolphin	400

The first three mammals on the list have not been seen for many years and may well be extinct.

TOP 10 ★

RAREST MARINE MAMMALS

	MAMMAL	ESTIMATED NO.
1	Caribbean monk seal	200
2	Mediterranean monk seal	400
3	Juan Fernandez fur seal	750
4	West Indian manatee	1,000
5	Guadeloupe fur seal	1,600
6	New Zealand fur seal	2,000
7 =	Hooker's sea lion	4,000
=	Right whale	4,000
9	Fraser's dolphin	7,800
10	Amazon manatee	8,000

The hunting of seals for their fur and of whales for oil and other products has resulted in a sharp fall in the population of many marine mammals.

TIGER IN DANGER

Of all the endangered big cats listed here, tigers are particularly under threat: there may be as few as 500 Siberian tigers, 400 Sumatran tigers, and only 20 to 30 South China tigers left in the world.

TOP 10 ★

MOST ENDANGERED SPIDERS

	SPIDER	COUNTRY
1	Kauai cave wolf spider	US
2	Doloff cave spider	US
3	Empire cave pseuoscorpion	US
4	Glacier Bay wolf spider	US
5	Great raft spider	Europe
6	Kocevje subterranean spider (*Troglohyphantes gracilis*)	Slovenia
7	Kocevje subterranean spider (*Troglohyphantes similis*)	Slovenia
8	Kocevje subterranean spider (*Troglohyphantes spinipes*)	Slovenia
9	Lake Placid funnel wolf spider	US
10	Melones cave harvestman	US

Source: *International Union for the Conservation of Nature*

The first spider on this list is considered by the IUCN as "endangered" (facing a very high risk of extinction in the wild in the near future), and the others as "vulnerable" (facing a high risk of extinction in the wild in the medium-term future).

TOP 10 ★

COUNTRIES WITH THE MOST ELEPHANTS

	COUNTRY	ESTIMATED NO.*
1	Tanzania	73,459
2	Dem. Rep. of Congo	65,974
3	Botswana	62,998
4	Gabon	61,794
5	Zimbabwe	56,297
6	Rep. of the Congo	32,563
7	India	20,000
8	Zambia	19,701
9	Kenya	13,834
10	South Africa	9,990

The difficulty of surveying animals in the wild means that the data are not always precise

The elephant has been associated with humans for thousands of years, used for hunting, in warfare, for travel, and in the logging industry.

background image: A 85-FT/26-M
SKELETON OF A DIPLODOCUS

TOP 10 ★
LARGEST DINOSAURS EVER DISCOVERED

DINOSAUR/DESCRIPTION	LENGTH/EST. WEIGHT
1 Seismosaurus	98–119 ft/30–36 m/ 55–88 tons

A skeleton of this colossal plant-eater was excavated in 1985 near Albuquerque, New Mexico, by US palaeontologist David Gillette and given a name that means "earth-shaking lizard". It is currently being studied by the New Mexico Museum of Natural History, which may confirm its position as the largest dinosaur yet discovered, with some claiming a length of up to 170 ft/52 m.

| **2 Supersaurus** | 80–98 ft/24–30 m/55 tons |

The remains of Supersaurus were found in Colorado in 1972. Some scientists have suggested a length of up to 138 ft/42 m and a weight of 83–110 tonnes for this massive dinosaur.

| **3 Antarctosaurus** | 60–98 ft/18–30 m/ 44–55 tons |

Named Antarctosaurus ("southern lizard") by German palaeontologist Friedrich von Huene in 1929, this creature's thigh bone alone measures 7 ft 6 in/2.3 m. Some authorities have put its weight as high as 88 tons.

| **4 Barosaurus** | 75–90 ft/23–27.5 m/uncertain |

Barosaurus (meaning "heavy lizard", so named by US palaeontologist Othniel C. Marsh in 1890) has been found in both North America and Africa, thus proving the existence of a land link in Jurassic times (205–140 million years ago).

| **5 Mamenchisaurus** | 89 ft/27 m/uncertain |

An almost complete skeleton discovered in 1972 showed that Mamenchisaurus had the longest neck of any known animal, comprising more than half its total body length – perhaps up to 49 ft/15 m. It was named by Chinese palaeontologist Yang Zhong-Jiun (known in palaeontological circles as "C.C. Young") after the place in China where it was found.

| **6 Diplodocus** | 75–89 ft/23–27 m/13 tons |

Because it was long and thin, Diplodocus was a relative lightweight in the dinosaur world. It was also probably one of the most stupid dinosaurs, having the smallest brain in relation to its body size. Diplodocus was given its name (which means "double beam") in 1878 by Othniel C. Marsh.

| **7 Ultrasauros** | Over 82 ft/25 m/55 tons |

Ultrasauros was discovered by US palaeontologist James A. Jensen in Colorado in 1979 but has not yet been fully studied. Some authorities have claimed its weight as 155 tons. It was originally called Ultrasaurus ("ultra lizard"), which was a name also given to another, smaller dinosaur; to avoid confusion its spelling has been altered.

| **8 Brachiosaurus** | 82 ft/25 m/55 tons |

Its name (given to it in 1903 by US palaeontologist Elmer S. Riggs) means "arm lizard". Some palaeontologists have put the weight of Brachiosaurus as high as 210 tons, but this seems improbable (if not impossible), in the light of theories of the maximum possible weight of terrestrial animals.

| **9 Pelorosaurus** | 80 ft/24 m/uncertain |

The first fragments of Pelorosaurus (meaning "monstrous lizard") were found in Sussex and named by British doctor and geologist Gideon Algernon Mantell as early as 1850.

| **10 Apatosaurus** | 66–70 ft/20–21 m/ 22–33 tons |

Apatosaurus (its name, coined by Othniel C. Marsh, means "deceptive lizard") is better known by its former name of Brontosaurus ("thunder lizard"). The bones of the first one ever found, in Colorado in 1879, caused great confusion for many years because its discoverer attached a head from a different species to the rest of the skeleton.

This Top 10 is based on the most reliable recent evidence of their lengths and indicates the probable ranges; as more and more information is assembled, these are undergoing constant revision. Lengths have often been estimated from only a few surviving fossilized bones, and there is much dispute even among experts about these and even more about the weights of most dinosaurs. Some, such as Diplodocus, had squat bodies but extended necks, which made them extremely long but not necessarily very heavy.

Everyone's favorite dinosaur, Tyrannosaurus rex ("tyrant lizard"), does not appear in the Top 10 list because, although it was one of the fiercest flesh-eating dinosaurs, it was not as large as many of the herbivorous ones. However, measuring a probable 39 ft/12 m and weighing more than 6.112 tons, it certainly ranks as one of the largest flesh-eating animals yet discovered. Bones of an earlier dinosaur called Epanterias were found in Colorado in 1877 and 1934, but incorrectly identified until recently, when studies suggested that this creature was possibly larger than Tyrannosaurus.

To compare these sizes with living animals, note that the largest recorded crocodile measured 20 ft 4 in/6.2 m and the largest elephant 35 ft/10.7 m.

WAITING FOR A MATE

This captive-bred female Spix's macaw, Cyanopsitta spixxi, awaits release into the wild, where it will meet the last surviving male Spix's macaw.

THE 10 COUNTRIES WITH THE MOST THREATENED SPECIES
(Country/species)

1 US, 854   **2** Australia, 483
3 Indonesia, 340   **4** Mexico, 247
5 Brazil, 240   **6** China, 213   **7** South Africa, 205   **8** India, 193   **9** Philippines, 188   **10** =Japan, 132;   = Tanzania, 132

Source: International Union for the Conservation of Nature

TOP 10 ★
RAREST BIRDS

BIRD/COUNTRY	ESTIMATED NO.*
1 =Spix's macaw, Brazil	1
=Cebu flower pecker, Philippines	1
3 Hawaiian crow, Hawaii	5
4 Black stilt, New Zealand	12
5 Echo parakeet, Mauritius	13
6 Imperial Amazon parrot, Dominica	15
7 Magpie robin, Seychelles	20
8 Kakapo, New Zealand	24
9 Pink pigeon, Mauritius	70
10 Mauritius kestrel, Mauritius	100

* Of breeding pairs reported since 1986

Several rare bird species are known from old records or from only one specimen, but must be assumed to be extinct in the absence of recent sightings or records of breeding pairs. Rare birds come under most pressure on islands like Mauritius, where the dodo met its fate.

LAND ANIMALS

TOP 10 ★
DEADLIEST SNAKES

SNAKE	MAXIMUM DEATHS PER BITE	MORTALITY RATE RANGE (PERCENT)
1 Black Mamba	200	75–100
2 Forest cobra	50	70–95
3 Russell's viper	150	40–92
4 Taipan	170	10–90
5 Common krait	60	70–80
6 Jararacussu	100	60–80
7 Terciopelo	40	Not known
8 Egyptian cobra	35	50
9 Indian cobra	40	30–35
10 Jararaca	30	25–35

TOP 10 ★
HEAVIEST CARNIVORES

CARNIVORE	LENGTH FT	M	WEIGHT LB	KG
1 Southern elephant seal	21	6.5	7,716	3,500
2 Walrus	12	3.8	2,646	1,200
3 Steller sea lion	9	3	2,425	1,100
4 Grizzly bear	9	3	1,720	780
5 Polar bear	8	2.6	1,323	600
6 Tiger	9	2.8	661	300
7 Lion	6	1.9	551	250
8 American black bear	6	1.8	500	227
9 Giant panda	5	1.5	353	160
10 Spectacled bear	6	1.8	309	140

Of the 273 mammal species in the order *Carnivora*, or meat eaters, many (including its largest representatives on land, bears) are, in fact, omnivorous and around 40 specialize in eating fish or insects. All, however, share a common ancestry indicated by the butcher's-knife form of their canine teeth. Because the Top 10 would otherwise consist exclusively of seals and related marine carnivores, only three have been included in order to enable the terrestrial heavyweight division to make an appearance. The polar bear is probably the largest land carnivore if shoulder height (when on all fours) is taken into account: it tops an awesome 5.3 ft/1.6 m, compared with the 4 ft/1.2 m of its nearest rival, the grizzly bear. The common weasel is probably the smallest carnivore at less than 7 in/17 cm long, not counting the tail.

KING OF THE JUNGLE
Second in size to the tiger in the cat family, the lion weighs in at an impressive 551 lb/250 kg. Lions sleep for 12 hours a day, and can run at 50 mph/80 km/h.

TOP 10 MAMMALS WITH THE SHORTEST GESTATION PERIODS
(Mammal/average gestation in days)

1 Short-nosed bandicoot, 12
2 Opossum, 13 3 Common shrew, 14
4 Golden hamster, 16 5 Lemming, 20
6 Mouse, 21 7 Rat, 22 8 Gerbil, 24
9 Rabbit, 30 10 Mole, 38

TOP 10 MAMMALS WITH THE LONGEST GESTATION PERIODS
(Mammal/average gestation in days)

1 African elephant, 660 2 Asiatic elephant, 600 3 Baird's beaked whale, 520 4 White rhinoceros, 490
5 Walrus, 480 6 Giraffe, 460 7 Tapir, 400 8 Arabian camel (dromedary), 390
9 Fin whale, 370 10 Llama, 360

TOP 10 ★
MOST VENOMOUS CREATURES

CREATURE*	TOXIN	FATAL AMOUNT MG#
1 Indian cobra	Peak V	0.009
2 Mamba	Toxin 1	0.02
3 Brown snake	Texilotoxin	0.05
4 = Inland taipan	Paradotoxin	0.10
= Mamba	Dendrotoxin	0.10
6 Taipan	Taipoxin	0.11
7 = Indian cobra	Peak X	0.12
= Poison arrow frog	Batrachotoxin	0.12
9 Indian cobra	Peak 1X	0.17
10 Krait	Bungarotoxin	0.50

* Excluding bacteria
# Quantity required to kill one average-sized human adult

The venom of these creatures is almost unbelievably powerful: 1 milligram of Mamba toxin 1 would be sufficient to kill 50 people. Such creatures as scorpions (0.5 mg) and black widow spiders (1.0 mg) fall just outside the Top 10.

Did You Know? Howler monkeys are the noisiest land animals. Their calls can be heard over 2 miles (3 km) away.

TOP 10 MOST INTELLIGENT MAMMALS

1 Man **2** Chimpanzee **3** Gorilla **4** Orangutan **5** Baboon **6** Gibbon
7 Monkey **8** Smaller toothed whale **9** Dolphin **10** Elephant

TOP 10 ★
HEAVIEST TERRESTRIAL MAMMALS

MAMMAL	LENGTH		WEIGHT	
	FT	M	LB	KG
1 African elephant	24	7.3	14,432	7,000
2 White rhinoceros	14	4.2	7,937	3,600
3 Hippopotamus	13	4.0	5,512	2,500
4 Giraffe	19	5.8	3,527	1,600
5 American bison	13	3.9	2,205	1,000
6 Arabian camel (dromedary)	12	3.5	1,521	690
7 Polar bear	8	2.6	1,323	600
8 Moose	10	3.0	1,213	550
9 Siberian tiger	11	3.3	661	300
10 Gorilla	7	2.0	485	220

The list excludes domesticated cattle and horses. It also avoids comparing close kin such as the African and Indian elephants, highlighting instead the sumo stars within distinctive large mammal groups such as the bears, deer, big cats, primates, and bovines (oxlike mammals). Sizes are not necessarily the top of the known range.

AFRICAN GIANTS

At a length of 24 ft/7.3 m and weighing 14, 432 lb/7,000 kg, the African elephant is by far the largest and heaviest of all the terrestrial mammals.

TOP 10 ★
FASTEST MAMMALS IN THE WORLD

MAMMAL	MAXIMUM RECORDED SPEED	
	MPH	KM/H
1 Cheetah	65	105
2 Pronghorn antelope	55	89
3 =Mongolian gazelle	50	80
=Springbok	50	80
5 =Grant's gazelle	47	76
=Thomson's gazelle	47	76
7 Brown hare	45	72
8 Horse	43	69
9 =Greyhound	42	68
=Red deer	42	68

These figures are based on controlled measurements of average speeds over a quarter of a mile (0.4 km).

TOP 10 SLEEPIEST ANIMALS*

(Animal/average hours of sleep)

1 Koala, 22 **2** Sloth, 20 **3** = Armadillo, 19; = Opossum, 19 **5** Lemur, 16 **6** = Hamster, 14; = Squirrel, 14 **8** = Cat, 13; = Pig, 13 **10** Spiny anteater, 12

* Excluding periods of hibernation

CLEVER CHIMP

Based on research conducted by Edward O. Wilson, Professor of Zoology at Harvard University, to assess speed and extent of learning performance over a wide range of tasks, the chimp ranks second in the world.

TOP 10 ★
HEAVIEST PRIMATES

PRIMATE	LENGTH*		WEIGHT	
	IN	CM	LB	KG
1 Gorilla	79	200	485	220
2 Man	70	177	170	77
3 Orangutan	54	137	165	75
4 Chimpanzee	36	92	110	50
5 =Baboon	39	100	99	45
=Mandrill	37	95	99	45
7 Gelada baboon	30	75	55	25
8 Proboscis monkey	30	76	53	24
9 Hanuman langur	42	107	44	20
10 Siamung gibbon	35	90	29	13

* Excluding tail

The longer, skinnier, and lighter forms of the langurs, gibbons, and monkeys, designed for serious monkeying around in trees, compare sharply with their heavier great ape cousins.

MARINE ANIMALS

HEAVIEST MARINE MAMMALS

MAMMAL	LENGTH FT	LENGTH M	WEIGHT TONS
1 Blue whale	110.0	33.5	143.3
2 Fin whale	82.0	25.0	49.6
3 Right whale	57.4	17.5	44.1
4 Sperm whale	59.0	18.0	39.7
5 Gray whale	46.0	14.0	36.0
6 Humpback whale	49.2	15.0	29.2
7 Baird's whale	18.0	5.5	12.1
8 Southern elephant seal	21.3	6.5	4.0
9 Northern elephant seal	19.0	5.8	3.7
10 Pilot whale	21.0	6.4	3.2

Probably the largest animal that ever lived, the blue whale, dwarfs even the other whales listed here, all but one of which far outweigh the biggest land animal, the elephant. Among the mammals that frequent inland waters, the dugong, a type of sea cow, is largest at 2,000 lb/907 kg and 13.5 ft/4.1 m.

TOP 10 FISHING COUNTRIES
(Country/annual catch in tons)

1 China, 36,559,962 2 Peru, 10,496,164
3 Chile, 8,367,586 4 Japan, 7,450,333
5 US, 6,188,964 6 India, 5,798,620
7 Indonesia, 4,852,308
8 Russia, 4,821,318
9 Thailand, 4,021,121
10 Norway, 3,094,795

SPECIES OF FISH MOST CAUGHT

SPECIES	TONS CAUGHT PER ANNUM
1 Anchoveta	13,113,986
2 Alaska pollock	4,738,416
3 Chilean jack mackerel	4,689,925
4 Silver carp	2,572,429
5 Atlantic herring	2,079,074
6 Grass carp	2,007,976
7 South American pilchard	1,976,912
8 Common carp	1,793,676
9 Chubb mackerel	1,661,730
10 Skipjack tuna	1,612,281

Among broader groupings of fish, some 3 million tons of shrimp and prawns, and a similar tonnage of squids, cuttlefish, and octopuses are caught annually.

HEAVIEST SHARKS

SHARK	WEIGHT LB	WEIGHT KG
1 Whale shark	46,297	21,000
2 Basking shark	32,000	14,515
3 Great white shark	7,300	3,314
4 Greenland shark	2,250	1,020
5 Tiger shark	2,070	939
6 Great hammerhead shark	1,860	844
7 Six-gill shark	1,300	590
8 Gray nurse shark	1,225	556
9 Mako shark	1,200	544
10 Thresher shark	1,100	500

As well as specimens that have been caught, estimates have been made of beached examples, but such is the notoriety of sharks that many accounts of their size are exaggerated, and this list should be taken as an approximate ranking based on the best available evidence.

SWIMMERS BEWARE!

The great white shark is not only large but is also very fast, notching up speeds of 30 mph/48 km/h with ease. Its teeth are a fearsome 5 in/12 cm long.

TOP 10 ★
FASTEST FISH

FISH	RECORDED SPEED MPH	KM/H
1 Sailfish	68	110
2 Marlin	50	80
3 Bluefin tuna	46	74
4 Yellowfin tuna	44	70
5 Blue shark	43	69
6 Wahoo	41	66
7 =Bonefish	40	64
=Swordfish	40	64
9 Tarpon	35	56
10 Tiger shark	33	53

Flying fish have a top speed in the water of only 23 mph/37 km/h, but when airborne they can reach 35 mph/56 km/h. Many sharks qualify for the list: only two are listed here to prevent the list becoming overly shark-infested.

TOP 10 ★
HEAVIEST TURTLES

TURTLE	WEIGHT LB	KG
1 Pacific leatherback turtle	1,908	865
2 Atlantic leatherback turtle	1,000	454
3 Green sea turtle	900	408
4 Loggerhead turtle	850	386
5 Alligator snapping turtle	403	183
6 Black sea turtle	278	126
7 Flatback turtle	185	84
8 Hawksbill turtle	150	68
9 =Kemps ridley turtle	50	110
=Olive ridley turtle	50	110

Both the sizes and longevity of turtles remain hotly debated by zoologists, and although the weights on which this Top 10 are ranked are from corroborated sources, there are many claims of even larger specimens of *Chelonia*.

STUPENDOUS TURTLE

This green sea turtle would be dwarfed in size by prehistoric monster turtles such as Stupendemys geographicus, which measured up to 10 ft/3 m in length and weighed over 4,497 lb/2,040 kg.

TOP 10 ★
HEAVIEST SPECIES OF FRESHWATER FISH CAUGHT

SPECIES	ANGLER/LOCATION/DATE	WEIGHT LB	OZ	KG
1 White sturgeon	Joey Pallotta III, Benicia, California, July 9, 1983	468	0	212.28
2 Alligator gar	Bill Valverde, Rio Grande, Texas, Dec 2, 1951	279	0	126.55
3 Beluga sturgeon	Merete Lehne, Guryev, Kazakhstan, May 3, 1993	224	13	101.97
4 Nile perch	Adrian Brayshaw, Lake Nasser, Egypt, Dec 18, 1997	213	0	96.62
5 Flathead catfish	Ken Paulie, Withlacoochee River, Florida, May 14, 1998	123	9	56.05
6 Blue catfish	William P. McKinley, Wheeler Reservoir, Tennessee, July 5, 1996	111	0	50.35
7 Chinook salmon	Les Anderson, Kenai River, Alaska, May 17, 1985	97	4	44.11
8 Giant tigerfish	Raymond Houtmans, Zaire River, Zaire, July 9, 1988	97	0	44.00
9 Smallmouth buffalo	Randy Collins, Athens Lake, Arkansas, June 6, 1993	82	3	37.28
10 Atlantic salmon	Henrik Henrikson, Tana River, Norway (date unknown) 1928	79	2	35.89

Source: *International Game Fish Association*

TOP 10 ★
HEAVIEST SPECIES OF SALTWATER FISH CAUGHT

SPECIES	ANGLER/LOCATION/DATE	WEIGHT LB	OZ	KG
1 Great white shark	Alfred Dean, Ceduna, South Australia, Apr 21, 1959	2,664	0	1,208.39
2 Tiger shark	Walter Maxwell, Cherry Grove, California, June 14, 1964	1,780	0	807.41
3 Greenland shark	Terje Nordtvedt, Trondheimsfjord, Norway, Oct 18, 1987	1,708	9	775.00
4 Black marlin	A.C. Glassell, Jr., Cabo Blanco, Peru, Aug 4, 1953	1,560	0	707.62
5 Bluefin tuna	Ken Fraser, Aulds Cove, Nova Scotia, Oct 26, 1979	1,496	0	678.59
6 Atlantic blue marlin	Paulo Amorim, Vitoria, Brazil, Feb 29, 1992	1,402	2	635.99
7 Pacific blue marlin	Jay W. de Beaubien, Kaaiwi Point, Kona, May 31, 1982	1,376	0	624.15
8 Swordfish	L. Marron, Iquique, Chile, May 7, 1953	1,182	0	536.16
9 Mako shark	Patrick Guillanton, Black River, Mauritius, Nov 16, 1988	1,115	0	505.76
10 Hammerhead shark	Allen Ogle, Sarasota, Florida, May 20, 1982	991	0	449.52

Source: *International Game Fish Association*

Which country produces most rubber?
see p.70 for the answer
A Malaysia
B Thailand
C Sri Lanka

BAT BOMBS

During World War II, the US Army Air Corps captured millions of bats. The plan was to make them carry tiny bombs, fly into buildings, and explode. Luckily for the bats, the war ended before the plan could be carried out.

TOP 10 ★
SMALLEST BATS

BAT/HABITAT	WEIGHT OZ	WEIGHT G	LENGTH IN	LENGTH CM
1 Kitti's hognosed bat (*Craseonycteris thonglongyai*), Thailand	0.07	2.0	1.10	2.9
2 Proboscis bat (*Rhynchonycteris naso*), Central and South America	0.09	2.5	1.50	3.8
3 = Banana bat (*Pipistrellus nanus*), Africa	0.11	3.0	1.50	3.8
= Smoky bat (*Furiptera horrens*), Central and South America	0.11	3.0	1.50	3.8
5 = Little yellow bat (*Rhogeessa mira*), Central America	0.12	3.5	1.57	4.0
= Lesser bamboo bat (*Tylonycteris pachypus*), Southeast Asia	0.12	3.5	1.57	4.0
7 Disc-winged bat (*Thyroptera tricolor*), Central and South America	0.14	4.0	1.42	3.6
8 Lesser horseshoe bat (*Rhynolophus hipposideros*), Europe and Western Asia	0.18	5.0	1.46	3.7
9 California myotis (*Myotis californienses*), North America	0.18	5.0	1.69	4.3
10 Northern blossom bat (*Macroglossus minimus*), Southeast Asia to Australia	0.53	15.0	2.52	6.4

This list focuses on the smallest example of 10 different bat families. The weights shown are typical, rather than extreme – and because a bat can eat more than half its own weight, the weights of individual examples may vary considerably. The smallest of all weighs less than a ping pong ball, and even the heaviest listed here weighs less than an empty aluminum drink can. Length is of head and body only, since tail lengths vary from zero (as in Kitti's hognosed bat and the Northern blossom bat) to long (as in the Proboscis bat and Lesser horseshoe bat).

TOP 10 ★
HEAVIEST FLIGHTED BIRDS

BIRD	WINGSPAN FT	WINGSPAN M	WEIGHT LB	WEIGHT OZ	WEIGHT KG
1 Great bustard	9	2.7	46	1	20.9
2 Trumpeter swan	11	3.4	37	1	16.8
3 Mute swan	10	3.1	35	15	16.3
4 = Albatross	12	3.7	34	13	15.8
= Whooper swan	10	3.1	34	13	15.8
6 Manchurian crane	7	2.1	32	14	14.9
7 Kori bustard	9	2.7	30	0	13.6
8 Gray pelican	10	3.1	28	11	13.0
9 Black vulture	10	3.1	27	8	12.5
10 Griffon vulture	7	2.1	26	7	12.0

Wing size does not necessarily correspond to weight in flighted birds. The 13-ft/4-m wingspan of the marabou stork beats all the birds listed here, even the mighty albatross, yet its body weight is normally no heavier than any of these. When laden with a meal of carrion, however, the marabou can double its weight and needs all the lift it can get to take off. It often fails altogether and has to put up with flightlessness until digestion takes its course.

TOP 10 ISLANDS WITH THE MOST ENDEMIC BIRD SPECIES*
(Island/species)

1 New Guinea, 195 **2** Jamaica, 26
3 Cuba, 23 **4** New Caledonia, 20
5 Rennell, Solomon Islands, 15 **6** São Tomé, 14 **7** = Aldabra, Seychelles, 13;
= Grand Cayman, Cayman Islands, 13 **9** Puerto Rico, 12 **10** New Britain, Papua New Guinea, 11

* Birds that are found uniquely on these islands
Source: United Nations

LOOKING FOR A MEAL

A native of the southern United States and the American tropics, the Black vulture lives on a diet of carrion.

TOP 10 ★
LARGEST BIRDS IN THE UK

BIRD	BEAK-TO-TAIL LENGTH IN	BEAK-TO-TAIL LENGTH CM
1 = Mute swan	57–63	145–160
= Whooper swan	57–63	145–160
3 Bewick's swan	46–50	116–128
4 Canada goose	up to 43	up to 110
5 Gray heron	35–39	90–100
6 Cormorant	33–39	84–98
7 Gannet	34–38	86–96
8 Golden eagle	30–36	76–91
9 White-tailed sea eagle	27–36	69–91
10 Capercaillie (male)	32–35	82–90

Because of its size, the mute swan (which weighs up to 26 lb/12 kg) needs very strong and long feathers to power its flight: its outer wing feathers can be up to 18 in/45 cm long, but even so each feather weighs only 0.5 oz/15 g. Pheasants sometimes measure 36 in/91 cm, but are not included in this list because more than half their total length is tail.

COMING IN TO LAND

A marabou stork approaching its nest in a tree in the Masai Mara Game Reserve in Kenya. It has long legs and a massive wingspan.

TOP 10 ★
BIRDS WITH THE LARGEST WINGSPANS

BIRD	WINGSPAN FT	M
1 Marabou stork	13	4.0
2 Albatross	12	3.7
3 Trumpeter swan	11	3.4
4 =Mute swan	10	3.1
=Whooper swan	10	3.1
=Gray pelican	10	3.1
=Californian condor	10	3.1
=Black vulture	10	3.1
9 =Great bustard	9	2.7
=Kori bustard	9	2.7

TOP 10 ★
FASTEST BIRDS

BIRD	RECORDED SPEED MPH	KM/H
1 Spine-tailed swift	106	171
2 Frigate bird	95	153
3 Spur-winged goose	88	142
4 Red-breasted merganser	80	129
5 White-rumped swift	77	124
6 Canvasback duck	72	116
7 Eider duck	70	113
8 Teal	68	109
9 =Mallard	65	105
=Pintail	65	105

Until airplane pilots cracked 190 mph/306 km/h in 1919, birds were the fastest animals on the Earth: stooping (diving) peregrine falcons clock up speeds approaching 185 mph/298 km/h.

TOP 10 ★
MOST COMMON NORTH AMERICAN GARDEN BIRDS

BIRD	PERCENTAGE OF FEEDERS VISITED
1 Dark-eyed junco	83
2 House finch	70
3 =American goldfinch	69
=Downy woodpecker	69
5 Blue jay	67
6 Mourning dove	65
7 Black-capped chickadee	60
8 House sparrow	59
9 Northern cardinal	56
10 European starling	52

Source: *Project FeederWatch/Cornell Lab of Ornithology*

These are the birds that watchers are most likely to see at their feeders in North America.

TOP 10 ★
MOST COMMON BREEDING BIRDS IN THE US

1	Red-winged blackbird
2	House sparrow
3	Mourning dove
4	European starling
5	American robin
6	Horned lark
7	Common grackle
8	American crow
9	Western meadowlark
10	Brown-headed cowbird

Source: *US Fish and Wildlife Service*

This list, based on research carried out by the Breeding Bird Survey of the US Fish and Wildlife Service, ranks birds breeding in the US, with the red-winged blackbird (*Agelaius phoeniceus*) heading the list. Found throughout the United States, except in extreme desert and mountain regions, its population has grown from 25.6 million estimated in 1983 to more than 30 million today.

TOP 10 LARGEST FLIGHTLESS BIRDS

(Bird/height in in/cm)

1 Ostrich, 108.0/274.3
2 Emu, 60.0/152.4; = Cassowary, 60.0/152.4; 4 Rhea, 54.0/137.1
5 Emperor penguin, 45.0/114.0
6 Flightless cormorant, 37.3/95.0
7 Flightless steamer, 33.0/84.0
8 Kakapo, 26.0/66.0 9 Kagu, 23.6/59.9
10 Kiwi, 22.0/55.9

Which country has more horses than people?
see p.69 for the answer
A Mongolia
B Ethiopia
C Brazil

TOP 10 ★
PETS IN THE US

PET	ESTIMATED NO.*
1 Cats	66,150,000
2 Dogs	58,200,000
3 Small animal pets#	12,740,000
4 Parakeets	11,000,000
5 Freshwater fish	10,800,000
6 Reptiles	7,540,000
7 Finches	7,350,000
8 Cockatiels	6,320,000
9 Canaries	2,580,000
10 Parrots	1,550,000

* *Number of households owning, rather than individual specimens*

\# *Includes small rodents: rabbits, ferrets, hamsters, guinea pigs, and gerbils*

Source: *Pet Industry Joint Advisory Council*

TOP 10 ★
MOST INTELLIGENT DOG BREEDS

1	Border collie
2	Poodle
3	German shepherd
4	Golden retriever
5	Doberman pinscher
6	Shetland sheepdog
7	Labrador retriever
8	Papillon
9	Rottweiler
10	Australian cattle dog

Source: *Stanley Coren,* The Intelligence of Dogs *(Scribner, 1994)*

American psychology professor and pet trainer Stanley Coren devised a ranking of 133 breeds of dogs after studying their responses to a range of IQ tests, as well as the opinions of judges in dog obedience tests. Dog owners who have criticized the results point out that dogs are bred for specialized abilities, such as speed or ferocity, and that obedience to their human masters is only one feature of their "intelligence."

TOP 10 DOGS' NAMES IN THE US

1 Max 2 Molly 3 Buddy 4 Maggie
5 Bailey 6 Jake 7 Lucy
8 Sam 9 Sadie 10 Shadow

Based on a database of 140,000 I.D. tag records
Source: *American Pet Classics*

SPOT ON

Although not a Top-10 dog for either intelligence or popularity, the Dalmatian is the star of the two highest-rated films starring dogs.

TOP 10 ★
FILMS STARRING DOGS

	FILM	YEAR
1	101 Dalmatians	1996
2	One Hundred and One Dalmatians*	1961
3	Lady and the Tramp*	1955
4	Oliver & Company*	1988
5	Turner & Hooch	1989
6	The Fox and the Hound*	1981
7	Beethoven	1992
8	Homeward Bound II: Lost in San Francisco	1996
9	Beethoven's 2nd	1993
10	K-9	1991

* *Animated*

Man's best friend has been stealing scenes since the earliest years of filmmaking, with the 1905 low-budget *Rescued by Rover,* outstanding as one of the most successful productions of the pioneer period. The numerous silent era films starring Rin Tin Tin, an ex-German army dog who emigrated to the US, and his successor Lassie, whose long series of feature and TV films date from the 1940s on, are among the most enduring in movie history.

TOP 10 ★
DOG BREEDS IN THE US

	BREED	NO. REGISTERED BY AMERICAN KENNEL CLUB, INC. (1998)
1	Labrador retriever	157,936
2	Golden Retriever	65,681
3	German shepherd	65,326
4	Rottweiler	55,009
5	Dachshund	53,896
6	Beagle	53,322
7	Poodle	51,935
8	Chihuahua	43,468
9	Yorkshire terrier	42,900
10	Pomeranian	38,540

The Labrador retriever tops the list for the eighth consecutive year. This breed is also No. 1 in the UK. New to this year's Top 10 is the Chihuahua.

Source: *The American Kennel Club*

TOP 10 ★
TRICKS PERFORMED BY DOGS IN THE US

	TRICK	PERCENT OF DOGS PERFORMING
1	Sit	21.0
2	Shake paw	15.0
3	Roll over	11.4
4	"Speak"	10.6
5 =	Lie down	7.4
=	Stand on hind legs	7.4
7	Beg	7.2
8	Dance	6.1
9	"Sing"	3.0
10	Fetch newspaper	1.7

A survey conducted by the Pet Food Institute and Frosty Paws, a novelty pet food manufacturer, concluded that 25,300,500 out of a total of more than 40,000,000 dogs were able to perform at least one trick.

TOP 10 ★
CAT BREEDS IN THE US

	BREED	NO. REGISTERED*
1	Persian	35,490
2	Maine coon	4,756
3	Siamese	2,492
4	Exotic	2,165
5	Abyssinian	2,012
6	Oriental	1,305
7	Scottish fold	1,102
8	American shorthair	1,001
9	Birman	896
10	Tonkinese	871

* Year ending December 31, 1998

Of the 36 different breeds of cats listed with the Cat Fancier's Association, these were the Top 10 registered in 1998 out of a total of 61,151 (a decrease from 65,183 the previous year).
Source: *Cat Fancier's Association*

TOP 10 CATS' NAMES IN THE US

1 Tiger **2** Sam **3** Max **4** Tigger
5 Smokey **6** Shadow **7** Sammy
8 Simba **9** Lucky **10** Misty

Source: *American Pet Classics*
Based on a database of 140,000 I.D. tag records

TOP 10 GOLDFISH NAMES IN THE US

1 Jaws **2** Goldie **3** Fred **4** Tom
5 Bubbles **6** George **7** Flipper
8 Ben **9** Jerry **10** Sam

INSECTS & CREEPY-CRAWLIES

DEADLIEST SPIDERS

SPIDER/LOCATION

1 **Banana spider** (*Phonenutria nigriventer*), Central and South America

2 **Sydney funnel web** (*Atrax robusteus*), Australia

3 **Wolf spider** (*Lycosa raptoria/erythrognatha*), Central and South America

4 **Black widow** (*Latrodectus species*), Worldwide

5 **Violin spider/Recluse spider**, Worldwide

6 **Sac spider**, Southern Europe

7 **Tarantula** (*Eurypelma rubropilosum*), Neotropics

8 **Tarantula** (*Acanthoscurria atrox*), Neotropics

9 **Tarantula** (*Lasiodora klugi*), Neotropics

10 **Tarantula** (*Pamphobeteus species*), Neotropics

This list ranks spiders according to their "lethal potential" – their venom yield divided by their venom potency. The Banana spider, for example, yields 6 mg of venom, with 1 mg the estimated lethal dose in man. However, few spiders are capable of killing humans – there were just 14 recorded deaths caused by black widows in the US in the whole of the 19th century.

LARGEST BUTTERFLIES

BUTTERFLY	WINGSPAN IN	MM
1 Queen Alexandra's birdwing	11.0	280
2 African giant swallowtail	9.1	230
3 Goliath birdwing	8.3	210
4 =*Trogonoptera trojana*	7.9	200
=*Buru opalescent birdwing*	7.9	200
=*Troides hypolitus*	7.9	200
7 =*Ornithoptera lydius*	7.5	190
=*Chimaera birdwing*	7.5	190
=*Troides magellanus*	7.5	190
=*Troides miranda*	7.5	190

KING-SIZED BUTTERFLY

Queen Alexandra's birdwing, the largest butterfly in the world, is a protected species found in south-east Papua New Guinea. The male (shown here) is smaller and more colorful than the female.

LARGEST SNAILS

SNAIL	LENGTH IN	MM
1 Californian sea hare (*Aplysia californica*)	30	750
2 Trumpet or baler conch (*Syrinx aruanus*)	28	700
3 Apple (*Pomacea scalaris*)	20	500
4 =*Dolabella dolabella*	15	400
=Trumpet shell (*Charonia tritorus*)	15	400
6 =African land (*Achatina achatina*)	10	300
=*Aplysia fasciata*	10	300
=*Carinaria mediterranea*	10	300
9 =Green turban (*Turbo marmoratus*)	5	200
=*Tetus niloticus*	5	200

This list includes both marine and land gastropods. Of these, the African land snail (*Achatina achatina*) is the largest land snail. The longest snail in the world is *Parenteroxenos doglieli*, which measures 50 in (1,300 mm) in length but is only 2 in/50 mm in diameter. It lives as a parasite in the body cavity of a sea cucumber.

MOST POPULAR US STATE INSECTS

INSECT/STATES	NO.
1 **Honey bee**, Arkansas, Georgia, Kansas, Louisiana, Maine, Mississippi, Missouri, Nebraska, New Jersey, North Carolina, South Dakota, Utah, Wisconsin	13
2 **Swallowtail butterfly**, Florida (giant), Georgia (tiger), Mississippi (spicebush), Ohio (tiger), Oklahoma (black), Oregon (Oregon), Virginia (tiger), Wyoming (western)	8
3 **Ladybird beetle/ladybug**, Delaware (convergent), Iowa, Massachusetts, New York (nine-spotted), New Hampshire, Ohio, Tennessee (ladybug)	7
4 **Monarch butterfly**, Alabama, Illinois, Texas, Vermont	4
5 **Firefly**, Pennsylvania, Tennessee	2
6 =**Baltimore checkerspot butterfly**, Maryland	1
=**California dogface butterfly**, California	1
=**Carolina mantis**, South Carolina	1
=**Colorado hairstreak butterfly**, Colorado	1
=**European praying mantis**, Connecticut	1
=**Four-spotted skimmer**, Alaska	1
=**Tarantula hawk wasp**, New Mexico	1
=**Viceroy butterfly**, Kentucky	1

Along with birds, trees, flowers, and other state symbols, most states have officially adopted an insect or butterfly. These are nominated by each state's residents.

TOP 10 COUNTRIES WITH THE MOST THREATENED INVERTEBRATES

(Country/threatened invertebrate species)

1 US, 594 **2** Australia, 281 **3** South Africa, 101 **4** Portugal, 67 **5** France, 61 **6** Spain, 57 **7** Tanzania, 46 **8** = Japan, 45; = Dem. Rep. of Congo, 45 **10** = Austria, 41; = Italy, 41

Source: International Union for the Conservation of Nature

Background image: **SPIDER'S WEB COVERED IN DEW**

BIG MOTH STRIKES AGAIN

The unusual shape and coloring of the Atlas moth's wings make it quite different from other moths. It is the largest moth in the world and is found from Indonesia and Sri Lanka to China and Malaysia.

TOP 10 ★
LARGEST MOTHS

MOTH	WINGSPAN IN	MM
1 Atlas moth (*Attacus atlas*)	11.8	300
2 Owlet moth (*Thysania agrippina*)*	11.4	290
3 *Haematopis grataria*	10.2	260
4 Hercules emperor moth (*Coscinocera hercules*)	8.3	210
5 Malagasy silk moth (*Argema mitraei*)	7.1	180
6 *Eacles imperialis*	6.9	175
7 =Common emperor moth (*Bunaea alcinoe*)	6.3	160
=Giant peacock moth (*Saturnia pyri*)	6.3	160
9 Gray moth (*Brahmaea wallichii*)	6.1	155
10 =Black witch (*Ascalapha odorata*)	5.9	150
=Regal moth (*Citheronia regalis*)	5.9	150
=Polyphemus moth (*Antheraea polyphemus*)	5.9	150

* Exceptional specimen measured at 308 mm/12.2 in

DISTINCT SPHINX

The Verdant sphinx moth takes its name from its incredible green forewings. It is found south of the Sahara Desert in Africa.

TOP 10 ★
FASTEST FLYING INSECTS

SPECIES	SPEED MPH	KM/H
1 Hawkmoth (*Sphingidaei*)	33.3	53.6
2 =West Indian butterfly (*Nymphalidae prepona*)	30.0	48.0
=Deer bot fly (*Cephenemyia pratti*)	30.0	48.0
4 Deer bot fly (*Chrysops*)	25.0	40.0
5 West Indian butterfly (*Hesperiidae sp.*)	18.6	30.0
6 Dragonfly (*Anax parthenope*)	17.8	28.6
7 Hornet (*Vespa crabro*)	13.3	21.4
8 Bumble bee (*Bombus lapidarius*)	11.1	17.9
9 Horsefly (*Tabanus bovinus*)	8.9	14.3
10 Honey bee (*Apis millefera*)	7.2	11.6

Few accurate assessments of these speeds have been attempted, and this list reflects only the results of those scientific studies recognized by entomologists.

TOP 10 ★
MOST COMMON INSECTS*

SPECIES	APPROXIMATE NO. OF KNOWN SPECIES
1 Beetles (*Coleoptera*)	400,000
2 Butterflies and moths (*Lepidoptera*)	165,000
3 Ants, bees, and wasps (*Hymenoptera*)	140,000
4 True flies (*Diptera*)	120,000
5 Bugs (*Hemiptera*)	90,000
6 Crickets, grasshoppers, and locusts (*Orthoptera*)	20,000
7 Caddisflies (*Trichoptera*)	10,000
8 Lice (*Phthiraptera/Psocoptera*)	7,000
9 Dragonflies and damselflies (*Odonata*)	5,500
10 Lacewings (*Neuroptera*)	4,700

* By number of known species

This list includes only species that have been discovered and named: it is believed that many thousands of species still await discovery.

TOP 10 CREATURES WITH THE MOST LEGS

(*Creature/average no. of legs*)

1 *Millipede Illacme plenipes*, 750 **2** *Centipede Himantarum gabrielis* 354 **3** *Centipede Haplophilus subterraneus*, 86 **4** Millipedes*, 30 **5** Symphylans, 24 **6** Caterpillars*, 16 **7** Woodlice, 14 **8** Crabs, shrimps, 10 **9** Spiders, 8 **10** Insects, 6

* Most species

"Centipede" means "100 feet" and "millipede" "1,000 feet." However, despite their names, centipedes, depending on their species, have anything from 28 to 354 legs, and millipedes up to 400, with the record standing at around 700. The other principal difference between them is that each body segment of a centipede has two legs, while that of a millipede has four.

PASSIONATE POSTMAN

This intimidating beast is the caterpillar of a butterfly known as the Postman. It is common from Central America to southern Brazil, and its food of choice is the passion flower.

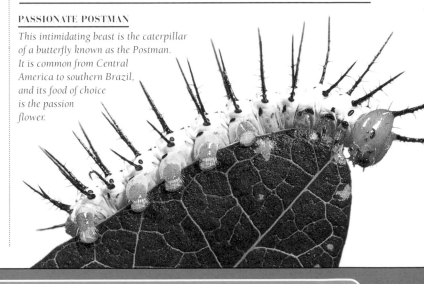

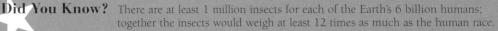

Did You Know? There are at least 1 million insects for each of the Earth's 6 billion humans; together the insects would weigh at least 12 times as much as the human race.

LIVESTOCK & FOOD CROPS

TOP 10 ★
MILK-PRODUCING COUNTRIES

	COUNTRY	1998 PRODUCTION TONS*
1	US	78,550,704
2	India	38,029,740
3	Russia	35,273,961
4	Germany	31,415,872
5	France	27,006,627
6	Brazil	22,281,018
7	UK	16,148,860
8	Ukraine	13,778,891
9	Poland	13,007,273
10	Netherlands	12,566,348
	World total	517,773,206

* Fresh cow's milk

TOP 10 ★
COFFEE-PRODUCING COUNTRIES

	COUNTRY	1998 PRODUCTION TONS
1	Brazil	1,822,142
2	Colombia	793,664
3	Indonesia	501,682
4	Vietnam	416,673
5	Côte d'Ivoire	366,358
6	Mexico	317,465
7	India	251,326
8	Ethiopia	224,871
9 =	Guatemala	198,416
=	Uganda	198,416
	US	3,747
	World total	6,946,681

Source: *Food and Agriculture Organization of the United Nations*

In recent years, there has been a decline in coffee production, from its former world peak of over 6.6 million tons. Kenya, perhaps surprisingly, does not appear in this list as its annual total of 63,000 tons places it at No. 21.

TOP 10 ★
RICE-PRODUCING COUNTRIES

	COUNTRY	1998 PRODUCTION TONS
1	China	212,714,446
2	India	134,750,943
3	Indonesia	51,026,497
4	Bangladesh	31,187,583
5	Vietnam	30,474,278
6	Thailand	23,148,537
7	Myanmar	18,298,367
8	Japan	13,813,063
9	Philippines	11,027,742
10	US	9,020,213
	World total	633,544,276

Source: *Food and Agriculture Organization of the United Nations*

World production of rice rose dramatically during the twentieth century. It remains the staple diet for a huge proportion of the global population, especially in Asian countries. Relatively small quantities are grown in the US and in Europe, where Italy is the leading producer with 1,537,157 tons.

TOP 10 ★
ORANGE-PRODUCING COUNTRIES

	COUNTRY	1998 PRODUCTION TONS
1	Brazil	25,376,198
2	US	13,857,155
3	Mexico	4,415,048
4	China	3,091,125
5	Spain	2,755,778
6	India	2,292,807
7	Italy	2,066,797
8	Iran	1,984,160
9	Egypt	1,730,628
10	Pakistan	1,554,258
	World total	73,118,931

Source: *Food and Agriculture Organization of the United Nations*

TOP 10 ★
WHEAT-PRODUCING COUNTRIES

	COUNTRY	1998 PRODUCTION TONS
1	China	121,254,464
2	US	76,725,276
3	India	72,752,546
4	France	43,940,333
5	Russia	27,337,320
6	Canada	25,527,325
7	Australia	24,091,013
8	Turkey	23,148,537
9	Germany	22,127,025
10	Pakistan	20,943,914
	World total	649,389,369

Source: *Food and Agriculture Organization of the United Nations*

TOP 10 ★
VEGETABLE-PRODUCING COUNTRIES*

	COUNTRY	1998 PRODUCTION TONS
1	China	261,398,025
2	India	60,590,745
3	US	38,541,951
4	Turkey	23,364,612
5	Japan	15,006,315
6	Italy	14,970,148
7	Egypt	13,498,331
8	Russia	13,335,211
9	South Korea	12,063,077
10	Spain	12,004,059
	World total	658,928,914

* Including watermelons; only vegetables grown for human consumption, but excluding crops from private gardens

Source: *Food and Agriculture Organization of the United Nations*

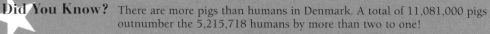

Did You Know? There are more pigs than humans in Denmark. A total of 11,081,000 pigs outnumber the 5,215,718 humans by more than two to one!

TOP 10 ★
PIG COUNTRIES

COUNTRY	PIGS (1998)
1 China	485,698,400
2 US	60,250,000
3 Brazil	35,900,000
4 Germany	24,782,200
5 Poland	19,240,000
6 Spain	18,155,000
7 Vietnam	18,060,000
8 Russia	16,579,000
9 India	16,005,000
10 Mexico	15,500,000
World total	938,944,200

The distribution of the world's pig population is determined by cultural, religious, and dietary factors. Few pigs are found in African and Islamic countries, for example, with the result that there is a disproportionate concentration of pigs in those countries that do not have such prohibitions: 74 percent of the world total is found in the Top 10 countries. Historically, pigs have been considered "unclean" by many religions because they do not chew the cud and because they have less-than-fastidious habits like wallowing in mud and eating garbage.

TOP 10 WOOL-PRODUCING COUNTRIES*

(Country/tons)

1 Australia, 757,287 **2** China, 316,363 **3** New Zealand, 279,987 **4** Uruguay, 90,220 **5** Russia, 77,161 **6** South Africa, 73,854 **7** UK, 71,650 **8** Argentina, 70,547 **9** Iran, 69,114 **10** Pakistan, 63,011

* 1998 production

HORSE POWER
The close relationship between men and their horses, shown here driving some long-horn cattle, has a special significance in Texas, the land of the cowboy.

TOP 10 ★
HORSE COUNTRIES

COUNTRY	HORSES (1998)
1 China	8,854,800
2 Brazil	6,394,140
3 Mexico	6,250,000
4 US	6,150,000
5 Argentina	3,300,000
6 Mongolia	2,900,000
7 Ethiopia	2,750,000
8 Colombia	2,450,000
9 Russia	2,200,000
10 Kazakhstan	1,082,700
Canada	395,000
World total	60,774,795

Mongolia makes an appearance in few Top 10 lists – but here it scores doubly since it is not only the sixth-largest rearer of horses in the world but also the only country in the world where the horse population is greater than its human population (2,363,000). Throughout the world, and especially in the US where there were once more than 10 million horses, the equine population has steadily declined as they have been replaced by motor vehicles. Horses are still used extensively in agriculture in many developing countries, but in the rest of the world they tend to be kept for sports and other recreational purposes.

TOP 10 ★
CATTLE COUNTRIES

COUNTRY	CATTLE (1998)
1 India	209,084,000
2 Brazil	161,000,000
3 US	99,501,000
4 China	96,192,530
5 Argentina	50,277,000
6 Russia	31,700,000
7 Ethiopia	29,900,000
8 Colombia	28,261,000
9 Australia	26,330,000
10 Mexico	25,580,000
Canada	13,157,300
World total	1,303,927,390

Source: *Food and Agriculture Organization of the United Nations*

TOP 10 CAMEL COUNTRIES

(Country/camels, 1998)

1 Somalia, 6,100,000 **2** Sudan, 2,950,000 **3** India, 1,520,000 **4** = Mauritania, 1,100,000; = Pakistan, 1,100,000 **6** Ethiopia, 1,030,000 **7** Kenya, 810,000 **8** Chad, 650,000 **9** Saudi Arabia, 422,000 **10** Niger, 392,000

Source: *Food and Agriculture Organization of the United Nations*

TREES & NONFOOD CROPS

LARGEST NATIONAL FORESTS IN THE US

	FOREST	LOCATION	AREA SQ MILES	SQ KM
1	Tongass National Forest	Sitka, Alaska	25,937	67,177
2	Chugach National Forest	Anchorage, Alaska	8,281	21,448
3	Toiyabe National Forest	Sparks, Nevada	5,000	12,950
4	Tonto National Forest	Phoenix, Arizona	4,531	11,735
5 =Gila National Forest		Silver City, New Mexico	4,218	10,925
=Boise National Forest		Boise, Idaho	4,218	10,925
7 =Challis National Forest		Challis, Idaho	3,906	10,116
=Humboldt National Forest		Elko, Nevada	3,906	10,116
9 =Shoshone National Forest		Cody, Wyoming	3,750	9,712
=Flathead National Forest		Kalispell, Montana	3,750	9,712

This list's No. 1 is actually larger than all 10 of the smallest states and the District of Columbia. Even the much smaller No. 2 is larger than Connecticut.

Source: *Land Areas of the National Forest System*

NONFOOD CROPS

	CROP	1998 PRODUCTION TONS
1	Cotton	20,028,681
2	Tobacco	7,646,760
3	Rubber	7,473,768
4	Jute	3,142,176
5	Castor beans	1,311,884
6	Coir	716,381
7	Flax	706,708
8	Sisal	366,467
9	Kapok	135,821
10	Hops	128,769

Source: *Food and Agriculture Organization of the United Nations*

COTTON PICKING

In a "snowy" field in Queensland, Australia, cotton is being harvested. As the No. 1 nonfood crop in the world, cotton is used mainly for clothing; world production reaches a massive 21,560,000 tons.

RUBBER-PRODUCING COUNTRIES

	COUNTRY	1998 PRODUCTION TONS
1	Thailand	2,383,650
2	Indonesia	1,724,372
3	Malaysia	1,193,141
4	India	597,452
5	China	496,040
6	Philippines	220,462
7	Vietnam	199,187
8	Côte d'Ivoire	127,502
9	Sri Lanka	116,608
10	Nigeria	99,208
	World total	7,473,768

Source: *Food and Agriculture Organization of the United Nations*

COTTON-PRODUCING COUNTRIES

	COUNTRY	1998 PRODUCTION TONS
1	China	4,409,245
2	US	3,175,758
3	India	2,998,286
4	Pakistan	1,721,810
5	Uzbekistan	1,074,753
6	Turkey	826,733
7	Australia	734,139
8 =Brazil		459,433
=Greece		459,433
10	Egypt	377,023
	World total	20,028,681

Source: *Food and Agriculture Organization of the United Nations*

Did You Know? The planet's total area of forests and woodland has barely fluctuated in the past quarter-century. In 1972 the forested proportion stood at just over 32 percent, and today it is just under 32 percent.

TOP 10 ★
MOST FORESTED COUNTRIES

	COUNTRY	PERCENTAGE FOREST COVER
1	Surinam	92
2	Papua New Guinea	91
3	Solomon Islands	85
4	French Guiana	81
5	Guyana	77
6	Gabon	74
7	Finland	69
8 =	Bhutan	66
=	Japan	66
10	North Korea	65

Source: *Food and Agriculture Organization of the United Nations*

REACH FOR THE SKY

This giant sequoia is the General Grant tree in King's Canyon National Park, California. Another Californian example, the General Sherman, at 275 ft/ 83.8 m high is the biggest tree in the US and the tallest living thing on the Earth.

TOP 10 ★
TIMBER-PRODUCING COUNTRIES

	COUNTRY	1998 PRODUCTION CU FT	CU M
1	US	17,491,532,624	495,305,000
2	China	11,051,973,179	312,957,000
3	India	10,747,631,353	304,339,000
4	Brazil	7,782,046,625	220,363,000
5	Indonesia	7,090,638,359	200,784,500
6	Canada	6,654,413,897	188,432,000
7	Nigeria	4,036,855,242	114,311,000
8	Russia	3,399,036,988	96,250,000
9	Sweden	1,992,594,940	56,424,000
10	Ethiopia	1,742,944,943	49,354,700
	World total	118,455,733,074	3,354,292,510

Source: *Food and Agriculture Organization of the United Nations*

TOP 10 ★
BIGGEST TREES IN THE US*

	TREE/LOCATION	POINTS#
1	**General Sherman giant sequoia**, Sequoia National Park, California	1,300
2	**Coast redwood**, Prairie Creek, California	1,205
3	**Western redcedar**, Olympic National Park, Washington	931
4	**Sitka spruce**, Olympic National Park, Washington	924
5	**Coast Douglas fir**, Coos County, Oregon	782
6	**Common baldcypress**, Cat Island, Louisiana	748
7	**Sycamore**, Jeromesville, Ohio	737
8	**Sugar pine**, Dorrington, California	681
9	**Port-Orford-cedar**, Siskiyou National Forest, Oregon	680
10	**Monterey express**, Pescadero County, California	656

* By species (i.e., the biggest known example of each)

The circumference in inches of the tree 4½ feet above the ground added to the height of the tree in feet and to ¼ of the average crown spread in feet

Source: *National Register of Big Trees, American Forestry Association*

TOP 10 ★
TALLEST TREES IN THE US*

	TREE	LOCATION	HEIGHT FT	M
1	Coast Douglas fir	Coos County, Oregon	329	100.3
2	Coast redwood	Prairie Creek Redwoods State Park, California	313	95.4
3	General Sherman, giant sequoia	Sequoia National Park, California	275	83.8
4	Noble fir	Mount St. Helens National Monument, Washington	272	82.9
5	Grand fir	Redwood National Park, California	257	78.3
6	Western hemlock	Olympic National Park, Washington	241	73.5
7	Sugar pine	Dorrington, California	232	70.7
8	Ponderosa pine	Plumas National Forest, California	223	68.0
9	Port-Orford cedar	Siskiyou National Forest, Oregon	219	66.8
10	Pacific silver fir	Forks, Washington	217	66.1

* By species (i.e., the tallest known example of each of the 10 tallest species)

THE HUMAN WORLD

TOP 10 ★
COUNTRIES THAT SPEND THE MOST ON HEALTH CARE

	COUNTRY	TOTAL SPENDING AS A PERCENTAGE OF GDP*
1	US	14.2
2	Argentina	10.6
3	Germany	10.4
4	Croatia	10.1
5	Switzerland	10.0
6	France	9.9
7=	Canada	9.6
=	Czech Republic	9.6
9=	Australia	8.9
=	Austria	8.9

* Gross Domestic Product

Source: World Bank, World Development Indicators 1998

The figures are for total health care spending, public and private. In some countries, private spending is greater than public spending on health (in the US, public spending is 6.3 percent of GDP, private spending is 7.9 percent). In other countries, government accounts for a much greater share (in Croatia, public spending is 8.5 percent of GDP; private spending is 1.6 percent). The UK spends less than half the proportion spent by the US (public spending is 5.8 percent of GDP; private spending is 1.1 percent).

THE 10 MOST COMMON HOSPITAL ER CASES

(Reason for visit/visits, 1997)

1 Stomach and abdominal pain, cramps and spasms, 5,527,000 **2** Chest pain and related symptoms, 5,315,000 **3** Fever, 4,212,000 **4** Headache, pain in head, 2,518,000 **5** Injury – upper extremity, 2,383,000 **6** Shortness of breath, 2,242,000 **7** Cough, 2,220,000 **8** Back symptoms, 2,073,000 **9** Pain, site not referable to a specific body system, 2,040,000 **10** Symptoms referable to throat, 1,953,000

Source: Center for Disease Control/National Center for Health Statistics

THE 10 ★
COUNTRIES WITH THE MOST PATIENTS PER DOCTOR

	COUNTRY	PATIENTS PER DOCTOR
1	Niger	53,986
2	Malawi	44,205
3	Mozambique	36,225
4	Burkina Faso	34,804
5	Ethiopia	32,499
6	Chad	30,030
7	Central African Republic	25,920
8	Rwanda	24,967
9	Lesotho	24,095
10	Angola	23,725
	US	421

Source: World Bank, World Development Indicators

THE 10 ★
MOST COMMON REASONS FOR VISITS TO A PHYSICIAN

	REASON FOR VISIT	VISITS, 1997
1	General medical examination	59,796,000
2	Progress visit, not otherwise specified	28,583,000
3	Cough	25,735,000
4	Routine prenatal examination	22,979,000
5	Postoperative visit	18,861,000
6	Symptoms referable to throat	17,151,000
7	Well baby examination	15,526,000
8	Vision dysfunctions	13,443,000
9	Earache or ear infection	13,359,000
10	Back symptoms	12,863,000

Source: National Ambulatory Medical Care Survey/Center for Disease Control/National Center for Health Statistics

A total of 787,372,000 visits were made in 1997.

TOP 10 ★
LONGEST BONES IN THE HUMAN BODY

	BONE	AVERAGE LENGTH IN	CM
1	Femur (thighbone – upper leg)	19.88	50.50
2	Tibia (shinbone – inner lower leg)	16.94	43.03
3	Fibula (outer lower leg)	15.94	40.50
4	Humerus (upper arm)	14.35	36.46
5	Ulna (inner lower arm)	11.10	28.20
6	Radius (outer lower arm)	10.40	26.42
7	7th rib	9.45	24.00
8	8th rib	9.06	23.00
9	Innominate bone (hipbone – half pelvis)	7.28	18.50
10	Sternum (breastbone)	6.69	17.00

These are average dimensions of the bones of an adult male measured from the extremities (ribs are curved, and the pelvis is measured diagonally). The same bones in the female skeleton are usually 6 to 13 percent smaller, with the exception of the sternum, which is virtually identical.

TOP 10 ★
MOST COMMON ELEMENTS IN THE HUMAN BODY

	ELEMENT	WEIGHT OZ	G*
1	Oxygen	1,608	45,500
2	Carbon	445	12,600
3	Hydrogen	247	7,000
4	Nitrogen	74	2,100
5	Calcium	37	1,050
6	Phosphorus	25	700
7	Sulfur	6	175
8	Potassium	5	140
9=	Chlorine	4	105
=	Sodium	4	105

* Average in a 154 lb/70 kg person

The remaining 1 percent comprises minute quantities of metallic elements.

Did You Know? Keraunothnetophobia is a fear of satellites falling to Earth. Other strange phobias include geniophobia (a fear of chins), linonophobia (a fear of string), and chrometophobia (a fear of money).

TOP 10 ★
LARGEST HUMAN ORGANS

ORGAN		AVERAGE WEIGHT OZ	G
1 Skin		384.0	10,886
2 Liver		55.0	1,560
3 Brain	male	49.7	1,408
	female	44.6	1,263
4 Lungs	right	20.5	580
	left	18.0	510
	total	38.5	1,090
5 Heart	male	11.1	315
	female	9.3	265
6 Kidneys	right	4.9	140
	left	5.3	150
	total	10.2	290
7 Spleen		6.0	170
8 Pancreas		3.5	98
9 Thyroid		1.2	35
10 Prostate (male only)		0.7	20

This list is based on average immediate post-mortem weights, as recorded by St. Bartholemew's Hospital, London, and other sources during a 10-year period. Various instances of organs far in excess of the average have been recorded, including male brains of over 70.6 oz/2,000 g. The Victorians believed that the heavier the brain, the greater the intelligence, and were impressed by recorded weights of 58 oz/1,658 g and 67 oz/1,907 g for William Makepeace Thackeray and Otto von Bismarck, respectively.

TOP 10 ★
MOST COMMON PHOBIAS

	OBJECT OF PHOBIA	MEDICAL TERM
1	Spiders	Arachnephobia or arachnophobia
2	People and social situations	Anthropophobia or sociophobia
3	Flying	Aerophobia or aviatophobia
4	Open spaces	Agoraphobia, cenophobia, or kenophobia
5	Confined spaces	Claustrophobia, cleisiophobia, cleithrophobia, or clithrophobia
6 =	Vomiting	Emetophobia or emitophobia
=	Heights	Acrophobia, altophobia, hypsophobia, or hypsiphobia
8	Cancer	Carcinomaphobia, carcinophobia, carcinomatophobia, cancerphobia, or cancerophobia
9	Thunderstorms	Brontophobia or keraunophobia
10 =	Death	Necrophobia or thanatophobia
=	Heart disease	Cardiophobia

A phobia is a morbid fear that is out of all proportion to the object of the fear. Many people would admit to being uncomfortable about these principal phobias, as well as others, such as snakes (ophiophobia) or ghosts (phasmophobia), but most do not become obsessive about them and allow such fears to rule their lives. Technophobia, the fear of modern technology such as computers, is increasingly reported.

HAIRY SCARY
A fear of spiders is not necessarily groundless: many spiders, such as black widows and hobo spiders are lethal. As for the house spider, look behind you! It can speed at 1 mph/1.9 km/h.

THE 10 ★
MOST COMMON CAUSES OF ILLNESS

	CAUSE	NEW CASES ANNUALLY
1	Diarrhea (including dysentery)	4,002,000,000
2	Malaria	up to 500,000,000
3	Acute lower respiratory infections	395,000,000
4	Occupational injuries	350,000,000
5	Occupational diseases	217,000,000
6	Trichomoniasis	170,000,000
7	Mood (affective) disorders	122,865,000
8	Chlamydial infections	89,000,000
9	Alcohol dependence syndrome	75,000,000
10	Gonococcal (bacterial) infections	62,000,000

Source: *World Health Organization*

SKIN DEEP

Considered the largest human organ, the human skin (seen here in closeup, with a hair follicle) accounts for an area of 21 sq ft/2 sq m. It averages 0.04–0.08 in (1–2 mm) thick, but may measure up to 0.2 in (6 mm) thick on the soles of the feet, while the eyelids may be as little as 0.02 in (0.5 mm) thick. Skin is constantly replaced: it takes 50 days for new tissue completely to replace the old, which sheds at a rate of some 50,000 microscopic flakes per minute. In a lifetime, a person loses a total of 40 lb/18 kg. The skin contains about 3 million sweat glands, which release 10 ounces (0.3 liters) of sweat per day on average – up to 3.7 quarts (3.5 liters) in hot climates.

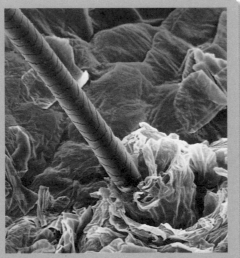

BIRTHS, MARRIAGES & DEATHS

THE 10 MOST SUICIDAL COUNTRIES

(Country/suicides per 100,000 population, 1997)

1. Lithuania, 45.8
2. Russia, 41.8
3. Estonia, 41.0
4. Latvia, 40.7
5. Hungary, 32.9
6. Slovenia, 28.4
7. Belarus, 27.9
8. Finland, 27.3
9. Kazakstan, 23.8
10. Croatia, 22.8

Source: United Nations

The lowest suicide rate recorded is in Egypt – fewer than one suicide per 1 million people.

THE 10 COUNTRIES WITH THE HIGHEST DIVORCE RATE

(Country/1997 divorce rate per 1,000)

1. Maldives, 10.75
2. Cuba, 5.95
3. China, 4.63
4. Russia, 4.60
5. US, 4.57
6. Belarus, 4.26
7. Surinam, 4.15
8. Ukraine, 4.00
9. Estonia, 3.74
10. Latvia, 3.20

Source: United Nations

The UK has the highest divorce rate in Europe (excluding republics of the former Soviet Union). According to UN statistics, the Isle of Man, if it was an independent country, would appear in seventh place in this list, with a divorce rate of 4.2 per 1,000 population.

TOP 10 COUNTRIES WITH THE HIGHEST FEMALE LIFE EXPECTANCY

COUNTRY	LIFE EXPECTANCY AT BIRTH (YEARS), 1997
1 Japan	82.5
2 Switzerland	81.2
3 Sweden	81.1
4 =France	80.8
=Iceland	80.8
6 Canada	80.7
7 =Australia	80.6
=Italy	80.6
9 Spain	80.5
10 Netherlands	80.4

Source: United Nations

TOP 10 COUNTRIES WITH THE HIGHEST MALE LIFE EXPECTANCY

COUNTRY	LIFE EXPECTANCY AT BIRTH (YEARS), 1997
1 Japan	76.4
2 Iceland	75.8
3 Sweden	75.4
4 Greece	75.0
5 Cyprus	74.8
6 =Australia	74.7
=Switzerland	74.7
8 =Israel	74.6
=Spain	74.6
10 Netherlands	74.4

Source: United Nations

TOP 10 COUNTRIES WITH THE HIGHEST MARRIAGE RATE

(Country/1997 marriage rate per 1,000, per annum)

1. Maldives, 19.7
2. Cuba, 17.7
3. Bermuda, 14.2
4. Liechtenstein, 12.9
5. Seychelles, 11.9
6. Barbados, 11.2
7. Bangladesh, 10.9
8. Tajikistan, 9.6
9. Mauritius, 9.5
10. Bahamas, 9.3

Source: United Nations

THE 10 COUNTRIES WITH THE LOWEST DIVORCE RATE

COUNTRY	1997 DIVORCE RATE PER 1,000
1 Guatemala	0.15
2 Macedonia	0.27
3 Mexico	0.35
4 =Chile	0.46
=Turkey	0.46
6 Italy	0.48
7 =Iran	0.50
=Libya	0.50
9 El Salvador	0.51
10 Jamaica	0.54

Source: United Nations

THE 10 COUNTRIES WITH THE LOWEST MARRIAGE RATE

COUNTRY	1997 MARRIAGE RATE PER 1,000
1 Andorra	2.0
2 Malaysia	3.2
3 South Africa	3.3
4 St. Lucia	3.4
5 =Dominican Republic	3.6
=Paraguay	3.6
7 Cape Verde	3.8
8 =Bulgaria	4.0
=United Arab Emirates	4.0
10 El Salvador	4.2

Source: United Nations

THE 10 COUNTRIES WITH THE HIGHEST DEATH RATE

COUNTRY	1997 DEATH RATE PER 1,000
1 Sierra Leone	25.1
2 Afghanistan	21.8
3 Guinea Bissau	21.3
4 Guinea	20.3
5 =Angola	19.2
=Uganda	19.2
7 Niger	18.9
8 The Gambia	18.8
9 =Mozambique	18.5
=Somalia	18.5
US	8.8

Source: United Nations

What is the most popular boy's name in the US?
see p.79 for the answer

A Jacob
B Michael
C Christopher

THE 10 ★
MOST COMMON CAUSES OF DEATH

	CAUSE	APPROXIMATE DEATHS PER ANNUM
1	Ischemic heart disease	7,200,000
2	Cancers	6,346,000
3	Cerebrovascular disease	4,600,000
4	Acute lower respiratory infection	3,905,000
5	Tuberculosis	3,000,000
6	Chronic obstructive pulmonary disease	2,888,000
7	Diarrhea (including dysentery)	2,473,000
8	Malaria	1,500,000–2,700,000
9	HIV/AIDS	1,500,000
10	Hepatitis B	1,156,000

Source: *World Health Organization*

SMOKERS' DISEASE

This magnification of the epithelium – the mucus membrane that lines the lung airways – shows the chaotic cell growth caused by lung cancer. Blood cells (in red) have also leaked out due to hemorrhage.

THE 10 ★
COUNTRIES WITH THE MOST DEATHS FROM HEART DISEASE

	COUNTRY	DEATH RATE PER 100,000
1	Czech Republic	314.4
2	Scotland	258.3
3	New Zealand	248.6
4	Finland	243.2
5	Hungary	240.0
6	Bulgaria	230.1
7	Denmark	211.1
8	England and Wales	210.0
9	Sweden	209.3
10	Australia	200.5
	US	188.1

TOP 10 ★
YEARS WITH THE MOST BIRTHS IN THE US

	YEAR	BIRTHS
1	1957	4,308,000
2	1961	4,268,000
3	1960	4,258,000
4	1958	4,255,000
5	1959	4,245,000
6	1956	4,218,000
7	1962	4,167,000
8	1990	4,158,000
9	1991	4,111,000
10	1955	4,104,000

The total number of births in the US first exceeded 3 million in 1921, but then remained below this figure throughout the 1920s and 1930s.

THE 10 COUNTRIES WITH THE HIGHEST BIRTH RATE

(Country/live births per 1,000 per annum)

1 Niger, 52.5 **2** Uganda, 51.8
3 Angola, 51.3 **4** Guinea, 50.6
5 = Afghanistan, 50.2; = Somalia, 50.2
7 Côte d'Ivoire, 49.8 **8** Yemen, 49.4
9 Sierra Leone, 49.1 **10** = Benin, 48.7; = Mali, 48.7

THE 10 COUNTRIES WITH THE LOWEST BIRTH RATE

(Country/live births per 1,000 per annum)

1 Bulgaria, 8.1 **2** Latvia, 8.5
3 Estonia, 8.8 **4** Spain, 9.1 **5** Italy, 9.2
6 = Czech Republic, 9.3; = Germany, 9.3; = Russia, 9.3 **9** Slovenia, 9.6
10 = Greece, 9.8; = San Marino, 9.8

Source: *United Nations*
If counted as an independent country, the Vatican City, with a birth rate of zero, would head this list.

BABY BOOM

The population is expanding fast, with more people being born and living longer than ever before. Experts predict that the world population will reach 10 billion by 2080.

WHAT'S IN A NAME?

TOP 10 MOST COMMON LAST NAMES IN THE UK

1 Smith **2** Jones **3** Williams **4** Brown **5** Taylor **6** Davies/Davis **7** Evans **8** Thomas **9** Roberts **10** Johnson

The list of top surnames in the UK has a number of entries in common with its US counterpart, reflecting the British ancestry of a high proportion of American citizens. Smith heads the list in both countries.

MASTER...?

One hundred years ago, this little boy would quite possibly have been called William, John, or George. None of the boys' names popular in the US then are still favored today, but in the UK Thomas and James remain perennial favorites.

TOP 10 ★ BOYS' NAMES IN ENGLAND AND WALES

1988		1998
Daniel	1	Jack
Christopher	2	Thomas
Michael	3	James
James	4	Daniel
Matthew	5	Joshua
Andrew	6	Matthew
Adam	7	Samuel
Thomas	8	Callum
David	9	Joseph
Richard	10	Jordan

TOP 10 MOST COMMON LAST NAMES IN THE US

(Name/percent of all US last names)

1 Smith, 1.006 **2** Johnson, 0.810 **3** Williams, 0.699 **4** = Jones, 0.621; = Brown, 0.621 **6** Davis, 0.480 **7** Miller, 0.424 **8** Wilson, 0.339 **9** Moore, 0.312 **10** = Anderson, 0.311; = Taylor, 0.311; = Thomas, 0.311

The Top 10 (or, in view of those in equal 10th place, 12) US last names together make up over 6 percent of the entire US population – in other words, one American in every 16 bears one of these names.

TOP 10 ★ GIRLS' AND BOYS' NAMES IN THE US 100 YEARS AGO

GIRLS		BOYS
Mary	1	John
Helen	2	William
Anna	3	James
Margaret	4	George
Ruth	5	Charles
Elizabeth	6	Joseph
Marie	7	Frank
Rose	8	Henry
Florence	9	Robert
Bertha	10	Harry

TOP 10 ★ GIRLS' AND BOYS' NAMES IN THE UK 100 YEARS AGO

GIRLS		BOYS
Florence	1	William
Mary	2	John
Alice	3	George
Annie	4	Thomas
Elsie	5	Charles
Edith	6	Frederick
Elizabeth	7	Arthur
Doris	8	James
Dorothy	9	Albert
Ethel	10	Ernest

TOP 10 ★ MOST COMMON LAST NAMES IN THE MANHATTAN TELEPHONE DIRECTORY

1	Smith
2	Brown
3	Williams
4	Cohen
5	Lee
6	Johnson
7	Rodriguez
8	Green
9	Davis
10	Jones

IT'S A GIRL!
Emily and Hannah are popular choices today on both sides of the Atlantic. Ten years ago, Sarah and Samantha were shared favorites.

TOP 10 ⭐
GIRLS' NAMES IN THE US

1988		1998
Ashley	1	Kaitlyn
Jessica	2	Emily
Amanda	3	Sarah
Jennifer	4	Hannah
Brittany	5	Ashley
Sarah	6	Brianna
Stephanie	7	Alexis
Samantha	8	Samantha
Heather	9	Taylor
Elizabeth	10	Madison

TOP 10 TERMS OF ENDEARMENT USED IN THE US

1 Honey **2** Baby **3** Sweetheart **4** Dear **5** Lover **6** Darling **7** Sugar **8** = Angel; = Pumpkin **10** = Beautiful; = Precious

A survey of romance conducted by a US champagne company concluded that 26 percent of American adults favored "honey" as their most frequently used term of endearment. Curiously, identical numbers were undecided whether to call their loved one an angel or a pumpkin ....

TOP 10 ⭐
BOYS' NAMES IN THE US

1988		1998
Michael	1	Michael
Christopher	2	Jacob
Matthew	3	Matthew
Joshua	4	Nicholas
David	5	Joshua
Daniel	6	Christopher
Andrew	7	Brandon
Justin	8	Austin
Robert	9	Tyler
Joseph	10	Zachary

TOP 10 ⭐
GIRLS' NAMES IN ENGLAND AND WALES

1988		1998
Rebecca	1	Chloe
Sarah	2	Emily
Emma	3	Megan
Laura	4	Jessica
Rachel	5	Sophie
Samantha	6	Charlotte
Charlotte	7	Hannah
Kirsty	8	Lauren
Nicola	9	Rebecca
Amy	10	Lucy

⭐ **Did You Know?** At least 800,000 people in England and Wales have Smith for their last name, which means that one person in every 61 is called Smith.

TOP 10 LONGEST-SERVING PRESIDENTS TODAY

	PRESIDENT	COUNTRY	TOOK OFFICE
1	General Gnassingbé Eyadéma	Togo	Apr 14, 1967
2	El Hadj Omar Bongo	Gabon	Dec 2, 1967
3	Colonel Mu'ammar Gadhafi	Libya	Sep 1, 1969
4	Lt.-General Hafiz al-Asad	Syria	Feb 22, 1971
5	Zayid ibn Sultan al-Nuhayyan	United Arab Emirates	Dec 2, 1971
6	Fidel Castro	Cuba	Dec 2, 1976
7	France-Albert René	Seychelles	Jun 5, 1977
8	Hassan Gouled Aptidon	Djibouti	Sep 30, 1977
9	Daniel Teroitich arap Moi	Kenya	Oct 14, 1978
10	Saddam Hussein	Iraq	Jul 16, 1979

All the presidents in this list have been in power for more than 20 – some for over 30 – years. Among those no longer in office, Félix Houhouët-Boigny, President of Côte d'Ivoire, died on December 7, 1993; he was, at 88, the oldest president in the world.

TOP 10 ★ US PRESIDENTS WITH THE MOST CHILDREN

	PRESIDENT	CHILDREN
1	John Tyler	14
2	William Henry Harrison	10
3	Rutherford Birchard Hayes	8
4	James Abram Garfield	7
5=	George Herbert Walker Bush	6
=	Thomas Jefferson	6
=	Franklin Delano Roosevelt	6*
=	Theodore Roosevelt	6
=	Zachary Taylor	6
10=	John Adams	5
=	Grover Cleveland	5
=	Andrew Johnson	5
=	Ronald Reagan	5

* Including one child deceased

THE 10 ★ FIRST COUNTRIES TO RATIFY THE UN CHARTER

	COUNTRY	DATE
1	Nicaragua	Jul 6, 1945
2	US	Aug 8, 1945
3	France	Aug 31, 1945
4	Dominican Republic	Sep 4, 1945
5	New Zealand	Sep 19, 1945
6	Brazil	Sep 21, 1945
7	Argentina	Sep 24, 1945
8	China	Sep 28, 1945
9	Denmark	Oct 9, 1945
10	Chile	Oct 11, 1945

In New York on June 26, 1945, barely weeks after the end of World War II in Europe (the Japanese did not surrender until September 3), 50 nations signed the World Security Charter, thereby establishing the United Nations as an international peacekeeping organization. The UN came into effect on October 24, which has since been celebrated as United Nations Day.

INTERNATIONAL RELIEF

The UN's Operation Lifeline Sudan brought food and medical supplies to thousands of starving Sudanese in 1994. One of the UN's most high-profile activities is its supply of relief aid.

TOP 10 ★
PARLIAMENTS WITH THE MOST WOMEN MEMBERS*

	PARLIAMENT/ ELECTION	WOMEN MEMBERS	TOTAL MEMBERS	% WOMEN
1	Sweden, 1998	149	349	42.7
2	Denmark, 1998	67	179	37.4
3	Norway, 1997	60	165	36.4
4	Netherlands, 1998	54	150	36.0
5	Finland, 1995	67	200	33.5
6	Germany, 1998	207	669	30.9
7	South Africa, 1994	118	400	29.6
8	New Zealand, 1996	35	120	29.2
9	=Argentina, 1997	71	257	27.6
	=Cuba, 1998	166	601	27.6

As at January 1, 1999, as a percentage
Source: *Inter-Parliamentary Union*

THE 10 ★
FIRST FEMALE PRIME MINISTERS AND PRESIDENTS

	PRIME MINISTER OR PRESIDENT	COUNTRY/ PERIOD IN OFFICE
1	Sirimavo Bandaranaike (PM)	Sri Lanka, 1960–64/1970–77
2	Indira Gandhi (PM)	India, 1966–84
3	Golda Meir (PM)	Israel, 1969–74
4	Maria Estela Perón (P)	Argentina, 1974–75
5	Elisabeth Domitien (PM)	Central African Republic, 1975–present
6	Margaret Thatcher (PM)	UK, May 1979–Nov 1990
7	Dr. Maria Lurdes Pintasilgo (PM)	Portugal, Aug–Nov 1979
8	Vigdís Finnbogadóttir (P)	Iceland, Jun 1980–present
9	Mary Eugenia Charles (PM)	Dominica, Jul 1980–present
10	Gro Harlem Brundtland (PM)	Norway, Feb–Oct 1981/ May 1986–Oct 1989

VOTES FOR WOMEN

Campaigners, such as Sylvia Pankhurst and Susan B. Anthony, were often jailed for their public demonstrations in support of the Women's Suffrage movement. As the movement gained momentum on both sides of the Atlantic, women were gradually allowed to vote in most Western countries, including Great Britain and Ireland in 1918 and the US in 1920. A number of European countries, such as France and Italy, did not permit women to vote until 1945. Liechtenstein was one of the last countries to relent, finally giving women the right to vote in 1984.

SNAP SHOTS★

THE 10 FIRST COUNTRIES TO GIVE WOMEN THE VOTE

(Country/year)

1 New Zealand, 1893 **2** Australia, 1902 (South Australia, 1894; Western Australia, 1898; Australia united, 1901) **3** Finland (then a Grand Duchy under the Russian Crown), 1906 **4** Norway, 1907 (restricted franchise; all women over 25 in 1913) **5** Denmark and Iceland (a Danish dependency until 1918), 1915 **6** = Netherlands, 1917; = USSR, 1917 **8** = Austria, 1918; = Canada, 1918; = Germany, 1918; = Great Britain and Ireland, 1918 (Ireland part of the United Kingdom until 1921; women over 30 only – lowered to 21 in 1928); = Poland, 1918

TOP 10 ★
YOUNGEST US PRESIDENTS

	PRESIDENT	AGE ON TAKING OFFICE YEARS	DAYS
1	Theodore Roosevelt	42	322
2	John F. Kennedy	43	236
3	William J. Clinton	46	154
4	Ulysses S. Grant	46	236
5	Grover Cleveland	47	351
6	Franklin Pierce	48	101
7	James A. Garfield	49	105
8	James K. Polk	49	122
9	Millard Fillmore	50	184
10	Chester A. Arthur	50	350

The US Constitution states that a president must be at least 35 years old on taking office.

TOP 10 ★
LONGEST-LIVED US PRESIDENTS

	PRESIDENT	AGE AT DEATH YEARS	MONTHS
1	John Adams	90	8
2	Herbert Clark Hoover	90	2
3	Harry S. Truman	88	7
4	James Madison	85	3
5	Thomas Jefferson	83	2
6	Richard M. Nixon	81	3
7	John Quincy Adams	80	7
8	Martin Van Buren	79	7
9	Dwight D. Eisenhower	78	5
10	Andrew Jackson	78	2

At 88 on February 6, 1999, Ronald Reagan is the oldest living former president.

Did You Know? The United Nations has grown from its 50 founding nations to a total of 184 nations.

81

AMUNDSEN AT THE POLE

Just 33 days separated the first two expeditions to reach the South Pole. While Scott's team struggled toward its goal, the Norwegians arrived first. The exhausted British team died on the return trip.

THE 10 ★
FIRST PEOPLE TO REACH THE SOUTH POLE

	NAME/NATIONALITY	DATE
1=	Roald Amundsen*, Norwegian	Dec 14, 1911
=	Olav Olavsen Bjaaland, Norwegian	Dec 14, 1911
=	Helmer Julius Hanssen, Norwegian	Dec 14, 1911
=	Helge Sverre Hassel, Norwegian	Dec 14, 1911
=	Oscar Wisting, Norwegian	Dec 14, 1911
6=	Robert Falcon Scott*, British	Jan 17. 1912
=	Henry Robertson Bowers, British	Jan 17, 1912
=	Edgar Evans, British	Jan 17, 1912
=	Lawrence Edward Oates, British	Jan 17, 1912
=	Edward Adrian Wilson, British	Jan 17, 1912

* Expedition leader

THE 10 ★
FIRST PEOPLE TO GO OVER NIAGARA FALLS AND SURVIVE

	NAME/METHOD	DATE
1	Annie Edson Taylor, Wooden barrel	Oct 24, 1901
2	Bobby Leach, Steel barrel	July 25, 1911
3	Jean Lussier, Steel and rubber ball fitted with oxygen cylinders	July 4, 1928
4	William Fitzgerald (aka Nathan Boya), Steel and rubber ball fitted with oxygen cylinders	July 15, 1961
5	Karel Soucek, Barrel	July 3, 1984
6	Steven Trotter, Barrel	Aug 18, 1985
7	Dave Mundy, Barrel	Oct 5, 1985
8=	Peter deBernardi, Metal container	Sept 28, 1989
=	Jeffrey Petkovich, Metal container	Sept 28, 1989
10	Dave Mundy, Diving bell	Sept 26, 1993

Source: *Niagara Falls Museum*

THE 10 ★
FIRST *TIME* MAGAZINE "MEN OF THE YEAR"

YEAR	RECIPIENT/DATES	DESCRIPTION
1927	Charles Lindbergh (1902–74)	US aviator
1928	Walter P. Chrysler (1875–1940)	US businessman
1929	Owen D. Young (1874–1962)	US lawyer
1930	Mahatma Gandhi (1869–1948)	Indian politician
1931	Pierre Laval (1883–1945)	French President
1932	Franklin D. Roosevelt (1882–1945)	US President
1933	Hugh S. Johnson (1882–1942)	US soldier
1934	Franklin D. Roosevelt (1882–1945)	US President
1935	Haile Salassie (1891–1975)	Emperor of Ethiopia
1936	Wallis Simpson (1896–1986)	Duchess of Windsor

The most newsworthy "Man of the Year," nominated annually by the editors of *Time* magazine, may be one man, a group of men, a couple, a woman (as in the case of No. 10 in this list), a group of women, a machine, or even, as in 1988, "Endangered Earth." The lives of two of the First 10 ended violently: Gandhi was assassinated, while Laval was executed by firing squad after being found guilty of treason.

THE 10 ★
CIRCUMNAVIGATION FIRSTS

	CIRCUMNAVIGATION/CRAFT	CAPTAIN(S)	RETURN DATE
1	**First**, *Vittoria*	Juan Sebastian de Elcano*	Sept 6, 1522
2	**First in less than 80 days**, Various	"Nellie Bly" #	Jan 25, 1890
3	**First solo**, *Spray*	Capt. Joshua Slocum	July 3, 1898
4	**First by air**, *Chicago* / *New Orleans*	Lt. Lowell Smith / Lt. Leslie P. Arnold	Sept 28, 1924
5	**First nonstop by air**, *Lucky Lady II*	Capt. James Gallagher	Mar 2, 1949
6	**First underwater**, *Triton*	Capt. Edward Latimer Beach	Apr 25, 1960
7	**First non-stop solo**, *Suhali*	Robin Knox-Johnston	Apr 22, 1969
8	**First helicopter**, *Spirit of Texas*	H. Ross Perot Jr. and Jay Coburn	Sept 30, 1982
9	**First air without refueling**, *Voyager*	Richard Ruttan and Jeana Yaeger	Dec 23, 1986
10	**First by balloon**, *Breitling Orbiter 3*	Brian Jones and Bertrand Piccard	Mar 21, 1999

* The expedition was led by Ferdinand Magellan, but he did not survive the voyage.

 # Real name Elizabeth Cochrane. This US journalist set out to beat the fictitious "record" established in Jules Verne's novel, Around the World in 80 Days.

 Did You Know? The youngest person to swim the English Channel was just 11 years old: Thomas Gregory, a British boy, took 11 hours 54 minutes to complete the crossing in 1988.

THE 10 ★
NORTH POLE FIRSTS

1 First to reach the Pole?
American adventurer Frederick Albert Cook claimed that he had reached the Pole, accompanied by two Inuits, on April 21, 1908, but his claim is disputed. It is more likely that Robert Edwin Peary, Matthew Alexander Henson (both Americans), and four Inuits were first at the Pole on April 6, 1909.

2 First to fly over the Pole in an airplane
Two Americans, Lt. Cdr. (later Admiral) Richard Evelyn Byrd (team-leader and navigator) and Floyd Bennett (pilot) traversed the Pole on May 9, 1926 in a three-engined Fokker F.VIII-3m named Josephine Ford after Henry Ford's granddaughter.

3 First to fly over the Pole in an airship
A team of 16 led by Roald Amundsen, the Norwegian explorer who first reached the South Pole in 1911, flew across the North Pole on May 12, 1926 in the Italian-built airship Norge.

4 First to land at the Pole in an aircraft
Soviets Pavel Afanaseyevich Geordiyenko, Mikhail Yemel'yenovich Ostrekin, Pavel Kononovich Sen'ko, and Mikhail Mikhaylovich Somov arrived at and departed from the Pole by air on April 23, 1948.

5 First solo flight over the Pole in a single-engined aircraft
Capt. Charles Francis Blair Jr. of the US flew a single-engined Mustang fighter, Excalibur III, on May 29, 1951, crossing from Bardufoss, Norway, to Fairbanks, Alaska.

6 First confirmed overland journey to the Pole
American explorer Ralph S. Plaisted, with companions Walter Pederson, Gerald Pitzel, and Jean Luc Bombardier, reached the Pole on April 18, 1968.

7 First woman at the Pole
Fran Phipps, a Canadian, arrived at the Pole by airplane on April 5, 1971.

8 First solo overland journey to the Pole
Japanese explorer Naomi Uemura reached the Pole on May 1, 1978, travelling by dog sled, and was then picked up by an airplane.

9 First crossing on a Pole-to-Pole expedition
Sir Ranulph Fiennes and Charles Burton walked over the North Pole on April 10, 1982, having crossed the South Pole on December 15, 1980.

10 First to reach the Pole on a motorcycle
Fukashi Kazami of Japan arrived at the Pole on April 20, 1987 on a specially adapted 250cc motorcycle, after which he was picked up by an airplane.

FIRST TO THE TOP
Edmund Hillary and Tenzing Norgay climbed the south col of Mount Everest, reaching the pinnacle at 11:30 a.m. on May 29, 1953. They planted the flags of Britain, Nepal, India, and the United Nations.

TOP 10 ★
FASTEST CROSS-CHANNEL SWIMMERS

	SWIMMER/NATIONALITY	YEAR	TIME HRS:MINS
1	Chad Hundeby, American	1994	7:17
2	Penny Lee Dean, American	1978	7:40
3	Tamara Bruce, Australian	1994	7:53
4	Philip Rush, New Zealander	1987	7:55
5	Hans van Goor, Dutch	1995	8:02
6	Richard Davey, British	1988	8:05
7	Irene van der Laan, Dutch	1982	8:06
8	Paul Asmuth, American	1985	8:12
9	Anita Sood, Indian	1987	8:15
10	John van Wisse, Australian	1994	8:17

THE 10 ★
FIRST MOUNTAINEERS TO CLIMB EVEREST

	MOUNTAINEER/NATIONALITY	DATE
1	Edmund Hillary, New Zealander	May 29, 1953
2	Tenzing Norgay, Nepalese	May 29, 1953
3	Jürg Marmet, Swiss	May 23, 1956
4	Ernst Schmied, Swiss	May 23, 1956
5	Hans-Rudolf von Gunten, Swiss	May 24, 1956
6	Adolf Reist, Swiss	May 24, 1956
7	Wang Fu-chou, Chinese	May 25, 1960
8	Chu Ying-hua, Chinese	May 25, 1960
9	Konbu, Tibetan	May 25, 1960
10=	Nawang Gombu, Indian	May 1, 1963
=	James Whittaker, American	May 1, 1963

Nawang Gombu and James Whittaker are 10th equal because they ascended the last feet to the summit side by side.

TOUCHDOWN
The first nonstop round-the-world balloon trip was completed by Bertrand Piccard (Switzerland) and Brian Jones (UK) on board the *Breitling Orbiter 3*. Launched from Château d'Oex, in the Swiss Alps, on March 1, 1999, the balloon flew around the globe for 19 days, 21 hours, and 55 minutes, breaking all previous records of distance and duration. During the trip, the crew endured dramatic changes in weather. After traveling 26,585 miles (42,810 km), they landed safely in southeast Egypt.

SNAP SHOTS ★

TOP 10 NOBEL PRIZE-WINNING COUNTRIES*

	COUNTRY	PHY	CHE	PH/MED	LIT	PCE	ECO	TOTAL
1	US	67	43	78	10	18	25	241
2	UK	21	25	24	8	13	7	98
3	Germany	20	27	15	6	4	1	73
4	France	12	7	7	12	9	1	48
5	Sweden	4	4	7	7	5	2	29
6	Switzerland	2	5	6	2	3	–	18
7	USSR	7	1	2	3	2	1	16
8	Italy	3	1	3	6	1	–	14
9	Netherlands	6	3	2	–	1	1	13
10	Denmark	3	–	5	3	1	–	12

Phy – Physics; Che – Chemistry; Ph/Med – Physiology or Medicine; Lit – Literature; Pce – Peace; Eco – Economic Sciences. Germany includes the united country before 1948, West Germany to 1990 and the united country since 1990

* In addition, institutions including the Red Cross have been awarded 16 Nobel Peace Prizes

TOP 10 ★ NOBEL PHYSICS PRIZE-WINNING COUNTRIES

	COUNTRY	PRIZES
1	US	67
2	UK	21
3	Germany	20
4	France	12
5	USSR	7
6	Netherlands	6
7	Sweden	4
8	=Austria	3
	=Denmark	3
	=Italy	3
	=Japan	3

TOP 10 ★ NOBEL PEACE PRIZE-WINNING COUNTRIES

	COUNTRY	PRIZES
1	US	18
2	International institutions	16
3	UK	13
4	France	9
5	Sweden	5
6	=Germany	4
	=South Africa	4
8	=Belgium	3
	=Israel	3
	=Switzerland	3

TOP 10 ★ NOBEL PHYSIOLOGY OR MEDICINE PRIZE-WINNING COUNTRIES

	COUNTRY	PRIZES
1	US	78
2	UK	24
3	Germany	15
4	=France	7
	=Sweden	7
6	Switzerland	6
7	Denmark	5
8	=Austria	4
	=Belgium	4
10	=Italy	3
	=Australia	3

TOP 10 ★ NOBEL LITERATURE PRIZE-WINNING COUNTRIES

	COUNTRY	PRIZES
1	France	12
2	US	10
3	UK	8
4	Sweden	7
5	=Germany	6
	=Italy	6
7	Spain	5
8	=Denmark	3
	=Ireland	3
	=Norway	3
	=Poland	3
	=USSR	3

TOP 10 NOBEL CHEMISTRY PRIZE-WINNING COUNTRIES
(Country/prizes)

1 US, 43 **2** Germany, 27 **3** UK, 25 **4** France, 17 **5** Switzerland, 5 **6** Sweden, 4 **7** = Canada, 3; = Netherlands, 3 **9** = Argentina, 1; = Austria, 1; = Belgium, 1; = Czechoslovakia, 1; = Finland, 1; = Hungary, 1; = Italy, 1; = Japan, 1; = Mexico, 1; = Norway, 1; = USSR, 1

Background image: THE TWO SIDES OF THE NOBEL PRIZE MEDAL

THE 10 ★
LATEST WINNERS OF THE NOBEL PRIZE FOR LITERATURE

	WINNER	COUNTRY	YEAR
1	José Saramago	Portugal	1998
2	Dario Fo	Italy	1997
3	Wislawa Szymborska	Poland	1996
4	Seamus Heaney	Ireland	1995
5	Kenzaburo Oe	Japan	1994
6	Toni Morrison	US	1993
7	Derek Walcott	Saint Lucia	1992
8	Nadine Gordimer	South Africa	1991
9	Octavio Paz	Mexico	1990
10	Camilo José Cela	Spain	1989

THE 10 ★
LATEST WINNERS OF THE NOBEL PRIZE FOR PHYSICS

	WINNER	COUNTRY	YEAR
1=	Robert B. Laughlin	US	1998
=	Horst L. Störmer	Germany	1998
=	Daniel C. Tsui	US	1998
4=	Steven Chu	US	1997
=	William D. Phillips	US	1997
=	Claude Cohen-Tannoudji	France	1997
7=	David M. Lee	US	1996
=	Douglas D. Osheroff	US	1996
=	Robert C. Richardson	US	1996
10=	Martin L. Perl	US	1995
=	Frederick Reines	US	1995

THE 10 ★
LATEST WINNERS OF THE NOBEL PRIZE FOR PHYSIOLOGY OR MEDICINE

	WINNER	COUNTRY	YEAR
1=	Robert F. Furchgott	US	1998
=	Louis J. Ignarro	US	1998
=	Ferid Murad	US	1998
4	Stanley B. Prusiner	US	1997
5=	Peter C. Doherty	Australia	1996
=	Rolf M. Zinkernagel	Switzerland	1996
7=	Christiane Nüsslein-Volhard	Germany	1995
=	Eric F. Wieschaus	US	1995
=	Edward B. Lewis	US	1995
10=	Alfred G. Gilman	US	1994
=	Martin Rodbell	US	1994

THE 10 LATEST WINNERS OF THE NOBEL PRIZE FOR CHEMISTRY

(Winner/country/year)

❶ =Walter Kohn, US, 1998; = John A. Pople, UK, 1998 **❸** = Paul D. Boyer, US, 1997; = John E. Walker, UK, 1997; = Jens C. Skou, Denmark, 1997 **❻** = Sir Harold W. Kroto, UK, 1996; = Richard E. Smalley, US, 1996 **❽** = Paul Crutzen, Netherlands, 1995; = Mario Molina, Mexico, 1995; = Frank Sherwood Rowland, US, 1995

THE 10 ★
LATEST WINNERS OF THE NOBEL PEACE PRIZE

	WINNER	COUNTRY	YEAR
1=	John Hume	UK	1998
=	David Trimble	UK	1998
3=	International Campaign to Ban Landmines	–	1997
=	Jody Williams	US	1997
5=	Carlos Filipe Ximenes Belo	East Timor	1996
=	José Ramos-Horta	East Timor	1996
7	Joseph Rotblat	UK	1995
8=	Yasir Arafat	Palestine	1994
=	Shimon Peres	Israel	1994
=	Itzhak Rabin	Israel	1994

PEACE AT LAST?
John Hume and David Trimble celebrate the signing of the Good Friday Agreement in 1998. All the parties at Stormont Castle agreed to work toward peace in Northern Ireland.

Who was the youngest US President?
see p.81 for the answer

A John F. Kennedy
B Theodore Roosevelt
C William J. Clinton

CRIMINAL RECORDS

THE 10 ★

FIRST ELECTROCUTIONS AT SING SING

	VICTIM	AGE	ELECTROCUTED
1	Harris A. Smiler	32	Jul 7, 1891
2	James Slocum	22	Jul 7, 1891
3	Joseph Wood	21	Jul 7, 1891
4	Schihick Judigo	35	Jul 7, 1891
5	Martin D. Loppy	51	Dec 7, 1891
6	Charles McElvaine	20	Feb 8, 1892
7	Jeremiah Cotte	40	Mar 28, 1892
8	Fred McGuire	24	Dec 19, 1892
9	James L. Hamilton	40	Apr 3, 1893
10	Carlyle Harris	23	May 8, 1893

THE 10 ★

COUNTRIES WITH THE MOST PRISONERS

	COUNTRY	PRISONERS*
1	US	1,630,940
2	Russia	1,051,515
3	Germany	71,047
4	Poland	57,320
5	England and Wales	55,537
6	France	54,014
7	Italy	48,747
8	Spain	42,105
9	Japan	40,389
10	Canada	33,785

* In latest year for which figures are available

If recast according to the incarceration rate per 1,000, Russia takes the lead with 7.1, and the US a close second on 6.2 per 1,000.

THE 10 ★

COUNTRIES WITH THE HIGHEST CRIME RATES

	COUNTRY	RATE*
1	Gibraltar	18,316
2	Surinam	17,819
3	St. Kitts and Nevis	15,468
4	Finland	14,799
5	Rwanda	14,550
6	New Zealand	13,854
7	Sweden	12,982
8	Denmark	10,525
9	Canada	10,451
10	US Virgin Islands	10,441
	US	5,376

* Reported crime per 100,000 population

THE 10 ★

FIRST EXECUTIONS BY LETHAL INJECTION IN THE US

	NAME	EXECUTED
1	Charles Brooks	Dec 7, 1982
2	James Autry	Mar 14, 1984
3	Ronald O'Bryan	Mar 31, 1984
4	Thomas Barefoot	Oct 30, 1984
5	Dovle Skillem	Jan 16, 1985
6	Stephen Morin	Mar 13, 1985
7	Jesse de la Rosa	May 15, 1985
8	Charles Milton	Jun 25, 1985
9	Henry M. Porter	Jul 9, 1985
10	Charles Rumbaugh	Sep 11, 1985

Source: *Death Penalty Information Center*

Although Oklahoma was the first state to legalize execution by lethal injection, the option was not taken there until 1990. All of the above were executed in Texas.

FINGER OF SUSPICION

In 1892 the first murder was solved by an incriminating fingerprint. Today, dusting a crime scene for prints is commonplace.

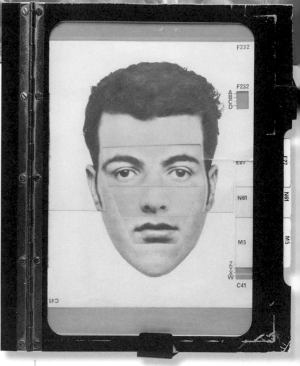

PHOTOFIT

The police's photofit method of depicting suspects is a more realistic development of the original identikit system, which was devised in Los Angeles in 1959.

THE 10 ★

COUNTRIES WITH THE FEWEST POLICE OFFICERS

	COUNTRY	POPULATION PER POLICE OFFICER
1	Maldives	35,710
2	Canada	8,640
3	Rwanda	4,650
4	Côte d'Ivoire	4,640
5	The Gambia	3,310
6	Benin	3,250
7	Madagascar	2,900
8	Central African Republic	2,740
9	Bangladesh	2,560
10	Niger	2,350*

* Including paramilitary forces

The saying "there's never a policeman when you need one" is nowhere truer than in these countries, where the police are few and far between. There are various possible and contradictory explanations for these ratios: countries may be so law-abiding that there is simply no need for large numbers of police officers, or the force may be so underfunded and inefficient that it is irrelevant.

THE 10 ⭐
LARGEST FEDERAL CORRECTIONAL INSTITUTIONS IN THE US

INSTITUTION/LOCATION	OCCUPANCY
1 Federal Correctional Institution, Fort Dix, New Jersey	3,566
2 US Penitentiary, Atlanta, Georgia	2,399
3 US Penitentiary, Leavenworth, Kansas	1,822
4 Federal Correctional Institution, Elkton, Ohio	1,764
5 Federal Correctional Institution (Low Security), Coleman, Florida	1,735
6 Correctional Institution*, Taft, California	1,730
7 Federal Correctional Institution, Forrest City, Arizona	1,712
8 Federal Detention Center, Miami, Florida	1,707
9 Federal Correctional Institution, Yazoo City, Mississippi	1,596
10 US Penitentiary, Lompoc, California	1,595

* Privately managed

Source: *Bureau of Federal Prisons*

THE 10 ⭐
STATES WITH THE MOST EXECUTIONS 1977–99*

STATE	EXECUTIONS
1 Texas	171
2 Virginia	62
3 Florida	43
4 Missouri	35
5 Louisiana	25
6 Georgia	23
7 South Carolina	22
8 Arkansas	18
9 Alabama	17
10 Arizona	16

* To March 10, 1999

Source: *Death Penalty Information Center*

THE 10 ⭐
FIRST COUNTRIES TO ABOLISH CAPITAL PUNISHMENT

COUNTRY	ABOLISHED
1 Russia	1826
2 Venezuela	1863
3 Portugal	1867
4 = Brazil	1882
= Costa Rica	1882
6 Ecuador	1897
7 Panama	1903
8 Norway	1905
9 Uruguay	1907
10 Colombia	1910

Some countries abolished capital punishment in peacetime only, or for all crimes except treason, and then extended it totally at a more recent date. However, several countries later reinstated it. Some countries retained capital punishment on their statute books, but effectively abolished it: the last execution in Liechtenstein, for example, took place in 1795; in Mexico in 1946 and in Belgium in 1950. Finland abolished the death penalty at the same time as Russia (under whose rule it was at the time), but reintroduced it in 1882 – although no criminal has been executed in that country since 1824. One US state, Michigan, abolished capital punishment in 1846 for every offense except treason.

THE 10 STATES WITH THE MOST PRISONERS ON DEATH ROW

(State/prisoners under death sentence*)

1 California, 519 **2** Texas, 441
3 Florida, 390 **4** Pennsylvania, 226
5 North Carolina, 209 **6** Ohio, 191
7 Alabama, 173 **7** Illinois, 162
9 Oklahoma, 151 **10** Georgia, 123

* As of January 1, 1999
Source: *Department of Justice*

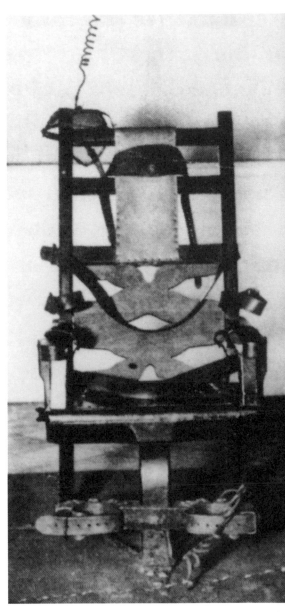

HOT SEAT

"An awful spectacle, far worse than hanging," was how the New York Times *described the electric chair, first used at Auburn Prison, New York, in 1890. A year later, the electric chair was installed in Sing Sing Prison, Ossining, New York. By 1963, when the chair was used for the last time, a total of 614 victims had been electrocuted at Sing Sing.*

Which country has the most submarines?
see p.90 for the answer
A US
B China
C Russia

MURDER FILE

THE 10 ★
COUNTRIES WITH THE HIGHEST MURDER RATES

COUNTRY	MURDERS P.A. PER 100,000 POPULATION
1 Swaziland	87.8
2 Bahamas	52.6
3 Monaco	36.0
4 Philippines	30.1
5 Guatemala	27.4
6 Jamaica	20.9
7 Russia	19.9*
8 Botswana	19.5
9 Zimbabwe	17.9
10 Netherlands	14.8
US	6.8

Includes attempted murder

THE 10 ★
COUNTRIES WITH THE LOWEST MURDER RATES

COUNTRY	MURDERS P.A. PER 100,000 POPULATION
1 =Argentina	0.1
=Brunei	0.1
3 =Burkina Faso	0.2
=Niger	0.2
5 =Guinea	0.5
=Guinea-Bissau	0.5
=Iran	0.5
8 =Finland	0.6
=Saudi Arabia	0.6
10 =Cameroon	0.7
=Ireland	0.7
=Mongolia	0.7

TOP 10 ★
RELATIONSHIPS OF MURDER VICTIMS TO PRINCIPAL SUSPECTS IN THE US

RELATIONSHIP	VICTIMS (1997)
1 Acquaintance	4,237
2 Stranger	2,067
3 Wife	583
4 Friend	432
5 Girlfriend	426
6 Son	274
7 Daughter	211
8 Husband	183
9 Boyfriend	156
10 Neighbor	154

These offenses – which remain in similar order from year to year – accounted for 8,723, or 57 percent, of the 15,289 murders committed in the US in 1997. In the year that these figures were gathered, FBI statistics also recorded 5,869 murders where the victim's relationship to the suspect was unknown, 311 "other family members" (those not specified elsewhere), 147 fathers, 120 brothers, 83 mothers, and 20 sisters.

THE 10 WORST YEARS FOR GUN MURDERS IN THE US
(Year/victims)

1 1993, 16,136 **2** 1994, 15,546 **3** 1992, 15,489 **4** 1991, 14,373 **5** 1980, 13,650
6 1990, 13,035 **7** 1981, 12,523 **8** 1974, 12,474 **9** 1975, 12,061 **10** 1989, 11,832

DNA FINGERPRINTING

DNA – deoxyribonucleic acid, which is found in all animal tissue, contains genetic information that is unique to the individual that produced it. In 1985 British scientist Professor Alec J. Jeffreys, head of the genetic laboratory at the University of Leicester, used this characteristic to develop the process of DNA fingerprinting in which cells taken from almost any sample of human tissue, including skin, blood, saliva, and hair, however small, can be analyzed for sequences of DNA. This "genetic identity card" has since been successfully used worldwide to identify both criminals and the victims of murders and has added a new and extremely accurate weapon to the law enforcement arsenal. The scientists who, in 1953, discovered the structure of DNA – Dr. James Watson, Dr. Francis Crick, and Dr. Maurice Wilkins – were awarded the Nobel Prize for Physiology or Medicine.

SNAP ★ SHOTS

Which country has the largest Buddhist population?
see p.92 for the answer
A Thailand
B Japan
C China

TOP 10 ★
RELATIONSHIPS OF MURDER VICTIMS TO PRINCIPAL SUSPECTS IN ENGLAND AND WALES

	RELATIONSHIP	VICTIMS (1997)
1	Male friend or acquaintance	134
2	Male stranger	115
3	Current or former wife, female cohabitant, or lover	105
4	Son	36
5	Current or former husband, male cohabitant, or lover	34
6	Female friend or acquaintance	25
7	Female stranger	22
8	Mother	21
9	Daughter	17
10	Father	6

In addition to these offenses, Home Office statistics record that in 1997, 12 murder victims were unspecified male and eight female family members, while seven men and five women are described as "other person in course of employment," such as security guards killed during holdups.

THE 10 ★
WORST STATES FOR MURDER IN THE US

	STATE	FIREARMS USED	TOTAL MURDERS (1997)
1	California	1,832	2,579
2	Texas	876	1,327
3	Illinois*	560	743
4	Michigan	477	717
5	New York	408	710
6	Louisiana	497	635
7	North Carolina	366	612
8	Pennsylvania	417	582
9	Maryland	389	502
10	Virginia	346	488

Provisional figures

THE 10 ★
MOST COMMON MURDER WEAPONS AND METHODS IN ENGLAND AND WALES

	WEAPON/METHOD	VICTIMS (1997)
1	Sharp instrument	203
2	Hitting and kicking	109
3	Blunt instrument	74
4	Strangulation and asphyxiation	70
5	Shooting	58
6	Burning	30
7	Poison or drugs	24
8	Motor vehicle	15
9	Drowning	7
10	Explosion	1

THE 10 ★
WORST CITIES FOR MURDER IN THE US

	CITY	MURDERS*
1	Chicago	335
2	New York	299
3	Los Angeles	193
4	Detroit	192
5	Baltimore	156
6	New Orleans	139
7	Dallas	133
8	Washington, DC	122
9	Houston	114
10	Atlanta	75

Provisional figures, January–June 1998; figure for Philadelphia not published

The identity of America's 10 murder capitals remains fairly consistent from year to year, with only some slight adjustment to the order.

THE 10 ★
MOST COMMON MURDER WEAPONS AND METHODS IN THE US

	WEAPON/METHOD	VICTIMS (1997)
1	Handguns	8,104
2	Knives or cutting instruments	1,963
3	Firearms (type not stated)	970
4	"Personal weapons" (hands, feet, fists, etc.)	964
5	Blunt objects (hammers, clubs, etc.)	702
6	Shotguns	637
7	Rifles	624
8	Strangulation	223
9	Fire	134
10	Asphyxiation	87

TOP 10 ★
REASONS FOR MURDER IN THE US

	REASON	MURDERS (1997)
1	Arguments (unspecified)	4,297
2	Robbery	1,458
3	Narcotic drug laws	786
4	Juvenile gang killings	780
5	Felony (unspecified)	325
6	Argument over money or property	286
7	Brawl due to influence of alcohol	240
8	Romantic triangle	171
9	Suspected felony	153
10	Brawl due to influence of narcotics	105

Source: *FBI Uniform Crime Reports*

A total of 15,289 murders were reported in 1997, including 1,424 without a specified reason and 4,790, which were unknown.

MILITARY MATTERS

THE 10 20TH-CENTURY WARS WITH THE MOST MILITARY FATALITIES

	WAR	YEARS	MILITARY FATALITIES
1	World War II	1939–45	15,843,000
2	World War I	1914–18	8,545,800
3	Korean War	1950–53	1,893,100
4 =	Sino Japanese War	1937–41	1,000,000
=	Biafra–Nigeria Civil War	1967–70	1,000,000
6	Spanish Civil War	1936–39	611,000
7	Vietnam War	1961–73	546,000
8 =	India–Pakistan War	1947	200,000
=	USSR invasion of Afghanistan	1979–89	200,000
=	Iran–Iraq War	1980–88	200,000

The statistics of warfare have always been an imperfect science. Not only are battle deaths seldom recorded accurately but figures are often deliberately inflated by both sides in a conflict. For political reasons and to maintain morale, each is anxious to enhance reports of its military success and low casualty figures, so that often quite contradictory reports of the same battle may be issued. These figures thus represent military historians' "best guesses" and fail to take into account the enormous toll of deaths among civilian populations during the many wars that have beset the 20th century.

TOP 10 ★ SMALLEST ARMED FORCES*

	COUNTRY	ESTIMATED TOTAL ACTIVE FORCES
1	Antigua and Barbuda	150
2	Seychelles	400
3	Barbados	610
4	The Gambia	800
5	Luxembourg	811
6	Bahamas	860
7	Belize	1,050
8	Cape Verde	1,100
9	Equatorial Guinea	1,320
10	Guyana	1,600

* Excluding countries not declaring a defense budget

TOP 10 COUNTRIES WITH THE MOST SUBMARINES

(Country/submarines)

1 Russia (and assoc. states), 98 **2** US, 84 **3** China, 63 **4** North Korea, 26 **5** India, 19 **6** = Japan, 16; = Turkey 16 **8** UK, 15 **9** France, 14; = Germany, 14; = South Korea, 14

TOP 10 COUNTRIES WITH THE LARGEST NAVIES

(Country/manpower*)

1 US, 380,600 **2** China, 260,000 **3** Russia, 180,000 **4** Taiwan, 68,000 **5** France, 63,300 **6** South Korea, 60,000 **7** India, 55,000 **8** Turkey, 51,000 **9** North Korea, 46,000 **10** UK, 44,500

* Including naval air forces and marines

TOP 10 ★ COUNTRIES WITH THE MOST CONSCRIPTED PERSONNEL

	COUNTRY	CONSCRIPTS
1	China	1,275,000
2	Turkey	528,000
3	Russia	381,000
4	Egypt	320,000
5	Iran	250,000
6	South Korea	159,000
7	Poland	141,600
8	Israel	138,500
9	Germany	137,500
10	Italy	134,100

Most countries have abolished peacetime conscription (the US did so in 1973), and recruit their armed forces on an entirely voluntary basis.

TOP 10 ★ COUNTRIES WITH THE LARGEST DEFENSE BUDGETS

	COUNTRY	BUDGET ($)
1	US	270,500,000,000
2	UK	37,200,000,000
3	Japan	35,200,000,000
4	Russia	34,000,000,000
5	France	30,400,000,000
6	Germany	26,400,000,000
7	Saudi Arabia	18,400,000,000
8	Italy	17,800,000,000
9	China	11,000,000,000
10	South Korea	10,200,000,000
	Canada	7,100,000,000
	Australia	6,900,000,000

The so-called "peace dividend" – the savings made as a consequence of the end of the Cold War between the West and the former Soviet Union – means that both the numbers of personnel and the defense budgets of many countries have been cut. That of the US has gone down from its 1989 peak of $303.6 billion.

Did You Know? Boomerang bullets were patented in the US in 1870. Designed to fire in a curved line, the obvious drawback lay in the danger of the bullet traveling in a complete circle!

TOP 10 ★
LARGEST ARMED FORCES

| COUNTRY | ARMY | ESTIMATED ACTIVE FORCES | | TOTAL |
		NAVY	AIR	
1 China	2,090,000	260,000	470,000	2,820,000
2 US	479,400	380,600	370,300	1,401,600*
3 India	980,000	55,000	140,000	1,175,000
4 Russia	420,000	180,000	210,000	1,159,000#
5 North Korea	923,000	46,000	85,000	1,054,000
6 South Korea	560,000	60,000	52,000	672,000
7 Turkey	525,000	51,000	63,000	639,000
8 Pakistan	520,000	22,000	45,000	587,000
9 Iran	350,000	20,600	45–50,000	540–545,600+
10 Vietnam	420,000	42,000	30,000★	484,000

* Includes 174,900 Marine Corps

Includes Strategic Deterrent Forces, Paramilitary, National Guard, etc.

+ Includes 120,000 Revolutionary Guards

★ Includes 15,000 Air Force and 15,000 Air Defense

In addition to the active forces listed here, many of the world's dominant countries have substantial reserves on standby: South Korea's has been estimated at some 4,500,000, Vietnam's at 3–4,000,000 and China's at 1,200,000. Russia's former total of 3 million has steadily dwindled as a result of both the end of the Cold War and the economic problems faced by the post-Soviet military establishment. China is also notable for having a massive arsenal of military equipment at its disposal, including some 8,500 tanks, and 3,740 combat aircraft.

TOP 10 ★
COUNTRIES WITH THE HIGHEST MILITARY/ CIVILIAN RATIO

COUNTRY	RATIO*
1 North Korea	421
2 Israel	296
3 United Arab Emirates	250
4 Singapore	236
5 Jordan	214
6 Qatar	205
7 Syria	202
8 Iraq	185
9 Bahrain	180
10 Taiwan	174
US	52

* Military personnel per 10,000 population

WAR OF FUTILITY

America's involvement in the Vietnam War was deeply unpopular with the people, who held large antiwar demonstrations in protest against the massive casualties.

WORLD RELIGIONS

TOP 10 ★
CHRISTIAN DENOMINATIONS

	DENOMINATION	MEMBERS
1	Roman Catholic	912,636,000
2	Orthodox	139,544,000
3	Pentecostal	105,756,000
4	Lutheran	84,521,000
5	Baptist	67,146,000
6	Anglican	53,217,000
7	Presbyterian	47,972,000
8	Methodist	25,599,000
9	Seventh Day Adventist	10,650,000
10	Churches of Christ	6,400,000

Source: *Christian Research*

TOP 10 ★
LARGEST CHRISTIAN POPULATIONS

	COUNTRY	TOTAL CHRISTIAN POPULATION
1	US	182,674,000
2	Brazil	157,973,000
3	Mexico	88,380,000
4	China	73,300,000
5	Philippines	65,217,000
6	Germany	63,332,000
7	Italy	47,403,000
8	France	45,624,000
9	Nigeria	38,969,000
10	Dem. Rep. of Congo	37,922,000
	World total	1,965,993,000

Source: *Christian Research Association*

As many as 30 million more Christians in the US may profess membership of this religion than actually practice it.

TOP 10 ★
LARGEST BUDDHIST POPULATIONS

	COUNTRY	TOTAL BUDDHIST POPULATION
1	China	104,000,000
2	Japan	90,510,000
3	Thailand	57,450,000
4	Vietnam	50,080,000
5	Myanmar	41,880,000
6	Sri Lanka	12,540,000
7	South Korea	11,110,000
8	Cambodia	9,870,000
9	India	7,000,000
10	Malaysia	3,770,000
	World total	356,875,000

TOP 10 RELIGIOUS BELIEFS

	RELIGION	MEMBERS*
1	Christianity	1,965,993,000
2	Islam	1,179,326,000
3	Hinduism	865,000,000
4	Nonreligious	766,672,000
5	Buddhism	356,875,000
6	Tribal religions	244,164,000
7	Atheism	146,406,000
8	New religions	99,191,000
9	Sikhism	22,874,000
10	Judaism	15,050,000

* Estimated total projections to mid-1998

HIS HOLINESS

Elected in 1978, John Paul II (born in Poland as Karol Wojtyia) became the first non-Italian Pope since the Dutch-born Hadrian VI in 1522.

BLUE MOSQUE

Istanbul's 17th-century mosque is one of Turkey's most magnificent centers of Muslim worship.

TOP 10 ★
LARGEST HINDU POPULATIONS

	COUNTRY	TOTAL HINDU POPULATION
1	India	814,632,942
2	Nepal	21,136,118
3	Bangladesh	14,802,899
4	Indonesia	3,974,895
5	Sri Lanka	2,713,900
6	Pakistan	2,112,071
7	Malaysia	1,043,500
8	US	798,582
9	South Africa	649,980
10	Mauritius	587,884
	World total	865,000,000

More than 99 percent of the world's Hindu population lives in Asia, with 94 percent in India.

TOP 10 ★
LARGEST MUSLIM POPULATIONS

	COUNTRY	TOTAL MUSLIM POPULATION
1	Pakistan	157,349,290
2	Indonesia	156,213,374
3	Bangladesh	133,873,621
4	India	130,316,250
5	Iran	74,087,700
6	Turkey	66,462,107
7	Russia	64,624,770
8	Egypt	57,624,098
9	Nigeria	46,384,120
10	Morocco	33,542,780
	World total	1,179,326,000

Historically, Islam spread as a result of missionary activity and through contacts with Muslim traders. In such countries as Indonesia, its appeal lay in part in its opposition to Western colonial influences, which, along with the concept of Islamic community and other tenets, has attracted followers worldwide.

TOP 10 ★
LARGEST JEWISH POPULATIONS

	COUNTRY	TOTAL JEWISH POPULATION
1	US	6,122,462
2	Israel	4,354,900
3	France	640,156
4	Russia	460,266
5	Ukraine	424,136
6	UK	345,054
7	Canada	342,096
8	Argentina	253,666
9	Brazil	107,692
10	Belarus	107,350
	World total	15,050,000

The Diaspora, or scattering of the Jews, has continued for nearly 2,000 years, and Jewish communities are found in virtually every country in the world. In 1939 the total world Jewish population was around 17,000,000. More than 6,000,000 fell victim to Nazi persecution, but numbers have since grown to 15,050,000.

Did You Know? One-fifth of the world's population is Muslim.

TOWN & COUNTRY

TOP 10 ★
COUNTRIES IN WHICH WOMEN MOST OUTNUMBER MEN

COUNTRY	WOMEN PER 100 MEN
1 Latvia	116.7
2 Ukraine	115.2
3 Russia	113.3
4 Belarus	112.9
5 =Estonia	112.5
=Lithuania	112.5
7 Georgia	109.6
8 Moldova	109.4
9 Hungary	108.8
10 Swaziland	108.7

TOP 10 ★
COUNTRIES IN WHICH MEN MOST OUTNUMBER WOMEN

COUNTRY	MEN PER 100 WOMEN
1 Qatar	197.1
2 United Arab Emirates	176.6
3 Bahrain	134.4
4 Saudi Arabia	125.8
5 Oman	110.4
6 Brunei	109.6
7 Libya	108.7
8 Pakistan	107.2
9 India	106.9
10 Papua New Guinea	106.6

TOP 10 ★
LONGEST BORDERS

COUNTRY	BORDERS MILES	KM
1 China	13,759	22,143
2 Russia	12,514	20,139
3 Brazil	9,129	14,691
4 India	8,763	14,103
5 US	7,611	12,248
6 Dem. Rep. of Congo	6,382	10,271
7 Argentina	6,006	9,665
8 Canada	5,526	8,893
9 Mongolia	5,042	8,114
10 Sudan	4,783	7,697

This list represents the total length of borders, compiled by adding together the lengths of individual land borders.

TOP 10 ★
MOST DENSELY POPULATED COUNTRIES

COUNTRY	AREA (SQ KM)	ESTIMATED POPULATION	POPULATION PER SQ MILE	SQ KM
1 Monaco	1*	27,000	14,917.0	38,620.0
2 Singapore	618	3,439,000	5,564.7	14,407.0
3 Malta	316	371,000	1,174.1	3,040.0
4 Maldives	298	273,000	916.1	2,371.8
5 Bangladesh	143,998	122,013,000	847.3	2,193.7
6 Bahrain	694	582,000	838.6	2,171.1
7 Mauritius	1,865	1,141,000	611.8	1,589.0
8 Barbados	430	262,000	609.3	1,577.5
9 South Korea	99,274	45,717,000	460.5	1,192.2
10 San Marino	61	25,000	409.8	1,061.0
US	9,169,389	271,648,000	29.6	76.6
World	135,807,000	5,847,465,000	43.1	111.6

* Rounded; precise area used for calculation of population density
Source: United Nations

RUSH HOUR IN THE SUBCONTINENT

Traffic congestion in Old Dacca, Bangladesh, illustrates the massive overcrowding experienced in some parts of this country. The population is unevenly spread, so some rural areas are relatively empty while the cities teem with life.

Background image: **POLITICAL MAP OF THE WORLD**

TOP 10 ★
LARGEST COUNTRIES IN EUROPE

	COUNTRY	SQ MILES	AREA SQ KM
1	Russia (in Europe)	1,818,629	4,710,227
2	Ukraine	233,090	603,700
3	France	211,208	547,026
4	Spain*	194,897	504,781
5	Sweden	173,732	449,964
6	Germany	137,838	356,999
7	Finland	130,119	337,007
8	Norway	125,182	324,220
9	Poland	120,725	312,676
10	Italy	116,304	301,226

* Including offshore islands

The UK falls just outside the Top 10 at 94,247 sq miles/244,101 sq km. Geographically, the total area of the British Isles (including the whole island of Ireland) is 121,383 sq miles/314,384 sq km.

THE 10 ★
LARGEST COUNTRIES

	COUNTRY	SQ MILES	AREA SQ KM
1	Russia	6,590,876	17,070,289
2	Canada	3,849,670	9,970,599
3	China	3,705,408	9,596,961
4	US	3,540,321	9,169,389
5	Brazil	3,286,488	8,511,965
6	Australia	2,967,909	7,686,848
7	India	1,269,346	3,287,590
8	Argentina	1,073,512	2,780,400
9	Kazakhstan	1,049,156	2,717,300
10	Sudan	967,500	2,505,813
	UK	94,247	244,101
	World total	52,740,700	136,597,770

The list of the world's largest countries, the Top 10 of which comprise more than 53 percent of the total Earth's surface, has undergone great revision of late. The breakup of the former Soviet Union has introduced two new countries, with Russia taking preeminent position, occupying a massive 12.5 percent of the total. At the other end of the list, Sudan accounts for a more modest, but still sizable, 1.8 percent.

SOCIALIZING AT A GREEK STREET CAFÉ

All of the Top 10 countries with the oldest populations are in Western Europe, implying that this region has lower death rates and a higher life expectancy than the rest of the world.

TOP 10 ★
COUNTRIES WITH THE YOUNGEST POPULATIONS

	COUNTRY	PERCENTAGE UNDER 15
1	Côte d'Ivoire	49.1
2	Uganda	48.8
3	Comoros	48.7
4	Niger	48.4
5	Dem. Rep. of Congo	48.0
6	Kenya	47.7
7	=Oman	47.5
	=Somalia	47.5
9	=Benin	47.4
	=Mali	47.4
	=Zambia	47.4
	US	22.0

Source: *World Health Organization*

Countries with high proportions of their people under the age of 15 are usually characterized by high birth rates and high death rates.

TOP 10 ★
COUNTRIES WITH THE OLDEST POPULATIONS

	COUNTRY	PERCENTAGE OVER 60
1	Sweden	17.3
2	Italy	16.0
3	=Greece	15.9
	=Norway	15.9
5	Belgium	15.8
6	UK	15.5
7	=Denmark	15.2
	=Germany	15.2
9	=Austria	14.9
	=France	14.9
	=Spain	14.9

Source: *World Health Organization*

All of these countries are in Western Europe, implying that this region has lower death rates and a higher life expectancy than the rest of the world. On average, one in every eight people in Europe is over the age of 54 (12.5 percent).

THE 10 ★
SMALLEST COUNTRIES

	COUNTRY	SQ MILES	AREA SQ KM
1	Vatican City	0.17	0.44
2	Monaco	0.7	1.81
3	Gibraltar	2.5	6.47
4	Macao	6.2	16.06
5	Nauru	8.2	21.23
6	Tuvalu	10.0	25.90
7	Bermuda	20.6	53.35
8	San Marino	23.0	59.57
9	Liechtenstein	61.0	157.99
10	Antigua	108.0	279.72

The "country" status of several of these micro-states is questionable, since their government, defense, currency, and other features are often intricately linked with those of larger countries, such as San Marino with Italy.

 Which country has the largest area of protected land? *see p.101 for the answer*   A Brazil   B Greenland   C US

TOP 10 ★
HIGHEST CITIES

CITY/COUNTRY	HEIGHT FT	M
1 **Wenchuan**, China	16,730	5,099
2 **Potosí**, Bolivia	13,045	3,976
3 **Oruro**, Bolivia	12,146	3,702
4 **Lhasa**, Tibet	12,087	3,684
5 **La Paz**, Bolivia	11,916	3,632
6 **Cuzco**, Peru	11,152	3,399
7 **Huancayo**, Peru	10,660	3,249
8 **Sucre**, Bolivia	9,301	2,835
9 **Tunja**, Colombia	9,252	2,820
10 **Quito**, Ecuador	9,249	2,819

Lhasa was formerly the highest capital city in the world, a role now occupied by La Paz, capital of Bolivia. Wenchuan is situated at more than half the elevation of Everest. Even the cities at the end of this list are more than one-third as high as Everest.

TOP 10 ★
OLDEST CITIES IN THE US

CITY	FOUNDED
1 **St. Augustine**, Florida	1565
2 **Santa Fe**, New Mexico	1609
3 **Hampton**, Virginia	1610
4 **Newport News**, Virginia	1621
5 =**Albany**, New York	1624
=**New York**, New York	1624
7 **Quincy**, Massachusetts	1625
8 **Salem**, Massachusetts	1626
9 =**Jersey City**, New Jersey	1629
=**Lynn**, Massachusetts	1629

The oldest permanently inhabited settlements in what is now the United States are the subject of much debate, but the founding years listed are those from which these cities are generally presumed to date. Some sources give Tallahassee, Florida as having been originally settled in 1539, but this date refers only to the winter camp (and the first Christmas Mass celebrated on American soil) of the Spanish explorer Hernando de Soto (c.1500–42) and his 600 companions. The city was not founded on this site until 1636.

TOP 10 ★
LARGEST NONCAPITAL CITIES

CITY/COUNTRY/CAPITAL CITY	POPULATION
1 **Shanghai**, China	13,400,000
Beijing	*10,940,000*
2 **Bombay**, India	12,596,243
New Delhi	*8,419,000*
3 **Calcutta**,* India	11,021,918
New Delhi	*8,419,000*
4 **São Paulo**, Brazil	9,394,000
Brasília	*1,601,094*
5 **Tianjin**, China	9,090,000
Beijing	*10,940,000*
6 **Istanbul**,* Turkey	7,774,169
Ankara	*2,782,200*
7 **New York**, US	7,380,906
Washington, DC	*567,094*
8 **Karachi**,* Pakistan	7,183,000
Islamabad	*320,000*
9 **Rio de Janeiro**,* Brazil	5,547,033
Brasília	*1,601,094*
10 **St. Petersburg**,* Russia	4,273,001
Moscow	*8,436,447*

* Former capital

ON TOP OF THE WORLD

Potosí in Bolivia is the highest city in the Americas, established in the 16th century after the discovery of silver and other minerals in Potosí mountain. Despite its susceptibility to floods and earthquakes, it remains the country's foremost industrial center.

TOP 10 ★
MOST DENSELY POPULATED CITIES*

CITY/COUNTRY	POPULATION PER SQ MILE	SQ KM
1 **Hong Kong**, China	253,957	98,053
2 **Lagos**, Nigeria	174,982	67,561
3 **Dhaka**, Bangladesh	165,500	63,900
4 **Jakarta**, Indonesia	146,724	56,650
5 **Bombay**, India	142,442	54,997
6 **Ahmadabad**, India	131,250	50,676
7 **Ho Chi Minh**, Vietnam	131,097	50,617
8 **Shenyang**, China	114,282	44,125
9 **Bangalore**, India	112,880	43,583
10 **Cairo**, Egypt	107,260	41,413

* Includes only cities with populations of over 2 million

Source: *US Bureau of the Census*

Did You Know? Hong Kong has a density equivalent to a cramped 113 sq ft/10.5 sq m per person. By comparison, London appears positively spacious with 2,673 sq ft/248 sq m per person.

TOP 10 ★
MOST POPULATED FORMER CAPITAL CITIES

	CITY/COUNTRY	CEASED TO BE CAPITAL	POPULATION*
1	Calcutta, India	1912	11,021,918
2	Istanbul, Turkey	1923	7,774,169
3	Karachi, Pakistan	1968	7,183,000
4	Rio de Janeiro, Brazil	1960	5,547,033
5	St. Petersburg, Russia	1980	4,273,001
6	Berlin, Germany	1949	3,472,009
7	Alexandria, Egypt	c.641	3,380,000
8	Melbourne, Australia	1927	3,189,200
9	Nanjiang, China	1949	2,610,594
10	Philadelphia, US	1800	1,524,249

* Within administrative boundaries

TOP 10 ★
LARGEST CITIES IN THE US

	CITY/STATE	POPULATION
1	New York, New York	7,380,906
2	Los Angeles, California	3,553,638
3	Chicago, Illinois	2,721,547
4	Houston, Texas	1,744,058
5	Philadelphia, Pennsylvania	1,478,002
6	San Diego, California	1,171,121
7	Phoenix, Arizona	1,159,014
8	San Antonio, Texas	1,067,816
9	Dallas, Texas	1,053,292
10	Detroit, Michigan	1,000,272

Source: *US Bureau of the Census*

These are estimates for central city areas only, not for the total metropolitan areas that surround them, which may be several times as large.

THE BIG APPLE

New York's vibrant character is largely due to the vast numbers of immigrants that have come to this city: Irish, Greeks, Italians, Russians, Canadians, English, Dutch, and Puerto Ricans have all made it their home.

LIFE IN THE CITY

Mahatma Ghandi Road in Calcutta, which teems with trams, cars, trucks, rickshaws, and people, epitomizes the colorful – and noisy – hustle and bustle of daily life in India's former capital city.

TOP 10 ★
LARGEST CITIES IN NORTH AMERICA

	CITY/COUNTRY	POPULATION*
1	New York, US	16,329,000
2	Mexico City, Mexico	15,643,000
3	Los Angeles, US	12,410,000
4	Chicago, US	6,846,000
5	Toronto, Canada	4,483,000
6	Philadelphia, US	4,304,000
7	Washington DC, US	4,111,000
8	San Fransisco, US	3,866,000
9	Detroit, US	3,725,000
10	Dallas, US	3,612,000

* Of urban agglomeration

Source: *United Nations*

TOP 10 LARGEST CITIES IN EUROPE
(City/country/population*)

1. **Paris**, France, 9,469,000
2. **Moscow**, Russia, 9,233,000
3. **London**, UK, 7,335,000
4. **Essen**, Germany, 6,481,000
5. **St. Petersburg**, Russia, 5,111,000
6. **Milan**, Italy, 4,251,000
7. **Madrid**, Spain, 4,072,000
8. **Athens**, Greece, 3,693,000
9. **Frankfurt**, Germany, 3,606,000
10. **Katowice**, Poland, 3,552,000

* Of urban agglomeration
Source: *United Nations*

TOP 10 ★
FASTEST-GROWING CITIES

	CITY/COUNTRY	RATE*
1	Tanjung Karang, Indonesia	6.52
2	Maputo, Mozambique	6.07
3	Esfahan, Iran	5.66
4	Kabul, Afghanistan	5.56
5	Conakry, Guinea	5.17
6	Nairobi, Kenya	5.16
7	Lagos, Nigeria	5.05
8	Dacca, Bangladesh	5.03
9	Luanda, Angola	4.99
10	Yaounde, Cameroon	4.94

* Population growth rate, percent per annum

Source: *United Nations*

NATIONAL PARKS

LARGEST NATIONAL PARKS IN THE US

	NATIONAL PARK/LOCATION	ESTABLISHED	AREA (ACRES)
1	Wrangell-St. Elias, Alaska	Dec 2, 1980	8,323,618
2	Gates of the Arctic, Alaska	Dec 2, 1980	7,523,888
3	Denali (formerly Mt McKinley), Alaska	Feb 26, 1917	4,741,910
4	Katmai, Alaska	Dec 2, 1980	3,674,794
5	Death Valley, California/Nevada	Oct 31, 1994	3,367,628
6	Glacier Bay, Alaska	Dec 2, 1980	3,224,794
7	Lake Clark, Alaska	Dec 2, 1980	2,619,859
8	Yellowstone, Wyoming/Montana/Idaho	Mar 1, 1872	2,219,791
9	Kobuk Valley, Alaska	Dec 2, 1980	1,750,737
10	Everglades, Florida	May 30, 1934	1,507,850

Yellowstone National Park was established on March 1, 1872, as the first national park in the world with its role "as a public park or pleasuring ground for the benefit and enjoyment of the people." There are now some 1,200 national parks in more than 100 countries. In the US, there are 54 National Parks with a total area of 83,906 sq miles/217,316 sq km, or 53,699,743 acres (more than double their area before 1980 – when large tracts of Alaska were added). With the addition of various National Monuments, National Historic Parks, National Preserves, and other specially designated areas under the aegis of the National Park Service, the total area is 129,688 sq miles/335,890 sq km (approximately 83 million acres), visited by almost 300 million people a year.

FIRST NATIONAL MONUMENTS IN THE US

	NATIONAL MONUMENT/LOCATION	ESTABLISHED
1	Little Big Horn Battlefield, Montana	Jan 29, 1879
2	Casa Grande Ruins, Arizona	Mar 2, 1889
3	Devils Tower, Wyoming	Sep 24, 1906
4=	El Morro, New Mexico	Dec 8, 1906
=	Montezuma Castle, Arizona	Dec 8, 1906
6	Gila Cliff Dwellings, New Mexico	Nov 16, 1907
7	Tonto, Arizona	Dec 19, 1907
8	Muir Woods, California	Jan 9, 1908
9	Grand Canyon, Arizona	Jan 11, 1908
10	Pinnacles, California	Jan 16, 1908

There are some 73 National Monuments in the US, covering a total of 3,226 sq miles/8,355 sq km, or 2,064,446 acres.

MOST VISITED NATIONAL PARKS IN THE US

	PARK	LOCATION	VISITORS (1997)
1	Great Smoky Mountains National Park	North Carolina/Tennessee	9,965,075
2	Grand Canyon National Park	Arizona	4,791,668
3	Olympic National Park	Washington	3,846,709
4	Yosemite National Park	California	3,669,970
5	Rocky Mountain National Park	California	2,965,354
6	Yellowstone National Park	Wyoming	2,889,513
7	Acadia National Park	Maine	2,760,306
8	Grand Teton National Park	Wyoming	2,658,762
9	Zion National Park	Utah	2,445,534
10	Mammoth Cave	Kentucky	1,997,658

The total number of visitors to US National Parks in 1997 was 275,236,335.

FIRST NATIONAL PARKS IN THE US

	NATIONAL PARK/LOCATION	ESTABLISHED
1	Yellowstone, Wyoming/Montana/Idaho	Mar 1, 1872
2	Sequoia, California	Sep 25, 1890
3=	Yosemite, California	Oct 1, 1890
=	General Grant, California*	Oct 1, 1890
5	Mount Rainier, Washington	Mar 2, 1899
6	Crater Lake, Oregon	May 22, 1902
7	Wind Cave, South Dakota	Jan 9, 1903
8	Mesa Verde, Colorado	Jun 29, 1906
9	Glacier, Montana	May 11, 1910
10	Rocky Mountain, Colorado	Jan 26, 1915

Name changed to Kings Canyon National Park, March 4, 1940

These are the first 10 National Parks established in the US, although several other National Parks may claim a place in the list by virtue of their having been founded under different appellations at earlier dates and subsequently redesignated as National Parks. Hot Springs, Arkansas, for example, which was established as early as April 20, 1832, as Hot Springs Reservation, became a public park on June 16, 1880, but did not become a National Park until March 4, 1921. Similarly, Petrified Forest, Arizona, was proclaimed a National Monument on December 8, 1906, but did not become a National Park until December 9, 1962.

THE 10 ★
FIRST NATIONAL BATTLEFIELDS IN THE US

	NATIONAL BATTLEFIELD/LOCATION	BATTLE	ESTABLISHED*
1	**Chickamauga and Chattanooga**, Georgia/Tennessee	Sep 19–20, 1863	Aug 19, 1890
2	**Antietam**, Maryland	Sep 17, 1862	Aug 30, 1890
3	**Shiloh**, Tennessee	Apr 6–7, 1862	Dec 27, 1894
4	**Gettysburg**, Pennsylvania	Jul 1–3, 1863	Feb 11, 1895
5	**Vicksburg**, Mississippi	Jan 9–Jul 4, 1863	Feb 21, 1899
6	**Big Hole**, Montana	Aug 9, 1877	Jun 23, 1910
7	**Guilford Courthouse**, North Carolina	Mar 15, 1781	Mar 2, 1917
8	**Kennesaw Mountain**, Georgia	Jun 20–Jul 2, 1864	Apr 22, 1917
9	**Moores Creek**, North Carolina	Feb 27, 1776	Jun 2, 1926
10	**Petersburg**, Virginia	Jun 15, 1864–Apr 3, 1865	Jul 3, 1926

* Dates include those for locations originally assigned other designations but later authorized as National Battlefields, National Battlefield Parks, and National Military Parks

THE 10 ★
FIRST NATIONAL HISTORIC SITES IN THE US

	NATIONAL HISTORIC SITE/LOCATION	ESTABLISHED*
1	**Ford's Theatre**, Washington, DC	Apr 7, 1866
2	**Abraham Lincoln Birthplace**, Kentucky	Jul 17, 1916
3	**Andrew Johnson**, Tennessee	Aug 29, 1935
4	**Jefferson National Expansion Memorial**, Missouri	Dec 20, 1935
5	**Whitman Mission**, Washington	Jun 29, 1936
6	**Salem Maritime**, Massachusetts	Mar 17, 1938
7	**Fort Laramie**, Wyoming	Jul 16, 1938
8	**Hopewell Furnace**, Pennsylvania	Aug 3, 1938
9	**Vanderbilt Mansion**, New York	Dec 18, 1940
10	**Fort Raleigh**, North Carolina	Apr 5, 1941

* Dates include those for locations originally assigned other designations but later authorized as Historic Sites

Among the most recent of the 72 locations established as Historic Sites was the Plains, Georgia, in 1987, birthplace and home of President Jimmy Carter.

ULURU
Once known as Ayers Rock, this giant block of red sandstone is the world's largest free-standing rock, and lies in one of Australia's protected areas. Its name means "giant pebble" in Aboriginal language.

TOP 10 COUNTRIES WITH THE LARGEST PROTECTED AREAS

	COUNTRY	PERCENT OF TOTAL AREA	DESIGNATED AREA SQ MILES	DESIGNATED AREA SQ KM
1	**Brazil**	16.8	552,191	1,430,167
2	**US**	10.6	383,611	993,547
3	**Greenland**	45.2	379,345	982,500
4	**Australia**	10.9	323,493	837,843
5	**Colombia**	71.9	316,158	818,346
6	**Canada**	5.6	214,092	554,369
7	**Venezuela**	60.7	213,706	553,496
8	**Tanzania**	38.9	140,972	365,115
9	**Indonesia**	17.2	127,437	330,059
10	**China**	3.2	119,294	308,970

Which world city has the most skyscrapers?
see p.106 for the answer
A Hong Kong
B New York
C Chicago

STATES OF THE US

TOP 10 ★
LARGEST STATES IN THE US

	STATE	AREA* SQ MILES	AREA* SQ KM
1	Alaska	615,230	1,593,438
2	Texas	267,277	692,244
3	California	158,869	411,469
4	Montana	147,046	380,847
5	New Mexico	121,598	314,937
6	Arizona	114,006	295,274
7	Nevada	110,567	286,367
8	Colorado	104,100	269,618
9	Wyoming	97,819	253,350
10	Oregon	97,131	251,568

* Total, including water

Source: US Bureau of the Census

TOP 10 ★
LARGEST NATIVE AMERICAN TRIBES

	TRIBE	POPULATION
1	Cherokee	308,132
2	Navajo	219,198
3	Chippewa	103,826
4	Sioux	103,255
5	Choctaw	82,299
6	Pueblo	52,939
7	Apache	50,051
8	Iroquois	49,038
9	Lumbee	48,444
10	Creek	43,550

The total Native American poulation as assessed by the 1990 Census was 1,878,285. Different authorities have estimated that the total North American population at the time of the first European arrivals in 1492 was anything from 1,000,000 to 10,000,000. This declined to a low in 1890 of some 90,000, but has experienced a substantial resurgence in the past century: according to successive censuses, it had risen to 357,000 in 1950, 793,000 in 1970, and 1,479,000 in 1980.

TOP 10 ★
SMALLEST STATES IN THE US

	STATE	AREA* SQ MILES	AREA* SQ KM
1	Rhode Island	1,545	4,002
2	Delaware	2,489	6,447
3	Connecticut	5,544	14,358
4	New Jersey	8,722	22,590
5	New Hampshire	9,351	24,219
6	Vermont	9,615	24,903
7	Massachusetts	10,555	27,337
8	Hawaii	10,932	28,313
9	Maryland	12,407	32,135
10	West Virginia	24,231	62,759

* Total, including water

TOP 10 ★
MOST HIGHLY POPULATED STATES IN THE US

	STATE	POPULATION 1990	POPULATION 1998*
1	California	1,485,053	32,666,550
2	Texas	3,048,710	19,759,614
3	New York	7,268,894	18,175,301
4	Florida	528,542	14,915,980
5	Illinois	4,821,550	12,045,326
6	Pennsylvania	6,302,115	12,001,451
7	Ohio	4,157,545	11,209,493
8	Michigan	2,420,982	9,817,242
9	New Jersey	1,883,669	8,115,011
10	Georgia	2,216,231	7,642,207

* Estimated

Source: US Bureau of the Census

The total population of the United States according to the 1900 Census was 75,994,575, compared to the US Bureau of the Census's 1998 estimate of 270,298,524. It has undergone a more than 68 times expansion in the 208 years since 1790, when it was just 3,929,214.

THE 10 ★
FIRST STATES OF THE US

	STATE	ENTERED UNION
1	Delaware	Dec 7, 1787
2	Pennsylvania	Dec 12, 1787
3	New Jersey	Dec 18, 1787
4	Georgia	Jan 2, 1788
5	Connecticut	Jan 9, 1788
6	Massachusetts	Feb 6, 1788
7	Maryland	Apr 28, 1788
8	South Carolina	May 23, 1788
9	New Hampshire	June 21, 1788
10	Virginia	June 25, 1788

The names of two of the first 10 American states commemorate early colonists. Delaware Bay (and hence the river, and later the state) was named after Thomas West, Lord De La Warr, a governor of Virginia. Pennsylvania was called "Pensilvania," or "Penn's woodland," in its original charter, issued in 1681 to the Quaker leader William Penn by King Charles II. Two states were named after places with which their founders had associations: New Jersey was the subject of a deed issued in 1644 by the Duke of York to John Berkeley and Sir George Carteret, who came from Jersey in the Channel Islands, and New Hampshire was called after the English county by settler Captain John Mason.

THE 10 ★
LAST STATES OF THE US

	STATE	ENTERED UNION
1	Hawaii	Aug 21, 1959
2	Alaska	Jan 3, 1959
3	Arizona	Feb 14, 1912
4	New Mexico	Jan 6, 1912
5	Oklahoma	Nov 16, 1907
6	Utah	Jan 4, 1896
7	Wyoming	July 10, 1890
8	Idaho	July 3, 1890
9	Washington	Nov 11, 1889
10	Montana	Nov 8, 1889

TOP 10 ⭐
US STATES WITH THE MOST COUNTIES

	STATE	COUNTIES
1	Texas	254
2	Georgia	159
3	Kentucky	120
4	Missouri	114
5	Kansas	105
6	Illinois	102
7	North Carolina	100
8	Iowa	99
9 =	Tennessee	95
=	Virginia	95

TOP 10 ⭐
US STATES WITH THE LONGEST SHORELINES

	STATE	SHORELINE MILES	KM
1	Alaska	33,904	54,904
2	Florida	8,426	13,560
3	Louisiana	7,721	12,426
4	Maine	3,478	5,597
5	California	3,427	5,515
6	North California	3,375	5,432
7	Texas	3,359	5,406
8	Virginia	3,315	5,335
9	Maryland	3,190	5,134
10	Washington	3,026	4,870

Pennsylvania's 890-mile/143-km shoreline is the shortest among states that have one – 26 states, plus the District of Columbia, have no shoreline.

TOP 10 ⭐
STATES WITH THE MOST FOREIGN-BORN RESIDENTS

	STATE	FOREIGN-BORN RESIDENTS
1	California	6,458,825
2	New York	2,851,861
3	Florida	1,662,601
4	Texas	1,524,436
5	New Jersey	966,610
6	Illinois	952,272
7	Massachusetts	573,733
8	Pennsylvania	369,316
9	Michigan	355,393
10	Washington	322,144

Source: *US Bureau of the Census*

TOP 10 ⭐
STATES WITH THE GREATEST AREA OF TRIBAL LAND

	STATE	ACRES
1	Arizona	20,087,538
2	New Mexico	7,882,619
3	Montana	5,574,835
4	South Dakota	4,520,719
5	Nevada	2,721,000
6	Washington	2,718,516
7	Utah	2,319,286
8	Wyoming	2,059,632
9	Alaska	1,352,205
10	Oklahoma	1,097,004

A total of 34 states contain 56,183,794 acres of tribal land (land owned by tribes and individuals and held in trust by the federal government at the time of the 1990 Census). Some have very small areas (Arkansas has just 3 acres). The remaining 16 states have no tribal land at all.

THE 10 FIRST UNESCO HERITAGE SITES IN THE US

	SITE	LOCATION	YEAR
1 =	Mesa Verde National Park	Colorado	1978
=	Yellowstone National Park	Wyoming/Idaho/Montana	1978
3 =	Everglades National Park	Florida	1979
=	Grand Canyon National Park	Arizona	1979
=	Independence Hall	Pennsylvania	1979
6	Redwood National Park	California	1980
7 =	Mammoth Cave National Park	Kentucky	1981
=	Olympic National Park	Washington State	1981
9	Cahokia Mounds State Historic Site	Illinois	1982
10	Great Smoky Mountains National Park	North Carolina/Tennessee	1983

Which country in the world is the most densely populated?
see p.96 for the answer
A Bangladesh
B Monaco
C Singapore

PLACE NAMES

TOP 10 ★

COUNTRIES WITH THE LONGEST OFFICIAL NAMES

	OFFICIAL NAME*	COMMON ENGLISH NAME	LETTERS
1	al-Jamāhīrīyah al-Arabīya al-Lībīyah ash-Sha bīyah al-Ishtirākīyah	Libya	56
2	al-Jumhūrīyah al-Jazā'irīyah ad-Dīmuqrāṭīyah ash-Sha bīyah	Algeria	49
3	United Kingdom of Great Britain and Northern Ireland	United Kingdom	45
4	Sri Lankā Prajathanthrika Samajavadi Janarajaya	Sri Lanka	43
5	'Jumhurīyat al-Qumur al-Ittihādīyah al-Islāmīyah	The Comoros	41
6	=al-Jumhūrīyah al-Islāmīyah al-Mūrītānīyah	Mauritania	36
	=The Federation of St. Christopher and Nevis	St. Kitts and Nevis	36
8	Jamhuuriyadda Dimuqraadiga Soomaaliya	Somalia	35
9	al-Mamlakah al-Urdunnīyah al-Hāshimīyah	Jordan	34
10	Repoblika Demokratika n'i Madagaskar	Madagascar	32

* Some official names have been transliterated from languages that do not use the Roman alphabet; their length may vary according to the method used.

TOP 10 MOST COMMON CITY NAMES IN THE US

(Name/occurrences)*

1 Fairview, 66 **2** Midway, 52
3 Oak Grove, 44 **4** = Franklin, 40;
= Riverside, 40 **6** Centerville, 39
7 Mount Pleasant, 38 **8** Georgetown, 37 **9** Salem, 36 **10** Greenwood, 34

* Incorporated city status only

TOP 10 ★

MOST COMMON STREET NAMES IN THE US

1	Second Street
2	Park Street
3	Third Street
4	Fourth Street
5	Fifth Street
6	First Street
7	Sixth Street
8	Seventh Street
9	Washington Street
10	Maple Street

CITY OF ANGELS

Bangkok, the city with the world's longest name, lies on the banks of the Chao Phraya River.

TOP 10 MOST COMMON PLACE NAMES IN THE US

(Name/occurrences)

1 Fairview, 287 **2** Midway, 252
3 Riverside, 180 **4** Oak Grove, 179
5 Five Points, 155 **6** Oakland, 149
7 Greenwood, 145 **8** = Bethel, 141;
= Franklin, 141 **10** Pleasant Hill, 140

Source: *US Geological Board*

TOP 10 ★
LONGEST PLACE NAMES*

NAME	LETTERS
1 Krung thep mahanakhon bovorn ratanakosin mahintharayutthaya mahadilok pop noparatratchathani burirom udomratchanivetmahasathan amornpiman avatarnsathit sakkathattiyavisnukarmprasit	167

When the poetic name of Bangkok, capital of Thailand, is used, it is usually abbreviated to "Krung Thep" (city of angels).

| **2** Taumatawhakatangihangakoauauotamateaturipukakapikimaungahoronu-kupokaiwhenuakitanatahu | 85 |

This is the longer version (the other has a mere 83 letters) of the Maori name of a hill in New Zealand. It translates as "The place where Tamatea, the man with the big knees, who slid, climbed, and swallowed mountains, known as land-eater, played on the flute to his loved one."

| **3** Gorsafawddacha'idraigodanheddogleddollônpenrhynareurdraethceredigion | 67 |

A name contrived by the Fairbourne Steam Railway, Gwynedd, North Wales, for publicity purposes and in order to outdo its rival, No. 4. It means "The Mawddach station and its dragon teeth at the Northern Penrhyn Road on the golden beach of Cardigan Bay."

| **4** Llanfairpwllgwyngyllgogerychwyrndrobwllllantysiliogogogoch | 58 |

This is the place in Gwynedd famed especially for the length of its train tickets. It means "St. Mary's Church in the hollow of the white hazel near to the rapid whirlpool of Llantysilio of the Red Cave." Questions have been raised about its authenticity, since its official name comprises only the first 20 letters, and the full name appears to have been invented as a hoax in the 19th century by a local poet, John Evans, known as Y Bardd Cocos. It also has Britain's longest Internet site name: http://www.llanfairpwllgwyngyllgogerychwyrndrobwllllantysilio-gogogoch.-wales.com/llanfair

| **5** El Pueblo de Nuestra Señora la Reina de los Angeles de la Porciuncula | 57 |

The site of a Franciscan mission and the full Spanish name of Los Angeles; it means "The town of Our Lady the Queen of the Angels of the Little Portion." Nowadays it is customarily known by its initial letters, "LA", making it also one of the shortest-named cities in the world.

| **6** Chargoggagoggmanchauggagoggchaubunagungamaugg | 45 |

America's longest place name, a lake near Webster, Massachusetts. Its Native American name, loosely translated, means "You fish on your side, I'll fish on mine, and no one fishes in the middle." It is said to be pronounced "Char-gogg-a-gogg (pause) man-chaugg-a-gogg (pause) chau-bun-a-gung-amaugg." It is, however, an invented extension of its real name (Chagungungamaug Pond, or "boundary fishing place"), devised in the 1920s by Larry Daly, the editor of the Webster Times.

| **7** = Lower North Branch Little Southwest Miramichi | 40 |

Canada's longest place name – a short river in New Brunswick.

| = Villa Real de la Santa Fe de San Francisco de Asis | 40 |

The full Spanish name of Santa Fe, New Mexico, translates as, "Royal city of the holy faith of St. Francis of Assisi."

| **9** Te Whakatakanga-o-te-ngarehu-o-te-ahi-a-Tamatea | 38 |

The Maori name of Hammer Springs, New Zealand; like the second name in this list, it refers to a legend of Tamatea, explaining how the springs were warmed by "the falling of the cinders of the fire of Tamatea." Its name is variously written either hyphenated or as a single word.

| **10** Meallan Liath Coire Mhic Dhubhghaill | 32 |

The longest multiple name in Scotland, a place near Aultanrynie, Highland, this is alternatively spelled Meallan Liath Coire Mhic Dhughaill (30 letters).

* Including single-word, hyphenated, and multiple-word names

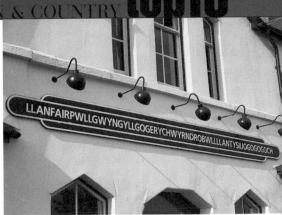

WELSH TONGUE TWISTER

This small village with a very long name on the island of Anglesey, in North Wales, is known to its residents as simply Llanfair.

TOP 10 ★
LONGEST PLACE NAMES IN THE UK*

NAME/LOCATION	LETTERS
1 Gorsafawddachaidraigddanhed-dogleddollônpenrhyn-areurdraethceredigion (see Top 10 Longest Place Names)	67
2 Llanfairpwllgwyngyllgogery-chwyrndrobwllllantysiliogo-gogoch (see Top 10 Longest Place Names)	58
3 Sutton-under-Whitestonecliffe, North Yorkshire	27
4 Llanfihangel-yng-Ngwynfa, Powys	22
5 = Llanfihangel-y-Creuddyn, Dyfed	21
= Llanfihangel-y-traethau, Gwynedd	21
7 Cottonshopeburnfoot, Northumberland	19
8 = Blakehopeburnhaugh, Northumberland	18
= Coignafeuinternich, Inverness-shire	18
10 = Claddach-baleshare, North Uist, Outer Hebrides	17
= Claddach-knockline, North Uist, Outer Hebrides	17

*Single and hyphenated only

STREETS AHEAD

Toward the end of the 1900s in America, civic authorities demanded that street names be made uniform, following a system that avoided duplication.

Did You Know? Kentucky has several two-letter place names, including Ed, Ep, Or, Oz, and Uz.

TALLEST HABITABLE BUILDINGS

BUILDING/YEAR/ LOCATION	STORIES	HEIGHT FT	M
1 Petronas Towers, 1996, Kuala Lumpur, Malaysia	96	1,482	452
2 Sears Tower, 1974, Chicago	110	1,454	443
with spires		1,707	520
3 World Trade Center,* 1973, New York City	110	1,368	417
4 Jin Mao Building, 1997, Shanghai, China	93	1,255	382
with spire		1,378	420
5 Empire State Building, 1931, New York City	102	1,250	381
with spire		1,472	449
6 T & C Tower, 1997, Kao-hsiung, Taiwan	85	1,142	348
7 Amoco Building, 1973, Chicago	80	1,136	346
8 John Hancock Center, 1968, Chicago	100	1,127	343
with spires		1,476	450
9 Shun Hing Square, 1996, Shenzen, China	80	1,082	330
with spires		1,263	384
10 Sky Central Plaza, 1996, Guangzhou, China	80	1,060	323
with spires		1,283	391

* Twin towers; the second tower is slightly smaller

TOP 10 TALLEST MASTS

(Mast/location/height in ft/m)

1 KTHI-TV Mast, Fargo, North Dakota, 2,063/629 **2** KSLA-TV Mast, Shreveport, Louisiana, 1,898/579 **3** = WBIR-TV Mast, Knoxville, Tennessee, 1,749/533; = WTVM & WRBL TV Mast, Columbus, Georgia, 1,749/533 **5** KFVS TV Mast, Cape Girardeau, Missouri, 1,676/511 **6** WPSD-TV Mast, Paducah, Kentucky, 1,638/499 **7** WGAN TV Mast, Portland, Maine, 1,619/493 **8** KWTV TV Mast, Oklahoma City, Oklahoma, 1,572/479 **9** BREN Tower, Area 25, Nevada Test Site, Nevada, 1,521/464 **10** Omega Base Navigational Mast, Gippsland, Victoria, Australia, 1,400/426

TALLEST REINFORCED CONCRETE BUILDINGS

BUILDING/YEAR/ LOCATION	STORIES	HEIGHT FT	M
1 Baiyoke II Tower, 1997, Bangkok, Thailand	89	1,046	319
2 Central Plaza, 1992, Hong Kong, China	78	1,015	309
with spire		1,228	374
3 311 South Wacker Drive, 1990, Chicago	65	970	296
4 2 Prudential Plaza, 1990, Chicago	64	901	275
with spire		978	298
5 NCNB, 1992, Charlotte	60	871	265
6 Water Tower Place, 1975, Chicago	74	859	262
7 Messeturm, 1990, Frankfurt, Germany	70	841	256
8 Citispire, 1989, New York City	72	802	245
9 Rialto Tower, 1985, Melbourne, Australia	60	794	242
10 Tun Abdul Rasak Building, 1985, Penang, Malaysia	61	761	232

Reinforced concrete was patented in France on March 16, 1867, by Joseph Monier (1823–1906) and developed by another Frenchman, François Hennebique (1842–1921). The first American buildings constructed from concrete date from a century ago, when it became one of the most important of all building materials. Steel bars set within concrete slabs expand and contract at the same rate as the concrete, providing great tensile strength and fire resistance. These qualities make it the ideal material for huge structures such as bridge spans and skyscrapers.

TOP HOTEL

At 1,046 ft/319 m, the Baiyoke II Tower is also the tallest hotel in the world. The second-tallest hotel – the Yu Kyong in North Korea – has a greater number of stories, however: 105 to the Baiyoke's 89.

TOP 10 CITIES WITH THE MOST SKYSCRAPERS*

(City/location/skyscrapers)

1 New York City, 140 **2** Chicago, 68 **3** = Hong Kong, China, 36; = Houston, 36 **5** Kuala Lumpur, Malaysia, 25 **6** Los Angeles, 24 **7** Dallas, 22 **8** = San Francisco, 20; = Shanghai, China, 20 **10** = Singapore, 18; = Sydney, Australia, 18

* Habitable buildings of more than 500 ft/152 m

TALLEST CYLINDRICAL BUILDINGS

BUILDING/YEAR/ LOCATION	STORIES	HEIGHT FT	M
1 Treasury Building, 1986, Singapore	52	770	235
2 Tun Abdul Prazak Building, 1985, Penang, Malaysia	61	760	232
3 Westin Peachtree Plaza, 1973, Atlanta	71	721	220
4 Renaissance Center, 1977, Detroit	73	718	219
5 Hopewell Center, 1980, Hong Kong, China	64	705	215
6 Marina City Apartments (twin towers), 1969, Chicago	61	588	179
7 Australia Square Tower, 1968, Sydney, Australia	46	560	170
8 Amartapura Condominium 1, 1996, Tangerang, Indonesia	54	535	163
9 Shenzen City Plaza, 1996, Shenzen, China	37	490	150
10 Amartapura Condominium 2, 1997, Tangerang, Indonesia	36	445	136

When completed in 1968, the misleadingly named Australia Square Tower in Sydney became the world's tallest cylindrical building as well as the tallest concrete building. It also claims the world's largest revolving restaurant, measuring 135 ft/41 m in diameter and situated at a dizzy 502 ft/153 m above street level.

TWIN TOWERS

The World Trade Center in New York has a staggering 3,140 stairs. In 1977, instead of taking this indoor route to the top, George Willig climbed up the outside of the center – without using any ropes.

TOP 10 ★
TALLEST APARTMENT BUILDINGS

	BUILDING/YEAR/LOCATION	STORIES	FT	M
1	**Lake Point Tower**, 1968, Chicago	70	645	197
2	**Central Park Place**, 1988, New York City	56	628	191
3	**Olympic Tower**, 1976, New York City	51	620	189
4	**May Road Apartments**, 1993, Hong Kong, China	58	590	180
5	**Marina City Apartments**, 1968, Chicago	61	588	179
6	**North Pier Apartments**, 1990, Chicago	61	581	177
7	**Onterie Center**, 1985, Chicago	58	570	174
8 =	**Triple Towers**, U/C, Mang Tzeng, China	57	564	172
=	**Newton Tower**, U/C, Hong Kong, China	43	564	172
10	**30 Broad Street**, 1980, New York City	48	562	171

U/C = under construction

TOP 10 ★
HIGHEST PUBLIC OBSERVATORIES

	BUILDING/LOCATION	OBSERVATORY	YEAR	FT	M
1	**CN Tower, Toronto**, Canada	Space deck	1975	1,465	447
2	**World Trade Center**, New York City	Rooftop Tower B	1973	1,360	415
3	**Sears Tower**, Chicago	103rd floor	1974	1,353	412
4	**Empire State Building**, New York City	102nd floor	1931	1,250	381
		Outdoor observatory		1,050	320
5	**Ostankino Tower**, Moscow, Russia	5th floor turret	1967	1,181	360
6	**Oriental Pearl Broadcasting Tower**, Shanghai, China	VIP observation level	1995	1,148	350
		Public observation level		863	263
7	**Jin Mao Building**, Shanghai, China	88th floor	1997	1,115	340
8	**John Hancock Center**, Chicago	94th floor	1968	1,030	314
9	**Sky Central Plaza**, Guanghshou, China	90th floor	1996	1,016	310
10	**KL Tower**, Kuala Lumpur, Malaysia	Revolving restaurant	1995	925	282
		Public observation level		907	276

TOP 10 ★
TALLEST TELECOMMUNICATIONS TOWERS

	TOWER/YEAR/LOCATION	FT	M
1	**CN Tower**, 1975, Toronto, Canada	1,821	555
2	**Ostankino Tower**, 1967, Moscow, Russia	1,762	537
3	**Oriental Pearl Broadcasting Tower**, 1995, Shanghai, China	1,535	468
4	**Menara Telecom Tower**, 1996, Kuala Lumpur, Malaysia	1,381	421
5	**Tianjin TV and Radio Tower**, 1991, Tianjin, China	1,362	415
6	**Central Radio and TV Tower**, 1994, Beijing, China	1,328	405
7	**TV Tower**, 1983, Tashkent, Uzbekistan	1,230	375
8	**Liberation Tower**, 1998, Kuwait City, Kuwait	1,220	372
9	**Alma-Ata Tower**, 1983, Kazakhstan	1,214	370
10	**TV Tower**, 1969, Berlin, Germany	1,198	365

All the towers listed are self-supporting, rather than masts braced with guy wires, and all have observation facilities, the highest being that in the CN Tower, Toronto, at 1,467 ft/447 m. The completion of the Telecom Tower, Kuala Lumpur, means that the Eiffel Tower dropped out of the Top 10.

PEARL OF THE ORIENT

Shanghai's Oriental Pearl, the highest tower in Asia, was designed by Chinese architect Jia Huan Cheng to represent a string of pearls.

Did You Know? The Menara Jakarta, a tower under construction in Jakarta, Indonesia, is intended to be 1,831 ft/558 m tall. When it is completed, it will be the tallest structure of any kind in the Southern Hemisphere.

BRIDGES & OTHER STRUCTURES

LONGEST CANTILEVER BRIDGES

BRIDGE/YEAR/LOCATION	LONGEST SPAN	
	FT	M
1 Pont de Québec, 1917, Canada	1,800	549
2 Firth of Forth, 1890, Scotland	1,710	521
3 Minato, Osaka, 1974, Japan	1,673	510
4 Commodore John Barry, 1974, New Jersey/Pennsylvania	1,622	494
5 =Greater New Orleans 1, 1958, Louisiana	1,575	480
=Greater New Orleans 2, 1988, Louisiana	1,575	480
7 Howrah, 1943, Calcutta, India	1,500	457
8 Gramercy, 1995, Louisiana	1,460	445
9 Transbay, 1936, San Francisco	1,400	427
10 Baton Rouge, 1969, Louisiana	1,235	376

LONGEST UNDERWATER TUNNELS*

TUNNEL/YEAR/LOCATION	LENGTH	
	MILES	KM
1 Seikan, 1988, Japan	33.49	53.90
2 Channel Tunnel, 1994, France/England	31.03	49.94
3 Dai–Shimizu, 1982, Japan	13.78	22.17
4 Shin–Kanmon, 1975, Japan	11.61	18.68
5 Great Belt Fixed Link, 1997, Eastern Tunnel, Denmark	4.97	8.00
6 Severn, 1886, UK	4.36	7.01
7 Haneda, 1971, Japan	3.72	5.98
8 BART, 1970, San Francisco	3.62	5.83
9 Kammon, 1942, Japan	2.24	3.60
10 Kammon, 1958, Japan	2.15	3.46

* All are rail tunnels, except No. 10, which is road

The need to connect the Japanese islands of Honshu, Kyushu, and Hokkaido has resulted in a wave of undersea tunnel building in recent years, with the Seikan the most ambitious project of all. Connecting Honshu and Hokkaido, 14.4 miles/23.3 km of the tunnel is 328 ft/100 m below the ocean bed. It took 24 years to complete.

HIGHEST DAMS

DAM/YEAR/RIVER/LOCATION	HEIGHT	
	FT	M
1 Rogun, U/C, Vakhsh, Tajikistan	1,099	335
2 Nurek, 1980, Vakhsh, Tajikistan	984	300
3 Grand Dixence, 1961, Dixence, Switzerland	935	285
4 Inguri, 1980, Inguri, Georgia	892	272
5 =Chicoasén, U/C, Grijalva, Mexico	856	261
=Tehri, U/C, Bhagirathi, India	856	261
7 Kishau, U/C, Tons, India	830	253
8 =Ertan, U/C, Yangtse-kiang, China	804	245
=Sayano–Shushensk, U/C, Yeniesei, Russia	804	245
10 Guavio, U/C, Guavio, Colombia	797	243

U/C = under construction

LONGEST CABLE-STAYED BRIDGES

BRIDGE/YEAR/LOCATION	LENGTH OF MAIN SPAN	
	FT	M
1 Tatara, 1999, Onomichi–Imabari, Japan	2,920	890
2 Pont de Normandie, 1994, Le Havre, France	2,808	856
3 Qunghzhou Minjiang, 1996, Fozhou, China	1,985	605
4 Yangpu, 1993, Shanghai, China	1,975	602
5 =Meiko–Chuo, 1997, Nagoya, Japan	1,936	590
=Xupu, 1997, Shanghai, China	1,936	590
7 Skarnsundet, 1991, Trondheim Fjord, Norway	1,739	530
8 =Ikuchi, 1994, Onomichi–Imabari, Japan	1,608	490
=Öresund, 2000, Copenhagen–Malmö, Denmark/Sweden)	1,608	490
10 Higashi–Kobe, 1992, Kobe, Japan	1,591	485

BRIDGE OF SIZE

Crossing the Seine estuary, the Pont de Normandie links Le Havre with the route westward.

Background image: FORTH RAIL BRIDGE, UK

108

TOP 10 ★
LONGEST SUSPENSION BRIDGES

BRIDGE/YEAR/LOCATION	LENGTH OF MAIN SPAN	
	FT	M
1 Akashi–Kaiko, 1998, Kobe–Naruto, Japan	6,529	1,990
2 =Great Belt, 1997, Denmark	5,328	1,624
=Jiangyin, 1998, China	5,328	1,624
4 Humber Estuary, 1980, UK	4,626	1,410
5 Tsing Ma, 1997, Hong Kong, China	4,518	1,377
6 Verrazano Narrows, 1964, New York	4,260	1,298
7 Golden Gate, 1937, San Francisco	4,200	1,280
8 Höga Kusten, 1997, Veda, Sweden	3,970	1,210
9 Mackinac Straits, 1957, Michigan,	3,800	1,158
10 Minami Bisan-seto, 1988, Kojima–Sakaide, Japan	3,609	1,100

The Messina Strait Bridge between Sicily and Calabria, Italy, remains a speculative project, but if constructed according to plan it will have by far the longest center span of any bridge at 10,892 ft/3,320 m. Although Japan's 12,828ft/3,910m Akashi–Kaiko bridge, completed in 1998 and with a main span of 6,528 ft/1,990 m, is the world's longest overall.

TOP 10 ★
LARGEST SPORTS STADIUMS

STADIUM/LOCATION	CAPACITY
1 Strahov Stadium, Prague, Czech Republic	240,000
2 Maracaña Municipal Stadium, Rio de Janeiro, Brazil	205,000
3 Rungnado Stadium, Pyongyang, South Korea	150,000
4 Estadio Maghalaes Pinto, Belo Horizonte, Brazil	125,000
5 =Estadio Morumbi, São Paulo, Brazil	120,000
=Estadio da Luz, Lisbon, Portugal	120,000
=Senayan Main Stadium, Jakarta, Indonesia	120,000
=Yuba Bharati Krirangan, Nr Calcutta, India	120,000
9 Estadio Castelão, Fortaleza, Brazil	119,000
10 =Estadio Arrudão, Recife, Brazil	115,000
=Estadio Azteca, Mexico City, Mexico	115,000
=Nou Camp, Barcelona, Spain	115,000

The Aztec Stadium, Mexico City, holds 107,000, and most of the seats are under cover. The New Orleans Superdome is the largest indoor stadium, with a capacity of 97,365. The Michigan Football Stadium, Ann Arbor, Michigan, built in 1927, is the largest outdoor stadium in the US, with a seating capacity of 107,501.

SUPER STADIUM

Brazil's giant Maracaña Municipal Stadium, named after the nearby river, holds up to 178,000 seated and 42,000 standing. It was begun in 1945 and completed in 1965.

TOP 10 ★
LONGEST ROAD TUNNELS

TUNNEL/YEAR	LOCATION	LENGTH	
		MILES	KM
1 St. Gotthard, 1980	Switzerland	10.14	16.32
2 Arlberg, 1978	Austria	8.69	13.98
3 =Fréjus, 1980	France/Italy	8.02	12.90
=Pinglin Highway, U/C	Taiwan	8.02	12.90
5 Mont-Blanc, 1965	France/Italy	7.21	11.60
6 Gudvangen, 1992	Norway	7.08	11.40
7 Leirfjord, U/C	Norway	6.90	11.11
8 Kan-Etsu, 1991	Japan	6.84	11.01
9 Kan-Etsu, 1985	Japan	6.79	10.93
10 Gran Sasso, 1984	Italy	6.32	10.17

U/C = under construction

TOP 10 ★
LONGEST STEEL ARCH BRIDGES

BRIDGE/YEAR/LOCATION	LONGEST SPAN	
	FT	M
1 New River Gorge, 1977, Fayetteville, West Virginia	1,700	518
2 Kill van Kull, 1931, Bayonne, New Jersey/ Staten Island, New York City	1,654	504
3 Sydney Harbour, 1932, Australia	1,650	503
4 Fremont, 1973, Portland, Oregon	1,257	383
5 Port Mann, 1964, Vancouver, Canada	1,200	366
6 Thatcher Ferry, 1962, Panama Canal	1,128	344
7 Laviolette, 1967, Quebec, Canada	1,100	335
8 =Runcorn–Widnes, 1961, UK	1,082	330
=Zdákov, 1967, Lake Orlík, Czech Republic	1,082	330
10 =Birchenough, 1935, Fort Victoria, Zimbabwe	1,080	329
=Roosevelt Lake, 1990, Arizona	1,080	329

Which is the highest city in the world?
see p.98 for the answer

A Wenchuan
B Sucre
C Potosi

CULTURE & LEARNING

TOP 10 ★
LONGEST WORDS IN THE ENGLISH LANGUAGE

WORD/MEANING — LETTERS

1 MethionylglutaminylarginyltyrosylglutamylserylleucylphenylalanylalanylglutaminylleucyllysylglutamylarginyllysylglutamylglycylalanylphenylalanylvalylprolylphenylalanylvalylthreonylleucylglycylaspartylprolylglycylisoleucylglutamylglutaminylserylleucyllysylisoleucylaspartylthreonylleucylisoleucylglutamylalanylglycylalanylaspartylalanylleucylglutamylleucylglycylisoleucylprolylphenylalanylserylaspartylprolylleucelalanylaspartylglycylprolylthreonylisoleucylglutaminylasparaginylalanylthreonylleucylarginylalanylphenylalanylalanylalanylglycylvalylthreonylprolylalanylglutaminylcysteinylphenylalanylglutamylmethionylleucyalanylleucylisoleucylarginylglutaminyllysylhistidylprolylthreonylisoleucylproIylisoleucylglycylleucylleucylmethionyltyrosylalanylasparaginylleucylvalylphenylalanylasparaginyllysylglycylisoleucylaspartylglutamylphenylalanyltyrosylalanylglutaminylcysteinylglutamyllysylvalylglycylvalylaspartylserylvalylleucylvalylalanylaspartylvalylprolylvalylglutaminylglutamylserylalanylprolylphenylalanylarginylglutaminylalanylalanylleucylarginylhistidylasparaginylvalylalanylprolylisoleucylphenylalanylisoleucylcysteinylprolylprolylaspartylalanylaspartylaspartylaspartylleucylleucylarginylglutaminylisoleucylalanylseryltyrosylglycylarginylglycyltyrosylthreonyltyrosylleucylleucylserylarginylalanylglycylvalylthreonylglycylalanylglutamylasparaginylarginylanylalanylleucylprolylleucylaspaaginylhistidylleucylvalylalanyllysylleucyllysylglutamyltyrosylasparaginylalanylalanylprolylprolylleucylglutaminylglycylphenylalanylglycylisoleucylserylalanylprolylaspartylglutaminylvalyllysylalanylalanylisoleucylaspartylalanylglycylalanylalanylglycylalanylisoleucylserylglycylserylalanylisoleucylbalyllysylisoleucylisoleucylglutamylglutaminylhistidylasparaginylisoleucylglutamylprolylglutamyllysylmethionylleucylalanylalanylleucyllysylvalylphenylalanylvalylglutaminylprolylmethionyllysylalanylalanylthreonylarginylserine — **1,909**

Tryptophan synthetase A protein, an enzyme consisting of 267 amino acids, stretches to a record 1,909 letters. It has actually appeared in print in various publications.

2 Acetylseryltyrosylserylisoleucylthreonylserylprolylserylglutaminylphenylalanylvalylphenylalanylleucylserylserylvalyltryptophylalanylaspartylprolylisoleucylglutamylleucylleucyllaspparaginylvalylcysteinylthreonylserylserylleucylglycllasparaginylglutaminylphenylalanylglutaminylthreonylglutaminylglutaminylalanylarginylthreonylthreonylglutaminylvalylglutaminylglutaminylphenylalanylserylglutaminylvalyltryptophyllysylprolylphenylalanylprolylglutaminylserylthreonylvalylarginylphenylalanylprolylglycylaspartylvalyltyrosyllsyslvalyltyrosylarginyltyrosylasparaginylalanylvalylleucylaspartylprolylleucylisoleucylthreonylalanylleucylleucylglycylthreonylphenylalanylaspartylthreonylarginylasparaginylarginylisoleucylisoleucylglutamylvalylglutamylasparaginylglutaminylglutaminylserylprolylthreonylthreonylalanylglutamylthreonylleucylaspartylalanylthreonylarginylarginylvalylaspartylaspartylalanylthreonylvalylalanylisoleucylarginylserylalanylasparaginylisoleucylasparaginylleucylvallasparaginylglutamylleucylvalylarginylglycylthreonylglycylleucyltyrosylasparaginylglutaminylasparaginylthreonylphenylalanylglutamylserylmethionylserylglycylleucylvalyltryptophylthreonylserylalanylprolylalanylserine — **1,185**

The word for the Tobacco Mosaic Virus, Dahlemense Strain, qualifies as the second longest word in English because it has actually been used in print (in the American Chemical Society's Chemical Abstracts).

3 Ornicopytheobibliopsychocrystarroscioaerogenethliometeoroaustrohieroanthropoichthyopyrosiderochpnomyoalectryoophiobotanopegohydrorhabdocrithoaleuroalphitohalomolybdoclerobeloaxinocoscinodactyliogeolithopessopsephocatoptrotephraoneirochiroonychodactyloarithstichooxogeloscogastrogyrocerobletonooenoscapulinaniac — **310**

Medieval scribes used this word (and variations of it) when writing about superstition, to refer to a deluded human who indulges in superstitious practices.

4 Lopadotemachoselachogaleokranioleipsanodrimhypotrimmatosilphioparaomelitokatakechymenokichlepikossyphophattoperisteralektryonoptekephalliokigklopeleiolagoiosiraiobaphetraganopterygon — **182**

The English transliteration of a 170-letter Greek word that appears in The Ecclesiazusae by the Greek playwright Aristophanes (c.448–380BC). It is used as a description of a 17-ingredient dish.

5 Aequeosalinocalcinosetaceoaluminosocupreovitriolic — **52**

Invented by a medical writer, Dr. Edward Strother (1675–1737), to describe the spa waters at Bath.

6 Osseocarnisanguineoviscericartilaginonervomedullary — **51**

Coined by writer and East India Company official Thomas Love Peacock (1785–1866), and used in his satire Headlong Hall (1816) as a description of the structure of the human body.

7 Pneumonoultramicroscopicsilicovolcanoconiosis — **45**

It first appeared in print (though ending in "koniosis") in F. Scully's Bedside Manna [sic] (1936). It is said to mean a lung disease caused by breathing fine dust.

8 Hepaticocholecystostcholecystenterostomies — **42**

Surgical operations to create channels of communication between gall bladders and hepatic ducts or intestines.

9 Praetertranssubstantiationalistically — **37**

The adverb describing surpassing the act of transubstantiation; the word is found in Mark McShane's novel Untimely Ripped (1963).

10 =Pseudoantidisestablishmentarianism — **34**

A word meaning "false opposition to the withdrawal of state support from a Church," derived from that perennial favorite long word, antidisestablishmentarianism (a mere 28 letters). Another composite made from it (though usually hyphenated) is ultra-antidisestablishmentarianism (33 letters)

=Supercalifragilisticexpialidocious — **34**

An invented word, but perhaps now eligible since it has appeared in the Oxford English Dictionary. It was popularized by the song of this title in the film Mary Poppins (1964), where it is used to mean "wonderful," but it was originally written in 1949 in an unpublished song by Parker and Young who spelled it "supercalafajalistickespialadojus" (32 letters). In 1965–66, Parker and Young unsuccessfully sued the makers of Mary Poppins, claiming infringement of copyright. In summarizing the case, the US court decided against repeating this mouthful, stating that "All variants of this tongue-twister will hereinafter be referred to collectively as 'the word'."

What is the most expensive painting by Andy Warhol?
see p.130 for the answer

A *Shot Red Marilyn*
B *Orange Marilyn*
C *Marilyn Monroe, twenty times*

TOP 10 ★
MOST WIDELY SPOKEN LANGUAGES

	LANGUAGE	APPROXIMATE NO. OF SPEAKERS
1	Chinese (Mandarin)	1,070,000,000
2	English	508,000,000
3	Hindustani	497,000,000
4	Spanish	392,000,000
5	Russian	277,000,000
6	Arabic	246,000,000
7	Bengali	211,000,000
8	Portuguese	191,000,000
9	Malay-Indonesian	159,000,000
10	French	129,000,000

According to 1998 estimates by Sidney S. Culbert of the University of Washington, in addition to those languages appearing in the Top 10, there are three more languages that are spoken by more than 100 million individuals: German (128 million), Japanese (126 million), and Urdu (105 million). Thirteen more languages are spoken by 50–100 million: Punjabi (94 million), Korean (77 million), Telugu (76 million), Tamil (74 million), Marathi (71 million), Cantonese (71 million), Wu (70 million), Vietnamese (67 million), Javanese (64 million), Italian (63 million), Turkish (61 million), Tagalog (58 million), and Thai (52 million).

ANCIENT SCRIPT
As early as 1390 BC writing made an appearance in China: the Shang people made inscriptions on oracle bones and bronze ritual vessels.

TOP 10 ★
LANGUAGES OFFICIALLY SPOKEN IN THE MOST COUNTRIES

	LANGUAGE	COUNTRIES
1	English	54
2	French	33
3	Arabic	24
4	Spanish	21
5	Portuguese	8
6	German	5
7	= Malay	4
	= Dutch	4
9	Chinese (Mandarin)	3
10	= Italian	2
	= Russian	2
	= Tamil	2

There are many countries in the world with more than one official language – both English and French are recognized officially in Canada, for example. English is also used in numerous countries as the lingua franca.

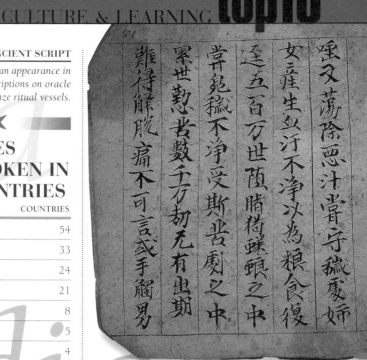

TOP 10 ★
COUNTRIES WITH THE MOST ENGLISH-LANGUAGE SPEAKERS

	COUNTRY	APPROXIMATE NO. OF SPEAKERS
1	US	230,8300,000
2	UK	57,320,000
3	Canada	18,448,000
4	Australia	15,027,000
5	South Africa	3,860,000
6	Irish Republic	3,580,000
7	New Zealand	3,321,000
8	Jamaica	2,380,000
9	Trinidad and Tobago	1,193,000
10	Guyana	746,000

This Top 10 represents the countries with the greatest numbers of inhabitants who speak English as their mother tongue. After the 10th entry, the figures dive to under 260,000 in the case of the Bahamas, Barbados, and Zimbabwe.

TOP 10 MOST STUDIED FOREIGN LANGUAGES IN THE US*

1 Spanish **2** French **3** German **4** Japanese **5** Italian
6 Chinese (Mandarin) **7** Latin **8** Russian **9** Ancient Greek **10** Hebrew

* In US institutions of higher education
Source: *Modern Language Association of America*

These rankings are from the most recent survey conducted every five years, from colleges and universities in the fall of 1995.

UNITED NATIONS
Members from around the world come together at the United Nations. Many different languages are represented here, and translators are kept busy relaying the necessary information to participants.

A REVOLUTION IN PRINTING

The Gutenberg Bible was printed by Johann Gutenberg, a 15th-century goldsmith who invented moveable type.

THE 10 FIRST PENGUIN PAPERBACKS

(Author/book)

1 André Maurois, *Ariel* **2** Ernest Hemingway, *A Farewell to Arms* **3** Eric Linklater, *Poet's Pub* **4** Susan Ertz, *Madame Claire* **5** Dorothy L. Sayers, *The Unpleasantness at the Bellona Club* **6** Agatha Christie, *The Mysterious Affair at Styles* **7** Beverley Nichols, *Twenty-five* **8** E.H. Young, *William* **9** Mary Webb, *Gone to Earth* **10** Compton Mackenzie, *Carnival*

TOP 10 CHILDREN'S HARDBACK BOOKS IN THE US

(Book/author/no. sold)

1 *The Pokey Little Puppy*, Janette Sebring Lowrey, 14,000,000 **2** *The Tale of Peter Rabbit*, Beatrix Potter, 9,331,266 **3** *Tootle*, Gertrude Crampton, 8,055,500 **4** *Saggy Baggy Elephant*, Kathryn and Byron Jackson, 7,098,000 **5** *Scuffy the Tugboat*, Gertrude Crampton, 7,065,000 **6** *Pat the Bunny*, Dorothy Kunhardt, 6,146,543 **7** *Green Eggs and Ham*, Dr. Seuss, 6,065,197 **8** *The Cat in the Hat*, Dr. Seuss, 5,643,731 **9** *The Littlest Angel*, Charles Tazewell, 5,424,709 **10** *One Fish, Two Fish, Red Fish, Blue Fish*, Dr. Seuss, 4,822,331   Source: *Publishers Weekly*

PICK UP A PENGUIN

The first Penguin paperback was published in 1935, the brainchild of Allen Lane. Legend has it that Lane was inspired to create a paperback collection after a weekend at Agatha Christie's house. On his way back to London, he was disappointed by the books available at Exeter station and realized that the market was in need of affordable versions of contemporary titles. In 1961, Penguin published the first unabridged version of D.H. Lawrence's *Lady Chatterley's Lover*. Charged under the British Obscene Publications Act, Penguin had to go to court to defend their rights to publish the infamous novel.

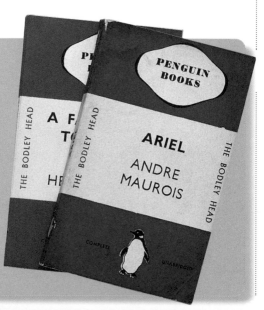

BOOK/MANUSCRIPT/SALE	PRICE ($)*
1 *The Codex Hammer*, Christie's, New York, Nov 11, 1994	30,800,000

This Leonardo da Vinci notebook was bought by Bill Gates, the billionaire founder of Microsoft.

2 *The Gospels of Henry the Lion*, c.1173–75, Sotheby's, London, Dec 6, 1983	10,846,000

At the time of its sale, this became the most expensive manuscript or book ever sold.

3 *The Canterbury Tales*, Geoffrey Chaucer, c.1476–77, Christie's, London, Jul 8, 1998	7,406,000

This is the world's most expensive printed book.

4 *The Gutenberg Bible*, 1455, Christie's, New York, Oct 22, 1987	5,390,000

This is one of the first books ever printed, by Johann Gutenberg and Johann Fust in 1455.

5 *The Northumberland Bestiary*, c.1250–60, Sotheby's, London, Nov 29, 1990	5,049,000

This holds the record for an English manuscript.

6 Autograph manuscript of nine symphonies by Wolfgang Amadeus Mozart, c.1773–74, Sotheby's, London, May 22, 1987	3,854,500

This holds the record for any music manuscript.

7 *The Birds of America*, John James Audubon, 1827–38, Sotheby's, New York, Jun 6, 1989	3,600,000

This holds the record for any natural history book.

8 *The Bible* in Hebrew, Sotheby's, London, Dec 5, 1989	2,932,000

This holds the record for any Hebrew manuscript.

9 *The Monypenny Breviary*, illuminated manuscript, c.1490–95, Sotheby's, London, Jun 19, 1989	2,639,000

This holds the record for any French manuscript.

10 *The Hours and Psalter of Elizabeth de Bohun, Countess of Northampton*, c.1340–45, Sotheby's, London, Jun 21, 1988	2,530,000

* *Excluding premiums*

TOP 10 ALLTIME BESTSELLING BOOKS

	BOOK	APPROXIMATE SALES
1	*The Bible*	6,000,000,000
2	*Quotations from the Works of Mao Tse-tung*	800,000,000
3	*American Spelling Book* by Noah Webster	100,000,000
4	*The Guinness Book of Records*	81,000,000*
5	*The McGuffey Readers* by William Holmes McGuffey	60,000,000
6	*A Message to Garcia* by Elbert Hubbard	40–50,000,000
7	World Almanac	over 40,000,000*
8	*The Common Sense Book of Baby and Child Care* by Benjamin Spock	over 39,200,000
9	*Valley of the Dolls* by Jacqueline Susann	30,000,000
10	*In His Steps: "What Would Jesus Do?"* by Rev. Charles Monroe Sheldon	28,500,000

* Aggregate sales of annual publication

It is extremely difficult to establish precise sales even of contemporary books, and virtually impossible to do so with books published long ago. How can one calculate how many copies of *The Complete Works of Shakespeare* have been sold in countless editions?

THE 10 ★
FIRST BOOKS PUBLISHED BY AVON BOOKS

	AUTHOR/BOOK
1	Sinclair Lewis, *Elmer Gantry*
2	Edward Fitzgerald, *The Rubáiyát of Omar Khayyam*
3	Agatha Christie, *The Big Four*
4	James Hilton, *Ill Wind*
5	John Rhode, *Dr. Priestly Investigates*
6	Wilkie Collins, *The Haunted Hotel and 25 Other Ghost Stories*
7	John Dickson Carr, *The Plague Court Murders*
8	R.A.J. Walling, *The Corpse in the Green Pajamas*
9	Freeman Wills Crofts, *Willful and Premeditated*
10	R. Austin Freeman, *Dr. Thorndyke's Discovery*

The first 13 numbered Avon paperbacks were issued in the US in November 1941.

THE 10 ★
FIRST BOOKS PUBLISHED BY BANTAM BOOKS

	AUTHOR/BOOK
1	Mark Twain, *Life on the Mississippi*
2	Frank Gruber, *The Gift Horse*
3	Zane Grey, *Nevada*
4	Elizabeth Daly, *Evidence of Things Seen*
5	Rafael Sabatini, *Scaramouche*
6	Robert George Dean, *A Murder by Marriage*
7	John Steinbeck, *The Grapes of Wrath*
8	F. Scott Fitzgerald, *The Great Gatsby*
9	Geoffrey Household, *Rogue Male*
10	Marjorie Kinnan Rawlings, *South Moon Under*

The first 20 numbered titles published as Bantam paperbacks went on sale in the US on January 3, 1946, priced at 25 cents each.

THE 10 ★
FIRST PUBLICATIONS PRINTED IN ENGLAND

	AUTHOR/BOOK
1	*Propositio ad Carolum ducem Burgundiae**
2	Cato, *Disticha de Morbidus*
3	Geoffrey Chaucer, *The Canterbury Tales*
4	*Ordinale seu Pica ad usem Sarum* ("Sarum Pie")
5	John Lydgate, *The Temple of Glass*
6	John Lydgate, *Stans puer mensam*
7	John Lydgate, *The Horse, the Sheep and the Goose*
8	John Lydgate, *The Churl and the Bird*
9	*Infanta Salvatoris*
10	William Caxton, advertisement for "Sarum Pie"

* This work was printed before September 1476; all the others were printed in either 1476 or 1477.

THE 10 ★
FIRST POCKET BOOKS

	AUTHOR/BOOK
1	James Hilton, *Lost Horizon*
2	Dorothea Brande, *Wake Up and Live!*
3	William Shakespeare, *Five Great Tragedies*
4	Thorne Smith, *Topper*
5	Agatha Christie, *The Murder of Roger Ackroyd*
6	Dorothy Parker, *Enough Rope*
7	Emily Brontë, *Wuthering Heights*
8	Samuel Butler, *The Way of All Flesh*
9	Thornton Wilder, *The Bridge of San Luis Rey*
10	Felix Salten, *Bambi*

All 10 Pocket Books were published in the US in 1939 (a single title, Pearl S. Buck's Nobel Prize-winning *The Good Earth*, had been test-marketed the previous year, but only in New York). Unlike Penguins, Pocket Books all had pictorial covers.

THE BARD

Almost 400 years after his death, William Shakespeare (1564–1616) remains one of the most translated, most written-about, and most widely read authors in the world. His plays are also among the most frequently performed, and, through a recent wave of enthusiasm for converting them into films, or basing films on them, such as the Oscar-winning *Shakespeare in Love*, are attracting growing audiences around the world. Shakespeare's own life remains tantalizingly enigmatic, his early career and development as a playwright an almost complete mystery. This has led to a range of theories about his true identity, and the authorship of his works has been ascribed to various contemporaries, from Francis Bacon to Queen Elizabeth I. It is even questioned if his remains occupy his tomb at his birthplace, Stratford-upon-Avon.

TOP 10 ★
LARGEST PUBLIC LIBRARIES IN THE US

LIBRARY/LOCATION/ BRANCHES/FOUNDED	BOOKS
1 New York Public Library, (The Branch Libraries), NY, 85, 1895*	11,445,971#
2 Queens Borough Public Library, Jamaica, NY, 62, 1896	9,237,300
3 Public Library of Cincinnati and Hamilton County, Cincinnati, OH, 41, 1853	8,582,637
4 Chicago Public Library, IL, 79, 1872	8,100,000
5 Free Library of Philadelphia, PA, 52, 1891	7,891,532
6 County of Los Angeles Public Library, CA, 85, 1872	7,425,092
7 Carnegie Library of Pittsburgh, PA, 19, 1895	6,582,144
8 Boston Public Library, MA, 25, 1852	6,581,736
9 Los Angeles Public Library, CA, 66, 1872	5,743,103
10 Houston Public Library, TX, 36, 1901	5,187,973

* Astor Library founded 1848; consolidated with Lenox Library and Tilden Trust to form New York Public Library, 1895

\# Lending library and reference library holdings in all branch libraries available for loan

Source: *Public Library Association*

THE 10 ★
FIRST PUBLIC LIBRARIES IN THE US

LIBRARY	FOUNDED
1 Peterboro Public Library, Peterboro, NH	1833
2 New Orleans Public Library, New Orleans, LA	1843
3 Boston Public Library, Boston, MA	1852
4 Public Library of Cincinnati and Hamilton County, Cincinnati, OH	1853
5 Springfield City Library, Springfield, MA	1857
6 Worcester Public Library, Worcester, MA	1859
7 Multnomah County Library, Portland, OR	1864
8 = Detroit Public Library, Detroit, MI	1865
= St. Louis Public Library, St. Louis, MO	1865
10 Atlanta-Fulton Public Library, Atlanta, GA	1867

Source: *Public Library Association*

Peterboro Public Library, founded on April 9, 1833, was the first truly public library, in that it was supported by local taxes, in the US.

TOP 10 ★
COUNTRIES WITH THE MOST PUBLIC LIBRARIES

COUNTRY	LIBRARIES
1 Russia	96,177
2 UK	24,869
3 Ukraine	21,857
4 US	15,900
5 Kazakhstan	15,055
6 Germany	13,032
7 Poland	9,505
8 Belarus	9,121
9 Czech Republic	7,986
10 Mexico	5,630

Source: *UNESCO*

The very high figure given for the former Soviet Union was probably due to the propaganda value attached to cultural status. Recent changes in these countries make such a high level of expenditure unlikely to continue. National literary traditions play a major role in determining the ratio of libraries to population. The Japanese do not customarily borrow books, and consequently the country has only 1,950 public libraries.

TOP 10 OLDEST PRESIDENTIAL LIBRARIES

(Library/founded)

1 Roosevelt, 1940   2 Truman, 1957
3 Hoover, 1962   4 Johnson, 1971
5 Eisenhower, 1972   6 Kennedy, 1979
7 Ford, 1981   8 Carter, 1986
9 Reagan, 1991   10 Bush, 1997

 Which country boasts the three best-selling newspapers in the world?
see p.120 for the answer

A Japan
B China
C UK

TOP 10 LARGEST UNIVERSITY LIBRARIES IN THE US
(Library/books)

1 **Harvard**, 13,617,133 **2** **Yale**, 9,932,080 **3** **Illinois-Urbana**, 9,024,298 **4** **California-Berkeley**, 8,628,028 **5** **Texas**, 7,495,275 **6** **California-Los Angeles**, 7,010,234 **7** **Michigan**, 6,973,162 **8** **Columbia**, 6,905,609 **9** **Stanford**, 6,863,158 **10** **Chicago**, 6,116,978   Source: *Association of Research Libraries*

TOP 10 ★
LARGEST LIBRARIES

	LIBRARY	LOCATION	FOUNDED	BOOKS
1	Library of Congress	Washington DC	1800	23,041,334
2	National Library of China	Beijing, China	1909	15,980,636
3	National Library of Canada	Ottawa, Canada	1953	14,500,000
4	Deutsche Bibliothek*	Frankfurt, Germany	1990	14,350,000
5	British Library#	London, UK	1753	13,000,000
6	Harvard University Library	Cambridge, Massachusetts	1638	13,617,133
7	Russian State Library+	Moscow, Russia	1862	11,750,000
8	New York Public Library	New York, New York	1895★	11,445,971
9	National Diet Library	Tokyo, Japan	1948	11,304,139
10	Yale University Library	New Haven, Connecticut	1701	9,932,080

* *Formed in 1990 through the unification of the Deutsche Bibliothek, Frankfurt (founded 1947) and the Deutsche Bücherei, Leipzig*

Founded as part of the British Museum, 1753; became an independent body in 1973

+ *Founded 1862 as Rumyantsev Library, formerly State V.I. Lenin Library*

★ *Astor Library founded 1848, consolidated with Lenox Library and Tilden Trust to form New York Public Library in 1895*

THE MASTER STORYTELLER

Dickens first came to public attention with his sketches of London life signed "Boz." His novels were published in monthly or weekly parts, and his readers waited with eager anticipation for each installment.

TOP 10 ★
MOST CITED AUTHORS OF ALL TIME

	AUTHOR	DATES
1	William Shakespeare	1564–1616
2	Charles Dickens	1812–70
3	Sir Walter Scott	1771–1832
4	Johann Goethe	1749–1832
5	Aristotle	384–322BC
6	Alexandre Dumas père	1802–70
7	Robert Louis Stevenson	1850–94
8	Mark Twain	1835–1910
9	Marcus Tullius Cicero	106–43BC
10	Honoré de Balzac	1799–1850

This Top 10 is based on a search of a major US library computer database, Citations, which includes books both by and about authors, with a total of more than 15,000 for Shakespeare alone.

READING ROOM

The Library of Congress contains more than 100 million cataloged items, has 532 miles/856 km of shelving, and approximately 4,600 employees. It moved to its present building in 1897, which cost $7 million.

117

THE 10 ★
LATEST BOOKER PRIZE WINNERS

YEAR	AUTHOR/TITLE
1998	Ian McEwan, *Amsterdam*
1997	Arundhati Roy, *The God of Small Things*
1996	Graham Swift, *Last Orders*
1995	Pat Barker, *The Ghost Road*
1994	James Kelman, *How Late It Was, How Late*
1993	Roddy Doyle, *Paddy Clarke Ha Ha Ha*
1992 =	Michael Ondaatje, *The English Patient*
=	Barry Unsworth, *Sacred Hunger*
1991	Ben Okri, *Famished Road*
1990	A.S. Byatt, *Possession: A Romance*

THE 10 ★
LATEST WINNERS OF THE PULITZER PRIZE FOR FICTION

YEAR	AUTHOR/TITLE
1999	Michael Cunningham, *The Hours*
1998	Philip Roth, *American Pastoral*
1997	Steven Millhauser, *Martin Dressler: The Tale of an American Dreamer*
1996	Richard Ford, *Independence Day*
1995	Carol Shields, *The Stone Diaries*
1994	E. Annie Proulx, *The Shipping News*
1993	Robert Olen Butler, *A Good Scent from a Strange Mountain: Stories*
1992	Jane Smiley, *A Thousand Acres*
1991	John Updike, *Rabbit at Rest*
1990	Oscar Hijuelos, *The Mambo Kings Play Songs of Love*

LITERARY FIRST

Richard Ford's sixth novel, Independence Day, *set during the 4th of July weekend, is the first novel to win both the Pulitzer Prize and the PEN/Faulkner Award for fiction.*

THE 10 ★
LATEST WINNERS OF THE NATIONAL BOOK CRITICS CIRCLE AWARD FOR FICTION

YEAR	AUTHOR/TITLE
1998	Alice Munro, *The Love of a Good Woman*
1997	Penelope Fitzgerald, *The Blue Flower*
1996	Gina Berriault, *Women in Their Beds*
1995	Stanley Elkin, *Mrs. Ted Bliss*
1994	Carol Shields, *The Stone Diaries*
1993	Ernest J. Gaines, *A Lesson Before Dying*
1992	Cormac McCarthy, *All the Pretty Horses*
1991	Jane Smiley, *A Thousand Acres*
1990	John Updike, *Rabbit at Rest*
1989	E.L. Doctorow, *Billy Bathgate*

The National Book Critics Circle was founded in 1974 and consists of almost 700 active reviewers. The Circle presents annual awards in five categories: fiction, general nonfiction, biography and autobiography, poetry, and criticism. Winners receive a scoll and citation.

THE 10 ★
LATEST WINNERS OF THE JOHN NEWBERY MEDAL

YEAR	AUTHOR/TITLE
1999	Louis Sachar, *Holes*
1998	Karen Hesse, *Out of the Dust*
1997	E.L. Konigsburg, *The View from Saturday*
1996	Karen Cushman, *The Midwife's Apprentice*
1995	Sharon Creech, *Walk Two Moons*
1994	Lois Lowry, *The Giver*
1993	Cynthia Rylant, *Missing May*
1992	Phyllis Reynolds Naylor, *Shiloh*
1991	Jerry Spinelli, *Maniac Magee*
1990	Lois Lowry, *Number the Stars*

The John Newbery Medal is awarded annually for "the most distinguished contribution to American literature for children." Its first winner in 1923 was Hugh Lofting's *The Voyages of Doctor Dolittle*. The medal is named after John Newbery (1713–67), a London bookseller and publisher who specialized in children's books.

THE 10 ★
LATEST WINNERS OF HUGO AWARDS FOR BEST SCIENCE FICTION NOVEL

YEAR	AUTHOR/TITLE
1998	Joe Haldeman, *Forever Peace*
1997	Kim Stanley Robinson, *Blue Mars*
1996	Neal Stephenson, *The Diamond Age*
1995	Lois McMaster Bujold, *Mirror Dance*
1994	Kim Stanley Robinson, *Green Mars*
1993	Vernor Vinge, *A Fire Upon the Deep*
1992	Connie Willis, *Doomsday Book*
1991	Lois McMaster Bujold, *Barrayar*
1990	Lois McMaster Bujold, *The Vor Game*
1989	Dan Simmons, *Hyperion*

Hugo Awards for science fiction novels, short stories, and other fiction and nonfiction works are presented by the World Science Fiction Society. They were established in 1953 as "Science Fiction Achievement Awards for the best science fiction writing".

TOP 10 US HARDBACK NONFICTION BESTSELLERS OF 1998

(Title/author/sales)

1 *The 9 Steps to Financial Freedom*, Suze Orman, 1,470,865 **2** *The Greatest Generation*, Tom Brokaw, 1,423,863 **3** *Sugar Busters!*, H. Leighton Steward, Morrison C. Bethea, Sam S. Andrews, and Luis A. Balart, 1,201,000 **4** *Tuesdays with Morrie*, Mitch Alborn, 1,150,000 **5** *The Guinness Book of Records 1999*, Guinness Media, 714,000 **6** *Talking to Heaven*, James Van Praagh, 696,816 **7** *Somthing More: Excavating Your Authentic Self*, Sarah Ban Breathnach, 682,958 **8** *In the Meantime*, Iyania Vanzant, 649,583 **9** *A Pirate Looks at Fifty*, Jimmy Buffett, 605,982 **10** *If Life Is a Game These Are the Rules*, Cherie Carter-Scott, 530,561

Source: Publishers' Weekly

THE 10 ⭐ LATEST WINNERS OF THE NATIONAL BOOK AWARD FOR FICTION

YEAR	AUTHOR/TITLE
1998	Alice McDermott, *Charming Billy*
1997	Charles Frazier, *Cold Mountain*
1996	Andrea Barrett, *Ship Fever and Other Stories*
1995	Philip Roth, *Sabbath's Theater*
1994	William Gaddis, *A Frolic of His Own*
1993	E. Annie Proulx, *The Shipping News*
1992	Cormac McCarthy, *All the Pretty Horses*
1991	Norman Rush, *Mating*
1990	Charles Johnson, *Middle Passage*
1989	John Casey, *Spartina*

The National Book Award is presented by the National Book Foundation as part of its program to foster reading in the United States. Award winners receive $10,000. Past recipients include books now regarded as modern classics, among them William Styron's *Sophie's Choice* and John Irving's *The World According to Garp*.

TOP 10 ⭐ US HARDBACK FICTION TITLES OF 1998

TITLE/AUTHOR	SALES
1 *The Street Lawyer*, John Grisham	2,550,000
2 *Rainbow Six*, Tom Clancy	2,000,000
3 *Bag of Bones*, Stephen King	1,496,520
4 *A Man in Full*, Tom Wolfe	1,260,000
5 *Mirror Image*, Danielle Steel	1,187,877
6 *The Long Road Home*, Danielle Steel	1,161,229
7 *The Klone and I*, Danielle Steel	1,152,681
8 *Point of Origin*, Patricia Cornwell	1,000,000
9 *Paradise*, Toni Morrison	804,862
10 *All Through the Night*, Mary Higgins Clark	775,000

Source: Publishers' Weekly

TRIPLE WINNER

National Book Award (1993) and Pulitzer Prize (1994) winner, Canadian writer E. Annie Proulx has also won the 1993 Irish Times *International Prize for* The Shipping News.

THE 10 ⭐ LATEST RANDOLPH CALDECOTT MEDAL WINNERS*

YEAR	AUTHOR/TITLE
1999	Jacqueline Briggs Martin (illustrated by MaryAzarian), *Snowflake Bentley*
1998	Paul O. Zelinsky, *Rapunzel*
1997	David Wisniewski, *Golem*
1996	Peggy Rathman, *Officer Buckle and Gloria*
1995	Eve Bunting (illustrated by David Diaz), *Smoky Night*
1994	Allen Say, *Grandfather's Journey*
1993	Emily Arnold McCully, *Mirette on the High Wire*
1992	David Wiesner, *Tuesday*
1991	David Macauley, *Black and White*
1990	Ed Young, *Lon Po Po*

* *The Randolph Caldecott Medal, named after the English illustrator (1846–86), has been awarded annually since 1938 "to the artist of the most distinguished American picture book for children published in the United States during the preceding year."*

TOP 10 ⭐ US CHILDREN'S BOOKS OF 1998

TITLE	SALES
1 *Pooh's Friendly Tale*	710,393
2 *Tigger's Friendly Tale*	653,871
3 *Thank You Pooh!*	628,870
4 *Eeyore's Friendly Tale*,	540,614
5 *Barney: Sharing Is Caring*	532,811
6 *Piglet's Friendly Tale*	530,200
7 *Pooh: The Grand and Wonderful Day*	506,866
8 *Blue's Clues: The Shape Detective*	488,753
9 *Blue's Clues: Blue's #1 Picnic*	470,532
10 *Barney: Twinkle, Twinkle, Little Star*	444,948

Source: Publishers' Weekly

What was the name of the most expensive teddy bear sold at auction?   A Teddy Girl
see p.123 for the answer   B Teddy Edward   C Happy

119

TOP 10 ★
LONGEST-RUNNING COMIC STRIPS IN THE US

	COMIC STRIP	FIRST PUBLISHED
1	*Gasoline Alley*	1918
2	*Winnie Winkle*	1920
3	*Tarzan*	1929
4	*Blondie*	1930
5	*Dick Tracy*	1931
6	*Alley Oop*	1933
7	*Li'l Abner*	1934
8	*The Phantom*	1936
9	*Prince Valiant*	1937
10	*Nancy*	1938

Source: *Gemstone Publishing*

TOP 10 ★
BESTSELLING AMERICAN COMICS OF ALL TIME

	COMIC	PUBLISHER
1	*Darkness* #11	Image
2	*Superman* #123 Collectors Ed.	DC
3	*Fantastic Four* #1	Marvel
4	*Captain America* #1	Marvel
5	*Avengers* #1	Marvel
6	*Iron Man* #1	Marvel
7	*Uncanny X-Men* #345	Marvel
8	*Uncanny X-Men* #350	Marvel
9	*Uncanny X-Men* #346	Marvel
10	*X-Men* #65	Marvel

Source: *Gemstone Publishing*

STOP THE PRESS!

Since 59BC, when the Acta Diurna *(Daily News) was posted daily in the Forum of Rome, news of political events, wars, and social affairs have been enjoyed by an ever-increasing readership.*

TOP 10 ★
COUNTRIES WITH THE MOST DAILY NEWSPAPERS PER CAPITA

	COUNTRY	SALES PER 1,000 INHABITANTS
1	Norway	596
2	Japan	576
3	Iceland	510
4	Finland	468
5	Sweden	460
6	South Korea	394
7	Kuwait	387
8	Switzerland	371
9	UK	344
10	Luxembourg	332

Source: *UNESCO*

The Vatican City's sole newspaper, *l'Osservatore Romano*, sells around 70,000 copies, which implies a daily sale of 95 copies per head. In fact, most of them are sent outside the Holy See.

YESTERDAY'S NEWS

Discarded newspapers provide a massive amount of waste: 31,000 tons of newsprint is dumped every day in the US, of which only 14,000 tons are recycled.

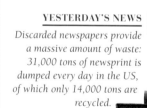

TOP 10 ★
DAILY NEWSPAPERS

	NEWSPAPER	COUNTRY	AVERAGE DAILY CIRCULATION
1	*Yomiuri Shimbun*	Japan	14,485,453
2	*Asahi Shimbun*	Japan	12,660,066
3	*Mainichi Shimbun*	Japan	5,867,224
4	*MZ Guangbo Dianshi*	China	5,348,000
5	*Xinmin Wanbao*	China	5,227,000
6	*Bild-Zeitung*	Germany	4,644,000
7	*Nihon Keizai Shimbun*	Japan	4,550,311
8	*Chunichi Shimbun*	Japan	4,394,849
9	*The Sun*	UK	3,767,941
10	*BJ Guangbo Dianshi*	China	3,372,000

Source: *World Association of Newspapers*

TOP 10 ★
ENGLISH-LANGUAGE DAILY NEWSPAPERS

	NEWSPAPER	COUNTRY	AVERAGE DAILY CIRCULATION
1	*The Sun*	UK	3,698,300
2	*The Mirror*	UK	2,351,815
3	*Daily Mail*	UK	2,343,494
4	*Wall Street Journal*	US	1,774,880
5	*USA Today*	US	1,629,665
6	*The Express*	UK	1,134,719
7	*The New York Times*	US	1,074,741
8	*The Daily Telegraph*	UK	1,062,853
9	*Los Angeles Times*	US	1,050,176
10	*Washington Post*	US	775,894

TOP 10 ★
OLDEST NATIONAL NEWSPAPERS PUBLISHED IN THE US

NEWSPAPER/PUBLISHED	YEAR ESTABLISHED
1 *The Hartford Courant*, Hartford, CT	1764
2 = *Poughkeepsie Journal*, Poughkeepsie, NY	1785
= *The Augusta Chronicle*, Augusta, GA	1785
= *Register-Star*, Hudson, NY	1785
5 = *Pittsburgh Post Gazette*, Northampton, MA	1786
= *Daily Hampshire Gazette*, Northampton, MA	1786
7 *The Berkshire Eagle*, Pittsfield, MA	1789
8 *Norwich Bulletin*, Norwich, CT	1791
9 *The Recorder*, Greenfield, MA	1792
10 *Intelligencer Journal*, Lancaster, PA	1794

Source: Editor & Publisher Year Book

TOP 10 DAILY NEWSPAPERS IN THE US
(Newspaper/average daily circulation*)

1 *USA Today*, 2,133,467
2 *Wall Street Journal*, 1,792,452 **3** *Los Angeles Times*, 1,098,347 **4** *The New York Times*, 1,048,460 **5** *Washington Post*, 809,059 **6** *New York Daily News*, 729,449 **7** *Chicago Tribune*, 673,171 **8** *New York Newsday*, 573,542 **9** *Houston Chronicle*, 541,782 **10** *Dallas Morning News*, 479,248
* Through March, 1999
Source: *Audit Bureau of Circulation*

PAPARAZZI
In the desperate search for that ultimate scoop, journalists will go to almost any lengths to take photographs of famous people. Their increasingly intrusive behavior has resulted in the introduction of new codes of conduct.

TOP 10 ★
LONGEST-RUNNING MAGAZINES IN THE US

MAGAZINE	FIRST PUBLISHED
1 *Scientific American*	1845
2 *Town & Country*	1846
3 *Harper's**	1850
4 *The Moravian*	1856
5 *The Atlantic*#	1857
6 *Armed Forces Journal*+	1863
7 *The Nation*	1865
8 *American Naturalist*	1867
9 *Harper's Bazaar*	1867
10 *Animals*★	1868

* *Originally* Harper's New Monthly Magazine
# *Originally* The Atlantic Monthly
+ *Originally* Army and Navy Journal
★ *Originally* Our Dumb Animals
Source: *Magazine Publishers of America*

TOP 10 ★
MAGAZINES IN THE US

MAGAZINE/YEARLY ISSUES	CIRCULATION*
1 *Modern Maturity*, 36	20,402,096
2 *NRTA/AARP Bulletin*, 10	20,360,798
3 *Reader's Digest*, 12	14,675,541
4 *TV Guide*, 52	13,085,971
5 *National Geographic Magazine*, 12	8,783,752
6 *Better Homes and Gardens*, 12	7,616,114
7 *Family Circle*, 17	5,005,084
8 *Ladies Home Journal*, 12	4,521,970
9 *Good Housekeeping*, 12	4,517,713
10 *McCall's*, 12	4,239,622

* *Average for Jan–June 1998*
Source: *Audit Bureau of Circulation*

TOP 10 ★
MOST LANDED-ON SQUARES IN MONOPOLY®*

US GAME		UK GAME
Illinois Avenue	1	Trafalgar Square
Go	2	Go
B. & O. Railroad	3	Fenchurch Street Station
Free Parking	4	Free Parking
Tennessee Avenue	5	Marlborough Street
New York Avenue	6	Vine Street
Reading Railroad	7	King's Cross Station
St. James Place	8	Bow Street
Water Works	9	Water Works
Pennsylvania Railroad	10	Marylebone Station

* Based on a computer analysis of the probability of landing on each square

Monopoly® is a registered trade mark of Parker Brothers division of Tonka Corporation, USA.

TOP 10 ★
BOARD GAMES IN THE US

	GAME	MANUFACTURER
1	Monopoly	Parker Brothers
2	Star Wars Trilogy Monopoly	Parker Brothers
3	Disney Wonderful World of Trivia	Mattel
4	Star Wars Monopoly	Parker Brothers
5	Sorry	Parker Brothers
6	Deluxe Monopoly	Parker Brothers
7	Clue	Parker Brothers
8	Life	Milton Bradley
9	Taboo	Milton Bradley
10	Jenga	Milton Bradley

Source: *The NPD Group – TRSTS*

TOP 10 TOYS OF 1999 IN THE US

(Toy/manufacturer)

1. **Teletubbies**, Playskool Eden
2. **Spice Girls fashion dolls**, Galoob
3. **World Wrestling Federation figures**, Jakks Pacific
4. **Barbie dolls**, Mattel
5. **Beanie Babies**, Ty
6. **= Nintendo**, Nintendo of America; **= PlayStation**, Sony
8. **Blue's Clues**, Fisher-Price
9. **Power Rangers in Space figures**, Bandai
10. **Small Soldiers figures**, Hasbro

Source: Playthings *magazine*
Beanie Babies were invented by Chicago toy designer H. Ty Warner, who introduced his first nine at a toy fair in 1993. They went on sale in Chicago the following year, and by 1995 – largely through word-of-mouth recommendation – became one of the country's most popular and sought-after toys. The company's policy of constantly "retiring" selected lines and introducing new products has kept them at the forefront of collectables.

TALKATIVE PET

A Furby is an interactive toy that can communicate with fellow Furbys in Furbish, but can also be taught to converse in English.

TOP 10 ★
HIGHEST-SCORING SCRABBLE®* WORDS

	WORD/PLAY	SCORE
1	QUARTZY	164/162

(i) Play across a triple-word-score (red) square with the Z on a double-letter-score (light blue) square
(ii) Play across two double-word-score (pink) squares with Q and Y on pink squares

| 2 | = BEZIQUE | 161/158 |

(i) Play across a red square with either the Z or the Q on a light blue square
(ii) Play across two pink squares with the B and second E on two pink squares

| | = CAZIQUE | 161/158 |

(i) Play across a red square with either the Z or the Q on a light blue square
(ii) Play across two pink squares with the C and E on two pink squares

| 4 | ZINKIFY | 158 |

Play across a red square with the Z on a light blue square

| 5 | = QUETZAL | 155 |

Play across a red square with either the Q or the Z on a light blue square

| | = JAZZILY | 155 |

(Using a blank as one of the Zs.) Play across a red square with the non-blank Z on a light blue square

| | = QUIZZED | 155 |

(Using a blank as one of the Zs.) Play across a red square with the non-blank Z or the Q on a light blue square

| 8 | = ZEPHYRS | 152 |

Play across a red square with the Z on a light blue square

| | = ZINCIFY | 152 |

Play across a red square with the Z on a light blue square

| | = ZYTHUMS | 152 |

Play across a red square with the Z on a light blue square

All the Top 10 words contain seven letters and therefore earn the premium of 50 for using all the letters in the rack. Being able to play them depends on there already being suitable words on the board to which they can be added. In an actual game, the face values of the perpendicular words to which they are joined would also be counted, but these are discounted here as the total score variations would be infinite.

Scrabble® is a registered trade mark of Hasbro Inc.

Did You Know? Twelve black "mourning" Steiff teddy bears were made to commemorate the sinking of the *Titanic* in 1912.

TOP 10 ★
MOST EXPENSIVE DOLLS SOLD AT AUCTION

DOLL/SALE	PRICE ($)
1 **Kämmer and Reinhardt doll**, Sotheby's, London, Feb 8, 1994	282,750
2 **Kämmer and Reinhardt bisque character doll**, German, c.1909, Sotheby's, London, Oct 17, 1996 *(Previously sold at Sotheby's, London, February 16, 1989 for $140,171)*	169,117
3 **Kämmer and Reinhardt bisque character doll**, German, c.1909, Sotheby's, London, Oct 17, 1996	143,327
4 **Albert Marque bisque character doll**, Sotheby's, London, Oct 17, 1996	112,380
5 **William and Mary wooden doll**, English, c.1690, Sotheby's, London, Mar 24, 1987	110,396
6 **Wooden doll, Charles II**, 17th century, Christie's, London, May 18, 1989	103,850
7 **Albert Marque bisque character doll**, Sotheby's, London, Oct 17, 1996	91,748
8= **Albert Marque bisque character doll**, Christie's, London, May 23, 1997	89,581
= **Pressed bisque swivel-head Madagascar doll**, Sotheby's, London, Oct 17, 1996	88,310
10 **Shellacked pressed bisque swivel-head doll**, Sotheby's, London, Oct 17, 1996	71,117

TOP 10 BESTSELLING PC & PLAYSTATION COMPUTER GAMES
(Game/manufacturer)

1 Gran Turismo (Sony) **2** Resident Evil 2 (Capcom) **3** Tekken 3 (Namco) **4** Madden NFL '99 (Konami) **5** Metal Gear Solid (Konami) **6** Crash Bandicoot 2 (Sony) **7** NFL Game Day '99 (Sony, 989 Studios) **8** WWF Warzone (Acclaim) **9** Crash Bandicoot: Warped (Sony) **10** Crash Bandicoot (Sony)

TOP 10 ★
MOST EXPENSIVE TOYS EVER SOLD AT AUCTION BY CHRISTIE'S EAST, NEW YORK

TOY/SALE	PRICE ($)
1 **"The Charles,"** a fire-hose-reel made by American manufacturer George Brown and Co., c.1875, Dec 1991	231,000
2 **Märklin fire station**, Dec 1991	79,200
3 **Horse-drawn double-decker tram**, Dec 1991	71,500
4 **Mikado mechanical bank**, Dec 1993	63,000
5 **Märklin ferris wheel**, June 1994	55,200
6 **Girl skipping rope mechanical bank**, June 1994	48,300
7 **Märklin battleship**, June 1994	33,350
8 **Märklin battleship**, June 1994	32,200
9= **Bing keywind open phaeton tinplate automobile**, Dec 1992	24,200
= **Märklin fire pumper**, Dec 1991	24,200

* Including 10 percent buyer's premium

Source: *Christie's East*

The fire-hose-reel at # 1 in this list is the record price paid at auction for a toy other than a doll. Models by the German tinplate maker Märklin, regarded by collectors as the Rolls-Royce of toys, similarly feature among the record prices of auction houses in the UK and other countries, where high prices have also been attained.

TOP 10 ★
MOST EXPENSIVE TEDDY BEARS SOLD AT AUCTION

BEAR/SALE	PRICE ($)*
1 **"Teddy Girl,"** Christie's, London, Dec 5, 1994	169,928
A 1904 Steiff formerly owned by Lt-Col. Bob Henderson, precisely doubled the previous world record for a teddy bear when it was acquired by Yoshiro Sekiguchi for display at his teddy bear museum near Tokyo.	
2 **"Happy,"** a dual-plush Steiff teddy bear, 1926, Sotheby's, London, Sept 19, 1989	85,470
Although estimated at $1100–$1400, competitive bidding pushed the price up to the then world record, when it was acquired by collector Paul Volpp.	
3 **"Elliot,"** a blue Steiff bear, 1908, Christie's, London, Dec 6, 1993	74,275
Produced as a sample for Harrods, but never manufactured commercially	
4 **Teddy Edward**, a golden mohair teddy bear, star of the TV show *Watch with Mother*, Christie's, London, Dec 9, 1996	53,924
5 **Black Steiff teddy bear**, c.1912, Sotheby's, London, May 18, 1990	45,327
6 **"Albert,"** a Steiff teddy bear c.1910, Christie's, London, Dec 9, 1996	28,759
7 **"Theodore,"** a miniature Steiff teddy bear, 3½ in/9 cm tall, c.1948, Christie's, London, Dec 11, 1995	22,705
8 **"Black Jack,"** a black Steiff teddy bear, Christie's, London, May 22, 1997	21,569
9 **White Steiff teddy bear**, c.1908, Christie's, London, June 1, 1995	19,212
10 **"Alfonzo,"** a red Steiff teddy bear, c.1906–09, once owned by Russian Princess Xenia, Christie's, London, May 18, 1989	18,803

* Prices include buyer's premium

Margarete Steiff, a German toymaker, began making her first toy bears in 1903.

SONY'S WINNER

The Sony PlayStation console is the best-selling games console on the market, and in the year 2000 the company will be launching PlayStation 2, an upgraded version of the product.

Pierre-Auguste Renoir's Au Moulin de la Galette, an animated panorama of a crowd under the trees at the pleasure resort of Montmartre, was first shown in 1876.

TOP 10 ★
MOST EXPENSIVE PAINTINGS BY WOMEN ARTISTS EVER SOLD AT AUCTION

PAINTING/ARTIST/SALE	PRICE ($)
1 *The Conversation*, Mary Cassatt, Christie's, New York, May 11, 1988	4,100,000
2 *In the Box*, Mary Cassatt, (American; 1844–1926), Christie's, New York, May 23, 1996	3,700,000
3 *Mother, Sara and the Baby*, Mary Cassatt, Christie's, New York, May 10, 1989	3,500,000
4 *From the Plains*, Georgia O'Keeffe (American; 1887–1986), Sotheby's, New York, Dec 3, 1997	3,300,000
5 *Après le déjeuner*, Berthe Morisot (French; 1841–95), Christie's, New York, May 14, 1997	3,250,000
6 *Autoretrato con chango y loro*, Frida Kahlo (Mexican; 1907–54), Sotheby's, New York, May 17, 1995	2,900,000
7 *Augusta Reading to her Daughter*, Mary Cassatt, Sotheby's, New York, May 9, 1989	2,800,000
8 *Children Playing with a Cat*, Mary Cassatt, Sotheby's, New York, Dec 3, 1998	2,700,000
9 *Sara Holding her Dog*, Mary Cassatt, Sotheby's, New York, Nov 11, 1988	2,500,000
10 *Calla Lily with Red Roses*, Georgia O'Keeffe, Sotheby's, New York, May 20, 1998	2,400,000

TOP 10 ARTISTS WITH MOST WORKS SOLD FOR MORE THAN ONE MILLION DOLLARS

(Artist/works sold)

1 Pablo Picasso (Spanish; 1881–1973), 232   **2** Claude Monet (French; 1888–1926), 178   **3** Pierre Auguste Renoir (French; 1841–1919), 172   **4** Edgar Degas (French; 1834–1917), 94   **5** Paul Cézanne (French; 1839–1906), 68   **6** Marc Chagall (Russian; 1887–1985), 67   **7** Henri Matisse (French; 1869–1954), 62   **8** Camille Pissaro (French; 1830–1903), 61   **9** Amedeo Modigliani (Italian; 1884–1920), 50   **10** Vincent van Gogh (Dutch; 1853–90), 48

SPANISH GENIUS

Pablo Picasso, one of the 20th century's greatest artists, photographed in April 1971, two years before his death.

TOP 10 ★
MOST EXPENSIVE PAINTINGS EVER SOLD AT AUCTION

PAINTING/ARTIST/SALE	PRICE ($)
1 *Portrait of Dr. Gachet*, Vincent van Gogh (Dutch; 1853–90), Christie's, New York, May 15, 1990	75,000,000
Both this painting and the one in No. 2 position were bought by Ryoei Saito, chairman of the Japanese firm Daishowa Paper Manufacturing.	
2 *Au Moulin de la Galette*, Pierre-Auguste Renoir (French; 1841–1919), Sotheby's, New York, May 17, 1990	71,000,000
3 *Portrait de l'artiste sans barbe*, Vincent van Gogh, Christie's, New York, Nov 19, 1998	65,000,000
4 *Les noces de Pierrette*, Pablo Picasso (Spanish; 1881–1973), Binoche et Godeau, Paris, Nov 30, 1989	51,671,920
This painting was sold by Swedish financier Fredrik Roos and bought by Tomonori Tsurumaki, a Japanese property developer, bidding from Tokyo by telephone.	
5 *Irises*, Vincent van Gogh, Sotheby's, New York, Nov 11, 1987	49,000,000
The Australian businessman Alan Bond was unable to pay for this painting in full, so its former status as the world's most expensive work of art has been disputed.	
6 *Le rêve*, Pablo Picasso, Christie's, New York, Nov 10, 1997	44,000,000
Victor and Sally Ganz had paid $7,000 for this painting in 1941.	
7 *Self Portrait: Yo Picasso*, Pablo Picasso, Sotheby's, New York, May 9, 1989	43,500,000
The purchaser has remained anonymous but unconfirmed reports have identified him as Stavros Niarchos, the Greek shipping magnate.	
8 *Au Lapin Agile*, Pablo Picasso, Sotheby's, New York, Nov 15, 1989	37,000,000
The painting depicts Picasso as a harlequin at the bar of the café Lapin Agile.	
9 *Sunflowers*, Vincent van Gogh, Christie's, London, Mar 30, 1987	36,225,000
At the time, this was the most expensive picture ever sold (and is still the most expensive sold in the UK).	
10 *Acrobate et Jeune Arlequin*, Pablo Picasso, Christie's, London, Nov 28, 1988	35,530,000

MOST EXPENSIVE OLD MASTER PAINTINGS EVER SOLD AT AUCTION*

PAINTING/ARTIST/SALE	PRICE ($)
1 *Portrait of Duke Cosimo I de Medici*, **Jacopo da Carucci (Pontormo)** (Italian; 1493–1558), Christie's, New York, May 31, 1989	32,000,000
2 *The Old Horse Guards, London, from St James's Park*, **Canaletto** (Italian; 1697–1768), Christie's, London, Apr 15, 1992	16,008,000 (£9,200,000)
3 *View of the Giudecca and the Zattere, Venice*, **Francesco Guardi** (Italian; 1712–93), Sotheby's, Monaco, Dec 1, 1989	13,943,218 (F.Fr85,000,000)
4 *Venus and Adonis*, **Titian** (Italian; c.1488–1576), Christie's, London, Dec 13, 1991	12,376,000 (£6,800,000)
5 *Le Retour du Bucentaure le Jour de l'Ascension*, **Canaletto**, Ader Tajan, Paris, Dec 15, 1993	11,316,457 (F.Fr66,000,000)
6 *Adoration of the Magi*, **Andrea Mantegna** (Italian; 1431–1506), Christie's, London, Apr 18, 1985	9,525,000 (£7,500,000)
7 *Portrait of a Girl Wearing a Gold-trimmed Cloak*, **Rembrandt** (Dutch; 1606–69), Sotheby's, London, Dec 10, 1986	9,372,000 (£6,600,000)
8 *Portrait of Bearded Man in Red Coat*, **Rembrandt**, Sotheby's, New York, Jan 30, 1998	8,250,000
9 Study for *Head and Hand of an Apostle*, **Raphael** (Italian; 1483–1520), Christie's, London, Dec 13, 1996	7,920,000 (£4,800,000)
10 *Venice, Molo from Bacino S. Marco*, **Canaletto**, Sotheby's, London, Dec 3, 1990	7,590,000 (£4,600,000)

UNDER THE HAMMER

One of Monet's water lily studies is offered for sale at Sotheby's. When the Impressionist painters first exhibited in Paris in 1874 their work attracted ridicule, but 178 of Monet's paintings alone have now sold for more than $1 million.

MOST EXPENSIVE AMERICAN PAINTINGS EVER SOLD AT AUCTION

PAINTING/ARTIST/SALE	PRICE ($)
1 =*Interchange*, **Willem de Kooning** (1904–97), Sotheby's, New York, Nov 8, 1989	18,000,000
=*Orange Marilyn*, **Andy Warhol** (1928–87), Sotheby's, New York, May 14, 1998	18,000,000
3 *False Start*, **Jasper Johns** (b.1930,) Sotheby's, New York, Nov 10, 1988	15,500,000
4 *Woman*, **Willem de Kooning**, Christie's, New York, Nov 20, 1996	14,200,000
5 *Two Flags*, **Jasper Johns**, Sotheby's, New York, Nov 8, 1989	11,000,000
6 *Number 8, 1950*, **Jackson Pollock** (1925–56), Sotheby's, New York, May 2, 1989	10,500,000
7 *July*, **Willem de Kooning**, Christie's, New York, Nov 7, 1990	8,000,000
8 *Corpse and Mirror*, **Jasper Johns**, Christie's, New York, Nov 10, 1997	7,600,000
9 *Home by the Lake: Scene in the Catskill Mountains*, **Frederick Edwin Church** (1826–1900), Sotheby's, New York, May 24, 1989	7,500,000
10 =*Flags, Afternoon on the Avenue*, **Childe Hassam** (1859–1935), Christie's, New York, May 21, 1998	7,200,000
=*White Numbers*, **Jasper Johns**, Christie's, New York, Nov 10, 1997	7,200,000

What is the most widely spoken language in the world?   A English
see p.113 for the answer   B Chinese (Mandarin)
C Arabic

125

TOP 10 ★
OLDEST OUTDOOR STATUES IN LONDON

	STATUE/LOCATION	DATE
1	**Sekhmet**, over Sotheby's, 34 Bond Street	c.1600 BC
2	**King Alfred** (?), Trinity Church Square	Late 14th century
3	**Queen Elizabeth I**, St. Dunstan in the West, Fleet Street	1586
4	**Charles I**, Trafalgar Square	1633
5	**Guy of Warwick**, corner of Newgate Street and Warwick Lane	1668
6=	**Robert Devereux, Earl of Essex**, above the Devereux Inn, Devereux Court	1676
=	**Charles II**, Chelsea Hospital	1676
8	**Charles II**, Soho Square	1681
9	**Pannier Boy**, Panyer Alley	1688
10	**Henry VIII**, over the gateway of St. Bartholemew's Hospital	1702

LADY LIBERTY

The Statue of Liberty consists of sheets of copper on an iron frame, which weighs 229 tonnes. It stands on a massive pedestal that more than doubles the overall height to 305 ft/93 m from the base to the torch.

TOP 10 ★
TALLEST FREE-STANDING STATUES

	STATUE/LOCATION	HEIGHT FT	M
1	**Chief Crazy Horse**, Thunderhead Mountain, South Dakota, US	563	172

Started in 1948 by Polish-American sculptor Korczak Ziolkowski, and continued after his death in 1982 by his widow and eight of his children, this gigantic equestrian statue is even longer than it is high (641 ft/195 m). It is being carved out of the granite mountain by dynamiting and drilling.

2	**Buddha**, Tokyo, Japan	394	120

This Japan–Taiwanese project, unveiled in 1993, took seven years to complete and weighs 1,000 tonnes.

3	**The Indian Rope Trick**, Riddersberg Säteri, Jönköping, Sweden	337	103

Sculptor Calle Ornemark's 144-tonne wooden sculpture depicts a long strand of "rope" held by a fakir, while another figure ascends.

4	**Motherland**, 1967, Volgograd, Russia	270	82

This concrete statue of a woman with a raised sword, designed by Yevgeniy Vuchetich, commemorates the Soviet victory at the Battle of Stalingrad (1942–43).

5	**Buddha**, Bamian, Afghanistan	173	53

This dates from the 3rd–4th centuries AD.

6	**Kannon**, Otsubo-yama, near Tokyo, Japan	170	52

The immense statue of the goddess of mercy was unveiled in 1961 in honour of the dead of World War II.

7	**Statue of Liberty**, New York, US	151	46

Designed by Auguste Bartholdi and presented to the US by the people of France, the statue was shipped in sections to Liberty (formerly Bedloes) Island where it was assembled, before being unveiled on October 28, 1886; it was restored on July 4, 1986.

8	**Christ**, Rio de Janeiro, Brazil	125	38

The work of sculptor Paul Landowski and engineer Heitor da Silva Costa, the figure of Christ was unveiled in 1931.

9	**Tian Tan (Temple of Heaven) Buddha**, Po Lin Monastery, Lantau Island, Hong Kong	112	34

This was completed after 20 years' work and unveiled on December 29, 1993.

10	**Colossi of Memnon**, Karnak, Egypt	70	21

This statue portrays two seated sandstone figures of Pharaoh Amenhotep III.

TOP 10 ★
MOST VISITED ART GALLERIES AND MUSEUMS IN THE US

	MUSEUM/GALLERY	VISITORS
1	**The Smithsonian Institution**, Washington, DC	27,000,000
2	**National Air & Space Museum**, Washington, DC	8,000,000
3	**National Museum of Natural History**, Washington, DC	6,300,000
4	**National Museum of American History**, Washington, DC	5,600,000
5	**Grand Canyon National Park Museum Collection**, Grand Canyon, AZ	5,000,000
6	**Metropolitan Museum of Modern Art**, New York, NY	4,900,000
7	**National Gallery of Art**, Washington, DC	4,500,000
8	**Statue of Liberty National Monument and Ellis Island Immigration Museum**, New York, NY	4,300,000
9=	**American Museum of Natural History**, New York, NY	3,000,000*
=	**United States Capitol Historical Society**,	3,000,000*
=	**United States Army Center of Military History, Museum Division**, Washington, DC	3,000,000

* *Estimated attendance*

Source: *The Official Museum Directory*

TOP 10 OLDEST MUSEUMS AND ART GALLERIES IN THE UK

(Museum or art gallery/founded)

1 **Ashmolean Museum**, Oxford, 1683
2 **British Museum**, London, 1753
3 **National Museum of Antiquities**, Edinburgh, 1780 **4** **Hunterian Museum**, Glasgow, 1807 **5** **Royal College of Surgeons Museum**, London, 1813
6 **Museum of Antiquities**, Newcastle upon Tyne, 1813 **7** **Dulwich Picture Gallery**, London, 1814 **8** **Fitzwilliam Museum**, Cambridge, 1816 **9** **Leeds City Museum**, 1820 **10** **Manchester Museum**, 1821

Did You Know? The Angel of the North, Gateshead, UK, with a wingspan of 177 ft/54 m, is the largest sculpture of an angel in the world.

THE ARTIST'S GARDEN

This painting of the garden at Giverny, Monet's home, is exhibited at the Musée d'Orsay in Paris, but also appears in touring exhibitions, such as the popular 1999 show at the Royal Academy in London.

TOP 10 ★
BEST-ATTENDED EXHIBITIONS AT THE BRITISH MUSEUM, LONDON

	EXHIBITION/YEAR	TOTAL ATTENDANCE
1	Treasures of Tutankhamun*, 1972–73	1,694,117
2	Turner Watercolours, 1975	585,046
3	The Vikings*, 1980	465,000
4	Thracian Treasures from Bulgaria, 1976	424,465
5	From Manet to Toulouse-Lautrec: French Lithographs 1860–1900, 1978	355,354
6	The Ancient Olympic Games, 1980	334,354
7	Treasures for the Nation*, 1988–89	297,837
8	Excavating in Egypt, 1982–83	285,736
9	Heraldry, 1978	262,183
10	Drawings by Michelangelo, 1975	250,000

* Admission charged

WELCOME TO THE LOUVRE

The Louvre Museum in Paris, which contains one of the most important art collections in the world, was given its imposing glass pyramid entrance in 1989.

TOP 10 BEST-ATTENDED EXHIBITIONS, 1998

	EXHIBITION/VENUE	TOTAL ATTENDANCE
1	**Monet in the 20th Century**, Museum of Fine Arts, Boston, US	586,000
2	**The Collection of Edgar Degas**, Metropolitan Museum, New York, US	528,000
3	**Van Gogh's van Goghs**, National Gallery, Washington, DC, US	480,000
4	**Gianni Versace**, Metropolitan Museum, New York, US	410,000
5	**Delacroix: The Late Works**, Museum of Art, Philadelphia, US	306,000
6	**René Magritte**, Musées Royaux des Beaux-Arts, Brussels, Belgium	302,000
7	**The Art of the Motorcycle**, Guggenheim Museum, New York, US	301,000
8	**Alexander Calder, 1898–1976**, Museum of Modern Art, San Francisco, US	300,000
9	**China: 5,000 Years**, Guggenheim Museum, New York, US	300,000
10	**Recognizing van Eyck**, Museum of Art, Philadelphia, US	153,000

TOP 10 ★
LARGEST PAINTINGS IN THE LOUVRE MUSEUM, PARIS

	PAINTING/ARTIST	SIZE (HEIGHT X WIDTH) FT	M
1	*Interior of Westminster Abbey*, Jean-Pierre Alaux	62 x 131	19.0 x 40.0
2	*Interior of St. Peter's, Rome*, Jean-Pierre Alaux	57 x 131	17.5 x 40.0
3	*Palace Ceiling*, Francesco Fontebasso	26 x 33	8.0 x 10.0
4	*The Marriage Feast at Cana*, Paolo Veronese	22 x 32	6.7 x 9.8
5	*The Coronation of Napoleon*, Jacques-Louis David	20 x 32	6.2 x 9.8
6	*The Battle of Arbela*, Charles Lebrun	15 x 42	4.7 x 13.1
7	*Alexander and Porus*, Charles Lebrun	15 x 41	4.7 x 12.6
8	*Crossing the Granicus*, Charles Lebrun	15 x 40	4.7 x 12.1
9	*The Battle of Eylau*, Antoine-Jean Gros	17 x 26	5.2 x 7.8
10	*Napoleon Visiting the Plague Victims of Jaffa*, Antoine-Jean Gros	17 x 24	5.2 x 7.2

ART ON SALE

MOST EXPENSIVE SCIENTIFIC INSTRUMENTS EVER SOLD AT AUCTION BY CHRISTIE'S, SOUTH KENSINGTON

	INSTRUMENT/DATE/SALE	PRICE ($)
1	Pair of globes, terrestrial and celestial, attributed to Gerard Mercator, 1579, 30 Oct 1991	1,723,755
2	Ptolemaic armillary sphere, c.1579, 9 Apr 1997	1,252,145
3	Astrolabe by Ersamus Habermel, c.1590, 11 Oct 1995	838,350
4	Astrolabe by Walter Arsenius, 1559, 29 Sep 1988	645,645
5	Ptolemaic armillary sphere, 8 Apr 1998	443,398
6	Gilt-brass universal rectilinear dial, c.1590, 8 Apr 1998	370,614
7	The Regiomontanus Astrolabe, 1462, 28 Sep 1989	324,786
8	Astrolabe quadrant by Christopher Schissler, 1576, 28 Sep 1989	290,598
9	Section of Difference Engine No. 1 by Charles and Henry Prevost Babbage, 16 Nov 1995	274,404
10	Arithmometre (mechanical calculator) by Thomas de Colmar, 1848, 9 Apr 1997	270,230

Astrolabes are instruments for calculating the altitude of heavenly bodies and were once used by astronomers, astrologers, and travellers. They were originally made by Islamic artisans, but during the Renaissance were manufactured by Western craftsmen, often for wealthy connoisseurs (the Habermel astrolabe at No.3, for example, was made for the Duke of Parma), and many skilfully made and richly decorated examples have survived. They are now so desirable among collectors that they dominate this Top 10. The "Difference Engine" designed by Charles Babbage (1791–1871), a precursor of the computer, was abandoned in 1833 and completed by his son Henry Prevost Babbage in 1879. Just outside the Top 10, high prices have also been paid for other astrolabes, globes, compasses, and calculating devices, and substantial prices have also been achieved for rare examples of microscopes.

CELESTIAL SPHERE

The armillary sphere is a type of sundial used by early astronomers to pinpoint the position of the stars.

RARE PAIR

Carved from porphyry and featuring lions, swags, and serpents, a pair of these Louis XV vases sold for nearly £2 million.

MOST EXPENSIVE ITEMS OF FURNITURE EVER SOLD AT AUCTION

	ITEM/SALE	PRICE ($)
1	18th-century "Badminton Cabinet", Christie's, London, July 5, 1990	16,070,340
2	1760s mahogany desk by John Goddard, Christie's, New York, June 3, 1989	12,100,000
3	Carved silver-mounted plum-pudding mahogany dome-top secretary bookcase by Nathaniel Appleton, Sotheby's, New York, January 17, 1999	8,252,500
4	Porcelain-mounted jewel coffer by Martin Carlin, Ader Picard & Tajan, Paris, November 7, 1991	4,349,650 (FrF.25,700,000)
5	Louis XIV bureau plat by A-C Boulle, Christie's, Monaco, December 4, 1993	3,217,549 (FrF.18,869,996)
6	Pair of Louis XV porphyry and gilt-bronze two-handled vases, Christie's, London, December 8, 1994	2,976,057
7	Louis XVI ormolu and Sèvres porcelain-mounted table, Sotheby's, New York, November 5, 1998	2,972,500
8	Porcelain-mounted commode by Martin Carlin, Ader Picard & Tajan, Paris, November 7, 1991	2,811,173 (FrF.16,600,000)
9	Early 17th-century Italian baroque inlaid marble tabletop, Sotheby's, New York, November 5, 1998	2,752,500
10	Le mobilier Crozat, a suite of Regency seat furniture, Christie's, Monaco, December 7, 1987	2,723,108 (FrF.16,836,735)

TOP 10 BESTSELLING POSTCARDS IN THE ART INSTITUTE OF CHICAGO

(Artist/painting)

1 *A Sunday on La Grande Jatte*, Georges Seurat **2** *Water Lilies*, Claude Monet **3** *Two Sisters (on the Terrace)*, Pierre Auguste Renoir **4** *Nighthawks*, Edward Hopper **5** *Paris Street; Rainy Day*, Gustave Caillebotte **6** *The Artist's House at Argenteuil*, Claude Monet **7** *The Bedroom at Arles*, Vincent Van Gogh **8** *American Gothic*, Grant Wood **9** *Cliff Walk at Pourville*, Claude Monet **10** *The Cry*, Edvard Munch

Source: *The Art Institute of Chicago*

TOP 10 ★
BESTSELLING POSTCARDS IN THE TATE GALLERY, LONDON

	ARTIST/PAINTING	DATE
1	John William Waterhouse, *The Lady of Shalott*	1888
2	John Everett Millais, *Ophelia*	1851–52
3	Henri Matisse, *Snail*	1953
4	Salvador Dali, *Lobster Telephone*	1936
5	Salvador Dali, *Metamorphosis of Narcissus*	1937
6	Pablo Picasso, *Weeping Woman*	1937
7	Andy Warhol, *Marilyn Diptych*	1962
8	Mark Rothko, *Light Red over Black*	1957
9	Arthur Hughes, *April Love*	1855–56
10	Salvador Dali, *Autumn Cannibalism*	1936

While the Spanish Surrealist Dali maintains his preeminence in this Top 10, the popularity of the Pre-Raphaelites (Waterhouse, Millais, and Hughes) remains as strong as ever, alongside such modern painters as Warhol and Rothko whose works have recently entered the list.

TOP 10 ★
BESTSELLING POSTCARDS IN THE NATIONAL GALLERY, LONDON

	ARTIST/PAINTING	QUANTITY 1998/99
1	Vincent van Gogh, *Sunflowers*	45,920
2	Claude Monet, *The Water-Lily Pond*	28,940
3	Pierre-Auguste Renoir, *The Umbrellas*	21,380
4	Vincent van Gogh, *A Cornfield with Cypresses*	20,890
5	Georges Pierre Seurat, *Bathers, Asnières*	17,800
6	Claude Monet, *The Thames Below Westminster*	17,090
7	Jan van Eyck, *The Marriage of Giovanni (?) Arnolfini and Giovanna Cenami (?)*	16,775
8	Vincent van Gogh, *Chair and Pipe*	15,800
9	George Stubbs, *Whistle Jacket*	15,400
10	Jean-Auguste-Dominique Ingres, *Mme. Moittessier*	15,300

MONET. MONET. MONET

The Water-Lily Pond, one of Monet's many water-lily studies, has become a bestselling postcard.

TOP 10 ★
BESTSELLING POSTCARDS IN THE BRITISH LIBRARY, LONDON

	IMAGE	DATE
1	Exterior of the new British Library	–
2	Interior of the new British Library	–
3	Exterior of the new British Library showing the Edouardo Paolozzi statue of Isaac Newton	–
4	Interior of the new British Library showing the R.B. Kitaj tapestry	–
5	View of the King's Library	–
6	*Magna Carta*	1215
7	St. Luke's Gospels, from the *Lindisfarne Gospels*	c.698
8	Decorated cross from page preceding St. Luke's Gospels, from the *Lindisfarne Gospels*	c.698
9	The *Codex Sinaiticus* (Greek Bible)	4th century AD
10	Manuscript of The Beatles' song *I Want to Hold your Hand*	1963

TOP 10 BESTSELLING POSTCARDS IN THE NATIONAL PORTRAIT GALLERY, LONDON

1 Elizabeth I **2** Henry VIII **3** William Shakespeare **4** Virginia Woolf **5** Oscar Wilde **6** A.A. Milne **7** Anne Boleyn **8** Mary I **9** The Brontë Sisters **10** Stan Laurel

---

Which van Gogh is the most expensive painting ever sold at auction? *see p.125 for the answer*   **A** *Sunflowers* **B** *Portrait of Dr Gachet* **C** *Irises*

TOP 10 ★

MOST EXPENSIVE PAINTINGS BY ANDY WARHOL

PAINTING*/SALE	PRICE ($)
1 *Orange Marilyn*, Sotheby's, New York, May 14, 1998	15,750,000
2 *Marilyn X 100*, Sotheby's, New York, Nov 17, 1992	3,400,000)
3 *Shot Red Marilyn*, Sotheby's, New York, May 3, 1989	3,700,000
4 *Shot Red Marilyn*, Sotheby's, New York, Nov 2, 1994	3,300,000
5 *Marilyn Monroe, twenty times*, Sotheby's, New York, Nov 10, 1988	3,600,000

PAINTING*/SALE	PRICE ($)
6 *Big Torn Campbell's Soup Can*, Christie's, New York, May 7, 1997	3,200,000
7 *Orange Marilyn*, Christie's, New York, Nov 19, 1998	2,500,000
8 *Self Portrait*, Christie's, New York, May 12, 1998	2,200,000
9 *Liz*, Christie's, New York, Nov 7, 1989	2,050,000
10 *Four Marilyns*, Sotheby's, New York, Nov 17, 1998	2,100,000

* Including silkscreen works

HIGH PRIEST OF POP ART

Andy Warhol is famous for turning everyday images into high art through repetitious silkscreen works.

TOP 10 ★

MOST EXPENSIVE PAINTINGS BY 20TH-CENTURY ARTISTS*

PAINTING/ARTIST	SALE	PRICE ($)
1 *Interchange*, Willem de Kooning (American/Dutch; 1904–97)	Sotheby's, New York, Nov 8, 1989	18,800,000
2 *Fugue*, Wassily Kandinsky (Russian; 1866–1944)	Sotheby's, New York, May 17, 1990	19,000,000
3 *Harmonie jaune*, Henri Matisse (French; 1869–1954)	Christie's, New York, Nov 11, 1992	13,200,000
4 *False Start*, Jasper Johns (American; b.1930)	Sotheby's, New York, November 10, 1988	15,500,000
5 *La pose Hindoue*, Henri Matisse	Sotheby's, New York, May 8, 1995	13,500,000
6 *Contrastes de Formes*, Fernand Léger (French; 1881–1955)	Christie's, London, Nov 27, 1989	13,430,000
7 *La Mulatresse Fatma*, Henri Matisse	Sotheby's, New York, May 11, 1993	13,000,000
8 *Woman*, Willem de Kooning	Christie's, New York, Nov 20, 1996	14,200,000
9 *La vis*, Henri Matisse	Sotheby's, New York, Nov 3, 1993	14,200,000
10 *Anniversaire*, Marc Chagall (French/Russian; 1887–1985)	Sotheby's, New York, May 17, 1990	13,500,000

* Excluding Picasso, who would otherwise comletely dominate the list

TOP 10 ★

MOST EXPENSIVE PAINTINGS BY ROY LICHTENSTEIN

PAINTING/SALE	PRICE ($)
1 *Kiss II*, Christie's, New York, May 7, 1990	5,500,000
2 *Torpedo... Los*, Christie's, New York, Nov 7, 1989	5,000,000
3 *Tex!*, Christie's, New York, Nov 20, 1996	3,600,000
4 *Blang*, Christie's, New York, May 7, 1997	2,600,000
5 *Kiss II*, Christie's, New York, May 3, 1995	2,300,000
6 *I I'm Sorry!*, Sotheby's, New York, Nov 1, 1994	2,250,000
7 *The Ring*, Sotheby's, New York, Nov 19, 1997	2,000,000
8 *Forest Scene*, Sotheby's, New York, Nov 19, 1996	1,900,000
9 *Girl with Piano*, Sotheby's, New York, Nov 17, 1992	1,650,000
10 *I can see the whole room and there's nobody in it*, Christie's, New York, Nov 9, 1988	1,900,000

Did You Know? Jasper Johns' *False Start* holds the current world record for the most expensive painting by a living artist.

TOP 10 ★
MOST EXPENSIVE PAINTINGS BY JACKSON POLLOCK

PAINTING*/SALE	PRICE ($)
1 *Number 8, 1950*, Sotheby's, New York, May 2, 1989	10,500,000
2 *Frieze*, Christie's, New York, Nov 9, 1988	5,200,000
3 *Search*, Sotheby's, New York, May 2, 1988	4,400,000
4 *Number 19, 1949*, Sotheby's, New York, May 2, 1989	3,600,000
5 *Number 31, 1949*, Christie's, New York, May 3, 1988	3,200,000
6 *Number 26, 1950*, Sotheby's, New York, May 4, 1987	2,500,000
7 *Something of the past*, Christie's, New York, May 7, 1996	2,200,000
8 *Number 19, 1948*, Christie's, New York, May 4, 1993	2,200,000
9 *Number 13*, Christie's, New York, Nov 7, 1990	2,800,000
10 *Number 20*, Sotheby's, New York, May 8, 1990	2,200,000

* Including mixed media compositions

TOP 10 MOST EXPENSIVE PAINTINGS BY JASPER JOHNS

(Work/sale date/price in $)

1 *False Start*, Nov 10, 1988, 15,500,000
2 *Two Flags*, Nov 8, 1989, 11,000,000
3 *Corpse and Mirror*, Nov 10, 1997, 7,600,000 4 *White Numbers*, Nov 10, 1987, 7,200,000 5 *White Flag*, Nov 9, 1988, 6,400,000 6 *Jubilee*, Nov 13, 1991, 4,500,000
7 = *Device Circle*, Nov 12, 1991, 4,000,000; = *Decoy*, Nov 10, 1997, 4,000,000 9 *Gray Rectangles*, Nov 10, 1988, 3,900,000
10 *Small False Start*, Nov 7, 1989, 3,700,000

SURREAL MEALS

As well as his surreal paintings, Salvador Dali promoted "Futurist" food, including herrings and raspberry jam, and sausage with nougat.

TOP 10 ★
MOST EXPENSIVE PAINTINGS BY SALVADOR DALI

PAINTING/SALE	PRICE ($)	PAINTING/SALE	PRICE ($)
1 *Assumpta corpuscularia lapislazulina*, Christie's, New York, May 15, 1990	3,700,000	6 *Printemps nécrophilique*, Christie's, London, Dec 10, 1998	1,984,000
2 *Cygnes reflétant des Elephants*, Sotheby's, New York, May 9, 1995	3,200,000	7 *Portrait de Paul Eluard*, Christie's, New York, Nov 14, 1989	1,900,000
3 *L'ascension de Christ – Pietà*, Christie's, New York, Nov 2, 1993	2,200,000	8 *Surrealist Composition*, Christie's, New York, May 12, 1998	1,000,000
4 *The Battle of Tetuan*, Sotheby's, New York, Nov 11, 1987	2,200,000	9 *Le Christ de Gala*, Christie's, New York, May 10, 1994	950,000
5 *La bataille de Tetouan*, Christie's, New York, May 10, 1994	2,000,000	10 *Bataille autour d'un pissenlit*, Guy Loudmer, Paris, Mar 21, 1988	917,782

MUSIC

CHART HITS

TOP 10 ALBUMS OF ALL TIME IN THE US

(Album/artist or group/sales)

1. = *Thriller*, Michael Jackson, 25,000,000;
   = *Their Greatest Hits 1971–1975*, The Eagles, 25,000,000
3. *The Wall*, Pink Floyd, 23,000,000
4. = *Greatest Hits Volumes I & II*, Billy Joel, 18,000,000;
   = *Rumours*, Fleetwood Mac, 18,000,000
6. = *The Beatles*, The Beatles, 17,000,000;
   = *Led Zeppelin IV*, Led Zeppelin, 17,000,000
8. = *Boston*, Boston, 16,000,000;
   = *Back in Black*, AC/DC, 16,000,000;
   = *No Fences*, Garth Brooks, 16,000,000;
   = *Jagged Little Pill*, Alanis Morissette, 16,000,000

Source: *RIAA*

TOP 10 ⭐ OLDEST ARTISTS TO HAVE A NO. 1 HIT SINGLE IN THE US

	ARTIST/SINGLE	AGE* YRS	MTHS
1	Louis Armstrong, *Hello Dolly!*	63	10
2	Lawrence Welk, *Calcutta*	57	11
3	Morris Stoloff, *Moonglow and Theme from Picnic*	57	10
4	Cher, *Believe*	52	7
5	Frank Sinatra#, *Somethin' Stupid*	51	4
6	Elton John, *Candle in the Wind (1997)/Something About the Way You Look Tonight*	50	6
7	Lorne Greene, *Ringo*	49	9
8	= Dean Martin, *Everybody Loves Somebody*	47	2
	= Bill Medley+, *(I've Had) the Time of My Life*	47	2
10	Sammy Davis, Jr., *The Candy Man*	46	6

* During first week of No. 1 US single
\# Duet with Nancy Sinatra
\+ Duet with Jennifer Warnes

Source: *The Popular Music Database*

TOP 10 ⭐ SINGLES THAT STAYED LONGEST IN THE US CHARTS

	SINGLE/ARTIST OR GROUP/YEAR	WEEKS IN CHARTS
1	*How Do I Live*, LeAnn Rimes, 1997	69
2	*Foolish Games, You Were Meant for Me*, Jewel, 1996	65
3	*Macarena (Bayside Boys Mix)*, Los Del Rio, 1996	60
4	*I Don't Want to Wait*, Paula Cole, 1997	56
5	= *Missing*, Everything But the Girl, 1996	55
	= *Barely Breathing*, Duncan Sheik, 1996	55
7	*December 1963 (Oh, What a Night)*, Four Seasons, 1976*	54
8	*Too Close*, Next, 1998	53
9	= *Truly Madly Deeply*, Savage Garden, 1997	52
	= *How's It Going to Be*, Third Eye Blind, 1997	52

* Re-charted in 1994

Source: *The Popular Music Database*

TOP 10 SINGLES OF ALL TIME

(Single/artist or group/sales exceed)

1. *Candle in the Wind (1997)/Something About the Way You Look Tonight*, Elton John, 37,000,000
2. *White Christmas*, Bing Crosby, 30,000,000
3. *Rock Around the Clock*, Bill Haley and His Comets, 17,000,000
4. *I Want to Hold Your Hand*, The Beatles, 12,000,000
5. = *Hey Jude*, The Beatles, 10,000,000;
   = *It's Now or Never*, Elvis Presley, 10,000,000;
   = *I Will Always Love You*, Whitney Houston, 10,000,000
8. = *Hound Dog/Don't Be Cruel*, Elvis Presley, 9,000,000;
   = *Diana*, Paul Anka, 9,000,000
10. = *I'm a Believer*, The Monkees, 8,000,000;
   = *(Everything I Do) I Do It for You*, Bryan Adams, 8,000,000

TOP 10 ⭐ SINGLES OF ALL TIME IN THE US

	SINGLE/ARTIST OR GROUP	EST. US SALES
1	*Candle in the Wind (1997)/Something About the Way You Look Tonight*, Elton John	11,000,000
2	= *We Are the World*, USA for Africa	4,000,000
	= *I Will Always Love You*, Whitney Houston	4,000,000
	= *Whoomp! (There It Is)*, Tag Team	4,000,000
5	= *Hound Dog*, Elvis Presley	3,000,000
	= *(Everything I Do) I Do It for You*, Bryan Adams	3,000,000
	= *Macarena*, Los Del Rio	3,000,000
	= *I'll Be Missing You*, Puff Duffy and Faith Evans (featuring 112)	3,000,000
	= *How Do I Live*, LeAnn Rimes	3,000,000
10	*Vogue*, Madonna	2,000,000

Source: *RIAA*

TOP 10 ⭐ ARTISTS WITH THE MOST WEEKS ON THE US SINGLES CHART*

	ARTIST OR GROUP	TOTAL WEEKS
1	Elvis Presley	1,586
2	Elton John	956
3	Stevie Wonder	770
4	Rod Stewart	724
5	James Brown	706
6	Pat Boone	697
7	Madonna	673
8	Michael Jackson	661
9	The Beatles	629
10	Fats Domino	604

* Up to December 31, 1998

Source: *The Popular Music Database*

Background image: SGT. PEPPER'S LONELY HEARTS CLUB BAND ALBUM COVER

Did You Know? It took 55 years for a record to overtake Bing Crosby's 1942 *White Christmas* as the top-selling single of all time.

TOP 10 ARTISTS WITH THE MOST CONSECUTIVE US TOP 10 ALBUMS

(Artist or group/period/albums)

1 **The Rolling Stones**, Nov 1964–Jul 1980, 26 **2** **Johnny Mathis**, Sep 1957–Dec 1960, 14 **3** **Frank Sinatra**, Feb 1958–Mar 1962, 12 **4** = **The Beatles**, June 1965–Mar 1970, 11; = **Elton John**, Nov 1971–Nov 1976, 11; = **Van Halen**, Apr 1979–Nov 1996, 11 **7** = **Led Zeppelin**, Feb 1969–Dec 1982, 10; = **Chicago**, Feb 1970–Oct 1977, 10; = **Bruce Springsteen**, Sept 1975–Mar 1995, 10; = **Garth Brooks**, Mar 1991–Dec 1998, 10

Source: *The Popular Music Database*

TOP 10 ALBUMS OF ALL TIME

(Album/artist or group)

1 *Thriller*, Michael Jackson
2 *Dark Side of the Moon*, Pink Floyd
3 *Their Greatest Hits 1971–1975*, The Eagles **4** *The Bodyguard*, Soundtrack
5 *Rumours*, Fleetwood Mac
6 *Sgt. Pepper's Lonely Hearts Club Band*, The Beatles **7** *Led Zeppelin IV*, Led Zeppelin **8** *Greatest Hits*, Elton John
9 *Jagged Little Pill*, Alanis Morissette
10 *Bat out of Hell*, Meat Loaf

Total worldwide sales of albums have traditionally been notoriously hard to gauge, but even with the huge expansion of the album market during the 1980s, and multiple-million sales of many major releases, this Top 10 is still élite territory.

STRUTTING HIS STUFF

Mick Jagger, lead singer for the Rolling Stones, formed the band with Keith Richards while still a student at the London School of Economics.

TOP 10 ★

ARTISTS WITH THE MOST CONSECUTIVE US TOP 10 HITS

ARTIST OR GROUP/PERIOD	HITS
1 Elvis Presley, 1956–62	30
2 The Beatles, 1964–76	20
3 Janet Jackson, 1989–98	18
4 = Michael Jackson, 1979–88	17
= Madonna, 1984–89	17
6 Pat Boone, 1956–58	14
7 = Whitney Houston, 1985–91	13
= Phil Collins, 1984–90	13
= Lionel Richie, 1981–87	13
10 = Mariah Carey, 1990–94	11

Source: *The Popular Music Database*

TOP 10 ★

ALBUMS WITH THE MOST WEEKS ON THE US ALBUM CHART

ALBUM/ARTIST OR GROUP		WEEKS
1 *The Dark Side of the Moon*, Pink Floyd		741
2 *Johnny's Greatest Hits*, Johnny Mathis		490
3 *My Fair Lady*, Original Cast		480
4 *Highlights from The Phantom of the Opera*, Original Cast		331
5 *Oklahoma!*, Soundtrack		305
6 *Tapestry*, Carole King		302
7 *Heavenly*, Johnny Mathis		295
8 *MCMXC AD*, Enigma		282
9 *Metallica*, Metallica	16	10
10 = *The King and I*, Soundtrack		277
= *Hymns*, Tennesse Ernie Ford		277

Source: *The Popular Music Database*

CHILD STAR

Michael Jackson's career started at the age of 5, when – along with four of his elder brothers – he was a member of the Jackson Five.

RECORD FIRSTS

THE 10 FIRST US CHART SINGLES
(Single/artist)

1 *I'll Never Smile Again*, Tommy Dorsey **2** *The Breeze and I*, Jimmy Dorsey
3 *Imagination*, Glenn Miller **4** *Playmates*, Kay Kyser **5** *Fools Rush in*, Glenn Miller
6 *Where Was I*, Charlie Barnet **7** *Pennsylvania 6-5000*, Glenn Miller **8** *Imagination*,
Tommy Dorsey **9** *Sierra Sue*, Bing Crosby **10** *Make-believe Island*, Mitchell Ayres

Source: Billboard

THE 10 ★ FIRST AMERICAN GROUPS TO HAVE A NO. 1 SINGLE IN THE UK

	GROUP/SINGLE	DATE AT NO. 1
1	Bill Haley and His Comets, *Rock Around the Clock*	Nov 25, 1955
2	Dream Weavers, *It's Almost Tomorrow*	Mar 16, 1956
3	Teenagers featuring Frankie Lymon, *Why Do Fools Fall in Love?*	Jul 20, 1956
4	The Crickets, *That'll Be the Day*	Nov 1, 1957
5	The Platters, *Smoke Gets in Your Eyes*	Mar 20, 1959
6	The Marcels, *Blue Moon*	May 4, 1961
7	The Highwaymen, *Michael*	Oct 12, 1961
8	B. Bumble and the Stingers, *Rocker*	May 17, 1962
9	The Supremes, *Baby Love*	Nov 19, 1964
10	The Byrds, *Mr. Tambourine Man*	Jul 22, 1965

Source: *The Popular Music Database*

THE 10 ★ FIRST MILLION-SELLING US SINGLES

	SINGLE/ARTIST	CERTIFICATION DATE
1	*Catch a Falling Star*, Perry Como	Mar 14, 1958
2	*He's Got the Whole World in His Hands*, Laurie London	July 18, 1958
3	*Hard Headed Woman*, Elvis Presley	Aug 11, 1958
4	*Patricia*, Perez Prado	Aug 18, 1958
5	*Tom Dooley*, Kingston Trio	Jan 21, 1959
6	*Calcutta*, Lawrence Welk	Feb 14, 1961
7	*Big Bad John*, Jimmy Dean	Dec 14, 1961
8	*The Lion Sleeps Tonight*, The Tokens	Jan 19, 1962
9	*Can't Help Falling in Love*, Elvis Presley	Mar 30, 1962
10	*I Can't Stop Loving You*, Ray Charles	July 19, 1962

Source: *RIAA*

THE 10 ★ FIRST BRITISH GROUPS TO HAVE A NO. 1 SINGLE IN THE US

	GROUP/SINGLE	DATE AT NO. 1
1	Tornados, *Telstar*	Dec 22, 1962
2	The Beatles, *I Want to Hold Your Hand*	Feb 1, 1964
3	The Animals, *House of the Rising Sun*	Sep 5, 1964
4	Manfred Mann, *Do Wah Diddy Diddy*	Oct 17, 1964
5	Freddie and the Dreamers, *I'm Telling You Now*	Apr 10, 1965
6	Wayne Fontana and the Mindbenders, *The Game of Love*	Apr 24, 1965
7	Herman's Hermits, *Mrs. Brown You've Got a Lovely Daughter*	May 1, 1965
8	The Rolling Stones, *(I Can't Get No) Satisfaction*	Jul 10, 1965
9	Dave Clark Five, *Over and Over*	Dec 25, 1965
10	Troggs, *Wild Thing*	Jul 30, 1966

Source: *The Popular Music Database*

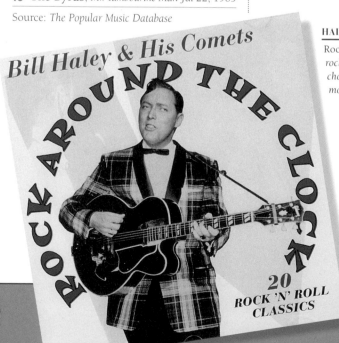

Bill Haley & His Comets
ROCK AROUND THE CLOCK
20 ROCK 'N' ROLL CLASSICS

HALEY'S CLOCK
Rock Around the Clock *became a rock 'n' roll anthem after being chosen as the theme song for the movie* Blackboard Jungle.

ANIMAL APPEAL
Formed in Newcastle, England, in 1962, the Animals had a string of hits including House of the Rising Sun *and* We Gotta Get out of This Place.

THE 10 ★
FIRST BRITISH SOLO ARTISTS TO HAVE A NO. 1 SINGLE IN THE US

	ARTIST/SINGLE	DATE AT NO. 1
1	Mr. Acker Bilk, *Stranger on the Shore*	May 26, 1962
2	Petula Clark, *Downtown*	Jan 23, 1965
3	Donovan, *Sunshine Superman*	Sep 3, 1966
4	Lulu, *To Sir with Love*	Oct 21, 1967
5	George Harrison, *My Sweet Lord*	Dec 26, 1970
6	Rod Stewart, *Maggie May*	Oct 2, 1971
7	Gilbert O'Sullivan, *Alone Again Naturally*	Jul 29, 1972
8	Elton John, *Crocodile Rock*	Feb 3, 1973
9	Ringo Starr, *Photograph*	Nov 24, 1973
10	Eric Clapton, *I Shot the Sheriff*	Sep 14, 1974

Source: *The Popular Music Database*

THE 10 ★
FIRST AMERICAN SOLO ARTISTS TO HAVE A NO. 1 SINGLE IN THE UK

	ARTIST/SINGLE	DATE AT NO. 1
1	Al Martino, *Here in My Heart*	Nov 14, 1952
2	Jo Stafford, *You Belong to Me*	Jan 16, 1953
3	Kay Starr, *Comes A-Long A-Love*	Jan 23, 1953
4	Eddie Fisher, *Outside of Heaven*	Jan 30, 1953
5	Perry Como, *Don't Let the Stars Get in Your Eyes*	Feb 6, 1953
6	Guy Mitchell, *She Wears Red Feathers*	Mar 13, 1953
7	Frankie Laine, *I Believe*	Apr 24, 1953
8	Doris Day, *Secret Love*	Apr 16, 1954
9	Johnnie Ray, *Such a Night*	Apr 30, 1954
10	Kitty Kallen, *Little Things Mean a Lot*	Sept 10, 1954

Source: *The Popular Music Database*

Clearly, in the 1950s, it was much easier for American solo artists to top the UK survey than it was for British artists to compete in the US market.

THE 10 ★
FIRST FEMALE SINGERS TO HAVE A NO. 1 HIT IN THE US DURING THE ROCK ERA

	ARTIST/SINGLE	DATE AT NO. 1
1	Joan Weber, *Let Me Go Lover*	Jan 1, 1955
2	Georgia Gibbs, *Dance with Me Henry (Wallflower)*	May 14, 1955
3	Kay Starr, *Rock and Roll Waltz*	Feb 18, 1956
4	Gogi Grant, *The Wayward Wind*	June 16, 1956
5	Debbie Reynolds, *Tammy*	Aug 19, 1957
6	Connie Francis, *Everybody's Somebody's Fool*	Jun 27, 1960
7	Brenda Lee, *I'm Sorry*	July 18, 1960
8	Shelley Fabares, *Johnny Angel*	Apr 7, 1962
9	Little Eva, *The Loco-motion*	Aug 25, 1962
10	Little Peggy March, *I Will Follow Him*	Apr 27, 1963

Source: *The Popular Music Database*

By the time Little Peggy March had her first No. 1, Connie Francis had had two more, and Brenda Lee one.

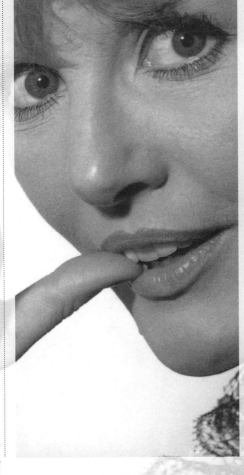

THE 10 ★
FIRST US CHART ALBUMS

	ALBUM	ARTIST OR GROUP
1	*Al Jolson (Volume III)*	Al Jolson
2	*A Presentation of Progressive Jazz*	Stan Kenton
3	*Emperor's Waltz*	Bing Crosby
4	*Songs of Our Times*	Carmen Cavallaro
5	*Wizard at the Organ*	Ken Griffin
6	*Glenn Miller Masterpieces*	Glenn Miller
7	*Busy Fingers*	Three Suns
8	*Songs of Our Times*	B. Grant Orchestra
9	*Glenn Miller*	Glenn Miller
10	*Theme Songs*	Various artists

Source: Billboard

This was the first albums Top 10 compiled by *Billboard* magazine, for its issue dated September 3, 1948.

PET'S STAYING POWER

Petula Clark was a child star during World War II. More recently she moved into musical theater, playing Norma Desmond in Sunset Boulevard.

Which opera house is largest in the world?
see p.163 for the answer
A Cincinnati Opera
B Lyric Opera of Chicago
C The Metropolitan Opera, New York

CHART TOPPERS

ARTISTS WITH THE MOST NO. 1 SINGLES IN THE US

ARTIST OR GROUP	NO. 1 SINGLES
1 The Beatles	20
2 Elvis Presley	18
3 = Michael Jackson	13
= Mariah Carey	13*
5 The Supremes	12
6 = Whitney Houston	11
= Madonna	11
8 = Stevie Wonder	10
9 = Paul McCartney/Wings	9
= Bee Gees	9
= Elton John	9

* Includes a duet with Boyz II Men

Source: *The Popular Music Database*

QUEEN OF THE CHARTS
Madonna burst onto the pop scene in 1984. Her constantly changing image and chart-topping records have made her a household name.

TOP 10 ★

SINGLES WITH MOST WEEKS AT NO. 1 IN THE US*

SINGLE/ARTIST OR GROUP/YEAR	WEEKS AT NO. 1
1 *One Sweet Today*, Mariah Carey and Boyz II Men, 1995	16
2 = *I Will Always Love You*, Whitney Houston, 1992	14
= *I'll Make Love to You*, Boyz II Men, 1994	14
= *Macarena (Bayside Boys Mix)*, Los Del Rio, 1995	14
= *Candle in the Wind (1997)/ Something About the Way You Look Tonight*, Elton John, 1997	14
6 = *End of the Road*, Boyz II Men, 1992	13
= *The Boy is Mine*, Brandy & Monica, 1998	13
8 = *Don't Be Cruel/Hound Dog*, Elvis Presley, 1956	11
= *I Swear*, All-4-One, 1994	11
= *Un-break My Heart*, Toni Braxton, 1996	11

* Based on Billboard charts

Source: *The Popular Music Database*

TOP 10 ★

YOUNGEST ARTISTS TO HAVE A NO. 1 SINGLE IN THE US*

ARTIST/SINGLE/YEAR	AGE* YRS	MTHS
1 Jimmy Boyd, *I Saw Mommy Kissing Santa Claus*, 1952	12	11
2 Stevie Wonder, *Fingertips*, 1963	13	1
3 Donny Osmond, *Go Away Little Girl*, 1971	13	7
4 Michael Jackson, *Ben*, 1972	13	11
5 Laurie London, *He's Got the Whole World in His Hands*, 1958	14	2
6 Little Peggy March, *I Will Follow Him*, 1963	15	0
7 Brenda Lee, *I'm Sorry*, 1960	15	5
8 Paul Anka, *Diana*, 1957	16	0
9 Tiffany, *I Think We're Alone Now*, 1987	16	10
10 Lesley Gore, *It's My Party*, 1963	17	0

* To March 1, 1999

\# During first week of debut No. 1 UK single

Source: *The Popular Music Database*

TOP 10 ★

LONGEST GAPS BETWEEN NO. 1 HIT SINGLES IN THE US

ARTIST OR GROUP	PERIOD	GAP YRS	MTHS
1 = Elton John	Nov 11, 1975–Oct 11, 1997	21	11
= The Beach Boys	Dec 10, 1966–Nov 5, 1988	21	11
3 Paul Anka	Jul 13, 1959–Aug 24, 1974	15	1
4 George Harrison	June 30, 1973–Jan 16, 1988	14	7
5 Neil Sedaka	Aug 11, 1962–Feb 1, 1975	12	6
6 Four Seasons	July 18, 1964–Mar 13, 1976	11	8
7 Herb Albert	June 22, 1968–Oct 20, 1979	11	4
8 Frank Sinatra	July 9, 1955–July 2, 1966	11	0
9 Stevie Wonder	Aug 10, 1963–Jan 27, 1973	10	5
10 Dean Martin	Jan 7, 1956–Aug 15, 1964	8	7

Source: *The Popular Music Database*

TOP 10 ★ ARTISTS WITH THE MOST CONSECUTIVE NO. 1 SINGLES IN THE US*

	ARTIST OR GROUP	PERIOD	NO. 1s
1	Elvis Presley	1956–58	10
2	Whitney Houston	1985–88	7
3 =	The Beatles	1964–66	6
=	Bee Gees	1977–79	6
=	Paula Abdul	1988–91	6
6 =	Michael Jackson	1987–88	5
=	The Supremes	1964–65	5
=	Mariah Carey	1990–91	5
=	Mariah Carey	1995–98	5
10 =	Jackson 5	1970	4
=	George Michael	1987–88	4

* To March 1, 1999

Source: *The Popular Music Database*

TOP 10 ★ OLDEST ARTISTS TO HAVE A NO. 1 SINGLE IN THE US*

	ARTIST OR GROUP/SINGLE	AGE# YRS	MTHS
1	Louis Armstrong, *Hello Dolly!*	67	10
2	Lawrence Welk, *Calcutta*	52	7
3	Morris Stoloff, *Moonglow and Theme from Picnic*	51	7
4	Frank Sinatra+, *Somethin' Stupid*	51	4
5	Elton John, *Candle in the Wind (1997)/ Something About the Way You Look Tonight*	51	1
6	Lorne Greene, *Ringo*	50	2
7	Dean Martin, *Everybody Loves Somebody*	50	1
8	Bill Medley★, *(I've Had) the Time of My Life*	50	1
9	Sammy Davis, Jr., *The Candy Man*	49	0
10	Tina Turner, *What's Love Got to Do with It*	48	5

* To Dec 31, 1998 # During first week of No. 1 single

+ Duet with Nancy Sinatra

★ Duet with Jennifer Warnes

Source: *The Popular Music Database*

TOP 10 ★ US ALBUMS WITH THE MOST CONSECUTIVE WEEKS AT NO. 1*

	SINGLE/ARTIST OR GROUP	WEEKS AT NO. 1
1	*Love Me or Leave Me*, Doris Day	25
2 =	*Calypso*, Harry Belafonte	24
=	*Saturday Night Fever*, Soundtrack	24
=	*Purple Rain (soundtrack)*, Prince	24
5	*Blue Hawaii (soundtrack)*, Elvis Presley	20
6	*Rumours*, Fleetwood Mac	19
7 =	*More of the Monkees*, The Monkees	18
=	*Please Hammer Don't Hurt 'Em*, MC Hammer	18
9 =	*Thriller*, Michael Jackson#	17
=	*Thriller*, Michael Jackson#	17
=	*Some Gave All*, Billy Ray Cyrus	17

* Based on Billboard charts, up to March 1, 1999

 # Two separate periods: Feb 26, 1983–Jul 18, 1983 and Dec 24, 1983–Apr 14, 1984

TOP 10 ★ TOP 10 ARTISTS WITH THE MOST WEEKS AT NO. 1 IN THE US

	ARTIST OR GROUP	WEEKS AT NO. 1
1	Elvis Presley	80
2	The Beatles	59
3	Mariah Carey	58*
4	Boyz II Men	50*
5	Michael Jackson	37
6	Elton John	32
7	Whitney Houston	31
8	Paul McCartney/Wings	30
9	Madonna	28
10	Bee Gees	27

* Boyz II Men and Mariah Carey share a 16-week run with a duet

Source: *The Popular Music Database*

TOP 10 SLOWEST US ALBUM CHART RISES TO NO. 1

(Album/artist or group/weeks to reach No. 1)

1 *First Take*, Roberta Flack, 118 **2** *You Don't Mess Around with Jim*, Jim Croce, 81 **3** *Forever Your Girl*, Paula Abdul, 64 **4** *Film Encores*, Mantovani & His Orchestra, 59 **5** *Fleetwood Mac*, Fleetwood Mac, 58 **6** *Hangin' Tough*, New Kids on the Block, 55 **7** *Nick of Time*, Bonnie Raitt, 52; = *Throwing Copper*, Live, 52 **9** *Appetite for Destruction*, Guns 'N Roses, 50; = *Whitney Houston*, Whitney Houston, 50

Source: *The Popular Music Database*

THE HILLBILLY CAT

Elvis Presley used this name while touring at the start of his career. He later became a worldwide sensation with hits like Love Me Tender *and* Hound Dog.

Did You Know? T. Rex's *My People Were Fair and Had Sky in Their Hair, but Now They're Content to Wear Stars on Their Brows* was the longest album title ever.

139

HIT SINGLES OF THE DECADES

TOP 10 ★
SINGLES OF THE 1950s IN THE US

	SINGLE/ARTIST OR GROUP	YEAR
1	*Hound Dog/Don't Be Cruel*, Elvis Presley	1956
2	*The Chipmunk Song*, The Chipmunks	1958
3	*Love Letters in the Sand*, Pat Boone	1957
4	*Rock Around the Clock*, Bill Haley and His Comets	1955
5	*Tom Dooley*, Kingston Trio	1958
6	*Love Me Tender*, Elvis Presley	1956
7	*Tennessee Waltz*, Patti Page	1951
8	*Nel Blu Dipinto Di Blu (Volare)*, Domenico Modugno	1958
9	*Jailhouse Rock*, Elvis Presley	1957
10	*All Shook Up*, Elvis Presley	1957

Rock 'n' Roll and Elvis Presley were the twin catalysts that ignited record sales in the United States in the middle of the 1950s, and both are represented strongly in the decade's biggest sellers, the former mostly in the person of the latter. While Presley's double-sider, topping 6 million, was the decade's top single by a wide margin, the fastest seller was the *Chipmunk Song*, which moved a remarkable 3,500,000 copies in five weeks.

THE FAB FOUR

The Beatles, together with Elvis Presley, are co-holders of the record for the greatest amount of UK No. 1 hit singles, which currently stands at 17. The majority of these hits were penned by John Lennon (second from right) and Paul McCartney (far left).

TOP 10 ★
SINGLES OF THE 1960s IN THE US

	SINGLE/ARTIST OR GROUP	YEAR
1	*I Want to Hold Your Hand*, The Beatles	1964
2	*It's Now or Never*, Elvis Presley	1960
3	*Hey Jude*, The Beatles	1968
4	*The Ballad of the Green Berets*, Sgt. Barry Sadler	1966
5	*Love Is Blue*, Paul Mauriat	1968
6	*I'm a Believer*, The Monkees	1966
7	*Can't Buy Me Love*, The Beatles	1964
8	*She Loves You*, The Beatles	1964
9	*Sugar Sugar*, The Archies	1969
10	*The Twist*, Chubby Checker	1960

Though the 1960s are recalled as the decade in which British music invaded America, the only UK representatives among the decade's 10 biggest sellers in the United States are by the leaders of that invasion, the Beatles – although they do completely dominate the list.

TOP 10 ★
SINGLES OF THE 1970s IN THE US

	SINGLE/ARTIST OR GROUP	YEAR
1	*You Light up My Life*, Debby Boone	1977
2	*Le Freak*, Chic	1978
3	*Night Fever*, Bee Gees	1978
4	*Stayin' Alive*, Bee Gees	1978
5	*Shadow Dancing*, Andy Gibb	1978
6	*Disco Lady*, Johnnie Taylor	1976
7	*I'll Be There*, Jackson 5	1970
8	*Star Wars Theme/Cantina Band*, Meco	1977
9	*Car Wash*, Rose Royce	1976
10	*Joy to the World*, Three Dog Night	1971

During the last four years of the 1970s, singles sales in the United States rose to their highest-ever level, and chart-topping records were almost routinely selling over 2 million copies.

TOP 10 ★
SINGLES OF THE 1980s IN THE US

	SINGLE/ARTIST OR GROUP	YEAR
1	*We Are the World*, USA for Africa	1985
2	*Physical*, Olivia Newton-John	1981
3	*Endless Love*, Diana Ross and Lionel Richie	1981
4	*Eye of the Tiger*, Survivor	1982
5	*I Love Rock 'n' Roll*, Joan Jett and The Blackhearts	1982
6	*When Doves Cry*, Prince	1984
7	*Celebration*, Kool and The Gang	1981
8	*Another One Bites the Dust*, Queen	1980
9	*Wild Thing*, Tone Loc	1989
10	*Islands in the Stream*, Kenny Rogers and Dolly Parton	1983

America's top-selling single of the 1980s was, rather fittingly, a record that included contributions from many of those artists who had become the recording elite during the decade – the charity single for Africa's famine victims, *We Are the World*.

Background image: **JUKEBOX**

TOP 10 SINGLES OF EACH YEAR OF THE 1960s IN THE US

(Year/single/artist or group)

1. 1960, *It's Now or Never*, Elvis Presley
2. 1961, *Runaway*, Del Shannon
3. 1962, *I Can't Stop Loving You*, Ray Charles
4. 1963, *Sugar Shack*, Jimmy Gilmer and The Fireballs
5. 1964, *I Want to Hold Your Hand*, The Beatles
6. 1965, *Help!*, The Beatles
7. 1966, *The Ballad of the Green Berets*, Sgt. Barry Sadler
8. 1967, *To Sir With Love*, Lulu
9. 1968, *Hey Jude*, The Beatles
10. 1969, *Sugar Sugar*, The Archies

TOP 10 SINGLES OF EACH YEAR OF THE 1970s IN THE US

(Year/single/artist or group)

1. 1970, *I'll Be There*, Jackson 5
2. 1971, *Joy to the World*, Three Dog Night
3. 1972, *The First Time Ever I Saw Your Face*, Roberta Flack
4. 1973, *Tie a Yellow Ribbon Round the Old Oak Tree*, Dawn
5. 1974, *The Way We Were*, Barbra Streisand
6. 1975, *Love Will Keep Us Together*, Captain and Tennille
7. 1976, *Disco Lady*, Johnnie Taylor
8. 1977, *You Light up My Life*, Debby Boone
9. 1978, *Night Fever*, Bee Gees
10. 1979, *I Will Survive*, Gloria Gaynor

TOP 10 SINGLES OF EACH YEAR OF THE 1980s IN THE US

(Year/single/artist or group)

1. 1980, *Another One Bites the Dust*, Queen
2. 1981, *Endless Love*, Diana Ross and Lionel Richie
3. 1982, *Eye of the Tiger*, Survivor
4. 1983, *Islands in the Stream*, Kenny Rogers and Dolly Parton
5. 1984, *When Doves Cry*, Prince
6. 1985, *We Are the World*, USA for Africa
7. 1986, *That's What Friends Are For*, Dionne Warwick and Friends
8. 1987, *I Wanna Dance With Somebody (Who Loves Me)*, Whitney Houston
9. 1988, *Kokomo*, The Beach Boys
10. 1989, *Wild Thing*, Tone Loc

TOP 10 ★
SINGLES OF THE 1990s IN THE US

	SINGLE/ARTIST OR GROUP	YEAR
1	*Candle in the Wind 1997/ Something About the Way You Look Tonight*, Elton John	1997
2	*I Will Always Love You*, Whitney Houston	1992
3	*Whoomp! (There it Is)*, Tag Team	1993
4	*Macarena*, Los Del Rio	1995
5	*(Everything I Do) I Do it For You*, Bryan Adams	1991
6	*I'll Be Missing You*, Puff Daddy and Faith Evans (featuring 112)	1997
7	*How Do I Live*, LeAnn Rimes	1997
8	*Gangsta's Paradise*, Coolio featuring L.V.	1995
9	*Dazzey Duks*, Duice	1993
10	*Fantasy*, Mariah Carey	1995

TOP 10 ★
SINGLES OF THE 1990s IN THE US (MALE)

	SINGLE/ARTIST	YEAR
1	*Candle in the Wind 1997/ Something About the Way You Look Tonight*, Elton John	1997
2	*(Everything I Do) I Do It For You*, Bryan Adams	1991
3	*Gangsta's Paradise*, Coolio featuring L.V.	1995
4	*How Do U Want It*, 2 Pac	1996
5	*I Believe I Can Fly*, R. Kelly	1996
6	*You Make Me Wanna ...*, Usher	1997
7	*Here Comes the Hotstepper*, Ini Kamoze	1994
8	*Ice Ice Baby*, Vanilla Ice	1990
9	*This Is How We Do It*, Montell Jordan	1995
10	*Twisted*, Keith Sweat	1996

BAD BOY

Puff Daddy, aka Sean "Puffy" Combs, was a highly acclaimed record producer for his own label, Bad Boy Records, before becoming a global superstar with I'll Be Missing You, a duet with Faith Evans.

TOP 10 ★
SINGLES OF THE 1990s IN THE US (FEMALE)

	SINGLE/ARTIST	YEAR
1	*I Will Always Love You*, Whitney Houston	1992
2	*How Do I Live*, LeAnn Rimes	1997
3	*Fantasy*, Mariah Carey	1995
4	*Vogue*, Madonna	1990
5	*You Were Meant For Me/ Foolish Games*, Jewel	1996
6	*The Power of Love*, Celine Dion	1993
7	*Hero*, Mariah Carey	1993
8	*You're Still the One*, Shania Twain	1998
9	*Baby One More Time*, Britney Spears	1999
10	*This Kiss*, Faith Hill	1998

Did You Know? Elton John's phenomenally successful double single *Candle in the Wind 1997/Something About the Way You Look Tonight* topped the lists of bestselling singles on both sides of the Atlantic.

TOP 10 ALBUMS OF THE 1990s IN THE US

	ALBUM/ARTIST OR GROUP	YEAR
1	*No Fences*, Garth Brooks	1990
2	*Jagged Little Pill*, Alanis Morissette	1995
3	*The Bodyguard*, Soundtrack	1992
4	*Cracked Rear View*, Hootie & the Blowfish	1994
5	*Ropin' the Wind*, Garth Brooks	1991
6	*Breathless*, Kenny G	1992
7	*Double Live*, Garth Brooks	1998
8	*II*, Boyz II Men	1994
9	*The Woman in Me*, Shania Twain	1995
10	*Metallica*, Metallica	1991

Source: *RIAA*

TOP 10 ★

ALBUMS OF EACH YEAR IN THE 1960s IN THE US

YEAR	ALBUM/ARTIST OR GROUP
1960	*The Sound of Music*, Original Cast
1961	*Judy at Carnegie Hall*, Judy Garland
1962	*West Side Story*, Soundtrack
1963	*John Fitzgerald Kennedy: A Memorial Album*, Documentary
1964	*Meet The Beatles*, The Beatles
1965	*Mary Poppins*, Soundtrack
1966	*Whipped Cream & Other Delights*, Herb Alpert & The Tijuana Brass
1967	*Sgt. Pepper's Lonely Hearts Club Band*, The Beatles
1968	*The Beatles ("White Album")*, The Beatles
1969	*Hair*, Broadway Cast

TOP 10 ★

ALBUMS OF EACH YEAR IN THE 1970s IN THE US

YEAR	ALBUM/ARTIST OR GROUP
1970	*Bridge Over Troubled Water*, Simon and Garfunkel
1971	*Tapestry*, Carole King
1972	*American Pie*, Don McLean
1973	*Dark Side of the Moon*, Pink Floyd
1974	*John Denver's Greatest Hits*, John Denver
1975	*Captain Fantastic and the Brown Dirt Cowboy*, Elton John
1976	*Frampton Comes Alive!*, Peter Frampton
1977	*Rumours*, Fleetwood Mac
1978	*Saturday Night Fever*, Soundtrack
1979	*Breakfast in America*, Supertramp

ISN'T IT IRONIC?

Canadian singer/songwriter Alanis Morissette was born in Ottawa in 1974. She released her first single at the age of 11.

TOP 10 ★
ALBUMS OF THE 1960s IN THE US

	ALBUM/ARTIST OR GROUP	YEAR
1	*West Side Story* (Original Soundtrack), Various	1961
2	*Blue Hawaii* (Original Soundtrack), Elvis Presley	1961
3	*The Sound of Music* (Original Soundtrack), Various	1965
4	*Sgt. Pepper's Lonely Hearts Club Band*, The Beatles	1967
5	*More of the Monkees*, The Monkees	1967
6	*Days of Wine and Roses*, Andy Williams	1963
7	*G.I. Blues*, Elvis Presley	1960
8	*The Button-Down Mind Of Bob Newhart*, Bob Newhart	1960
9	*Whipped Cream & Other Delights*, Herb Alpert & The Tijuana Brass	1965
10	*A Hard Day's Night* (Original Soundtrack), The Beatles	1964

TOP 10 ★
ALBUMS OF THE 1970s IN THE US

	ALBUM/ARTIST OR GROUP	YEAR
1	*Rumours*, Fleetwood Mac	1977
2	*Their Greatest Hits, 1971–1975*, The Eagles	1976
3	*The Dark Side of the Moon*, Pink Floyd	1973
4	*Tapestry*, Carole King	1971
5	*Saturday Night Fever* (Original Soundtrack), Various	1977
6	*Led Zeppelin IV* (Untitled), Led Zeppelin	1971
7	*Boston*, Boston	1976
8	*Grease* (Original Soundtrack), Various	1978
9	*Frampton Comes Alive!*, Peter Frampton	1976
10	*Songs in the Key of Life*, Stevie Wonder	1976

TOP 10 ★
ALBUMS OF THE 1980s IN THE US

	ALBUM/ARTIST OR GROUP	YEAR
1	*Thriller*, Michael Jackson	1982
2	*Born in the USA*, Bruce Springsteen	1984
3	*Dirty Dancing* (Original Soundtrack), Various	1987
4	*Purple Rain* (Original Soundtrack), Prince & The Revolution	1984
5	*Can't Slow Down*, Lionel Richie	1983
6	*Whitney Houston*, Whitney Houston	1985
7	*Hysteria*, Def Leppard	1987
8	*Slippery When Wet*, Bon Jovi	1986
9	*Appetite For Destruction*, Guns N' Roses	1988
10	*The Wall*, Pink Floyd	1979

On October 30, 1984, *Thriller* became the first album to receive its 20th platinum sales certificate for sales of 20 million copies in the United States alone (for comparison, the next bestselling album of the 1980s, Bruce Springsteen's *Born in the USA*, sold 11 million copies).

TOP 10 ★
ALBUMS OF EACH YEAR IN THE 1980s IN THE US

YEAR	ALBUM/ARTIST OR GROUP
1980	*The Wall*, Pink Floyd
1981	*Hi Infidelity*, REO Speedwagon
1982	*Asia*, Asia
1983	*Thriller*, Michael Jackson
1984	*Purple Rain*, Prince & The Revolution
1985	*Like a Virgin*, Madonna
1986	*Whitney Houston*, Whitney Houston
1987	*Slippery When Wet*, Bon Jovi
1988	*Faith*, George Michael
1989	*Girl You Know It's True*, Milli Vanilli

RECORD BREAKER

The eponymous album by Whitney Houston sold 14 million copies and was the first album by a female artist to enter the US Billboard chart at No. 1.

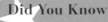

WOMEN IN THE CHARTS

VOCAL VIRTUOSO
Whitney Houston's first album spawned three No. 1 hit singles and went straight into the record books as the best-selling debut album by a female solo singer.

Background image: **MADONNA**

TOP 10 ★
FEMALE GROUPS OF ALL TIME IN THE US*

	GROUP	NO. 1	TOP 10	TOP 20
1	The Supremes	12	20	24
2	The Pointer Sisters	–	7	13
3	= Expose	1	8	9
	= The McGuire Sisters	2	4	9
5	The Fontane Sisters	2	2	8
6	= The Shirelles	2	6	7
	= TLC	–	7	7
	= Martha & The Vandellas	–	6	7
	= En Vogue	–	5	7
	= Spice Girls	–	4	7

* Ranked according to total number of Top 20 singles

Source: *The Popular Music Database*

The Supremes also had three other Top 20 hits, not included here, in partnership with Motown male groups the Four Tops and the Temptations.

TOP 10 ★
FEMALE SINGERS WITH THE MOST TOP 10 HITS IN THE US*

	SINGER	HITS
1	Madonna	32
2	Janet Jackson (including one duet with Michael Jackson)	23
3	Whitney Houston (including one duet with CeCe Winans)	18
4	= Aretha Franklin (including one duet with George Michael)	17
	= Mariah Carey (including one duet with Boyz II Men and one with Luther Vandross)	17
6	Connie Francis	16
7	Olivia Newton-John (including two duets with John Travolta and one with the Electric Light Orchestra)	15
8	Donna Summer	14
9	= Brenda Lee	12
	= Diana Ross (including one duet with Marvin Gaye and one with Lionel Richie)	12
	= Dionne Warwick (including one duet with the Detroit Spinners and one with "Friends" Stevie Wonder, Gladys Knight, and Elton John)	12

* To December 31, 1998

The hitmaking careers of many of these artists – most noticeably Diana Ross, Connie Francis, and Olivia Newton-John – have either slowed down or ceased altogether in recent years. In contrast, Madonna's career is still going strong.

TOP 10 ★
YOUNGEST FEMALE SINGERS TO HAVE A NO. 1 SINGLE IN THE US

	SINGER	AGE YEARS	AGE MONTHS	AGE DAYS
1	Little Peggy March	15	1	20
2	Brenda Lee	15	7	7
3	Tiffany	16	1	5
4	Lesley Gore	17	0	30
5	Little Eva	17	1	27
6	Britney Spears	17	1	29
7	Monica	17	11	9
8	Shelley Fabares	18	2	19
9	Debbie Gibson	18	6	4
10	Joan Weber*	18	?	?

*Birthdate unknown, but was aged between 18 years and 6 months and 19 years

Source: *The Popular Music Database*

FAMILY FORTUNES
The youngest of the talented Jackson siblings, Janet Jackson became the highest-paid singer in the world, surpassing even her megastar brother Michael, when she signed a $70 million deal with Virgin Records in 1997.

TOP 10 ★
OLDEST FEMALE SINGERS TO HAVE A NO. 1 SINGLE IN THE US

SINGER	YEARS	AGE MONTHS	DAYS
1 Cher	52	9	15
2 Tina Turner	45	9	5
3 Bette Midler	44	8	24
4 Kim Carnes	35	9	26
5 Dolly Parton	35	1	2
6 Georgie Gibbs	34	8	18
7 Deniece Williams	33	11	23
8 Kay Starr	33	6	15
9 Anne Murray	33	4	15
10 Roberta Flack	33	2	5

Source: *The Popular Music Database*

TOP 10 ★
ALBUMS BY FEMALE GROUPS IN THE US

TITLE/GROUP	YEAR
1 *Crazysexycool*, TLC	1994
2 *Spice*, Spice Girls	1997
3 *Wilson Phillips*, Wilson Phillips	1990
4 *Very Necessary*, Salt 'N Pepa	1993
5 *Ooooooohhh ... On the TLC Tip*, TLC	1992
6 *Wide Open Spaces*, Dixie Chicks	1998
7 *Spiceworld*, Spice Girls	1997
8 *Funky Divas*, En Vogue	1992
9 *It's That Time*, SWV	1993
10 *A Different Light*, Bangles	1986

Source: *The Popular Music Database*

TOP 10 ★
SINGLES BY FEMALE SINGERS IN THE US

TITLE/ARTIST	YEAR
1 *I Will Always Love You*, Whitney Houston	1992
2 *How Do I Live*, LeAnn Rimes	1997
3 *Fantasy*, Mariah Carey	1995
4 *Vogue*, Madonna	1990
5 *Mr. Big Stuff*, Jean Knight	1971
6 *You Light up My Life*, Debby Boone	1977
7 *The Power of Love*, Celine Dion	1993
8 *Because You Loved Me*, Celine Dion	1996
9 *You Were Meant for Me*, Jewel	1996
10 *Physical*, Olivia Newton-John	1981

Source: *The Popular Music Database*

Among these blockbusters, all of them platinum sellers, it is fitting that Whitney Houston's multiplatinum success from *The Bodyguard Original Soundtrack* was also written by a woman – Dolly Parton.

TOP 10 ALBUMS BY FEMALE SINGERS IN THE US
(Title/group/year)

1 *Jagged Little Pill*, Alanis Morissette 1995 **2** *The Bodyguard* (soundtrack), Whitney Houston 1992 **3** *Whitney Houston*, Whitney Houston 1985 **4** *The Woman in Me*, Shania Twain 1995 **5** = *Tapestry*, Carole King 1971; = *Falling Into You*, Celine Dion 1996; = *Music Box*, Mariah Carey 1993 **8** = *Whitney*, Whitney Houston 1987; = *Like a Virgin*, Madonna 1984; = *Daydream*, Mariah Carey 1995

Source: *The Popular Music Database*

TOP 10 ★
SINGLES BY FEMALE GROUPS IN THE US

TITLE/GROUP	YEAR
1 *Don't Let Go*, En Vogue	1996
2 *Hold On*, En Vogue	1990
3 *Wannabe*, Spice Girls	1997
4 *Whatta Man*, Salt 'N Pepa	1994
5 *Expressions*, Salt 'N Pepa	1990
6 *Push It*, Salt 'N Pepa	1987
7 *Waterfall*, TLC	1995
8 *Creep*, TLC	1994
9 *Weak*, SWV	1993
10 *Baby, Baby, Baby*, TLC	1992

Source: *The Popular Music Database*

CHART-TOPPER
Since the massive success of her single Think Twice, *Celine Dion has become increasingly popular. In 1999 she won 10 prestigious music awards.*

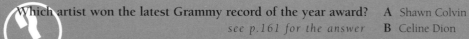

Which artist won the latest Grammy record of the year award?
see p.161 for the answer

A Shawn Colvin
B Celine Dion
C Eric Clapton

SUPERGROUPS

ALBUMS OF ALL TIME BY GROUPS IN THE US

	ALBUM/GROUP	YEAR
1	*Their Greatest Hits, 1971–1975*, The Eagles	1976
2	*The Wall,* Pink Floyd	1979
3	*Rumours,* Fleetwood Mac	1977
4	*Led Zeppelin IV,* Led Zeppelin	1971
5	*The Beatles ("White Album"),* The Beatles	1968
6	*Boston,* Boston	1976
7	*Back in Black,* AC/DC	1980
8	*Dark Side of the Moon,* Pink Floyd	1973
9	*Hotel California,* The Eagles	1977
10	*Cracked Rear View,* Hootie and the Blowfish	1995

This list has changed considerably in recent times, with official sales figures being updated in the US on several perennially big-selling albums – most notably those by the recently resurrected Eagles.

TOP 10 ★

ALBUMS OF ALL TIME IN THE UK

	ALBUM/GROUP OR ARTIST	YEAR
1	*Sgt. Pepper's Lonely Hearts Club Band,* The Beatles	1967
2	*(What's the Story?) Morning Glory,* Oasis	1995
3	*Bad,* Michael Jackson	1987
4	*Brothers in Arms,* Dire Straits	1985
5	*Stars,* Simply Red	1991
6	*Thriller,* Michael Jackson	1982
7	*Greatest Hits,* Queen	1981
8	*Spice,* Spice Girls	1996
9	*The Immaculate Collection,* Madonna	1990
10	*The Very Best of Elton John,* Elton John	1990

Source: BPI

TOP 10 ★

GROUPS OF THE 1990s IN THE US

1	Boyz II Men
2	Guns N' Roses
3	Pearl Jam
4	The Beatles
5	Spice Girls
6	U2
7	Aerosmith
8	Hootie and The Blowfish
9	Wilson Phillips
10	Backstreet Boys

This "biggest so far" listing for the current decade is based on comparative US single and album chart performances of the 1990s.

TOP 10 ★

SINGLES OF ALL TIME BY GROUPS IN THE UK

	SINGLE/GROUP	YEAR
1	*Bohemian Rhapsody,* Queen	1975
2	*Mull of Kintyre,* Wings	1977
3	*Rivers of Babylon/Brown Girl in the Ring,* Boney M	1978
4	*Relax,* Frankie Goes to Hollywood	1984
5	*She Loves You,* The Beatles	1963
6	*Mary's Boy Child/ Oh My Lord,* Boney M	1978
7	*Love Is All Around,* Wet Wet Wet	1994
8	*I Want to Hold Your Hand,* The Beatles	1963
9	*Can't Buy Me Love,* The Beatles	1964
10	*Two Tribes,* Frankie Goes to Hollywood	1984

The Beatles appear three times in this Top 10, with Paul McCartney scoring a bonus entry via the Wings single.

SLASH N' BURN

Lead guitarist of Guns N' Roses from 1985, Saul "Slash" Hudson (b. 1965) left the band in 1996, citing musical differences with frontman Axl Rose. Although the guitar hero grew up in Los Angeles, he was born in Stoke on Trent, England.

TOP 10 GROUPS OF THE 1960s IN THE US

1 The Beatles **2** The Supremes **3** The Four Seasons
4 The Beach Boys **5** The Rolling Stones **6** The Miracles
7 The Temptations **8** Tommy James and The Shondells
9 Dave Clark Five **10** Herman's Hermits

Based on comparative US singles chart performance

TOP 10 GROUPS OF THE 1970s IN THE US

1 Bee Gees **2** The Carpenters **3** Chicago
4 Jackson 5/Jacksons **5** Three Dog Night **6** Gladys Knight and the Pips **7** Dawn **8** Earth, Wind and Fire
9 The Eagles **10** Fleetwood Mac

Based on comparative US singles chart performance

TOP 10 GROUPS OF THE 1980s IN THE US

1 Wham! **2** Kool and the Gang **3** Huey Lewis and the News **4** Journey **5** Duran Duran **6** U2
7 The Rolling Stones **8** Alabama **9** The Pointer Sisters
10 Jefferson Starship/Starship

Based on comparative US singles and albums chart performance

TOP 10 GROUPS OF THE 1960s IN THE UK

1 The Beatles **2** The Rolling Stones **3** The Shadows
4 The Hollies **5** The Beach Boys **6** The Kinks
7 The Four Tops **8** Manfred Mann **9** The Seekers
10 The Bachelors

Based on comparative UK singles chart performance

TOP 10 GROUPS OF THE 1970s IN THE UK

1 Abba **2** Slade **3** T. Rex **4** Bay City Rollers
5 The Sweet **6** Showaddywaddy **7** Mud **8** Wings
9 The Electric Light Orchestra **10** The Osmonds

Based on comparative UK singles chart performance

TOP 10 GROUPS OF THE 1980s IN THE UK

1 Police **2** Wham! **3** Dire Straits **4** U2 **5** Queen
6 Simple Minds **7** Pet Shop Boys **8** Duran Duran
9 Adam and the Ants **10** Madness

Based on comparative UK singles and albums chart performance

It should be noted that apart from U2, who are from Ireland, all 10 of these groups are British. With the exception of Queen, none of them had achieved any success prior to the tail-end of the 1970s.

TOP 10 ★
GROUPS OF THE 1990s IN THE UK

1	Spice Girls
2	Oasis
3	Manic Street Preachers
4	Take That
5	Blur
6	Simply Red
7	Wet Wet Wet
8	Lighthouse Family
9	Verve
10	Boyzone

... THANK YOU, MA'AM!
Wham! (George Michael and Andrew Ridgeley) had their first hit in 1982; they split in 1986.

 Which female singer has had the most hits in the US?
see p.144 for the answer

A Janet Jackson
B Madonna
C Whitney Houston

STAR SINGLES & ALBUMS

TOP 10 ★
ELTON JOHN SINGLES IN THE US

	SINGLE	YEAR
1	Candle in the Wind (1997)/ Something About the Way You Look Tonight	1997
2	Crocodile Rock	1972
3	Goodbye Yellow Brick Road	1973
4	Island Girl	1975
5	Philadelphia Freedom	1975
6	Can You Feel the Love Tonight	1994
7	Lucy in the Sky with Diamonds	1974
8	Little Jeannie	1980
9	Daniel	1973
10	The Bitch is Back	1974

Source: *The Popular Music Database*

TOP 10 ★
FLEETWOOD MAC ALBUMS IN THE US

	ALBUM	YEAR
1	Rumours	1977
2	Fleetwood Mac	1975
3	The Dance	1997
4	Greatest Hits	1988
5	Tango in the Night	1987
6	Mirage	1982
7	Bare Trees	1972
8	Tusk	1979
9	Behind the Mask	1990
10	Mystery to Me	1973

Source: *The Popular Music Database*

TOP 10 ★
ROLLING STONES ALBUMS IN THE US

	ALBUM	YEAR
1	Hot Rocks 1964–1971	1972
2	Some Girls	1978
3	Tattoo You	1981
4	Big Hits (High Tide and Green Grass)	1966
5	Let It Bleed	1969
6	Steel Wheels	1989
7	Voodoo Lounge	1994
8	Bridges to Babylon	1997
9	Out of Our Heads	1965
10	Emotional Rescue	1980

Source: *The Popular Music Database*

TOP 10 ★
BRUCE SPRINGSTEEN ALBUMS IN THE US

	ALBUM	YEAR
1	Born in the U.S.A.	1984
2	Bruce Springsteen & the E Street Band Live/1975–85	1986
3	Born to Run	1975
4	The River	1980
5	Tunnel of Love	1987
6	Greatest Hits	1995
7	Darkness on the Edge of Town	1978
8	Greetings from Asbury Park, N.J.	1975
9	Nebraska	1982
10	The Wild, the Innocent & the E Street Shuffle	1975

Source: *The Popular Music Database*

TOP 10 ★
BEATLES SINGLES IN THE US

	SINGLE	YEAR
1	Hey Jude	1968
2	Get Back	1969
3	Something	1969
4	Let It Be	1970
5	The Long and Winding Road	1970
6	I Want to Hold Your Hand	1964
7	Can't Buy Me Love	1964
8	She Loves You	1964
9	I Feel Fine	1964
10	Help!	1965

Source: *The Popular Music Database*

The top four titles here were all certified with 2 million-plus sales in 1999.

THE BOSS

Bruce Springsteen was inducted into the Rock and Roll Hall of Fame in 1999 after 25 years of recording.

TOP 10 ★
JOHN LENNON SINGLES IN THE US

	SINGLE	YEAR
1	*(Just Like) Starting Over*	1980
2	*Woman*	1981
3	*Whatever Gets You Thru the Night*	1974
4	*Imagine*	1971
5	*Instant Karma (We All Shine on)*	1970
6	*Give Peace a Chance*	1969
7	*Happy Xmas (War is Over)*	1971
8	*Nobody Told Me*	1984
9	*#9 Dream*	1974
10	*Power to the People*	1971

Source: MRIB

John Lennon began his extracurricular recording projects during the year before the Beatles actually split up: *Give Peace a Chance* appeared in 1969, credited to the Plastic Ono Band. *Imagine* was a hit twice, the second occasion being immediately after Lennon's death. *Nobody Told Me* was a posthumous Top 10 chart entry just over four years after he died.

JOHN LENNON

Born during a Nazi bombing of Liverpool, John Lennon grew to condemn the insanity of war in pacifistic songs such as Give Peace a Chance.

TOP 10 ★
ELVIS PRESLEY SINGLES IN THE US

	SINGLE	YEAR
1	*Don't Be Cruel/Hound Dog*	1956
2	*It's Now or Never*	1960
3	*Love Me Tender*	1956
4	*Heartbreak Hotel*	1956
5	*Jailhouse Rock*	1957
6	*All Shook Up*	1957
7	*(Let Me Be Your) Teddy Bear*	1957
8	*Are You Lonesome Tonight?*	1960
9	*Don't*	1958
10	*Too Much*	1957

Source: *MRIB*

Elvis had dozens of million-selling singles, scattered throughout his career, but most of his absolute monster hits were during his 1950s heyday when he was the spearhead of rock 'n roll music. The inspired coupling of *Don't Be Cruel* and *Hound Dog*, which held the No. 1 spot for almost a quarter of 1956, sold some 6 million copies in the US alone.

TOP 10 ★
MADONNA ALBUMS IN THE US

	ALBUM	YEAR
1	*Like a Virgin*	1984
2	*True Blue*	1986
3	*The Immaculate Collection*	1990
4	*Like a Prayer*	1989
5	*Ray of Light*	1998
6	*Madonna*	1983
7	*Erotica*	1992
8	*Bedtime Stories*	1994
9	*Something to Remember*	1990
10	*I'm Breathless*	1987

Source: *The Popular Music Database*

Did You Know? The top five Fleetwood Mac albums all date from the years 1974–87 and feature Lindsey Buckingham. After he left in 1987, the band never achieved quite the same level of success.

POP STARS OF THE '90S

BOYZ II MEN SINGLES IN THE US

SINGLE	YEAR
1 I'll Make Love to You	1994
2 End of the Road	1992
3 On Bended Knee	1994
4 4 Seasons of Loneliness	1997
5 It's So Hard to Say Goodbye to Yesterday	1991
6 Motownphilly	1991
7 In the Still of the Nite	1992
8 Water Runs Dry	1995
9 A Song for Mama	1997
10 Uhh Ahh	1991

TOP 10 ★

PRINCE SINGLES IN THE US

SINGLE	YEAR
1 Cream	1991
2 The Most Beautiful Girl in the World	1994
3 7	1992
4 Thieves in the Temple	1990
5 Gett Off	1991
6 Diamonds and Pearls	1991
7 I Hate U	1995
8 Money Don't Matter 2 Night	1992
9 Letitgo	1994
10 My Name Is Prince	1992

TOP 10 ★

CELINE DION SINGLES IN THE US

SINGLE	YEAR
1 The Power of Love	1993
2 Because You Loved Me	1996
3 It's All Coming Back to Me	1996
4 My Heart Will Go On	1998
5 Where Does My Heart Beat Now	1990
6 If You Asked Me To	1992
7 All by Myself	1997
8 Beauty and the Beast	1992
9 When I Fall in Love	1993
10 Misled	1994

TOP 10 ★

WHITNEY HOUSTON SINGLES IN THE US

SINGLE	YEAR
1 I Will Always Love You	1992
2 Exhale (Shoop Shoop)	1995
3 I'm Your Baby Tonight	1990
4 All the Man That I Need	1990
5 I'm Every Woman	1993
6 I Have Nothing	1993
7 I Believe in You and Me	1996
8 Miracle	1991
9 My Name Is Not Susan	1991
10 Run to You	1993

TOP 10 ★

MICHAEL BOLTON SINGLES IN THE US

SINGLE	YEAR
1 Said I Loved You ... But I Lied	1993
2 When a Man Loves a Woman	1991
3 Time, Love and Tenderness	1991
4 To Love Somebody	1992
5 Love Is a Wonderful Thing	1991
6 How Can We Be Lovers	1990
7 When I'm Back on My Feet Again	1990
8 Missing You Now	1992
9 Go the Distance	1997
10 Can I Touch You ... There?	1995

TOP 10 ★

JANET JACKSON SINGLES IN THE US

SINGLE	YEAR
1 Again	1993
2 That's the Way Love Goes	1993
3 Together Again	1997
4 Love Will Never Do Without You	1990
5 Escapade	1990
6 Black Cat	1990
7 Runaway	1995
8 If	1993
9 You Want This	1994
10 Any Time, Any Place	1994

TOP 10 SPICE GIRLS SINGLES IN THE UK

(Single/year)

1 Wannabe, 1996 2 2 Become 1, 1996
3 Too Much, 1997 4 Goodbye, 1998
5 Say You'll Be There, 1996 6 Spice up Your Life, 1997 7 Viva Forever, 1998
8 Mama/Who Do You Think You Are, 1997
9 Stop, 1998 10 When You're Gone
(Bryan Adams featuring Melanie C), 1998

TOP 10 GEORGE MICHAEL SINGLES OF THE 1990s IN THE UK

(Single/year)

1 Outside, 1998 2 Fast Love, 1996
3 Jesus to a Child, 1996 4 You Have Been Loved/The Strangest Thing '97, 1997
5 Star People '97, 1997 6 Spinning the Wheel, 1996
7 Older/I Can't Make You Love Me, 1997 8 Too Funky, 1992
9 Praying for Time, 1990 10 Freedom, 1990

Background image: FENDER STRATOCASTER GUITAR

TOP 10 ★
MADONNA SINGLES IN THE US

	SINGLE	YEAR
1	Vogue	1990
2	Justify My Love	1990
3	Take a Bow	1994
4	This Used to Be My Playground	1992
5	Erotica	1992
6	Secret	1994
7	I'll Remember	1994
8	You'll See	1995
9	Ray of Light	1998
10	Frozen	1998

TOP 10 ★
MARIAH CAREY SINGLES IN THE US

	SINGLE	YEAR
1	Hero	1993
2	Always Be My Baby	1996
3	Fantasy	1995
4	My All	1997
5	Honey	1997
6	Dreamlover	1993
7	Love Takes Time	1990
8	Vision of Love	1990
9	Someday	1991
10	Without You	1994

TOP 10 ★
CHER SINGLES OF THE 1990s IN THE UK

	SINGLE	YEAR
1	Believe	1998
2	The Shoop Shoop Song (It's in His Kiss)	1991
3	One by One	1996
4	Love and Understanding	1991
5	Walking in Memphis	1995
6	Just Like Jesse James	1990
7	Oh No Not My Baby	1992
8	Love Hurts	1991
9	Could've Been You	1992
10	The Sun Ain't Gonna Shine Anymore	1996

THANKS FOR CHER-ING

The ability to reinvent herself and change her style to match the times is surely the reason why Cher's musical career has spanned four decades and shows no signs of slowing. She is also an Oscar-winning actress.

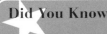

Did You Know? The original lineup of the band Pulp formed in 1979 while its leader, Jarvis Cocker, was still at school. Early shows were performed during lunch breaks in the school cafeteria.

151

MUSIC GENRES

★ TOP 10 ★

GREATEST HITS ALBUMS IN THE US

ALBUM	ARTIST OR GROUP	APPROX. SALES
1 Their Greatest Hits, 1971–1975	The Eagles	25,000,000
2 Greatest Hits	Elton John	15,000,000
3 Greatest Hits	Kenny Rogers	12,000,000
4 James Taylor's Greatest Hits	James Taylor	11,000,000
5 = Best of The Doobies	The Doobie Brothers	10,000,000
= The Hits	Garth Brooks	10,000,000
= Greatest Hits	Journey	10,000,000
8 = Aerosmith's Greatest Hits	Aerosmith	9,000,000
= Greatest Hits Volumes I & II	Billy Joel	9,000,000
= Greatest Hits, Volume II	The Eagles	9,000,000
= Legend	Bob Marley & The Wailers	9,000,000

Source: *RIAA*

STARTING YOUNG

Kenny Rogers' first million-seller was Crazy Feeling *in 1957, when he was only 19, but* Lucille *was the hit that made him an international country star.*

JAZZ GIANT

Harry Connick, Jr.'s combination of jazz with Big Band, American classics, and New Orleans funk has won nominations for Oscars, Grammys, and Emmys, as well as ensuring a high place on both jazz and pop charts.

★ TOP 10 ★

JAZZ ALBUMS OF ALL TIME IN THE US

ALBUM/ARTIST OR GROUP	YEAR
1 *Time Out Featuring Take Five*, Dave Brubeck Quartet.	1960
2 *Hello Dolly*, Louis Armstrong	1991
3 *Getz & Gilberto*, Stan Getz and Joao Gilberto	1992
4 *Sun Goddess*, Ramsey Lewis	1979
5 *Jazz Samba*, Stan Getz and Charlie Byrd	1977
6 *Bitches Brew*, Miles Davies	1987
7 *In the Crowd*, Ramsey Lewis Trio	1962
8 *Time Further Out*, Dave Brubeck Quartet.	1963
9 *Mack the Knife – Ella in Berlin*, Ella Fitzgerald	1963
10 *Exodus to Jazz*, Eddie Harris	1960

Source: *MRIB*

Dave Brubeck's *Time Out* album spent 86 weeks in the American Top 40 between 1960 and 1962, an unprecedented achievement for a jazz album during the era and due, not least, to the huge popularity of the track featured in its full title, *Take Five*, which hit US No. 25 on the pop chart. The quartet comprised Brubeck (b. David Warren) on piano, Joe Morello (drums), Eugene Wright (bass), and Paul Desmond (alto sax).

★ TOP 10 ★

COUNTRY SINGLES IN THE US

SINGLE	ARTIST
1 *How Do I Live*	LeAnn Rimes
2 *Islands in the Stream*	Kenny Rogers and Dolly Parton
3 *This Kiss*	Faith Hill
4 *You're Still the One*	Shania Twain
5 *Elvira*	Oak Ridge Boys
6 *Achy Breaky Heart*	Billy Ray Cyrus
7 *The Devil Went Down to Georgia*	Charlie Daniels Band
8 *Always on My Mind*	Willie Nelson
9 *It's Your Love*	Tim McGraw with Faith Hill
10 *Convoy*	C.W. McCall

Source: *The Popular Music Database*

★ TOP 10 ★

RAP SINGLES IN THE US

SINGLE	ARTIST OR GROUP	APPROX. SALES
1 *Whoomp! (There It Is)*	Tag Team	4,000,000
2 *I'll be Missing You*	Puff Daddy & Faith Evans (featuring 112)	3,000,000
3 *How Do U Want It*	2Pac	2,000,000
= *Tha Crossroads*	Bone Thugs-N-Harmony	2,000,000
= *Gangsta's Paradise*	Coolio featuring L.V.	2,000,000
= *Dazzey Duks*	Duice	2,000,000
= *O.P.P.*	Naughty By Nature	2,000,000
= *Baby Got Back*	Sir Mix-A-Lot	2,000,000
= *Wild Thing*	Tone Loc	2,000,000
= *Jump*	Kris Kross	2,000,000
= *Rump Shaker*	Wreckx-N-Effect	2,000,000

Source: *RIAA*

 What was the bestselling album in the world in 1998?
see p.155 for the answer

A *Titanic* (Soundtrack)
B *Ray of Light* (Madonna)
C *Hello Nasty* (Beastie Boys)

TOP 10 ORIGINAL SOUNDTRACK ALBUMS IN THE US

1 *Saturday Night Fever* 2 *The Bodyguard* 3 *Purple Rain* 4 *Dirty Dancing* 5 *Titanic* 6 *The Lion King* 7 *Footloose* 8 *Waiting to Exhale* 9 *Top Gun* 10 *The Big Chill*

Source: *The Popular Music Database*

TOP 10 ORIGINAL SOUNDTRACK ALBUMS IN THE UK

(Album/year)

1 *The Sound of Music*, 1965 2 *Saturday Night Fever*, 1978 3 *The Bodyguard*, 1992 4 *Grease*, 1978 5 *Dirty Dancing*, 1987 6 *South Pacific*, 1958 7 *West Side Story*, 1962 8 *Top Gun*, 1986 9 *A Star is Born*, 1977 10 *Fame*, 1980

Source: *MRIB*

TOP 10 ★
COUNTRY ALBUMS IN THE US

	ALBUM	ARTIST	APPROX. SALES
1	*No Fences*	Garth Brooks	16,000,000
2	*Ropin' the Wind*	Garth Brooks	14,000,000
3	*Greatest Hits*	Kenny Rogers	12,000,000
4	*The Woman in Me*	Shania Twain	11,000,000
5	*The Hits*	Garth Brooks	10,000,000
6 =	*Some Gave All*	Billy Ray Cyrus	9,000,000
=	*Garth Brooks*	Garth Brooks	9,000,000
8 =	*Greatest Hits*	Patsy Cline	8,000,000
=	*Come on Over*	Shania Twain	8,000,000
=	*In Pieces*	Garth Brooks	8,000,000
=	*The Chase*	Garth Brooks	8,000,000

Source: *RIAA*

MELODIC METAL

Bon Jovi, fronted by singer-turned-actor Jon Bon Jovi, has moved from tuneful heavy metal to pop and ballads, and achieved multiplatinum sales with Slippery When Wet.

TOP 10 ★
HEAVY METAL ALBUMS IN THE US

	ALBUM	ARTIST OR GROUP	APPROX. SALES
1 =	*Back in Black*	AC/DC	16,000,000
=	*Boston*	Boston	16,000,000
3	*Bat out of Hell*	Meat Loaf	13,000,000
4 =	*Slippery When Wet*	Bon Jovi	12,000,000
=	*Hysteria*	Def Leppard	12,000,000
6	*Metallica*	Metallica	11,000,000
7 =	*Van Halen*	Van Halen	10,000,000
=	*Eliminator*	ZZ Top	10,000,000
9 =	*Pyromania*	Def Leppard	9,000,000
=	*Aerosmith's Greatest Hits*	Aerosmith	9,000,000
=	*1984*	Van Halen	9,000,000

Source: *RIAA*

TOP 10 ★
HEAVY METAL SINGLES IN THE US

	SINGLE	ARTIST OR GROUP
1	*Eye of the Tiger*	Survivor
2	*Keep on Loving You*	REO Speedwagon
3	*I Love Rock 'n' Roll*	Joan Jett & the Blackhearts
4	*Always*	Bon Jovi
5	*I'd Do Anything for Love (But I Won't Do That)*	Meat Loaf
6	*Blaze of Glory*	Jon Bon Jovi
7	*Sweet Child O' Mine*	Guns 'N Roses
8	*Jump*	Van Halen
9	*You Ain't Seen Nothing Yet/Free Wheelin'*	Bachman Turner Overdrive
10	*Dr. Feelgood*	Motley Crue

Source: *The Popular Music Database*

WORLD MUSIC

TOP 10 ★
IRISH ALBUMS IN THE UK

ALBUM/GROUP	YEAR
1 *The Joshua Tree*, U2	1987
2 *Where We Belong*, Boyzone	1998
3 *Watermark*, Enya	1988
4 *Shepherd Moons*, Enya	1991
5 *Rattle and Hum*, U2	1988
6 *Achtung Baby!*, U2	1991
7 *Said and Done*, Boyzone	1995
8 *U2 Live – Under a Blood Red Sky*, U2	1983
9 *No Need to Argue*, Cranberries	1994
10 *A Different Beat*, Boyzone	1996

Source: *The Popular Music Database*

PERFECT POP

Together since 1977, U2, the sincere stadium rockers, have had consistently huge record sales since their first album Boy in the early 1980s – though critical acclaim has been patchy.

TOP 10 ★
REGGAE ALBUMS IN THE US, 1998

ALBUM	ARTIST OR GROUP
1 *Many Moods of Moses*	Beenie Man
2 *Reggae Gold 1998*	Various
3 *Pure Reggae*	Various
4 *Inna Heights*	Buju Banton
5 *Best of Bob Marley*	Bob Marley
6 *Strictly the Best 19*	Various
7 *Reggae Gold 1997*	Various
8 *Maverick a Strike*	Finley Quaye
9 *Think Like a Girl*	Diana King
10 *Midnight Lover*	Shaggy

Source: *Billboard*

TOP 10 ★
TROPICAL/SALSA ALBUMS IN THE US, 1998

ALBUM	ARTIST OR GROUP
1 *Buena Vista Social Club*	Buena Vista Social Club
2 *Contra La Corriente*	Marc Anthony
3 *Dance with Me*	Soundtrack
4 *Suavemente*	Elvis Crespo
5 *Sentimientos*	Charlie Zaa
6 *Un Segundo Sentimiento*	Charlie Zaa
7 *Sobre El Fuego*	India
8 *Ironias*	Victor Manuelle
9 *Alto Honor*	Grupo Mania
10 *A Toda Cuba Le Gusta*	Afro-Cuban All Stars

Source: *Billboard*

TOP 10 LATIN POP ALBUMS IN THE US, 1998

(Album/artist or group)

1 *Me Estoy Enamorando*, Alejandro Fernández 2 *Vuelve*, Ricky Martin 3 *Suenos Liquidos*, Maná 4 *Romances*, Luis Miguel 5 *Mas*, Alejandro Sanz 6 *Inolvidable*, Jose Luis Rodriguez with Los Panchos 7 *Cosas Del Amor*, Enrique Iglesias 8 *Donde Estan Los Ladrones?*, Shakira 9 *Lo Mejor De Mi*, Cristian 10 *Compas*, Gipsy Kings

Source: *Billboard*

TOP 10 ⭐
ALBUMS IN THE WORLD, 1998*

ALBUM	ARTIST OR GROUP
1 Ray of Light	Madonna
2 Hello Nasty	Beastie Boys
3 Armageddon	Soundtrack
4 Adore	Smashing Pumpkins
5 Titanic	Soundtrack
6 Let's Talk About Love	Celine Dion
7 Vuelve	Ricky Martin
8 Back for Good	Modern Talking
9 City of Angels	Soundtrack
10 Talk on Corners	The Corrs

* Based on CNN's "Worldbeat" album chart, launched on June 6, 1998

Source: *The Popular Music Database*

TOP 10 ⭐
MUSIC MARKETS

COUNTRY	SALES 1998 ($)
1 US	13,193,400,000
2 Japan	6,521,000,000
3 UK	2,855,600,000
4 Germany	2,832,500,000
5 France	2,134,800,000
6 Brazil	1,055,700,000
7 Canada	969,300,000
8 Spain	680,700,000
9 Australia	606,700,000
10 Italy	597,700,000

Source: *International Federation of the Phonographic Industry*

BRAT ROCKERS
The ultimate middle-class rebels, the Beastie Boys are known for their loud, brash mixture of rap, punk, and heavy metal.

TOP 10 ⭐
WORLD MUSIC ALBUMS IN THE US, 1998

ALBUM	ARTIST OR GROUP
1 Romanza	Andrea Bocelli
2 The Book of Secrets	Loreena McKennitt
3 Buena Vista Social Club	Buena Vista Social Club
4 Celtic Christmas III	Various
5 Celtic Moods	Various
6 Riverdance	Bill Whelan
7 Michael Flatley's Lord of the Dance	Ronan Hardiman
8 Deep Forest III – Comparasa	Deep Forest
9 Compas	Gipsy Kings
10 Mamaloshen	Mandy Patinkin

Source: Billboard

SIMPLY ADORABLE
Adore has been the Smashing Pumpkins' biggest seller since their 1995 double-CD album Mellon Collie and the Infinite Sadness.

What was the first ever Grammy Record of the Year?
see p.161 for the answer

A *Moon River* (Henry Mancini)
B *Mack the Knife* (Bobby Darin)
C *Nel Blu Dipinto di Blu (Volare)* (Domenico Modugno)

GOLD & PLATINUM DISCS

FEMALE ARTISTS WITH THE MOST GOLD ALBUMS IN THE US

ARTIST	GOLD ALBUMS
1 Barbra Streisand	40
2 Reba McEntire	19
3 Linda Ronstadt	17
4 Olivia Newton-John	15
5 =Aretha Franklin	13
=Madonna	13
=Dolly Parton	13
8 =Gloria Estefan*	12
=Anne Murray	12
=Tanya Tucker	12

* Includes hits with Miami Sound Machine
Source: RIAA

MALE ARTISTS WITH THE MOST GOLD ALBUMS IN THE US

ARTIST	GOLD ALBUMS
1 Elvis Presley	62
2 Neil Diamond	35
3 Elton John	32
4 Kenny Rogers	28
5 Frank Sinatra	26
6 Bob Dylan	24
7 =George Strait	23
=Willie Nelson	23
9 Hank Williams, Jr.	21
10=Paul McCartney/Wings	20
=Rod Stewart	20

Source: RIAA

SYMBOLISM

Born Prince Rogers Nelson in Minneapolis, one of The Artist's previous incarnations was as ... Prince. A talented musician, he played almost all the instruments on his debut album.

FEMALE ARTISTS WITH THE MOST PLATINUM ALBUMS IN THE UK

ARTIST	PLATINUM ALBUMS
1 Madonna	34
2 Celine Dion	19
3 Whitney Houston	18
4 Tina Turner	17
5 =Enya	12
=Gloria Estefan	12
7 =Kylie Minogue	10
=Mariah Carey	10
=Alanis Morissette	10
10 Kate Bush	9

Source: BPI

TOP 10 MALE ARTISTS WITH THE MOST GOLD ALBUMS IN THE UK

(Artist/gold albums)

❶ = Elton John, 20; = Cliff Richard, 20 ❸ Rod Stewart, 19 ❹ = Neil Diamond, 17; = James Last, 17; = Paul McCartney*, 17 ❼ Mike Oldfield, 16 ❽ = David Bowie, 15; = Elvis Presley, 15 ❿ Prince, 13

* Including gold albums with Wings
Source: RIAA

TOP 10 FEMALE ARTISTS WITH THE MOST GOLD ALBUMS IN THE UK

(Artist/gold albums)

❶ Diana Ross, 17 ❷ = Barbra Streisand, 12; = Madonna, 12 ❹ Donna Summer, 9 ❺ Mariah Carey, 8 ❻ = Kate Bush, 7; = Tina Turner, 7 ❽ = Joan Armatrading, 6; = Janet Jackson, 6; = Cher, 6; = Celine Dion, 6

Source: BPI

TOP 10 ★
FEMALE ARTISTS WITH THE MOST PLATINUM ALBUMS IN THE US

	ARTIST	PLATINUM ALBUMS
1	Barbra Streisand	49
2	Madonna	47
3 =	Whitney Houston	45
=	Mariah Carey	45
5	Celine Dion	34
6	Reba McEntire	24
7	Linda Ronstadt	23
8 =	Janet Jackson	19
=	Shania Twain	19
10 =	Sade	18
=	Gloria Estefan	18

Source: *RIAA*

TOP 10 ★
MALE ARTISTS WITH THE MOST PLATINUM ALBUMS IN THE US

	ARTIST	PLATINUM ALBUMS
1	Garth Brooks	95
2	Billy Joel	69
3	Elton John	58
4	Michael Jackson	51
5	Bruce Springsteen	49
6	Kenny Rogers	45
7	Elvis Presley	43
8	Kenny G	40
9	George Strait	37
10	Neil Diamond	35

A US platinum award represents a ratio of one sale per 266 inhabitants. In the UK, it represents approximately one sale per 195 inhabitants.
Source: *BPI*

PRESIDENTIAL CHOICE
Famous for their ever-changing lineup, Fleetwood Mac derives their name from the only two consistent members of the band: drummer Mick Fleetwood and bass player John McVie. The band played at President Bill Clinton's inauguration in January 1993.

TOP 10 ★
GROUPS WITH THE MOST PLATINUM ALBUMS IN THE US

	GROUP	PLATINUM ALBUMS
1	The Beatles	90
2	Led Zeppelin	80
3	Pink Floyd	66
4	The Eagles	62
5	Aerosmith	51
6	Van Halen	50
7	Fleetwood Mac	46
8	Alabama	44
9 =	AC/DC	42
=	U2	42

Source: *The Popular Music Database*

TOP 10 ★
GROUPS WITH THE MOST GOLD ALBUMS IN THE US

	GROUP	GOLD ALBUMS
1	The Beatles	39
2	The Rolling Stones	37
3	Kiss	23
4	Rush	22
5	Aerosmith	21
6 =	Alabama	20
=	Chicago	20
=	Jefferson Airplane/Starship	20
9	The Beach Boys	18
10	AC/DC	17

Source: *BPI*

Which song from a film won the Oscar for "Best Song" in 1989?
see p.159 for the answer

A *Take My Breath Away (Top Gun)*
B *Under the Sea (The Little Mermaid)*
C *Let the River Run (Working Girl)*

MOVIE MUSIC

THE 10 ★ "BEST SONG" OSCAR WINNERS OF THE 1950s

YEAR	TITLE/MOVIE
1950	*Mona Lisa*, Captain Carey
1951	*In the Cool, Cool, Cool of the Evening*, Here Comes the Groom
1952	*High Noon (Do Not Forsake Me, Oh My Darling)*, High Noon
1953	*Secret Love*, Calamity Jane
1954	*Three Coins in the Fountain*, Three Coins in the Fountain
1955	*Love is a Many-Splendored Thing*, Love is a Many-Splendored Thing
1956	*Whatever Will Be, Will Be (Que Sera, Sera)*, The Man Who Knew Too Much
1957	*All the Way*, The Joker is Wild
1958	*Gigi*, Gigi
1959	*High Hopes*, A Hole in the Head

Doris Day benefited strongly from these Oscars, scoring million-selling singles with *Secret Love* and *Whatever Will Be, Will Be*, both from movies in which she starred.

GREASE IS THE WORD
Olivia Newton-John and John Travolta starred in the film Grease, *as well as scoring several hit singles from the movie's soundtrack, including* Sandy *and* Hopelessly Devoted (to You).

THE 10 ★ "BEST SONG" OSCAR WINNERS OF THE 1960s

YEAR	TITLE/MOVIE
1960	*Never on Sunday*, Never on Sunday
1961	*Moon River*, Breakfast at Tiffany's
1962	*Days of Wine and Roses*, Days of Wine and Roses
1963	*Call Me Irresponsible*, Papa's Delicate Condition
1964	*Chim Chim Cheree*, Mary Poppins
1965	*The Shadow of Your Smile*, The Sandpiper
1966	*Born Free*, Born Free
1967	*Talk to the Animals*, Dr. Dolittle
1968	*The Windmills of Your Mind*, The Thomas Crown Affair
1969	*Raindrops Keep Fallin' on My Head*, Butch Cassidy and the Sundance Kid

Both *The Windmills of Your Mind* and *Raindrops Keep Fallin' on My Head* hit the US Top 10. Sacha Distel's cover version of the 1969 Oscar winner charted five times in the UK in 1970.

TOP 10 ★ MUSICAL MOVIES*

	TITLE	YEAR
1	*Grease*	1978
2	*Saturday Night Fever*	1977
3	*The Sound of Music*	1965
4	*Footloose*	1984
5	*American Graffiti*	1973
6	*Mary Poppins*	1964
7	*Flashdance*	1983
8	*The Rocky Horror Picture Show*	1975
9	*Coal Miner's Daughter*	1980
10	*My Fair Lady*	1964

* Traditional musicals (in which the cast actually sing) and movies in which a musical soundtrack is a major component of the movie are included

The era of the blockbuster musical may be over, but in recent years animated movies with a strong musical content appear to have taken over, such as *Aladdin* and *The Lion King*.

THE 10 "BEST SONG" OSCAR WINNERS OF THE 1970s

(Year/title/movie)

1 1970, *For All We Know*, Lovers and Other Strangers **2** 1971, *Theme from "Shaft"*, Shaft **3** 1972, *The Morning After*, The Poseidon Adventure **4** 1973, *The Way We Were*, The Way We Were **5** 1974, *We May Never Love Like This Again*, The Towering Inferno **6** 1975, *I'm Easy*, Nashville **7** 1976, *Evergreen*, A Star is Born **8** 1977, *You Light up My Life*, You Light up My Life **9** 1978, *Last Dance*, Thank God It's Friday **10** 1979, *It Goes Like It Goes*, Norma Rae

TINA'S TRIUMPH
What's Love Got to Do with It is based on the life of Tina Turner. In the 1993 movie, actress Angela Bassett offered a convincing portrayal of the pop star.

TOP 10 POP MUSIC MOVIES

1 *The Blues Brothers*, 1980 **2** *Purple Rain*, 1984 **3** *La Bamba*, 1987 **4** *The Doors*, 1991 **5** *What's Love Got to Do with It*, 1993 **6** *Xanadu*, 1980 **7** *The Jazz Singer*, 1980 **8** *Sgt. Pepper's Lonely Hearts Club Band*, 1978 **9** *Lady Sings the Blues*, 1972 **10** *Pink Floyd – The Wall*, 1982

THE 10 ★
"BEST SONG" OSCAR WINNERS OF THE 1980s

YEAR	TITLE/MOVIE
1980	*Fame*, Fame
1981	*Up Where We Belong*, An Officer and a Gentleman
1982	*Arthur's Theme (Best That You Can Do)*, Arthur
1983	*Flashdance What a Feeling*, Flashdance
1984	*I Just Called to Say I Love You*, The Woman in Red
1985	*Say You, Say Me*, White Nights
1986	*Take My Breath Away*, Top Gun
1987	*(I've Had) The Time of My Life*, Dirty Dancing
1988	*Let the River Run*, Working Girl
1989	*Under the Sea*, The Little Mermaid

TOP 10 ★
ARTISTS WITH THE MOST "BEST SONG" OSCAR NOMINATIONS

	ARTIST/WINS/YEARS	NOMINATIONS
1	Sammy Cahn, 4, 1942–75	26
2	Johnny Mercer, 4, 1938–71	18
3 =	Paul Francis Webster, 3, 1944–76	16
=	Alan and Marilyn Bergman, 2, 1968–95	16
5	James Van Heusen, 4, 1944–68	14
6 =	Henry Warren, 3, 1935–57	11
=	Henry Mancini, 2, 1961–86	11
=	Ned Washington, 1, 1940–61	11
9	Alan Menken, 4, 1986–97	10
=	Sammy Fain, 2, 1937–77	10
=	Leo Robin, 1, 1934–53	10
=	Jule Styne, 1, 1940–68	10

It was not until 1934 that the category of "Best Song" was added to the many accolades bestowed on movies. The awards are often multiple, including the writers of the music and the lyrics.

THE 10 ★
LATEST "BEST SONG" OSCAR WINNERS

YEAR	TITLE/MOVIE
1998	*When You Believe*, Prince of Egypt
1997	*My Heart Will Go On*, Titanic
1996	*You Must Love Me*, Evita
1995	*Colors of the Wind*, Pocahontas
1994	*Can You Feel the Love Tonight*, The Lion King
1993	*Streets of Philadelphia*, Philadelphia
1992	*A Whole New World*, Aladdin
1991	*Beauty and the Beast*, Beauty and the Beast
1990	*Sooner or Later (I Always Get My Man)*, Dick Tracy
1989	*Under the Sea*, The Little Mermaid

TOP 10 ★
"BEST SONG" OSCAR-WINNING SINGLES IN THE US

	TITLE/ARTIST OR GROUP	YEAR
1	*You Light up My Life*, Debby Boone	1977
2	*Up Where We Belong*, Joe Cocker and Jennifer Warnes	1982
3	*Love Theme* from *A Star is Born (Evergreen)*, Barbra Streisand	1976
4	*My Heart Will Go On*, Celine Dion	1997
5	*I Just Called to Say I Love You*, Stevie Wonder	1984
6	*Arthur's Theme (Best That You Can Do)*, Christopher Cross	1981
7	*The Way We Were*, Barbra Streisand	1973
8	*A Whole New World*, Peabo Bryson and Regina Belle	1992
9	*Raindrops Keep Fallin' on My Head*, B.J. Thomas	1969
10	*(I've Had) The Time of My Life*, Bill Medley and Jennifer Warnes	1987

Source: *The Popular Music Database*

OSCAR-WINNING SINGER
Pop star and actress Madonna has won Oscars for two songs from movies in which she also starred: Evita (pictured here) and Dick Tracy.

TOP 10 ★
JAMES BOND MOVIE THEMES IN THE US

	TITLE/ARTIST OR GROUP	YEAR
1	*A View To A Kill*, Duran Duran	1985
2	*Nobody Does it Better* (from *The Spy Who Loved Me*), Carly Simon	1977
3	*Live and Let Die*, Paul McCartney and Wings	1973
4	*For Your Eyes Only*, Sheena Easton	1981
5	*Goldfinger*, Shirley Bassey	1965
6	*Thunderball*, Tom Jones	1966
7	*All Time High* (from *Octopussy*)	1983
8	*You Only Live Twice*, Nancy Sinatra	1967
9	*Diamonds Are Forever*, Shirley Bassey	1972
10	*Goldfinger*, John Barry	1965

Did You Know? The movie soundtrack of *Titanic* is the bestselling soundtrack album of all time.

MUSIC AWARDS

THE 10 ★ LATEST RECIPIENTS OF THE SONGWRITERS HALL OF FAME SAMMY CAHN LIFETIME ACHIEVEMENT AWARD

YEAR	ARTIST
1998	Berry Gordy
1997	Vic Damone
1996	Frankie Laine
1995	Steve Lawrence and Eydie Gorme
1994	Lena Horne
1993	Ray Charles
1992	Nat "King" Cole
1991	Gene Autry
1990	B.B. King
1989	Quincy Jones

Source: *National Academy of Popular Music*

THE 10 ★ LATEST INDUCTEES INTO THE ROCK 'N' ROLL HALL OF FAME

1 **Charles Brown** (Early influence category)
2 **Billy Joel**
3 **Paul McCartney**
4 **George Martin** (Non-performer category)
5 **Curtis Mayfield**
6 **Del Shannon**
7 **Dusty Springfield**
8 **Bruce Springsteen**
9 **The Staple Singers**
10 **Bob Wills and his Texas Playboys**

The latest inductees into the Rock 'n' Roll Hall of Fame received the accolade on March 15, 1999, at the Waldorf Astoria Hotel in New York City. They are listed here alphabetically.

THE 10 ★ LATEST INDUCTEES INTO THE COUNTRY MUSIC HALL OF FAME

YEAR	ARTIST*
1998	George Morgan
1998	Elvis Presley
1998	E.W. "Bud" Wendell
1998	Tammy Wynette
1997	Harlan Howard
1997	Cindy Walker
1997	Brenda Lee
1996	Patsy Montana
1996	Buck Owens
1996	Ray Price

* *Listed alphabetically by year*

Source: *Country Music Association*

THE 10 ★ LATEST RECIPIENTS OF THE GRAMMY LIFETIME ACHIEVEMENT AWARD

YEAR	ARTIST*
1999	Johnny Cash
1999	Sam Cooke
1999	Otis Redding
1999	William "Smokey" Robinson
1999	Mel Torme
1998	Bo Diddley
1998	The Mills Brothers
1998	Roy Orbison
1998	Paul Robeson
1998	Frank Zappa

* *Listed alphabetically by year*

Source: *NARAS*

TOP 10 ★ ARTISTS WITH MOST GRAMMY AWARDS

	ARTIST	AWARDS
1	Sir George Solti	31
2	Quincy Jones	26
3	Vladimir Horowitz	25
4	Pierre Boulez	22
5 =	Henry Mancini	20
=	Stevie Wonder	20
7	John Williams	17
8	Leonard Bernstein	16
9 =	Aretha Franklin	15
=	Itzhak Perlman	15

The Grammy Awards ceremony has been held annually in the US since its inauguration on May 4, 1959. The awards are considered to be the most prestigious award in the music industry. The proliferation of classical artists in this Top 10 (not least conductor Sir George Solti) is largely attributable to the large number of classical award categories at the Grammys.

WONDERFUL TALENT

Stevie Wonder is regarded by many as a musical genius. His unique style reflects his gospel background, as well as the influence of jazz, rock, and African rhythms.

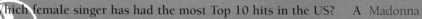
Which female singer has had the most Top 10 hits in the US? *see p.144 for the answer*
A Madonna
B Whitney Houston
C Janet Jackson

STYLISH SINGER

Formerly a backup singer, Sheryl Crow has achieved enormous success and critical acclaim as a singer/songwriter and musician through her creative and soul-baring approach to lyrics and melody.

THE 10 ★
FIRST GRAMMY RECORDS OF THE YEAR

YEAR	RECORD/ARTIST OR GROUP
1958	*Nel Blu Dipinto di Blu (Volare)*, Domenico Modugno
1959	*Mack the Knife*, Bobby Darin
1960	*Theme from A Summer Place*, Percy Faith
1961	*Moon River*, Henry Mancini
1962	*I Left My Heart in San Francisco*, Tony Bennett
1963	*The Days of Wine and Roses*, Henry Mancini
1964	*The Girl from Ipanema*, Stan Getz and Astrud Gilberto
1965	*A Taste of Honey*, Herb Alpert and the Tijuana Brass
1966	*Strangers in the Night*, Frank Sinatra
1967	*Up Up and Away*, 5th Dimension

THE 10 ★
LATEST GRAMMY RECORDS OF THE YEAR

YEAR	RECORD/ARTIST
1999	*My Heart Will Go On*, Celine Dion
1998	*Sunny Came Home*, Shawn Colvin
1997	*Change the World*, Eric Clapton
1996	*Kiss from a Rose*, Seal
1995	*All I Wanna Do*, Sheryl Crow
1994	*I Will Always Love You*, Whitney Houston
1993	*Tears in Heaven*, Eric Clapton
1992	*Unforgettable*, Natalie Cole with Nat "King" Cole
1991	*Another Day in Paradise*, Phil Collins
1990	*The Wind Beneath My Wings*, Bette Midler

TOP 10 MTV VIDEO MUSIC AWARDS WINNERS, 1984–98
(Artist/awards)

1 Madonna, 16* **2** R.E.M., 12*
3 Peter Gabriel, 11* **4** = Aerosmith, 9;
= Janet Jackson, 9* **6** = a-ha, 8;
= Michael Jackson, 8* **8** Smashing
Pumpkins, 7 **9** = Beck, 6; = En Vogue, 6

* Includes Video Vanguard Award

TOP 10 COUNTRY MUSIC AWARDS WINNERS
(Artist/awards)

1 Vince Gill, 15 **2** George Strait, 12
3 Garth Brooks, 11 **4** Roy Clark, 10
5 = Alabama, 9; = Chet Atkins, 9;
= Brooks and Dunn, 9; = Judds, 9
9 = Loretta Lynn, 8; = Ronnie Milsap, 8;
= Willie Nelson, 8; = Dolly Parton, 8;
= Ricky Skaggs, 8

The Country Music Awards are the most prestigious Country awards, held as an annual ceremony since 1967. Veteran Country instrumentalist Roy Clark netted the Instrumentalist of the Year award for seven consecutive years between 1974 and 1980.

SEAL OF APPROVAL

Kiss from a Rose, *used on the* Batman Forever *soundtrack, sent Seal's album,* Seal, *multiplatinum, selling 4 million copies in the US alone, and remaining in the charts for 45 weeks.*

CLASSICAL & OPERA

THE 10 ★
LATEST WINNERS OF THE "BEST CLASSICAL ALBUM" GRAMMY AWARD

YEAR	COMPOSER/TITLE	CONDUCTOR/SOLOIST/ORCHESTRA
1999	Barber, *Prayers of Kierkegaard*/ Vaughan Williams, *Dona Nobis Pacem*/ Bartók, *Cantata Profana*	Robert Shaw, Richard Clement, Nathan Gunn, Atlanta Symphony Orchestra and chorus
1998	Danielpour, Kirchner, Rouse, *Premières – Cello Concertos*	Yo-Yo Ma, David Zinman, Philadelphia Orchestra
1997	Corigliano, *Of Rage and Remembrance*	Leonard Slatkin, National Symphony Orchestra
1996	Claude Debussy, *La Mer*	Pierre Boulez, Cleveland Orchestra
1995	Béla Bartók, *Concerto for Orchestra; Four Orchestral Pieces, Op. 12*	Pierre Boulez, Chicago Symphony Orchestra
1994	Béla Bartók, *The Wooden Prince*	Pierre Boulez, Chicago Symphony Orchestra and Chorus
1993	Gustav Mahler, *Symphony No. 9*	Leonard Bernstein, Berlin Philharmonic Orchestra
1992	Leonard Bernstein, *Candide*	Leonard Bernstein, London Symphony Orchestra
1991	Charles Ives, *Symphony No. 2* (and *Three Short Works*)	Leonard Bernstein, New York Philharmonic Orchestra
1990	Béla Bartók, *Six String Quartets*	Emerson String Quartet

Source: *NARAS*

The three consecutive awards to Leonard Bernstein in 1991–93 brought his overall Grammy tally to 16.

THREE OF THE BEST

The Three Tenors – Placido Domingo, José Carreras, and Luciano Pavarotti – have brought excerpts of opera and other popular pieces to an audience of billions worldwide.

THE 10 ★
LATEST WINNERS OF THE "BEST OPERA RECORDING" GRAMMY AWARD

YEAR	COMPOSER/TITLE	SOLOISTS/ORCHESTRA
1999	Béla Bartók, *Bluebeard's Castle*	Jessye Norman, Laszlo Polgar, Karl-August Naegler, Chicago Symphony Orchestra
1998	Richard Wagner, *Die Meistersinger von Nürnberg*	Ben Heppner, Herbert Lippert, Karita Mattila, Alan Opie, Rene Pape, Jose van Dam, Iris Vermillion, Chicago Symphony Chorus, Chicago Symphony Orchestra
1997	Benjamin Britten, *Peter Grimes*	Philip Langridge, Alan Opie, Janice Watson, Opera London, London Symphony Chorus, City of London Sinfonia
1996	Hector Berlioz, *Les Troyens*	Charles Dutoit, Orchestra Symphonie de Montreal
1995	Carlisle Floyd, *Susannah*	Jerry Hadley, Samuel Ramey, Cheryl Studer, Kenn Chester
1994	George Handel, *Semele*	Kathleen Battle, Marilyn Horne, Samuel Ramey, Sylvia McNair, Michael Chance
1993	Richard Strauss, *Die Frau Ohne Schatten*	Placido Domingo, Jose Van Dam, Hildegard Behrens
1992	Richard Wagner, *Götterdämmerung*	Hildegard Behrens, Ekkehard Wlashiha
1991	Richard Wagner, *Das Rheingold*	James Morris, Kurt Moll, Christa Ludwig
1990	Richard Wagner, *Die Walküre*	Gary Lakes, Jessye Norman, Kurt Moll

Source: *NARAS*

TOP 10 LONGEST OPERAS PERFORMED AT THE ROYAL OPERA HOUSE, COVENT GARDEN

(Opera/composer/running time* in hrs:mins)

1. **Götterdämmerung**, Richard Wagner, 6:0
2. **Die Meistersinger von Nürnberg**, Richard Wagner, 5:40
3. **Siegfried**, Richard Wagner, 5:25
4. **Tristan und Isolde**, Richard Wagner, 5:19
5. **Die Walküre**, Richard Wagner, 5:15
6. **Parsifal**, Richard Wagner, 5:09
7. **Donnerstag aus Licht**, Karlheinz Stockhausen, 4:42
8. **Lohengrin**, Richard Wagner, 4:26
9. **Der Rosenkavalier**, Richard Strauss, 4:25
10. **Don Carlo**, Giuseppe Verdi, 4:19

* *Including intermissions*

TOP 10 MOST PROLIFIC CLASSICAL COMPOSERS

(Composer/nationality/hours of music)

1 Joseph Haydn (1732–1809), Austrian, 340 **2** George Handel (1685–1759), German–English, 303 **3** Wolfgang Amadeus Mozart (1756–91), Austrian, 202 **4** Johann Sebastian Bach (1685–1750), German, 175 **5** Franz Schubert (1797–1828), German, 134 **6** Ludwig van Beethoven (1770–1827), German, 120 **7** Henry Purcell (1659–95), English, 116 **8** Giuseppe Verdi (1813–1901), Italian, 87 **9** Anton Dvořák (1841–1904), Czech, 79 **10** = Franz Liszt (1811–86), Hungarian, 76; = Peter Tchaikovsky (1840–93), Russian, 76

This list is based on a survey conducted by *Classical Music*, which ranked classical composers by the total number of hours of music each composed.

TOP 10 LARGEST OPERA HOUSES

(Opera house/location/total capacity)*

1 The Metropolitan Opera, New York, 4,065 **2** Cincinnati Opera, Cincinnati, 3,630 **3** Lyric Opera of Chicago, Chicago, 3,563 **4** San Francisco Opera, San Francisco, 3,476 **5** The Dallas Opera, Dallas, 3,420 **6** Canadian Opera Company, Toronto, Canada, 3,167 **7** Los Angeles Music Center Opera, Los Angeles, 3,098 **8** San Diego Opera, San Diego, 3,076 **9** Seattle Opera, Seattle, 3,017 **10** L'Opéra de Montréal, Montreal, Canada, 2,874

* Seating plus standing, where applicable

CLASSICAL SOUNDTRACK
The Philadelphia Orchestra's conductor, Leopold Stokowski, led the recording of the 1939 soundtrack of Fantasia; it was digitally remastered for the film's 50th anniversary.

TOP 10 ⭐ CLASSICAL ALBUMS IN THE UK

TITLE/PERFORMER/ORCHESTRA

1 *The Essential Pavarotti*, Luciano Pavarotti

2 *The Three Tenors in Concert*, Carreras, Domingo, Pavarotti

3 *Vivaldi: The Four Seasons*, Nigel Kennedy/English Chamber Orchestra

4 *The Essential Mozart*, Various

5 *Essential Opera*, Various

6 *The Three Tenors – In Concert 1994*, Pavarotti, Mehta, Carreras, Domingo

7 *Mendelssohn/Bruch Violin Concertos*, Nigel Kennedy/English Chamber Orchestra

8 *Brahms: Violin Concerto*, Nigel Kennedy/New Philharmonia Orchestra

9 *Górecki: Symphony No. 3*, London Sinfonia/David Zinman

10 *The Essential Pavarotti, 2*, Luciano Pavarotti

Source: *MRIB*

TOP 10 ⭐ CLASSICAL ALBUMS IN THE US

TITLE/PERFORMER/ORCHESTRA

1 *The Three Tenors in Concert*, Carreras, Domingo, Pavarotti

2 *Chant*, Benedictine Monks of Santo Domingo De Silos

3 *In Concert*, Carreras, Domingo, Pavarotti

4 *Tchaikovsky: Piano Concerto No. 1*, Van Cliburn

5 *Fantasia (50th Anniversary Edition)*, Soundtrack, Philadelphia Orchestra

6 *Perhaps Love*, Placido Domingo

7 *Amadeus*, Neville Marriner

8 *O Holy Night*, Luciano Pavarotti

9 *Tchaikovsky: 1812 Overture/Capriccio Italien*, Antal Dorati/Minneapolis Symphony Orchestra

10 *Switched-On Bach*, Walter Carlos

The *Fantasia* soundtrack contained short pieces or excerpts by a number of composers, including Bach, Beethoven, and Stravinsky. According to some criteria, the soundtrack album of *Titanic* is regarded as a "classical" album; if accepted as such, it would appear at No. 1 in this Top 10.

STAGE & SCREEN

ALL THE WORLD'S A STAGE

MOVIES OF SHAKESPEARE PLAYS

	MOVIE	YEAR
1	William Shakespeare's Romeo & Juliet	1996
2	Romeo and Juliet	1968
3	Much Ado About Nothing	1993
4	Hamlet	1990
5	Henry V	1989
6	Hamlet	1996
7	Richard III	1995
8	Othello	1995
9	The Taming of the Shrew	1967
10	Hamlet	1948

The romantic appeal of Romeo and Juliet has ensured its appearance in first and second places, with movies directed by Baz Luhrmann and Franco Zeffirelli respectively. If all the films of his plays are considered, William Shakespeare could be regarded as the most prolific movie writer of all time, with well over 300 cinematic versions made in a period of almost 100 years.

MOST PRODUCED PLAYS BY SHAKESPEARE

	PLAY	PRODUCTIONS
1	Twelfth Night	75
2	Hamlet	74
3 =	As You Like It	72
=	The Taming of the Shrew	72
5 =	Much Ado About Nothing	68
=	The Merchant of Venice	68
7	A Midsummer Night's Dream	66
8	Macbeth	60
9	The Merry Wives of Windsor	58
10	Romeo and Juliet	56

This Top 10 list, based on analyses of productions staged during the period from December 31, 1878 to April 30, 1998 at Stratford-upon-Avon, and by the Royal Shakespeare Company in London and on tour, provides a reasonable picture of Shakespeare's most popular plays.

STAR-CROSSED LOVERS
Clare Danes and Leonardo DiCaprio starred as the doomed lovers in the 1996 movie version of Romeo and Juliet, directed by Baz Luhrmann.

TOP 10 MOST-FILMED PLAYS BY SHAKESPEARE

1. Hamlet 2. Romeo and Juliet
3. Macbeth 4. A Midsummer Night's Dream 5. Julius Caesar 6. Othello
7. Richard III 8. Henry V
9. The Merchant of Venice
10. Antony and Cleopatra

Counting modern versions, including those in foreign languages, but discounting made-for-TV movies, parodies, and derivative stories, Hamlet appears to be the most-filmed of Shakespeare's works (70 releases to date), while Romeo and Juliet has been remade on at least 40 occasions.

LATEST WINNERS OF THE LAURENCE OLIVIER AWARD FOR BEST PLAY*

YEAR	PLAY	PLAYWRIGHT
1999	The Weir	Conor McPherson
1998	Closer	Patrick Marber
1997	Stanley	Pam Gems
1996	Skylight	David Hare
1995	Broken Glass	Arthur Miller
1994	Arcadia	Tom Stoppard
1993	Six Degrees of Separation	John Guare
1992	Death and the Maiden	Ariel Dorfman
1991	Dancing at Lughnasa	Brian Friel
1990	Racing Demon	David Hare

* "BBC Award for Best Play" until 1996; "Best New Play" thereafter

 Did You Know? If stories derived from Shakespeare's plays were taken into account, West Side Story (1961), based on Romeo and Juliet, would be second in the list of Top 10 movies made of his plays; Shakespeare in Love (1998), which focuses on the same play, would come first.

TOP 10 ★
LONGEST-RUNNING SHOWS ON BROADWAY

	SHOW	PERFORMANCES
1	*Cats* (1982–)	6,880*
2	*A Chorus Line* (1975–90)	6,137
3	*Oh! Calcutta!* (1976–89)	5,959
4	*Les Misérables* (1987–)	4,962*
5	*The Phantom of the Opera* (1988–)	4,692*
6	*42nd Street* (1980–89)	3,486
7	*Grease* (1972–80)	3,338
8	*Miss Saigon* (1991–)	3,303*
9	*Fiddler on the Roof* (1964–72)	3,242
10	*Life with Father* (1939–47)	3,224

* *Still running; total as at March 31, 1999*
Source: Playbill

Cats became the longest running Broadway show of all time on June 19, 1997 when it notched up its 6,138th performance.

TOP 10 ★
LONGEST-RUNNING MUSICALS ON BROADWAY

	SHOW	PERFORMANCES
1	*Cats* (1982–)	6,880*
2	*A Chorus Line* (1975–90)	6,137
3	*Les Misérables* (1987–)	4,962*
4	*The Phantom of the Opera* (1988–)	4,692*
5	*42nd Street* (1980–89)	3,486
6	*Grease* (1972–80)	3,388
7	*Miss Saigon* (1991–)	3,303*
8	*Fiddler on the Roof* (1964–72)	3,242
9	*Hello Dolly!* (1964–71)	2,844
10	*My Fair Lady* (1956–62)	2,717

* *Still running; total as at March 31, 1999*
Source: Playbill

THE 10 ★
LATEST WINNERS OF THE AMERICAN EXPRESS AWARD FOR BEST NEW MUSICAL*

YEAR	MUSICAL
1999	*Kat and the Kings*
1998	*Beauty and the Beast*
1997	*Martin Guerre*
1996	*Jolson*
1995	*Once on this Island*
1994	*City of Angels*
1993	*Crazy for You*
1992	*Carmen Jones*
1991	*Sunday in the Park with George*
1990	*Return to the Forbidden Planet*

* *Originally called the Laurence Olivier "Musical of the Year" Award*

FELINE SUCCESS

The now-famous poster for the musical Cats, based on Old Possum's Book of Practical Cats *by T.S. Eliot.*

TM© 1981 RUG LTD

CATS
MUSIC BY ANDREW LLOYD WEBBER
BASED ON 'OLD POSSUM'S BOOK OF PRACTICAL CATS' BY T.S. ELIOT
NOW AND FOREVER

MOVIE HITS & MISSES

TOP 10 HIGHEST-GROSSING MOVIES OF ALL TIME

	MOVIE	YEAR	GROSS INCOME ($) US	WORLD TOTAL
1	Titanic	1998	600,800,000	1,814,800,000
2	Jurassic Park	1993	357,100,000	920,100,000
3	Independence Day	1996	306,200,000	811,200,000
4	Star Wars	1977/97	461,000,000	783,700,000
5	The Lion King	1994	312,900,000	766,900,000
6	E.T.: The Extra-Terrestrial	1982	399,800,000	704,800,000
7	Forrest Gump	1994	329,700,000	679,700,000
8	The Lost World: Jurassic Park	1997	229,100,000	614,100,000
9	Men in Black	1997	250,100,000	586,100,000
10	Return of the Jedi	1983/97	309,100,000	572,900,000

TOP 10 ★ MOVIE OPENINGS OF ALL TIME IN THE US

	MOVIE/RELEASE DATE	OPENING WEEKEND GROSS ($)
1	The Lost World: Jurassic Park*, May 23, 1997	92,729,064
2	Star Wars Episode I: The Phantom Menace, May 21, 1999	61,800,000
3	Mission: Impossible*, May 22, 1996	56,811,602
4	Godzilla, May 20, 1998	55,726,951
5	Batman Forever, June 16, 1995	52,784,433
6	Men in Black, July 2, 1997	51,068,455
7	Independence Day, July 3, 1996	50,228,264
8	Jurassic Park, June 11, 1993	50,159,460
9	Batman Returns, June 19, 1992	45,687,711
10	Batman & Robin, June 20, 1997	42,872,606

* Estimate based on four-day holiday weekend

TOP 10 HIGHEST-GROSSING MOVIES OF ALL TIME IN THE UK

(Movie/year/UK gross in £)

❶ Titanic, 1998, 68,532,000 ❷ The Full Monty, 1997, 51,992,000 ❸ Jurassic Park, 1993, 47,140,000 ❹ Independence Day, 1996, 36,800,000 ❺ Men in Black, 1997, 35,400,000 ❻ Four Weddings and a Funeral, 1994, 27,800,000 ❼ The Lost World: Jurassic Park, 1997, 25,300,000 ❽ Ghost, 1990, 23,300,000 ❾ The Lion King, 1994, 23,100,000 ❿ A Bug's Life, 1998, 22,894,000

From the nadir of the late 1960s and 1970s, today's movies are both more widely viewed (even excluding video) than those of 15 to 25 years ago, as well as grossing considerably more at the box office.

ADULATION AHOY

The phenomenal success of Titanic catapulted its two young stars, Kate Winslet and Leonardo DiCaprio, into the stratosphere of movie megastardom, making them the darlings of Tinseltown.

TOP 10 ★ HIGHEST-GROSSING MOVIES OF ALL TIME IN THE US

	MOVIE	YEAR	US GROSS ($)
1	Titanic	1998	600,800,000
2	Star Wars	1977/97	461,000,000
3	E.T.: The Extra-Terrestrial	1982	399,800,000
4	Jurassic Park	1993	357,100,000
5	Forrest Gump	1994	329,700,000
6	The Lion King	1994	312,900,000
7	Return of the Jedi	1983/97	309,100,000
8	Independence Day	1996	306,200,000
9	The Empire Strikes Back	1980/97	290,200,000
10	Home Alone	1990	285,800,000

Inevitably, bearing inflation in mind, the top-grossing movies of all time are releases from the 1990s, although it is also true that US movie admissions have risen sharply in recent years.

TOP 10 ⭐
MOVIE SEQUELS THAT EARNED THE GREATEST AMOUNT MORE THAN THE ORIGINAL*

	ORIGINAL	OUTEARNED BY
1	*The Terminator*	*Terminator 2: Judgment Day*
2	*First Blood*	*Rambo: First Blood Part II / Rambo III*
3	*Die Hard*	*Die Hard With a Vengeance*
4	*Lethal Weapon*	*Lethal Weapon 2/3/4*
5	*Ace Ventura: Pet Detective*	*Ace Ventura: When Nature Calls*
6	*Raiders of the Lost Ark*	*Indiana Jones and the Last Crusade*
7	*Star Trek: The Motion Picture*	*Star Trek IV/VI/ Star Trek: First Contact*
8	*Patriot Games*	*Clear and Present Danger*
9	*The Karate Kid*	*The Karate Kid, Part II*
10	*A Nightmare on Elm Street*	*A Nightmare on Elm Street 3/4/5*

* Ranked by greatest differential between original and highest-earning sequel

---

THE 10 BIGGEST MOVIE FLOPS OF ALL TIME

(Movie/year/estimated loss in $)

① *Cutthroat Island*, 1995, 81,000,000
② *The Adventures of Baron Munchausen*, 1988, 48,100,000 ③ *Ishtar*, 1987, 47,300,000 ④ *Hudson Hawk*, 1991, 47,000,000 ⑤ *Inchon*, 1981, 44,100,000 ⑥ *The Cotton Club*, 1984, 38,100,000 ⑦ *Santa Claus – The Movie*, 1985, 37,000,000 ⑧ *Heaven's Gate*, 1980, 34,200,000 ⑨ *Billy Bathgate*, 1991, 33,000,000 ⑩ *Pirates*, 1986, 30,300,000

Since the figures shown here are based upon North American earnings balanced against the movies' original production cost, some may eventually recoup their losses via overseas earnings, video, and TV revenue, while for *Inchon* and *Pirates*, time has run out.

TOP 10 ⭐
MOVIE SERIES OF ALL TIME

	MOVIE SERIES	YEARS
1	*Star Wars/The Empire Strikes Back/Return of the Jedi/Star Wars Episode I: The Phantom Menace*	1977–99
2	*Jurassic Park/The Lost World: Jurassic Park*	1993–97
3	*Batman/Batman Returns/Batman Forever/Batman & Robin*	1989–97
4	*Raiders of the Lost Ark/ Indiana Jones and the Temple of Doom/Indiana Jones and the Last Crusade*	1981–89
5	*Star Trek: The Motion Picture/ Star Trek II/III/IV/V/VI/ Generations/First Contact*	1979–96
6	*Home Alone/Home Alone 2: Lost in New York*	1990–92
7	*Back to the Future/II/III*	1985–90
8	*Die Hard/2/Die Hard with a Vengeance*	1988–95
9	*Jaws/2/3(-D)/: The Revenge*	1975–87
10	*Rocky/II/III/IV/V*	1976–90

TOP 10 ⭐
MOST EXPENSIVE MOVIES EVER MADE

	MOVIE	YEAR	ESTIMATED COST ($)
1	*Titanic*	1997	200,000,000
2	*Waterworld*	1995	175,000,000
3 =	*Armageddon*	1998	140,000,000
=	*Lethal Weapon 4*	1998	140,000,000
5	*Godzilla*	1998	125,000,000
6	*Dante's Peak*	1997	116,000,000
7 =	*Star Wars Episode I: The Phantom Menace*	1999	110,000,000
=	*Batman and Robin*	1997	110,000,000
=	*Speed 2: Cruise Control*	1997	110,000,000
=	*Tomorrow Never Dies*	1997	110,000,000
=	*True Lies*	1994	110,000,000

THE CAPED CRUSADER

In the movies, the colorful comic-book treatment of the original TV series gives way to a darker style in which Batman is portrayed as an avenging vigilante whose life is cursed by his endless fight against crime.

What is the most popular time travel movie? A *Back to the Future*
see p.172 for the answer **B** *Back to the Future II*
C *Terminator II: Judgment Day*

169

ADORABLE ALIEN

Steven Spielberg's touching tale of E.T. – an alien creature stranded on Earth and befriended by a young boy – charmed children and adults alike.

TOP 10 ★
MOVIES OF THE 1930s

1	Gone with the Wind*	1939
2	Snow White and the Seven Dwarfs	1937
3	The Wizard of Oz	1939
4	The Woman in Red	1935
5	King Kong	1933
6	San Francisco	1936
7=	Hell's Angels	1930
=	Lost Horizon	1937
=	Mr. Smith Goes to Washington	1939
10	Maytime	1937

* Winner of "Best Picture" Academy Award

Gone with the Wind and Snow White and the Seven Dwarfs have generated more income than any other pre-war movies.

BIG GUNS

New York secret agents Tommy Lee Jones and Will Smith were the Men in Black who, with some futuristic weaponry and their own razor-sharp wits, saved the Earth from intergalactic terrorists.

TOP 10 ★
MOVIES OF THE 1940s

1	Bambi	1942
2	Pinocchio	1940
3	Fantasia	1940
4	Cinderella	1949
5	Song of the South	1946
6	The Best Years of Our Lives*	1946
7	The Bells of St. Mary's	1945
8	Duel in the Sun	1946
9	Mom and Dad	1948
10	Samson and Delilah	1949

* Winner of "Best Picture" Academy Award

With the top four movies of the decade classic Disney cartoons, the 1940s may be regarded as the "golden age" of the animated movie.

TOP 10 ★
MOVIES OF THE 1950s

1	Lady and the Tramp	1955
2	Peter Pan	1953
3	Ben-Hur*	1959
4	The Ten Commandments	1956
5	Sleeping Beauty	1959
6	Around the World in 80 Days*	1956
7=	The Robe	1953
=	The Greatest Show on Earth*	1952
9	The Bridge on the River Kwai*	1957
10	Peyton Place	1957

* Winner of "Best Picture" Academy Award

While the popularity of animated movies continued, the 1950s was outstanding as the decade of the "big" picture (in cast and scale).

TOP 10 MOVIES OF THE 1960s

1 *One Hundred and One Dalmatians*, 1961 **2** *The Jungle Book*, 1967 **3** *The Sound of Music**, 1965 **4** *Thunderball*, 1965 **5** *Goldfinger*, 1964 **6** *Doctor Zhivago*, 1965 **7** *You Only Live Twice*, 1967 **8** *The Graduate*, 1968 **9** *Mary Poppins*, 1964 **10** *Butch Cassidy and the Sundance Kid*, 1969

* Winner of "Best Picture" Academy Award

TOP 10 ★
MOVIES OF THE 1970s

1	*Star Wars*	1977/97
2	*Jaws*	1975
3	*Close Encounters of the Third Kind*	1977/80
4	*Moonraker*	1979
5	*The Spy Who Loved Me*	1977
6	*The Exorcist*	1973
7	*The Sting**	1973
8	*Grease*	1978
9	*The Godfather**	1972
10	*Saturday Night Fever*	1977

* Winner of "Best Picture" Academy Award

In the 1970s the arrival of Steven Spielberg and George Lucas set the scene for the high-adventure blockbusters whose domination has continued ever since. Lucas wrote and directed *Star Wars*, formerly the highest-earning movie of all time. Spielberg directed *Jaws* and wrote and directed *Close Encounters of the Third Kind*.

TOP 10 ★
MOVIES OF THE 1980s

1	*E.T.: The Extra-Terrestrial*	1982
2	*Indiana Jones and the Last Crusade*	1989
3	*Batman*	1989
4	*Rain Man*	1988
5	*Return of the Jedi*	1983
6	*Raiders of the Lost Ark*	1981
7	*The Empire Strikes Back*	1980
8	*Who Framed Roger Rabbit*	1988
9	*Back to the Future*	1985
10	*Top Gun*	1986

The 1980s was clearly the decade of the adventure movie, with George Lucas and Steven Spielberg continuing to assert their control of Hollywood, carving up the Top 10 between them, with Lucas as producer of 5 and 7 and Spielberg director of 1, 2, 6, 8, and 9. The 10 highest-earning movies scooped in more than $4 billion between them at the global box office.

WHEN DINOSAURS ROAMED THE EARTH...
A monster movie in more ways than one, The Lost World: Jurassic Park, with its breathtaking dinosaur creations, grossed $611 million.

TOP 10 ★
MOVIES OF THE 1990s

1	*Titanic**	1997
2	*Jurassic Park*	1993
3	*Independence Day*	1996
4	*The Lion King*	1994
5	*Forrest Gump**	1994
6	*The Lost World: Jurassic Park*	1997
7	*Men in Black*	1997
8	*Home Alone*	1990
9	*Ghost*	1990
10	*Terminator 2: Judgment Day*	1991

* Winner of "Best Picture" Academy Award

Each of the Top 10 movies of the present decade has earned more than $500 million around the world, a total of almost $8 billion between them.

Did You Know? If the income of *Gone with the Wind* was adjusted to allow for inflation in the period since its release, it could be regarded as the most successful movie ever.

MOVIE GENRES

TOP 10 ★
TIME TRAVEL MOVIES

1	Terminator 2: Judgment Day	1991
2	Back to the Future	1985
3	Back to the Future III	1990
4	Back to the Future II	1989
5	Timecop	1994
6	The Terminator	1984
7	Time Bandits	1981
8	Bill and Ted's Excellent Adventure	1989
9	Highlander III: The Sorcerer	1994
10	Highlander	1986

TOP 10 ★
VAMPIRE MOVIES

1	Interview with the Vampire	1994
2	Bram Stoker's Dracula	1992
3	Love at First Bite	1979
4	The Lost Boys	1987
5	Dracula	1979
6	Fright Night	1985
7	Vampire in Brooklyn	1995
8	Buffy the Vampire Slayer	1992
9	Dracula: Dead and Loving It	1995
10	Transylvania 6-5000	1985

TOP 10 ★
HORROR MOVIES

1	Jurassic Park	1993
2	The Lost World: Jurassic Park	1997
3	Jaws	1975
4	Godzilla	1998
5	The Exorcist	1973/98
6	Interview with the Vampire	1994
7	Jaws II	1978
8	Bram Stoker's Dracula	1992
9	Scream	1996
10	Scream 2	1997

TOP 10 ★
COMEDY MOVIES

1	Forrest Gump	1994
2	Home Alone	1990
3	Ghost	1990
4	Pretty Woman	1990
5	Mrs. Doubtfire	1993
6	The Flintstones	1994
7	Who Framed Roger Rabbit	1988
8	There's Something About Mary	1998
9	The Mask	1994
10	Beverly Hills Cop	1984

TOP 10 ★
GHOST MOVIES

1	Ghost	1990
2	Ghostbusters	1984
3	Casper	1995
4	Ghostbusters II	1989
5	Beetlejuice	1988
6	Scrooged	1988
7	The Frighteners	1996
8	Ghost Dad	1990
9	Hamlet	1990
10	The Sixth Man	1997

TOP 10 ★
SCIENCE-FICTION MOVIES

1	Jurassic Park	1993
2	Independence Day	1996
3	Star Wars	1977/97
4	E.T.: The Extra-Terrestrial	1982
5	The Lost World: Jurassic Park	1997
6	Men in Black	1997
7	The Empire Strikes Back	1980/97
8	Terminator 2: Judgment Day	1991
9	Return of the Jedi	1983/97
10	Batman	1989

DOUBLE-ACT WITH A DIFFERENCE

The adventures of C-3P0, the pessimistic robot diplomat, and his sidekick, R2-D2, were a central element of the Star Wars movies. Their endearing personalities made them as popular as their human co-stars.

TOP 10 ★
WAR MOVIES

1	Saving Private Ryan	1998
2	Platoon	1986
3	Good Morning, Vietnam	1987
4	Apocalypse Now	1979
5	M*A*S*H	1970
6	Patton	1970
7	The Deer Hunter	1978
8	Full Metal Jacket	1987
9	Midway	1976
10	The Dirty Dozen	1967

Until the hugely successful and Oscar-winning *Saving Private Ryan*, surprisingly few war movies appeared in the high-earning bracket in the late 1990s, which led some to consider that the days of big-budget movies in this genre were over. The release of *The Thin Red Line* in 1998 to critical acclaim, however, helped to put this genre firmly back on the map. This list excludes successful movies that are not technically "war" movies but have military themes.

TOP 10 ★
COP MOVIES

1	Die Hard with a Vengeance	1995
2	The Fugitive	1993
3	Basic Instinct	1992
4	Se7en	1995
5	Lethal Weapon 3	1993
6	Beverly Hills Cop	1984
7	Beverly Hills Cop II	1987
8	Lethal Weapon 4	1998
9	Speed	1994
10	Lethal Weapon 2	1989

Although movies in which one of the central characters is a policeman have never been among the most successful movies of all time, many have earned respectable amounts at the box office. They are divided between those with a comic slant, such as all three *Beverly Hills Cop* movies, and darker police thrillers, such as *Basic Instinct*. Movies featuring FBI and CIA agents have been excluded here, thus eliminating blockbusters such as *Mission: Impossible* and *The Silence of the Lambs*.

EXPLOSIVE ACTION
Die Hard with a Vengeance, *the third in the series, outgrossed its two predecessors in terms of both box office revenues and graphically portrayed violence.*

TOP 10 ★
DISASTER MOVIES

1	Titanic	1997
2	Twister	1996
3	Die Hard with a Vengeance	1995
4	Apollo 13	1995
5	Outbreak	1995
6	Dante's Peak	1997
7	Daylight	1996
8	Die Hard	1988
9	Volcano	1997
10	Die Hard 2	1990

Disasters involving blazing buildings, natural disasters such as volcanoes, earthquakes, and tidal waves, train and air crashes, sinking ships, and terrorist attacks, have long been a high-earning staple of Hollywood movies.

Which was the most successful Tom Cruise movie? A *Top Gun*
see p.180 for the answer   B *Mission: Impossible*
C *Jerry Maguire*

173

OSCAR-WINNING MOVIES

TOP 10 ★
HIGHEST-EARNING "BEST PICTURE" OSCAR WINNERS

	MOVIE	YEAR
1	Titanic	1997
2	Forrest Gump	1994
3	Dances with Wolves	1990
4	Rain Man	1988
5	Schindler's List	1993
6	The English Patient	1996
7	Braveheart	1995
8	Gone with the Wind	1939
9	The Sound of Music	1965
10	The Sting	1973

Winning the Academy Award for "Best Picture" is no guarantee of box-office success: the award is given for a picture released the previous year – by the time the Oscar ceremony takes place, the moviegoing public has already effectively decided the winning picture's fate. Receiving the Oscar may enhance a picture's continuing earnings, but it is generally too late to revive a movie that may already have been judged mediocre.

TOP 10 MOVIES TO WIN THE MOST OSCARS*

	MOVIE	YEAR	NOMINATIONS	AWARDS
1 =	Ben-Hur	1959	12	11
=	Titanic	1997	14	11
3	West Side Story	1961	11	10
4 =	Gigi	1958	9	9
=	The Last Emperor	1987	9	9
=	The English Patient	1996	12	9
7 =	Gone with the Wind	1939	13	8#
=	From Here to Eternity	1953	13	8
=	On the Waterfront	1954	12	8
=	My Fair Lady	1964	12	8
=	Cabaret	1972	10	8
=	Gandhi	1982	11	8
=	Amadeus	1984	11	8

* Oscar® is a Registered Trade Mark

\# Plus two special awards

VOYAGE OF DOOM
The enormous global success of Titanic ensured it a place in cinematic history. Despite the enormous cost of making the movie, the profits were huge.

TOP 10 MOVIES NOMINATED FOR THE MOST OSCARS
(Movie/year/awards/nominations)

1 = All About Eve, 1950, 6, 14; = Titanic, 1997, 11, 14 **3** Gone with the Wind, 1939 ,8*, 13; = From Here to Eternity, 1953, 8, 13; = Mary Poppins, 1964, 5, 13; = Who's Afraid of Virginia Woolf?, 1966, 5, 13; = Forrest Gump, 1994, 6, 13; = Shakespeare in Love, 1998, 7, 13 **9** = Mrs. Miniver, 1942, 6, 12; = The Song of Bernadette, 1943, 4, 12; = Johnny Belinda, 1948, 1, 12; = A Streetcar Named Desire, 1951, 4, 12; = On the Waterfront, 1954, 8, 12; = Ben-Hur, 1959, 11, 12; = Becket, 1964, 1, 12; = My Fair Lady, 1964, 8, 12; = Reds, 1981, 3, 12; = Dances with Wolves, 1990, 7, 12; = Schindler's List, 1993, 7, 12; = The English Patient, 1996 , 9, 12

* Plus two special awards

Dame Judi Dench, as Queen Elizabeth in Shakespeare in Love, warns Colin Firth about his future wife's attraction to the playhouse.

THE 10 "BEST PICTURE" OSCAR WINNERS OF THE 1950s

(Year/movie)

1950 *All About Eve* 1951 *An American in Paris* 1952 *The Greatest Show on Earth* 1953 *From Here to Eternity* 1954 *On the Waterfront* 1955 *Marty* 1956 *Around the World in 80 Days* 1957 *The Bridge on the River Kwai* 1958 *Gigi* 1959 *Ben-Hur*

THE 10 "BEST PICTURE" OSCAR WINNERS OF THE 1960s

(Year/movie)

1960 *The Apartment* 1961 *West Side Story* 1962 *Lawrence of Arabia* 1963 *Tom Jones* 1964 *My Fair Lady* 1965 *The Sound of Music* 1966 *A Man for All Seasons* 1967 *In the Heat of the Night* 1968 *Oliver!* 1969 *Midnight Cowboy*

THE 10 ⭐ "BEST PICTURE" OSCAR WINNERS OF THE 1970s

YEAR	MOVIE
1970	Patton
1971	The French Connection
1972	The Godfather
1973	The Sting
1974	The Godfather Part II
1975	One Flew Over the Cuckoo's Nest*
1976	Rocky
1977	Annie Hall
1978	The Deer Hunter
1979	Kramer vs. Kramer

* *Winner of Oscars for "Best Director," "Best Actor," "Best Actress," and "Best Screenplay"*

THE 10 ⭐ "BEST PICTURE" OSCAR WINNERS OF THE 1980s

YEAR	MOVIE
1980	Ordinary People
1981	Chariots of Fire
1982	Gandhi
1983	Terms of Endearment
1984	Amadeus
1985	Out of Africa
1986	Platoon
1987	The Last Emperor
1988	Rain Man
1989	Driving Miss Daisy

THE 10 ⭐ LATEST "BEST PICTURE" OSCAR WINNERS

YEAR	MOVIE
1998	Shakespeare in Love
1997	Titanic
1996	The English Patient
1995	Braveheart
1994	Forrest Gump
1993	Schindler's List
1992	Unforgiven
1991	The Silence of the Lambs
1990	Dances with Wolves
1989	Driving Miss Daisy

TOP 10 STUDIOS WITH THE MOST "BEST PICTURE" OSCARS

(Studio/awards)

1 United Artists, 13 **2** Columbia, 12 **3** Paramount, 11 **4** MGM, 9 **5** Twentieth Century Fox, 7 **6** Warner Bros, 6 **7** Universal, 5 **8** Orion, 4 **9** RKO, 2 **10** Miramax, 1

Did You Know? Both *The Turning Point* (1977) and *The Color Purple* (1985) suffered the ignominy of receiving 11 Oscar nominations without a single win.

OSCAR-WINNING STARS

THE 10 ★
"BEST ACTOR" OSCAR WINNERS OF THE 1970s

YEAR	ACTOR/MOVIE
1970	George C. Scott, *Patton**
1971	Gene Hackman, *The French Connection**
1972	Marlon Brando, *The Godfather**
1973	Jack Lemmon, *Save the Tiger*
1974	Art Carney, *Harry and Tonto*
1975	Jack Nicholson, *One Flew Over the Cuckoo's Nest**#
1976	Peter Finch, *Network*
1977	Richard Dreyfuss, *The Goodbye Girl*
1978	John Voight, *Coming Home*
1979	Dustin Hoffman, *Kramer vs. Kramer***

* *Winner of "Best Picture" Oscar*

Winner of "Best Director," "Best Actress," and "Best Screenplay" Oscars

THE 10 ★
"BEST ACTRESS" OSCAR WINNERS OF THE 1970s

YEAR	ACTRESS/MOVIE
1970	Glenda Jackson, *Women in Love*
1971	Jane Fonda, *Klute*
1972	Liza Minelli, *Cabaret*
1973	Glenda Jackson, *A Touch of Class*
1974	Ellen Burstyn, *Alice Doesn't Live Here Any More*
1975	Louise Fletcher, *One Flew Over the Cuckoo's Nest**#
1976	Faye Dunaway, *Network*
1977	Diane Keaton, *Annie Hall**
1978	Jane Fonda, *Coming Home*
1979	Sally Field, *Norma Rae*

* *Winner of "Best Picture" Oscar*

Winner of "Best Director," "Best Actor," and "Best Screenplay" Oscars

FIGHTING FOR SUCCESS

Robert De Niro won the 1980 Best Actor award for his role in Raging Bull. *The movie marked his fourth collaboration with director Martin Scorsese.*

TOP 10 ★
OLDEST OSCAR-WINNING ACTORS AND ACTRESSES

	ACTOR OR ACTRESS	AWARD/MOVIE (WHERE SPECIFIED)	YEAR	AGE*
1	Jessica Tandy	"Best Actress" (*Driving Miss Daisy*)	1989	80
2	George Burns	"Best Supporting Actor" (*The Sunshine Boys*)	1975	80
3	Melvyn Douglas	"Best Supporting Actor" (*Being There*)	1979	79
4	John Gielgud	"Best Supporting Actor" (*Arthur*)	1981	77
5	Don Ameche	"Best Supporting Actor" (*Cocoon*)	1985	77
6	Peggy Ashcroft	"Best Supporting Actress" (*A Passage to India*)	1984	77
7	Henry Fonda	"Best Actor" (*On Golden Pond*)	1981	76
8	Katharine Hepburn	"Best Actress" (*On Golden Pond*)	1981	74
9	Edmund Gwenn	"Best Supporting Actor" (*Miracle on 34th Street*)	1947	72
10	Ruth Gordon	"Best Supporting Actress" (*Rosemary's Baby*)	1968	72

* *At the time of the Award ceremony; those of apparently identical age have been ranked according to their precise age in days at the time of the ceremony*

TOP 10 ★
YOUNGEST OSCAR-WINNING ACTORS AND ACTRESSES

	ACTOR OR ACTRESS	AWARD/FILM (WHERE SPECIFIED)	YEAR	AGE*
1	Shirley Temple	Special Award – outstanding contribution during 1934	1934	6
2	Margaret O' Brien	Special Award (*Meet Me in St. Louis*)	1944	8
3	Vincent Winter	Special Award (*The Little Kidnappers*)	1954	8
4	Ivan Jandl	Special Award (*The Search*)	1948	9
5	Jon Whiteley	Special Award (*The Little Kidnappers*)	1954	10
6	Tatum O'Neal	"Best Supporting Actress" (*Paper Moon*)	1973	10
7	Anna Paquin	"Best Supporting Actress" (*The Piano*)	1993	11
8	Claude Jarman, Jr.	Special Award (*The Yearling*)	1946	12
9	Bobby Driscoll	Special Award (*The Window*)	1949	13
10	Hayley Mills	Special Award (*Pollyanna*)	1960	13

* *At the time of the Award ceremony; those of apparently identical age have been ranked according to their precise age in days at the time of the ceremony*

The Academy Awards ceremony usually takes place at the end of March in the year following that in which eligible movies were released in the US, so the winners are generally at least a year older when they receive their Oscars than when they acted in their award-winning movies.

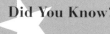

Did You Know? Peter Finch was the first "Best Actor" to be honored posthumously: he died on January 14, 1977, and the award was announced on March 28, 1977.

THE 10 ★
"BEST ACTOR" OSCAR WINNERS OF THE 1980s

YEAR	ACTOR/MOVIE
1980	Robert De Niro, *Raging Bull*
1981	Henry Fonda, *On Golden Pond* *
1982	Ben Kingsley, *Gandhi* #
1983	Robert Duvall, *Tender Mercies*
1984	F. Murray Abraham, *Amadeus* #
1985	William Hurt, *Kiss of the Spider Woman*
1986	Paul Newman, *The Color of Money*
1987	Michael Douglas, *Wall Street*
1988	Dustin Hoffman, *Rain Man* #
1989	Daniel Day-Lewis, *My Left Foot*

* Winner of "Best Actress" Oscar
# Winner of "Best Picture" Oscar

THE 10 ★
"BEST ACTRESS" OSCAR WINNERS OF THE 1980s

YEAR	ACTRESS/MOVIE
1980	Sissy Spacek, *Coal Miner's Daughter*
1981	Katharine Hepburn, *On Golden Pond* *
1982	Meryl Streep, *Sophie's Choice*
1983	Shirley MacLaine, *Terms of Endearment* #
1984	Sally Field, *Places in the Heart*
1985	Geraldine Page, *The Trip to Bountiful*
1986	Marlee Matlin, *Children of a Lesser God*
1987	Cher, *Moonstruck*
1988	Jodie Foster, *The Accused*
1989	Jessica Tandy, *Driving Miss Daisy* #

* Winner of "Best Actor" Oscar
# Winner of "Best Picture" Oscar

THE 10 ★
LATEST "BEST ACTOR" OSCAR WINNERS

YEAR	ACTOR/MOVIE
1998	Roberto Benigni, *La vita è bella* (Life Is Beautiful)
1997	Jack Nicholson, *As Good As It Gets* #
1996	Geoffrey Rush, *Shine*
1995	Nicolas Cage, *Leaving Las Vegas*
1994	Tom Hanks, *Forrest Gump* *
1993	Tom Hanks, *Philadelphia*
1992	Al Pacino, *Scent of a Woman*
1991	Anthony Hopkins, *The Silence of the Lambs* *#
1990	Jeremy Irons, *Reversal of Fortune*
1989	Daniel Day-Lewis, *My Left Foot*

* Winner of "Best Picture" Oscar
# Winner of "Best Actress" Oscar

Tom Hanks shares the honor of consecutive wins with Spencer Tracy, who was awarded an Oscar in 1937 and 1938. Only three other actors have won twice: Marlon Brando (1954; 1972), Gary Cooper (1941; 1952), and Dustin Hoffman (1977; 1988).

THE 10 LATEST "BEST ACTRESS" OSCAR WINNERS

(Year/actress/movie)

1998 Gwyneth Paltrow, *Shakespeare in Love* **1997** Helen Hunt, *As Good As It Gets* * **1996** Frances McDormand, *Fargo* **1995** Susan Sarandon, *Dead Man Walking* **1994** Jessica Lange, *Blue Sky* **1993** Holly Hunter, *The Piano* **1992** Emma Thompson, *Howards End* **1991** Jodie Foster, *The Silence of the Lambs* *# **1990** Kathy Bates, *Misery* **1989** Jessica Tandy, *Driving Miss Daisy* #

* Winner of "Best Actor" Oscar
# Winner of "Best Picture" Oscar

OSCAR CEREMONY

Some of the winners for 1998 movies: Roberto Benigni, Dame Judi Dench, Gwyneth Paltrow, and James Coburn.

177

AND THE WINNNER IS...

LATEST GOLDEN GLOBE AWARDS FOR "BEST PERFORMANCE BY AN ACTRESS IN A MOTION PICTURE – MUSICAL OR COMEDY"

YEAR	ACTRESS/MOVIE
1998	Gwyneth Paltrow, *Shakespeare in Love*
1997	Helen Hunt, *As Good As It Gets*
1996	Madonna, *Evita*
1995	Nicole Kidman, *To Die For*
1994	Jamie Lee Curtis, *True Lies*
1993	Angela Bassett, *What's Love Got to Do with It*
1992	Miranda Richardson, *Enchanted April*
1991	Bette Midler, *For the Boys*
1990	Julia Roberts, *Pretty Woman*
1989	Jessica Tandy, *Driving Miss Daisy*

Among the most recent winners, Jessica Tandy also went on to win the "Best Actress" Academy Award for her starring role in *Driving Miss Daisy*.

LATEST GOLDEN GLOBE AWARDS FOR "BEST PERFORMANCE BY AN ACTOR IN A MOTION PICTURE – MUSICAL OR COMEDY"

YEAR	ACTOR/MOVIE
1998	Michael Caine, *Little Voice*
1997	Jack Nicholson, *As Good As It Gets*
1996	Tom Cruise, *Jerry Maguire*
1995	John Travolta, *Get Shorty*
1994	Hugh Grant, *Four Weddings and a Funeral*
1993	Robin Williams, *Mrs. Doubtfire*
1992	Tim Robbins, *The Player*
1991	Robin Williams, *The Fisher King*
1990	Gerard Depardieu, *Green Card*
1989	Morgan Freeman, *Driving Miss Daisy*

The "Musical or Comedy" awards tend to be presented to movies that have received popular and commercial success, but seldom also receive the critical accolade of an Academy Award.

THE 10 FIRST GOLDEN GLOBE AWARDS FOR "BEST PICTURE"

(Year/movie)

1943 *The Song of Bernadette* 1944 *Going My Way** 1945 *The Lost Weekend** 1946 *The Best Years of Our Lives** 1947 *Gentleman's Agreement** 1948 *Treasure of Sierra Madre* and *Johnny Belinda*# 1949 *All the King's Men** 1950 *Sunset Boulevard* 1951 *A Place in the Sun* 1952 *The Greatest Show on Earth**

* Also won "Best Picture" Academy Award
# Joint winners

THE 10 LATEST GOLDEN GLOBE AWARDS FOR "BEST MOTION PICTURE – DRAMA"

(Year/movie)

1998 *Saving Private Ryan* 1997 *Titanic* 1996 *The English Patient* 1995 *Sense and Sensibility* 1994 *Forrest Gump* 1993 *Schindler's List* 1992 *Scent of a Woman* 1991 *Bugsy* 1990 *Dances with Wolves* 1989 *Born on the Fourth of July*

OFF TO CHURCH
Four Weddings and a Funeral *was a low-budget movie that shot to success and made Hugh Grant a household name.*

THE 10 ⭐ LATEST WINNERS OF THE CANNES PALME D'OR FOR "BEST FILM"

YEAR	MOVIE/COUNTRY
1998	*Eternity and a Day* (Greece)
1997	*The Eel* (Japan)/ *The Taste of Cherries* (Iran)
1996	*Secrets and Lies* (UK)
1995	*Underground* (Yugoslavia)
1994	*Pulp Fiction* (US)
1993	*Farewell My Concubine* (China)/ *The Piano* (Australia)
1992	*Best Intentions* (Denmark)
1991	*Barton Fink* (US)
1990	*Wild at Heart* (US)
1989	*sex, lies, and videotape* (US)

In the early years of the Cannes Film Festival there was no single "Best Film" award. Several films were honored jointly, including such unlikely bedfellows as David Lean's *Brief Encounter* and Walt Disney's *Dumbo*. The "Grand Prize" is now known as the "Palme d'Or."

THE 10 ⭐ LATEST GOLDEN GLOBE AWARDS FOR "BEST PERFORMANCE BY AN ACTRESS IN A MOTION PICTURE – DRAMA"

YEAR	ACTRESS/MOVIE
1998	Cate Blanchett, *Elizabeth*
1997	Judi Dench, *Mrs. Brown*
1996	Brenda Blethyn, *Secrets and Lies*
1995	Sharon Stone, *Casino*
1994	Jessica Lange, *Blue Sky*
1993	Holly Hunter, *The Piano*
1992	Emma Thompson, *Howards End*
1991	Jodie Foster, *The Silence of the Lambs*
1990	Kathy Bates, *Misery*
1977	Michelle Pfeiffer, *The Fabulous Baker Boys*

FEMME FATALE
Uma Thurman plays an enigmatic temptress in Quentin Tarantino's *Pulp Fiction*. The movie won the Palme d'Or at Cannes in 1994.

THE 10 ⭐ LATEST GOLDEN GLOBE AWARDS FOR "BEST DIRECTOR"

YEAR	DIRECTOR/MOVIE
1998	Steven Spielberg, *Saving Private Ryan*
1997	James Cameron, *Titanic*
1996	Milos Forman, *The People vs. Larry Flynt*
1995	Mel Gibson, *Braveheart*
1994	Robert Zemeckis, *Forrest Gump*
1993	Steven Spielberg, *Schindler's List*
1992	Clint Eastwood, *Unforgiven*
1991	Oliver Stone, *JFK*
1990	Kevin Costner, *Dances with Wolves*
1989	Oliver Stone, *Born on the Fourth of July*

THE 10 LATEST GOLDEN GLOBE AWARDS FOR "BEST MOTION PICTURE – MUSICAL OR COMEDY"

(Year/movie)

1998 *Saving Private Ryan* 1997 *As Good As It Gets* 1996 *Evita* 1995 *Babe* 1994 *The Lion King* 1993 *Mrs. Doubtfire* 1992 *The Player* 1991 *Beauty and the Beast* 1990 *Green Card* 1989 *Driving Miss Daisy*

TOP 10 ⭐ LATEST GOLDEN GLOBE AWARDS FOR "BEST PERFORMANCE BY AN ACTOR IN A MOTION PICTURE – DRAMA"

YEAR	ACTOR/MOVIE
1998	Jim Carrey, *The Truman Show*
1997	Peter Fonda, *Ulee's Gold*
1996	Geoffrey Rush, *Shine*
1995	Nicolas Cage, *Leaving Las Vegas*
1994	Tom Hanks, *Forrest Gump*
1993	Tom Hanks, *Philadelphia*
1992	Al Pacino, *Scent of a Woman*
1991	Nick Nolte, *The Prince of Tides*
1990	Jeremy Irons, *Reversal of Fortune*
1989	Tom Cruise, *Born on the Fourth of July*

THE 10 LATEST RECIPIENTS OF THE AMERICAN FILM INSTITUTE LIFETIME ACHIEVEMENT AWARD

(Year/recipient)

1999 Dustin Hoffman 1998 Robert Wise 1997 Martin Scorsese 1996 Clint Eastwood 1995 Steven Spielberg 1994 Jack Nicholson 1993 Elizabeth Taylor 1992 Sidney Poitier 1991 Kirk Douglas 1990 David Lean

Did You Know? Although the Cannes Film Festival was established in 1939, World War II delayed its inaugural ceremony until 1946.

MOVIE ACTORS

TOP 10 ★ BRAD PITT MOVIES

1	Se7en	1995
2	Interview with the Vampire	1994
3	Sleepers	1996
4	Legends of the Fall	1994
5	Twelve Monkeys	1995
6	The Devil's Own	1997
7	Seven Years in Tibet	1997
8	Meet Joe Black	1998
9	Thelma & Louise	1991
10	A River Runs Through It	1992

TOP 10 ★ TOM CRUISE MOVIES

1	Mission: Impossible	1996
2	Rain Man	1988
3	Top Gun	1986
4	Jerry Maguire	1996
5	The Firm	1993
6	A Few Good Men	1992
7	Interview with the Vampire	1994
8	Days of Thunder	1990
9	Cocktail	1988
10	Born on the Fourth of July*	1989

* Nominated for Academy Award for "Best Actor"

TOP 10 ★ ARNOLD SCHWARZENEGGER MOVIES

1	Terminator 2: Judgment Day	1991
2	True Lies	1994
3	Total Recall	1990
4	Eraser	1996
5	Twins	1988
6	Kindergarten Cop	1990
7	Jingle All the Way	1996
8	Last Action Hero	1993
9	Junior	1994
10	The Terminator	1984

TOP 10 JACK NICHOLSON MOVIES

1 *Batman*, 1989 **2** *A Few Good Men*, 1992 **3** *As Good As It Gets**, 1997 **4** *Terms of Endearment#*, 1983 **5** *Wolf*, 1994 **6** *One Flew Over the Cuckoo's Nest**, 1975 **7** *Mars Attacks!*, 1996 **8** *The Witches of Eastwick*, 1987 **9** *The Shining*, 1980 **10** *Broadcast News*, 1987

* Academy Award for "Best Actor"
# Academy Award for "Best Supporting Actor"

TOP 10 TOM HANKS MOVIES

1 *Forrest Gump**, 1994 **2** *Saving Private Ryan*, 1998 **3** *Apollo 13*, 1995 **4** *Sleepless in Seattle*, 1993 **5** *Philadelphia**, 1993 **6** *Big*, 1998 **7** *You've Got Mail*, 1998 **8** *A League of Their Own*, 1992 **9** *Turner & Hooch*, 1989 **10** *Splash!*, 1984

Academy Award for "Best Actor"

TOP 10 ★
SAMUEL L. JACKSON MOVIES

1	*Jurassic Park*	1993
2	*Die Hard with a Vengeance*	1995
3	*Coming to America*	1988
4	*Pulp Fiction*	1994
5	*Patriot Games*	1992
6	*A Time to Kill*	1996
7	*Sea of Love*	1989
8	*Jackie Brown*	1997
9	*The Long Kiss Goodnight*	1996
10	*Sphere*	1998

TOP 10 ★
MEL GIBSON MOVIES

1	*Lethal Weapon 4*	1998
2	*Lethal Weapon 2*	1989
3	*Lethal Weapon 3*	1992
4	*Braveheart**	1995
5	*Ransom*	1996
6	*Forever Young*	1992
7	*Maverick*	1994
8	*Bird on a Wire*	1990
9	*Lethal Weapon*	1987
10	*Tequila Sunrise*	1988

* Academy Award for "Best Director"

TOP 10 NICOLAS CAGE MOVIES

1 *The Rock*, 1996 **2** *Face/Off*, 1997 **3** *Con Air*, 1997 **4** *City of Angels*, 1998 **5** *Snake Eyes*, 1998 **6** *Moonstruck*, 1987 **7** *Leaving Las Vegas*, 1995 **8** *Peggy Sue Got Married*, 1986 **9** *It Could Happen to You*, 1994 **10** *Honeymoon in Vegas*, 1992

DISCO MANIA

John Travolta in Saturday Night Fever wowed 1970s moviegoers with his energetic dance routines and that famous white suit.

TOP 10 ★
JOHN TRAVOLTA MOVIES

1	*Face/Off*	1997
2	*Grease*	1978
3	*Look Who's Talking*	1989
4	*Saturday Night Fever**	1977
5	*Pulp Fiction*	1994
6	*Phenomenon*	1996
7	*Broken Arrow*	1996
8	*Staying Alive*	1983
9	*Get Shorty*	1995
10	*Michael*	1996

* Nominated for Academy Award for "Best Actor"

GRIM REALISM

Despite the overwhelming critical acclaim for Saving Private Ryan, and for Tom Hanks' profoundly moving performance, neither "Best Picture" nor "Best Actor" were among the five Academy Awards won by this movie.

TOP 10 JOHNNY DEPP MOVIES

1 *Platoon*, 1986 **2** *Donnie Brasco*, 1997 **3** *Edward Scissorhands*, 1990 **4** *Don Juan DeMarco*, 1995 **5** *Freddy's Dead: The Final Nightmare**, 1991 **6** *A Nightmare on Elm Street*, 1984 **7** *Fear and Loathing in Las Vegas*, 1998 **8** *What's Eating Gilbert Grape*, 1993 **9** *Cry-Baby*, 1990 **10** *Nick of Time*, 1995

* Uncredited appearance

HOLLYWOOD HEART-THROB

Despite his pin-up image, Johnny Depp tends to be associated with movies with artistic integrity such as the quietly poignant What's Eating Gilbert Grape.

Which Jim Carrey movie has been the most successful? **A** *The Mask*
see p.185 for the answer **B** *Liar Liar*
C *Batman Forever*

MOVIE ACTRESSES

TOP 10 ★
JODIE FOSTER MOVIES

1	The Silence of the Lambs*	1990
2	Maverick	1994
3	Contact	1997
4	Sommersby	1993
5	Nell#	1994
6	The Accused*	1988
7	Taxi Driver#	1976
8	Freaky Friday	1976
9	Little Man Tate+	1991
10	Home for the Holidays★	1995

* Academy Award for "Best Actress"

\# Academy Award nomination

\+ Acted and directed

★ Directed only

After a career as a child TV star, Jodie Foster (born November 19, 1962, Los Angeles, California) moved into movies at the age of 10, varying roles between childish innocence and street-wise "bad girl." She won Best Actress Oscars for *The Accused* and *The Silence of the Lambs*; she then launched into directing with *Little Man Tate*.

TOP 10 ★
WINONA RYDER MOVIES

1	Bram Stoker's Dracula	1992
2	Alien: Resurrection	1997
3	Edward Scissorhands	1990
4	Beetlejuice	1988
5	Little Women	1994
6	Mermaids	1990
7	The Age of Innocence	1993
8	How to Make an American Quilt	1995
9	Reality Bites	1994
10	The Crucible	1996

TOP 10 ★
UMA THURMAN MOVIES

1	Batman & Robin	1997
2	Pulp Fiction	1994
3	The Truth About Cats & Dogs	1996
4	The Avengers	1998
5	Dangerous Liaisons	1988
6	Final Analysis	1992
7	Beautiful Girls	1996
8	Johnny Be Good	1988
9	Gattaca	1997
10	Les Misérables	1998

TOP 10 DEMI MOORE MOVIES

1 *Ghost*, 1990 **2** *Indecent Proposal*, 1993 **3** *A Few Good Men*, 1992 **4** *Disclosure*, 1995 **5** *Striptease*, 1996 **6** *G.I. Jane*, 1997 **7** *The Juror*, 1996 **8** *About Last Night*, 1986 **9** *St. Elmo's Fire*, 1985 **10** *Young Doctors in Love*, 1982

Demi Moore has progressed from working as a teenage model through the TV soap *General Hospital* to Hollywood movies. She provided the voice of Esmeralda in the animated movie *The Hunchback of Notre Dame* (1996). If included in her Top 10, it would be in second place. Although uncredited, her voice appears in *Beavis and Butt-head Do America* (1996), which would also merit a place in her Top 10.

TOP 10 ★
GWYNETH PALTROW MOVIES

1	Se7en	1995
2	Hook	1991
3	Shakespeare in Love*	1998
4	A Perfect Murder	1998
5	Great Expectations	1998
6	Malice	1993
7	Emma	1996
8	Sliding Doors	1998
9	Hush	1998
10	Flesh and Bone	1993

* Academy Award for "Best Actress"

HONORARY ENGLISHWOMAN

Gwyneth Paltrow's impeccable accent convinces many that she is the quintessential English rose.

TOP 10 ★
MICHELLE PFEIFFER MOVIES

1	Batman Returns	1992
2	Dangerous Minds	1995
3	Wolf	1994
4	Up Close & Personal	1996
5	One Fine Day	1996
6	The Witches of Eastwick	1987
7	Tequila Sunrise	1988
8	Scarface	1983
9	Dangerous Liaisons	1988
10	The Age of Innocence	1993

Michelle Pfeiffer provided the voice of Tzipporah in the animated movie *Prince of Egypt* (1998). If included in her Top 10, it would feature in second place.

NICOLE'S ROLE

With her husband Tom Cruise, Nicole Kidman stars in Stanley Kubrick's controversial movie Eyes Wide Shut, which was completed shortly before the director's death in 1999.

TOP 10 ★
NICOLE KIDMAN MOVIES

1	*Batman Forever*	1995
2	*Days of Thunder*	1990
3	*The Peacemaker*	1997
4	*Practical Magic*	1998
5	*Far and Away*	1992
6	*Malice*	1993
7	*My Life*	1993
8	*To Die For*	1995
9	*Billy Bathgate*	1991
10	*Dead Calm*	1989

TOP 10
JULIA ROBERTS MOVIES

1 *Pretty Woman**, 1990 **2** *My Best Friend's Wedding*, 1997 **3** *The Pelican Brief*, 1993 **4** *Six Days, Seven Nights*, 1998 **5** *Sleeping with the Enemy*, 1991 **6** *Conspiracy Theory*, 1997 **7** *Hook*, 1991 **8** *Steel Magnolias*#, 1989 **9** *Stepmom*, 1998 **10** *Flatliners*, 1990

* Academy Award nomination for "Best Actress"
 # Academy Award nomination for "Best Supporting Actress"

TOP 10 ★
SHARON STONE MOVIES

1	*Basic Instinct*	1992
2	*Total Recall*	1990
3	*The Specialist*	1995
4	*Last Action Hero*	1993
5	*Sliver*	1993
6	*Sphere*	1998
7	*Casino**	1995
8	*Diabolique*	1996
9	*Police Academy 4: Citizens on Patrol*	1987
10	*Intersection*	1994

 # Academy Award nomination

Sharon Stone's part in *Last Action Hero* amounted to no more than a brief cameo. If discounted, *Action Jackson* (1988) would occupy 10th place. She provided the voice of Bala in *Antz* (1998).

TOP 10 ★
DREW BARRYMORE MOVIES

1	*E.T.: The Extra-Terrestrial*	1982
2	*Batman Forever*	1995
3	*Scream*	1996
4	*The Wedding Singer*	1998
5	*Ever After*	1998
6	*Wayne's World 2*	1993
7	*Everyone Says I Love You*	1996
8	*Boys on the Side*	1995
9	*Mad Love*	1995
10	*Bad Girls*	1994

TROUBLESOME TEENAGER

Drew Barrymore has cast aside her notorious wild-child image to become a sophisticated and successful movie star.

TOP 10 ★
MEG RYAN MOVIES

1	*Top Gun*	1986
2	*Sleepless in Seattle*	1993
3	*City of Angels*	1998
4	*You've Got Mail*	1998
5	*French Kiss*	1995
6	*Courage under Fire*	1996
7	*When Harry Met Sally*	1989
8	*Addicted to Love*	1997
9	*When a Man Loves a Woman*	1994
10	*Joe Versus the Volcano*	1990

Meg Ryan provided the voice of Anastasia in the 1997 movie of that title. If included, it would appear in seventh place.

What was the most successful animated movie?   A *Bambi*
see p.190 for the answer   B *Toy Story*
C *The Lion King*

THE FUNNIES

TOP 10 ★
WHOOPI GOLDBERG MOVIES

1	Ghost	1990
2	Sister Act	1992
3	The Color Purple*	1985
4	Star Trek: Generations	1994
5	Made in America	1993
6	In & Out	1997
7	Sister Act 2: Back in the Habit	1993
8	The Little Rascals	1994
9	Eddie	1996
10	How Stella Got Her Groove Back	1998

* Academy Award nomination for "Best Actress"

Whoopi Goldberg provided the voice of Shenzi in *The Lion King* (1994). If that were taken into the reckoning, it would appear in No. 1 position in her Top 10. Her voice was also that of Ranger Margaret in *The Rugrats Movie* (1998), which would appear in 6th position.

DIVINE COMEDY

From intergalactic agony aunt to the singing "nun" on the run in Sister Act, Whoopi Goldberg, real name Caryn Johnson, is one of America's most well-loved and highly paid actresses.

TOP 10 BILL MURRAY MOVIES

1 *Ghostbusters*, 1984 **2** *Tootsie*, 1982 **3** *Ghostbusters II*, 1989 **4** *Stripes*, 1981 **5** *Groundhog Day*, 1993 **6** *What About Bob?*, 1991 **7** *Scrooged*, 1988 **8** *Meatballs*, 1979 **9** *Caddyshack*, 1980 **10** *Little Shop of Horrors*, 1986

TOP 10 ★
STEVE MARTIN MOVIES

1	Parenthood	1989
2	The Jerk*	1979
3	Father of the Bride	1991
4	Father of the Bride Part II	1995
5	Housesitter	1992
6	Planes, Trains & Automobiles	1987
7	Dirty Rotten Scoundrels	1988
8	Roxanne	1987
9	¡Three Amigos!*	1986
10	Little Shop of Horrors	1986

*Also co-writer

Steve Martin provided the voice of Hotep in *Prince of Egypt*, which would head his Top 10. He was one of the many guest stars in *The Muppet Movie*.

TOP 10 ★
DAN AYKROYD MOVIES

1	Indiana Jones and the Temple of Doom	1984
2	Ghostbusters	1984
3	Casper	1995
4	Ghostbusters II	1989
5	Driving Miss Daisy	1989
6	Trading Places	1983
7	Spies Like Us	1985
8	My Girl	1991
9	Dragnet	1987
10	The Blues Brothers	1980

Aykroyd's directorial debut with *Nothing but Trouble* (1991), in which he also starred, was one of his least commercially successful movies.

TOP 10 ★
EDDIE MURPHY MOVIES

1	Beverly Hills Cop	1984
2	Beverly Hills Cop II	1987
3	Coming to America	1988
4	The Nutty Professor	1996
5	Doctor Dolittle	1998
6	Boomerang	1992
7	Harlem Nights*	1989
8	Trading Places	1983
9	Another 48 Hrs.	1990
10	The Golden Child	1986

* Also director

Eddie Murphy also provided the voice of Mushu in the animated movie *Mulan* (1998), which would rank third in his Top 10.

Did You Know? The most successful comedy movie of all time is *Forrest Gump* starring Tom Hanks.

TOP 10 ★
BETTE MIDLER MOVIES

1	*The First Wives Club*	1996
2	*Get Shorty*	1995
3	*Ruthless People*	1986
4	*Down and Out in Beverly Hills*	1986
5	*Beaches**	1988
6	*Outrageous Fortune*	1987
7	*The Rose*	1979
8	*Big Business*	1988
9	*Hocus Pocus*	1993
10	*Hawaii*	1966

* *Also producer*

Bette Midler's role in *Get Shorty* is no more than a cameo, and that in *Hawaii*, her first movie part, is as an extra. If these were excluded, *Stella* (1990) and *For the Boys* (1991), which she also produced, would join the list. Her voice appears as that of the character Georgette in the animated movie *Oliver & Company* (1988).

TOP 10 ★
ROBIN WILLIAMS MOVIES

1	*Mrs. Doubtfire*	1993
2	*Hook*	1991
3	*Jumanji*	1995
4	*Dead Poets Society*	1989
5	*The Birdcage*	1996
6	*Good Will Hunting**	1997
7	*Nine Months*	1995
8	*Good Morning, Vietnam*	1987
9	*Jack*	1996
10	*Patch Adams*	1998

* *Academy Award for "Best Supporting Actor"*

Robin Williams (born July 21, 1952, Chicago, Illinois) first came to public attention on TV through his appearances in *Rowan and Martin's Laugh-In* and as the alien Mork in *Mork and Mindy*. Since then he has made 15 movies, typically playing crazed individuals – such as the DJ in *Good Morning, Vietnam*, and the certifiable down-and-out in *The Fisher King*. Williams has also played some impressive dramatic roles, as in *Dead Poets Society* and *Awakenings*.

TOP 10 ★
CHEVY CHASE MOVIES

1	*National Lampoon's Christmas Vacation*	1989
2	*National Lampoon's Vacation*	1983
3	*Spies Like Us*	1985
4	*Foul Play*	1978
5	*National Lampoon's European Vacation*	1985
6	*Fletch*	1985
7	*Seems Like Old Times*	1980
8	*Caddyshack*	1980
9	*Man of the House*	1995
10	*¡Three Amigos!*	1986

Chevy Chase (real name Cornelius Crane) was born on October 8, 1943. He made his name as a comedian on the anarchic TV show *Saturday Night Live* before starring in comedy movies such as the hugely successful *National Lampoon* series.

TOP 10 ★
JIM CARREY MOVIES

1	*Batman Forever*	1995
2	*The Mask*	1994
3	*Liar Liar*	1997
4	*The Truman Show*	1998
5	*Dumb & Dumber*	1994
6	*Ace Ventura: When Nature Calls*	1995
7	*The Cable Guy*	1996
8	*Ace Ventura: Pet Detective*	1994
9	*Peggy Sue Got Married*	1986
10	*The Dead Pool*	1988

RUBBER FEATURES

Jim Carrey's extraordinary repertoire of facial expressions, with or without the help of special effects, combined with his split-second comic timing, has helped to make him one of the '90s' most successful comedy actors.

TOP 10 ★
DANNY DEVITO MOVIES

1	*Batman Returns*	1992
2	*Get Shorty*	1995
3	*Romancing the Stone*	1984
4	*One Flew Over the Cuckoo's Nest*	1975
5	*Twins*	1988
6	*Terms of Endearment*	1983
7	*Mars Attacks!*	1996
8	*Junior*	1994
9	*The War of the Roses**	1989
10	*Ruthless People*	1986

* *Also director*

Danny DeVito had a relatively minor role in *One Flew Over the Cuckoo's Nest*. If this is discounted from the reckoning, his 10th most successful movie becomes *L.A. Confidential* (1997). He provided the voices of Whiskers in *Last Action Hero* (1993), Rocks in *Look Who's Talking Now* (1993), and Swackhammer in *Space Jam* (1996), and directed, appeared in, and narrated *Matilda* (1996), which just fails to make his own Top 10.

THE DIRECTORS

RETURN TO *CAPE FEAR*

Scorsese directed Cape Fear 30 years after the original movie by J. Lee Thompson. His cast included two of the original actors: Gregory Peck and Robert Mitchum.

TOP 10 ★
MOVIES DIRECTED BY ACTORS

	MOVIE/YEAR	DIRECTOR
1	*Pretty Woman*, 1990	Garry Marshall
2	*Dances with Wolves*, 1990	Kevin Costner
3	*3 Men and a Baby*, 1987	Leonard Nimoy
4	*Rocky IV*, 1985	Sylvester Stallone
5	*A Few Good Men*, 1992	Rob Reiner
6	*Rocky III*, 1982	Sylvester Stallone
7	*On Golden Pond*, 1981	Mark Rydell
8	*Dick Tracy*, 1990	Warren Beatty
9	*Stir Crazy*, 1980	Sidney Poitier
10	*Star Trek IV: The Voyage Home*, 1986	Leonard Nimoy

The role of actor-director has a long movie tradition, numbering such luminaries as Orson Welles and John Huston among its ranks. Heading this list, *Pretty Woman* director Garry Marshall is the brother of actress-director Penny Marshall, who only just misses a place in this Top 10 herself.

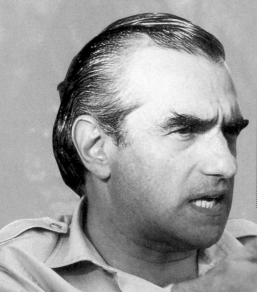

TOP 10 ★
MOVIES DIRECTED BY MARTIN SCORSESE

1	Cape Fear	1991
2	The Color of Money	1986
3	GoodFellas	1990
4	Casino	1995
5	The Age of Innocence	1993
6	Taxi Driver	1976
7	Raging Bull	1980
8	Alice Doesn't Live Here Anymore	1975
9	New York New York	1977
10	New York Stories*	1989

* Part only; other segments directed by Francis Ford Coppola and Woody Allen

TOP 10 ★
MOVIES DIRECTED BY JOHN CARPENTER

1	Halloween	1978
2	Escape from L.A.	1996
3	Starman	1984
4	Escape from New York	1981
5	The Fog	1980
6	Christine	1983
7	Vampires	1998
8	Memoirs of an Invisible Man	1992
9	Prince of Darkness	1987
10	They Live	1988

THE ITALIAN CONNECTION

Martin Scorsese was born into an Italian-American family in New York, the city that provides the backdrop for most of his movies.

What is Nicole Kidman's most successful movie?   A *Days of Thunder*
see p.183 for the answer   B *Batman Forever*
   C *The Peacemaker*

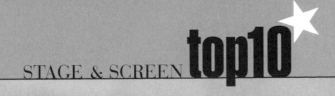

top10

TOP 10 ★
MOVIES DIRECTED BY STEVEN SPIELBERG

1	Jurassic Park	1993
2	E.T.: The Extra-Terrestrial	1982
3	Indiana Jones and the Last Crusade	1989
4	Jaws	1975
5	Saving Private Ryan	1998
6	Raiders of the Lost Ark	1981
7	Schindler's List	1993
8	Close Encounters of the Third Kind*	1977/80
9	Indiana Jones and the Temple of Doom	1984
10	The Lost World: Jurassic Park	1997

Re-edited and re-released as "Special Edition"

Steven Spielberg has directed some of the most successful movies of all time: the top five in this list appear among the top 22 movies of all time, while the cumulative world box-office gross of his Top 10 amounts to almost $4.5 billion.

TOP 10 MOVIES DIRECTED BY STANLEY KUBRICK

1 *The Shining*, 1980 2 *2001: A Space Odyssey*, 1968 3 *Full Metal Jacket*, 1987 4 *A Clockwork Orange*, 1971 5 *Spartacus*, 1960; = *Barry Lyndon*, 1975 7 *Dr. Strangelove or: How I Learned to Stop Worrying and Love the Bomb*, 1964 8 *Lolita*, 1962 9 *Paths of Glory*, 1957 10 *The Killing*, 1956

TOP 10 MOVIES DIRECTED BY ROBERT ZEMECKIS

1 *Forrest Gump*, 1994 2 *Who Framed Roger Rabbit*, 1988 3 *Back to the Future*, 1985 4 *Back to the Future Part III*, 1990 5 *Back to the Future Part II*, 1989 6 *Contact*, 1997 7 *Death Becomes Her*, 1992 8 *Romancing the Stone*, 1984 9 *Used Cars*, 1980 10 *I Wanna Hold Your Hand*, 1978

TOP 10 ★
MOVIES DIRECTED BY WOMEN

	MOVIE/YEAR	DIRECTOR
1	Look Who's Talking, 1989	Amy Heckerling
2	Sleepless in Seattle, 1993	Nora Ephron
3	Wayne's World, 1992	Penelope Spheeris
4	Big, 1988	Penny Marshall
5	A League of Their Own, 1992	Penny Marshall
6	The Prince of Tides, 1991	Barbra Streisand
7	Pet Sematary, 1989	Mary Lambert
8	Clueless, 1995	Amy Heckerling
9	Michael, 1996	Nora Ephron
10	National Lampoon's European Vacation, 1985	Amy Heckerling

TOP 10 MOVIES DIRECTED BY FRANCIS FORD COPPOLA

1 *Bram Stoker's Dracula*, 1992 2 *The Godfather*, 1972 3 *Jack*, 1996 4 *The Godfather Part III*, 1990 5 *Apocalypse Now*, 1979 6 *The Godfather Part II*, 1974 7 *The Rainmaker*, 1997 8 *Peggy Sue Got Married*, 1986 9 *The Cotton Club*, 1984 10 *The Outsiders*, 1983

TOP 10 ★
MOVIES DIRECTED OR PRODUCED BY GEORGE LUCAS

1	Star Wars*	1977/97
2	The Empire Strikes Back#	1980/97
3	Indiana Jones and the Last Crusade#	1989
4	Return of the Jedi#	1983
5	Raiders of the Lost Ark#	1981
6	Indiana Jones and the Temple of Doom#	1984
7	American Graffiti*	1973
8	Willow#	1988
9	The Land Before Time#	1988
10	Tucker: The Man and His Dream#	1988

* Director

Producer

STANLEY KUBRICK

Born in New York in 1928, Stanley Kubrick moved to England in the early 1960s. He never shied away from tackling controversial issues in his movies, from the dangers of a nuclear war (*Dr Strangelove or: How I Learned to Stop Worrying and Love the Bomb*) to the portrayal of a society where violence is the prerogative of both the government and the individual (*A Clockwork Orange*). He died in March 1999, just after completing his last movie, *Eyes Wide Shut*.

SNAP ★
SHOTS

TOP 10 ★
MOVIES WITH THE MOST EXTRAS

	MOVIE/COUNTRY/YEAR	EXTRAS
1	*Gandhi*, UK, 1982	300,000
2	*Kolberg*, Germany, 1945	187,000
3	*Monster Wang-Magwi*, South Korea, 1967	157,000
4	*War and Peace*, USSR, 1967	120,000
5	*Ilya Muromets*, USSR, 1956	106,000
6	*Tonko*, Japan, 1988	100,000
7	*The War of Independence*, Romania, 1912	80,000
8	*Around the World in 80 Days*, US, 1956	68,894
9=	*Intolerance*, US, 1916	60,000
=	*Dny Zrady*, Czechoslovakia, 1972	60,000

TOP 10 ★
COUNTRIES WITH THE MOST MOVIE THEATERS

	COUNTRY	THEATERS
1	US	23,662
2	Ukraine	14,960
3	India	8,975
4	China	4,639
5	France	4,365
6	Italy	3,816
7	Germany	3,814
8	Belarus	3,780
9	Uzbekistan	2,365
10	Spain	2,090

Source: Screen Digest

TOP 10 MOST PROLIFIC MOVIE-PRODUCING COUNTRIES
(Country/average no. of movies produced per annum in 1991–96)

❶ India, 851 ❷ US, 569 ❸ Japan, 252 ❹ Russia, 192 ❺ France, 143 ❻ China, 137 ❼ Italy, 107 ❽ South Korea, 80 ❾ Turkey, 71 ❿ UK, 65

Source: Screen Digest

TOP 10 MOVIEGOING COUNTRIES
(Country/total annual attendance)

❶ China, 14,428,400,000 ❷ India, 4,297,500,000 ❸ US, 981,900,000 ❹ Russia, 140,100,000 ❺ Japan, 130,700,000 ❻ France, 130,100,000 ❼ Germany, 124,500,000 ❽ UK, 114,600,000 ❾ Australia, 69,000,000 ❿ Lebanon, 99,200,000

Source: UNESCO

Did You Know? The longest-ever movie was the 85-hour *The Cure for Insomnia*, which was not released commercially.

TOP 10 MOVIE ATTENDERS

(Country/annual attendance per inhabitant)

1 Lebanon, 35.3 **2** China, 12.3 **3** Georgia, 5.6 **4** India, 5.0
5 Iceland, 4.5 **6** = Australia, 3.9; = New Zealand, 3.9;
= US, 3.9 **9** Monaco, 3.7 **10** Canada, 2.8
Source: *UNESCO*

TOP 10 ★
YEARS WITH MOST MOVIE VISITS IN THE US, 1946–98

	YEAR	NO. OF MOVIES RELEASED	BOX OFFICE GROSS ($)	ADMISSIONS
1	1946	400	1,692,000,000	4,067,300,000
2	1947	426	1,594,000,000	3,664,400,000
3	1948	444	1,506,000,000	3,422,700,000
4	1949	490	1,448,000,000	3,168,500,000
5	1950	483	1,379,000,000	3,017,500,000
6	1951	433	1,332,000,000	2,840,100,000
7	1952	389	1,325,000,000	2,777,700,000
8	1953	404	1,339,000,000	2,630,600,000
9	1954	369	1,251,000,000	2,270,400,000
10	1955	319	1,204,000,000	2,072,300,000

Source: *Motion Picture Association of America, Inc.*

From 1956, admissions continued to decline, reaching an all-time low of 820,300,000 in 1971. Since 1991, admissions have increased each year.

TOP 10 ★
LONGEST MOVIES EVER SCREENED

	MOVIE	COUNTRY/YEAR	DURATION HRS	MINS
1	The Longest and Most Meaningless Movie in the World	UK, 1970	48	0
2	The Burning of the Red Lotus Temple	China, 1928–31	27	0
3	****	US, 1967	25	0
4	Heimat	West Germany, 1984	15	40
5	Berlin Alexanderplatz	West Germany/Italy, 1980	15	21
6	The Journey	Sweden, 1987	14	33
7	The Old Testament	Italy, 1922	13	0
8	Comment Yukong déplace les montagnes	France, 1976	12	43
9	Out 1: Noli me Tangere	France, 1971	12	40
10	Ningen No Joken (The Human Condition)	Japan, 1958–60	9	29

The list includes commercially screened films, but not "stunt" films created solely to break endurance records (particularly those of their audiences).

TOP 10 ★
MOST EXPENSIVE ITEMS OF MOVIE MEMORABILIA EVER SOLD AT AUCTION

	ITEM/SALE	PRICE ($)
1	Vivien Leigh's Oscar for *Gone With the Wind*, Sotheby's, New York, Dec 15, 1993	562,500
2	Clark Gable's Oscar for *It Happened One Night*, Christie's, Los Angeles, Dec 15, 1996	607,500
3	Poster for *The Mummy, 1932*, Sotheby's, New York, Mar 1, 1997	453,500
4	James Bond's Aston Martin DB5 from *Goldfinger*, Sotheby's, New York, June 28, 1986	275,000
5	Clark Gable's personal script for *Gone With the Wind*, Christie's, Los Angeles, Dec 15, 1996	244,500
6	"Rosebud" sled from *Citizen Kane*, Christie's, Los Angeles, Dec 15, 1996	233,500
7	Herman J. Mankiewicz's scripts for *Citizen Kane* and *The American*, Christie's, New York, June 21, 1989	231,000
8	Judy Garland's ruby slippers from *The Wizard of Oz*, Christie's, New York, June 21, 1988	165,000
9	Piano from the Paris scene in *Casablanca*, Sotheby's, New York, Dec 16, 1988	154,000
10	Charlie Chaplin's hat and cane, Christie's, London, Dec 11, 1987 (resold at Christie's, London, Dec 17, 1993, for $86,900)	130,350*

* $/£ conversion at rate then prevailing

This list excludes animated film celluloids or "cels" – the individually painted scenes that are shot in sequence to make up cartoon films – which are now attaining colossal prices: just one of the 150,000 color cels from *Snow White and the Seven Dwarfs* (1937) was sold in 1991 for $209,000, and in 1989 $286,000 was reached for a black-and-white cel depicting Donald Duck in *Orphan's Benefit* (1934).

SILENT STAR

Chaplin's trademark hat and the cane that he twirled on screen made him the most instantly recognizable of the silent movie stars.

ANIMATION

TOP 10 ANIMATED MOVIES

1	The Lion King	1994
2	Aladdin	1992
3	A Bug's Life	1998
4	Toy Story	1995
5	Beauty and the Beast	1991
6	Who Framed Roger Rabbit*	1988
7	Pocahontas	1995
8	The Hunchback of Notre Dame	1996
9	Mulan	1998
10	Casper*	1995

* Part animated, part live action

The 1990s have already provided nine of the 10 most successful animated movies of all time, which have ejected a number of their high-earning predecessors – such as *Bambi*, *Fantasia*, and *Snow White and the Seven Dwarfs* – from this Top 10. Animated movies stand out among the leading moneymakers of each decade.

THE 10 ★
FIRST FULL-LENGTH SIMPSONS EPISODES

	EPISODE	FIRST SCREENED
1	Simpsons Roasting on an Open Fire	Dec 17, 1989
2	Bart the Genius	Jan 14, 1990
3	Homer's Odyssey	Jan 21, 1990
4	There's No Disgrace Like Homer	Jan 28, 1990
5	Bart the General	Feb 4, 1990
6	Moaning Lisa	Feb 11, 1990
7	The Call of the Simpsons	Feb 18, 1990
8	The Telltale Head	Feb 25, 1990
9	Life in the Fast Lane	Mar 18, 1990
10	Homer's Night Out	Mar 25, 1990

THE 10 ★
FIRST OSCAR-WINNING ANIMATED MOVIES*

YEAR	FILM	DIRECTOR#
1933	Flowers and Trees	Walt Disney
1934	The Three Little Pigs	Walt Disney
1935	The Tortoise and the Hare	Walt Disney
1936	Three Orphan Kittens	Walt Disney
1937	The Country Cousin	Walt Disney
1938	The Old Mill	Walt Disney
1939	Ferdinand the Bull	Walt Disney
1940	The Ugly Duckling	Walt Disney
1941	The Milky Way	Rudolf Ising
1942	Lend a Paw	Walt Disney

* In the category "Short Films (Cartoons)"
 # All US

THE 10 ★
LATEST OSCAR-WINNING ANIMATED MOVIES*

YEAR	FILM	DIRECTOR/COUNTRY
1998	Bunny	Chris Wedge, US
1997	Geri's Game	Jan Pinkava, US
1996	Quest	Tyron Montgomery, UK
1995	A Close Shave	Nick Park, UK
1994	Bob's Birthday	David Fine and Alison Snowden, UK
1993	The Wrong Trousers	Nick Park, UK
1992	Mona Lisa Descending a Staircase	Joan C. Gratz, US
1991	Manipulation	Daniel Greaves, UK
1990	Creature Comforts	Nick Park, UK
1989	Balance	Christoph and Wolfgang Lauenstein, West Germany

* In the category "Short Films (Animated)"

TOP 10 PART ANIMATION/PART LIVE ACTION FILMS

1 Who Framed Roger Rabbit, 1988 **2** Casper, 1995 **3** Space Jam, 1996 **4** 9 to 5, 1980 **5** Mary Poppins, 1964 **6** Song of the South, 1946 **7** Pete's Dragon, 1977 **8** Fletch Lives, 1989 **9** Bedknobs and Broomsticks, 1971 **10** Xanadu, 1980

TOP 10 WALT DISNEY ANIMATED FILMS

1 *The Lion King*, 1994 **2** *Aladdin*, 1992
3 *A Bug's Life*, 1998 **4** *Toy Story*, 1995
5 *Beauty and the Beast*, 1991
6 *Who Framed Roger Rabbit*, 1988
7 *Pocahontas*, 1995 **8** *The Hunchback of Notre Dame*, 1996 **9** *Mulan*, 1998
10 *Bambi*, 1942

In 1923, having started his business in Kansas City, Walt Disney moved to California, where he experienced modest success with his animated movies, until the advent of sound made a notable commercial success of *Steamboat Willie* (1928).

"YOU'RE NOT REAL!"

Woody tries unsuccessfully to convince Buzz that he is only a toy, not a real spaceman, in Toy Story, *the first-ever completely computer-generated animated film.*

TOP 10 ★ NON-DISNEY ANIMATED FEATURE FILMS

1	Prince of Egypt	1998
2	Antz	1998
3	The Rugrats Movie	1998
4	The Land Before Time	1988
5	An American Tail	1986
6	The Lord of the Rings	1978
7	All Dogs Go to Heaven	1989
8	Heavy Metal	1981
9	FernGully: The Last Rainforest	1992
10	Jetsons: The Movie	1990

THE 10 ★ FIRST DISNEY ANIMATED FEATURES

1	Snow White and the Seven Dwarfs	1937
2	Pinocchio	1940
3	Fantasia	1940
4	Dumbo	1941
5	Bambi	1942
6	Victory Through Air Power	1943
7	The Three Caballeros	1945
8	Make Mine Music	1946
9	Fun and Fancy Free	1947
10	Melody Time	1948

Excluding part-animated fims such as *Song of the South* and *Mary Poppins*, and films made specially for television serialization, Disney has made a total of 37 full-length animated feature films up to its 1998 release, *Mulan*.

THE 10 ★ FIRST TOM AND JERRY CARTOONS

	CARTOON	RELEASE DATE
1	Puss Gets the Boot*	Feb 20, 1940
2	The Midnight Snack	Jul 19, 1941
3	The Night Before Christmas*	Dec 6, 1941
4	Fraidy Cat	Jan 17, 1942
5	Dog Trouble	Apr 18, 1942
6	Puss 'N' Toots	May 30, 1942
7	The Bowling Alley-Cat	Jul 18, 1942
8	Fine Feathered Friend	Oct 10, 1942
9	Sufferin' Cats!	Jan 16, 1943
10	The Lonesome Mouse	May 22, 1943

* Academy Award nomination

The duo were created by William Hanna and Joseph Barbera and have been perennially popular during six decades.

What was the most successful Martin Scorsese film?
see p.186 for the answer
A *Cape Fear*
B *GoodFellas*
C *The Color of Money*

ON THE RADIO

MOST LISTENED-TO RADIO STATIONS IN THE US

	STATION	FORMAT	AQH*
1	WSKQ – FM	Hispanic Hits	156,600
2	WLTW – FM	Soft AC#	156,300
3	WQHT – FM	Top 40/Urban	151,900
4	WHTZ – FM	CHR	135,200
5	WCBS – FM	Oldies	122,000
6	KLVE – FM	Hispanic AC#	117,400
7	WRKS – FM	Black AC#	114,500
8	WKTU – FM	Urban Hits	113,400
9	KSCA – FM	Hispanic	110,800
10	WXRK – FM	Howard Stern/ New Rock	108,100

Average Quarter Hour statistic based on no. of listeners aged 12+ listening between Monday and Sunday 6.00 am to midnight, from Arbitron data

Adult Contemporary

Source: *Duncan's American Radio*

THE 10 ★
LATEST MOST LISTENED-TO RADIO STATIONS IN THE US

YEAR	STATION*
1998	WSKQ – FM
1997	WQHT – FM
1996	WKTU – FM
1995	WRKS – FM
1994	WLTW – FM
1993	WRKS – FM
1992	WRKS – FM
1991	WCBS – FM
1990	WRKS – FM
1989	WHTZ – FM

All New York-based

Source: *Duncan's American Radio*

TOP 10 ★
STATES WITH THE MOST NPR MEMBER STATIONS

	STATE	NPR STATIONS
1	New York	39
2	California	34
3	Ohio	26
4	Wisconsin	24
5	Michigan	22
6	Alaska	20
7	Texas	18
8	Florida	17
9	Colorado	16
10=	Illinois	15
=	Minnesota	15
=	North Carolina	15

Source: *National Public Radio*

TOP 10 ★
US RADIO STATIONS BY AUDIENCE SHARE

	STATION	FORMAT	PERCENTAGE SHARE
1	WFGY – FM	Country	24.6
2=	WXBQ – FM	Country	22.3
=	WZID – FM	AC/Soft AC*	22.3
4	WIVK – FM	Country	21.6
5	WTHI – FM	Country	21.1
6	WOVK – FM	Country	20.6
7	WDRM – FM	Country	20.5
8	WIKY – FM	AC*	20.3
9=	WKEE – FM	CHR/AC*	18.8
=	WIBW – FM	Country	18.8

Adult Contemporary

Source: *Duncan's American Radio, spring 1998 Arbitron data*

HER FATHER'S DAUGHTER
Zoe Ball hosts the Breakfast Show on Britain's BBC Radio 1 every weekday. Until recently one of the hosts of children's TV show Live and Kicking, she followed the career of her father, TV personality Johnny Ball.

Background Image: PORTABLE RADIO

TOP 10 ★
LONGEST-RUNNING PROGRAMS ON NPR

PROGRAM	FIRST BROADCAST
1 All Things Considered	1971
2 Weekend All Things Considered	1974
3 Fresh Air with Terry Gross	1977
4 Piano Jazz with Marion McPartland	1978
5 Morning Edition	1979
6 Weekend Edition/ Saturday with Scott Simon	1985
7 Performance Today	1987
8 Weekend Edition/ Sunday with Liane Hansen	1987
9 Car Talk	1987
10 Talk of the Nation	1991

Source: National Public Radio

TOP 10 ★
RADIO-OWNING COUNTRIES

COUNTRY	RADIO SETS PER 1,000 POPULATION
1 US	2,093
2 UK	1,433
3 Australia	1,304
4 Canada	1,053
5 Denmark	1,034
6 South Korea	1,024
7 Monaco	1,019
8 Finland	1,008
9 New Zealand	997
10 Germany	944

Source: UNESCO

In addition to the countries on this list, many small island communities have very high numbers of radios to enable people to maintain regular contact with the outside world.

THE 10 ★
LATEST GEORGE FOSTER PEABODY AWARDS FOR BROADCASTING WON BY NPR*

YEAR	AWARD
1998	Coverage of Africa/I Must Keep Fighting: The Art of Paul Robeson/Performance Today
1997	Jazz from Lincoln Center
1996	Remorse: The 14 Stories of Eric Morse
1995	Wynton Marsalis: Making the Music/ Marsalis on Music
1994	Tobacco Stories/Wade in the Water: African American Sacred Music Traditions (NPR/Smithsonian Institution)
1993	Health Reform Coverage 1993
1992	Prisoners in Bosnia
1991	The Coverage of the Judge Clarence Thomas Confirmation
1990	Manicu's Story: The War in Mozambique
1989	Scott Simon's Radio Essays on Weekend Edition Saturday

* Includes programs made or co-produced by NPR

Source: Peabody Awards

THE 10 ★
LATEST NAB HALL OF FAME INDUCTEES

YEAR	INDUCTEE/CATEGORY
1999	Wolfman Jack, radio personality
1998	Rush Limbaugh, radio personality
1997	Wally Phillips, radio personality
1996	Don Imus, radio personality
1995	Gary Owens, radio personality
1994	Harry Caray, radio sportscaster
1993	Grand Ole Opry, radio program
1992	Larry King, radio personality
1991	Douglas Edwards, radio correspondent
1990	Red Barber, radio sportscaster/Nathan Safir, Spanish broadcasting pioneer

Since 1977, the US National Association of Broadcasters' Hall of Fame has honored radio personalities and programs that have earned a place in US broadcasting history. Among its earlier inductees were Orson Welles and Bing Crosby, while two US Presidents have also been inducted: Herbert Hoover in 1977, and former radio sportscaster Ronald Reagan in 1981.

THE 10 ★
LATEST NAB NETWORK/ SYNDICATED PERSONALITIES OF THE YEAR

YEAR	PERSONALITY/NETWORK
1998	Paul Harvey, ABC Radio Networks
1997	Dr. Laura Schlessinger, Synergy Broadcasting
1996	Paul Harvey, ABC Radio Networks
1995	Rush Limbaugh, EFM Media Management
1994	Don Imus, Westwood One Radio Networks
1993	Charles Osgood, CBS Radio Networks
1992	Rush Limbaugh, EFM Media Management
1991	Paul Harvey, ABC Radio Networks
1990	Larry King, Mutual Broadcasting System
1989	Paul Harvey, ABC Radio Networks

The US National Association of Broadcasters presents annual awards in 22 different categories. They are known as the Marconi Awards in honor of radio pioneer and inventor Guglielmo Marconi.

TOP 10 ★
RADIO FORMATS IN THE US BY NO. OF STATIONS

FORMAT	NO. OF STATIONS
1 Country	2,491
2 News/Talk	1,111
3 AC	902
4 Oldies	755
5 Adult Standards	551
6 Spanish	474
7 Religion (teaching and variety*)	404
8 CHR (Top 40)	358
9 Soft AC	346
10 Rock	262

* Excluding Gospel and Contemporary Christian

Source: M Street

Did You Know? The very first radio broadcast in the US was sent on Dec 24, 1906, from Brant Rock, MA, by Professor Reginald Aubrey Essenden.

TOP TV

TALK PROGRAMS ON US TV, 1997–98

	PROGRAM	HOUSEHOLDS
1	Oprah Winfrey Show	7,180,000
2	Jerry Springer	6,270,000
3	Montel Williams Show	4,260,000
4	Salley Jessy Raphael	4,010,000
5	Live – Regis and Kathie Lee	3,950,000
6	Jenny Jones Show	3,901,000
7	Ricki Lake	3,390,000
8	Meet the Press	3,280,000
9	Maury Povich Show	3,080,000
9	Siskel and Ebert	2,640,000

© 1999 Nielsen Media Research

JUST GOOD FRIENDS
The coffee-loving stars of the internationally top-rated TV show Friends have all gone on to launch successful film careers in their own right.

TOP 10 ★

SYNDICATED PROGRAMS ON US TV, 1997–98

	PROGRAM	HOUSEHOLDS
1	Wheel of Fortune	15,930,000
2	Jeopardy!	13,090,000
3	Portfolio XV	11,360,000
4	WCW Wrestling	11,040,000
5	Home Improvement	10,520,000
6	X–Files	10,030,000
7	Buena Vista I	9,750,000
8	Seinfeld	9,500,000
9	ESPN NFL Football	9,160,000
10	ESPN NFL Regular Season	9,140,000

© 1999 Nielsen Media Research

TOP 10 ★

DAYTIME DRAMAS ON US TV, 1997–98

	PROGRAM	HOUSEHOLDS
1	The Young and the Restless	6,690,000
2	The Days of Our Lives	4,970,000
3	The Bold and the Beautiful	4,740,000
4	General Hospital	4,590,000
5	All My Children	4,290,000
6	As the World Turns	4,070,000
7	Guiding Light	3,920,000
8	One Life to Live	3,640,000
9	Another World	2,600,000
10	Port Charles	2,080,000

© 1999 Nielsen Media Research

TOP 10 ★

MOST WATCHED PROGRAMS OF ALL TIME ON PBS TV*

	PROGRAM/BROADCAST	AVERAGE AUDIENCE
1	The Civil War, Sept 1990	8.8
2	Life on Earth, Jan 1982	7.9
3	The Living Planet: A Portrait of the Earth, Feb 1985	7.8
4	The American Experience: The Kennedys, Sept 1992	7.0
5	Nature: Kingdom of the Ice Bear, Feb 1986	6.9
6	Cosmos, Sept 1980	6.5
7	=Planet Earth, Jan 1986	6.3
	=Lewis and Clark: The Journey of the Corps of Discovery, Nov 1997	6.3
9	Baseball, Sept 1994	5.5
10	The Dinosaurs!, Nov 1992	5.3

* As of April 1999

Source: PBS Research Department

TOP 10 ★
TV MOVIES IN THE US, 1997–98

	MOVIE	NETWORK	HOUSEHOLDS
1	Sunday Movie: *What the Deaf Man Heard*	CBS	22,530,000
2	Sunday Night Movie: *Merlin, Part I*	NBC	21,260,000
3	Movie of the Week: *Merlin, Part II*	NBC	20,170,000
4	Sunday Night Movie: *Before Women Had Wings*	ABC	18,380,000
5	Wonderful World of Disney: *Cinderella*	ABC	18,350,000
6	Sunday Movie: *Borrowed Hearts*	CBS	18,010,000
7	Sunday Night Movie: Oprah Winfrey Presents: *Wedding, Part I*	ABC	16,450,000
8	Sunday Movie: *Ellen Foster*	CBS	16,130,000
9	Sunday Movie: *The Echo of Thunder*	CBS	16,050,000
10	Sunday Movie: *The Long Way Home*	CBS	15,380,000

© 1999 Nielsen Media Research

TOP 10 TELEVISION-WATCHING COUNTRIES
(Country/average daily viewing time in hrs:mins)

1 US, 3:59   **2** = Italy, 3:36; = Turkey, 3:36   **4** UK, 3:35   **5** Spain, 3:34   **6** Hungary, 3:33   **7** Japan, 3:25   **8** Greece, 3:22   **9** Canada, 3:12   **10** Argentina, 3:11

Source: *Screen Digest/Eurodate TV*

TOP 10 ★
TV AUDIENCES OF ALL TIME IN THE US

	PROGRAM	DATE	HOUSHOLDS VIEWING TOTAL	%
1	*M*A*S*H* Farewell Special	Feb 28, 1983	50,150,000	60.2
2	*Dallas*	Nov 21, 1980	41,470,000	53.3
3	*Roots* Part 8	Jan 30, 1977	36,380,000	51.1
4	Super Bowl XVI	Jan 24, 1982	40,020,000	49.1
5	Super Bowl XVII	Jan 30, 1983	40,480,000	48.6
6	XVII Winter Olympics	Feb 23, 1994	45,690,000	48.5
7	Super Bowl XX	Jan 26, 1986	41,490,000	48.3
8	*Gone With the Wind* Pt. 1	Nov 7, 1976	33,960,000	47.7
9	*Gone With the Wind* Pt. 2	Nov 8, 1976	33,750,000	47.4
10	Super Bowl XII	Jan 15, 1978	34,410,000	47.2

© 1999 Nielsen Media Research

TOP 10 CABLE TELEVISION COUNTRIES
(Country/subscribers)

1 US, 67,011,180   **2** Germany, 18,740,260   **3** Netherlands, 6,227,472   **4** Russia, 5,784,432   **5** Belgium, 3,945,342   **6** Poland, 3,830,788   **7** Romania, 3,000,000   **8** UK, 2,666,783   **9** France, 2,478,630   **10** Switzerland, 2,156,120

Source: *The Phillips Group*

Although the US is the world's most cabled country, its services are fragmented between numerous operators, with TCI the foremost company, followed by Time Warner Cable. In Europe, a smaller number of large companies dominate the market, with Germany's Deutsche Telekom providing service to more homes than any single US operator.

THE 10 FIRST COUNTRIES TO HAVE TELEVISION*
(Country/year#)

1 UK, 1936   **2** US, 1939   **3** USSR, 1939   **4** France, 1948   **5** Brazil, 1950   **6** Cuba, 1950   **7** Mexico, 1950   **8** Argentina, 1951   **9** Denmark, 1951   **10** Netherlands, 1951

* High-definition regular public broadcasting service
 # Countries sharing the same year are ranked by month

TOP 10 ★
MOVIES OF ALL TIME ON PRIME-TIME NETWORK TV

	MOVIE/YEAR RELEASED	BROADCAST	RATING (%)*
1	*Gone With the Wind* Pt. 1, 1939	Nov 7, 1976	47.7
2	*Gone With the Wind* Pt. 2, 1939	Nov 8, 1976	47.4
3	= *Love Story*, 1970	Oct, 1 1972	42.3
	= *Airport*, 1970	Nov 11, 1973	42.3
5	*The Godfather, Part II*, 1974	Nov 18, 1974	39.4
6	*Jaws*, 1975	Nov 4, 1979	39.1
7	*The Poseidon Adventure*, 1972	Oct 27, 1974	39.0
8	= *True Grit*, 1969	Nov 12, 1972	38.9
	= *The Birds*, 1963	Jan 6, 1968	38.9
10	*Patton*, 1970	Nov 19, 1972	38.5

* Of households viewing

© 1999 Nielsen Media Research

All the movies listed are dramas made for theatrical release, but if made-for-TV productions were included, then the controversial 1983 post-nuclear war movie, *The Day After* (screened on Nov 20, 1983), would rank in third place with a rating of 46.0 percent. It is significant that all the most watched movies on TV were broadcast before the dawn of the video-era.

Background image: 1970s SPACE-AGE TELEVISION

Did You Know? The first demonstration of television was given by John Logie Baird in 1926, but his mechanical "Televisor" could not transmit pictures and sound at the same time.

TV OF THE DECADES

TV SERIES OF THE 1990s IN THE US

SERIES	NETWORK	SEASON	RATING (%)*
1 = The Cosby Show	NBC	1989/90	23.1
= Roseanne	ABC	1989/90	23.1
3 Cheers	NBC	1989/90	22.7
4 = ER	NBC	1995/96	22.0
= Seinfeld	NBC	1997/98	22.0
6 A Different World	NBC	1989/90	21.1
7 = 60 Minutes	CBS	1991/2;1992/3	21.9
= Home Improvement	ABC	1993/94	21.9
9 America's Funniest Home Videos	ABC	1989/90	20.9
10 The Golden Girls	NBC	1989/90	20.1

*Highest rated season during decade for each series only

© 1999 Nielsen Media Research

TV SERIES OF THE 1980s IN THE US

SERIES	NETWORK	SEASON	RATING (%)*
1 The Cosby Show	NBC	1986/87	34.9
2 Dallas	CBS	1980/81	34.5
3 Family Ties	NBC	1985/86	32.7
4 60 Minutes	CBS	1979/80	28.4
5 The Dukes of Hazard	CBS	1980/81	27.3
6 Cheers	NBC	1986/87	27.2
7 Three's Company	ABC	1979/80	26.3
8 That's Incredible	ABC	1979/80	25.8
9 M*A*S*H	CBS	1980/81	25.7
10 Murder, She Wrote	CBS	1986/87	25.4

*Highest rated season during decade for each series only

© 1999 Nielsen Media Research

TV SERIES OF THE 1970s IN THE US

SERIES	NETWORK	SEASON	RATING (%)*
1 All in the Family	CBS	1971/72	34.0
2 Laverne & Shirley	ABC	1977/78	31.6
3 Happy Days	ABC	1976/77	31.5
4 Three's Company	ABC	1978/79	30.3
5 Marcus Welby, MD	ABC	1970/71	29.6
6 Sanford and Son	NBC	1974/75	29.6
7 Chico and the Man	NBC	1974/75	28.5
8 60 Minutes	CBS	1979/80	28.4
9 The Flip Wilson Show	CBS	1971/72	28.2
10 The Waltons	CBS	1973/74	28.1

*Highest rated season during decade for each series only

© 1999 Nielsen Media Research

TV SERIES OF THE 1960s IN THE US

SERIES	NETWORK	SEASON	RATING (%)*
1 The Beverly Hillbillies	CBS	1963/64	39.1
2 Bonanza	CBS	1963/64	36.9
3 The Dick Van Dyke Show	CBS	1963/64	33.3
4 Rowan & Martin's Laugh-In	NBC	1968/69	31.8
5 Bewitched	ABC	1964/65	31.0
6 Gomer Pyle, USMC	CBS	1964/65	30.7
7 Petticoat Junction	CBS	1963/64	30.3
8 The Andy Griffith Show	CBS	1963/64	29.4
9 The Red Skelton Hour	CBS	1966/67	28.2
10 The Lucy Show	CBS	1963/64	28.1

*Highest rated season during decade for each series only

© 1999 Nielsen Media Research

TOP 10 TV SERIES OF THE 1950s IN THE US

(Series/network/season/rating %*)

1 I Love Lucy, CBS, 1952/53, 67.3 **2** Texaco Star Theater, NBC, 1950/51, 61.6 **3** Arthur Godfrey's Talent Scouts, CBS, 1952/53, 54.7 **4** Dragnet, NBC, 1953/54, 53.6 **5** Fireside Theater, NBC, 1950/51, 52.6 **6** The Red Skelton Show, NBC, 1951/52, 50.2 **7** The $64,000 Question, CBS, 1955/56, 47.5 **8** Arthur Godfrey and His Friends, CBS, 1952/53, 47.1 **9** The Buick Circus Hour, NBC, 1952/53, 46.0 **10** Philco TV Playhouse, NBC, 1950/51, 45.3

*Highest rated season during decade for each series only   © 1999 Nielsen Media Research

Background image: SCENE FROM DALLAS

THE 10 LATEST WINNERS OF THE "OUTSTANDING DRAMA" EMMY AWARD

(Season ending/program)

1 1998, *The Practice*   **2** 1997, *Law & Order*   **3** 1996, *ER*   **4** 1995, *NYPD Blues*
5 1994, *Picket Fences*   **6** 1993, *Picket Fences*   **7** 1992, *Northern Exposure*
8 1991, *LA Law*   **9** 1991, *LA Law*   **10** 1991, *LA Law*

THE 10 ★ LATEST WINNERS OF THE "LEAD ACTOR IN A DRAMA SERIES" EMMY AWARD

SEASON ENDING	ACTOR	PROGRAM
1998	Andre Braugher	*Homicide: Life on the Street*
1997	Dennis Franz	*NYPD Blue*
1996	Dennis Franz	*NYPD Blue*
1995	Mandy Patinkin	*Chicago Hope*
1994	Dennis Franz	*NYPD Blue*
1993	Tom Skerritt	*Picket Fences*
1992	Christoper Lloyd	*Avonlea*
1991	James Earl Jones	*Gabriel's Fire*
1990	Peter Falk	*Colombo*
1989	Carroll O'Connor	*In the Heat of the Night*

THE 10 ★ LATEST WINNERS OF THE "LEAD ACTOR IN A COMEDY SERIES" EMMY AWARD

SEASON ENDING	ACTOR	PROGRAM
1998	Kelsey Grammer	*Frasier*
1997	John Lithgow	*3rd Rock from the Sun*
1996	John Lithgow	*3rd Rock from the Sun*
1995	Kelsey Grammer	*Frasier*
1994	Kelsey Grammer	*Frasier*
1993	Ted Danson	*Cheers*
1992	Craig T. Nelson	*Coach*
1991	Burt Reynolds	*Evening Shade*
1990	Ted Danson	*Cheers*
1989	Richard Mulligan	*Empty Nest*

THE 10 ★ LATEST WINNERS OF THE "LEAD ACTRESS IN A COMEDY SERIES" EMMY AWARD

SEASON ENDING	ACTRESS	PROGRAM
1998	Helen Hunt	*Mad About You*
1997	Helen Hunt	*Mad About You*
1996	Helen Hunt	*Mad About You*
1995	Candice Bergen	*Murphy Brown*
1994	Candice Bergen	*Murphy Brown*
1993	Roseanne	*Roseanne*
1992	Candice Bergen	*Murphy Brown*
1991	Kirstie Alley	*Cheers*
1990	Candice Bergen	*Murphy Brown*
1989	Candice Bergen	*Murphy Brown*

THE 10 ★ LATEST WINNERS OF THE "LEAD ACTRESS IN A DRAMA SERIES" EMMY AWARD

SEASON ENDING	ACTRESS	PROGRAM
1998	Christine Lahti	*Chicago Hope*
1997	Gillian Anderson	*The X–Files*
1996	Kathy Baker	*Picket Fences*
1995	Kathy Baker	*Picket Fences*
1994	Sela Ward	*Sisters*
1993	Kathy Baker	*Picket Fences*
1992	Dana Delany	*China Beach*
1991	Patricia Wettig	*Thirtysomething*
1990	Patricia Wettig	*Thirtysomething*
1989	Dana Delany	*China Beach*

GEORGE CLOONEY

After years as a struggling actor in failed TV pilots and low-budget films, George Clooney finally made the big time playing heartthrob pediatrician Doug Ross in Michael Crichton's medical drama *ER*. He has gone on to star in a series of major movies, including *One Fine Day*, *Out of Sight*, and Quentin Tarantino's *From Dusk Till Dawn*; he also took the title role in Tim Burton's *Batman*. *ER* is one of the top-rated shows in the US, pulling in audiences of 18 million households. In the UK, although popular, it enjoys more of a cult status. His army of fans mourned his departure from *ER* in May 1999.

SNAP SHOTS

Which was the first country to have television?
see p.195 for the answer

A US
B UK
C USSR

197

CHILDREN'S TV & VIDEO

LATEST WINNERS OF THE DAYTIME EMMY AWARD FOR A CHILDREN'S PROGRAM

SEASON	PROGRAM
1998/99	*The Island on Bird Street*
1997/98	*In His Father's Shoes*
1996/97	*Elmo Saves Christmas*
1995/96	*Stand up*
1994/95	*A Child Betrayed: The Calvin Mire Story*
1993/94	*Dead Drunk: The Kevin Tunnel Story*
1992/93	*ABC Afterschool Special: Shades of a Single Protein*
1991/92	*Vincent and Me*
1990/91	*Lost in the Barrens*
1989/90	*CBS Schoolbreak Special: A Matter of Conscience*

LATEST WINNERS OF THE DAYTIME EMMY AWARD FOR A CHILDREN'S ANIMATED PROGRAM

SEASON	PROGRAM
1998/99	*Steven Spielberg Presents: Pinky and the Brain*
1997/98	*Arthur*
1996/97	*Animaniacs*
1995/96	*Animaniacs*
1994/95	*Where on Earth is Carmen Sandiego*
1993/94	*Rugrats*
1992/93	*Tiny Toon Adventures*
1991/92	*Rugrats*
1990/91	*Tiiny Toon Adventures*
1989/90	*Beetlejuice/The New Adventures of Winnie the Pooh (tie)*

LATEST WINNERS OF THE DAYTIME EMMY AWARD FOR A CHILDREN'S SERIES

SEASON	SERIES
1998/99	Preschool: *Sesame Street* School age: *Bill Nye the Science Guy*
1997/98	*Sesame Street*
1996/97	Preschool: *Sesame Street* School age: *Reading Rainbow*
1995/96	*Reading Rainbow*
1994/95	*Nick News*
1993/94	*Sesame Street*
1992/93	*Reading Rainbow*
1991/92	*Sesame Street*
1990/91	*Sesame Street*
1989/90	*Reading Rainbow*

GLUED TO THE TV

When asked to rank their favorite activities, children tend to put watching TV a long way down the list. However, research shows that they spend, on average, between 4 and 6 hours a day in front of the TV.

TOP 10 ★
TELEVISION PROGRAMS WATCHED BY MOST CHILDREN IN THE US, 1997–98

	PROGRAM	NETWORK	VIEWERS AGED 2–12
1	Sabrina the Teenage Witch	ABC	3,330,000
2	Boy Meets World	ABC	3,060,000
3	Wonderful World of Disney	ABC	2,990,000
4 =	Teen-Angel	ABC	2,950,000
=	You Wish	ABC	2,950,000
6	King of the Hill	Fox	2,660,000
7	Simpsons	Fox	2,560,000
8	Seinfeld	NBC	2,100,000
9	Home Improvement	ABC	1,840,000
10	Friends	NBC	1,800,000

© 1999 Nielsen Media Research

TOP 10 ★
CHILDREN'S VIDEOS IN THE US, 1998

	VIDEO	LABEL
1	The Lion King II – Simba's Pride	Buena Vista
2	Pocahontas – Journey to a New World	Disney
3	The Land Before Time VI: The Secret of Saurus Rock	Universal
4	Dr. Seuss: How the Grinch Stole Christmas	MGM
5	The Land Before Time V: The Mysterious Island	Universal
6	Billboard Dad	Warner
7	Blue's Clues Storytime	Paramount
8	Scooby Doo on Zombie Island	Turner
9	Dance with the Teletubbies	PBS
10	Elmopalooza	Sony Wonder

Source: *Videoscan, Inc.*

TOP 10 ★
BESTSELLING CHILDREN'S VIDEOS IN THE UK*

1	The Jungle Book
2	The Lion King
3	Snow White and the Seven Dwarfs
4	Toy Story
5	Fantasia
6	One Hundred and One Dalmatians
7	Lady and the Tramp
8	Beauty and the Beast
9	Aladdin
10	Cinderella

* To April 30, 1999

TOP 10 ★
CHILDREN'S VIDEOS IN THE UK, 1998

1	Lady and the Tramp
2	Hercules
3	Peter Pan
4	Anastasia
5	The Little Mermaid
6	Rudolph the Red-Nosed Reindeer
7	Beauty and the Beast: Enchanted Christmas
8	Cinderella
9	Teletubbies – Nursery Rhymes
10	Teletubbies – Happy Xmas

Source: *British Video Association*

VIRTUAL VIDEO

The story of Woody the Cowboy and his rival, Buzz Lightyear the Space Ranger, was the first entirely computer-generated full-length feature film. Its stunningly realistic animation won its creator John Lasseter an Oscar.
© DISNEY

What is the bestselling non-Disney animated feature film?
see p.191 for the answer

A *Antz*
B *The Land Before Time*
C *Prince of Egypt*

TAPE LEISURE

The advent of the video age has revolutionized television viewing habits. No longer constrained by the program schedules, people can now watch what they want, when it suits them.

TOP 10 ★
BESTSELLING MUSIC VIDEOS OF 1998 IN THE US

	VIDEO	ARTIST
1	Tulsa, Tokyo and the Middle of Nowhere	Hanson
2	All Access Video	Backstreet Boys
3	One Hour of Girl Power	Spice Girls
4	Rage Against the Machine	Rage Against the Machine
5	MP Da Lost Don	Master P
6	Tribute	Yanni
7	The Dance	Fleetwood Mac
8	Girl Power! Live in Istanbul	Spice Girls
9	Garth Live from Central Park	Garth Brooks
10	Closure	Nine Inch Nails

Source: Billboard

TOP 10 ★
COUNTRIES WITH THE MOST VIDEO RENTAL OUTLETS

	COUNTRY	EST. NO. OF RENTAL OUTLETS
1	US	27,944
2	Pakistan	25,000
3	China	20,000
4	South Korea	19,000
5	Romania	15,000
6	=Bulgaria	10,000
	=India	10,000
	=Japan	10,000
	=Poland	10,000
10	Brazil	9,710

Source: Screen Digest

TOP 10 ★
BESTSELLING SPORTS VIDEOS OF 1998 IN THE US

	VIDEO	SPORT
1	The Official 1997 World Series Video	Baseball
2	Michael Jordan: Above and Beyond	Basketball
3	Denver Broncos: Super Bowl XXXII Champions	Football
4	Gretzky: The Great One and the Next Ones	Hockey
5	This Week in Baseball: 20 Years of Unforgettable Plays and Bloopers	Hockey
6	Pure Payton	Football
7	Michael Jordan's Playground	Basketball
8	The Ultimate Fighting Championship 4	Boxing
9	Tiger Woods: Son, Hero and Champion	Golf
10	Michael Jordan: Air Time	Basketball

Source: Billboard

TOP 10 ★
COUNTRIES WITH THE MOST VIDEO RENTAL OUTLETS PER 1,000,000 POPULATION

	COUNTRY	OUTLETS PER 1,000,000 POPULATION
1	Bulgaria	1,186.5
2	Iceland	697.1
3	Romania	663.5
4	South Korea	415.6
5	Denmark	323.9
6	Ireland	311.0
7	Canada	267.2
8	Poland	258.8
9	Sri Lanka	231.6
10	Hungary	200.2

Source: Screen Digest

What has been Whoopi Goldberg's most successful film?
see p.184 for the answer
A *The Color Purple*
B *Sister Act*
C *Ghost*

TOP 10 ★
DVD SALES IN THE US, 1998

	TITLE	LABEL
1	Tomorrow Never Dies	MGM
2	Godzilla	Columbia
3	Air Force One	Columbia
4	US Marshals	Warner
5	Lost in Space	New Line
6	Lethal Weapon 4	Warner
7	Starship Troopers	Columbia
8	Mask of Zorro	Columbia
9	Gone With the Wind	MGM
10	LA Confidential	Warner

Source: Videoscan Inc.

TOP 10 MOST RENTED VIDEOS IN THE US, 1998

	TITLE	LABEL
1	LA Confidential	Warner
2	Face/Off	Paramount
3	As Good As It Gets	Columbia TriStar
4	Good Will Hunting	Miramax/Buena Vista
5	The Devil's Advocate	Warner
6	Boogie Nights	New Line/Warner
7	The Full Monty	Fox Video
8	The Game	Polygram
9	Wag the Dog	New Line/Warner
10	Austin Powers: International Man of Mystery	New Line/Warner

Source: Billboard

TOP 10 MOVIE SALES ON VIDEO IN THE US, 1998

1 Titanic 2 The Lion King II: Simba's Pride 3 The Little Mermaid 4 Lady and the Tramp 5 Peter Pan 6 Armageddon 7 Hercules 8 Dr. Dolittle 9 Anastasia 10 Austin Powers: International Man of Mystery

Source: Videoscan, Inc.

TOP 10 ★
COUNTRIES WITH THE MOST VCRs

	COUNTRY/PERCENT OF HOMES	VCRs
1	US, 89.6	86,825,000
2	China, 13.3	40,000,000
3	Japan, 80.4	34,309,000
4	Germany, 71.8	26,328,000
5	UK, 81.7	18,848,000
6	Brazil, 37.2	15,488,000
7	France, 70.4	15,483,000
8	Italy, 60.2	13,161,000
9	Russia, 20.6	10,315,000
10	Mexico, 56.7	8,540,000

Source: Screen Digest

SPECIAL DELIVERY

Will Smith, one of the Men in Black, takes a break from blasting extraterrestrials into oblivion to assist at the birth of an alien baby.

THE COMMERCIAL WORLD

WORKERS & INVENTORS

WORKERS OF THE WORLD
Migrant workers at this clothing factory in Guangdong province account for just some of China's massive work force.

TOP 10 ★
COUNTRIES WITH THE MOST WORKERS

	COUNTRY	WORKERS (1998)*
1	China	709,000,000
2	India	398,000,000
3	US	133,000,000
4	Indonesia	89,000,000
5	Russia	77,000,000
6	Brazil	71,000,000
7	Japan	66,000,000
8	Bangladesh	60,000,000
9	Pakistan	46,000,000
10	Nigeria	44,000,000
	UK	29,000,000

* Based on people aged 15–64 who are currently employed; unpaid groups are not included.
Source: World Bank

THE 10 ★
FIRST PATENTS IN THE US

	PATENTEE	PATENT	DATE
1	Samuel Hopkins	Making pot and pearl ash	Jul 31, 1790
2	Joseph S. Sampson	Candle making	Aug 6, 1790
3	Oliver Evans	Flour and meal making	Dec 18, 1790
4 =	Francis Bailey	Punches for type	Jan 29, 1791
=	Aaron Putnam	Improvement in distilling	Jan 29, 1791
6	John Stone	Driving piles	Mar 10, 1791
7 =	Samuel Mullikin	Threshing machine	Mar 11, 1791
=	Samuel Mullikin	Breaking hemp	Mar 11, 1791
=	Samuel Mullikin	Polishing marble	Mar 11, 1791
=	Samuel Mullikin	Raising nap on cloth	Mar 11, 1791

A patent is an exclusive license to manufacture and exploit a unique product or process for a fixed period. The world's first patent, by which the architect Filippo Brunelleschi was granted the exclusive license to make a barge crane to transport marble, was issued in Florence in 1421. Of the most prolific patentees in the US, Thomas Edison tops the bill with a massive 1,093 patents. Electricity, radio, and television feature prominently among the many patents credited to the most prolific patentees in the US, but their inventions also cover the Polaroid camera and the tape drive used in the Sony Walkman.

Did You Know? In 1596, Queen Elizabeth I issued a patent to Sir John Harington for a water closet.

THE 10 ★
FIRST TRADEMARKS ISSUED IN THE US

	ISSUED TO	PRODUCT
1	Averill Chemical-Paint Co.	Liquid paint
2	J.B. Baldy & Co.	Mustard
3	Ellis Branson	Retail coal
4	Tracy Coit	Fish
5	William Lanfair Ellis & Co.	Oyster packing
6	Evans, Clow, Dalzell & Co.	Wrought-iron pipe
7	W.E. Garrett & Sons	Snuff
8	William G. Hamilton	Cartwheel
9	John K. Hogg	Soap
10	Abraham P. Olzendam	Woolen hose

All of these trademarks were registered on the same day, October 25, 1870, and are ranked only by the trademark numbers assigned to them.

TOP 10 ★
OCCUPATIONS IN THE US

	JOB SECTOR*	EMPLOYEES#
1	Machine operators, assemblers, and inspectors	7,406,000
2	Sales workers (retail and personal services)	6,689,000
3	Food service	6,134,000
4	Construction trades	5,539,000
5	Teachers (except college and university)	5,371,000
6	Mechanics and repairers	5,025,000
7	Sales supervisors and proprietors	4,968,000
8	Handlers, equipment cleaners, helpers, and laborers	4,944,000
9	Management-related	4,800,000
10	Motor vehicle operators	4,085,000

* Excluding general and miscellaneous group categories; # As of February 1999

Source: *U.S. Bureau of Labor Statistics*

THE 10 ★
FIRST WOMEN PATENTEES IN THE US

	PATENTEE	PATENT	DATE
1	Mary Kies	Straw weaving with silk or thread	May 5, 1809
2	Mary Brush	Corset	Jul 21, 1815
3	Sophia Usher	Carbonated liquid	Sep 11, 1819
4	Julia Planton	Foot stove	Nov 4, 1822
5	Lucy Burnap	Weaving grass hats	Feb 16, 1823
6	Diana H. Tuttle	Accelerating spinning-wheel heads	May 17, 1824
7	Catharine Elliot	Manufacturing moccasins	Jan 26, 1825
8	Phoebe Collier	Sawing wheel-fellies (rims)	May 20, 1826
9	Elizabeth H. Buckley	Sheet-iron shovel	Feb 28, 1828
10	Henrietta Cooper	Whitening leghorn straw	Nov 12, 1828

TOP 10 EMPLOYERS IN THE US

(Company/employees, 1998)

1 U.S. Postal Service, 898,384   **2** Wal-Mart Stores, 825,000   **3** General Motors, 608,000   **4** Ford Motor, 363,892   **5** United Parcel Service, 331,000   **6** Sears Roebuck, 296,000   **7** Columbia/HCA Healthcare, 285,000   **8** General Electric, 276,000   **9** IBM, 269,565   **10** J.C. Penney, 260,000

Source: *Fortune 500*

PRODUCTION LINE

A Ford worker at the Halewood factory near Liverpool, UK. Car manufacturing is still big business, but some plants have had to close due to falling sales.

TOP 10 ★
CORPORATIONS IN THE US

	CORPORATION	1998 REVENUE ($)
1	General Motors	161,315,000,000
2	Ford Motor Company	144,416,000,000
3	Wal-Mart Stores	139,208,000,000
4	Exxon Corp.	100,697,000,000
5	General Electric	100,469,000,000
6	IBM	81,667,000,000
7	Citigroup	76,431,000,000
8	Philip Morris	57,813,000,000
9	Boeing	56,154,000,000
10	AT&T	53,588,000,000

Source: *Fortune 500*

TOP 10 ★
OLDEST ESTABLISHED BUSINESSES IN THE US

	COMPANY	BUSINESS	FOUNDED
1	J.E. Rhoads & Sons	Conveyor belts,	1702
2	Covenant Life Assurance	Insurance,	1717
3	Philadelphia Contributorship	Insurance,	1752
4	Dexter Corporation	Adhesives, etc.,	1767
5=	D. Landreth Seed	Seeds,	1784;
=	Bank of New York	Banking,	1784
=	Mutual Assurance	Insurance,	1784
=	Bank of Boston	Banking,	1784
9=	Burns & Russell	Building materials,	1789
=	George R. Ruhl & Sons	Bakery supplies,	1789

SHARE DEALING

Trading is brisk at the Petroleum Exchange in London. The traders' different colored jackets denote the company to which they belong.

TOP 10 ★
SUPERMARKET GROUPS IN THE US

COMPANY	ANNUAL SALES ($)
1 Kroger Co.	43,100,000,000
2 Albertson's	35,700,000,000
3 Wal-Mart Supercenters	32,000,000,000
4 Safeway	25,000,000,000
5 Ahold USA	19,700,000,000
6 Supervalu	17,800,000,000
7 Fleming Cos.	15,100,000,000
8 Winn-Dixie Stores	13,900,000,000
9 Publix Super Markets	12,100,000,000
10 A&P	10,500,000,000

Source: *Food Marketing Institute*

TOP 10 ★
INTERNATIONAL INDUSTRIAL COMPANIES

COMPANY/ LOCATION/SECTOR	ANNUAL SALES ($)
1 General Motors Corp., US, Transport	178,174,000,000
2 Ford Motor Co., US, Transport	153,627,000,000
3 Mitsui and Co. Ltd., Japan, Trading	142,688,000,000
4 Mitsubishi Corp., Japan, Trading	128,922,000,000
5 Royal Dutch/Shell Group, UK/Netherlands, Oil, gas, fuel	128,142,000,000
6 Itochu Corp., Japan, Trading	126,632,000,000
7 Exxon Corp., US, Oil, gas, fuel	122,379,000,000
8 Wal-Mart Stores, Inc., US, Retailing	119,299,000,000
9 Marubeni Corp., Japan, Trading	111,121,000,000
10 Sumitomo Corp., Japan, Trading	102,395,000,000

Source: *Fortune Global 500*

TOP 10 ★
US COMPANIES MAKING THE GREATEST PROFIT PER SECOND

COMPANY	PROFIT PER SEC ($)
1 Ford Motor Co.	699
2 General Electric	294
3 AT&T	202
4 Exxon Corp.	201
5 IBM	200
6 Intel Corp.	192
7 Citigroup	184
8 Philip Morris Companies, Inc.	170
9 Merck	166
10 BankAmerica Corp.	163

TOP 10 ★
RICHEST COUNTRIES

COUNTRY	GDP PER CAPITA ($)
1 = Liechtenstein	42,416
= Switzerland	42,416
3 Japan	41,718
4 Luxembourg	35,109
5 Norway	33,734
6 Denmark	33,191
7 Germany	29,632
8 Austria	29,006
9 Belgium	26,582
10 Monaco	26,470
US	*26,037*

Source: *United Nations*

GDP (Gross Domestic Product) is the total value of all the goods and services produced annually within a country (Gross National Product, GNP, also includes income from overseas). Dividing GDP by the country's population produces GDP per capita, which is often used as a measure of how "rich" a country is.

THE 10 ★
COUNTRIES MOST IN DEBT

COUNTRY	TOTAL EXTERNAL DEBT ($)
1 Mexico	165,743,000,000
2 Brazil	159,139,000,000
3 Russia	120,461,000,000
4 China	118,090,000,000
5 Indonesia	107,831,000,000
6 India	93,766,000,000
7 Argentina	89,747,000,000
8 Turkey	73,592,000,000
9 Thailand	56,789,000,000
10 Poland	42,291,000,000

Source: *World Bank*

The World Bank's annual debt calculations estimate the total indebtedness of low and middle income countries at $2,177,000,000,000 in 1996.

THE 10 ★
POOREST COUNTRIES

COUNTRY	GDP PER CAPITA ($)
1 Sudan	36
2 São Tomé and Principe	49
3 Mozambique	77
4 = Eritrea	96
= Ethiopia	96
6 Dem. Rep. of Congo	117
7 Somalia	119
8 Tajikistan	122
9 Cambodia	130
10 Guinea-Bissau	131

Source: *United Nations*

It is hard to imagine living on as little as $36 per year, but $1 in Sudan, for example, purchases far more than in the US and UK.

Who is the youngest $ billionaire in the US?
see p.219 for the answer

A Daniel Morton Ziff
B Michael Dell
C Robert David Ziff

IMPORTS & EXPORTS

TOP 10 ★ DUTY-FREE COUNTRIES

	COUNTRY	ANNUAL SALES ($)
1	UK	2,452,000,000
2	US	1,652,000,000
3	Finland	962,000,000
4	South Korea	908,000,000
5	Germany	864,000,000
6	France	683,000,000
7	Denmark	646,000,000
8	US Virgin Islands	611,000,000
9	Australia	570,000,000
10	Japan	568,000,000

In 1997 the UK led the world in duty- and tax-free shopping, accounting for 11.7 percent of total sales. Europe as a whole took almost half (46.6 percent) of global sales.

TOP 10 ★ DUTY-FREE AIRPORTS

	AIRPORT/LOCATION	ANNUAL SALES ($)
1	London Heathrow, UK	*
2	Honolulu, Hawaii	360,000,000
3	Amsterdam Schiphol, Netherlands	353,300,000
4	Singapore Changi	310,000,000
5	Paris Charles De Gaulle, France	309,800,000
6	Frankfurt, Germany	260,300,000
7	Hong Kong, China	250,000,000
8	Manila N. Aquino, Philippines	242,800,000
9	Tokyo Narita, Japan	220,000,000
10	São Paulo, Brazil	*

Precise figure confidential but accurate for ranking

TOP 10 ★ DUTY-FREE SHOPS

	SHOP/LOCATION
1	London Heathrow Airport, UK
2	Silja Ferries, Finland
3	Honolulu Airport, Hawaii
4	Amsterdam Schiphol Airport, Netherlands
5	Singapore Changi Airport, Singapore
6	Paris Charles De Gaulle Airport, France
7	Viking Line Ferries, Finland
8	Frankfurt Airport, Germany
9	London Gatwick Airport, UK
10	Stena Line UK, UK

In 1997 total global duty- and tax-free sales were worth $21 billion. Sales of several of those outlets featured in the Top 10 are confidential, but industry insiders have ranked them and place them in the range of over $270 million at the bottom of the list to over $500 million at the top. Although London Heathrow Airport achieves the greatest total sales, Honolulu Airport has the highest average sales, amounting in 1997 to $95.41 per passenger.

TOP 10 DUTY-FREE PRODUCTS

(Product/sales in $)

1 Women's fragrances, 2,250,000,000 **2** Cigarettes, 2,235,000,000 **3** Women's cosmetics, 1,767,000,000 **4** Scotch whisky, 1,663,000,000 **5** Cognac, 1,235,000,000 **6** Men's fragrances and toiletries, 1,109,000,000 **7** Accessories, 1,050,000,000 **8** Confectionery, 1,049,000,000 **9** Leather goods (handbags, belts, etc.), 902,000,000 **10** Watches, 703,000,000

TOP 10 ★ DUTY-FREE FERRY OPERATORS

	FERRY OPERATOR/LOCATION	ANNUAL SALES ($)
1	Silja Ferries, Finland	245,000,000
2	Eurotunnel, UK/France	225,000,000
3	P&O European Ferries, UK	220,000,000
4	Stena Line, UK	190,900,000
5	Viking Line Ferries, Finland	190,000,000
6	Stena Line, Sweden	168,100,000
7	Scandlines, Denmark	*
8	Color Line, Norway	119,900,000
9	Hoverspeed, UK	80,900,000
10	Brittany Ferries, France	*

Precise figure confidential, but accurate for ranking

END OF AN ERA

Under new EC laws, duty-free sales in member countries were axed in July 1999, much to the disappointment of millions of travelers.

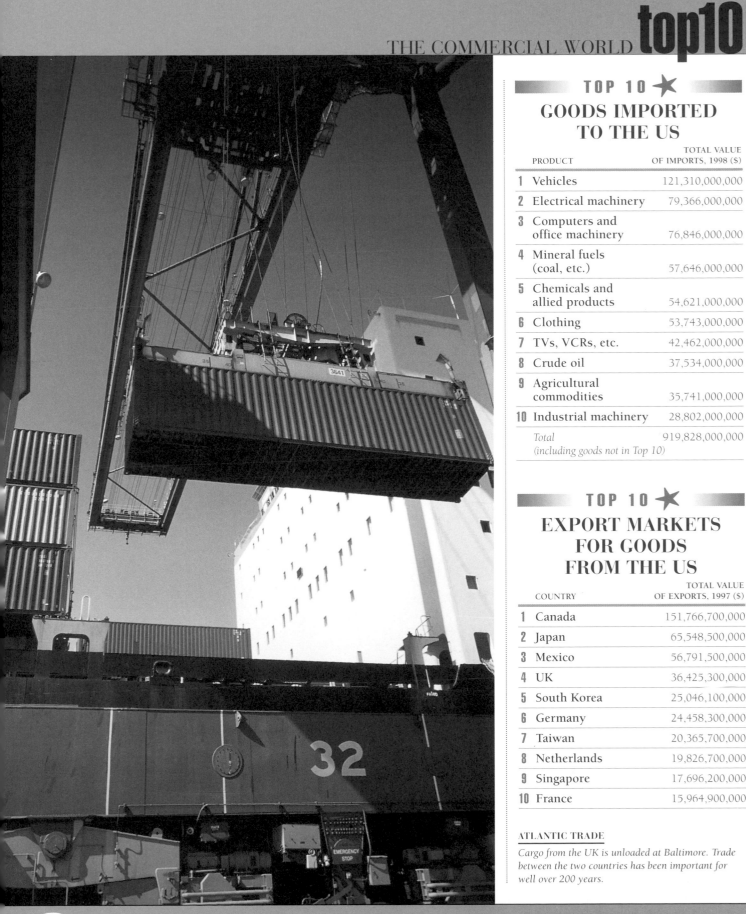

GOODS IMPORTED TO THE US

	PRODUCT	TOTAL VALUE OF IMPORTS, 1998 ($)
1	Vehicles	121,310,000,000
2	Electrical machinery	79,366,000,000
3	Computers and office machinery	76,846,000,000
4	Mineral fuels (coal, etc.)	57,646,000,000
5	Chemicals and allied products	54,621,000,000
6	Clothing	53,743,000,000
7	TVs, VCRs, etc.	42,462,000,000
8	Crude oil	37,534,000,000
9	Agricultural commodities	35,741,000,000
10	Industrial machinery	28,802,000,000
	Total (including goods not in Top 10)	919,828,000,000

EXPORT MARKETS FOR GOODS FROM THE US

	COUNTRY	TOTAL VALUE OF EXPORTS, 1997 ($)
1	Canada	151,766,700,000
2	Japan	65,548,500,000
3	Mexico	56,791,500,000
4	UK	36,425,300,000
5	South Korea	25,046,100,000
6	Germany	24,458,300,000
7	Taiwan	20,365,700,000
8	Netherlands	19,826,700,000
9	Singapore	17,696,200,000
10	France	15,964,900,000

ATLANTIC TRADE

Cargo from the UK is unloaded at Baltimore. Trade between the two countries has been important for well over 200 years.

Which country has the most internet users?
see p.211 for the answer
A New York
B Zurich
C Geneva

COMMUNICATION MATTERS

COUNTRIES WITH THE HIGHEST RATIO OF CELLULAR MOBILE PHONE USERS

	COUNTRY	SUBSCRIBERS	SUBSCRIBERS PER 1,000 INHABITANTS
1	Finland	2,148,000	418.7
2	Norway	1,685,000	383.0
3	Sweden	3,187,000	358.1
4	Australia	4,400,000	291.9
5	Denmark	1,489,000	282.0
6	Singapore	710,000	229.0
7	Japan	28,800,000	228.5
8	US	55,000,000	205.5
9	Italy	11,500,000	200.4
10	New Zealand	600,000	165.7
	World total	205,000,000	35.0

Source: *Siemens AG*

COUNTRIES MAKING THE MOST INTERNATIONAL PHONE CALLS*

	COUNTRY	CALLS PER HEAD PER ANNUM	TOTAL CALLS PER ANNUM
1	US	9.0	2,847,633,000
2	Germany	17.0	1,420,300,000
3	UK	9.1	528,000,000#
4	Italy	8.7	503,990,000
5	China	0.3	497,000,000
6	Switzerland	60.0	488,764,000
7	Netherlands	26.5	462,000,000
8	Canada	11.9	332,750,000#
9	Austria	38.9	314,571,000
10	Spain	7.5	295,450,000

* For latest year for which figures are available

Estimated

Source: *Siemens AG*

COUNTRIES WITH THE MOST TELEPHONES

	COUNTRY	TELEPHONES PER 100 INHABITANTS
1	Sweden	68.54
2	Switzerland	66.20
3	Denmark	62.88
4	US	62.56
5	Luxembourg	61.02
6	Norway	60.91
7	Iceland	60.00
8	France	58.36
9	Canada	57.88
10	Germany	56.16

The world average "teledensity" is 13.47 phones per 100 inhabitants. On a continental basis, Oceania (Australia, New Zealand, and their neighbors) has the highest ratio of telephones per 100 people – an average of 40.33 – followed by Europe with 35.64. The Americas as a whole have an average of 30.35, because even the high US figure fails to compensate for the much lower numbers in Central and South American countries. Asia's average is 6.70, and Africa's the lowest at 2.05, with many countries falling well below even this level: Tanzania has just 0.3.

ITEMS BOUGHT ON THE INTERNET

	ITEM	PERCENTAGE OF INTERNET USERS WHO HAVE PURCHASED
1	Computer software	43
2	Computer hardware	37
3	Books	23
4	Music CDs	17
5=	Consumer electronics	14
=	Travel	14
7	Games	11
8	Clothing	8
9	Flowers	7
10	Information	6

Source: *NOP survey*

In terms of value of sales, travel has emerged as the No. 1 online commodity, followed by computer hardware and books. Sectors of the online marketplace that are currently relatively small, but for which phenomenal growth has been predicted by industry forecasters, include grocery, entertainment tickets, and toys.

MOBILE PHONES

The first mobile phone system was a simple walkie-talkie device developed in 1921 by the Detroit Police Department. Originally used only by emergency services and utility companies, mobile telephony finally became a commercial enterprise in 1946. Just over 50 years later, in 1998, the European Global System for Mobile Communications (GSM) boasted 100 million subscribers and 5 million new users every month. Portable phones have gone through many changes in technology and design. Today's phones are fashionable accessories which, it is believed, will one day cause the disappearance of "land-line" phones.

SNAP ★ SHOTS

TOP 10 ★
COUNTRIES WITH THE MOST COMPUTERS

	COUNTRY	NO. OF COMPUTERS
1	US	129,000,000
2	Japan	32,800,000
3	Germany	21,100,000
4	UK	18,250,000
5	France	15,350,000
6	Canada	11,750,000
7	Italy	10,550,000
8	China	8,260,000
9	Australia	7,680,000
10	South Korea	6,650,000

Computer industry estimates put the number of computers in the world at 98,000,000 in 1990, and 364,400,000 at the end of 1998. By the year 2000, the total is predicted to rise to 579,000,000.

Source: *Computer Industry Almanac, Inc.*

TOP 10 ★
COUNTRIES WITH THE MOST INTERNET USERS

	COUNTRY	PERCENTAGE OF POPULATION	INTERNET USERS*
1	US	29	76,500,000
2	Japan	8	9,750,000
3	UK	14	8,100,000
4	Germany	9	7,140,000
5	Canada	22	6,490,000
6	Australia	24	4,360,000
7	France	5	2,790,000
8	Sweden	29	2,580,000
9	Italy	4	2,140,000
10	Spain	5	1,980,000
	World total	2.5	147,800,000

* Estimates for weekly usage as at end of 1998

One of the principal functions of the Internet is the dissemination of information. It is ironic that information about the number of users should be so patchy and erratic.

Source: *Computer Industry Almanac, Inc.*

SURFING THE NET

More than 150 million people all over the world are connected to the Internet. It gives users access to an amazing array of information and services.

TOP 10 ★
BESTSELLING US COMMEMORATIVE STAMPS

	ISSUE	DATE
1	Elvis Presley	1993
2	Wildflowers	1992
3	Rock 'n' Roll	1993
4	Moon Landing	1994
5	Civil War	1995
6	Legends of the West	1994
7	Marilyn Monroe	1995
8	Bugs Bunny	1997
9	Summer Olympics	1992
10	Centennial Olympic Games	1996

Source: *United States Postal Service*

TOP 10 ★
COUNTRIES WITH THE MOST POST OFFICES

	COUNTRY	POST OFFICES*
1	India	153,021
2	China	129,455
3	US	44,619
4	Russia	43,900
5	Japan	24,680
6	Germany	20,567
7	Turkey	19,063
8	UK	18,993
9	France	17,148
10	Ukraine	15,786

* 1997 or latest year available

Which country has the most workers?
see p.204 for the answer
A India
B China
C Russia

FUEL & POWER

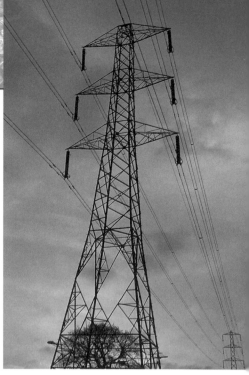

TOP 10 ★ NATURAL GAS-CONSUMING COUNTRIES

	COUNTRY	1997 CONSUMPTION BILLION CU FT	BILLION CU M
1	US	22,336.5	632.5
2	Russia	11,692.7	331.1
3	UK	3,030.0	85.8
4	Germany	2,789.9	79.0
5	Canada	2,645.1	74.9
6	Ukraine	2,549.7	72.2
7	Japan	2,299.0	65.1
8	Italy	1,903.5	53.9
9	Saudi Arabia	1,550.3	43.9
10	Iran	1,515.0	42.9
	World total	77,575.7	2,196.7

Source: BP Statistical Review of World Energy 1998

TOP 10 ★ OIL-CONSUMING COUNTRIES

	COUNTRY	1997 CONSUMPTION (TONS)
1	US	933,100,000
2	Japan	293,650,000
3	China	204,580,000
4	Germany	150,460,000
5	Russia	141,090,000
6	South Korea	116,730,000
7	Italy	104,270,000
8	France	101,302,000
9	Brazil	91,271,000
10	Canada	90,499,000

Source: BP Statistical Review of World Energy 1998

MIGHTY PYLONS

The list of Top 10 electricity-consuming countries is virtually synonymous with those countries listed below, because relatively little electricity is transmitted across national borders.

TOP 10 COUNTRIES WITH THE MOST NUCLEAR REACTORS

(Country/reactors)*

1 US, 110 **2** France, 57 **3** Japan, 53 **4** UK, 35 **5** Russia, 29 **6** Canada, 21 **7** Germany, 20 **8** Ukraine, 16 **9** Sweden, 12 **10** South Korea, 11

* Civilian nuclear power reactors only, excluding those devoted to military purposes

Source: International Atomic Energy Agency

TOP 10 COAL-CONSUMING COUNTRIES

(Country/consumption in tons of oil equivalent)

1 China, 751,550,000 **2** USA, 581,910,000 **3** India, 161,370,000 **4** Russia, 124,560,000 **5** Japan, 98,980,000 **6** Germany, 95,680,000 **7** South Africa, 91,600,000 **8** Poland, 78,484,000 **9** Australia, 51,477,000 **10** UK, 44,533,000

Source: BP Statistical Review of World Energy 1998

TOP 10 ★ ELECTRICITY-PRODUCING COUNTRIES

	COUNTRY	PRODUCTION KW/HR
1	US	3,145,892,000,000
2	Russia	956,587,000,000
3	Japan	906,705,000,000
4	China	839,453,000,000
5	Canada	527,316,000,000
6	Germany	525,721,000,000
7	France	471,448,000,000
8	India	356,519,000,000
9	UK	323,029,000,000
10	Brazil	251,484,000,000

TIMBER!

Logging mahogany trees in Brazil. From 1990–95, 18,568 sq miles/ 47,740 sq km of tropical forest were lost in South America each year.

TOP 10 DEFORESTING COUNTRIES

(Country/average annual forest loss 1990–95 in sq miles)

1 Brazil, 9,860 **2** Indonesia, 4,180 **3** Dem. Rep. of the Congo, 2,850 **4** Bolivia, 2,240 **5** Mexico, 1,960 **6** Venezuela, 1,940 **7** Malaysia, 1,540 **8** Myanmar, 1,490 **9** Sudan, 1,360 **10** Thailand, 1,270

Source: Food and Agriculture Organization of the United Nations

Did You Know? The world produces almost 10 million tons of oil every day.

TOP 10 ⭐
ENERGY-CONSUMING COUNTRIES

COUNTRY	1997 ENERGY CONSUMPTION*					
	OIL	GAS	COAL	NUCLEAR	HYDRO	TOTAL
1 US	933.1	627.5	581.9	188.4	32.6	2,363.6
2 China	204.6	19.2	751.5	4.1	17.9	997.3
3 Russia	141.1	328.5	124.6	30.8	14.9	639.8
4 Japan	293.7	64.6	99.0	91.9	8.9	558.1
5 Germany	150.5	78.4	95.7	48.4	2.0	374.9
6 India	91.6	24.3	161.4	2.8	6.8	286.8
7 France	101.3	34.4	14.6	112.5	6.4	269.2
8 Canada	90.5	74.3	29.2	23.5	33.1	250.6
9 UK	89.5	85.1	44.5	28.1	0.6	247.8
10 South Korea	116.7	16.3	37.5	21.9	0.6	193.0
World	3,557.0	2,076.3	2,436.9	657.4	240.9	8,968.4

* Millions of tons of oil equivalent

Source: *BP Statistical Review of World Energy 1998*

TOP 10 ⭐
ITEMS OF DOMESTIC GARBAGE IN THE US

ITEM	TONS PER ANNUM
1 Yard trimming	29,750,000
2 Corrugated boxes	28,800,000
3 Food waste	14,000,000
4 Newspapers	13,100,000
5 Miscellaneous durables	12,000,000
6 Wood packaging	10,600,000
7 Furniture and furnishings	7,200,000
8 Other commercial printing	7,100,000
9 Office-type papers	6,800,000
10 Paper folding cartons	5,300,000

Source: *Environmental Protection Agency*

THE 10 ⭐
SULFUR DIOXIDE-EMITTING COUNTRIES

COUNTRY	ANNUAL SO$_2$ EMISSIONS PER HEAD		
	LB	OZ	KG
1 Czech Republic	329	6	149.4
2 Former Yugoslavia	304	11	138.2
3 Bulgaria	257	8	116.8
4 Canada	229	4	104.0
5 Hungary	179	7	81.4
6 =Romania	174	10	79.2
=US	174	10	79.2
8 Poland	156	12	71.1
9 Slovakia	154	5	70.0
10 Belarus	126	12	57.5

Source: *World Resources Institute*

THE 10 ⭐
CARBON DIOXIDE-EMITTING COUNTRIES

COUNTRY	ANNUAL CO$_2$ EMISSIONS PER HEAD (TONS)
1 Qatar	57.52
2 United Arab Emirates	39.90
3 Kuwait	26.72
4 Luxembourg	22.18
5 US	21.69
6 Singapore	21.44
7 Bahrain	20.43
8 Trinidad and Tobago	18.89
9 Australia	18.70
10 Brunei	18.62

Source: *Carbon Dioxide Information Analysis Center*

AIR POLLUTION

Carbon-dioxide emissions have increased drastically since World War II as a result of industrialization. Most countries are actively trying to reverse this trend.

213

THE 10 ★
MOST COMMON PRODUCTS INVOLVED IN ACCIDENTS IN US HOMES

PRODUCT GROUP	ACCIDENTS
1 Sports activities and equipment	3,431,390
2 Home structures	2,499,588
3 Home furnishings and fixtures	1,933,937
4 Household containers	274,690
5 Personal use items	260,862
6 Home workshop tools	257,806
7 Heating and air conditioning	256,323
8 Yard and garden equipment	206,717
9 Household appliances	142,471
10 Toys	136,399

Source: *US Consumer Product Safety Commission/NEISs (National Electronic Injury Surveillance System)*

A survey of injuries caused by some 15,000 products, based on a sample of 101 US hospitals during 1997, showed that their ERs were kept busy with patients suffering from injuries caused by these broad products groups and several others. Within the sports category, basketball stood out as the most likely to produce sports injury (644,921 cases), followed by bicycles (567,002). In the home, stairs, ramps, landings, and floors were the most dangerous places, with a total of 1,753,031 injuries, while beds resulted in 411,689 accidents, clothing 122,782, and refrigerators and freezers 29,964. In the yard, fences were also involved in 110,731 cases, and lawnmowers 61,088.

FIRESTARTER
Most house fires result from the negligence of homeowners. In the words of Benjamin Franklin: "An ounce of prevention is worth a pound of cure."

THE 10 ★
MOST COMMON ANIMALS INVOLVED IN ACCIDENTS IN THE UK

ANIMAL OR INSECT	INJURIES CAUSED PER ANNUM
1 Dog	3,271
2 Bee, wasp	1,057
3 Cat	721
4 Unspecified insect	431
5 Rabbit, hamster, etc.	176
6 Horse, pony, donkey	164
7 "Other insect"	118
8 Wild animal	37
9 Chicken, swan, duck	32
10 "Other domestic animal"	30

THE 10 ★
MOST COMMON CAUSES OF DOMESTIC FIRES IN THE US*

CAUSE	APPROX. NO. OF FIRES PER ANNUM
1 Cooking equipment	99,300
2 Heating equipment	74,400
3 Incendiary or suspicious causes	55,000
4 Other equipment	44,500
5 Electrical distribution system	39,400
6 Appliance, tool, or air conditioning	30,700
7 Smoking materials	23,800
8 Child playing	21,900
9 Open flame, torch	20,800
10 Exposure to other hostile fire	17,200

* *Survey conducted by the NFIRS and NFPA covering the period 1991–95*

Source: *National Fire Protection Association*

THE 10 ⭐
MOST COMMON CAUSES OF ACCIDENTAL DEATH IN THE US

	CAUSE	DEATHS
1	Traffic accidents	43,363
2	Falls	13,986
3	Poisoning by drugs and medicines	8,000
4	Drowning	3,790
5	Fires and flames	3,761
6	Inhalation and ingestion of objects	3,185
7	Complications due to medical procedures	2,712
8	Firearms	1,215
9	Poisoning by solids, liquids, and gases	1,072
10	Nontraffic motor vehicle accidents	1,032

Source: *National Safety Council*

THE 10 ⭐
ARTICLES MOST FREQUENTLY INVOLVED IN ACCIDENTS IN THE HOME

	ARTICLE	ACCIDENTS PER ANNUM*
1	Construction feature	775,000
2	Furniture	329,000
3	Person	230,000
4	Outdoor surface	194,000
5	Clothing/footwear	191,000
6	Building/raw materials	159,000
7	Furnishings	145,000
8	Cooking/kitchen equipment	134,000
9	Animal/insect	113,000
10	Food/drink	109,000
	Total	2,502,000

* National estimates based on actual Home Accident Surveillance System figures for sample population

THE 10 MOST DANGEROUS JOBS IN THE US
(Job sector/fatalities per year)

1 Agriculture, forestry, fishing, 830
2 Special trade contractors, 648
3 Trucking and warehousing, 569
4 Heavy construction, other than building, 252
5 Wholesale trade, 241
6 Lumber and wood products, 199
7 General building contractors, 194
8 Food stores, 189
9 Business services, 181
10 Mining, 158

Source: *US Bureau of Labor Statistics*
In 1997 a total of 6,218 people received fatal occupational injuries. Of these, 5,594 were employed in private industry, and 624 by state or federal governments.

THE 10 ⭐
INDUSTRIES WITH THE MOST INJURIES IN THE US

	INDUSTRY	INJURY RATE*
1	Meat packing	36.6
2	Shipbuilding and repairing	32.7
3	Motor vehicles and car bodies	31.5
4	Truck trailers	31.2
5=	Gray and ductile iron foundries	29.2
=	Iron foundries	29.2
7	Secondary nonferrous metals	26.1
8	Malleable iron foundries	26.0
9	Mobile homes	24.3
10	Automotive stampings	23.8

* Nonfatal, per 100 employees
Source: *US Bureau of Labor Statistics*

THE 10 MOST ACCIDENT-PRONE COUNTRIES
(Country/accidental death rate per 100,000 population)

1 Estonia, 153.5
2 Lithuania, 120.7
3 South Africa, 99.4
4 Hungary, 74.3
5 Moldova, 72.1
6 Latvia, 71.7
7 Czech Republic, 60.7
8 South Korea, 59.9
9 Romania, 57.1
10 Slovenia, 55.2

Source: *United Nations*

THE 10 ⭐
MOST COMMON CAUSES OF INJURY AT WORK IN THE UK

	CAUSE	FATALITIES	INJURIES*
1	Handling, lifting, or carrying	–	47,889
2	Slip, trip, or fall on same level	3	32,343
3	Struck by moving (including flying or falling) object	43	22,335
4	Fall from height	56	13,220
5	Struck against something fixed or stationary	3	8,713
6	Contact with moving machinery	15	7,266
7	Exposure to or contact with a harmful substance	4	4,641
8	Acts of violence	2	4,374
9	Struck by moving vehicle	32	3,647
10	Animal	1	901
	Total (including causes not in Top 10)	210	151,741

* Resulting in work absence of more than three days, employees only (excluding self-employed), 1996/97 provisional figures

"Acts of violence" is a new category included for the first time in the 1996/97 statistics, and appears as the eighth most common cause of injury at work.

Which country is visited by most tourists?
see p.224 for the answer

A Italy
B US
C France

INDUSTRIAL & OTHER DISASTERS

MISERY IN BHOPAL
Lethal gas escaping from an underground storage tank at the Union Carbide factory brought death and sickness to thousands of local residents. Many awoke with burning eyes, vomiting, and dizziness; others simply died in their sleep.

THE 10 ★ WORST EXPLOSIONS*

	LOCATION/DATE	TYPE	NO. KILLED
1	**Rhodes**, Greece, 1856#	Lightning strike of gunpowder store	4,000
2	**Breschia**, Italy, 1769#	Arsenal	over 3,000
3	**Lanchow**, China, Oct 26, 1935	Arsenal	2,000
4	**Halifax**, Nova Scotia, Dec 6, 1917	Ammunition ship *Mont Blanc*	1,963
5	**Memphis**, Apr 27, 1865	*Sultana* boiler explosion	1,547
6	**Bombay**, India, Apr 14, 1944	Ammunition ship *Fort Stikine*	1,376
7	**Cali**, Colombia, Aug 7, 1956	Ammunition trucks	up to 1,200
8	**Salang Tunnel**, Afghanistan, Nov 2, 1982	Gasoline tanker collision	over 1,100
9	**Chelyabinsk**, USSR, Jun 3, 1989	Liquid gas beside railway	up to 800
10	**Texas City**, Texas, Apr 16, 1947	Ammonium nitrate on cargo ships	576

* *Excluding mining disasters, terrorist and military bombs, and natural explosions, such as volcanoes*

\# *Precise date unknown*

THE 10 ★ WORST FIRES*

	LOCATION/DATE	TYPE	NO. KILLED
1	**Kwanto**, Japan, Sept 1, 1923	Following earthquake	60,000
2	**London**, UK, July 11, 1212	London Bridge	3,000#
3	**Peshtigo**, Wisconsin, Oct 8, 1871	Forest	2,682
4	**Santiago**, Chile, Dec 8, 1863	Church of La Compañia	2,500
5	**Chungking**, China, Sept 2, 1949	Docks	1,700
6	**Hakodate**, Japan, Mar 22, 1934	City	1,500
7	**Constantinople**, Turkey, June 5, 1870	City	900
8	**San Francisco**, Apr 18, 1906	Following earthquake	600–700
9	**Cloquet**, Minnesota, Oct 12, 1918	Forest	559
10=	**Lagunillas**, Venezuela, Nov 14, 1939	Oil refinery and city	over 500
=	**Mandi Dabwali**, India, Dec 23, 1995	School tent	over 500

* *Excluding sports and entertainment venues, mining disasters, and the results of military action*

\# *Burned, crushed, and drowned in ensuing panic*

THE 10 ★ WORST FIRES OF THE 20TH CENTURY*

	LOCATION/DATE	TYPE	NO. KILLED
1	**Kwanto**, Japan, Sept 1, 1923	Following earthquake	60,000
2	**Chungking**, China, Sept 2, 1949	Docks	1,700
3	**Hakodate**, Japan, Mar, 22 1934	City	1,500
4	**San Francisco**, California, Apr 18, 1906	Following earthquake	600–700
5	**Cloquet**, Minnesota, Oct 12, 1918	Forest	559
6=	**Lagunillas**, Venezuela, Nov 14, 1939	Oil refinery and city	over 500
=	**Mandi Dabwali**, India, Dec 23, 1995	School tent	over 500
8	**Hoboken**, New Jersey, June 30,1900	Docks	326
9	**Brussels**, Belgium, May 22, 1967	Department store	322
10	**Columbus**, Ohio, April 21, 1930	State Penitentiary	320

* *Excluding sports and entertainment venues, mining disasters, and the results of military action*

THE 10 WORST MINING DISASTERS
(Location/date/no.killed)

1 **Hinkeiko**, China, Apr 26, 1942, 1,549 2 **Courrières**, France, Mar 10, 1906, 1,060 3 **Omuta**, Japan, Nov 9, 1963, 447 4 **Senghenydd**, UK, Oct 14, 1913, 439 5 **Coalbrook**, South Africa, Jan 21, 1960, 437 6 **Wankie**, Rhodesia, June 6, 1972, 427 7 **Dhanbad**, India, May 28, 1965, 375 8 **Chasnala**, India, Dec 27, 1975, 372 9 **Monongah**, West Virginia, Dec 6, 1907, 362 10 **Barnsley**, UK, Dec 12, 1866, 361*

* *Including 27 killed the following day while searching for survivors*

Which country has the most nuclear reactors?
see p.212 for the answer

A France
B Japan
C US

THE 10 ★
WORST COMMERCIAL AND INDUSTRIAL DISASTERS*

LOCATION/DATE/TYPE	NO. KILLED
1 Bhopal, India, Dec 3, 1984, Methylisocyanate gas escape at Union Carbide plant	up to 3,000
2 Seoul, Korea, June 29, 1995, Collapse of Sampoong Department Store	640
3 Oppau, Germany, Sept 21, 1921, Chemical plant explosion	561
4 Mexico City, Mexico, Nov 20, 1984, Explosion at a PEMEX liquified petroleum gas plant	540
5 Brussels, Belgium, May 22, 1967, Fire in L'Innovation department store	322
6 Novosibirsk, USSR, Apr 1979#, Anthrax infection following accident at biological and chemical warfare plant	up to 300
7 Guadalajara, Mexico, Apr 22, 1992, Explosions caused by gas leak into sewers	230
8 São Paulo, Brazil, Feb 1, 1974, Fire in Joelma bank and office building	227
9 Oakdale, California, May 18, 1918, Chemical plant explosion	193
10 Bangkok, Thailand, May 10, 1993, Fire engulfed a four-story doll factory	187

* Including industrial sites, factories, offices, and stores; excluding military, mining, marine, and other transport disasters

\# Precise date unknown

THE 10 ★
WORST DISASTERS AT SPORTS VENUES IN THE 20TH CENTURY

LOCATION/DATE/TYPE	NO. KILLED
1 Hong Kong Jockey Club, Feb 26, 1918, Stand collapse and fire	604
2 Lenin Stadium, Moscow, Oct 20, 1982, Crush in soccer stadium	340
3 Lima, Peru, May 24, 1964, Riot in soccer stadium	320
4 Sinceljo, Colombia, Jan 20, 1980, Bullring stand collapse	222
5 Hillsborough, Sheffield, UK, Apr 15, 1989, Crush in soccer stadium	96
6 Guatemala City, Guatemala, Oct 16, 1996, Stampede in Mateo Flores National Stadium	83
7 Le Mans, France, June 11, 1955, Racing car crash	82
8 Katmandu, Nepal, Mar 12, 1988, Stampede in soccer stadium	80
9 Buenos Aires, Argentina, May 23, 1968, Riot in soccer stadium	74
10 Ibrox Park, Glasgow, Scotland, Jan 2, 1971, Barrier collapse in soccer stadium	66

THE 10 ★
WORST FIRES AT THEATER AND ENTERTAINMENT VENUES*

LOCATION/DATE/TYPE	NO. KILLED
1 Canton, China, May 25, 1845, Theater	1,670
2 Shanghai, China, June 1871, Theater	900
3 Vienna, Austria, Dec 8, 1881, Ring Theater	640–850
4 St. Petersburg, Russia, Feb 14, 1836, Lehmann Circus	800
5 Antoung, China, Feb 13, 1937, Movie theater	658
6 Chicago, Illinois, Dec 30, 1903, Iroquois Theater	591
7 Boston, Massachusetts, Nov 28, 1942, Cocoanut Grove Night Club	491
8 Abadan, Iran, Aug 20, 1978, Theater	422
9 Niteroi, Brazil, Dec 17, 1961, Circus	323
10 Brooklyn Theater, New York, Dec 5, 1876,	295

* Nineteenth and twentieth centuries, excluding sports stadiums and race tracks

The figure given for the first entry is a conservative estimate; some sources put the figure as high as 2,500.

MELTDOWN

On April 30, 1986 the Soviet Union admitted that a major accident had occurred at the Chernobyl nuclear generating plant in the Ukraine. The immediate death toll was said to be 31 people, but it has been suggested that by 1992 some 6,000–8,000 people had died as a result of radioactive contamination, a toll that will continue for many years. Since the accident, Soviet scientists have been monitoring the effects on plant life in the area. The persistence of radioactive particles in the soil will contaminate future crops and the animals and people that eat them.

SNAP SHOTS

WEALTH & RICHES

TOP 10 ★
RICHEST RULERS

RULER/COUNTRY/ IN POWER SINCE	ESTIMATED WEALTH ($)
1 Sultan Haji Hassanal Bolkiah, Brunei, 1967	36,000,000,000
2 King Fahd bin Abdul Aziz Al Saud, Saudi Arabia, 1982	25,000,000,000
3= Presdient Sheikh Zayed bin Sultan al-Nahyan, United Arab Emirates, 1971	15,000,000,000
= Sheikh Jaber al-Ahmed al Jaber Al-Sabah, Kuwait, 1977	15,000,000,000
5= Amir Hamad bin Khalifa Al-Thani, Qatar, 1995	5,000,000,000
= President Saddam Hussein, Iraq, 1979	5,000,000,000
7 Queen Beatrix*, Netherlands, 1980	4,700,000,000
8 Prime Minister Rafic Al-Hariri#, Lebanon, 1992	3,600,000,000
9 President Hafez Al-Assad, Syria, 1971	2,000,000,000
10 President Fidel Castro, Cuba, 1959	100,000,000

Jointly with her mother, Princess Juliana

 # Officially deputy to President, but de facto ruler

Source: Forbes *magazine*

RICHEST RULER
Ruler of the small state of Brunei since 1967, the Sultan's colossal wealth derives from his country's oil and natural gas resources.

TOP 10 RICHEST PEOPLE IN THE US
(Name/source of wealth/assets in $)

1 Bill Gates, Computer software, 72,900,000,000 **2 Warren Edward Buffett**, Textiles, etc., 29,400,000,000 **3 Paul Gardner Allen**, Computer software, 21,000,000,000 **4 Michael Dell**, Computers, 13,000,000,000 **5 Steven Ballmer**, Computer software, 12,000,000,000 **6** = **Helen R. Walton**, Retailing, 11,000,000,000; = **John T. Walton**, Retailing, 11,000,000,000; = **Alice L. Walton**, Retailing, 11,000,000,000; = **S. Robson Walton**, Retailing, 11,000,000,000; = **Jim C. Walton**, Retailing, 11,000,000,000

Source: Forbes *magazine*

TOP 10 ★
COUNTRIES WITH THE MOST DOLLAR BILLIONAIRES*

COUNTRY	BILLIONAIRES
1 US	70
2 Germany	18
3 Japan	12
4 China (Hong Kong)	8
5= France	7
= Mexico	7
= Saudi Arabia	7
8= Switzerland	6
= UK	6
10= Philippines	5
= Taiwan	5

* *Individuals and families with a net worth of $1,000,000,000 or more*

Source: Forbes *magazine*

PERFECT GEM
The world's most expensive diamond was bought at auction in 1995 by Sheikh Ahmed Fitahi, the owner of a chain of Saudi Arabian jewelry shops.

TOP 10 ★
MOST EXPENSIVE SINGLE DIAMONDS SOLD AT AUCTION

DIAMOND/SALE	PRICE ($)
1 Pear-shaped 100.10-carat "D" Flawless diamond, Sotheby's, Geneva, May 17, 1995	16,548,750 (SF19,958,500)
2 The Mouawad Splendor pear-shaped 11-sided 101.84-carat diamond, Sotheby's, Geneva, Nov 14, 1990	12,760,000 (SF15,950,000)
3 Rectangular-cut 100.36-carat diamond, Sotheby's, Geneva, Nov 17, 1993	11,882,333 (SF17,823,500)
4 Fancy blue emerald-cut 20.17-carat diamond ring, Sotheby's, New York, Oct 18, 1994	9,902,500
5 Unnamed pear-shaped 85.91-carat pendant, Sotheby's, New York, Apr 19, 1988	9,130,000
6 Rectangular-cut fancy deep blue 13.49-carat diamond ring, Christie's, New York, Apr 13, 1995	7,482,500
7 Rectangular-cut 52.59-carat diamond ring, Christie's, New York, Apr 20, 1988	7,480,000
8 Fancy pink rectangular-cut 19.66-carat diamond, Christie's, Geneva, Nov 17, 1994	7,421,318 (SF9,573,500)
9 The Jeddah Bride rectangular-cut 80.02-carat diamond, Sotheby's, New York, Oct 24, 1991	7,150,000
10 The Agra Diamond Fancy light pink cushion-shaped 32.24-carat diamond, Christie's, London, June 20, 1990	6,959,700 (£4,070,000)

TOP 10 ★ LARGEST ROUGH DIAMONDS

DIAMOND/DESCRIPTION	CARATS
1 Cullinan	3,106.00

Measuring roughly 4 x 2½ x 2 in/10 x 6.5 x 5 cm, and weighing 1 lb 6 oz/621 g, the Cullinan was unearthed in 1905 and bought by the Transvaal Government for $240,000. It was presented to King Edward VII, who had it cut; the most important of the separate gems are among the British Crown Jewels.

2 Excelsior	995.20

Found at the Jagersfontein Mine on June 30, 1893, it was cut by the celebrated Amsterdam firm of Asscher in 1903, producing 21 superb stones.

3 Star of Sierra Leone	968.80

Found in Sierra Leone on St. Valentine's Day, 1972, the rough diamond weighed 8 oz/225 g and measured 2½ x 1⅛ in/63.5 x 38.1 mm.

4 Incomparable	890.00

Discovered in 1980 at Mbuji-Mayi, Dem. Rep. of Congo (then Zaïre).

5 Great Mogul	787.50

When found in 1650 in the Gani Mine, India, it was presented to Shah Jehan, the builder of the Taj Mahal.

6 Woyie River	770.00

Found in 1945 beside the Woyie River in Sierra Leone, it was cut into 30 stones. The largest of these, known as Victory and weighing 31.35 carats, was auctioned at Christie's, New York in 1984 for $880,000.

7 Golden Jubilee	755.50

Found in 1986 in the Premier Mine (the home of the Cullinan), the polished diamond cut from it is, at 545.67 carats, the largest in the world.

8 Presidente Vargas	726.60

Discovered in the Antonio River, Brazil, in 1938, it was named after the then President Getulio Vargas.

9 Jonker	726.00

In 1934 Jacobus Jonker found this massive diamond after it had been exposed by a heavy storm. Acquired by Harry Winston, it was exhibited in the American Museum of Natural History to enormous crowds.

10 Jubilee	650.80

Like the Excelsior, it was found in the Jagersfontein Mine in South Africa in 1895. The largest polished stone cut from it is called the Reitz.

The weight of diamonds is measured in carats (the word derives from the carob bean, which was once used as a measure). There are approximately 142 carats to the ounce. Fewer than 1,000 rough diamonds weighing more than 100 carats have ever been recorded.

TOP 10 GOLD-PRODUCING COUNTRIES

(Country/1997 production in tons)

1. **South Africa**, 539.3
2. **US**, 387.4
3. **Australia**, 343.3
4. **Canada**, 185.7
5. **China**, 172.8
6. **Russia**, 151.0
7. **Indonesia**, 111.8
8. **Uzbekistan**, 90.1
9. **Peru**, 82.5
10. **Brazil**, 65.1

As reported by Gold Fields Mineral Services Ltd, world-dominating gold producer South Africa saw its output fall again for the fifth consecutive year. Australia's output has increased dramatically over recent years: the country's record annual production had stood at 131 tons since 1903, but in 1988 it rocketed to 168 tons, and in 1992 for the first time overtook that of Russia.

TOP 10 ★ YOUNGEST BILLIONAIRES IN THE US

NAME/SOURCE OF WEALTH	ASSETS ($)	AGE
1 Daniel Morton Ziff, Ziff Brothers Investments	1,200,000,000	26
2 Robert David Ziff, Ziff Brothers Investments	1,200,000,000	32
3 Michael Dell, Dell Computer Corp.	13,000,000,000	33
4 = Jeffrey P. Bezos, Amazon.com	1,600,000,000	34
= Dirk Edward Ziff, Ziff Brothers Investments	1,200,000,000	34
6 Theodore W. Waitt, Gateway 2000 Computers	3,200,000,000	35
7 Abigail Johnson, Fidelity Investments	4,200,000,000	36
8 = Steven Anthony Ballmer, Microsoft Corp.	12,000,000,000	42
= Lee Marshall Bass, Oil, investments	3,300,000,000	42
= Bill Gates, Microsoft Corp.	58,400,000,000	42

Source: Forbes *magazine*

WINFREY'S WEALTH

Through international syndication of her TV shows, as well as bestselling books and acting roles, Oprah Winfrey has become one of the world's richest entertainers.

TOP 10 ★ HIGHEST-EARNING ENTERTAINERS*

ENTERTAINER/PROFESSION	1998 INCOME ($)
1 Jerry Seinfeld, TV performer	225,000,000
2 Larry David, Co-creator of *Seinfeld* TV show	200,000,000
3 Steven Spielberg, Film producer/director	175,000,000
4 Oprah Winfrey, TV host/producer	125,000,000
5 James Cameron, Film director	115,000,000
6 Michael Crichton, Novelist/screenwriter	65,000,000
7 = Mike Judge	53,000,000
= Greg Daniels, Co-creators of *Beavis & Butt-head* cartoon	53,000,000
9 Chris Carter, TV writer (*X-Files*)	52,000,000
10 David Copperfield, Illusionist	49,500,000

* *Other than movie actors and pop stars*

Source: Forbes *magazine*

Did You Know? The song *Diamonds Are a Girl's Best Friend* celebrates the famous New York diamond dealer Harry Winston, who acquired the Star of Sierra Leone.

219

FOOD FOR THOUGHT

CALORIE-CONSUMING COUNTRIES

	COUNTRY	AVERAGE DAILY PER CAPITA CONSUMPTION
1	Denmark	3,808
2	Portugal	3,658
3	US	3,642
4	Ireland	3,636
5	Greece	3,575
6	Turkey	3,568
7	France	3,551
8	Belgium/Luxembourg	3,543
9	Italy	3,504
10	Malta	3,417
	World average	2,745

Source: *Food and Agriculture Organization of the United Nations*

While people in most countries in Western Europe consume more than 3,000 calories per head, the consumption in some of the poorest African nations falls below 2,000: in Somalia it is 1,532 – less than half that of the countries in the Top 10. The daily calorie requirement of the average man is 2,700 and of a woman 2,500. Inactive people need less, while those engaged in heavy labor might require to increase, perhaps even to double, these figures. Calories that are not consumed as energy turn into fat, which is why calorie-counting is one of the key aspects in most diets. The high calorie intake of certain countries reflects the high proportion of starchy foods, such as potatoes, bread, and pasta, in the national diet.

TOP 10 CANDY BRANDS IN THE US

(Brand/sales in $ for first quarter of 1998)

1. **M&Ms**, 26,128,204   2. **Hershey**, 18,721,350   3. **Reeses**, 16,876,411
4. **Snickers**, 15,565,099   5. **York Peppermint Patty**, 6,971,883
6. **Butterfinger**, 5,645,239   7. **Three Musketeers**, 5,283,848   8. **Nestlé Crunch**, 5,1213,076   9. **Russell Stover**, 4,615,111
10. **Peter Paul Almond Joy**, 4,358,023

Source: *The Manufacturing Confectioner*

US CONFECTIONERY MANUFACTURERS

	BRAND MARKET	SHARE (%)	SALES ($)
1	Hershey	25.09	245,374,812
2	M&Ms/Mars	18.57	181,573,178
3	Wrigley	10.83	105,870,543
4	Adams	8.01	78,347,762
5	Lifesavers	7.05	68,347,762
6	Nestlé	6.12	59,800,013
7	Sunmark	5.19	50,765,532
8	Sathers	2.84	27,793,564
9	Tootsie Roll Industries	1.85	18,043,473
10	Ferrero US	1.60	15,611,205

Source: *American Wholesale Marketers Association*

FIRST MARS PRODUCTS

	PRODUCT	YEAR INTRODUCED
1	= Milky Way bar	1923
	= Snickers bar (non-chocolate)	1923
3	Snickers bar (chocolate)	1930
4	3 Musketeers bar	1932
5	Maltesers	1937
6	Kitekat (catfood; now a Whiskas product)	1939
7	Mars almond bar	1940
8	M&M's plain chocolate candies	1941
9	Uncle Ben's Converted brand rice	1942
10	= M&M's peanut chocolate candies	1954
	= Pal (dogfood)	1954

Candy manufacturer Franklin C. Mars established his first business in Tacoma, Washington, in 1911, and formed the Mar-O-Bar company in Minneapolis (later moving it to Chicago) in 1922, with the first of its products, the Milky Way bar. The founder's son Forrest E. Mars set up in the UK in 1932, merging the firm with its American counterpart in 1964.

SUGAR-CONSUMING COUNTRIES

	COUNTRY	ANNUAL CONSUMPTION PER CAPITA		
		KG	LB	OZ
1	Israel	98	216	1
2	= Belize	71	156	8
	= US	71	156	8
4	Iceland	63	138	14
5	= Barbados	61	134	8
	= Cuba	61	134	8
	= New Zealand	61	134	8
8	= Costa Rica	60	132	4
	= Malaysia	60	132	4
10	= Swaziland	59	130	1
	= Trinidad and Tobago	59	130	1

Source: *Food and Agriculture Organization of the United Nations*

TOP 10 COUNTRIES WITH THE MOST McDONALD'S RESTAURANTS

(Country/no. of restaurants)

1 US, 12,094 **2** Japan, 2,004
3 Canada, 992 **4** Germany, 743
5 UK, 650 **6** Australia, 608 **7** France, 541 **8** Brazil, 337 **9** Taiwan, 163
10 Netherlands, 151

TOP 10 FISH-CONSUMING COUNTRIES

	COUNTRY	ANNUAL CONSUMPTION PER CAPITA		
		KG	LB	OZ
1	Japan	66.9	147	8
2	Norway	45.0	99	3
3	Portugal	43.0	94	13
4	=Spain	30.0	66	2
	=Sweden	30.0	66	2
6	Belgium	19.0	41	14
7	=Germany	14.0	30	14
	=Italy	14.0	30	14
	=Netherlands	14.0	30	14
	=Poland	14.0	30	14

Source: *Food and Agriculture Organization of the United Nations*

TOP 10 CONSUMERS OF KELLOGG'S CORNFLAKES*

1 Ireland **2** UK **3** Australia
4 Denmark **5** Sweden **6** Norway
7 Canada **8** US **9** Mexico
10 Venezuela

* Based on per capita consumption

In 1894 the brothers Will Keith Kellogg and Dr. John Harvey Kellogg discovered, by accident, that boiled and rolled wheat dough turned into flakes if left overnight; once baked, they turned into a tasty cereal. In 1898 they replaced wheat with corn, thereby creating the cornflakes we know today. Will Keith Kellogg went into business manufacturing cornflakes, with his distinctive signature on the packet. Today, cornflakes remain Kellogg's bestselling product.

THE 10 FIRST HEINZ'S "57 VARIETIES"

	PRODUCT	YEAR PRODUCTS INTRODUCED
1	Horseradish	1869
2	=Sour gherkins	1870
	=Sour mixed pickles	1870
	=Chowchow pickle	1870
	=Sour onions	1870
	=Prepared mustard	1870
	=Sauerkraut in crocks	1870
8	=Heinz and Noble ketchup	1873
	=Vinegar	1873
10	=Green pepper sauce	1879
	=Red pepper sauce	1879
	=Worcestershire sauce	1879

The company that Henry John Heinz launched in 1869 with horseradish rapidly expanded. In 1896, inspired by a sign he saw on the New York Third Avenue Railway advertising "21 Styles" of shoe, he counted his products and then relaunched them as his famous "57 Varieties."

TOP 10 MEAT-EATING COUNTRIES

	COUNTRY	ANNUAL CONSUMPTION PER CAPITA		
		LB	OZ	KG
1	US	261	0	118.4
2	New Zealand	259	4	117.6
3	Australia	239	4	108.5
4	Cyprus	235	14	107.0
5	Uruguay	230	6	104.5
6	Austria	229	4	104.0
7	Saint Lucia	222	7	100.9
8	Denmark	219	5	99.5
9	Spain	211	3	95.8
10	Canada	210	15	95.7

Figures from the Meat and Livestock Commission show a huge range of consumption around the world, ranging from the US at No. 1, to very poor countries such as India, where consumption may be as little as 7 lb 8 oz/3.4 kg per person per year.

TOP 10 HOTTEST CHILLIES

	EXAMPLES OF CHILLIES	SCOVILLE UNITS
1	Datil, Habanero, Scotch Bonnet	100,000–350,000
2	Chiltepin, Santaka, Thai	50,000–100,000
3	Aji, Cayenne, Piquin, Tabasco	30,000–50,000
4	de Arbol	15,000–30,000
5	Serrano, Yellow Wax	5,000–15,000
6	Chipolte, Jalapeno, Mirasol	2,500–5,000
7	Cascabel, Sandia, Rocotillo	1,500–2,500
8	Ancho, Espanola, Pasilla, Poblano	1,000–1,500
9	Anaheim, New Mexico	500–1,000
10	Cherry, Peperoncini	100–500

Hot peppers contain substances called capsaicinoids, which determine how "hot" they are. In 1912 pharmacist Wilbur Scoville pioneered a test, based on which chillies are ranked by Scoville units. According to this scale, one part of capsaicin (the principal capsaicinoid) per million equals 15,000 Scoville units. Pure capsaicin registers 16 million on the Scoville scale – one drop diluted with 100,000 drops of water will still blister the tongue – while at the other end of the scale, bell peppers and pimentos register zero.

Did You Know? The value of the Kellogg's brand is rated second in the world after Coca-Cola.

221

ALCOHOLIC & SOFT DRINKS

FIRST COCA-COLA PRODUCTS

PRODUCT	YEAR INTRODUCED
1 Coca-Cola	May 1886
2 Fanta	June 1960
3 Sprite	Feb 1961
4 TAB	May 1963
5 Fresca	Feb 1966
6 Mr. PiBB*	June 1972
7 Hi-C Soft Drinks	Aug 1977
8 Mello Yello	Mar 1979
9 Ramblin' Root Beer	June 1979
10 Diet Coke	July 1982

* Mr. PiBB without Sugar launched Sep 1974; changed name to Sugar-free Mr. PiBB, 1975

TOP 10 BRANDS OF DOMESTIC BEER IN THE US

1 Budweiser 2 Bud Light
3 Miller Lite 4 Coors Light
5 Busch 6 Natural Light
7 Miller Genuine Draft
8 Miller High Life 9 Busch
Light Draft 10 Old Milwaukee

TOP 10 ★

ALCOHOL-CONSUMING COUNTRIES

COUNTRY	ANNUAL CONSUMPTION PER CAPITA (100 PERCENT ALCOHOL) GALLONS
1 Portugal	2.98
2 Luxembourg	2.95
3 France	2.87
4 =Hungary	2.66
=Spain	2.66
6 Czech Republic	2.64
7 Denmark	2.61
8 =Germany	2.50
=Austria	2.50
10 Switzerland	2.43
US	1.74

After heading this list for many years – with an annual consumption that peaked at 4.67 gallons per head in 1961 – France was first overtaken by Luxembourg, and then by Portugal.

TOP 10 ★

BEER-DRINKING COUNTRIES

COUNTRY	ANNUAL CONSUMPTION PER CAPITA QUARTS
1 Czech Republic	167.85
2 Ireland	147.98
3 Germany	138.57
4 Denmark	120.18
5 Austria	119.65
6 Luxembourg	117.11
7 UK	109.50
8 Belgium	107.81
9 Slovak Republic	100.21
10 Australia	100.09

Despite its position as the world's leading producer of beer, the US misses being in the Top 10 list – it is ranked in 14th place.

MONKS' BREW

Beer used to be brewed in households and monasteries for private consumption until the late middle ages, when it became a commercial product.

TOP 10 ★

CHAMPAGNE-IMPORTING COUNTRIES

COUNTRY	BOTTLES IMPORTED (1998)
1 UK	24,247,123
2 Germany	19,312,910
3 US	16,949,417
4 Belgium	9,474,456
5 Switzerland	8,387,721
6 Italy	8,157,053
7 Japan	2,975,680
8 Netherlands	2,370,322
9 Spain	1,425,927
10 Canada	1,360,935

In 1998 France consumed 179,004,405 bottles of champagne and exported 113,453,686. In that year Canada increased its imports by a record 45 percent, entering the global Top 10 list for the first time.

THE ART OF FERMENTATION

Champagne first became available in 1698, when Dom Pierre Perignon perfected the art of fermenting wine in the bottle at the abbey of Hautvillers in Champagne, France. Cork stoppers replaced the rag seals previously used, and strong English glass was used to withstand the pressure of fermentation.

CHEERS!

France produces 15,000 tons of wine every day – that's 20 million bottles a day.

TOP 10 ★
WINE-DRINKING COUNTRIES

COUNTRY	ANNUAL CONSUMPTION PER CAPITA GALLONS
1 Portugal	16.11
2 France	15.85
3 Italy	14.13
4 Luxembourg	13.73
5 Switzerland	11.49
6 Argentina	10.56
7 Greece	9.21
8 Spain	9.19
9 Uruguay	8.98
10 Austria	7.92
US	7.3

The US still does not make it into the Top 10 or even Top 30 wine-drinking countries in the world, but consumption of wine has become more and more popular over the last 25 years. Between 1970 and 1997, wine consumption increased by 48.5 percent. By contrast, in France, people have been drinking less.

TOP 10 ★
SOFT DRINK-CONSUMING COUNTRIES*

COUNTRY	ANNUAL CONSUMPTION PER CAPITA GALLONS
1 US	54.68
2 Bahrain	38.83
3 Iceland	35.66
4 Norway	34.87
5 Mexico	34.34
6 =Australia	29.05
=Canada	29.05
=Israel	29.05
9 Ireland	27.73
10 Chile	26.15

* Carbonated only

Source: *Zenith International*

As one might expect, affluent Western countries feature prominently in this list and, despite the spread of so-called "Coca-Cola culture," former Eastern Bloc and Third World countries rank very low – some African nations recording extremely low consumption figures of less than 1.76 pints/1 liter per year.

TOP 10 ★
SOFT DRINK BRANDS IN THE US, 1998

DRINK	ANNUAL SALES (GALLONS)
1 Coca-Cola Classic	3,192,100,000
2 Pepsi	2,199,200,000
3 Diet Coke	1,303,400,000
4 Mountain Dew	1,017,600,000
5 Sprite	992,800,000
6 Dr. Pepper	899,100,000
7 Diet Pepsi	759,600,000
8 Seven-Up	316,400,000
9 Caffeine-Free Diet Coke	272,800,000
10 Minute Maid Regular and Diet	189,400,000

Source: *Beverage Marketing Corporation*

TOP 10 ★
COFFEE-DRINKING COUNTRIES

COUNTRY	ANNUAL CONSUMPTION PER CAPITA		
	LB	OZ	CUPS*
1 Finland	24	4	1,650
2 Netherlands	20	4	1,379
3 Norway	20	4	1,377
4 Denmark	19	12	1,346
5 Sweden	18	10	1,269
6 Austria	17	12	1,209
7 Germany	15	12	1,071
8 Switzerland	13	4	905
9 France	12	8	852
10 Italy	11	3	762

* Based on 150 cups per 2 lb 3 oz

Source: *International Coffee Organization*

TOP 10 MILK-DRINKING COUNTRIES

(Country/annual consumption per capita in quarts)*

① Ireland, 164.46 **②** Finland, 162.14
③ Iceland, 160.87 **④** Norway, 158.65
⑤ Ukraine, 141.95 **⑥** Luxembourg, 137.51 **⑦** UK, 134.34 **⑧** Sweden, 132.65 **⑨** Australia, 117.74
⑩ Spain, 110.77

* Only those reporting to the International Dairy Federation
Source: *National Dairy Council*

MEDICINE MAN

Coca-Cola was created by John Styth Pemberton, a pharmacist from Atlanta, Georgia, in 1886.

Which country is the most accident prone?
see p.215 for the answer
A South Africa
B Lithuania
C Estonia

WORLD TOURISM

TOP 10 ★
SPENDING TOURISTS

	COUNTRY OF ORIGIN	PERCENTAGE OF WORLD TOTAL	TOTAL EXPENDITURE $ (1997)
1	US	13.6	51,220,000,000
2	Germany	12.2	46,200,000,000
3	Japan	8.7	33,041,000,000
4	UK	7.3	27,710,000,000
5	Italy	4.4	16,631,000,000
6	France	4.4	16,576,000,000
7	Canada	3.0	11,304,000,000
8	Austria	2.9	10,992,000,000
9	Netherlands	2.7	10,232,000,000
10	China	2.7	10,166,000,000

Source: *World Tourism Organization*

In 1997, the world spent $377,776 million on tourism.

TOP 10 ★
TOURIST COUNTRIES

	COUNTRY	PERCENTAGE OF WORLD TOTAL	VISITS 1997*
1	France	10.9	66,800,000
2	US	8.0	49,038,000
3	Spain	7.1	43,403,000
4	Italy	5.6	34,087,000
5	UK	4.2	25,960,000
6	China	3.9	23,770,000
7	Poland	3.2	19,514,000
8	Mexico	3.2	19,351,000
9	Canada	2.9	17,610,000
10	Czech Republic	2.8	17,400,000

* *International tourist arrivals, excluding same-day visitors*

Source: *World Tourism Organization*

In 1997, it was reckoned that 613,488,000 people – almost one in 10 of the world's population – traveled as tourists to another country. Of these, more than half (51.8 percent) visited these Top 10 destinations.

© *DISNEY*

GOTHIC CASTLE
The Gothic spires of the Château de la Belle au Bois Dormant – Sleeping Beauty's castle – in Disneyland® Paris, provide an impressive centerpiece for the park.

TOP 10 ★
AMUSEMENT AND THEME PARKS*

	PARK/LOCATION	VISITS (1998)
1	Tokyo Disneyland®, Tokyo, Japan	16,686,000
2	Disneyland® Paris, Marne-La-Vallée, France	12,500,000#
3	Everland, Kyonggi-Do, South Korea	7,326,000
4	Blackpool Pleasure Beach, Blackpool, UK	6,600,000#
5	Lotte World, Seoul, South Korea	5,800,000
6	Yokohama Hakkeijima Sea Paradise, Yokohama, Japan	5,737,000
7	Huis Ten Bosch, Sasebo, Japan	4,130,300
8	Suzuka Circuit, Suzuka, Japan	3,238,000
9	Nagashima Spa Land, Kuwana, Japan	3,200,000
10	Paramount Canada's Wonderland, Maple, Canada	3,025,000#

* *Excluding US*

Estimated attendance

Source: Amusement Business

TOP 10 MOST VISITED ZOOS IN THE US
(Zoo/location/visits 1998)

❶ = **San Diego Zoo**, San Diego, CA, 5,000,000; = **San Diego Wild Animal Park**, Escondido, CA, 5,000,000 ❸ **Busch Gardens Tampa Bay Zoo**, Tampa, FL, 4,000,000 ❹ = **National Zoological Park**, Washington, D.C., 3,000,000; = **Lincoln Park Zoo**, Chicago, IL, 3,000,000 ❻ **St. Louis Zoological Park**, St. Louis, MO, 2,906,359 ❼ **Brookfield Zoo**, Chicago, IL, 2,204,609 ❽ **Bronx Zoo**, Bronx, NY, 2,201,444 ❾ **Denver Zoological Gardens**, Denver, CO, 1,560,000 ❿ **Los Angeles Zoo**, Los Angeles, CA, 1,302,223

Source: *American Zoo & Aquarium Association*

TOP 10 ★
OLDEST ROLLER COASTERS*

ROLLER COASTER/LOCATION	YEAR FOUNDED
1 Scenic Railway, Luna Park, Melbourne, Australia	1912
2 Rutschbanen, Tivoli, Copenhagen, Denmark	1914
3 Jack Rabbit, Clementon Amusement Park, Clementon, NJ	1919
4 = Jack Rabbit, Sea Breeze Park, Rochester, NY	1920
= Scenic Railway, Dreamland, Margate, UK	1920
6 = Jack Rabbit, Kennywood, West Mifflin, PA	1921
= Roller Coaster, Lagoon, Farmington, UT	1921
8 = Zippin Pippin, Libertyland, Memphis, TN	1923
= Big Dipper, Blackpool Pleasure Beach, Blackpool, UK	1923
10 Giant Dipper, Santa Cruz Beach Boardwalk, Santa Cruz, CA	1924

* In operation at same location since founded

TOP 10 ★
DESTINATIONS OF TOURISTS FROM THE US

COUNTRY	VISITORS
1 Mexico	19,616,000
2 Canada	12,909,000
3 United Kingdom	2,869,000
4 France	1,860,000
5 Germany	1,642,000
6 The Bahamas	1,504,000
7 Italy	1,385,000
8 Jamaica	1,029,000
9 Japan	871,000
10 Netherlands	772,000

Source: *Tourism Industries, International Trade Administration*

TOP 10 ★
OLDEST AMUSEMENT PARKS IN THE US

PARK/LOCATION	YEAR FOUNDED
1 Lake Compounce Amusement Park, Bristol, CT	1846
2 Cedar Point, Sandusky, OH	1870
3 Idlewild Park, Ligonier, PA	1878
4 Sea Breeze Amusement Park, Rochester, NY	1879
5 Dorney Park, Allentown, PA	1884
6 Pullen Park, Raleigh, NC	1887
7 Beech Bend Park, Bowling Green, KY	1888
8 Geauga Lake, Aurora, OH	1888
9 Arnold's Park, Arnold's Park, IA	1889
10 Carousel Gardens – City Park, New Orleans, LA	1891

TOP 10 ★
US AMUSEMENT AND THEME PARKS

PARK/LOCATION	ATTENDANCE (1998)*
1 The Magic Kingdom at Walt Disney World, Lake Buena Vista, FL	15,640,000
2 Disneyland, Anaheim, CA	13,680,000
3 Epcot at Walt Disney World, Lake Buena Vista, FL	10,596,000
4 Disney-MGM Studios at Walt Disney World, Lake Buena Vista, FL	9,473,750
5 Universal Studios Florida, Orlando, FL	8,900,000
6 Disney's Animal Kingdom at Walt Disney World, Lake Buena Vista, FL	6,000,000
7 Universal Studios Hollywood, Universal City, CA	5,100,000
8 Sea World of Florida, Orlando, FL	4,900,000
9 Busch Gardens Tampa Bay, FL	4,200,000
10 Sea World of California, San Diego, CA	3,700,000

* All estimated attendances except Epcot
Source: *Amusement Business*

KEEP ON TURNING
Vienna's amusement park, the Prater, is symbolized by the giant Ferris wheel, which is 213 ft (65 m) high. It was built in 1896–97.

TOP 10 ★
OLDEST AMUSEMENT PARKS

PARK/LOCATION	YEAR FOUNDED
1 Bakken, Klampenborg, Denmark	1583
2 The Prater, Vienna, Austria	1766
3 Blackgang Chine Cliff Top Theme Park, Ventnor, Isle of Wight, UK	1842
4 Tivoli, Copenhagen, Denmark	1843
5 Lake Compounce Amusement Park, Bristol, CT	1846
6 Hanayashiki, Tokyo, Japan	1853
7 Grand Pier, Teignmouth, UK	1865
8 Blackpool Central Pier, Blackpool, UK	1868
9 Cedar Point, Sandusky, OH	1870
10 Clacton Pier, Clacton, UK	1871

Who is the biggest consumer of Kellogg's cornflakes?
see p.221 for the answer
A Australia
B UK
C Ireland

ON THE MOVE

SPEED RECORDS

FIRST AMERICAN HOLDERS OF THE LAND SPEED RECORD

	DRIVER*/CAR/LOCATION	DATE	MPH	KM/H
1	**William Vanderbilt**, *Mors*, Albis, France	Aug 5, 1902	76.08	121.72
2	**Henry Ford**, *Ford Arrow*, Lake St. Clair, Michigan	Jan 12, 1904	91.37	146.19
3	**Fred Marriott**, *Stanley Rocket*, Daytona Beach, Florida	Jan 23, 1906	121.57	194.51
4	**Barney Oldfield**, *Benz*, Daytona Beach, Florida	Mar 16, 1910	131.27	210.03
5	**Bob Burman**, *Benz*, Daytona Beach, Florida	Apr 23, 1911	141.37	226.19
6	**Ralph de Palma**, *Packard*, Daytona Beach, Florida	Feb 17, 1919	149.87	239.79
7	**Tommy Milton**, *Duesenberg*, Daytona Beach, Florida	Apr 27, 1920	156.03	249.64
8	**Ray Keech**, *White Triplex*, Daytona Beach, Florida	Apr 22, 1928	207.55	332.08
9	**Craig Breedlove**, *Spirit of America*, Bonneville Salt Flats, Utah	Aug 5, 1963	407.45	651.92
10	**Tom Green**, *Wingfoot Express*, Bonneville Salt Flats, Utah	Oct 2, 1964	413.20	661.12

* *Excluding those who subsequently broke their own records*

FIRST HOLDERS OF THE LAND SPEED RECORD

	DRIVER/CAR/LOCATION*	DATE	MPH	KM/H
1	**Gaston de Chasseloup-Laubat**, *Jeantaud*, Achères	Dec 18, 1898	39.24	62.78
2	**Camile Jenatzy**, *Jenatzy*, Achères	Jan 17, 1899	41.42	66.27
3	**Gaston de Chasseloup-Laubat**, *Jeantaud*, Achères	Jan 17, 1899	43.69	69.90
4	**Camile Jenatzy**, *Jenatzy*, Achères	Jan 27, 1899	49.92	79.37
5	**Gaston de Chasseloup-Laubat**, *Jeantaud*, Achères	Mar 4, 1899	57.60	92.16
6	**Camile Jenatzy**, *Jenatzy*, Achères	Apr 29, 1899	65.79	105.26
7	**Leon Serpollet**, *Serpollet*, Nice	Apr 13, 1902	75.06	120.09
8	**William Vanderbilt**, *Mors*, Albis	Aug 5, 1902	76.08	121.72
9	**Henri Fournier**, *Mors*, Dourdan	Nov 5, 1902	76.60	122.56
10	**M. Augières**, *Mors*, Dourdan	Nov 17, 1902	77.130	123.4

* *All locations in France*

The first official records were all broken within three years, the first six of them by rival racers Comte Gaston de Chasseloup-Laubat and Camile Jenatzy.

LATEST HOLDERS OF THE LAND SPEED RECORD

	DRIVER/CAR/LOCATION	DATE	MPH	KM/H
1	**Andy Green**, UK, *Thrust SSC*, Black Rock Desert, Nevada	Oct 15, 1997	763.04	1,227.99
2	**Richard Noble**, UK, *Thrust 2*, Black Rock Desert, Nevada	Oct 4, 1983	633.47	1,013.47
3	**Gary Gabelich**, US, *The Blue Flame*, Bonneville Salt Flats, Utah	Oct 23, 1970	622.41	995.85
4	**Craig Breedlove**, US, *Spirit of America – Sonic 1*, Bonneville Salt Flats, Utah	Nov 15, 1965	600.60	960.96
5	**Art Arfons**, US, *Green Monster*, Bonneville Salt Flats, Utah	Nov 7, 1965	576.55	922.48
6	**Craig Breedlove**, US, *Spirit of America – Sonic 1*, Bonneville Salt Flats, Utah	Nov 2, 1965	555.48	888.76
7	**Art Arfons**, US, *Green Monster*, Bonneville Salt Flats, Utah	Oct 27, 1964	536.71	858.73
8	**Craig Breedlove**, US, *Spirit of America*, Bonneville Salt Flats, Utah	Oct 15, 1964	526.28	842.04
9	**Craig Breedlove**, US, *Spirit of America*, Bonneville Salt Flats, Utah	Oct 13, 1964	468.72	749.95
10	**Art Arfons**, US, *Green Monster*, Bonneville Salt Flats, Utah	Oct 5, 1964	434.02	694.43

FASTER THAN THE SPEED OF SOUND

Fifty years after an aircraft broke the sound barrier, Thrust SSC became the first vehicle to do so on land.

*Background image: **THRUST SSC** BREAKING THE LAND SPEED RECORD IN BLACK ROCK DESERT, NEVADA*

THE 10 ★

FIRST HOLDERS OF THE MOTORCYCLE SPEED RECORD

	RIDER/MOTORCYCLE	YEAR	MPH	KM/H
1	Ernest Walker, 994 cc Indian	1920	104.19	167.67
2	Claude F. Temple, 996 cc British Azani	1923	108.48	174.58
3	Herbert Le Vack, 867 cc Brough Superior	1924	118.05	191.59
4	Claude F. Temple, 996 cc OEC Temple	1926	121.37	195.33
5	Oliver M. Baldwin, 996 cc Zenith JAP	1928	124.62	200.56
6	Herbert Le Vack, 995 cc Brough Superior	1929	128.33	207.33
7	Joseph S. Wright, 994 cc OEC Temple	1930	137.32	220.99
8	Ernest Henne, 735 cc BMW	1930	137.66	221.54
9	Joseph S. Wright, 995 cc OEC Temple JAP	1930	150.68	242.50
10	Ernest Henne, 735 cc BMW	1932	151.86	244.86

The Fédération Internationale Motorcycliste, the first organization officially to ratify motorcycle speed records, did not begin doing so until 1920.

THE 10 ★

LATEST HOLDERS OF THE MOTORCYCLE SPEED RECORD

	RIDER/MOTORCYCLE	YEAR	MPH	KM/H
1	Dave Campos, Twin 1,491 cc/91 cu in Ruxton Harley-Davidson Easyriders	1990	322.15	518.45
2	Donald A. Vesco, Twin 1,016 cc Kawasaki LightningBolt	1978	318.60	512.73
3	Donald A. Vesco, 1,496 cc Yamaha Silver Bird	1975	302.93	487.50
4	Calvin Rayborn, 1,480 cc Harley-Davidson	1970	264.96	426.40
5	Calvin Rayborn 1,480 cc Harley-Davidson	1970	254.99	410.37
6	Donald A. Vesco, 700 cc Yamaha	1970	251.82	405.25
7	Robert Leppan, 1,298 cc Triumph	1966	245.62	395.27
8	William A. Johnson, 667 cc Triumph	1962	224.57	361.40
9	Wilhelm Herz, 499 cc NSU	1956	210.08	338.08
10	Russell Wright, 998 cc Vincent HRD	1955	184.95	297.64

All the records listed here were achieved at the Bonneville Salt Flats, with the exception of No. 10, which was attained at Christchurch, New Zealand. To break a Fédération Internationale Motorcycliste record, the motorcycle has to cover a measured distance, making two runs within one hour and taking the average of the two. American Motorcycling Association records require a turnround within two hours. Although all those listed were specially adapted for their record attempts, the two most recent had two engines and were stretched to 21 ft/6.4 m and 23 ft/7 m respectively.

TOP 10 ★

FASTEST PRODUCTION CARS

	MODEL *	MPH #	KM/H #
1	Lamborghini Diablo 5.7	202	325
2	Ferrari 550M	199	320
3	Aston Martin V8 Vantage	186	299
4	Dodge Viper	185	298
5	Venturi Atlantique Twin-turbo	176	283
6	Lotus Esprit 3.5	175	282
7	Porsche 911	174	280
8 =	Bentley Continental T	170	274
=	Honda NSX 3.2	170	274
=	Marcos Mantis	170	274
=	Shelby Series 1	170	274
=	TVR Cerbera 4.5	170	274

* Fastest of each manufacturer

\# May vary according to specification modifications to meet national legal requirements

ITALIAN SPEED
This Bimota SB6R and its fellow YB11, both Italian-made 1,000 cc-plus superbikes, appear among the world's 10 fastest.

TOP 10 FASTEST PRODUCTION MOTORCYCLES
(Model/mph/km/h)

❶ Suzuki GSX1300R Hayabusa, 186/299 ❷ Honda CBR1100XX Blackbird, 181/291 ❸ Bimota SBR, 180/290 ❹ Bimota YB11, 175/282 ❺ Kawasaki ZZ-R1100, 174/280 ❻ Yamaha YZF-R1, 173/278 ❼ MV Agusta M4, 171/275 ❽ Kawasaki Ninja ZX-9R, 170/274 ❾ = Kawasaki Ninja ZX-7RR, 169/272; = Kawasaki Ninja ZX-6R, 169/272

Did You Know? The reason why Malcolm and Donald Campbell called both of their cars *Bluebird* was because of a play of the same name by Maurice Maeterlink in which the bird symbolized the unattainable.

CARS & ROAD TRANSPORTATION

TOP 10 ★
MOTOR VEHICLE-OWNING COUNTRIES

	COUNTRY	CARS	COMMERCIAL VEHICLES	TOTAL
1	US	134,981,000	65,465,000	200,446,000
2	Japan	44,680,000	22,173,463	66,853,463
3	Germany	40,499,442	3,061,874	43,561,316
4	Italy	30,000,000	2,806,500	32,806,500
5	France	25,100,000	5,195,000	30,295,000
6	UK	24,306,781	3,635,176	27,941,957
7	Russia	13,638,600	9,856,000	23,494,600
8	Spain	14,212,259	3,071,621	17,283,880
9	Canada	13,182,996	3,484,616	16,667,612
10	Brazil	12,000,000	3,160,689	15,160,689
	World total	477,010,289	169,748,819	646,759,108

Source: *American Automobile Manufacturers Association*

TOP 10 ★
COUNTRIES PRODUCING THE MOST MOTOR VEHICLES

	COUNTRY	CARS	COMMERCIAL VEHICLES	TOTAL
1	US	6,083,227	5,715,678	11,798,905
2	Japan	7,863,763	2,482,023	10,345,786
3	Germany	4,539,583	303,326	4,842,909
4	France	3,147,622	442,965	3,590,587
5	South Korea	2,264,709	548,005	2,812,714
6	Spain	2,213,102	199,207	2,412,309
7	Canada	1,279,312	1,117,731	2,397,043
8	UK	1,686,134	238,263	1,924,397
9	Brazil	1,466,900	345,700	1,812,600
10	Italy	1,317,995	227,370	1,545,365
	World total	37,318,281	14,194,882	51,513,163

Source: *American Automobile Manufacturers Association*

AF-FORD-ABLE

Launched in 1908, the Model T Ford became immediately popular, thanks to its affordable price and reliability. It remained on the market until 1927.

TOP 10 BESTSELLING CARS OF 1998 IN THE US

(Car/1998 sales)

1. Toyota Camry, 429,575
2. Honda Accord, 401,071
3. Ford Taurus, 371,074
4. Honda Civic, 334,562
5. Ford Escort, 291,9936
6. Chevrolet Cavalier, 256,099
7. Toyota Corolla, 250,501
8. Saturn, 231,522
9. Chevrolet Malibu, 223,703
10. Pontiac Grand Am, 180,428

Source: *Ward's AutoInfoBank*

TOP 10 ★
BESTSELLING CARS OF ALL TIME

	MODEL	FIRST YEAR PRODUCED	ESTIMATED NO. MADE
1	Toyota Corolla	1966	23,000,000
2	Volkswagen Beetle	1937*	21,376,331
3	Lada Riva	1972	19,000,000
4	Volkswagen Golf	1974	18,453,646
5	Ford Model T	1908	16,536,075
6	Nissan Sunny/Pulsar	1966	13,571,100
7 =	Ford Escort/Orion	1967	12,000,000
=	Honda Civic	1972	12,000,000
9	Mazda 323	1977	9,500,000
10	Renault 4	1961	8,100,000

* *Original model still produced in Mexico and Brazil*

Estimates of manufacturers' output of their bestselling models vary from the vague to the unusually precise: 16,536,075 of the Model T Ford, with 15,007,033 produced in the US and the rest in Canada and the UK in 1908–27.

Which port is the busiest in the world?
see p.237 for the answer

A Singapore
B Hong Kong
C Rotterdam

TOP 10 ★
MOST COMMON TYPES OF PROPERTY LOST ON THE NEW YORK TRANSIT AUTHORITY, 1997–98

	TYPE
1	Backpacks
2	Radios/Walkmans
3	Eyeglasses
4	Wallets and purses
5	Cameras
6	Keys
7	Cellular phones
8	Watches
9	Inline skates
10	Jewelry

Source: *New York City Transit Authority*

TOP 10 LIGHT TRUCKS OF 1998 IN THE US

(Truck/sales)

1 Ford F-series, 787,552 **2** Chevrolet C/K, Silverado, 538,254 **3** Ford Explorer, 431,488 **4** Dodge Ram, 410,130 **5** Ford Ranger, 328,136 **6** Dodge Caravan, 293,819 **7** Jeep Grand Cherokee, 229,135 **8** Chevrolet S-10, 228,093 **9** Ford Expedition, 225,703 **10** Chevrolet Blazer, 219,710

Source: *Ward's AutoInfoBank*

ON THE ROAD

The network of roads in the US is so vast that you could drive around the country at top speed night and day for four years and still not cover it all.

THE 10 ★
FIRST COUNTRIES TO MAKE SEAT BELTS COMPULSORY

	COUNTRY	INTRODUCED
1	Czechoslovakia	Jan 1969
2	Ivory Coast	Jan 1970
3	Japan	Dec 1971
4	Australia	Jan 1972
5 =	Brazil	June 1972
=	New Zealand	June 1972
7	Puerto Rico	Jan 1974
8	Spain	Oct 1974
9	Sweden	Jan 1975
10 =	Netherlands	June 1975
=	Belgium	June 1975
=	Luxembourg	June 1975

Seat belts, long in use in airplanes, were not designed for use in private cars until the 1950s. Ford was the first manufacturer in Europe to fit anchor-points, and belts were first fitted as standard equipment in Swedish Volvos from 1959.

THE BIRTH OF THE BEETLE

The Volkswagen – literally "people's car" – was the brainchild of Ferdinand Porsche. In Germany in 1934, only one person in 49 owned a car: Porsche recognized the need for a small car that the masses could afford. Construction of the first Volkswagen factory started in 1938 at Fahensleben. It was opened officially by Adolf Hitler, then switched from producing cars to armaments and military vehicles when World War II broke out. It was not until 1941 that the production of the first series Beetle was completed. Since then the car has come to be regarded as a design icon.

SNAP SHOTS

ROAD DISASTERS & ACCIDENTS

LOCATION/DATE/INCIDENT	NO. KILLED

1 Afghanistan, Nov 3, 1982 — over 2,000
Following a collision with a Soviet army truck, a gasoline tanker exploded in the 1.7-mile/2.7-km Salang Tunnel. Some authorities have put the death toll from the explosion, fire, and fumes as high as 3,000.

2 Colombia, Aug 7, 1956 — 1,200
Seven army ammunition trucks exploded at night in the center of Cali, destroying eight city blocks, including a barracks where 500 soldiers were sleeping.

3 Thailand, Feb 15, 1990 — over 150
A dynamite truck exploded.

4 Nepal, Nov 23, 1974 — 148
Hindu pilgrims were killed when a suspension bridge over the Mahahali River collapsed.

5 Egypt, Aug 9, 1973 — 127
A bus drove into an irrigation canal.

6 Togo, Dec 6, 1965 — over 125
Two trucks collided with dancers during a festival at Sotouboua.

7 Spain, Jul 11, 1978 — over 120
A liquid gas tanker exploded in a camp site at San Carlos de la Rapita.

8 South Korea, Apr 28, 1995 — 110
An undergound explosion destroyed vehicles and caused about 100 cars and buses to plunge into the pit it created.

9= The Gambia, Nov 12, 1992 — c.100
After brake failure, a bus carrying passengers to a dock plunged into a river.

= Kenya, early Dec 1992 — c.100
A bus carrying 112 people skidded, hit a bridge, and plunged into a river.

The worst-ever motor racing accident occurred on June 13, 1955, at Le Mans, France, when, in attempting to avoid other cars, French driver Pierre Levegh's Mercedes-Benz 300 SLR went out of control, hit a wall, and exploded in midair, showering wreckage into the crowd and killing 82. It is believed that the worst-ever accident involving a single car occurred on Dec 17, 1956, when eight adults and four children were killed when their car was hit by a train near Phoenix, Arizona.

CARNAGE ON THE ROADS
Although fatal crashes are common, road accidents resulting in very large numbers of deaths are, thankfully, comparatively rare.

TOP 10 SAFEST CAR COLORS

(Color/light reflection percentage)

1 White, 84.0 **2** Cream, 68.8 **3** Ivory, 66.7 **4** Light pink, 66.5 **5** Yellow, 57.0 **6** Pink, 51.6 **7** Buff, 51.5 **8** Light gray, 51.5 **9** Light green, 45.2 **10** Aluminum gray, 41.0

Source: *Mansell Color Company Inc, published by the National Safety Council*

THE 10 ★
COUNTRIES WITH THE MOST DEATHS BY MOTOR ACCIDENTS

COUNTRY	DEATH RATE PER 100,000 POPULATION
1 South Africa	99.4
2 Latvia	35.3
3 South Korea	33.1
4 Estonia	26.7
5 Russia	23.6
6 Portugal	22.8
7 Lithuania	22.1
8 Greece	21.3
9 Venezuala	20.7
10=El Salvador	20.3
=Kuwait	20.3

Source: *United Nations*

THE 10 ★
STATES WITH THE MOST MOTOR VEHICLE FATALITIES

STATE	TOTAL FATALITIES (1997)
1 California	3,688
2 Texas	3,510
3 Florida	2,782
4 New York	1,643
5 Georgia	1,577
6 Pennsylvania	1,557
7 North Carolina	1,483
8 Michigan	1,446
9 Ohio	1,441
10 Illinois	1,395

Most of these states are also among the nation's foremost vehicle users; taking this into account, they have fatality rates below the national average.

THE 10 ★
COUNTRIES WITH THE HIGHEST NUMBER OF ROAD DEATHS

COUNTRY	TOTAL DEATHS*
1 US	41,907
2 Thailand	15,176
3 Japan	11,674
4 South Korea	10,087
5 Germany	8,758
6 France	8,541
7 Brazil	6,759
8 Poland	6,744
9 Italy	6,688
10 Turkey	6,108

* In latest year for which figures are available

THE 10 ★
MOST COMMON COLLISIONS IN THE US

OBJECT/EVENT	COLLISIONS (1997)
1 Another vehicle, at an angle	2,438,000
2 Another vehicle, rear end	1,921,000
3 Parked motor vehicle	365,000
4 Another vehicle, sideswipe	294,000
5 Animal	265,000
6 Pole or post	210,000
7 Culvert/curb/ditch	188,000
8 Shrubbery/tree	155,000
9 Rollover	129,000
10 Guard rail	111,000

Out of 6,764,000 crashes recorded in 1997 (omitting those described as "other" or "unknown"), the next most common event is a head-on collision, with 105,000 cases. Collisions with pedestrians and bicyclists accounted for 78,000 and 63,000 cases respectively.

BEWARE!

Skidding and collisions with other objects or vehicles account for most road accidents; people from ages 16–20 are most at risk of being killed or injured.

THE 10 ★
MOST VULNERABLE AGES FOR ROAD FATALITIES IN THE US

AGE GROUP	1997 DEATHS	POPULATION	DEATH RATE PER 100,000
1 16–20	5,757	18,936,000	30.40
2 21–24	3,781	13,774,000	27.45
3 74+	4,123	15,577,000	26.47
4 25–34	7,365	39,610,000	18.59
5 65–74	3,203	18,499,000	17.31
6 35–44	6,432	43,988,000	14.62
7 55–64	3,137	21,813,000	14.38
8 45–54	4,667	33,633,000	13.88
9 10–15	1,554	22,910,000	6.78
10 5–9	815	19,738,000	4.13

Source: *National Highway Traffic Safety Administration*

THE 10 WORST YEARS FOR FATAL MOTOR VEHICLE ACCIDENTS IN THE US

(Year/fatalities)*

1 1972, 54,589 **2** 1973, 54,052
3 1969, 53,543 **4** 1968, 52,725
5 1970, 52,627 **6** 1971, 52,542
7 1979, 51,093 **8** 1980, 51,091
9 1966, 50,894 **10** 1967, 50,724

* *Traffic fatalities occurring within 30 days of accident*

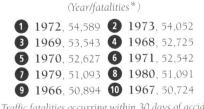

What was the biggest airship ever built?
see p.239 for the answer

A *Graf Zeppelin II*
B *Hindenburg*
C *Graf Zeppelin*

RAIL TRANSPORTATION

THE 10 ★
WORST RAIL DISASTERS

LOCATION/DATE/INCIDENT	NO. KILLED

1 Bagmati River, India, June 6, 1981   *c.*800
The carriages of a train traveling from Samastipur to Banmukhi in Bihar plunged off a bridge over the Bagmati River near Mansi – when the driver braked, apparently to avoid hitting a sacred cow. Although the official death toll was said to have been 268, many authorities have claimed that the train was so massively overcrowded that the actual figure was in excess of 800, making it probably the worst rail disaster of all time.

2 Chelyabinsk, Russia, June 3, 1989   up to 800
Two passenger trains, laden with vacationers heading to and from Black Sea resorts, were destroyed when liquid gas from a nearby pipeline exploded.

3 Guadalajara, Mexico, Jan 18, 1915   over 600
A train derailed on a steep incline, but political strife in the country meant that full details of the disaster were suppressed.

4 Modane, France, Dec 12, 1917   573
A troop-carrying train ran out of control and was derailed. It has been claimed that the train was overloaded and that as many as 1,000 may have died.

5 Balvano, Italy, Mar 2, 1944   521
A heavily-laden train stalled in the Armi Tunnel and many passengers were asphyxiated. Like the disaster at Torre (No. 6), wartime secrecy prevented full details from being published.

6 Torre, Spain, Jan 3, 1944   over 500
A double collision and fire in a tunnel resulted in many deaths – some have put the total as high as 800.

7 Awash, Ethiopia, Jan 13, 1985   428
A derailment hurled a train carrying some 1,000 passengers into a ravine.

8 Cireau, Romania, Jan 7, 1917   374
An overcrowded passenger train crashed into a military train and was derailed.

9 Quipungo, Angola, May 31, 1993   355
A trail was derailed by UNITA guerrilla action.

10 Sangi, Pakistan, Jan 4, 1990   306
A train was diverted onto the wrong line, resulting in a fatal collision.

RAIL WRECKAGE
The sparks from two trains traveling through the Ural mountains ignited gas leaking from the nearby Trans-Siberian Pipeline.

THE 10 ★
WORST RAIL DISASTERS IN THE US

LOCATION/DATE/INCIDENT	NO. KILLED

1 Nashville, Tennessee, July 9, 1918   101
On the Nashville, Chattanooga, and St. Louis Railroad, a head-on collision resulted in a deathtoll that remains the worst in US history, with 171 injured.

2 Brooklyn, New York, Nov 2, 1918   97
A subway train was derailed in the Malbone Street tunnel.

3 =Eden, Colorado, Aug 7, 1904   96
A bridge washed away during a flood smashed Steele's Hollow Bridge as the World's Fair Express was crossing.

=Wellington, Washington, Mar 1, 1910   96
An avalanche swept two trains into a canyon.

5 Bolivar, Texas, Sept 8, 1900   85
A train traveling from Beaumont encountered the hurricane that destroyed Galveston, killing 6,000. Attempts to load the train onto a ferry were abandoned, and it set back, but was destroyed by the storm.

6 Woodbridge, New Jersey, Feb 6, 1951   84
A Pennsylvania Railroad commuter train crashed while speeding through a sharply curving detour.

7 Chatsworth, Illinois, 10 Aug, 1887   82
A trestle bridge caught fire and collapsed as the Toledo, Peoria & Western train was passing over. As many as 372 were injured.

8 Ashtabula, Ohio, Dec 29, 1876   80
A bridge collapsed in a snow storm and the Lake Shore train fell into the Ashtabula river. The death toll may have been as high as 92.

9 =Frankford Junction, Pennsylvania, Sept 6, 1943   79
Pennsylvania's worst railway accident (since that at Camp Hill on July 17, 1856, when two trains crashed head-on, resulting in the deaths of 66 school children on a church picnic outing).

=Richmond Hill, New York, Nov 22, 1950   79
A Long Island Rail Road commuter train rammed into the rear of another, leaving 79 dead and 363 injured.

TOP 10 BUSIEST RAIL NETWORKS
(Country/passenger miles per annum*/passenger km per annum*)

1 Japan, 246,269,000,000/396,332,000,000   **2 China**, 219,965,000,000/354,700,000,000
3 India, 198,500,000,000/319,400,000,000   **4 Russia**, 119,200,000,000/191,900,000,000
5 Ukraine, 47,200,000,000/75,900,000,000   **6 France**, 36,276,000,000/58,380,000,000
7 Germany, 36,041,000,000/58,003,000,000   **8 Egypt**, 29,821,000,000/47,992,000,000
9 Italy, 29,270,000,000/47,100,000,000   **10 South Korea**, 18,775,000,000/30,216,000,000

US 13,138,000,000/21,144,000,000

* Number of passengers multiplied by distance carried

TOP 10 LONGEST RAIL NETWORKS

(Location/total rail length in miles/km)

1 US, 149,129/240,000 **2** Russia, 95,691/154,000 **3** Canada, 45,337/72,963 **4** China, 40,327/64,900 **5** India, 38,935/62,660 **6** Germany, 27,319/43,966 **7** Australia, 23,962/38,563 **8** Argentina, 23,556/37,910 **9** France, 19,901/32,027 **10** Brazil, 16,712/26,895

THE 10 FIRST CITIES IN NORTH AMERICA TO HAVE SUBWAY SYSTEMS

(City/year opened)

1 New York, 1867 **2** Chicago, 1892 **3** Boston, 1901 **4** Philadelphia, 1908 **5** Toronto, 1954 **6** Cleveland, 1955 **7** Montreal, 1966 **8** San Francisco, 1972 **9** Washington, DC, 1976 **10** Atlanta, 1979

FAST AS A BULLET

The Shinkansen, *or Bullet Train, is the world's fastest train. It debuted in 1964 and currently covers the 120 miles (190 km) between the stations at Hiroshima and Kokura in 44 minutes.*

TOP 10 ★ BUSIEST UNDERGROUND RAIL NETWORKS

CITY	YEAR OPENED	TRACK LENGTH MILES	KM	STATIONS	PASSENGERS PER ANNUM
1 Moscow	1935	153	243.6	150	3,183,900,000
2 Tokyo	1927	106	169.1	154	2,112,700,000
3 Mexico City	1969	112	177.7	154	1,422,600,000
4 Seoul	1974	84	133.0	112	1,354,000,000
5 Paris	1900	127	201.4	372	1,170,000,000
6 New York	1867	249	398.0	469	1,100,000,000
7 Osaka	1933	66	105.8	99	988,600,000
8 St. Petersburg	1955	58	91.75	50	850,000,000
9 Hong Kong	1979	27	43.2	38	804,000,000
10 London	1863	247	392.0	245	784,000,000

TOP 10 ★ FASTEST RAIL JOURNEYS*

JOURNEY/LOCATION/TRAIN	SPEED MPH	KM/H
1 Hiroshima–Kokura, Japan, *Nozomi 503/508*	162.7	261.8
2 Lille–Roissy, France, *TGV 538/9*	158.0	254.3
3 Madrid–Seville, Spain, *AVE 9616/9617*	129.9	209.1
4 Würzburg–Fulda, Germany, *ICE*	124.1	199.7
5 London–York, UK, *Scottish Pullman*	112.0	180.2
6 Hässleholm–Alvesta, Sweden, *X2000*	104.4	168.0
7 Rome–Florence, Italy, *10 Pendolini*	102.5	164.9
8 Baltimore–Wilmington, US, *Metroliner 110*	97.7	137.3
9 Salo–Karjaa, Finland, *S220 132*	94.3	151.7
10 Toronto–Dorval, Canada, *Metropolis*	87.6	141.0

* Fastest journey for each country; all those in the Top 10 have other similarly or equally fast services   Source: Railway Gazette International

Background image: **KOMSOMOLSKAYA STATION, MOSCOW**

Which is the largest cruise ship in the world?
see p.236 for the answer

A *Grand Princess*
B *Disney Magic*
C *Voyager of the Seas*

235

THE 10 ★
WORST OIL TANKER SPILLS

	TANKER(S)/LOCATION/DATE	APPROX. SPILLAGE TONNES
1	*Atlantic Empress* and *Aegean Captain*, Trinidad, July 19, 1979	330,000
2	*Castillio de Bellver*, Cape Town, South Africa, Aug 6, 1983	281,000
3	*Olympic Bravery*, Ushant, France, Jan 24, 1976	275,000
4	*Showa-Maru*, Malacca, Malaya, June 7, 1975	261,000
5	*Amoco Cadiz*, Finistère, France, Mar 16, 1978	245,000
6	*Odyssey*, Atlantic, off Canada, Nov 10, 1988	154,000
7	*Torrey Canyon*, Isles of Scilly, UK, Mar 18, 1967	132,000
8	*Sea Star*, Gulf of Oman, Dec 19, 1972	126,000
9	*Irenes Serenada*, Pilos, Greece, Feb 23, 1980	112,000
10	*Urquiola*, Corunna, Spain, May 12, 1976	111,000

In addition to these major slicks, it is estimated that an average of 2 million tons is spilled into the world's seas annually. All these accidents were caused by collision, grounding, fire, or explosion.

CARNIVAL DESTINY
The Carnival Destiny, the world's fourth largest cruise ship, is 892 ft (271 m) long, and contains a theater, a library, a gymnasium, and four outdoor pools.

THE 10 ★
WORST PASSENGER FERRY DISASTERS OF THE 20TH CENTURY

	FERRY/LOCATION/DATE	NO. KILLED
1	*Dona Paz*, Philippines, Dec 20, 1987	up to 3,000
2	*Neptune*, Haiti, Feb 17, 1992	1,800
3	*Toya Maru*, Japan, Sept 26, 1954	1,172
4	*Don Juan*, Philippines, Apr 22, 1980	over 1,000
5	*Estonia*, Baltic Sea, Sept 28, 1994	909
6	*Samia*, Bangladesh, May 25, 1986	600
7	*MV Bukoba*, Lake Victoria, Tanzania, May 21, 1996	549
8	*Salem Express*, Egypt, Dec 14, 1991	480
9	*Tampomas II*, Indonesia, Jan 27, 1981	431
10	*Nam Yung Ho*, South Korea, Dec 15, 1970	323

The *Dona Paz* sank in the Tabias Strait, Philippines, after the ferry was struck by the oil tanker *MV Victor*. The loss of life may have been much higher than the official figure (up to 4,386 has been suggested by some authorities).

TOP 10 ★
LARGEST CRUISE SHIPS

	SHIP/YEAR/COUNTRY BUILT	PASSENGER CAPACITY	GROSS TONNAGE
1	*Voyager of the Seas*, 1999, Finland	3,840	156,526
2	*Grand Princess*, 1998, Italy	3,300	119,936
3	*Carnival Triumph*, 1999, Italy	3,300	112,073
4	*Carnival Destiny*, 1996, Italy	3,336	111,721
5	*Disney Magic*, 1998, Italy	2,500	91,863
6	*Rhapsody of the Seas*, 1997, France	2,416	86,520
7	*Vision of the Seas*, 1997, France	2,416	86,350
8 =	*Dawn Princess*, 1997, Italy	1,950	85,363
=	*Sea Princess*, 1998, Italy	2,185	85,363
=	*Sun Princess*, 1995, Italy	2,272	85,363

Source: *Lloyd's Register of Shipping, MIPG/PPMS*

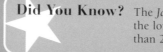

Did You Know? The *Jahre Viking* oil tanker, at 1,504 ft/485.45 m long, is the longest vessel ever built. Its length is equal to more than 20 tennis courts end-to-end.

THE 10 ⭐
WORST MARINE DISASTERS OF THE 20TH CENTURY

LOCATION/DATE/INCIDENT	APPROX. NO. KILLED

1 Off Danzig (Gdansk), Poland, Jan 30, 1945 — up to 7,800
The German liner Wilhelm Gustloff, laden with refuges, was torpedoed by a Soviet submarine S-13. The precise death toll remains uncertain, but is in the range of 5,348 to 7,800.

2 Off Cape Rixhöft (Rozeewie), Poland, Apr 16, 1945 — 6,800
The German ship Goya, carrying evacuees from Gdansk, was torpedoed in the Baltic.

3 Off Yingkow, China, Nov 1947 — over 6,000
An unidentified Chinese troop ship carrying Nationalist soldiers from Manchuria.

4 Lübeck, Germany, May 3, 1945 — 5,000
The German ship Cap Arcona, carrying concentration camp survivors, was bombed and sunk by British aircraft.

5 Off St. Nazaire, France, June 17, 1940 — 3,050
The British troop ship Lancastria sank.

6 Off Stolpmünde (Ustka), Poland, Feb 9, 1945 — 3,000
German war-wounded and refugees were lost when the Steuben was torpedoed by the same Soviet submarine that had sunk the Wilhelm Gustloff.

7 Tabias Strait, Philippines, Dec 20, 1987 — up to 3,000
The ferry Dona Paz was struck by oil tanker MV Victor.

8 Woosung, China, Dec 3, 1948 — over 2,750
The overloaded steamship Kiangya, carrying refugees, struck a Japanese mine.

9 Lübeck, Germany, May 3, 1945 — 2,750
The refugee ship Thielbeck sank during the British bombardment of Lübeck Harbor in the closing weeks of World War II.

10 South Atlantic, Sept 12, 1942 — 2,279
The British passenger vessel Laconia, carrying Italian prisoners-of-war, was sunk by German U-boat U-156.

Recent reassessments of the death tolls in some of the World War II marine disasters means that the most famous marine disaster of all no longer ranks in the Top 10. The *Titanic* was a British liner that struck an iceberg in the North Atlantic and sank on April 15, 1912, with the loss of 1,517 lives. The *Titanic* tragedy remains one of the worst-ever peacetime disasters.

TOP 10 ⭐
BUSIEST PORTS

PORT/LOCATION	GOODS HANDLED PER ANNUM (TONS)
1 Rotterdam, Netherlands	385,800,000
2 Singapore	319,600,000
3 Chiba, Japan	191,400,000
4 Kobe, Japan	188,400,000
5 Hong Kong	162,200,000
6 Houston, US	156,500,000
7 Shanghai, China	153,800,000
8 Nagoya, Japan	151,300,000
9 Yokohama, Japan	141,400,000
10 Antwerp, Belgium	120,700,000

The only other world port handling more than 100 million tons is Kawasaki, Japan (115,900,000 tons per annum).

DOCK OF THE BAY
Many docks perform functions besides serving freight on passenger ships. These include dredging and public recreational facilities.

AIR RECORDS

FIRST PEOPLE TO FLY IN HEAVIER-THAN-AIR AIRCRAFT

	PILOT/COUNTRY/AIRCRAFT	DATE
1	**Orville Wright**, US, *Wright Flyer I*	Dec 17, 1903
2	**Wilbur Wright**, US, *Wright Flyer I*	Dec 17, 1903
3	**Alberto Santos-Dumont**, Brazil, *No. 14-bis*	Oct 23, 1906
4	**Charles Voisin**, France, *Voisin-Delagrange I*	Mar 30, 1907
5	**Henri Farman**, UK, later France, *Voisin-Farman I-bis*	Oct 7, 1907
6	**Léon Delagrange**, France, *Voisin-Delagrange I*	Nov 5, 1907
7	**Robert Esnault-Pelterie**, France, *REP No. 1*	Nov 16, 1907
8	**Charles W. Furnas***, US, *Wright Flyer III*	May 14, 1908
9	**Louis Blériot**, France, *Blériot VIII*	June 29, 1908
10	**Glenn Hammond Curtiss**, US, *AEA June Bug*	July 4, 1908

* As a passenger in a plane piloted by Wilbur Wright, Furnass was the first airplane passenger in the US.

THE WRIGHT BROTHERS

Following Orville Wright's first-ever flight at Kitty Hawk, North Carolina, he (right) and his brother Wilbur dominated the air for the next few years.

FIRST TRANSATLANTIC FLIGHTS

	AIRCRAFT/CREW/COUNTRY	CROSSING	DATE
1	**US Navy/Curtiss flying boat** *NC-4*, Lt.-Cdr. Albert Cushing Read and crew of five, US	Trepassy Harbor, Newfoundland, to Lisbon, Portugal	May 16–27, 1919*
2	**Twin Rolls-Royce-engined converted Vickers Vimy bomber#**, Capt. John Alcock and Lt. Arthur Whitten Brown, UK	St John's, Newfoundland, to Galway, Ireland	June 14–15, 1919
3	**British *R-34* airship+**, Maj. George Herbert Scott and crew of 30, UK	East Fortune, Scotland, to Roosevelt Field, New York	July 2–6, 1919
4	**Fairey IIID seaplane *Santa Cruz***, Adm. Gago Coutinho and Cdr. Sacadura Cabral, Portugal	Lisbon, Portugal, to Recife, Brazil	Mar 30–June 5, 1922
5	**Two Douglas seaplanes, *Chicago* and *New Orleans***, Lt. Lowell H. Smith and Leslie P. Arnold/ Erik Nelson and John Harding, US	Orkneys, Scotland, to Labrador, Canada	Aug 2–31, 1924
6	***Los Angeles*, a renamed German-built *ZR 3* airship**, Dr. Hugo Eckener, with 31 passengers and crew, Germany	Friedrichshafen, Germany, to Lakehurst, New Jersey	Oct 12–15, 1924
7	***Plus Ultra*, a Dornier Wal twin-engined flying boat**, Capt. Julio Ruiz and crew, Spain	Huelva, Spain, to Recife, Brazil	Jan 22–Feb 10, 1926
8	***Santa Maria*, a Savoia-Marchetti S.55 flying boat**, Francesco Marquis de Pinedo, Capt. Carlo del Prete, and Lt. Vitale Zacchetti, Italy	Cagliari, Sardinia, to Recife, Brazil	Feb 8–24, 1927
9	**Dornier Wal flying boat**, Sarmento de Beires and Jorge de Castilho, Portugal	Lisbon, Portugal, to Natal, Brazil	Mar 16–17, 1927
10	**Savoia-Marchetti flying boat**, João De Barros and crew, Brazil	Genoa, Italy, to Natal, Brazil	Apr 28–May 14, 1927

* All dates refer to the actual Atlantic legs of the journeys; some started earlier and ended beyond their first transatlantic landfalls

\# First nonstop flight

\+ First east–west flight

THE 10 FIRST FLIGHTS OF MORE THAN ONE HOUR

(Pilot/duration in hrs:mins:secs/date)

❶ Orville Wright, 1:2:15, Sept 9, 1908 **❷ Orville Wright**, 1:5:52, Sept 10, 1908
❸ Orville Wright, 1:10:0, Sept 11, 1908 **❹ Orville Wright**, 1:15:20, Sept 12, 1908
❺ Wilbur Wright, 1:31:25, Sept 21, 1908 **❻ Wilbur Wright**, 1:7:24, Sept 28, 1908
❼ Wilbur Wright*, 1:4:26, Oct 6, 1908 **❽ Wilbur Wright**, 1:9:45, Oct 10, 1908
❾ Wilbur Wright, 1:54:53, Dec 18, 1908 **❿ Wilbur Wright**, 2:20:23, Dec 31, 1908

* First ever flight of more than one hour with a passenger (M.A. Fordyce)

*Background image: **ARTIST'S IMPRESSION OF AN EARLY FLIGHT BY THE WRIGHT BROTHERS AT KITTY HAWK, US***

TOP 10 ★
FASTEST X-15 FLIGHTS

	PILOT/DATE	MACH*	SPEED MPH	KM/H
1	William J. Knight, Oct 3, 1967	6.70	4,520	7,274
2	William J. Knight, Nov 18, 1966	6.33	4,261	6,857
3	Joseph A. Walker, June 27, 1962	5.92	4,105	6,606
4	Robert M. White, Nov 9, 1961	6.04	4,094	6,589
5	Robert A. Rushworth, Dec 5, 1963	6.06	4,018	6,466
6	Neil A. Armstrong, June 26, 1962	5.74	3,989	6,420
7	John B. McKay, June 22, 1965	5.64	3,938	6,388
8	Robert A. Rushworth, July 18, 1963	5.63	3,925	6,317
9	Joseph A. Walker, June 25, 1963	5.51	3,911	6,294
10	William H. Dana, Oct 4, 1967	5.53	3,910	6,293

* Mach no. varies with altitude – the list is ranked on actual speed

THE 10 ★
FIRST ROCKET AND JET AIRCRAFT

	AIRCRAFT/COUNTRY	FIRST FLIGHT
1	Heinkel He 176*, Germany	June 20, 1939
2	Heinkel He 178, Germany	Aug 27, 1939
3	DFS 194*, Germany	Aug 1940#
4	Caproni-Campini N-1, Italy	Aug 28, 1940
5	Heinkel He 280V-1, Germany	Apr 2, 1941
6	Gloster E.28/39, UK	May 15, 1941
7	Messerschmitt Me 163 Komet*, Germany	Aug 13, 1941
8	Messerschmitt Me 262V-3, Germany	July 18, 1942
9	Bell XP-59A Airacomet, US	Oct 1, 1942
10	Gloster Meteor F Mk 1, UK	Mar 5, 1943

* Rocket-powered
 # Precise date unknown

GRAF ZEPPELIN II

Sister ship of the ill-fated Hindenburg, *the equally gigantic Graf Zeppelin II airship flew successfully, but in March 1940, on the orders of Herman Goering, it was dismantled at Frankfurt, Germany, and its aluminum frame used in the construction of Luftwaffe fighter aircraft.*

TOP 10 ★
BIGGEST AIRSHIPS EVER BUILT

	AIRSHIP	COUNTRY	YEAR	VOLUME CU FT	CU M	LENGTH FT	M
1 =	Hindenburg	Germany	1936	7,062,934	200,000	804	245
=	Graf Zeppelin II	Germany	1938	7,062,934	200,000	804	245
3 =	Akron	US	1931	6,500,000	184,060	785	239
=	Macon	US	1933	6,500,000	184,060	785	239
5	R101	UK	1930	5,500,000	155,744	777	237
6	Graf Zeppelin	Germany	1928	3,708,040	105,000	776	237
7	L72	Germany	1920	2,419,055	68,500	743	226
8	R100	UK	1929	5,500,000	155,743	709	216
9	R38	UK*	1921	2,724,000	77,136	699	213
10 =	L70	Germany	1918	2,418,700	62,200	694	212
=	L71	Germany	1918	2,418,700	62,200	694	212

* UK-built, but sold to US Navy

Although several of the giant airships in this list traveled long distances carrying thousands of passengers, they all ultimately suffered unfortunate fates: six (the *Hindenburg, Akron, Macon, R101, L72,* and *R38*) crashed with the loss of many lives, the *L70* was shot down, and the *L71*, both *Graf Zeppelins*, and the *R100* were broken up for scrap.

Did You Know? The speeds attained by the rocket-powered X-15 and X-15A-2 aircraft are the greatest ever attained by piloted vehicles in the Earth's atmosphere.

239

THE 10 ★
WORST AIRSHIP DISASTERS

LOCATION/DATE/INCIDENT	NO. KILLED
1 Off the Atlantic coast, US, Apr 4, 1933 *US Navy airship Akron crashed into the sea in a storm, leaving only three survivors in the world's worst airship tragedy.*	73
2 Over the Mediterranean, Dec 21, 1923 *French airship Dixmude is presumed to have been struck by lightning, broke up, and crashed into the sea; wreckage believed to be from the airship was found off Sicily 10 years later.*	52
3 Near Beauvais, France, Oct 5, 1930 *British airship R101 crashed into a hillside leaving 48 dead, with two dying later, and six survivors.*	50
4 Off the coast near Hull, UK, Aug 24, 1921 *Airship R38, sold by the British Government to the US and renamed USN ZR-2, broke in two on a training and test flight.*	44
5 Lakehurst, New Jersey, US, May 6, 1937 *German Zeppelin Hindenburg caught fire while mooring.*	36
6 Hampton Roads, Virginia, US, Feb 21, 1922 *Roma, an Italian airship bought by the US Army, crashed, killing all but 11 men on board.*	34
7 Berlin, Germany, Oct 17, 1913 *German airship LZ18 crashed after engine failure during a test flight at Berlin-Johannisthal.*	28
8 Baltic Sea, Mar 30, 1917 *German airship SL9 was struck by lightning on a flight from Seerappen to Seddin and crashed into the sea.*	23
9 Mouth of the River Elbe, Germany, Sept 3, 1915 *German airship L10 was struck by lightning and plunged into the sea.*	19
10=Off Heligoland, North Sea, Sept 9, 1913 *German Navy airship L1 crashed into the sea, leaving six survivors.*	14
=Caldwell, Ohio, US, Sept 3, 1925 *US Navy dirigible Shenandoah, the first airship built in the US and the first to use safe helium instead of inflammable hydrogen, broke up in a storm, scattering sections over a large area of the Ohio countryside.*	14

THE 10 ★
WORST AIRPLANE DISASTERS

LOCATION/DATE/INCIDENT	NO. KILLED
1 Tenerife, Canary Islands, Mar 27, 1977 *Two Boeing 747s (Pan Am and KLM, carrying 364 passengers and 16 crew and 230 passengers and 11 crew, respectively) collided and caught fire on the runway of Los Rodeos Airport after the pilots received incorrect control-tower instructions.*	583
2 Mt. Ogura, Japan, Aug 12, 1985 *A JAL Boeing 747 on an internal flight from Tokyo to Osaka crashed, killing all but four on board in the worst-ever disaster involving a single aircraft.*	520
3 Charkhi Dadrio, India, Nov 12, 1996 *Soon after taking off from New Delhi's Indira Gandhi International Airport, a Saudi Airways Boeing 747 collided with a Kazakh Airlines Ilyushin IL76 cargo aircraft on its descent and exploded, killing all 312 on the Boeing and 37 on the Ilyushin in the world's worst mid-air crash.*	349
4 Paris, France, Mar 3, 1974 *A Turkish Airlines DC-10 crashed at Ermenonville, north of Paris, immediately after takeoff for London, with many English rugby fans among the dead.*	346
5 Off the Irish coast, June 23, 1985 *An Air India Boeing 747 on a flight from Vancouver to Delhi exploded in mid-air, perhaps as a result of a terrorist bomb.*	329
6 Riyadh, Saudi Arabia, Aug 19, 1980 *A Saudia (Saudi Arabian) Airlines Lockheed Tristar caught fire during an emergency landing.*	301
7 Kinshasa, Zaïre, Jan 8, 1996 *A Zaïrean Antonov-32 cargo plane crashed shortly after takeoff, killing shoppers in a city-center market.*	298
8 Off the Iranian coast, July 3, 1988 *An Iran Air A300 airbus was shot down in error by a missile fired by the US warship Vincennes.*	290
9 Chicago, US, May 25, 1979 *The worst air disaster in the US occurred when an engine fell off a DC-10 as it took off from Chicago O'Hare Airport and the plane plunged out of control, killing all 271 on board and two on the ground.*	273
10 Lockerbie, Scotland, Dec 21, 1988 *Pan Am Flight 103 from London Heathrow to New York exploded in mid-air as a result of a terrorist bomb, killing 243 passengers, 16 crew, and 11 on the ground in the UK's worst-ever air disaster.*	270

TOP 10 AIRLINE-USING COUNTRIES

(Country/passenger miles per annum*/passenger km per annum*)

❶ US, 571.547 billion/919.816 billion **❷ UK**, 100.269 billion/161.366 billion **❸ Japan**, 88.118 billion/141.812 billion **❹ France**, 50.700 billion/81.594 billion **❺ Germany**, 48.321 billion/77.765 billion **❻ Australia**, 45.108 billion/72.594 billion **❼ China**, 43.872 billion/70.605 billion **❽ Netherlands**, 38.772 billion/62.397 billion **❾ Canada**, 34.808 billion/56.018 billion **❿ Rep. of Korea**, 34.642 billion/55.751 billion

* *Total distance traveled by scheduled aircraft of national airlines multiplied by number of passengers carried*
Source: *International Civil Aviation Organization*

TOP 10 COUNTRIES WITH THE MOST AIRPORTS

(Country/airports)

❶ US, 14,574 **❷ Brazil**, 3,291 **❸ Russia**, 2,517 **❹ Mexico**, 1,810 **❺ Argentina**, 1,411 **❻ Canada**, 1,393 **❼ Bolivia**, 1,153 **❽ Colombia**, 1,136 **❾ Paraguay**, 948 **❿ South Africa**, 770

Source: *Central Intelligence Agency*

Airports, as defined by the CIA (which monitors them for strategic reasons), range in size from those with paved runways over 10,000 ft/3,048 m in length to those with only short landing strips. Among European countries with the most airports are Germany (613), France (460), and the UK (387).

Which country has the longest rail network?
see p.235 for the answer

A India
B Russia
C US

TOP 10 ★
BUSIEST INTERNATIONAL AIRPORTS

AIRPORT/LOCATION	PASSENGERS PER ANNUM
1 London Heathrow, London, UK	48,275,000
2 Frankfurt, Frankfurt, Germany	30,919,000
3 Hong Kong, Hong Kong, China	29,543,000
4 Charles de Gaulle, Paris, France	28,665,000
5 Schiphol, Amsterdam, Netherlands	27,085,000
6 Singapore International, Singapore	23,130,000
7 New Tokyo International (Narita), Tokyo, Japan	22,666,000
8 London Gatwick, Gatwick, UK	22,029,000
9 J.F. Kennedy International, New York City	17,453,000
10 Bangkok, Bangkok, Thailand	16,380,000

Source: *International Civil Aviation Organization*

AIRSHIP TRAGEDY

US airship Akron was named after the Ohio city known as America's rubber capital. Built in 1931, it crashed into the sea only two years later.

THE 10 ★
WORST AIR DISASTERS IN THE US

LOCATION/DATE/INCIDENT	NO. KILLED
1 Chicago, Illinois, May 25, 1979 *(See Worst Air Disasters, No. 9)*	275
2 Off Long Island, New York, July 17, 1996 — *Soon after takeoff from JFK, a TWA Boeing 747-100 en route for Paris exploded in midair and crashed into the Atlantic Ocean, killing all on board.*	230
3 Romulus, Michigan, Aug 16, 1987 — *A Northwest Airlines McDonnell Douglas DC-9 crashed onto a road following an engine fire after takeoff from Detroit. Only one passenger survived.*	156
4 Kenner, Louisiana, July 9, 1982 — *A Pan Am Boeing 747 crashed after takeoff from New Orleans for Las Vegas, killing all on board and eight on the ground.*	153
5 San Diego, California, Sept 25, 1978 — *A Pacific Southwest Airline Boeing 727 collided in the air with a Cessna 172 light aircraft, killing 135 in the plane, two in the Cessna, and seven on the ground.*	144
6 Dallas-Ft Worth Airport, Texas, Aug 2, 1985 — *A Delta Airlines TriStar crashed when a severe downdraft affected it during landing, killing 136 on board and the driver of a truck on the ground.*	137
7 New York, Dec 16, 1960 — *A United Airlines DC-8 with 77 passengers and crew of seven and a TWA Super Constellation with 39 passengers and five crew collided in a snowstorm. The DC-8 crashed in Brooklyn, killing six on the ground; the Super Constellation crashed into New York Harbor, killing all on board.*	134
8 Pittsburgh, Pennsylvania, Sept 8, 1994 — *A USAir Boeing 737-400 enroute from Chicago to West Palm Beach crashed, killing all on board.*	132
9 Grand Canyon, Arizona, June 30, 1956 — *A United Airlines DC-7 and a TWA Super Constellation collided in the air, killing all on board.*	128
10 JFK Airport, New York, June 24, 1975 — *An Eastern Air Lines Boeing 727 on a flight from New Orleans crashed while attempting to land.*	115

FLYING BOEING

First flown in 1981, the Boeing 737-300 can accommodate up to 126 passengers, and reaches speeds of 495 mph/801 km/h.

SPORTS

OLYMPIC RECORDS

OLYMPIC SPORTS IN WHICH THE US HAS WON THE MOST MEDALS

	SPORT	GOLD	SILVER	BRONZE	TOTAL
			MEDALS		
1	Athletics	299	216	177	692
2	Swimming	230	176	137	543
3	Diving	46	40	41	127
4	Wrestling	46	38	25	109
5	Boxing	47	21	34	102
6	Shooting	45	26	21	92
7	Gymnastics	26	23	28	77
8	Rowing	29	28	19	76
9	Yachting	16	19	16	51
10	Speed skating	22	16	10	48

OLYMPIC SPORTS IN WHICH THE UK HAS WON THE MOST MEDALS

	SPORT	GOLD	SILVER	BRONZE	TOTAL
1	Athletics	47	79	57	183
2	Swimming	18	23	30	71
3 =	Cycling	9	21	16	46
=	Tennis	16	14	16	46
5	Shooting	13	14	18	45
6	Boxing	12	10	21	43
7	Rowing	19	15	7	41
8	Yachting	14	12	9	35
9	Equestrianism	5	7	9	21
10	Wrestling	3	4	10	17

SUMMER OLYMPICS ATTENDED BY THE MOST COMPETITORS, 1896–1996

	CITY/YEAR	COUNTRIES REPRESENTED	COMPETITORS
1	Atlanta, 1996	197	10,310
2	Barcelona, 1992	172	9,364
3	Seoul, 1988	159	9,101
4	Munich, 1972	122	7,156
5	Los Angeles, 1984	141	7,058
6	Montreal, 1976	92	6,085
7	Mexico City, 1968	112	5,530
8	Rome, 1960	83	5,346
9	Moscow, 1980	81	5,326
10	Tokyo, 1964	93	5,140

The first games in 1896 were attended by just 311 competitors, all men, representing 13 countries. Women took part for the first time four years later at the Paris games.

WOMEN'S MOVEMENT

Over 3,500 female competitors took part in the 1996 Atlanta Olympics – 40 percent more than at the previous games in Barcelona in 1992.

Background image: **OLYMPIC RINGS**

SPECTACULAR ACHIEVEMENT

Larissa Latynina dominated gymnastics for over a decade. In Olympic, World, and European championships she won a total of 44 medals, 24 of them gold.

THE 10 OLYMPIC DECATHLON EVENTS

① 100 meters ② Long jump ③ Shot put ④ High jump
⑤ 400 meters ⑥ 110 meters hurdles ⑦ Discus
⑧ Pole vault ⑨ Javelin ⑩ 1500 meters

TOP 10 ★
LONGEST-STANDING CURRENT OLYMPIC TRACK AND FIELD RECORDS

	EVENT	WINNING DISTANCE, TIME OR SCORE	COMPETITOR/ COUNTRY	DATE SET
1	Men's long jump	8.90 m	Bob Beamon, US	Oct 18, 1968
2	Women's shot	22.41 m	Ilona Slupianek, East Germany	Jul 24, 1980
3	Women's 800 meters	1 min 53.43 sec	Nadezhda Olizarenko, USSR	Jul 27, 1980
4=	Women's 4 x 100 meters	41.60 sec	East Germany	Aug 1, 1980
=	Men's 1500 meters	3 min 32.53 sec	Sebastian Coe, UK	Aug 1, 1980
6	Women's marathon	2 hr 24 min 52 sec	Joan Benoit, US	Aug 5, 1984
7	Decathlon	8,847 points	Daley Thompson, UK	Aug 9, 1984
8	Men's 5,000 meters	13 min 05.59 sec	Said Aouita, Morocco	Aug 11, 1984
9	Men's marathon	2 hr 9 min 21 sec	Carlos Lopes, Portugal	Aug 12, 1984
10=	Men's shot	22.47 m	Ulf Timmermann, East Germany	Sep 23, 1988
=	Men's 20 km walk	1 hr 19 min 57 sec	Jozef Pribilinec, Czechoslovakia	Sep 23, 1988

TOP 10 ★
COUNTRIES WITH THE MOST SUMMER OLYMPICS MEDALS, 1896–1996

	COUNTRY	GOLD	SILVER	BRONZE	TOTAL
1	US	833	634	548	2,015
2	Soviet Union*	485	395	354	1,234
3	UK	177	233	225	635
4	France	176	181	205	562
5	Germany#	151	181	184	516
6	Sweden	134	152	173	459
7	Italy	166	136	142	444
8	Hungary	142	128	155	425
9	East Germany	153	130	127	410
10	Australia	87	85	122	294

Medals shown as MEDALS GOLD SILVER BRONZE.

* Includes Unified Team of 1992; does not include Russia since

Not including West/East Germany 1968–88

TOP 10 ★
MEDAL WINNERS IN A SUMMER OLYMPICS CAREER

	MEDALLIST	COUNTRY	SPORT	YEARS	GOLD	SILVER	BRONZE	TOTAL
1	Larissa Latynina	USSR	Gymnastics	1956–64	9	5	4	18
2	Nikolay Andrianov	USSR	Gymnastics	1972–80	7	5	3	15
3=	Edoardo Mangiarotti	Italy	Fencing	1936–60	6	5	2	13
=	Takashi Ono	Japan	Gymnastics	1952–64	5	4	4	13
=	Boris Shakhlin	USSR	Gymnastics	1956–64	7	4	2	13
6=	Sawao Kato	Japan	Gymnastics	1968–76	8	3	1	12
=	Paavo Nurmi	Finland	Athletics	1920–28	9	3	0	12
8=	Viktor Chukarin	USSR	Gymnastics	1952–56	7	3	1	11
=	Vera Cáslavská	Czechoslovakia	Gymnastics	1964–68	7	4	0	11
=	Carl Osborn	US	Shooting	1912–24	5	4	2	11
=	Mark Spitz	US	Swimming	1968–72	9	1	1	11
=	Matt Biondi	US	Swimming	1984–92	8	2	1	11

Medals shown as MEDALS GOLD SILVER BRONZE TOTAL.

How quick was the fastest knockout in a world title fight?
see p.255 for the answer

A 18 sec
B 19 sec
C 20 sec

SPORTS HEROES

MOST POINTS SCORED BY MICHAEL JORDAN IN A GAME

	TEAM	DATE	POINTS
1	Cleveland Cavaliers	Mar 28, 1990	69
2	Orlando Magic	Jan 16, 1993	64
3	Boston Celtics	Apr 20, 1986	63
4=	Detroit Pistons	Mar 4, 1987	61
=	Atlanta Hawks	Apr 16, 1987	61
6	Detroit Pistons	Mar 3, 1988	59
7	New Jersey Nets	Feb 6, 1987	58
8	Washington Bullets	Dec 23, 1992	57
9=	Philadelphia 76ers	Mar 24, 1987	56
=	Miami Heat	Apr 29, 1992	56

Source: NBA

LONGEST LONG JUMPS BY CARL LEWIS

	STADIUM/LOCATION	DATE	DISTANCE M
1	Tokyo, Japan	Aug 30, 1991	8.87
2=	Indianapolis, US	June 19, 1983	8.79
=	New York, US*	Jan 27, 1984	8.79
4=	Indianapolis, US	July 24, 1982	8.76
=	Indianapolis, US	July 18, 1888	8.76
6	Indianapolis, US	Aug 16, 1987	8.75
7	Seoul, Korea	Sept 26, 1888	8.72
8=	Westwood, US	May 13, 1984	8.71
=	Los Angeles, US	June 19, 1884	8.71
10	Barcelona, Spain	Aug 5, 1992	8.68

* Indoor performance

THE MAGIC TOUCH

Nicknamed June Bug as a child, because he was always hopping around on court, Magic Johnson went on to become one of America's best-loved sport stars.

FASTEST 100-METRE RUNS BY LINFORD CHRISTIE

	STADIUM/LOCATION	DATE	TIME SECS
1	Stuttgart, Germany	Aug 15, 1993	9.87
2	Victoria, Canada	Aug 23, 1994	9.91
3	Tokyo, Japan	Aug 25, 1991	9.92
4	Barcelona, Spain	Aug 1, 1992	9.96
5=	Seoul, Korea	Sept 24, 1988	9.97
=	Stuttgart, Germany	Aug 15, 1993	9.97
=	Johannesburg, SA	Sept 23, 1995	9.97
8	Victoria, Canada	Aug 23, 1994	9.98
9	Tokyo, Japan	Aug 25, 1991	9.99
10=	Barcelona, Spain	Aug 1, 1992	10.00
=	Stuttgart, Germany	Aug 14, 1993	10.00

HIGHEST POLE VAULTS BY SERGEI BUBKA

	STADIUM/LOCATION	DATE	HEIGHT M
1	Donetsk, Ukraine*	Feb 21, 1993	6.15
2=	Lievin, France*	Feb 13, 1993	6.14
=	Sestriere, Italy	July 31, 1994	6.14
4=	Berlin, Germany*	Feb 21, 1992	6.13
=	Tokyo, Japan	Sept 19, 1992	6.13
6=	Grenoble, France*	Mar 23, 1991	6.12
=	Padua, Italy	Aug 30, 1992	6.12
8=	Donetsk, Ukraine*	Mar 19, 1991	6.11
=	Dijon, France	June 13, 1992	6.11
10=	San Sebastian, Spain*	Mar 15, 1991	6.10
=	Malmo, Sweden	Aug 5, 1991	6.10

* Indoor performance

LATEST WINNERS OF THE JESSE OWENS INTERNATIONAL TROPHY

YEAR	WINNER/SPORT
1999	Marion Jones, athletics
1998	Haile Gebrselassie, athletics
1997	Michael Johnson, athletics
1996	Michael Johnson, athletics
1995	Johann Olav Koss, speed skating
1994	Wang Junxia, athletics
1993	Vitaly Scherbo, gymnastics
1992	Mike Powell, athletics
1991	Greg LeMond, cycling
1990	Roger Kingdom, athletics

The Jesse Owens International Trophy has been presented by the Amateur Athletic Association since 1981, when it was won by speed skater Eric Heiden. It is named in honor of American Olympic athlete Jesse (James Cleveland) Owens (1913–80). Michael Johnson is the only athlete to have won on two occasions, while Marion Jones, the most recent winner, is only the fourth woman to receive the award.

Who is the top male tennis player in the world?
see p.273 for the answer

A Marcelo Rios
B Pete Sampras
C Alex Corretja

THE 10 LATEST WINNERS OF THE *SPORTS ILLUSTRATED* SPORTSMAN OF THE YEAR AWARD

(Year/winner(s)/sport)

1 1998, Mark McGwire and Sammy Sosa, baseball **2** 1997, Dean Smith, basketball coach **3** 1996, Tiger Woods, golf **4** 1995, Cal Ripken, Jr., baseball **5** 1994, Johan Olav Koss and Bonnie Blair, ice skating **6** 1993, Don Shula, football coach **7** 1992, Arthur Ashe, tennis **8** 1991, Michael Jordan, basketball **9** 1990, Joe Montana, football **10** 1989, Greg LeMond, cycling

First presented in 1954, when it was won by British runner Roger Bannister, this annual award honors the sportsman or sportswoman who in that year, in the opinion of the editors of *Sports Illustrated*, most "symbolizes in character and performance the ideals of sportsmanship."

THE 10 LATEST WINNERS OF THE BBC SPORTS PERSONALITY OF THE YEAR AWARD

(Year/winner/sport)

1 1998, Michael Owen, soccer **2** 1997, Greg Rusedski, tennis **3** 1996, Damon Hill, motor racing **4** 1995, Jonathan Edwards, athletics **5** 1994, Damon Hill, motor racing **6** 1993, Linford Christie, athletics **7** 1992, Nigel Mansell, motor racing **8** 1991, Liz McColgan, athletics **9** 1990, Paul Gascoigne, soccer **10** 1989, Nick Faldo, golf

This annual award is based on a poll of BBC television viewers.

TOP 10 ★
SEASONS BY WAYNE GRETZKY

	SEASON	GOALS	ASSISTS	POINTS
1	1985–86	52	163	215
2	1981–82	92	120	212
3	1984–85	73	135	208
4	1983–84	87	118	205
5	1982–83	71	125	196
6	1986–87	62	121	183
7	1988–89	54	114	168
8	1980–81	55	109	164
9	1990–91	41	122	163
10	1987–88	40	109	149

Wayne Gretzky, who retired in 1999 after 20 seasons in the NHL, is considered the greatest ice hockey player of all time. He gained more records than any player in history, including the most goals, assists, and points in a career. All his best seasons were achieved with his original team, Edmonton, with the exception of 1988–89, which was with Los Angeles. His last three playing seasons were spent with the New York Rangers.

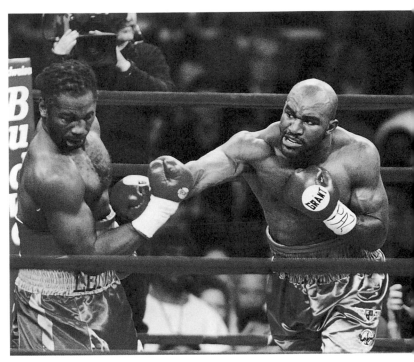

TAKE THAT!

In the 1999 Undisputed World Heavyweight Championship fight at Madison Square Garden, WBC champion Lennox Lewis appeared to dominate IBF/WBA champion Evander Holyfield. The controversial decision by the judges to declare the match a draw led to accusations of bribery and conspiracy, and calls for a rematch.

THE 10 ★
LATEST EVANDER HOLYFIELD WINS BY KNOCKOUT

	OPPONENT	ROUND	LOCATION	DATE
1	Michael Moorer	8	Las Vegas	Nov 8, 1997
2	Mike Tyson	11*	Las Vegas	Nov 9, 1996
3	Bobby Czyz	5	New York	May 10, 1996
4	Riddick Bowe	8*	Las Vegas	Nov 4, 1995
5	Bert Cooper	7	Atlanta	Nov 23, 1991
6	Buster Douglas	3	Las Vegas	Oct 25, 1990
7	Seamus McDonagh	4*	Atlantic City	June 1, 1990
8	Alex Stewart	8*	Atlantic City	Nov 4, 1989
9	Adilson Rodrigues	2	Lake Tahoe	July 15, 1989
10	Michael Dokes	10*	Las Vegas	Mar 11, 1989

* Technical knockout

Born October 19, 1962, boxer Evander Holyfield won his first undisputed heavyweight title in 1990 when he defeated Buster Douglas. His 1993 defeat of Riddick Bowe (when Holyfield won on points) and his 1996 victory over Mike Tyson established him as the only fighter apart from Muhammad Ali to win the heavyweight title on three occasions.

FOOTBALL

LONGEST CAREERS OF CURRENT NFL PLAYERS

PLAYER	TEAM	YEARS
1 Dave Krieg	Tennessee Titans	19
2 =Steve DeBerg	Atlanta Falcons	18
=Wade Wilson	Oakland Raiders	18
4 =Morten Andersen	Atlanta Falcons	17
=Gary Anderson	Minnesota Vikings	17
=Norm Johnson	Pittsburgh Steelers	17
7 =Henry Ellard	Washington Redskins	16
=John Elway	Denver Broncos	16
=Darrell Green	Washington Redskins	16
=Trey Junkin	Arizona Cardinals	16
=Dan Marino	Miami Dolphins	16
=Bruce Matthews	Tennessee Titans	16
=Reggie Roby	San Francisco 49ers	16
=Albert Lewis	Oakland Raiders	16

Source: *National Football League*

TOP 10 ★

BIGGEST WINNING MARGINS IN THE SUPER BOWL

WINNER/YEAR	SCORE	LOSERS/ MARGIN
1 San Francisco 49ers, 1990	55–10	Denver, 45
2 Chicago Bears, 1986	46–10	New England, 36
3 Dallas Cowboys, 1993	52–17	Buffalo, 35
4 Washington Redskins, 1988	42–10	Denver, 32
5 Los Angeles Raiders, 1984	38–9	Washington, 29
6 Green Bay Packers, 1967	35–10	Kansas City, 25
7 San Francisco 49ers, 1995	49–26	San Diego, 23
8 San Francisco 49ers, 1985	38–16	Miami, 22
9 Dallas Cowboys, 1972	24–3	Miami, 21
10 =Green Bay Packers, 1968	33–14	Oakland, 19
=New York Giants, 1987	39–20	Denver, 19

TOP 10 PLAYERS WITH THE MOST PASSING YARDS IN AN NFL CAREER*

(Player/passing yards)

1 Dan Marino#, 58,913 **2** John Elway, 51,475 **3** Warren Moon#, 49,097 **4** Fran Tarkenton, 47,003 **5** Dan Fouts, 43,040 **6** Joe Montana, 40,551 **7** Johnny Unitas ,40,239 **8** Dave Krieg, 37,946 **9** Boomer Esiason, 37,920 **10** Jim Kelly, 35,467

* To end of 1998–99 season
 # Still active 1998–99 season
Source: *National Football League*

ATTACK OF THE QUARTERBACK

During his impressive career, John Elway has taken the Denver Broncos to the Superbowl four times and to the AFC championships three additional times.

TOP 10 ★

POINT SCORERS IN AN NFL SEASON

PLAYER/TEAM/YEAR	GAMES WON
1 Paul Hornung, Green Bay Packers, 1960	176
2 Gary Anderson, Minnesota Vikings, 1998	164
3 Mark Moseley, Washington Redskins,1983	161
4 Gino Cappelletti, Boston Patriots, 1964	155*
5 Emmitt Smith, Dallas Cowboys, 1995	150
6 Chip Lohmiller, Washington Redskins, 1991	149
7 Gino Cappelletti, Boston Patriots, 1961	147
8 Paul Hornung, Green Bay Packers, 1961	146
9= Jim Turner, New York Jets, 1968	145
=John Kasay, Carolina Panthers, 1996	145

* Including a two-point conversion
Source: *National Football League*

TOP 10 ★

LARGEST NFL STADIUMS

STADIUM/HOME TEAM	CAPACITY
1 Pontiac Silverdrome, Detroit Lions	80,311
2 Jack Cooke Stadium, Washington Redskins	80,116
3 Rich Stadium, Buffalo Bills	80,024
4 Giants Stadium, New York Giants*	79,593
5 Arrowhead Stadium, Kansas City Chiefs	79,409
6 Mile High Stadium, Denver Broncos	76,082
7 Pro Player Stadium, Miami Dolphins	74,916
8 Sun Devil Stadium, Arizona Cardinals	73,273
9 Alltel Stadium, Jacksonville Jaguars	73,000
10 Ericsson Stadium, Carolina Panthers	72,250

* Seating reduced to 77,803 for New York Jets games
Source: *National Football League*

Did You Know? The first professional football game was played in Pennsylvania in 1895.

TOUCHDOWN!

The football is made of pebbled brown leather and has distinctive white lacing.

TOP 10 PLAYERS WITH THE MOST CAREER POINTS

(Player/points)

1 George Blanda, 2,002 **2** Gary Anderson*, 1,845 **3** Morten Andersen*, 1,761 **4** Nick Lowery, 1,71 **5** Jan Stenerud, 1,699 **6** Norm Johnson*, 1,657 **7** Eddie Murray, 1,532 **8** Pat Leahy, 1,470 **9** Jim Turner, 1,439 **10** Matt Bahr, 1,422

* Still active 1998–99 season
Source: *National Football League*

TOP 10 ★
COACHES IN AN NFL CAREER

	COACH	GAMES WON
1	Don Shula	347
2	George Halas	324
3	Tom Landry	270
4	Curly Lambeau	229
5	Chuck Noll	209
6	Chuck Knox	193
7=	Paul Brown	170
=	Dan Reeves*	170
9	Bud Grant	168
10	Marv Levy	154

* Still active 1999–2000 season
Source: *National Football League*

TOP 10 ★
PLAYERS WITH THE MOST CAREER TOUCHDOWNS

	PLAYER	TOUCHDOWNS
1	Jerry Rice*	175
2	Marcus Allen	145
3	Emmitt Smith*	134
4	Jim Brown	126
5	Walter Payton	125
6	John Riggins	116
7	Lenny Moore	113
8	Don Hutson	105
9	Steve Largent	101
10	Franco Harris	100

* Still active 1998–99 season
Source: *National Football League*

TOP 10 ★
NFL TEAMS*

	TEAM	WINS	LOSSES	PTS
1	Dallas Cowboys	5	3	13
2	San Francisco 49ers	5	0	10
3	Pittsburgh Steelers	4	1	10
4	Washington Redskins	3	2	8
5	Denver Broncos	2	4	8
6=	Green Bay Packers	3	1	7
=	Oakland/L.A. Raiders	3	1	7
8	Miami Dolphins	2	3	7
9	New York Giants	2	0	4
10=	Buffalo Bills	0	4	4
=	Minnesota Vikings	0	4	4

* Based on two points for a Superbowl win and one for a loss; wins take precedence in determining ranking.

Source: *National Football League*

THE WINNING TEAM

In addition to their five World Championship wins, the Dallas Cowboys are also the only team to win three Superbowls in a four-year period.

RUNAROUND

First run in 1970, the original course of the New York Marathon consisted simply of circuits of Central Park. In 1976, it was redesigned to take in all five boroughs – and several bridges – of New York City.

TOP 10 ★
FASTEST TIMES IN THE BOSTON MARATHON

MEN

	RUNNER/COUNTRY	YEAR	TIME
1	Cosmas Ndeti, Kenya	1994	2:07:15
2	Andres Espinosa, Mexico	1994	2:07:19
3	Moses Tanui, Kenya	1998	2:07:34
4	Joseph Chebet, Kenya	1998	2:07:37
5	Rob de Castella, Australia	1986	2:07:51
6	Gert Thys, South Africa	1998	2:07:51
7	Jackson Kipngok, Kenya	1994	2:08:08
8	Hwang Young-Jo, Korea	1994	2:08:09
9	Ibrahim Hussein, Kenya	1992	2:08:14
10	Gelindo Bordin, Italy	1990	2:08:19

WOMEN

	RUNNER/COUNTRY	YEAR	TIME
1	Uta Pippig, Germany	1994	2:21:45
2	Joan Benoit, US	1983	2:22:43
3	Fatuma Roba, Ethiopia	1998	2:23:21
4	Valentina Yegorova, Russia	1994	2:23:33
5	Olga Markova, CIS	1992	2:23:43
6	Wanda Panfil, Poland	1991	2:24:18
7	Rosa Mota, Portugal	1988	2:24:30
8	Ingrid Kristiansen, Norway	1989	2:24:33
9	Ingrid Kristiansen, Norway	1986	2:24:55
10	Uta Pippig, Germany	1995	2:25:11

Source: *Boston Athletic Association*

TOP 10 ★
FASTEST TIMES IN THE NEW YORK MARATHON

MEN

	RUNNER/COUNTRY	YEAR	TIME
1	Juma Ikangaa, Tanzania	1989	2.08.01
2	Alberto Salazar, US	1981	2.08.13
3	Steve Jones, UK	1988	2.08.20
4	John Kagwe, Kenya	1998	2.08.45
5	Joseph Chebet, Kenya	1998	2.08.48
6	Zebedayo Bayo, Tanzania	1998	2.08.51
7	Rod Dixon, New Zealand	1983	2.08.59
8	Geoff Smith, UK	1983	2.09.08
9	Salvador Garcia, Mexico	1991	2.09.28
10=	Alberto Salazar, US	1982	2.09.29
=	Willie Mtolo, South Africa	1992	2.09.29

WOMEN

	RUNNER/COUNTRY	YEAR	TIME
1	Lisa Ondieki, Australia	1992	2.24.40
2	Franca Fiacconi, Italy	1998	2.25.17
3	Allison Roe, New Zealand	1981	2.25.29
4	Ingrid Kristiansen, Norway	1989	2.25.30
5	Grete Waitz, Norway	1980	2.25.41
6	Uta Pippig, Germany	1993	2.26.24
7	Adriana Fernandez, Mexico	1998	2.26.33
8	Olga Markova, Russia	1992	2.26.38
9	Grete Waitz, Norway	1983	2.27.00
10	Grete Waitz, Norway	1982	2.27.14

Source: *New York Road Runners Club*

TOP 10 HIGHEST HIGH JUMPS*

(Athlete/country/year/height in meters)

1 Javier Sotomayor, Cuba, 1993, 2.45 **2** = Patrik Sjöberg, Sweden, 1987, 2.42; = Carlo Thränhardt[#], West Germany, 1988, 2.42 **4** Igor Paklin, USSR, 1985, 2.41 **5** = Rudolf Povarnitsyn, USSR, 1985, 2.40; = Sorin Matei, Romania, 1990, 2.40; = Charles Austin, US, 1991, 2.40; = Hollis Conway, US, 1991, 2.40 **9** = Zhu Jianhua, China, 1984, 2.39; = Hollis Conway[#], US, 1989, 2.39; = Dietmar Mögenburg[#], West Germany, 1985, 2.39; = Ralph Sonn[#], Germany, 1991, 2.39

* Highest by each athlete only # Indoor

TOP 10 HIGHEST POLE VAULTS*

(Athlete/country/year/height in meters)

1 Sergey Bubka[#], Ukraine, 1993, 6.15 **2** Okkert Brits, South Africa, 1995, 6.03 **3** Rodion Gataullin[#], USSR, 1989, 6.02 **4** = Igor Trandenkov, Russia, 1996, 6.01; = Jeff Hartwig, US, 1998, 6.01 **6** = Dmitri Markov, Belarus, 1998, 6.00; = Tim Lobinger, Germany, 1997, 6.00; = Maxim Tarasov, Russia, 1997, 6.00; = Jeane Galfione, France, 1999, 6.00 **10** Lawrence Johnson, US, 1996, 5.98

* Highest by each athlete only # Indoor

THE 10 ★
FIRST ATHLETES TO RUN A MILE IN UNDER FOUR MINUTES

	ATHLETE/COUNTRY	LOCATION	MIN:SEC	DATE
1	Roger Bannister, UK	Oxford	3:59.4	May 6, 1954
2	John Landy, Australia	Turku, Finland	3:57.9	June 21, 1954
3	Laszlo Tabori, Hungary	London	3:59.0	May 28, 1955
4 =	Chris Chataway, UK	London	3:59.8	May 28, 1955
=	Brian Hewson, UK	London	3:59.8	May 28, 1955
6	Jim Bailey, Australia	Los Angeles	3:58.6	May 5, 1956
7	Gunnar Nielsen, Denmark	Los Angeles	3:59.1	June 1, 1956
8	Ron Delany, Ireland	Los Angeles	3:59.4	June 1, 1956
9	Derek Ibbotson, UK	London	3:59.4	Aug 6, 1956
10	István Rózsavölgyi, Hungary	Budapest	3:59.0	Aug 26, 1956

FASTEST MILE

Just over two years after Roger Bannister's shattering of the four-minute-mile record, nine more athletes had achieved this goal.

ON TRACK

Merlene Ottey is the sportsperson with the most silver and bronze Olympic medals who has yet to win gold.

TOP 10 ★
FASTEST WOMEN ON EARTH*

	ATHLETE/COUNTRY	YEAR	TIME
1	Florence Griffith-Joyner, US	1988	10.49
2	Marion Jones, US	1998	10.65
3	Christine Arron, France	1998	10.73
4	Merlene Ottey, Jamaica	1996	10.74
5	Evelyn Ashford, US	1984	10.76
6	Irina Privalova, Russia	1994	10.77
7	Dawn Sowell, US	1989	10.78
7	Marlies Göhr, East Germany	1983	10.81
9 =	Gail Devers, US	1992	10.82
=	Gwen Torrence, US	1994	10.82

* Based on fastest time for the 100 meters

TOP 10 ★
FASTEST MEN ON EARTH*

	ATHLETE/COUNTRY	YEAR	TIME
1	Donovan Bailey, Canada	1996	9.84
2	Leroy Burrell, US	1994	9.85
3 =	Carl Lewis, US	1991	9.86
=	Frank Fredericks, Namibia	1996	9.86
5	Ato Boldon, Trinidad	1997	9.86
6 =	Linford Christie, UK	1993	9.87
=	Obadele Thompson, Barbados	1997	9.87
8	Bruny Surin, Canada	1996	9.89
9	Maurice Green, US	1997	9.90
10 =	Dennis Mitchell, US	1997	9.91

* Based on fastest time for the 100 meters

TOP 10 LONGEST LONG JUMPS*

(Athlete/country/year/distance in meters)

1 Mike Powell, US, 1991, 8.95 **2** Bob Beamon, US, 1968, 8.90 **3** Carl Lewis, US, 1991, 8.87 **4** Robert Emmiyan, USSR, 1987, 8.86 **5** = Larry Myricks, US, 1988, 8.74; = Eric Walder, US, 1994, 8.74 **7** Ivan Pedroso, Cuba, 1995, 8.71 **8** Kareem Streete-Thompson, US, 1994, 8.63 **9** James Beckford, Jamaica, 1997, 8.62 **10** Lutz Dombrowski, East Germany, 1990 8.54

* Longest by each athlete only

Did You Know? The current world record for running a mile is held by Noureddine Morceli, with a time of 3 minutes 44.39 seconds; 15.01 seconds faster than Bannister.

251

BASKETBALL BESTS

TOP 10 ★

MOST SUCCESSFUL DIVISION 1 NCAA TEAMS

COLLEGE	DIVISION 1 WINS
1 Kentucky	1,742
2 North Carolina	1,731
3 Kansas	1,684
4 =St. John's	1,577
=Duke	1,577
6 Temple	1,515
7 Syracuse	1,496
8 Oregon State	1,475
9 Pennsylvania	1,469
10 Indiana	1,452

Source: *NCAA*

TOP 10 NCAA COACHES
(Coach/wins)

1 Dean Smith, 879 2 Adolph Rupp, 876
3 Jim Phelan*, 797 4 Henry Iba, 767
5 Ed Diddle, 759 6 Phog Allen, 746
7 Bob Knight*, 742 8 Ray Meyer, 724
9 Norm Stewart*, 731
10 Don Haskins*, 719

* Still active 1998–99 season   Source: NCAA

PLAYERS TO HAVE PLAYED MOST GAMES IN THE NBA AND ABA

PLAYER	GAMES PLAYED
1 Robert Parish	1,611
2 Kareem Abdul-Jabbar	1,560
3 Moses Malone	1,455
4 Buck Williams*	1,348
5 Artis Gilmore	1,329
6 Elvin Hayes	1,303
7 Caldwell Jones	1,299
8 John Havlicek	1,270
9 Paul Silas	1,254
10 Julius Erving	1,243

* Retired mid-season, January 27,1999

Source: *NBA*

The ABA (American Basketball Association) was established as a rival to the NBA in 1968 and survived until 1976. Because many of the sport's top players "defected," their figures are still included in this list. Robert Parish moved to the top of this list by playing his 1,561st game on April 6, 1996 at the Gateway Arena in Cleveland, between the Charlotte Hornets and the Cleveland Cavaliers.

TOP POINT SCORER

Kareem Abdul-Jabbar, the greatest point scorer in NBA history, turned professional in 1970, playing for Milwaukee. His career spanned 20 seasons before he retired at the end of the 1989 season.

BIGGEST ARENAS IN THE NBA

ARENA/LOCATION	HOME TEAM	CAPACITY
1 **Georgia Dome**, Atlanta, Georgia	Atlanta Hawks	34,821
2 **The Alamodome**, San Antonio, Texas	San Antonio Spurs	34,215
3 **Charlotte Coliseum**, Charlotte, North Carolina	Charlotte Hornets	24,042
4 **United Center**, Chicago, Illinois	Chicago Bulls	21,711
5 **The Rose Garden**, Portland, Oregon	Portland Trailblazers	21,538
6 **The Palace of Auburn Hills**, Auburn Hills, Michigan	Detroit Pistons	21,454
7 **Gund Arena**, Cleveland, Ohio	Cleveland Cavaliers	20,562
8 **CoreStates Center**, Philadelphia, Pennsylvania	Philadelphia 76ers	20,444
9 **SkyDome**, Toronto	Toronto Raptors	20,125
10 **Byrne Meadowlands Arena**, East Rutherford, New Jersey	New Jersey Nets	20,049

The smallest arena is the 15,200-capacity Miami Arena, home of the Miami Heat. The largest ever, the Louisiana Superdome, used by New Orleans (now Utah) Jazz from 1975 to 1979, held 47,284 people.

Source: *The Sporting News Official NBA Guide*

POINT SCORERS IN AN NBA CAREER*

PLAYER	TOTAL POINTS
1 Kareem Abdul-Jabbar	38,387
2 Wilt Chamberlain	31,419
3 Michael Jordan	29,277
4 Karl Malone#	28,946
5 Moses Malone	27,409
6 Elvin Hayes	27,313
7 Oscar Robertson	26,710
8 Dominique Wilkins	26,534
9 John Havlicek	26,395
10 Alex English	25,613

* Regular season games only

 # Still active at end of 1998–99 season

Source: *NBA*

TOP 10 ★
POINT AVERAGES IN AN NBA SEASON

PLAYER/CLUB	SEASON	AVERAGE
1 Wilt Chamberlain, Philadelphia 76ers	1961–62	50.4
2 Wilt Chamberlain, San Francisco Warriors	1962–63	44.8
3 Wilt Chamberlain, Philadelphia 76ers	1960–61	38.4
4 Elgin Baylor, Los Angeles Lakers	1961–62	38.3
5 Wilt Chamberlain, Philadelphia 76ers	1959–60	37.6
6 Michael Jordan, Chicago Bulls	1986–87	37.1
7 Wilt Chamberlain, San Francisco Warriors	1963–64	36.9
8 Rick Barry, San Francisco Warriors	1966–67	35.6
9 Michael Jordan, Chicago Bulls	1987–88	35.0
10=Elgin Baylor, Los Angeles Lakers	1960–61	34.8
=Kareem Abdul-Jabbar, Milwaukee Bucks	1971–72	34.8

Source: *NBA*

TOP 10 ★
FREE THROW PERCENTAGES

PLAYER	ATTEMPTS	BASKETS	%
1 Mark Price	2,362	2,135	90.4
2 Rick Barry	4,243	3,818	90.0
3 Calvin Murphy	3,864	3,445	89.2
4 Scott Skiles	1,741	1,548	88.9
5 Larry Bird	4,471	3,960	88.6
6 Bill Sharman	3,559	3,143	88.3
7 Reggie Miller*	5,284	4,642	87.8
8 Ricky Pierce	3,871	3,389	87.5
9 Kiki Vandeweghe	3,997	3,484	87.2
10 Jeff Malone	3,383	2,947	87.1

* Still active, 1998–99 season

Source: *NBA*

TOP 10 ★
MOST SUCCESSFUL NBA COACHES

COACH	GAMES WON*
1 Lenny Wilkens #	1,120
2 Bill Fitch #	944
3 Red Auerbach	938
4 Dick Motta	935
5 Pat Riley #	914
6 Don Nelson #	867
7 Jack Ramsay	864
8 Cotton Fitzsimmons	832
9 Gene Shue	784
10 John MacLeod	707

* Regular season games only
# Still active 1998–99 season

Source: *NBA*

Lenny Wilkens reached his 1,000th win on March 1, 1996 when the Atlanta Hawks beat the Cleveland Cavaliers 74–68 at The Omni. Pat Riley acquired the best percentage record with 914 wins from 1,301 games, a 70.2 percent success rate.

TOP 10 POINTS SCORED IN THE WNBA
(Game/score)*

1 Utah Starzz vs Los Angeles Sparks, 102–89 **2** Cleveland Rockers vs Utah Starzz, 95–68 **3** = Sacramento Monarchs vs Utah Starzz, 93–78; = Los Angeles Sparks vs Sacramento Monarchs, 93–73 **5** Los Angeles Sparks vs Utah Starzz, 91–69 **6** = Cleveland Rockers vs Los Angeles Sparks, 89–85; = Houston Comets vs Sacramento Monarchs, 89–61 **8** Los Angeles Sparks vs Sacramento Monarchs, 88–77 **9** = Los Angeles Sparks vs Cleveland Rockers, 87–84; = Charlotte Sting vs New York Liberty, 87–69

* Ranked by winning score
Source: *STATS Inc.*

TOP 10 PLAYERS WITH THE MOST CAREER ASSISTS
(Player/assists)

1 John Stockton*, 13,087 **2** Magic Johnson, 10,141 **3** Oscar Robertson, 9,887 **4** Isiah Thomas, 9,061 **5** Mark Jackson*, 7,924 **6** Maurice Cheeks, 7,392 **7** Lenny Wilkens, 7,211 **8** Bob Cousy, 6,995 **9** Guy Rodgers, 6,917 **10** Nate Archibald, 6,476

* Still active at end of 1998–99 season
Source: *NBA*

JAZZ MAN
As well as breaking records while playing with his team, Utah Jazz, John Stockton was a member of the dream teams that won Gold at the '92 and '96 Olympics.

COMBAT SPORTS

OLYMPIC FENCING COUNTRIES

	COUNTRY	MEN'S MEDALS			WOMEN'S MEDALS			
		GOLD	SILVER	BRONZE	GOLD	SILVER	BRONZE	TOTAL
1	France	34	32	30	4	2	2	104
2	Italy	32	32	20	5	4	4	97
3	Hungary	27	14	20	5	6	6	78
4	Soviet Union*	14	14	15	5	3	3	54
5=	Poland	4	7	7	0	0	1	19
=	US	2	6	11	0	0	0	19
7	Germany	4	3	3	2	3	3	18
8	West Germany#	4	6	0	3	2	1	16
9	Belgium	5	3	5	0	0	0	13
10	Romania	1	0	2	1	3	4	11
	Great Britain	0	6	4	0	1	3	0	10

* Including United Team of 1992; excludes Russia since then

 # Not including West Germany or East Germany 1968–88

THE 10 LATEST WORLD HEAVYWEIGHT BOXING CHAMPIONS*

(Years/boxer)

1 1997, Evander Holyfield **2** 1996–97, Mike Tyson
3 1995–96, Bruce Seldon **4** 1994–95, George Foreman
5 1994, Michael Moorer **6** 1993–94, Evander Holyfield
7 1992–93, Riddick Bowe **8** 1990–92, Evander Holyfield
9 1990, James Douglas **10** 1989–90, Mike Tyson

* WBA only

THE BOXING MINISTER

Thulane Malinga, or Sugarboy as he is usually nicknamed, is a Pentecostal minister from South Africa. In two years, between 1996 and 1998, he won and lost the WBC Super Middleweight title twice. In March 1996 Sugarboy won the title in a fight against Nigel Benn. However, he was dethroned only a few months later, in July 1996, by the Italian Vincenzo Nardiello in a 12-round split decision. In December 1997, the South African boxer regained his title in a fight against Robin Reid, only to see it being snatched away again by Britain's Richie Woodhall just months later in March 1998.

SNAP ★ SHOTS

HEAVIEST BOXING WEIGHT DIVISIONS

	WEIGHT	LIMIT	
		LB	KG
1	Heavyweight	over 190	over 86
2	Cruiserweight	190	86
3	Light-heavyweight	175	79
4	Super-middleweight	168	76
5	Middleweight	160	73
6	Junior-middleweight/Super-welterweight	154	70
7	Welterweight	147	67
8	Junior-welterweight/Super-lightweight	140	65
9	Lightweight	135	61
10	Junior-lightweight/Super-featherweight	130	59

TOP 10 OLYMPIC JUDO COUNTRIES

(Country/medals)

1 Japan, 40 **2** Soviet Union*, 27 **3** France, 26 **4** South Korea, 25 **5** = Cuba, 15; = Great Britain, 15 **7** Netherlands, 10 **8** = Germany#, 9; = East Germany, 9 **10** = US, 8; = Poland, 8; = West Germany, 8; = Hungary, 8; = Brazil, 8

* Including United Team of 1992; excludes Russia since then
 # Not including West Germany or East Germany 1968–88

BOXERS WITH THE MOST KNOCKOUTS IN A CAREER

	BOXER*	CAREER	KO'S
1	Archie Moore	1936–63	129
2	Young Stribling	1921–63	126
3	Billy Bird	1920–48	125
4	Sam Langford	1902–26	116
5	George Odwell	1930–45	114
6	Sugar Ray Robinson	1940–65	110
7	Sandy Saddler	1944–65	103
8	Henry Armstrong	1931–45	100
9	Jimmy Wilde	1911–23	99
10	Len Wickwar	1928–47	93

* All from the US except Jimmy Wilde, who was Welsh

Did You Know? With 17 weight divisions in boxing, and four major bodies recognizing world champions, there could be 68 world champions at any one time.

THE 10 ★
WRESTLING WEIGHT DIVISIONS

	WEIGHT	LIMIT LB	LIMIT KG
1	Heavyweight plus	over 220	over 100
2	Heavyweight	220	100
3	Light-heavyweight	198	90
4	Middleweight	181	82
5	Welterweight	163	74
6	Lightweight	150	68
7	Featherweight	137	62
8	Bantamweight	126	57
9	Flyweight	115	52
10	Light-flyweight	106	48

TOP 10 ★
OLYMPIC WRESTLING COUNTRIES/FREESTYLE

	COUNTRY	GOLD	MEDALS SILVER	BRONZE	TOTAL
1	US	38	31	19	88
2	USSR	27	14	14	55
3	Japan	16	9	6	31
4	Turkey	15	10	5	30
5	Bulgaria	6	14	8	28
6	Sweden	8	10	8	26
7	Finland	8	7	10	25
8	Iran	3	7	9	19
9	Great Britain	3	4	10	17
10	Hungary	3	4	7	14

STRANGLEHOLD

Zafar Golyou (Russia) and Hiroshi Kadj (Japan) battle it out at the Men's Greco-Roman prelims in Georgia.

TOP 10 ★
OLYMPIC WRESTLING COUNTRIES/ GRECO-ROMAN

	COUNTRY	GOLD	MEDALS SILVER	BRONZE	TOTAL
1	USSR	34	19	10	63
2	Finland	19	19	18	56
3	Sweden	19	15	17	51
4	Hungary	13	9	11	33
5	Bulgaria	8	14	7	29
6 =	Romania	6	8	12	26
=	West Germany	4	14	8	26
8	Italy	5	3	9	17
9	Turkey	8	3	2	13
10 =	Yugoslavia	3	5	4	12
=	Poland	2	5	5	12

The US has won two Gold, five Silver, and three Bronze medals in this event.

TOP 10 ★
FASTEST KNOCKOUTS IN WORLD TITLE FIGHTS

	FIGHT (WINNERS FIRST)	WEIGHT	DATE	SEC*
1	Gerald McClellan vs Jay Bell	Middleweight	Aug 7, 1993	20
2	James Warring vs James Pritchard	Cruiserweight	Sep 6, 1991	24
3	Lloyd Honeyghan vs Gene Hatcher	Welterweight	Aug 30, 1987	45
4	Mark Breland vs Lee Seung-soon	Welterweight	Feb 4, 1989	54
5	Emile Pladner vs Frankie Genaro	Flyweight	Mar 2, 1929	58
6 =	Jackie Paterson vs Peter Kane	Flyweight	Jun 19, 1943	61
=	Bobby Czyz vs David Sears	Light-heavyweight	Dec 26, 1986	61
8	Michael Dokes vs Mike Weaver	Heavyweight	Dec 10, 1982	63
9	Tony Canzoneri vs Al Singer	Lightweight	Nov 14, 1930	66
10	Marvin Hagler vs Caveman Lee	Middleweight	Mar 7, 1982	67

* Duration of fight

Some authorities claim that Al McCoy defeated George Chip in a middleweight contest on April 7, 1914 in 45 seconds. Lightweight world champion Al Singer engaged in only two world title bouts in his career. The first was when he beat Sammy Mandell for the title on July 1, 1930. The fight lasted one minute 46 seconds. He lost the title four months later to Tony Canzoneri in a bout lasting one minute six seconds.

BASEBALL TEAMS

AVERAGE ATTENDANCES IN 1998

	TEAM	ATTENDANCE
1	Colorado Rockies	46,782
2	Baltimore Orioles	45,496
3	Arizona Diamondbacks	44,480
4	Cleveland Indians	42,806
5	Atlanta Braves	41,498
6	St. Louis Cardinals	39,938
7	Los Angeles Dodgers	38,139
8	New York Yankees	36,872
9	Texas Mariners	36,141
10	Chicago Cubs	32,788

Source: *Major League Baseball*

BIGGEST SINGLE GAME WINS IN THE WORLD SERIES

	TEAMS (WINNERS FIRST)/GAME	DATE	SCORE
1	New York Yankees vs New York Giants (Game 2)	Oct 2, 1936	18–4
2	New York Yankees vs Pittsburgh Pirates (Game 2)	Oct 6, 1960	16–3
3=	New York Yankees vs New York Giants (Game 5)	Oct 9, 1951	13–1
=	New York Yankees vs Pittsburgh Pirates (Game 6)	Oct 12, 1960	12–0
=	Detroit Tigers vs St. Louis Cardinals (Game 6)	Oct 9, 1968	13–1
=	New York Yankees vs Milwaukee Brewers (Game 6)	Oct 19, 1982	13–1
7=	New York Yankees vs Philadelphia Athletics (Game 6)	Oct 26, 1911	13–2
=	Atlanta Braves vs New York Yankees (Game 1)	Oct 20, 1996	12-1
=	St. Louis Cardinals vs Detroit Tigers (Game 7)	Oct 9, 1934	11–0
=	Chicago White Sox vs Los Angeles Dodgers (Game 1)	Oct 1, 1959	11–0
=	Kansas City Royals vs St. Louis Cardinals (Game 7)	Oct 27, 1985	11–0

Source: *Major League Baseball*

TEAMS WITH THE MOST WORLD SERIES WINS

	TEAM*	WINS
1	New York Yankees	24
2=	St. Louis Cardinals	9
=	Philadelphia/Kansas City/Oakland Athletics	9
4	Brooklyn/Los Angeles Dodgers	6
5=	New York/San Francisco Giants	5
=	Boston Red Sox	5
=	Cincinnati Reds	5
=	Pittsburgh Pirates	5
9	Detroit Tigers	4
10=	Boston/Milwaukee/Atlanta Braves	3
=	St. Louis/Baltimore Orioles	3
=	Washington Senators/Minnesota Twins	3

* Teams separated by / indicate changes of franchise and are regarded as the same team for Major League record purposes

Source: *Major League Baseball*

Major League baseball started in the United States with the forming of the National League in 1876. The rival American League was started in 1901, and two years later Pittsburgh, champions of the National League, invited American League champions Boston to take part in a best-of-nine games series to establish the "real" champions. Boston won 5–3. The following year the National League champions, New York, refused to play Boston and there was no World Series, but it was resumed in 1905.

BASEBALL TEAM PAYROLLS, 1999

	TEAM	AVERAGE SALARY	TOTAL PAYROLL
1	New York Yankees	3,037,656	85,054,360
2	Los Angeles Dodgers	2,730,378	79,180,952
3	Baltimore Orioles	2,906,872	78,485,547
4	Texas Rangers	2,882,113	74,934,931
5	Atlanta Braves	2,449,500	73,485,000
6	Cleveland Indians	2,459,487	68,865,628
7	Arizona Diamondbacks	2,440,963	65,906,000
8	New York Mets	2,269,182	63,537,096
9	Boston Red Sox	2,253,611	60,847,500
10	Chicago Cubs	2,075,552	60,191,000

Source: *Associated Press*

THE 10 LATEST YEARS OF MAJOR LEAGUE PLAYERS' SALARIES

(Year/average salary in $)

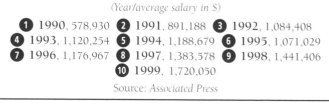

❶ 1990, 578,930 ❷ 1991, 891,188 ❸ 1992, 1,084,408
❹ 1993, 1,120,254 ❺ 1994, 1,188,679 ❻ 1995, 1,071,029
❼ 1996, 1,176,967 ❽ 1997, 1,383,578 ❾ 1998, 1,441,406
❿ 1999, 1,720,050

Source: *Associated Press*

TOP 10 ★
OLDEST STADIUMS IN MAJOR LEAGUE BASEBALL

STADIUM	HOME CLUB	FIRST GAME
1 =Fenway Park	Boston Red Sox	Apr 20, 1912
=Tiger Stadium	Detroit Tigers	Apr 20, 1912
3 Wrigley Field	Chicago Cubs	Apr 20, 1916
4 Yankee Stadium	New York Yankees	Apr 18, 1923
5 County Stadium	Milwaukee Brewers	Apr 6, 1953
6 3Com Park at Candlestick Point*	San Francisco Giants	Apr 12, 1960
7 Network Associates Coliseum#	Oakland Athletics	Apr 17, 1960
8 Dodger Stadium	Los Angeles Dodgers	Apr 11, 1962
9 Shea Stadium	New York Mets	Apr 17, 1964
10 The Astrodome	Houston Astros	Apr 9, 1965

* Formerly known as Candlestick Park
# Formerly known as Oakland-Alameda County Coliseum

Source: Major League Baseball

THE 10 ★
LATEST WINNERS OF THE WORLD SERIES

YEAR*	WINNER/LEAGUE#	LOSER/LEAGUE#	SCORE
1998	New York, AL	San Diego, NL	4–0
1997	Florida, NL	Cleveland, AL	4–3
1996	New York, AL	Atlanta, NL	4–2
1995	Atlanta, NL	Cleveland, AL	4–2
1993	Toronto, AL	Philadelphia, NL	4–2
1992	Toronto, AL	Atlanta, NL	4–2
1991	Minnesota, AL	Atlanta, NL	4–2
1990	Cincinnati, NL	Oakland, AL	4–0
1989	Oakland, AL	San Francisco, NL	4–0
1988	Los Angeles, NL	Oakland, AL	4–1

* The 1994 event was cancelled due to a players' strike

# AL = American League
  NL = National League

TOP 10 ★
NEWEST MAJOR LEAGUE TEAMS

TEAM	LEAGUE*	1ST SEASON
1 =Arizona Diamondbacks	NL	1998
=Tampa Bay Devil Rays	AL	1998
3 =Colorado Rockies	NL	1993
=Florida Marlins	NL	1993
5 =Seattle Mariners	AL	1977
=Toronto Blue Jays	AL	1977
7 =Kansas City Royals	AL	1969
=Montreal Expos	NL	1969
=Seattle Pilots/ Milwaukee Brewers	AL	1969
10 =Houston Astros	NL	1962
=New York Mets	NL	1962

* AL = American League
  NL = National League

Source: Major League Baseball

TOP 10 ★
LARGEST MAJOR LEAGUE BALLPARKS*

STADIUM	HOME TEAM	CAPACITY
1 3Com Park at Candlestick Point	San Francisco Giants	63,000
2 Veterans Stadium	Philadelphia Phillies	62,409
3 Qualcomm Stadium	San Diego Padres	56,133
4 Dodger Stadium	Los Angeles Dodgers	56,000
5 Shea Stadium	New York Mets	55,775
6 Yankee Stadium	New York Yankees	55,070
7 The Astrodome	Houston Astros	54,699
8 County Stadium	Milwaukee Brewers	53,192
9 Cinergy Field	Cincinnati Reds	52,953
10 SkyDome	Toronto Blue Jays	50,516

* By capacity

Source: Major League Baseball

Stadium capacities vary constantly, some being adjusted according to the event: Veterans Stadium, for example, holds fewer for baseball games than for football games. The Colorado Rockies formerly played at the Mile High Stadium, Denver, Colorado, which holds 76,100, but now play at Coors Field, which has a capacity of only 50,381.

Who was the best paid player in the NHL in 1998–99?
see p.271 for the answer
A Eric Lindros
B Paul Kariya
C Sergei Fedorov

BASEBALL STARS

TOP 10 ★
PLAYERS WITH THE MOST CAREER STRIKEOUTS

	PLAYER	STRIKEOUTS
1	Nolan Ryan	5,714
2	Steve Carlton	4,136
3	Bert Blyleven	3,701
4	Tom Seaver	3,640
5	Don Sutton	3,574
6	Gaylord Perry	3,534
7	Walter Johnson	3,508
8	Phil Niekro	3,342
9	Ferguson Jenkins	3,192
10	Roger Clemens*	3,153

* Still active in 1999 season

Source: *Major League Baseball*

TOP 10 ★
PLAYERS WITH THE HIGHEST CAREER BATTING AVERAGES

	PLAYER	AT BAT	HITS	AVERAGE*
1	Ty Cobb	11,434	4,189	.366
2	Rogers Hornsby	8,173	2,930	.358
3	Joe Jackson	4,981	1,772	.356
4	Ed Delahanty	7,505	2,597	.346
5	Tris Speaker	10,195	3,514	.345
6	=Billy Hamilton	6,268	2,158	.344
	=Ted Williams	7,706	2,654	.344
8	=Dan Brouthers	6,711	2,296	.342
	=Harry Heilmann	7,787	2,660	.342
	=Babe Ruth	8,399	2,873	.342

* Calculated by dividing the number of hits by the number of times a batter was at bat

Source: *Major League Baseball*

TOP 10 ★
PLAYERS WITH THE MOST RUNS IN A CAREER*

	PLAYER	RUNS
1	Ty Cobb	2,245
2	=Babe Ruth	2,174
	=Hank Aaron	2,174
4	Pete Rose	2,165
5	Willie Mays	2,062
6	Rickey Henderson#	2,014
7	Stan Musial	1,949
8	Lou Gehrig	1,888
9	Tris Speaker	1,882
10	Mel Ott	1,859

* Regular season only, excluding World Series

 # Still active in 1999 season

Source: *Major League Baseball*

TOP 10 ★
PLAYERS WITH THE MOST CONSECUTIVE GAMES PLAYED

	PLAYER	GAMES
1	Cal Ripken, Jr.	2,600
2	Lou Gehrig	2,130
3	Everett Scott	1,307
4	Steve Garvey	1,207
5	Billy Williams	1,117
6	Joe Sewell	1,103
7	Stan Musial	895
8	Eddie Yost	829
9	Gus Suhr	822
10	Nellie Fox	798

Source: *Major League Baseball*

Cal Ripken took himself out of the starting line-up on September 21, 1998, in a game between the Orioles and the Yankees, having played in every game since May 30, 1982.

TOP 10 ★
PLAYERS WHO PLAYED THE MOST GAMES IN A CAREER

	PLAYER	GAMES
1	Pete Rose	3,562
2	Carl Yastrzemski	3,308
3	Hank Aaron	3,298
4	Ty Cobb	3,034
5	=Stan Musial	3,026
	=Eddie Murray	3,026
7	Willie Mays	2,992
8	Dave Winfield	2,973
9	Rusty Staub	2,951
10	Brooks Robinson	2,896

Source: *Major League Baseball*

TOP 10 ★
PITCHERS WITH THE MOST CAREER WINS

	PLAYER	WINS
1	Cy Young	509
2	Walter Johnson	417
3	=Grover Alexander	373
	=Christy Mathewson	373
5	Warren Spahn	363
6	=Kid Nichols	361
	=Pud Galvin	361
8	Tim Keefe	344
9	Steve Carlton	329
10	=Eddie Plank	326
	=John Clarkson	326

Source: *Major League Baseball*

Which country has won the most table-tennis world championships?
see p.275 for the answer
A China
B Hungary
C Czechoslovakia

HIGHEST PAID PLAYERS IN MAJOR LEAGUE BASEBALL, 1998

	PLAYER	TEAM	SALARY ($)
1	Gary Sheffield	Florida Marlins	14,936,000
2	Albert Belle*	Chicago White Sox	10,000,000
3	Greg Maddux	Atlanta Braves	9,600,000
4	Mark McGwire	St. Louis Cardinals	8,928,000
5	Barry Bonds	San Francisco Giants	8,916,667
6	Roger Clemens#	Toronto Blue Jays	8,550,000
7	Andres Galarraga	Atlanta Braves	8,400,000
8	Sammy Sosa	Chicago Cubs	8,325,000
9	Bernie Williams	New York Yankees	8,300,000
10	Ken Griffey, Jr.	Seattle Mariners	8,203,000

* Now plays for the Baltimore Orioles

 # Now plays for the New York Yankees

Source: *Major League Baseball Players' Association*

FIRST PITCHERS TO THROW PERFECT GAMES

	PLAYER	MATCH	DATE
1	Lee Richmond	Worcester *vs* Cleveland	June 12, 1880
2	Monte Ward	Providence *vs* Buffalo	June 17, 1880
3	Cy Young	Boston *vs* Philadelphia	May 5, 1904
4	Addie Joss	Cleveland *vs* Chicago	Oct 2, 1908
5	Charlie Robertson	Chicago *vs* Detroit	Apr 30, 1922
6	Don Larsen*	New York *vs* Brooklyn	Oct 8, 1956
7	Jim Bunning	Philadelphia *vs* New York	June 21, 1964
8	Sandy Koufax	Los Angeles *vs* Chicago	Sept 9, 1965
9	Catfish Hunter	Oakland *vs* Minnesota	May 8, 1968
10	Len Barker	Cleveland *vs* Toronto	May 15, 1981

* Larsen's perfect game was, uniquely, in the World Series

Fourteen pitchers have thrown perfect games; that is, they have pitched in all nine innings, dismissing 27 opposing batters, and without giving up a hit. The last player to pitch a perfect game was David Wells, for the New York Yankees against the Minnesota Twins, on May 17, 1998.

Source: *Major League Baseball*

PLAYERS MOST AT BAT IN A CAREER

	PLAYER	AT BAT
1	Pete Rose	14,053
3	Hank Aaron	12.364
3	Carl Yastrzemski	11,988
4	Ty Cobb	11,434
5	Eddie Murray	11,336
6	Robin Yount	11,008
7	Dave Winfield	11,003
8	Stan Musial	10,906
9	Willie Mays	10,881
10	Paul Molitor	10,835

LOWEST EARNED RUN AVERAGES IN A CAREER

	PLAYER	EARNED RUN AVERAGES
1	Ed Walsh	1.82
2	Addie Joss	1.89
3	Three Finger Brown	2.06
4	John Ward	2.10
5	Christy Mathewson	2.13
6	Rube Waddell	2.16
7	Walter Johnson	2.17
8	Orval Overall	2.23
9	Tommy Bond	2.25
10	Ed Reulbach	2.28

Source: *Major League Baseball*

FIRST PLAYERS TO HIT FOUR HOME RUNS IN ONE GAME

	PLAYER	CLUB	DATE
1	Bobby Lowe	Boston	May 30, 1884
2	Ed Delahanty	Philadelphia	July 13, 1896
3	Lou Gehrig	New York	June 3, 1932
4	Chuck Klein	Philadelphia	July 10, 1936
5	Pat Seerey	Chicago	July 18, 1948
6	Gil Hodges	Brooklyn	Aug 31, 1950
7	Joe Adcock	Milwaukee	July 31, 1954
8	Rocky Colavito	Cleveland	June 10, 1959
9	Willie Mays	San Francisco	Apr 30, 1961
10	Mike Schmidt	Philadelphia	Apr 17, 1976

The only other players to score four homers in one game are Bob Horner, who did so for Atlanta on July 6, 1986, and Mark Whitten, for St. Louis on September 7, 1993.

INTERNATIONAL SOCCER

WORLD CUP WINNERS

Brazil has taken part in all the final phases of the World Cup since its inception in 1930, and has won four times. In the 1998 Championships Brazil lost the final to France, the host nation and first-time winners.

TOP 10 ★
WORLD CUP ATTENDANCES

	MATCH (WINNERS FIRST)	VENUE	YEAR	ATTENDANCE
1	Brazil v Uruguay	Rio de Janeiro*	1950	199,854
2	Brazil v Spain	Rio de Janeiro	1950	152,772
3	Brazil v Yugoslavia	Rio de Janeiro	1950	142,409
4	Brazil v Sweden	Rio de Janeiro	1950	138,886
5	Mexico v Paraguay	Mexico City	1986	114,600
6	Argentina v West Germany	Mexico City*	1986	114,590
7 =	Mexico v Bulgaria	Mexico City	1986	114,580
=	Argentina v England	Mexico City	1986	114,580
9	Argentina v Belgium	Mexico City	1986	110,420
10	Mexico v Belgium	Mexico City	1986	110,000

* Final tie

TOP 10 COUNTRIES WITH THE MOST PLAYERS SENT OFF IN THE FINAL STAGES OF THE WORLD CUP

(Country/dismissals)

① = Brazil, 8; = Argentina, 8 **③** = Uruguay, 6;
= Cameroon, 6 **⑤** = Germany/West Germany, 5;
= Hungary, 5 **⑦** = Czechoslovakia, 4; = Holland, 4;
= Italy, 4; = Mexico, 4

A total of 97 players have received their marching orders in the final stages of the World Cup since 1930. The South American nations account for 27 of them. Brazil, Czechoslovakia, Denmark, Hungary, and South Africa have each had three players sent off in a single game – Brazil twice (1938 and 1954).

TOP 10 ★
GOAL SCORERS IN THE FINAL STAGES OF THE WORLD CUP

	PLAYER/COUNTRY	YEARS	GOALS
1	Gerd Müller, West Germany	1970–74	14
2	Just Fontaine, France	1958	13
3	Pelé, Brazil	1958–70	12
4 =	Sandor Kocsis, Hungary	1954	11
=	Jürgen Klinsman, Germany	1990–98	11
6 =	Helmut Rahn, West Germany	1954–58	10
=	Teófilo Cubillas, Peru	1970–78	10
=	Grzegorz Lato, Poland	1974–82	10
=	Gary Lineker, England	1986–90	10
10 =	Leónidas da Silva, Brazil	1934–38	9
=	Ademir Marques de Menezes, Brazil	1950	9
=	Vavà, Brazil	1958–62	9
=	Uwe Seeler, West Germany	1958–70	9
=	Eusébio, Portugal	1966	9
=	Jairzinho, Brazil	1970–74	9
=	Paolo Rossi, Italy	1978–82	9
=	Karl-Heinz Rummenigge, West Germany	1978–86	9
=	Roberto Baggio, Italy	1990–98	9
=	Gabriel Batistuta, Argentina	1994–98	9

TOP 10 ★
TRANSFER FEES

	PLAYER	FROM	TO	YEAR	FEE (£)
1	Christian Vieri	Lazio	Inter Milan	1999	24,000,000
2	Denilson	São Paulo	Real Betis	1998	22,000,000
3 =	Christian Vieri	Atletico Madrid	Lazio	1998	17,000,000
=	Rivaldo	Deportivo la Coruna	Barcelona	1997	17,000,000
5	Ronaldo	Barcelona	Inter Milan	1997	16,800,000
6	A. Schevchenko	Dynamo Kiev	AC Milan	1999	15,700,000
7	Vincenzo Montella	Sampdoria	Roma	1999	15,300,000
8	Alan Shearer	Blackburn Rovers	Newcastle Utd.	1995	15,000,000
9	Gianluigi Lentini	Torino	AC Milan	1992	13,000,000
10	Dwight Yorke	Aston Villa	Manchester Utd.	1998	12,600,000

FOOTBALL FACT
Fédération Internationale de Football Association (FIFA) rules state that the weight of a soccer ball at the start of the game should be 14–16 oz/369–453 g.

TOP 10 ⭐ RICHEST SOCCER CLUBS

	CLUB	COUNTRY	INCOME (£)
1	Manchester United	England	87,939,000
2	Barcelona	Spain	58,862,000
3	Real Madrid	Spain	55,659,000
4	Juventus	Italy	53,223,000
5	Bayern Munich	Germany	51,619,000
6	AC Milan	Italy	47,480,000
7	Borussia Dortmund	Germany	42,199,999
8	Newcastle United	England	41,134,000
9	Liverpool	England	39,153,000
10	Inter Milan	Italy	39,071,000

A survey conducted by accountants Deloitte & Touche and the magazine *FourFourTwo* compared incomes of the world's top soccer clubs during the 1997/8 season. It revealed the extent to which soccer has become a major business enterprise, with many clubs generating considerably more revenue from commercial activities such as the sale of merchandise and income from TV rights than they receive from admissions to matches.

TOP 10 ⭐ HIGHEST-SCORING WORLD CUP FINALS

	YEAR	GAMES	GOALS	AVERAGE PER GAME
1	1954	26	140	5.38
2	1938	18	84	4.66
3	1934	17	70	4.11
4	1950	22	88	4.00
5	1930	18	70	3.88
6	1958	35	126	3.60
7	1970	32	95	2.96
8	1982	52	146	2.81
9	1998	64	179	2.80
10=	1962	32	89	2.78
=	1966	32	89	2.78

TOP 10 ⭐ MOST GAMES PLAYED BY INTERNATIONAL PLAYERS

	PLAYER	COUNTRY	GAMES
1	Thomas Ravelli	Sweden	143
2	Majed Abdullah	Saudi Arabia	140
3	Lothar Matthäus*	W. Germany/ Germany	135
4	Andoni Zubizarreta	Spain	126
5=	Marcelo Balboa*	US	125
=	Peter Shilton	England	125
7	Masami Ihara*	Japan	121
8	Pat Jennings	Northern Ireland	119
9	Heinz Hermann	Switzerland	117
10=	Gheorghe Hagi*	Romania	115
=	Björn Nordqvist	Sweden	115

* Still active 1998–99 season

Some sources quote Héctor Chumpitaz of Peru and Brazilian player Rivelino as having appeared in 150 and 120 Internationals respectively, but many of these were won in matches not recognized by FIFA.

TOP 10 ⭐ EUROPEAN CUP WINNERS

	COUNTRY	YEARS*	WINS
1=	England	1968–99	9
=	Italy	1961–96	9
3	Spain	1956–98	8
4	Holland	1970–95	6
5	Germany	1974–97	5
6	Portugal	1961–87	3
7=	France	1993	1
=	Romania	1986	1
=	Scotland	1967	1
=	Yugoslavia	1991	1

* Of first and last win

The European Cup, now known as the European Champions' League Cup, has been competed for annually since 1956. It was won that year, and the next four, by Real Madrid (who also won it in 1966 and 1998, making a total of seven times).

FOUL!

Every player in the World Cup is required to sign a declaration of fair play, underlining FIFA's belief that the world's top teams and players have a responsibility as role models to their young supporters. However, the pressure to succeed often leads to moments of madness. The France98 World Cup saw 256 yellow cards handed out for rule-breaking and foul play. Of the 22 red cards shown, the one with arguably the most disastrous consequence was awarded to England's David Beckham. Many felt that his display of aggression during the game against Argentina prevented England from going on into the final phase.

SNAP SHOTS

Did You Know? The lowest-scoring World Cup was Italia '90, which produced 115 goals from 52 matches at an average of 2.21 per game.

261

ON TWO WHEELS

TOP 10 ★
FASTEST WINNING SPEEDS OF THE DAYTONA 200

	RIDER/COUNTRY*	BIKE	YEAR	AVERAGE SPEED MPH	KM/H
1	Kenny Roberts	Yamaha	1984	113.84	182.09
2	Kenny Roberts	Yamaha	1983	110.93	178.52
3	Graeme Crosby, New Zealand	Yamaha	1982	109.10	175.58
4	Steve Baker	Yamaha	1977	108.85	175.18
5	Johnny Cecotto, Venezuela	Yamaha	1976	108.77	175.05
6	Dale Singleton	Yamaha	1981	108.52	174.65
7	Kenny Roberts	Yamaha	1978	108.37	174.41
8	Kevin Schantz	Suzuki	1988	107.80	173.49
9	Dale Singleton	Yamaha	1979	107.69	173.31
10	Patrick Pons, France	Yamaha	1980	107.55	173.09

* From the US unless otherwise stated

TOP 10 ★
FASTEST WORLD CHAMPIONSHIP RACES OF ALL TIME

	RIDER/COUNTRY	BIKE*	YEAR	AVERAGE SPEED MPH	KM/H
1	Barry Sheene, UK	Suzuki	1977	135.07	217.37
2	John Williams, UK	Suzuki	1976	133.49	214.83
3	Phil Read, UK	MV Agusta	1975	133.22	214.40
4	Wil Hartog, Holland	Suzuki	1978	132.90	213.88
5	Phil Read, UK	MV Agusta	1974	131.98	212.41
6	Giacomo Agostini, Italy	MV Agusta	1973	128.51	206.81
7	Walter Villa, Italy	Harley-Davidson	1977	127.03	204.43
8	Walter Villa, Italy	Harley-Davidson	1976	126.08	202.90
9	Giacomo Agostini, Italy	MV Agusta	1969	125.85	202.53
10	Kevin Schwartz, US	Suzuki	1991	125.34	201.72

* 500cc, except for Nos. 7 and 8, which were 250cc

All races except for No. 10 were during the Belgian Grand Prix at the Spa-Francorchamps circuit. No. 10 was the German Grand Prix at Hockenheim.

TOP 10 RIDERS WITH THE MOST GRAND PRIX RACE WINS

(Rider/country/years/race wins)

1 Giacomo Agostini, Italy, 1965–76, 122 **2** Angel Nieto, Spain, 1969–85, 90 **3** Mike Hailwood, UK, 1959–67, 76 **4** Rolf Biland, Switzerland, 1975–90, 56 **5** Mick Doohan, Australia, 1990–98, 54 **6** Phil Read, UK, 1961–75, 52 **7** Jim Redman, Southern Rhodesia, 1961–66, 45 **8** Anton Mang, West Germany, 1976–88, 42 **9** Carlo Ubbiali, Italy, 1950–60, 39 **10** John Surtees, UK, 1955–60, 38

All except Biland were solo machine riders. Britain's Barry Sheene won 23 races during his career, and is the only man to have won Grands Prix at 50 and 500cc.

TOP 10 WORLD SUPERBIKE RIDERS, 1998

(Rider/country/points)

1 Carl Fogarty, UK, 351.5 **2** Aaron Slight, New Zealand, 347 **3** Troy Corser, Australia, 328.5 **4** Pierfrancesco Chilli, Italy, 293.5 **5** Colin Edwards, US, 279.5 **6** Noriyuki Haga, Japan, 258 **7** Akira Yanagawa, Japan, 210 **8** Jamie Witham, UK, 173 **9** Peter Goddard, Australia, 155 **10** Scott Russell, US, 130.5

UNBEATEN RECORD HOLDER

The most successful motorcycle racer of all time, Giacomo Agostini won the 500cc world title for seven consecutive years.

MOTORCYCLISTS WITH THE MOST WORLD TITLES

RIDER/COUNTRY		YEARS	TITLES
1	Giacomo Agostini, Italy	1966–75	15
2	Angel Nieto, Spain	1969–84	13
3 =	Carlo Ubbiali, Itay	1951–60	9
=	Mike Hailwood, UK	1961–67	9
5 =	John Surtees, UK	1956–60	7
=	Phil Read, UK	1964–74	7
7 =	Geoff Duke, UK	1951–55	6
=	Jim Redman, Southern Rhodesia	1962–65	6
=	Klaus Enders, W. Germany	1967–74	6
10	Anton Mang, W. Germany	1980–87	5

OLYMPIC CYCLING COUNTRIES

COUNTRY		MEDALS		
		GOLD	SILVER	BRONZE	TOTAL
1	France	32	19	22	73
2	Italy	32	15	6	53
3	Great Britain	9	21	16	46
4	US	11	13	16	40
5	Netherlands	10	14	7	31
6	Germany*	8	9	9	26
7	Australia	6	11	8	25
8	Soviet Union#	11	4	9	24
9	Belgium	6	6	10	22
10	Denmark	6	6	10	21

* Not including West or East Germany 1968–88

 # Including United Team of 1992, exludes Russia since

TOP 10 COUNTRIES WITH MOST TOUR DE FRANCE WINNERS

(Country/winners)

1 France, 36 **2** Belgium, 18 **3** Italy, 9 **4** Spain, 8
5 Luxembourg, 4 **6** US, 3 **7** = Switzerland, 2; =
Holland, 2 **9** = Denmark, 1; = Germany, 1; = Ireland, 1

RIDERS WITH THE MOST AMA GRAND NATIONAL SERIES RACE WINS

RIDER/COUNTRY		YEARS	RACE WINS
1	Jay Springsteen	1975–85	40
2	Bubba Shobert	1982–88	38
3	Scott Parker	1979–90	37
4	Kenny Roberts	1974–84	33
5	Bart Markel	1960–71	28
6	Joe Leonard	1953–61	27
7 =	Dick Mann	1958–72	24
=	Ricky Graham	1980–86	24
9 =	Carol Resweber	1957–62	19
=	Gary Nixon	1963–74	19
=	Gary Scott	1972–82	19

The AMA (American Motocyclist Association) was founded in Chicago in 1924. For many years motocycle sport in the US revolved around dirt-track racing, and the AMA Grand National Series, which was launched in 1954, is the premier dirt-track series in the world.

TOUR DE FRANCE WINNERS

RIDER/COUNTRY	WINS
1= Jacques Anquetil, France	5
= Eddy Merckx, Belgium	5
= Bernard Hinault, France	5
= Miguel Indurain, Spain	5
5= Philippe Thys, Belgium	3
= Louison Bobet, France	3
= Greg LeMond, US	3
8= Lucien Petit-Breton, France	2
= Firmin Lambot, Belgium	2
= Ottavio Bottecchia, Italy	2
= Nicholas Frantz, Luxembourg	2
= André Leducq, France	2
= Antonin Magne, France	2
= Gino Bartali, Italy	2
= Sylvere Maës, Belgium	2
= Fausto Coppi, Italy	2
= Bernard Thevenet, France	2
= Laurent Fignon, France	2

Gino Bartali won the race in 1938 and 1948. He is the only cyclist to have won both before and after World War II.

BIG MIG

For five years from 1990 to 1995, Miguel Indurain dominated the Tour de France. His seemingly unbeatable combination of strength, skill, and stamina made him the focus of media attention and public expectation.

AUTO RACING

FASTEST WINNING SPEEDS OF THE DAYTONA 500

	DRIVER*	CAR	YEAR	MPH	KM/H
1	Buddy Baker	Oldsmobile	1980	177.602	285.823
2	Bill Elliott	Ford	1987	176.263	283.668
3	Dale Earnhardt	Chevrolet	1998	172.712	277.953
4	Bill Elliott	Ford	1985	172.265	277.234
5	Dale Earnhardt	Chevrolet	1998	172.071	276.921
6	Richard Petty	Buick	1981	169.651	273.027
7	Derrike Cope	Chevrolet	1990	165.761	266.766
8	Jeff Gordon	Chevrolet	1999	161.551	259.992
9	A.J. Foyt	Mercury	1972	161.550	259.990
10	Richard Petty	Plymouth	1966	160.627	258.504#

* All winners from the US

Race reduced to 495 miles/797 km

TOP 10 ★

FASTEST WINNING SPEEDS OF THE INDIANAPOLIS 500

	DRIVER/COUNTRY*	CAR YEAR	MPH	KM/H
1	Arie Luyendyk, Holland	Lola-Chevrolet 1990	185.984	299.307
2	Rick Mears	Chevrolet-Lumina 1991	176.457	283.980
3	Bobby Rahal	March-Cosworth 1986	170.722	274.750
4	Emerson Fittipaldi, Brazil	Penske-Chevrolet 1989	167.581	269.695
5	Rick Mears	March-Cosworth 1984	163.612	263.308
6	Mark Donohue	McLaren-Offenhauser 1972	162.962	262.619
7	Al Unser	March-Cosworth 1987	162.175	260.995
8	Tom Sneva	March-Cosworth 1983	162.117	260.902
9	Gordon Johncock	Wildcat-Cosworth 1982	162.029	260.760
10	Al Unser	Lola-Cosworth 1978	161.363	259.689

* All from the US unless otherwise stated

Source: Indianapolis Motor Speedway

The first Indianapolis 500, known affectionately as the "Indy," was held on Memorial Day, May 30, 1911, and was won by Ray Harroun driving a bright yellow 447-cu in six-cylinder Marmon Wasp at an average speed of 74.59 mph/120.04 km/h. The race takes place over 200 laps of the 2½-mile Indianapolis Raceway, which from 1927 to 1945 was owned by World War I flying ace Eddie Rickenbacker. Over the years, the speed has steadily increased: Harroun's race took 6 hours 42 minutes 6 seconds to complete, while Arie Luyendyk's record-breaking win was achieved in just 2 hours 18 minutes 18.248 seconds. The track record, set in the 1990 qualifying competition, is 225.301 mph/362.587 kp/h by Emerson Fittipaldi.

MONEY WINNERS AT THE INDIANAPOLIS 500, 1998

	DRIVER*	CHASSIS/ENGINE	TOTAL PRIZES ($)
1	Eddie Cheever	Dallara-Aurora	1,433,000
2	Buddy Lazier	Dallara-Aurora	483,200
3	Steve Knapp	G-Force-Aurora	338,750
4	Davey Hamilton	G-Force-Aurora	301,650
5	Robby Unser	G-Force-Aurora	209,400
6	Kenny Brack	Dallara-Aurora	310,750
7	John Paul, Jr.	Dallara-Aurora	216,350
8	Andy Michner	Dallara-Aurora	182,050
9	J. J. Veley	Dallara-Aurora	198,550
10	Buzz Calkins	G-Force-Aurora	248,500

Source: Indianapolis Motor Speedway

* Drivers are ranked here according to their finishing order, but as the list indicates prize money – which in 1998 totaled $8,642,450 – their placement does not follow precisely, varying according to such designations as first using a particular brand of tire. Even losers can be high earners in the Indy: Tony Stewart, who finished in 33rd and last position, earned $220,250.

TOP 10 CART DRIVERS WITH THE MOST RACE WINS

(Driver/years/wins)

1 A.J. Foyt, Jr., 1960–81, 67 **2** Mario Andretti, 1965–93, 52
3 Al Unser, 1965–87, 39 **4** Michael Andretti, 1986–98, 37
5 Bobby Unser, 1966–81, 35 **6** Al Unser, Jr., 1984–95, 31
7 Rick Mears, 1978–91, 29 **8** Johnny Rutherford, 1965–86, 27
9 Rodger Ward, 1953–66, 26 **10** Gordon Johncock, 1965–83, 25

Source: Championship Auto Racing Teams

TOP 10 WINNERS OF THE INDIANAPOLIS 500 WITH THE HIGHEST STARTING POSITIONS

(Driver/year/starting position)

1 = Ray Harroun, 1911, 28; = Louis Meyer, 1936, 28
3 Fred Frame, 1932, 27 **4** Johnny Rutherford, 1974, 25
5 = Kelly Petillo, 1935, 22; = George Souders, 1927, 22
7 L.L. Corum and Joe Boyer, 1924, 21 **8** = Frank Lockart, 1926, 20; = Tommy Milton, 1921, 20; = Al Unser, Jr., 1987, 20

Of the 75 winners of the Indianapolis 500, 44 have started from a position between 1 and 5 on the starting grid. The Top 10 is of those winners who have started from furthest back in the starting lineup.

TOP 10 ⭐
DRIVERS WITH THE MOST WINSTON CUP WINS*

DRIVER	YEARS	VICTORIES
1 Richard Petty	1958–92	200
2 David Pearson	1960–86	105
3 =Bobby Allison	1975–88	84
=Darrell Waltrip#	1972–98	84
5 Cale Yarborough	1957–88	83
6 Dale Earnhardt#	1975–98	71
7 Lee Petty	1949–64	55
8 =Ned Jarrett	1953–66	50
=Junior Johnson	1953–66	50
10 Rusty Wallace#	1986–99	49

* To April 11, 1999

Still driving at end of 1999 season

Source: NASCAR

The Winston Cup is a season-long series of races organized by the National Association of Stock Car Auto Racing, Inc. (NASCAR). Races, which take place over enclosed circuits such as the Daytona Speedway, are among the most popular motor races in the United States. The series started in 1949 (when it was won by Red Byron) as the Grand National series, but changed its style to the Winston Cup in 1970 when sponsored by the R.J. Reynolds tobacco company, manufacturers of Winston cigarettes. Cale (William Caleb) Yarborough, who also won the Daytona 500 on four occasions, is the only driver to win three successive titles. He, and all the other drivers in the Top 10, are all from the US.

TOP 10 NASCAR MONEY WINNERS OF ALL TIME*
(Driver/total prizes in $)

1 Dale Earnhardt, 34,343,913 **2** Jeff Gordon, 28,744,377
3 Bill Elliott, 19,881,229 **4** Terry Labonte, 19,648,501
5 Rusty Wallace, 19,438,938 **6** Mark Martin, 19,426,419
7 Darrell Waltrip, 17,498,446 **8** Dale Jarrett, 16,051,543
9 Ricky Rudd, 15,468,776 **10** Geoffrey Bodine, 13,083,743

* To April 11, 1999

Source: NASCAR

TOP 10 CARS IN THE LE MANS 24-HOUR RACE
(Car/wins)

1 Porsche, 15 **2** Ferrari, 9 **3** Jaguar, 7 **4** Bentley, 5
5 = Alfa Romeo, 4; = Ford, 4 **7** Matra-Simca, 3 **8** = Bugatti, 2;
= La Lorraine, 2; = Mercedes-Benz, 2; = Peugeot, 2

TOP 10 ⭐
FASTEST LE MANS 24-HOUR RACES

DRIVER/COUNTRY	CAR	YEAR	AVERAGE SPEED MPH	KM/H
1 Helmut Marko, Austria, Gijs van Lennep, Holland	Porsche	1971	138.133	222.304
2 Jan Lammers, Holland, Johnny Dumfries, Andy Wallace, UK	Jaguar	1988	137.714	221.630
3 Jochen Mass, Manuel Reuter, West Germany, Stanley Dickens, Sweden	Mercedes	1989	136.696	219.991
4 Dan Gurney, A. J. Foyt, US	Ford	1967	135.479	218.033
5 Geoff Brabham, Australia, Christophe Bouchot, Eric Hélary, France	Peugeot	1993	132.574	213.358
6 Klaus Ludwig, "John Winter," West Germany, Paulo Barilla, Italy	Porsche	1985	131.744	212.021
7 Vern Schuppan, Austria, Hurley Haywood, Al Holbert, US	Porsche	1983	130.693	210.330
8 Jean-Pierre Jassaud, Didier Pironi, France	Renault Alpine	1978	130.606	210.190
9 Jacky Ickx, Belgium, Jackie Oliver, UK	Ford	1969	129.401	208.250
10 Johnny Herbert, UK, Bertrand Gachot, Belgium, Volker Wendler, Germany	Mazda	1991	206.530	128.332

TOP 10 DRIVERS IN THE LE MANS 24-HOUR RACE
(Driver/country/years/wins)

1 Jacky Ickx, Belgium, 1969–82, 6 **2** Derek Bell, UK, 1975–87, 5
3 = Olivier Gendebien, Belgium, 1958–62, 4; = Henri Pescarolo, France, 1972–84, 4 **5** = Woolf Barnato, UK, 1928–30, 3; = Luigi Chinetti, Italy/US, 1932–49, 3; = Phil Hill, US, 1958–62, 3; = Klaus Ludwig, West Germany, 1979–85, 3; = Al Holbert, US, 1983–87, 3; = Yannick Dalmas, France, 1992–95, 3

Did You Know? The average speed of the first Le Mans race in 1923 was 57.205 mph/92.065 km/h.

GOLFING GREATS

TOP 10 PLAYERS TO WIN THE MOST MAJORS IN A CAREER

PLAYER/COUNTRY*	BRITISH OPEN	US OPEN	MASTERS	PGA	TOTAL
1 Jack Nicklaus	3	4	6	5	18
2 Walter Hagen	4	2	0	5	11
3 = Ben Hogan	1	4	2	2	9
= Gary Player, South Africa	3	1	3	2	9
5 Tom Watson	5	1	2	0	8
6 = Harry Vardon, UK	6	1	0	0	7
= Gene Sarazen	1	2	1	3	7
= Bobby Jones	3	4	0	0	7
= Sam Snead	1	0	3	3	7
= Arnold Palmer	2	1	4	0	7

* From the US unless otherwise stated

TOP 10 ★ BEST WINNING SCORES IN THE US MASTERS

PLAYER/COUNTRY*	YEAR	SCORE
1 Tiger Woods	1997	270
2 = Jack Nicklaus	1965	271
= Raymond Floyd	1976	271
4 = Ben Hogan	1953	274
= Ben Crenshaw	1995	274
6 = Severiano Ballesteros, Spain	1980	275
= Fred Couples	1992	275
8 = Arnold Palmer	1964	276
= Jack Nicklaus	1975	276
= Tom Watson	1977	276
= Nick Faldo, UK	1996	276

* From the US unless otherwise stated

The US Masters is the only major played on the same course each year, at Augusta, Georgia. The course was built on the site of an old nursery, and the abundance of flowers, shrubs, and plants is a reminder of its former days, with each of the holes named after the plants growing adjacent to it.

TOP 10 ★ MONEY-WINNING GOLFERS OF ALL TIME

PLAYER/COUNTRY*	CAREER WINNINGS ($)#
1 Greg Norman, Australia	12,015,443
2 Fred Couples	10,806,573
3 Mark O'Meara	10,730,943
4 Payne Stewart	10,551,358
5 Davis Love III	10,548,501
6 Tom Kite	10,447,472
7 Nick Price	10,039,234
8 Tom Watson	9,395,292
9 Scott Hoch	9,388,207
10 Mark Calcavecchia	9,120,814

* From the US unless otherwise stated
 # As at March 14, 1999

GOLF'S SHOWMAN

A flamboyant character, Walter Hagen helped raise the status of professional golfers by refusing to accept the limitations imposed by the game's establishment.

TOP 10 ★ MONEY-WINNING GOLFERS, 1998

PLAYER/COUNTRY*	WINNINGS ($)
1 David Duval	2,680,489
2 Vijay Singh, Fiji	2,398,782
3 Tiger Woods	2,077,197
4 Jim Furyk	2,054,334
5 Lee Westwood, UK	2,022,213
6 Mark O'Meara	2,014,039
7 Hal Sutton	1,838,740
8 Phil Mickelson	1,837,246
9 Davis Love III	1,703,001
10 Colin Montgomerie, UK	1,684,449

* From the US unless otherwise stated

This list is based on winnings on the world's five top tours: US PGA Tour, European PGA Tour, PGA Tour of Japan, Australasian PGA Tour, and FNB Tour of South Africa.

TOP 10 ⭐
PLAYERS WITH THE MOST CAREER WINS ON THE US TOUR

PLAYER*	TOUR WINS
1 Sam Snead	81
2 Jack Nicklaus	70
3 Ben Hogan	63
4 Arnold Palmer	60
5 Byron Nelson	52
6 Billy Casper	51
7 =Walter Hagen	40
=Cary Midlecoff	40
9 Gene Sarazen	38
10 Lloyd Mangrum	36

* All from the US

For many years Sam Snead's total of wins was held to be 84, but the PGA Tour amended his figure in 1990 after discrepancies were found in their previous lists. They deducted 11 wins from his total, but added eight others which should have been included, giving a revised total of 81. The highest-placed current member of the regular tour is Tom Watson, in joint 11th place with 32 wins. The highest-placed overseas player is Gary Player (South Africa), with 22 wins. Sam Snead, despite being the most successful golfer on the US Tour, has never won the US Open. However, he has finished 2nd on four occasions.

TOP 10 ⭐
WINS IN A US SEASON

PLAYER	YEAR	WINS
1 Byron Nelson	1945	18
2 Ben Hogan	1946	13
3 Sam Snead	1950	11
4 Ben Hogan	1948	10
5 Paul Runyan	1933	9
6 =Horton Smith	1929	8
=Gene Sarazen	1930	8
=Harry Cooper	1937	8
=Sam Snead	1938	8
=Henry Picard	1939	8
=Byron Nelson	1944	8
=Lloyd Mangrum	1948	8
=Arnold Palmer	1960	8
=Johnny Miller	1974	8

Having won eight Tour events in 1944, Byron Nelson went on to shatter the US record the following year with a stunning 18 wins. His remarkable year started on January 14, when he won the Phoenix Open, and by the time he won the Miami Four Ball at Palm Springs on March 11, he had achieved his fourth success of the season. This victory at Miami sparked off a run of 11 consecutive tournament wins, which is also a US record. Included in his 11-tournament winning streak was the PGA Championship and the Canadian Open.

TOP 10 ⭐
BEST WINNING TOTALS IN THE US OPEN

PLAYER/COUNTRY*/VENUE		YEAR	SCORE
1 =Jack Nicklaus,	Baltusrol	1980	272
=Lee Janzen,	Baltusrol	1993	272
3 David Graham,	Australia, Merion	1981	273
4 =Jack Nicklaus,	Baltusrol	1967	275
=Lee Trevino,	Oak Hill	1968	275
6 =Ben Hogan,	Riviera	1948	276
=Fuzzy Zoeller,	Winged Foot	1984	276
=Ernie Els,	South Africa, Congressional	1997	276
9 =Jerry Pate,	Atlanta	1976	277
=Scott Simpson,	Olympic Club	1987	277

* From the US unless otherwise stated

Winning the 1980 US Open at Baltusrol, 18 years after his first success in the tournament, Jack Nicklaus did so in record-breaking style: his total of 204 established yet another new record.

TOP 10 ⭐
WINNERS OF WOMEN'S MAJORS

PLAYER*	TITLES
1 Patty Berg	16
2 =Mickey Wright	13
=Louise Suggs	13
4 Babe Zaharias	12
5 Betsy Rawls	8
6 JoAnne Carner	7
7 =Kathy Whitworth	6
=Pat Bradley	6
=Julie Inkster	6
=Glenna Collett Vare	6

* All from the US

TIGER ON TOP

Tiger Woods is golf's current phenomenon. Playing since the age of 2, Tiger has had a massive impact on the game, and he looks set for a great future.

Who was the 1997 world heavyweight boxing champion?
see p.254 for the answer
A Evander Holyfield
B Mike Tyson
C George Foreman

267

Horse Racing

FASTEST WINNING TIMES OF THE KENTUCKY DERBY

	HORSE	YEAR	MINS	TIME SECS
1	Secretariat	1973	1	59.2
2	Northern Dancer	1964	2	00.0
3	Spend A Buck	1985	2	00.2
4	Decidedly	1962	2	00.4
5	Proud Clarion	1967	2	00.6
6	Grindstone	1996	2	01.0
7 =Lucky Debonair	1965	2	01.2
=Affirmed	1978	2	01.2
=Thunder Gulch	1995	2	01.2
10	Whirlaway	1941	2	01.4

Source: *The Jockey Club*

The Kentucky Derby is held on the first Saturday in May at Churchill Downs, Louisville, Kentucky. The first leg of the Triple Crown, it was first raced in 1875 over a distance of 1 mile 4 furlongs, but after 1896 was reduced to 1 mile 2 furlongs. It is said that the hat, known in England as a "bowler," became popular attire at the first Kentucky Derbys, thereby acquiring the name "derby."

TOP 10 ★

JOCKEYS IN THE BREEDERS CUP

	JOCKEY	YEARS	WINS
1	Pat Day	1984–97	9
2	Mike Smith	1992–97	8
3 =Eddie Delahoussaye	1984–93	7
=Laffit Pincay Jr.	1985–93	7
=Chris McCarron	1985–96	7
6 =Pat Valenzuela	1986–92	6
=Jerry Bailey	1991–96	6
=Jose Santos	1986–97	6
9 =Angel Cordero Jr.	1985–89	4
=Craig Perret	1984–96	4
=Gary Stevens	1990–96	4

Source: *The Breeders Cup*

Held at a different venue each year, the Breeders Cup is an end-of-season gathering with seven races run during the day, with the season's best throughbreds competing in each category. Staged in October or November, there is $10,000,000 prize money on offer, with $3,000,000 going to the winner of the day's senior race, the Classic.

THE SPORT OF KINGS

Although racing is classified as an equestrian sport, many would argue that it is a huge multinational industry in which betting is the central element.

TOP 10 ★

MONEY-WINNING NORTH AMERICAN JOCKEYS

	JOCKEY	EARNINGS ($)
1	Chris McCarron	226,021,526
2	Pat Day	206,850,832
3	Laffit Pincay Jr.	201,712,132
4	Gary Stevens	179,802,072
5	Eddie Delahoussaye	170,706,626
6	Jerry Bailey	166,160,174
7	Angel Cordero Jr.	164,561,227
8	Jose Santos	127,137,965
9	Jorge Velasquez	125,544,379
10	Bill Shoemaker	123,375,524

Source: *NTRA Communications*

TOP 10 ★

US JOCKEYS WITH THE MOST WINS IN A CAREER

	JOCKEY	YEARS RIDING	WINS
1	Willie Shoemaker	42	8
2	Laffit Pincay Jr.	35	4
3 =Pat Day	26	3
=David Gall	42	3
=Angel Cordero Jr.	35	3
=Jorge Velasquez	35	3
=Chris McCarron	25	3
=Russell Baze	25	3
9 =Sandy Hawley	31	2
=Larry Snyder	37	2

Source: *NTRA Communications*

TOP 10 ★

OLYMPIC EQUESTRIAN COUNTRIES

	COUNTRY	MEDALS GOLD	SILVER	BRONZE	TOTAL
1	West Germany/ Germany	31	17	20	68
2	Sweden	17	8	14	39
3	US	8	17	13	38
4	France	11	12	11	34
5	Italy	7	9	7	23
6	Great Britain	5	7	9	21
7	Switzerland	4	9	7	20
8 =Holland	6	7	2	15
=USSR	6	5	4	15
10	Belgium	4	2	5	11

TOP 10 ★
JOCKEYS IN THE TRIPLE CROWN RACES

	JOCKEY	KENTUCKY	PREAKNESS	BELMONT	TOTAL
1	Eddie Arcaro	5	6	6	17
2	Bill Shoemaker	4	2	5	11
3 =	Bill Hartack	5	3	1	9
=	Earle Sande	3	1	5	9
5 =	Pat Day	1	5	2	8
=	Jimmy McLaughlin	1	1	6	8
7 =	Angel Cordero Jr.	3	2	1	6
=	Chas Kurtsinger	2	2	2	6
=	Ron Turcotte	2	2	2	6
=	Gary Stevens	3	1	2	6

The US Triple Crown consists of the Kentucky Derby, Preakness Stakes, and Belmont Stakes. Since 1875, only 11 horses have won all three races in one season. The only jockey to complete the Triple Crown twice is Eddie Arcaro on Whirlaway in 1941 and Citation in 1948.

TOP 10 ★
MONEY-WINNING PACERS IN A HARNESS-RACING CAREER*

	HORSE	WINNINGS ($)
1	Nihilator	3,225,653
2	Artsplace	3,085,083
3	Presidential Ball	3,021,363
4	Matt's Scooter	2,944,591
5	On the Road Again	2,819,102
6	Beach Towel	2,570,357
7	Western Hanover	2,541,647
8	Cam's Card Shark	2,498,204
9	Pacific Rocket	2,333,401
10	Precious Bunny	2,281,142

* A pacer's legs are extended laterally and with a "swinging motion"; pacers usually travel faster than trotters

Unlike racehorses, harness-racing horses are trained to trot and pace, but do not gallop.

TOP 10 ★
MONEY-WINNING TROTTERS IN A HARNESS-RACING CAREER*

	HORSE	WINNINGS ($)
1	Peace Corps	5,506,443
2	Ourasi	4,010,105
3	Mack Lobell	3,917,594
4	Reve d'Udon	3,611,351
5	Sea Cove	2,818,693
6	Ideal du Gazeau	2,744,777
7	Vrai Lutin	2,612,429
8	Grades Singing	2,607,552
9	Embassy Lobell	2,566,370
10	Napoletano	2,467,878

* A trotter is a horse whose diagonally opposite legs move forward together

Harness racing is one of the oldest sports in the US, its origins going back to the Colonial period, when many races were held along the turnpikes of New York and the New England colonies. While widespread in the United States, harness racing is also popular in Australia and New Zealand and, increasingly, elsewhere in the world. Harness-racing horses pull a jockey on a two-wheeled "sulky" around an oval track.

THE 10 LATEST TRIPLE CROWN-WINNING HORSES*
(Horse/year)

1 Affirmed, 1978 **2** Seattle Slew, 1977 **3** Secretariat, 1973 **4** Citation, 1948 **5** Assault, 1946 **6** Count Fleet, 1943 **7** Whirlaway, 1941 **8** War Admiral, 1937 **9** Omaha, 1935 **10** Gallant Fox, 1930

* Horses that have won the Kentucky Derby, the Preakness, and Belmont Stakes in the same season

TOP 10 MONEY-WINNING HORSES, 1998
(Horse/winnings in $)

1 Silver Charm, 4,696,506 **2** Awesome Charm, 3,845,990 **3** Skip Away, 2,740,000 **4** Escena, 2,032,425 **5** Victory Gallop, 1,981,720 **6** Buck's Boy, 1,874,020 **7** Real Quiet, 1,788,800 **8** Coronado's Quest, 1,739,950 **9** Banshee Breeze, 1,425,980 **10** Silverbulletday, 1,114,110

Source: The Jockey Club

Did You Know? The fastest ever racehorse was Big Rocket, who ran at 43.26 mph/69.62 kmph in Mexico City in 1945.

ICE HOCKEY

TOP 10 ★
WINNERS OF THE HART TROPHY

	PLAYER	YEARS	WINS
1	Wayne Gretzky	1980–89	9
2	Gordie Howe	1952–63	6
3	Eddie Shore	1933–38	4
4	=Bobby Clarke	1973–76	3
	=Howie Morenz	1928–32	3
	=Bobby Orr	1970–72	3
	=Mario Lemieux	1988–96	3
8	=Jean Beliveau	1956–64	2
	=Bill Cowley	1941–43	2
	=Phil Esposito	1969–74	2
	=Bobby Hull	1965–66	2
	=Guy Lafleur	1977–78	2
	=Mark Messier	1990–92	2
	=Stan Mikita	1967–68	2
	=Nels Stewart	1926–30	2

Source: National Hockey League

TOP 10 POINT SCORERS
IN STANLEY CUP PLAY-OFF GAMES
(Player/total points)

1 Wayne Gretzky*, 382 **2** Mark Messier*, 295 **3** Jari Kurri*, 233
4 Glenn Anderson, 214 **5** Paul Coffey*, 195 **6** Bryan Trottier, 184
7 Jean Beliveau, 176 **8** Denis Savard, 175 **9** = Doug Gilmour*, 164;
= Denis Potvin, 164

* Still active 1997–98 season

TOP 10 TEAMS WITH THE MOST
STANLEY CUP WINS
(Team/wins)

1 Montreal Canadiens, 23 **2** Toronto Maple Leafs, 13 **3** Detroit Red Wings, 8
4 = Boston Bruins, 5; = Edmonton Oilers, 5 **6** = New York Islanders, 4;
= New York Rangers, 4 **8** Chicago Black Hawks, 3 **9** = Philadelphia Flyers, 2;
= Pittsburgh Penguins, 2

Source: National Hockey League

TOP 10 ★
ASSISTS IN AN NHL CAREER*

	PLAYER	SEASONS	ASSISTS
1	Wayne Gretzky#	19	1,910
2	Paul Coffey#	8	1,090
3	Gordie Howe	26	1,049
4	Marcel Dionne	18	1,040
5	Ray Bourque#	19	1,036
6	Mark Messier#	19	1,015
7	Ron Francis#	17	1,006
8	Stan Mikita	22	926
9	Bryan Trottier	18	901
10	Dale Hawerchuk	17	891

* Regular season only
 # Still active at end of 1997–98 season

TOP 10 ★
GOAL TENDERS IN AN NHL CAREER*

	PLAYER	SEASONS	GAMES WON
1	Terry Sawchuk	21	447
2	Jacques Plante	18	434
3	Tony Esposito	16	423
4	Glen Hall	18	407
5	Grant Fuhr#	16	382
6	Patrick Roy#	12	380
7	Andy Moog#	17	372
8	Rogie Vachie	16	355
9	Gump Worsley	21	334
10	Harry Lumley	16	333

* Regular season only
 # Still active at end of 1997–98 season

TOP 10 ★
GOAL SCORERS IN AN NHL CAREER*

	PLAYER	SEASONS	GOALS
1	Wayne Gretzky#	19	885
2	Gordie Howe	26	801
3	Marcel Dionne	18	731
4	Phil Esposito	18	717
5	Mike Gartner#	19	708
6	Mario Lemieux	12	613
7	Bobby Hull	16	610
8	Dino Ciccarelli#	18	602
9	Jari Kurri#	17	601
10	Mark Messier#	18	597

* Regular season only
 # Still active at end of 1997–98 season

TOP 10 ★
BEST PAID PLAYERS
IN THE NHL, 1998-1999

	PLAYER	TEAM	SALARY
1	Sergei Fedorov	Detroit Red Wings	14,000,000
2 =	Paul Kariya	Anaheim Mighty Ducks	8,500,000
=	Eric Lindros	Philadelphia Flyers	8,500,000
4	Dominik Hasek	Buffalo Sabres	8,000,000
5	Pavel Bure	Florida Panthers	6,400,000
6	Mats Sundin	Toronto Maple Leafs	6,347,164
7 =	Peter Forsberg	Colorado Avalanche	6,000,000
=	Doug Gilmour	Chicago Blackhawks	6,000,000
=	Wayne Gretzky	New York Rangers	6,000,000
=	Mark Messier	Vancouver Canucks	6,000,000

Source: *National Hockey League Players' Association*

TOP 10 ★
POINT SCORERS
IN AN NHL CAREER*

	PLAYER	SEASONS	GOALS	ASSISTS	TOTAL POINTS
1	Wayne Gretzky#	19	885	1,910	2,795
2	Gordie Howe	26	801	1,049	1,850
3	Marcel Dionne	18	731	1,040	1,771
4	Mark Messier#	19	597	1,015	1,612
5	Phil Esposito	18	717	873	1,590
6	Mario Lemieux	12	613	881	1,494
7	Stan Mikita	22	541	926	1,467
8	Paul Coffey#	18	380	1,085	1,465
9	Ron Francis	17	428	1,006	1,434
10	Bryan Trottier	18	524	901	1,425

* *Regular season only*

Still active at end of 1997-98 season

TOP 10 ★
GOAL SCORERS
IN AN NHL SEASON

	PLAYER/TEAM	SEASON	GOALS
1	Wayne Gretzky, Edmonton Oilers	1981–82	92
2	Wayne Gretzky, Edmonton Oilers	1983–84	87
3	Brett Hull, St. Louis Blues	1990–91	86
4	Mario Lemieux, Pittsburgh Penguins	1988–89	85
5 =	Phil Esposito, Boston Bruins	1970–71	76
=	Alexander Mogilny, Buffalo Sabres	1992–93	76
=	Teemu Selanne, Winnipeg Jets	1992–93	76
8	Wayne Gretzky, Edmonton Oilers	1984–85	73
9	Brett Hull, St. Louis Blues	1989–90	72
10 =	Wayne Gretzky, Edmonton Oilers	1982–83	71
=	Jari Kurri, Edmonton Oilers	1984–85	71

TOP 10 ★
GOAL SCORERS, 1997–98

	PLAYER/TEAM	GOALS
1 =	Peter Bondra, Washington Capitals	52
=	Teemu Selanne, Anaheim Mighty Ducks	52
3 =	Pavel Bure, Vancouver Canucks	51
=	John LeClair, Philadelphia Flyers	51
5	Zigmund Palffy, New York Islanders	45
6	Keith Tkachuk, Phoenix Coyotes	40
7	Joe Nieuwendyk, Dallas Stars	39
8	Rod Brind'Amour, Philadelphia Flyers	36
9	Jaromir Jagr, Pittsburgh Penguins	35
10 =	Jason Allison, Boston Bruins	33
=	Mats Sundin, Toronto Maple Leafs	33
=	Ray Whitney, Edmonton Oilers/Florida Panthers	33
=	Alexei Yashin, Ottawa Senators	33

Source: *National Hockey League*

TENNIS TRIUMPHS

PLAYERS WITH THE MOST US SINGLES TITLES

	PLAYER/COUNTRY*	YEARS	TITLES
1	Molla Mallory	1915–26	8
2 =	Richard Sears	1881–87	7
=	William Larned	1901–11	7
=	Bill Tilden	1920–29	7
=	Helen Wills-Moody	1923–31	7
=	Margaret Court, Australia#	1962–70	7
7	Chris Evert-Lloyd	1975–82	6
8 =	Jimmy Connors	1974–83	5
=	Steffi Graf, Germany	1988–96	5
10 =	Robert Wrenn	1893–97	4
=	Elisabeth Moore	1896–1905	4
=	Hazel Wightman	1909–19	4
=	Helen Jacobs	1932–35	4
=	Alice Marble	1936–40	4
=	Pauline Betz	1942–46	4
=	Maria Bueno, Brazil	1959–66	4
=	Billie Jean King	1967–74	4
=	John McEnroe	1979–84	4
=	Martina Navratilova	1983–87	4
=	Pete Sampras	1990–96	4

* From the US unless otherwise stated
\# Includes two wins in Amateur Championships of 1968 and 1969, which were held alongside the Open Championship

LEFT-HANDED WINNER
Martina Navratilova, a Czech-born tennis player who defected to the United States in 1975, retired in 1994, after winning 167 titles.

TOP 10 FEMALE PLAYERS*

(Player/country)

1. **Lindsay Davenport**, US 2. **Martina Hingis**, Switzerland 3. **Jana Novotna**, Czech Republic 4. **Arantxa Sanchez-Vicario**, Spain 5. **Venus Williams**, US 6. **Monica Seles**, US 7. **Mary Pierce**, France 8. **Conchita Martinez**, Spain 9. **Steffi Graf**, Germany 10. **Nathalie Tauziat**, France

* Based on 1999 WTA rankings

TOP 10 CAREER MONEY-WINNING WOMEN*

(Player/country/winnings in $)

1. **Steffi Graf**, Germany, 20,614,142
2. **Martina Navratilova**, US, 20,283,727
3. **Arantxa Sanchez-Vicario**, Spain, 14,029,452
4. **Monica Seles**, US, 10,878,024
5. **Jana Novotna**, Czech Republic, 10,297,692
6. **Chris Evert**, US, 8,896,195
7. **Gabriela Sabatini**, Argentina, 8,785,850
8. **Martina Hingis**, Switzerland, 8,124,248
9. **Conchita Martinez**, Spain, 7,737,227
10. **Natasha Zvereva**, Belarus, 7,014,631

* To end of 1998

DAVIS CUP WINNING TEAMS

	COUNTRY	WINS
1	United States	31
2	Australia	20
3	France	8
4	Sweden	7
5	Australasia	6
6	British Isles	5
7	Great Britain	4
8	West Germany	2
9 =	Germany	1
=	Czechoslovakia	1
=	Italy	1
=	South Africa	1

The UK was represented by the British Isles from 1900 to 1921, England from 1922 to 1928, and Great Britain since 1929. The combined Australia/New Zealand team took part as Australasia between 1905 and 1922. Australia first entered a separate team in 1923 and New Zealand in 1924. South Africa's sole win was gained when, for political reasons, India refused to meet them in the 1974 final.

MEN WITH THE MOST WIMBLEDON TITLES

	PLAYER/COUNTRY	YEARS	S	D	M	TOTAL
1	William Renshaw, UK	1880–89	7	7	0	14
2	Lawrence Doherty, UK	1897–1905	5	8	0	13
3	Reginald Doherty, UK	1897–1905	4	8	0	12
4	John Newcombe, Australia	1965–74	3	6	0	9
5 =	Ernest Renshaw, UK	1880–89	1	7	0	8
=	Tony Wilding, New Zealand	1907–14	4	4	0	8
7 =	Wilfred Baddeley, UK	1891–96	3	4	0	7
=	Bob Hewitt, Australia/S. Africa	1962–79	0	5	2	7
=	Rod Laver, Australia	1959–69	4	1	2	7
=	John McEnroe, US	1979–84	3	4	0	7

S – singles; D – doubles; M – mixed

Background image: **WIMBLEDON**

TOP 10 ⭐
WINNERS OF WOMEN'S GRAND SLAM SINGLES TITLES

PLAYER/COUNTRY	A	F	W	US	TOTAL
1 Margaret Court, Australia	11	5	3	5	24
2 Steffi Graf, Germany	4	5	7	5	21
3 Helen Wills-Moody, US	0	4	8	7	19
4 =Chris Evert-Lloyd, US	2	7	3	6	18
=Martina Navratilova, Czechoslovakia/US	3	2	9	4	18
6 Billie Jean King, US	1	1	6	4	12
7 =Maureen Connolly, US	1	2	3	3	9
=Monica Seles, Yugoslavia/US	4	3	0	2	9
9 =Suzanne Lenglen, France	0	2	6	0	8
=Molla Mallory, US	0	0	0	8	8

A – Australian Open; F – French Open; W – Wimbledon; US – US Open

TOP 10 ⭐
WINNERS OF MEN'S GRAND SLAM SINGLES TITLES

PLAYER/COUNTRY	A	F	W	US	TOTAL
1 Roy Emerson, Australia	6	2	2	2	12
2 =Björn Borg, Sweden	0	6	5	0	11
=Rod Laver, Australia	3	2	4	2	11
=Pete Sampras, US	2	0	5	4	11
5 =Jimmy Connors, US	1	0	2	5	8
=Ivan Lendl, Czechoslovakia	2	3	0	3	8
=Fred Perry, UK	1	1	3	3	8
=Ken Rosewall, Australia	4	2	0	2	8
9 =René Lacoste, France	0	3	2	2	7
=William Larned, US	0	0	0	7	7
=John McEnroe, US	0	0	3	4	7
=John Newcombe, Australia	2	0	3	2	7
=William Renshaw, UK	0	0	7	0	7
=Richard Sears, US	0	0	0	7	7
=Mats Wilander, Sweden	3	3	0	1	7

A – Australian Open; F – French Open; W – Wimbledon; US – US Open

THE 10 ⭐
LATEST WINNERS OF THE US OPEN MEN'S CHAMPIONSHIP

YEAR	WINNER	COUNTRY
1998	Patrick Rafter	Australia
1997	Patrick Rafter	Australia
1996	Pete Sampras	US
1995	Pete Sampras	US
1994	Andre Agassi	US
1993	Pete Sampras	US
1992	Stefan Edberg	Sweden
1991	Stefan Edberg	Sweden
1990	Pete Sampras	US
1989	Pete Sampras	US

TOP 10 ⭐
MALE PLAYERS*

PLAYER	COUNTRY
1 Pete Sampras	US
2 Marcelo Rios	Chile
3 Alex Corretja	Spain
4 Patrick Rafter	Australia
5 Carlos Moya	Spain
6 Andre Agassi	US
7 Tim Henman	UK
8 Karol Kucera	Slovak Republic
9 Greg Rusedski	UK
10 Richard Krajicek	Netherlands

* Based on 1999 WTA rankings

A SWEDISH HERO

The tennis player Björn Borg is such a popular sportsman in Sweden, his home country, that in 1996 a Björn Borg Day was organized.

Which woman won the 1998 New York Marathon?   **A** Lisa Ondieki
see p.250 for the answer   **B** Allison Roe
C Franca Fiacconi

TEAM GAMES

TOP 10 AUSTRALIAN FOOTBALL LEAGUE TEAMS

(Team/grand final wins)

1 Carlton, 16 **2** Essendon, 15
3 Collingwood, 14 **4** Melbourne, 12
5 Richmond, 10 **6** Hawthorn, 9
7 Fitzroy, 8 **8** Geelong, 6
9 = South Melbourne, 3;
= North Melbourne, 3

Australian Rules Football is an 18-a-side game that dates from the mid-19th century. The Australian Football League was formed in 1896.

TOP 10 ★ OLYMPIC SHOOTING COUNTRIES

	COUNTRY	GOLD	MEDALS SILVER	BRONZE	TOTAL
1	US	45	26	21	92
2	Soviet Union	22	17	81	57
3	Sweden	13	23	19	55
4	Great Britain	13	14	18	45
5	France	13	16	13	42
6	Norway	16	9	11	36
7	Switzerland	11	11	12	34
8	Italy	8	5	10	23
9	Greece	5	7	7	19
10	=China	7	5	5	17
	=Finland	3	5	9	17

TOP 10 COUNTIES IN THE ALL-IRELAND HURLING CHAMPIONSHIPS

(Country/wins)

1 Cork, 27 **2** Kilkenny, 25
3 Tipperary, 24 **4** Limerick, 7
5 = Dublin, 6; = Wexford, 6
7 = Galway, 4; = Offaly, 4 **9** Clare, 3
10 Waterford, 2

Hurling, one of the world's fastest sports, has a history dating back to prehistoric times.

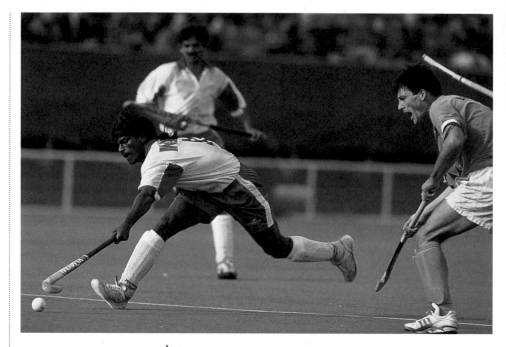

THE 10 ★ LATEST WINNERS OF THE ROLLER HOCKEY WORLD CHAMPIONSHIP

YEAR	WINNER
1997	Italy
1995	Argentina
1993	Portugal
1991	Portugal
1989	Spain
1988	Spain
1986	Spain
1984	Argentina
1982	Portugal
1980	Spain

Roller hockey, a five-a-side game formerly called rink hockey, has been played for more than 100 years. The first international tournament was held in Paris in 1910, the first European Championships in Britain in 1926, and the men's World Championship biennially since 1936 (odd-numbered years since 1989). Portugal is the overall winner, with 14 titles to its credit; Spain has won 10 times, Italy four, Argentina three, and England twice. The women's World Championship has been held since 1992 and has been won twice by Spain and once by Canada.

HOCKEY HEROES

Controversial and outspoken hockey star Dhanraj Pillay is shown here playing in the men's Olympic qualifying match in 1996. India has accumulated a record number of Olympic Gold medals for hockey.

TOP 10 ★ OLYMPIC HOCKEY COUNTRIES

	COUNTRY	GOLD	MEDALS SILVER	BRONZE	TOTAL
1	India	8	1	2	11
2	Great Britain*	3	2	5	10
3	Netherlands	2	2	5	9
4	Pakistan	3	3	2	8
5	Australia	2	3	2	7
6	Germany#	1	2	2	5
7	=Spain	1	2	1	4
	=West Germany	1	3	–	4
9	=South Korea	–	2	–	2
	=US	–	–	2	2
	=Soviet Union	–	–	2	2

* Including England, Ireland, Scotland, and Wales, which competed separately in the 1908 Olympics

 # Not including West Germany or East Germany 1968–88

OLYMPIC ARCHERY COUNTRIES

COUNTRY	GOLD	MEDALS SILVER	BRONZE	TOTAL
1 US	13	7	7	27
2 France	6	10	6	22
3 South Korea	10	6	3	19
4 Soviet Union	1	3	5	9
5 Great Britain	2	2	4	8
6 Finland	1	1	2	4
7 =China	0	3	0	3
=Italy	0	0	3	3
9 =Sweden	0	2	0	2
=Japan	0	1	1	2
=Poland	0	1	1	2

Archery was introduced as an Olympic sport at the second Modern Olympics, held in Paris in 1900. The format has changed considerably over succeeding games, with such events as shooting live birds being discontinued in favor of target shooting. Individual and team events for men and women are now included in the program.

WINNERS OF THE TABLE TENNIS WORLD CHAMPIONSHIP

COUNTRY	MEN'S	WOMEN'S	TOTAL
1 China	12	12	24
2 Japan	7	8	15
3 Hungary	12	–	12
4 Czechoslovakia	6	3	9
5 Romania	–	5	5
6 Sweden	4	–	4
7 =England	1	2	3
=US	1	2	3
9 Germany	–	2	2
10 =Austria	1	–	1
=North Korea	–	1	1
=South Korea	–	1	1
=USSR	–	1	1

Originally a European event, this was later extended to a world championship. Since 1959, the championship has been held biennially.

TOP 10 POLO TEAMS WITH THE MOST BRITISH OPEN CHAMPIONSHIP WINS

(Team/wins)

1 = Stowell Park, 5; = Tramontana, 5
3 = Ellerston, 3; = Cowdray Park, 3;
 = Pimms, 3; = Windsor Park, 3
7 = Casarejo, 2; = Jersey Lillies, 2;
 = Woolmer's Park, 2; = Falcons, 2;
 = Southfield, 2

The British Open Championship, which was first held in 1956 (replacing the Champion Cup, which was played at Hurlingham, London, from 1876 to 1939), is played at Cowdray Park, West Sussex. The winning team receives the Veuve Clicquot Gold Cup.

OLYMPIC VOLLEYBALL COUNTRIES

COUNTRY	GOLD	MEDALS SILVER	BRONZE	TOTAL
1 Soviet Union*	7	5	1	13
2 Japan	3	3	2	8
3 US	2	1	2	5
4 =Cuba	2	–	1	3
=Brazil	1	1	1	3
=China	1	1	1	3
=Poland	1	–	2	3
8 =Netherlands	1	1	–	2
=East Germany	–	2	–	2
=Bulgaria	–	1	1	2
=Czechoslovakia	–	1	1	2
=Italy	–	1	1	2

* Includes United Team of 1992; excludes Russia since

This list encompasses men's and women's volleyball in the Olympics of 1964–96, but excludes beach volleyball, first competed in 1996.

OVER THE NET
Originally known as mintonette, volleyball originated in the United States in 1895 when William G. Morgan decided to blend elements of basketball, baseball, tennis, and handball to create a game that would demand less physical contact than basketball.

Who has won the most medals in a summer Olympics career?
see p.245 for the answer

A Nikolay Andrianov
B Edoardo Mangiarotti
C Larissa Latynina

275

WATER SPORTS

TOP 10 ★
OLYMPIC YACHTING COUNTRIES

	COUNTRY	GOLD	MEDALS SILVER	BRONZE	TOTAL
1	US	16	19	16	51
2	Great Britain	14	12	9	35
3	Sweden	9	12	9	30
4	Norway	16	11	2	29
5	France	12	6	9	27
6	Denmark	10	8	4	22
7	Germany/West Germany	6	5	6	17
8	Netherlands	4	5	6	15
9	New Zealand	6	4	3	13
10=	Australia	3	2	7	12
=	Soviet Union*	4	5	3	12
=	Spain	9	2	1	12

* Includes United Team of 1992; excludes Russia since

TOP 10 POWERBOAT DRIVERS WITH MOST RACE WINS
(Owner/country/wins)

1 Bill Seebold, US, 912 **2** Jumbo McConnell, US, 217 **3** Chip Hanuer, US, 203 **4** Steve Curtis, UK, 183 **5** Mikeal Frode, Sweden, 152 **6** Neil Holmes, UK, 147 **7** Peter Bloomfield, UK, 126 **8** Renato Molinari, Italy, 113 **9** Cees Van der Valden, Netherlands, 98 **10** Bill Muney, US, 96

Source: Raceboat International

MAKING A SPLASH
The US Women's swimming team show their delight after winning the 4 x 100 meters relay at the 1996 Olympics in Atlanta, Georgia.

TOP 10 ★
OLYMPIC SWIMMING COUNTRIES

	COUNTRY	GOLD	MEDALS SILVER	BRONZE	TOTAL
1	US	230	176	137	543
2	Australia	41	37	47	125
3	East Germany	40	34	25	99
4	Soviet Union*	24	32	38	94
5	Germany#	19	33	34	86
6=	Great Britain	18	23	30	71
=	Hungary	29	23	19	71
8	Sweden	13	21	21	55
9	Japan	15	18	19	52
10	Canada	11	17	20	48

* Includes United Team of 1992; excludes Russia since
 # Not including West Germany or East Germany 1968–88

TOP 10 COLLEGES IN THE INTERCOLLEGIATE ROWING ASSOCIATION REGATTA*
(College/first to last winning years/wins)

1 Cornell, 1896–1982, 24 **2** Navy, 1921–84, 12 **3** = California, 1928–76, 10; = Washington, 1923–97, 10 **5** Pennsylvania, 1898–1989, 8 **6** = Wisconsin, 1951–90, 7; = Brown, 1979–95, 7 **8** Syracuse, 1904–78, 6 **9** Columbia, 1895–1929, 4 **10** Princeton, 1985–98, 3

* Men's varsity eight-oared shells event

SAIL ON
The US is consistently outstanding in yachting – one of the most physically demanding Olympic sports.

TOP 10 ★
OLYMPIC CANOEING COUNTRIES

COUNTRY	MEDALS			
	GOLD	SILVER	BRONZE	TOTAL
1 =Hungary	10	23	20	53
=Soviet Union*	30	13	10	53
3 Germany#	18	15	12	45
4 Romania	9	10	12	31
5 East Germany	14	7	9	30
6 Sweden	14	10	4	28
7 France	2	6	14	22
8 =Bulgaria	4	3	8	15
=US	5	4	6	15
10 Canada	3	7	4	14

* Includes United Team of 1992; excludes Russia since

 # Not including West or East Germany 1968–88

TOP 10 ★
WINNERS OF MOST SURFING WORLD CHAMPIONSHIPS

SURFER/COUNTRY	WINS
1 Kelly Slater, US	6
2 Mark Richards, Australia	4
3 Tom Curren, US	3
4 =Tom Carroll, Australia	2
=Damien Hardman, Australia	2
6 =Wayne Bartholemew, Australia	1
=Derek Ho, US	1
=Barton Lynch, Australia	1
=Martin Potter, UK	1
=Shaun Tomson, South Africa	1
=Peter Townend, Australia	1

TOP 10 ★
OLYMPIC ROWING COUNTRIES

COUNTRY	MEDALS			
	GOLD	SILVER	BRONZE	TOTAL
1 US	29	28	19	76
2 East Germany	33	7	8	48
3 Soviet Union*	12	20	11	43
4 Germany#	19	12	11	42
5 Great Britain	19	15	7	41
6 =Italy	12	11	9	32
=Canada	8	12	12	32
8 France	4	14	12	30
9 Romania	12	10	7	29
10 Switzerland	6	7	9	22

* Includes United Team of 1992; excludes Russia since

 # Not including West or East Germany 1968–88

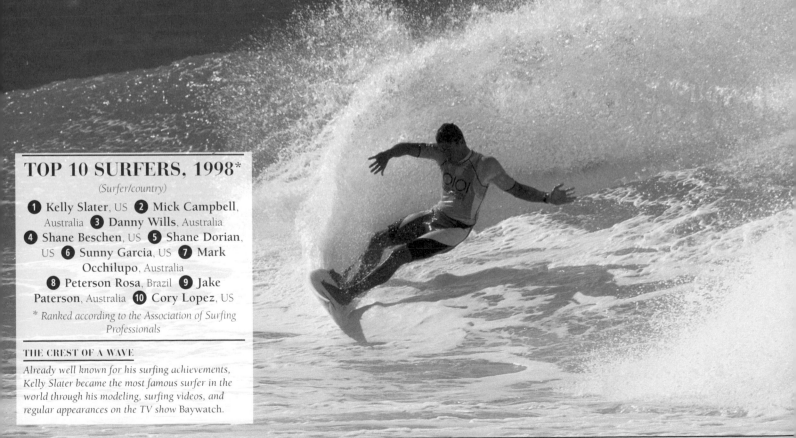

TOP 10 SURFERS, 1998*
(Surfer/country)

1 Kelly Slater, US **2** Mick Campbell, Australia **3** Danny Wills, Australia **4** Shane Beschen, US **5** Shane Dorian, US **6** Sunny Garcia, US **7** Mark Occhilupo, Australia **8** Peterson Rosa, Brazil **9** Jake Paterson, Australia **10** Cory Lopez, US

* Ranked according to the Association of Surfing Professionals

THE CREST OF A WAVE
Already well known for his surfing achievements, Kelly Slater became the most famous surfer in the world through his modeling, surfing videos, and regular appearances on the TV show Baywatch.

Who is the highest-earning athelete in the world?
see p.281 for the answer

A Mike Tyson
B Tiger Woods
C Michael Jordan

WINTER SPORTS

TOP 10 ★
SKATERS WITH THE MOST WORLD TITLES

SKATER/COUNTRY/EVENT	YEARS	TITLES
1 =Ulrich Salchow, Sweden, Men	1901–11	10
=Sonja Henie, Norway, Women	1927–36	10
=Irina Rodnina, USSR, Pairs	1969–78	10
4 =Karl Schäfer, Austria, Men	1930–36	7
=Herma Jaross-Szabo, Austria, Women/Pairs	1922–27	7
6 =Alexandr Zaitsev, USSR, Pairs	1973–78	6
=Lyudmila Pakhomova, USSR, Dance	1970–76	6
=Alexandr Gorshkov, USSR, Dance	1970–76	6
=Carol Heiss, US, Women	1956–61	6
10 Richard Button, US, Men	1948–52	5

The British pair of Jean Westwood and Lawrence Demmy won five successive ice dance titles from 1951 to 1955, but the 1951 event is not regarded as an official championship.

TOP 10 ★
WOMEN'S WORLD AND OLYMPIC FIGURE SKATING TITLES

SKATER/COUNTRY	YEARS	TITLES
1 Sonja Henie, Norway	1927–36	13
2 = Carol Heiss, US	1956–60	6
=Herma Planck Szabo, Austria	1922–26	6
=Katarina Witt, E. Germany	1984–88	6
5 =Lily Kronberger, Hungary	1908–11	4
=Sjoukje Dijkstra, Holland	1962–64	4
=Peggy Fleming, US	1966–68	4
8 =Meray Horvath, Hungary	1912–14	3
=Tenley Albright, US	1953–56	3
=Annett Poetzsch, E. Gemany	1978–80	3
=Beatrix Schuba, Austria	1971–72	3
=Barbara Ann Scott, Canada	1947–48	3
= Kristi Yamaguchi, US	1991–92	3
=Madge Sayers, UK	1906–08	3

TOP 10 WINTER OLYMPIC MEDAL-WINNING COUNTRIES
(Country/medals)

1 Norway, 239
2 Soviet Union*, 217 **3** US, 159
4 Austria, 145 **5** Finland, 135
6 Germany#, 116 **7** East Germany, 110
8 Sweden, 102 **9** Switzerland, 92
10 Canada, 79

* Includes United Team of 1992; excludes Russia since
 # Not including West or East Germany 1968–88

ARTISTIC ATHLETE
By the time she finished competitive skating in 1993, Kristi Yamaguchi's combination of athletic ability and artistic interpretation had made her America's favorite figure skater.

TOP 10 OLYMPIC FIGURE SKATING COUNTRIES
(Country/medals)

1 US, 39 **2** Soviet Union*, 29
3 Austria, 20 **4** Canada, 18
5 UK, 15 **6** France, 11 **7** = Sweden, 10; = East Germany, 10 **9** Germany#, 9
10 =Norway, 6; = Hungary, 6

* Includes United Team of 1992; excludes Russia since
 # Not including West or East Germany 1968–88

TOP 10 ★
MEN'S WORLD AND OLYMPIC FIGURE SKATING TITLES

SKATER/COUNTRY	YEARS	TITLES
1 Ulrich Salchow, Sweden	1901–11	11
2 Karl Schäfer, Austria	1930–36	9
3 Richard Button, US	1948–52	7
4 Gillis Grafstrom, Sweden	1920–29	6
5 =Hayes Jenkins, US	1953–56	5
=Scott Hamilton, US	1981–84	5
7 =Willy Bockl, Austria	1925–28	4
=David Jenkins, US	1957–60	4
=Ondrej Nepela, Czechoslovakia	1971–73	4
=Kurt Browning, Canada	1989–93	4

FANCY FOOTWORK
Despite being hospitalized four times for injuries caused while performing the hair-raising triple lutz, Kurt Browning exudes showmanship, technical prowess, style, and charisma.

Did You Know? The Iditarod dog sled race – from Anchorage to Nome, Alaska – commemorates an emergency operation in 1925 to get medical supplies to Nome following a diptheria epidemic.

TOP 10 ★
FASTEST WINNING TIMES OF THE IDITAROD DOG SLED RACE

				TIME	
WINNER	YEAR	DAY	HR	MIN	SEC
1 Doug Swingley	1995	9	2	42	19
2 Jeff King	1996	9	5	43	19
3 Jeff King	1998	9	5	52	26
4 Martin Buser	1997	9	8	30	45
5 Doug Swingley	1999	9	14	31	7
6 Martin Buser	1994	10	13	2	39
7 Jeff King	1993	10	15	38	15
8 Martin Buser	1992	10	19	17	15
9 Susan Butcher	1990	11	1	5	13
10 Susan Butcher	1987	11	2	53	28

Source: *Iditarod Trail Committee*

TOP 10 OLYMPIC BOBSLEDDING COUNTRIES
(Country/medals)

1 Switzerland, 26 **2** US, 14 **3** East Germany, 13 **4** = Germany*, 11; = Italy, 11 **6** West Germany, 6 **7** UK, 4 **8** = Austria, 3; = Soviet Union#, 3 **10** = Canada, 2; = Belgium, 2

* Not including West or East Germany 1968–88
 # Includes United Team of 1992; excludes Russia since

TOP 10 ★
MEN'S ALPINE SKIING WORLD CUP TITLES

NAME/COUNTRY		YEARS	TITLES
1 Marc Girardelli,	Luxembourg	1985–93	5
2 = Gustavo Thoeni,	Italy	1971–75	4
= Pirmin Zurbriggen,	Switzerland	1984–90	4
4 = Ingemar Stenmark,	Sweden	1976–78	3
= Phil Mahre,	US	1981–83	3
6 = Jean Claude Killy,	France	1967–68	2
= Karl Schranz,	Austria	1969–70	2
8 = Piero Gross,	Italy	1974	1
= Peter Lüscher,	Switzerland	1979	1
= Andreas Wenzel,	Leichtenstein	1980	1
= Paul Accola,	Switzerland	1992	1
= Kjetil-Andre Aamodt,	Norway	1994	1
= Alberto Tomba,	Italy	1995	1
= Lasse Kjus,	Norway	1996	1
= Luc Alphand,	France	1997	1

SKI WHIZZ!

Thought by many to be the greatest skier of all time, Marc Girardelli was forced to retire from competitive skiing, on doctor's orders, in 1997.

TOP 10 ★
WOMEN'S ALPINE SKIING WORLD CUP TITLES

NAME/COUNTRY		YEARS	TITLES
1 Annemarie Moser-Pröll,	Austria	1971–79	6
2 = Vreni Schneider,	Switzerland	1989–95	3
= Petra Kronberger,	Austria	1990–92	3
4 = Nancy Greene,	Canada	1967–68	2
= Hanni Wenzel,	Liechtenstein	1978–80	2
= Erika Hess,	Switzerland	1982–84	2
= Michela Figini,	Switzerland	1985–88	2
= Maria Walliser,	Switzerland	1986–87	2
= Kajta Seizinger,	Germany	1996–98	2
10 = Gertrude Gabl,	Austria	1969	1
= Michèle Jacot,	France	1970	1
= Rosi Mittermeier,	West Germany	1976	1
= Lise-Marie Morerod,	Switzerland	1977	1
= Marie-Thérèse Nadig,	Switzerland	1981	1
= Tamara McKinney,	US	1983	1
= Anita Wachter,	Austria	1993	1
= Pernilla Wiberg,	Sweden	1997	1

THIS SPORTING LIFE

THE IRONMAN CHALLENGE

The Hawaii Ironman Triathlon came into being in 1978, after John Collins, a Navy man stationed in Honolulu, threw a challenge to settle an argument on who the fittest athletes were – runners, swimmers, or cyclists. 15 people took part in the first race. At just over 140 miles/226 km, the triathlon includes a swim in the ocean, a long cycle ride, and a marathon, an especially gruelling combination, even without the extreme external factors of scorching sun and strong winds. The Ironman Triathlon has become the benchmark against which all extreme sporting challenges are now measured.

SNAP SHOTS

TOP 10 ★

FASTEST WINNING TIMES FOR THE HAWAII IRONMAN

	WINNER/COUNTRY*	YEAR	TIME HRS:MINS:SECS
1	Luc Van Lierde, Belgium	1996	8:04:08
2	Mark Allen	1993	8:07:45
3	Mark Allen	1992	8:09:08
4	Mark Allen	1989	8:09:15
5	Mark Allen	1991	8:18:32
6	Greg Welch, Australia	1994	8:20:27
7	Mark Allen	1995	8:20:34
8	Peter Reid, Canada	1998	8:24:20
9	Mark Allen	1990	8:28:17
10	Dave Scott	1986	8:28:37

* From the US unless otherwise stated

This is perhaps one of the most gruelling of all sporting contests, in which competitors engage in a 2.4-mile/3.9-km swim, followed by a 112-mile/180-km cycle race, ending with a full marathon. The first Hawaii Ironman was held at Waikiki Beach in 1978, but since 1981 the event's home has been at Kailua-Kona. Dave Scott and Mark Allen have dominated the race, each winning on a total of six occasions.

MOST COMMON SPORTING INJURIES

	COMMON NAME	MEDICAL TERM
1	Bruise	A soft tissue contusion
2	Sprained ankle	Sprain of the lateral ligament
3	Sprained knee	Sprain of the medial collateral ligament
4	Low back strain	Lumbar joint dysfunction
5	Hamstring tear	Muscle tear of the hamstrings
6	Jumper's knee	Patella tendinitis
7	Achilles tendinitis	Tendinitis of the Achilles tendon
8	Shin splints	Medial periostitis of the tibia
9	Tennis elbow	Lateral epicondylitis
10	Shoulder strain	Rotator cuff tendinitis

Many sporting injuries, such as tennis or golfer's elbow, are so closely associated with the repetitive actions of players of these sports that they are named after them. To this catalog of common injuries may be added less familiar afflictions such as soccer player's migraine, which results from heading soccer balls, and turf toe, caused by slipping on an Astroturf surface. Some authorities reckon that as many as 75 percent of all serious sports injuries involve the knee.

TOP 10 ★

MOVIES WITH SPORTING THEMES*

	MOVIE	SPORT
1	*Days of Thunder* (1990)	Stock car racing
2	*Rocky IV* (1985)	Boxing
3	*Rocky III* (1982)	Boxing
4	*Rocky* (1976)	Boxing
5	*A League of Their Own* (1992)	Baseball
6	*Rocky II* (1979)	Boxing
7	*Tin Cup* (1996)	Golf
8	*White Men Can't Jump* (1992)	Basketball
9	*Cool Runnings* (1993)	Bobsleighing
10	*Field of Dreams* (1989)	Baseball

* Based on worldwide box office income

Led by Sylvester Stallone's *Rocky* series, the boxing ring, a natural source of drama and thrills, dominates Hollywood's most successful sports-based epics.

TOP 10 ★

PARTICIPATION SPORTS, GAMES, AND PHYSICAL ACTIVITIES IN THE US

	ACTIVITY	NO. PARTICIPATING*
1	Exercise walking	77,600,000
2	Swimming	58,200,000
3	Camping	46,500,000
4	Exercise with equipment	46,100,000
5	Fishing	43,600,000
6	Cycling	43,500,000
7	Bowling	49,100,000
8	Billiards/pool	32,300,000
9	Basketball	29,400,000
10	Golf	27,500,000

* On more than one occasion by persons aged 7 and older

Source: *National Sporting Goods Association*

MOST DANGEROUS AMATEUR SPORTS

	SPORT	RISK FACTOR*
1	Powerboat racing	15
2	Ocean yacht racing	10
3	Cave diving	7
4	Spelunking	6
5 =	Drag racing	5
=	Go-karting	5
7	Ultralight flying	4
8 =	Hang gliding	3
=	Motor racing	3
=	Mountaineering	3

* Risk factor refers to the premium that insurance companies place on insuring someone for that activity – the higher the risk factor, the higher the premium

Source: *General Accident*

TOP 10 MOST EFFECTIVE FITNESS ACTIVITIES

1 Swimming 2 Cycling 3 Rowing
4 Gymnastics 5 Judo 6 Dancing
7 Football 8 Jogging 9 Walking
(briskly!) 10 Squash

TOP 10 CATEGORIES OF ATHLETES WITH THE LARGEST HEARTS*

1 Tour de France cyclists
2 Marathon runners 3 Rowers
4 Boxers 5 Sprint cyclists
6 Middle-distance runners
7 Weightlifters 8 Swimmers
9 Sprinters 10 Decathletes

* Based on average medical measurements

FERRARI WINNER
Michael Schumacher started his career in Formula 1 in 1991. After only one race with Jordan, he moved to the Benetton team, then in 1996 to Ferrari.

TOP 10 ★
SPORTING EVENTS WITH THE LARGEST TV AUDIENCES IN THE US

	EVENT	DATE	RATING
1	Super Bowl XVI	Jan 24, 1982	49.1
2	Super Bowl XVII	Jan 30, 1983	48.6
3	XVII Winter Olympics	Feb 23, 1994	48.5
4	Super Bowl XX	Jan 26, 1986	48.3
5	Super Bowl XII	Jan 15, 1978	47.2
6	Super Bowl XIII	Jan 21, 1979	47.1
7 =	Super Bowl XVIII	Jan 22, 1984	46.4
=	Super Bowl XIX	Jan 20, 1985	46.4
9	Super Bowl XIV	Jan 20, 1980	46.3
10	Super Bowl XXX	Jan 28, 1996	46.0

© 1999 *Nielsen Media Research*

TOP 10 ★
HIGHEST-EARNING ATHLETES

	NAME	SPORT	TEAM	INCOME ($)
1	Michael Jordan	Basketball	Chicago Bulls	69,000,000
2	Michael Schumacher*	Motor racing	Ferrari	38,000,000
3	Sergei Federov	Ice hockey	Detroit Red Wings	30,000,000
4	Tiger Woods	Golf	–	27,000,000
5	Dale Earnhardt	Stock car racing	–	24,000,000
6	Grant Hill	Basketball	Detroit Pistons	22,000,000
7 =	Oscar De La Hoya	Boxing	–	18,000,000
=	Arnold Palmer	Golf	–	18,000,000
=	Patrick Ewing	Basketball	New York Knicks	18,000,000
10	Gary Sheffield	Baseball	LA Dodgers	17,000,000

* From Germany, all others from the US

Source: Forbes *magazine*

Forbes' most recent analysis of the world's highest-earning athletes lists some 40 with total incomes of $10 million or more. Some have retired from active sports, and many earn the lion's share of their income from endorsements of sporting products. Among those falling just outside the Top 10 are tennis players Andre Agassi ($16 million) and recently retired ice-hockey superstar Wayne Gretzky ($15 million). With an income of $10 million, Czech-born tennis player Martina Hingis is the only woman among this elite group.

Who is the No. 1 surfer in the world?
see p.277 for the answer
A Mick Campbell
B Kelly Slater
C Danny Wills

INDEX

ACKNOWLEDGMENTS

Special US research: Dafydd Rees

UK research assistants: Harriet Hart, Lucy Hemming, Aylla Macphail

Thanks to the individuals, organizations, and publications listed below who kindly supplied information to enable me to prepare many of the lists.

Caroline Ash, Mark Atterto, John Bardsley, Richard Braddish, Catharine Burt, Pete Compton, Luke Crampton, Bonnie Fanstasia, Tonya Farden, Christopher Forbes, Darryl Francis, Russell E. Gough, Stan Greenberg, William Hartston, Andrew Hellawell, Gary Hemphil, Duncan Hislop, Alan Jeffreys, Robert Lamb, Anthony Lipmann, Dr. Benjamin Lucas, John Malam, Thom Moon, Ian Morrison, Vincent Nasso, Craig Noble, Roger Payne, Christiaan Rees, Linda Rees, Adrian Room, Lisa Smith, Tony Waltham.

Academy of Motion Picture Arts and Sciences, American Automobile Manufacturers Association, American Film Institute, American Forestry Association, American Kennel Club, American Music Conference, American Wholesale Marketers Association, American Zoo and Aquarium Association, *Amusement Business, Art Newspaper*, Art Institute of Chicago, Art Sales Index, Associated Press, Association of Surfing Professionals, ATP, Audit Bureau of Circulations, BabyCenter Inc., Beverage Marketing Corporation, *Billboard*, Boston Athletic Association, BPI, *BP Statistical Review of World Energy*, Breeders Cup, British Library, British Video Association, Bureau of Federal Prisons, Bureau of Justice Statistics, Carbon Dioxide Information Analysis Center, Cat Fancier's Association, Center for Disease Control, Central Intelligence Agency, Champagne Bureau, Championship Auto Racing Teams, Channel Swimming Association, Christian Research Association, Christie's, Christie's East, *Classical Music*, Coca-Cola, Computer Industry Almanac, Inc., Country Music Association, *Crime in the United States*, Death Penalty Information Center, De Beers, Duncan's American Radio, *Economist, Editor & Publisher Year Book*, Electoral Reform Society, Emmy Awards, Euromonitor, *FBI Uniform Crime Reports*, Feste Catalogue Index Database/Alan Somerset, *Financial Times*, Fine Arts Museum, Boston, *Flight International*, Food and Agriculture Organization of the United Nations, Food Marketing Institute, *Forbes, Fortune*, Gemstone Publishing, General Accident, Generation AB, Golden Globe Awards, Gold Fields Mineral Services Ltd., H.J. Heinz, Indianapolis Motor Speedway, Iditarod Trail Committee, International Atomic Energy Agency, International Civil Aviation Organization, International Coffee Organization, International Federation of the Phonographic Industry, International Game Fish Association, International Union for the Conservation of Nature, Inter-Parliamentary Union, Interpol, Jockey Club, Kellogg's, Korbel Champagne Cellars, Lipmann Walton & Co., Lloyds Register of Shipping/MIPG/PPMS, *London Metal Bulletin*, Magazine Publishers of America, Major League Baseball, Mansell Color Company, Inc., Manufacturing Confectioner, Mars, Inc., McDonald's, Meat and Livestock Commission, Metropolitan Museum of Art, New York, Modern Language Association of America, MORI, Motion Picture Association of America, Inc., MRIB, M Street, NARAS, NASA, NASCAR, National Academy of Popular Music, National Ambulatory Medical Care Survey, National Association of Broadcasters, National Basketball Association (NBA), National Book Critics Circle, National Center for Health Statistics, National Climatic Data Center, National Dairy Council, National Fire Protection Association, National Football League (NFL), National Highway Traffic Safety Administration, National

Hockey League (NHL), National Hockey League Players Association, National Ice Skating Association, National Park Service, National Pet Register, National Public Radio, National Safety Council, National Sporting Goods Association, NCAA, New York City Transit Authority, New York Road Runners Club, Niagara Falls Museum, Nielsen Media Research, Nobel Foundation, NOP, NTRA Communications, Nua Ltd., Office of National Statistics, UK, Official Museum Directory, Peabody Awards, Pet Industry Joint Advisory Council, Phillips Group, Phobics Society, *Playbill*, Popular Music Database, Produktschap voor Gedistilleerde Dranken, Project Feeder Watch/ Cornell Lab of Ornithology, Public Broadcasting System, Public Library Association, *Publishers' Weekly, Raceboat International, Railway Gazette International*, Really Useful Group, Recording Industry Association of America (RIAA), Royal Aeronautical Society, Royal Opera House, Covent Garden, *Screen Digest*, Siemens AG, Sotheby's, *Spaceflight, Sporting News, Sports Illustrated, Statistical Abstract of the United States*, STATS Inc., Tourism Industries, International Trade Administration, UNESCO, United Nations, Universal Postal Union, *USA Today*, US Board on Geographic Names, US Bureau of the Census, US Bureau of Labor Statistics, US Consumer Product Safety Commission, US Department of Justice, US Department of the Interior, US Fish and Wildlife Service, US Geological Survey, US Patent Office, US Social Security Administration, *Variety*, Videoscan, Inc., Ward's Automotive, *Wavelength*, World Association of Newspapers, World Bank, World Health Organization, World Meteorological Organization, World Resources Institute, World Tourism Organization, Zenith International.

PICTURE CREDITS

The publisher would like to thank the following for their kind permission to reproduce their photographs: (t=top, b=bottom, r=right, l=left, c=center)

Jacket photography: Allsport; Associated Press; Bruce Coleman Ltd.; Mary Evans Picture Library; LAT Photographic; Rex Features; The Stock Market

AKG London: 9cr, 17tl, 20br, 25tl, 27br; Erich Lessing 9tl, 10tl, 15b, 18tr, 21tc; S. Domingie 8l, 14tl. **Bryan and Cherry Alexander Photography:** 43b. **Allsport:** 246bl, 251bl, 252tr, 262br, 276; Agence Vandystadt 278bl; Andrew Redington 267bl; Bob Martin 278tr; Clive Brunskill 243tr, 260tl, 279b; Clive Mason 281tr; Darrell Ingham 250tl; David Cannon 261bc; David Leah 255bl; Gary M. Prior 272; Gary Newkirk 280–81, 280tc; Hulton 242tr, 245tl, 251tr, 266bl; IOC Olympic Museum 24cr; Jed Jacobsohn 247tr, 275bl; John Gichigi 244bl; Jonathan Daniel 253b; Mark Thompson 254bc; Mike Cooper 274tr; Mike Hewitt 242c, 243bl, 268, 276tr; MSI 262tl; Phil Cole 242bl, 263br; Stephen Dunn 249b; Steve Powell 273br; Vincent Laforet 248bl. **All Action:** Dreamworks/Paramount 180b; Duncan Raban 147b; Foto Blitz 175tr; Harry Goodwin 137c, 149 bl; Jean Cummings 182tl, 183br; Justin Thomas 142l; Paul Smith 144br, 145br, 160br, 161tl, 162bl; Phil Ramey 141r, 177b; Suzan Moore 144tl. **Apple Computer Inc.:** 8c, 31tl, 202bl, 211tr. **Associated Press AP:** 83b, 234br. **Bimota S.p.A.:** 227cl, 229cr. **The Boeing Company:** 227tl, 241bl. **Beaulieu Motor Museum:** 24br. **British Film Institute:** 170tl, 181tl. **British Library, London:** 111tl, 111bl, 113tr, 114tc. **Camera Press:** 27tl, 81tr, 92bl; David Sillitoe 119bc. **Cameron Mackintosh Ltd.** ™ © RUG LTD., designed by Dewynters Plc London: 167br. **Capital Records:** 155tr. **Channel 4 Television Corporation:** 197br. **Christie's Images Ltd.:** 8br, 22tl, 128bl, 128tr, 189br. **The Coca-Cola Company:** 203tl, 223r. **Bruce Coleman Ltd.:** David Austen 70b; Jen & Des Bartlett 59b; Kim Taylor 66–7; Michael Fogden

101b. **Columbia University, New York, USA:** 118. **The Commissioner for the City of London Police:** 86tr. **Corbis UK Ltd.:** 104b; Chloe Johnson/Eye Ubiquitous 188l; David Lees 14bl; Gail Mooney 26bc; George Hall 214–15; Jennie Woodcock 200l; Jim Sugar 198b; Leonard de Selva 19tr; Ludovic Maisant 12br; Rick Doyle 277b. **Anton Corbijn:** 153cl. **James Davis Travel Photography:** 99t, 107tl, 108br. **Disney:** 190–91, 199r, 224c. **Educational & Scientific Products Ltd./UK:** 73tl, 74. **EMI Records UK:** 136br. **Equity Cruises:** 227b, 236tr. **E.T. Archive:** 11tl, 17br. **Mary Evans Picture Library:** 8tr, 12tr, 13br, 19tc, 53tl, 72br, 78l, 84, 110br, 116tl, 117tr, 227tr, 238bl, 238, 239tr, 241tl. **Eye Ubiquitous:** Bennett Dean 98t. **Galaxy Picture Library:** Chris Livingstone 39t; Mt. Stromlo Observatory 38bl. **Robert Harding Picture Library:** A. Evrard 33tl; D. Jacobs 42tl; K. Gillham 107br; Paul van Riel 235tr; Simon Harris 105tr; Thomas Laird 46tr. **Hulton Getty:** 10b, 26tr, 49tl, 231bc. **Image Bank:** Barros & Barros 89. **Kobal Collection:** Amblin/Universal 171t; Columbia 170br, 201br; Fox/Paramount 168bl, 174bl; Lucas Films/C20th 172bl. **Magnum:** Ara Guler 124bl; Bruno Barbey 91b; F. Mayer 217br; Philippe Halsman 130tl, 131br; R. Rai 216tr. **Johnson Mathey:** 35tr, 48bl. **Moviestore Collection:** 139br, 187bl; United Artists 176tr. **NASA:** 34r, 35tl, 36, 39br, 40, 46; JPL 36tl. **Peter Newark's Pictures:** 8tl, 19br, 23br. **Nokia/ The Red Consultancy:** 203cla, 210br. **Novosti:** 41br. **Oxford Scientific Films:** Richard Packwood 55r, 63t, 71c; Rick Price 60. **PA News Photo Library:** Michael Stephens 32b; Roslin Institute 9bl, 33bl. **The Philadelphia Orchestra:** Don Tracy 162–3. **Popperfoto:** 9tr, 25br, 30bl, 31b, 82tl; Reuter 8bc, 28br, 32tl, 113bl, 118tr. **Rex Features:** 34bl, 40tc, 109br, 125t, 140bc, 208bl, 237br; Albert Facelly 85bc; Charles Ommanney 228bl, 228; Charles Sykes 219br; Denis Cameron 202br, 206. **Royal Geographical Society Picture Library:** Gregory 83tl. **SCALA:** 16tl. **Science & Society Picture Library:** Science Museum 9br, 21bc. **Science Photo Library:** Eye of Science 77bl; Geoff Tompkinson 88b; Ken Eward 29bl; NASA 30tl, 33br, 44tl; NIBSC 35br, 52tl; Quest 75bc. **Sony UK Ltd.:** 123bc, 196–97. **Sotheby's Transparency Library:** bought by Sheik Ahmed Fitaihi 218tr. **Frank Spooner Pictures:** Gamma 31tr, 203bl, 218bl. **Steiner Marzen:** 203tcl, 222bl. **Still Pictures:** Adrian Arbib 212tr; Carlos Guartia 205b; Gil Moti 52br, 95br, 96bl; Harmut Schwarzbach 80br; John Maier 57br; Julio Etchart 204t; Mark Edwards 51bl, 212bl; Ray Pfortner 203br, 213b. **The Stock Market:** 69t, 232r; Zefa-KALT 42; Peter Stone: 154–55, 154bl. **Telegraph Colour Library:** 45br, 47br, 117bl, 121br, 127br, 209l; C. Roessler 60bl. **Tiger Electronics UK Ltd.:** 111br, 122bl. **Topham Picturepoint:** 87tr. **Touchstone:** 158rc. **Warner Bros** © 1992: 143br. **Worldvision Enterprises Inc.:** 196–97.

PICTURE RESEARCH
Anna Grapes and Jo Open

INDEX
Patricia Coward

PUBLISHER'S ACKNOWLEDGMENTS
Dorling Kindersley would like to thank the following for their participation in this project: Editorial: Nicola Munro, Jane Simmonds, Sylvia Tombesi-Walton; Design: Austin Barlow, Jamie Hanson, Nigel Morris, Laura Watson; DTP: Rob Campbell; Administration: Christopher Gordon.

PACKAGER'S ACKNOWLEDGMENTS
Cooling Brown would like to thank Rachel Hagen, Lucinda Hawksley and Sean O'Connor for editorial assistance; Peter Cooling for technical support.